W9-DIU-797

ANALYSIS AND DESIGN OF INFORMATION SYSTEMS

ANALYSIS AND DESIGN OF INFORMATION SYSTEMS

James A. Senn
State University of New York

McGraw-Hill Book Company
New York St. Louis San Francisco Auckland Bogotá
Hamburg Johannesburg London Madrid Mexico
Montreal New Delhi Panama Paris São Paulo
Singapore Sydney Tokyo Toronto

ANALYSIS AND DESIGN OF INFORMATION SYSTEMS

234567890DOCDOC8987654

ISBN 0-07-056221-0

Library of Congress Cataloging in Publication Data

Senn, James A.
Analysis and design of information systems.

Bibliography: p.
Includes index.
1. System design. 2. System analysis. 3. Management information systems. I. Title.
QA76.9.S88S46 1984 003 83-22180
ISBN 0-07-056221-0

This book was set in Century Schoolbook by Black Dot, Inc.
The editors were Eric M. Munson and Linda A. Mittiga;
the designer was Joan E. O'Connor;
the production supervisor was Marietta Breitwieser.
The photo editor was Lorinda Morris/Photoquest;
the cover illustration was done by Colos.
The drawings were done by Fine Line Illustrations, Inc.
R. R. Donnelley & Sons Company was printer and binder.

CONTENTS

PREFACE

TO THE STUDENT

Although the computer is now commonplace in industry, government, medicine, and even politics, people still stand in awe of it. And they also tend to turn to persons who understand the power of the computer.

Systems analysts exert a significant influence over the organization in which they work. Based on their recommendations, new systems are installed and old ones displaced. Through information generated as a result of the systems that analysts develop, managers may decide the course of action for a new or existing product. The analyst may also be responsible for reports used in selecting a strategy determining the fate of the entire organization. On some days, an experienced systems analyst may touch a portion of each of these situations.

In this book, we will discuss each of the activities associated with developing a computer-based information system. You will see how to identify system requirements, including methods of collecting requirements data, interaction with managers and users, and documentation of system details through various methods. We will discuss the design of such new system features as reports and displays, including the use of color and graphics. Together, we will examine methods for detecting errors in input data and for preventing unexpected user activities from producing unintentional results. This text does not teach computer programming, but it does describe the responsibilities of the systems analyst who will later turn design specifications over to a programmer for development of the necessary software.

Not all systems require computer data processing. Similarly, not all user requests for information systems work should lead to a system development project. This book shows both how to analyze organization and business systems to determine whether improvement or change is needed and how to determine whether computer assistance is desirable.

It is not assumed that you have an extensive business background or that you even intend to pursue a career in information systems. You may be a business person who expects to interact with systems analysts or computer programmers and want to have a better understanding of their work so that you can work more effectively with them. Or you may want to collect knowledge so you can manage analysts responsible for a project in your department.

Some of you might also be computer programmers or computer engineers planning to move into the area of systems analysis in the future. In the latter case, your expertise in computer programming will be a useful supplement to the methods of systems analysis and design as we will discuss them.

Among the tools built into the book, you will find a set of questions at the beginning of each chapter that addresses the most important issues in the chapter. You can use the questions to guide your reading. After finishing the chapter, look back and see if you can answer the questions. Keywords and a summary are at the end of every chapter to highlight further the main points of the reading. By this time, you should be able to answer the review questions which follow.

Throughout the book there are many examples and over two hundred illustrations that demonstrate what systems analysts do to determine the feasibility of developing a computer-based system. Sometimes, their decisions are against developments altogether. These examples are based on real situations in which the author has been involved as a consultant, analyst, or designer of a system. Programmers have also taken specifications of the designs discussed in the chapter and turned them into working systems.

The concepts and theories underlying systems analysis and design are woven through the book so that you develop an understanding of why certain questions must be addressed or how various decisions are made. Emphasis is placed on practical aspects of system development—decisions that analysts must face every day when working on a project. Through the many examples and illustrations, you will gain a detailed understanding of the work of the systems analysts. If you take the time to work through the application problems at the end of each chapter you will acquire principles that will stay with you, and gain experience in making some of the decisions that can help you in actual business situations in the future. Developing the answers to the questions which are based on real life problems will not always be easy and may involve more than just a minute or two of thought. For that there is no apology. The amount of time you invest will determine the future payoff you can gain.

TO THE INSTRUCTOR

Systems analysis is one of the most difficult activities to teach students in a classroom environment. So much of systems analysis and design depends on tools, experience, and situations that are difficult to recreate in the typical classroom. Frequently when this area is taught in a college or university classroom the emphasis is on theory, and insufficient attention is given to applications.

This book is intended to go beyond classroom theory and concepts. It is practice-oriented with examples, applications, and proven techniques that *demonstrate* systems analysis and design. In addition, actual organization and business settings are used in the examples to show how systems concepts can apply to many different types of enterprises.

The text is designed to be used in a semester or quarter course in systems analysis and design. Although your students may not be computer or information systems majors, they should have had a course in either computer programming or introduction to computers. Therefore, basic operations of computer systems are not discussed.

The text is written in a fashion that is most logical for the student. The early chapters focus on feasibility studies and requirements determination, the later chapters are oriented toward design specification and implementation. Software design and testing specification are discussed in detail with repeated emphasis on maintaining the goal objectives.

Questions in project management and the selection of computer hardware and software, discussed in Chapters 14 and 15, are raised in virtually every aspect of systems development, and students may find it helpful to refer to these chapters repeatedly throughout the course.

Particular emphasis is placed on the problems of design involving online systems, the use of microcomputers, and small business systems. Another aspect considered is the development of formal database systems. Data communication and teleprocessing, increasingly common in information systems of all sizes, distributed or not, are examined in detail. A separate chapter is devoted to the design decisions the analyst must address in selecting equipment, choosing communication lines, and acquiring communication facilities.

It is important for the students to follow the development of lifelike systems as they study different analysis and design concepts. To assist you in achieving this objective, I have captured a live systems project and included portions of it through the text. The case study, which has been classroom tested repeatedly, involves an order entry/accounts receivable system that is common in many organizations. After each major topic in the text, the concepts and techniques are applied to the case study which include a feasibility study and a detailed investigation. Data flow diagrams, data dictionary entries, and decision tables are assembled to document the system. In the output and input design areas, reports, display screens, and interactive menus are shown to indicate how the previous user-requirements are translated into design specifications. Master and transaction file specifications and processing methods are also shown in detail. Since the system requires data communication, the design assembled to provide necessary transmission is also shown. By the time the students read the implementation of the system, they will have a good understanding of how the principles and practices of systems analysis and design are applied. As an aside, they will also have learned about the order and accounts receivable side of businesses as well.

A single case study is not sufficient to meet most instructor requirements. Consequently, a companion applications guide has been prepared to accompany the text. The guide has additional self-testing questions and problems to assist your students in mastering the material. But in addition, several other case studies are included for student use. They may be used in several ways. You may choose to use them as discussion vehicles throughout your course. After each major topic, your class may be asked to describe how they would deal with a specific aspect of the situation, using ideas, tools, techniques, and methods they have read about or discussed in class.

Another popular method of using the cases is to divide your class into 5- to 8-person project groups. Each project then works independently throughout the quarter or semester to develop a system to meet the user-requirements described in the case. I have found that the teams become very competitive and put in more time and effort on their own than you might expect. Many times they visit vendors to obtain equipment specification and pricing details. They also visit other computer installations to see how similar systems have been handled. At the end of the course, they present their system design to the class in a formal manner, complete with visuals and even prototype demonstrations in some cases. It is an effective teaching method, but more than that, it is rewarding to see how far they have progressed in a single course.

Accompanying software (for selected microcomputers) will be available with this text. Two types of software have been prepared. One type is a computer assisted instruction set. Through an interactive program, students are prompted with multiple-choice questions or system situations and asked to respond using information from specific text chapters. A question set has been developed for each chapter in the text. This self-instructional package will allow students to assess their understanding of each text chapter while freeing the instructors' time for work with the project teams or with individual students.

The other type of software demonstrates computer-based systems. For instance, students can interact with an on-line system to see first-hand menus, top-down operation, input validation, error trapping, and output generation. The software is intended to allow your classes to be independent of any campus computer facilities. It will be updated continually based on comments from persons using it in classroom environments.

The entire text and its accompanying tools have been developed to give the students a practical, applications-oriented understanding of systems analysis and design. It applies equally well to large main-frame and small personal computers. The up-to-date analyst should be familiar with both.

I would like to thank the following reviewers for their helpful comments and suggestions: Gordon B. Davis, University of Minnesota; Robert I. Mann, University of Georgia; Bruce Saulnier, Quinnipiac College; Michael Goldberg, Pace University; Skip Walter, U.S. Area Software Services, Digital Equipment Corporation; Susan Traynor, Clarion State College; John F. Schrage, Southern Illinois University at Edwardsville; and James H. Liskey, El Paso Community College.

The staff at McGraw-Hill Book Company was invaluable. Eric Munson, sponsor of the project, pulled out all stops to ensure it was a quality production. Elisa Adams worked diligently on early drafts of the manuscript. Her suggestions improved rough drafts and produced a readable manuscript. I especially want to thank Linda Mittiga, Dennis Conroy, Marietta Breitwieser, and the rest of the production crew who coordinated the preparation of illustrations and the manufacture of the book so that there were no loose ends.

Elaine, Marlene, and Kathy—my family—gave up many days on the sands at Myrtle Beach while this book was in process. Without their support, this project would still just be an idea and a sheath of notes.

James A. Senn

ANALYSIS AND DESIGN OF INFORMATION SYSTEMS

PART ONE

INTRODUCTION TO INFORMATION SYSTEMS DEVELOPMENT

CHAPTER 1 INTRODUCTION TO INFORMATION SYSTEMS DEVELOPMENT

QUESTIONS TO GUIDE YOU THROUGH THE CHAPTER

- What is systems analysis and design?
- What activities make up the systems development process?
- How do the responsibilities of systems analysts vary?
- What principles guide the analysis and design effort?
- Are there alternate methods for developing information systems?
- Do development methods change depending on whether the system is automated?
- Who are the systems users? How do their interactions with the system vary?

Computing technology abounds. We use it in many ways, from visible to invisible; spectacular to routine; video games and special effects for film and television to microwave ovens, electronic cameras, and automobile ignition systems. In business, too, computers and information systems occupy a special place, for they make possible the smooth and efficient operation of airline reservations offices, hospital records departments, accounting and payroll functions, electronic banking, telephone switching systems, and countless other applications, both large and small. These applications used to require painstaking hours of human labor, if they were possible at all.

How do such complex information systems come into existence? In a word, through people. Technology has developed at a soaring rate, but the most important aspect of any system is the human know-how and use of ideas to harness the computer so that it performs the required task. This process is essentially what systems development is all about. To be of any use, a computer-based information system must function properly, be easy to use, and suit the organization for which it has been designed. If it helps people to do their jobs better and more efficiently, they will use it. If it is not helpful, they will surely avoid it. To design and develop a system takes various skills, some of which you may already have. Others you will develop as you read this text and work through the cases and problems. What are some of these skills?

1 The ability to examine someone's request for computer assistance and determine whether the opportunity to draw on computers should be pursued.
2 The know-how to gather and interpret facts that assist in diagnosing a business problem as it relates to computing and information systems.
3 The understanding to determine, after examining a business situation, where computer assistance is desirable and where manual systems and procedures are more effective.
4 The ability to design and develop specifications for an information system as determined by an examination of the present system.
5 The knowledge to select the best methods for data input, file storage and access, processing, and output for a given situation.
6 An insight into software development, testing methods, and implementation strategies.

7 The ability to communicate effectively with others.
8 Experience in each of the above through application development problems and case studies.

Before we examine in detail the processes involved in systems analysis and design, we need to answer some basic questions to determine what systems analysis and design is, what principles guide the effort to develop a computer-based information system, and what the systems development life cycle is.

The remainder of this chapter will focus on three areas. The first part will describe the meaning of systems analysis and design. You will learn basic terms used in systems development and the responsibilities of personnel in information systems development. The second section will present general systems concepts as they apply to business in general and information systems in particular. The ideas in this section are universal and can be applied across many different types of organizations and situations.

The last part of this chapter will describe the actual development activities associated with information systems applications. It will familiarize you with the major topics that will be examined throughout the remainder of the text.

WHAT IS SYSTEMS ANALYSIS AND DESIGN?

Generally speaking, in business, systems analysis and design refers to the process of examining a business situation with the intent of improving it through better procedures and methods. This section overviews systems analysis and design. It also describes the work of systems analysts and the different types of users that participate in the development process.

Overview of Systems Analysis and Design

Systems development can generally be thought of as having two major components, systems analysis and systems design. Systems design is the process of planning a new business system to replace or complement the old. But before this can be done, of course, we must thoroughly understand the old system and determine how the computer can best be used (if at all) to make its operation more effective. *Systems analysis*, then, is the process of gathering and interpreting facts, diagnosing problems, and using the facts to improve the system. This is the job of the *systems analyst.*

Consider, for example, the stockroom of a clothing store. In order to better control its inventory and have more up-to-date information about stock levels and reordering, the store asks you to "computerize" the stockroom operation. Before you could design a system for the capture of data, update of files, and production of reports, you would need to know more about how the store now handles its operations. For instance, you would want to know what forms are being used to store information manually, such as requisitions, purchase orders, and invoices. You would want to know what reports, if any, are now being produced and what they are being used for. Therefore you would seek out information about such reports as lists of reorder notices, outstanding purchase orders, stock on hand, and so on. You would also need to find out where this information originates: the purchasing department, stockroom, or accounting department. In other words, you must understand the way the system presently works and, more specifically, what the flow of information through the system looks like. It is also important to learn why the store wants to change its current operations. Does it have problems tracking orders, merchandise, or money? Does it seem to fall behind in handling inventory "paperwork"? Does it need a more efficient system before it can expand operations?

Only after you have collected these facts can you begin to determine how and where a computer information system can benefit all the users of the system. This accumulation of information is called a *systems study*, and it must precede all other analysis activities.

Systems analysts do more than solve current problems. They are frequently called upon to help handle the planned expansion of a business. In this case, the systems study is future-oriented, since no present system exists. The analysts assess as carefully as possible what the future needs of the business will be and where changes should be considered to meet these needs. In this and most instances, the analysts may recommend alternative ways to improve the situation. Usually more than one strategy is possible.

Working with managers and employees in the organization, the systems analysts recommend which alternative solution to adopt. The choice should be based on such concerns as the suitability of the solution to the particular organization and setting, as well as the support it should have from employees. If the intended users of the system are not comfortable with it, it will fail in its purpose of improving the organization. Sometimes the time it takes to develop one alternative, compared with others, will be the most critical issue. Financial costs and benefits are also important determinants. Management in the end chooses which alternative to accept. The systems analysts can recommend, but management, which will pay for and use the result, actually decides.

Once this decision is made, a plan is developed to implement the recommendation. The plan includes all systems design features, such as new data capture needs, file specifications, operating procedures, and equipment and personnel needs. The systems design is like the blueprint for a building: it specifies all the features that are to be in the finished product.

Designs for the stockroom will provide ways to capture data about orders and sales to customers. They will also specify the way the data is stored, whether on paper forms or a computer readable medium, such as magnetic tape or disk. In fact, the designs will state which work people will do and which computers will do. Designs will vary in the division of people and computer tasks.

The stockroom personnel will also need information about the business.

Each design describes reports, documents, and other output to be produced by the system. Probable outputs include inventory reports, sales analyses, purchasing summaries, and invoices, but the systems analysts will actually decide that, as well as how to produce them.

Analysis specifies *what* the system should do. Design states *how* to accomplish the objective.

You probably noticed that each of the processes above involves people. Managers and employees have good ideas about what works and what does not, about what flows smoothly and what causes problems, about where change is needed and where it is not, and especially about where change will be accepted and where it will not. Even though technology abounds in many business organizations, people are still the keys that make the organizations work. Thus communicating and dealing with people are very important parts of the systems analysts' job.

What Systems Analysis Is NOT

You have an idea of what systems analysis is—studying business systems to learn current methods and assess effectiveness. It is also helpful to know what systems analysis is NOT:

It is NOT:

Studying a business to see which existing processes should be handled by computer and which should be done by noncomputer methods. The emphasis is on understanding the details of a situation and deciding whether improvement is desired or feasible. The selection of computer and noncomputer methods is secondary.

It is NOT:

Determining what changes should be made. The intent of the systems investigation is to study a business process and evaluate it. Sometimes change is not needed or possible. Change should be a *result*, not an *intent*.

It is NOT:

Determining how best to solve a systems problem. Regardless of the organization, the analyst works on *business* problems. It would be a mistake to distinguish between business and systems problems. Or, stated differently, there are no systems problems that are not first business problems. Any suggestion should be considered first in light of whether it will improve or harm the business. Technically attractive ideas should not be pursued unless they will improve the business system.

The Systems Analysts' Work

The description of systems analysis gives a good idea of what analysts do. However, organizations vary the responsibilities of their analysts, as well as their title. Listed below are the most common sets of responsibilities assigned to systems analysts. (Other names given to analysts are shown in parentheses.)

1 Systems analysis only. These analysts' entire responsibility is conducting systems studies to learn relevant facts about a business activity. The emphasis is on determining information and processing requirements. Their responsibilities do not include systems design. (Information analysts)
2 Systems analysis and design. These individuals carry out complete systems studies, but also have the added responsibility of designing the new system. People who are responsible for both systems analysis and design will work on fewer projects but spend more time on each one for a greater interval of time. (Systems designers, applications developers)
3 Systems analysis, design, and programming. These people conduct the systems investigation, develop design specifications, and program software to implement the design. (Programmer analysts)

You should not conclude that one type of analyst is better than another, since the size of the organization often dictates the nature of the analysts' work. In smaller firms, the analysts take on more roles than in large firms, which hire people who specialize in, say, systems design and work on nothing else. In many organizations, the actual programming is performed by persons who specialize in this part of the systems development effort. Most often they are called *application programmers*. Many analysts start as programmers and then become systems analysts after they gain experience.

Responsibility for Computer Programming

Do systems analysts write computer programs? As pointed out, it is part of the job description for some people; they are frequently called programmer analysts. Do most analysts *actually do* computer programming? That varies from firm to firm. However, one thing is very clear. The best and most valuable systems analysts *know how to program*. Systems analysts who have this knowledge are usually much more valuable to organizations since their added knowledge enables them to formulate better and more complete new application specifications. Not only do they know what can and cannot be built into a program, they also know what has to be communicated to the programmer. The result almost always is higher-quality software and less development time. That helps everyone.

Figure 1.1 shows the expected demand for information systems personnel.

How Have the Systems Analysts' Responsibilities Changed?

At one time all systems analysts were specialists in computing, not business. Consequently they had to be trained in business functions before

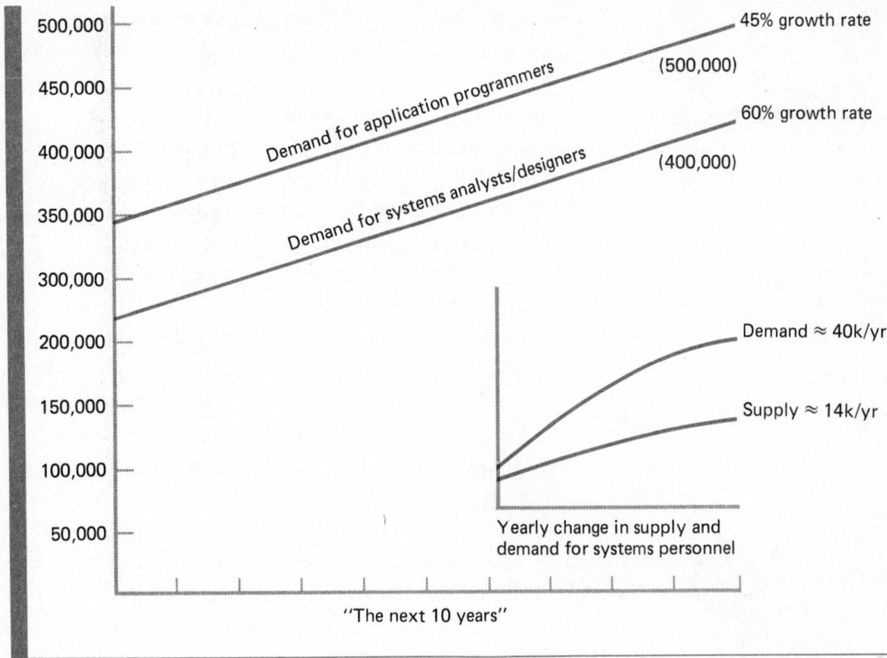

Figure 1.1. Ten-year projected demand for systems analysts and programmers.

they could develop systems for an organization department. Since the details of the business functions they were working with were relatively well understood (for example, capturing sales data or processing basic accounting statements), it was easier to train computer people about business than to train business people about computing.

The situation is changing as business people learn more about computing. Users (meaning managers and employees in business) are becoming highly involved in systems development. This is occurring for several reasons:

1 Users have accumulated experience from working with earlier applications that were developed for them. They have better insight into what information systems help means and how it can be achieved. If they experienced systems failures, they also formed ideas about what problems to avoid.
2 Users entering business organizations today have frequently received college or university training in various aspects of information systems. Many business majors have taken courses focusing specifically on systems analysis and design.
3 The applications being developed in organizations that have experience in information systems are becoming complex. Systems analysts need the continual involvement of users to understand the business functions being studied.

4 Better systems development tools are emerging. Some allow users to design and develop applications without involving trained systems analysts.

Who Are the Users?

We have been referring to *users* in the preceding discussion. These are, of course, the managers and employees in an organization who interact with information systems. The degree of their involvement may vary, depending on the type of user (Figure 1.2).

Direct users actually interact with the system. They feed in (input) data or receive output, perhaps using a terminal. Airline reservations agents, for example, use a terminal to query the system about passengers, flights, and tickets.

Indirect users benefit from the results or reports produced by the system, but do not directly interact with the hardware or software. These users may be managers of business functions using the system (say, marketing managers responsible for sales analysis applications that result in monthly reports).

Still a third type, *administrative users,* have management responsibilities for application systems. These users may be upper-level managers for business functions that make heavy use of information systems. While these people may not use the systems directly or indirectly, they retain authority to approve or disapprove investment in the development of applications. They also have the organizational responsibility for the effectiveness of the systems (in the same way that a vice president of marketing is responsible

TYPE OF MANAGEMENT USER		CHARACTERISTICS
Hands-on user		Operates the system. Direct interaction through systems equipment.
Indirect user		Uses reports or information produced by system but does not operate equipment.
Administratively responsible user		Oversees investment in development or use of the system. Has organization responsibility for control of system activities.

Figure 1.2. Categories of management users.

for the success of all sales and marketing programs). Clearly these upper-level users must be involved in major systems development efforts. This idea will be emphasized repeatedly throughout the chapters that follow

All three types of users are important. Each has essential information about the organization—how it functions and where it is going. However, the systems analysts are often the ones who supply the ideas—the imagination—about ways to use computers effectively. The information the analysts collect about a business system forms the basis from which the design for a new or changed system results.

BUSINESS SYSTEMS CONCEPTS

The word "system" has been used repeatedly. This section discusses its meaning in more detail. It first defines the term and looks at the components of systems. Then it applies the concepts to business in general and information systems in particular. Systems have a special meaning for analysts and designers, that guides every facet of their job. This meaning is the basis for the remainder of the book.

What Is a System?

In the broadest sense, a *system* is simply a set of components that interact to accomplish some purpose. Systems are, in fact, all around us. For example, you feel physical sensations by means of a complex nervous system, a set of parts, including your brain, spinal cord, nerves, and special sensitive cells under your skin, that work together to make you feel hot, cold, itchy, and so on. You communicate by means of language, a highly developed system of words and symbols that convey meanings to you and to others. You live according to an economic system, in which goods and services are exchanged for other goods and services of comparable value and by which (at least in theory) the participants to the exchange benefit.

You may not often realize it, but a business is a system too. Its parts have such titles as marketing, manufacturing, sales, research, shipping, accounting, and personnel. These parts all work together to create a profit that benefits the employees and stockholders of the firm. Each of these parts is a system itself. The accounting department, for example, may consist of accounts payable, accounts receivable, billing, auditing, and so on.

When you begin to see how pervasive systems are, it will not surprise you to realize that every business system depends on a more or less abstract entity called an *information system*. This system is the means by which data flows from one person or department to another, and it can encompass everything from interoffice mail and telephone links to a computer system that generates periodic reports for various users. Information systems, in fact, serve all the systems of a business, as we shall see. They link the different components together in such a way that they can effectively work toward the same purpose.

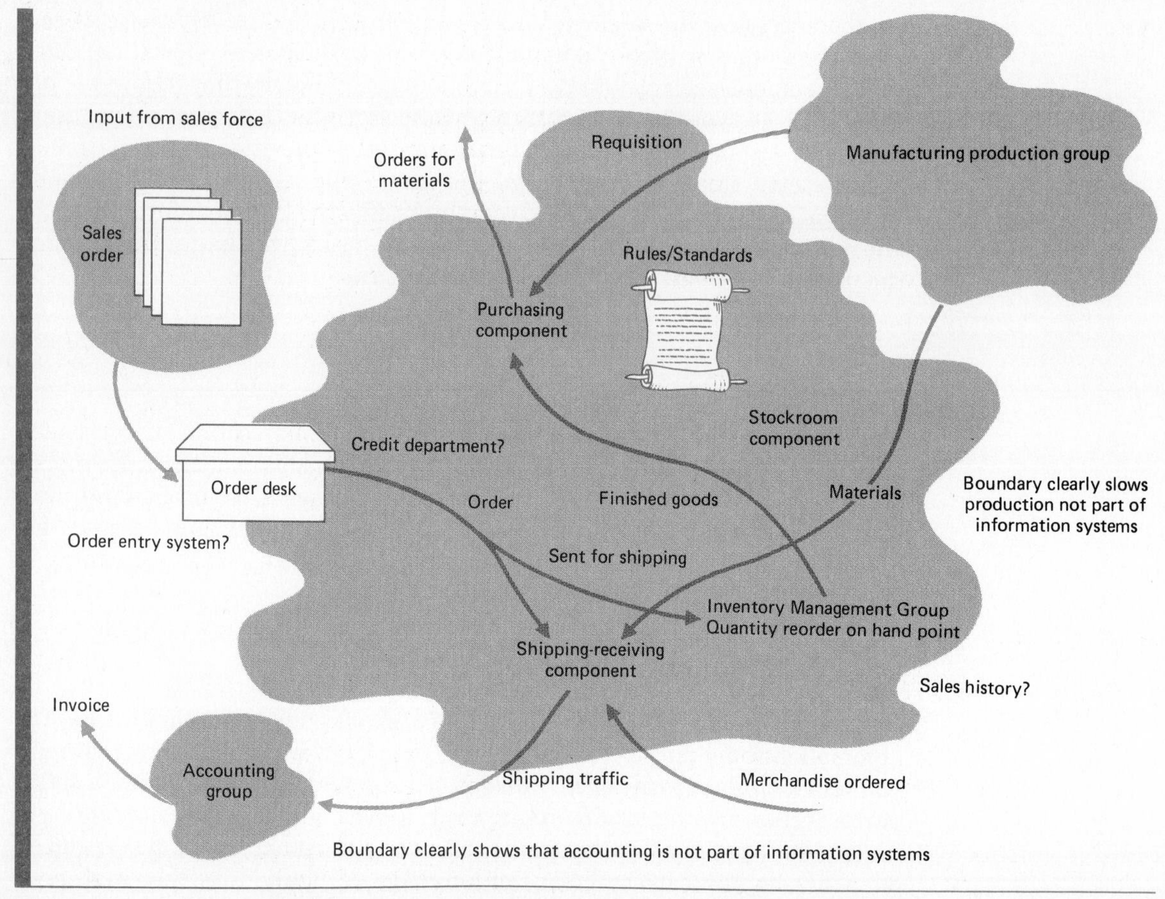

Figure 1.3. Open system example: inventory control system.

Figure 1.3 illustrates systems concepts applied to a familiar business situation. Notice the interrelations between the elements. These are important to successful systems operation.

Important Systems Characteristics

The system's purpose is its reason for existing. A legislative system, for example, exists to study problems facing voters and citizens and to pass legislation that eliminates the problems. The ignition system in an automobile has a clearly stated purpose of burning fuel that can be transformed into energy, used by the automobile's other systems.

To achieve their purposes, systems interact with their *environments*, any entities that lie outside the boundaries of the systems. The *boundaries* separate the systems from their environments.

Systems that interact with their environments, receive input and produce output, are *open systems*. In contrast, systems that do not interact with their surroundings are called *closed systems*. All ongoing systems are open. Thus closed systems exist as a concept only, but an important one as we will see in a moment.

The element of *control* is related to whether systems are open or closed. Systems work best when they operate within tolerable performance levels. For example, people function best when body temperature, measured by a thermometer, is 98.6 degrees, the normal Fahrenheit temperature. A slight deviation from 98.6 degrees, say to 99.0 degrees, probably will not affect performance too much, although some difference may be noticeable. However, a high variation, such as running a 103-degree fever, will change bodily functioning drastically. The system will become rundown and sluggish until the condition is corrected. If the condition continues too long, the result can be fatal. The system can die.

This example also demonstrates the importance of *control* in systems of every type. There are acceptable levels of performance, called *standards*. Actual performances are compared against the standards. Activities too far above or below standards should be noted, so that they can be studied and adjustments made. The information supplied by comparing results with standards and informing the control elements about the differences is termed *feedback* (Figure 1.4).

To summarize, systems use a basic control model consisting of:

1 A *standard* for acceptable performance
2 A method of *measuring* actual performance
3 A means for *comparing* actual performance against the standard
4 A method for *feedback*

Systems that can adjust their activities to acceptable levels continue to function. Those that cannot, stop.

The concept of interaction with the environment, which characterizes open systems, is essential for control. By receiving input and evaluating it, a system can determine how well it is operating. If a business, for example, produces as output products or services that are high priced and low quality, people probably will not continue to buy them. Low sales figures are feedback, telling management it needs to adjust the products and the way

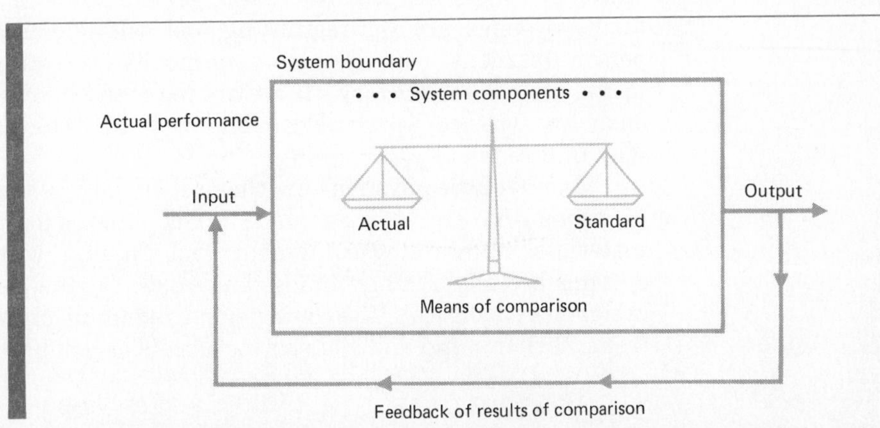

Figure 1.4. Basic system model control elements.

they are produced to improve performance and bring it into line with expectations.

In contrast, closed systems, which do not interact with the environment, sustain their operation only as long as they have adequate regulatory information and do not need anything from the environment. Since this condition cannot exist for long, we do not have closed systems. The concept is important, however, because it demonstrates a systems design objective: We strive to build systems that need as little outside intervention as possible to maintain acceptable performance. *Self-regulation* and *self-adjustment*, therefore, are design objectives in all systems environments.

The components that make up systems may actually be other smaller systems. That is, systems may contain levels of systems, or *subsystems*. The human body, for example, contains such subsystems as the respiratory and circulatory systems. An automobile includes combustion, electric, and emission control systems. Multiple levels of systems, interacting with each other, are common in virtually any systems situation.

Business Systems

Organizations consist of many business systems, each having the features of the general system discussed in the preceding section. For example, all manufacturing systems have similarities. Their purpose is to produce goods or products that fulfill a demand for them in the market. To achieve this objective, the systems interact with their environments to acquire the necessary materials, people, and knowledge to manufacture the goods. None of these inputs can be omitted for manufacturing to continue: manufacturing systems would not be able to produce many items if raw materials or workers were missing. The manufacturing systems also produce outputs, consisting of finished products, waste, production technology, and so on.

To keep going, manufacturing systems must be under control. For example, they must meet performance standards. The quantity of products manufactured must meet budgeted quotas and achieve acceptable quality and cost levels.

Managers and employees continually monitor actual performances and compare them against planned productivity. If there are differences or efficiency is below expectations, changes are made. In this sense manufacturing systems are self-regulating and self-adjusting; they will replace persons, purchase new equipment, or modify procedures. If internal adjustments are not satisfactory—there are too many injuries, quality is dangerously low, or prices are unreasonable—regulatory forces in the environment may intercede.

Manufacturing systems are themselves subsystems within larger organizations and are in turn made up of other subsystems for acquiring materials, maintaining equipment, and training workers. Manufacturing systems are one of many kinds that exist. Yet the general features of all systems are identical. You could begin to examine any one system with this framework in mind and add specific details as you need or learn of them. It is this flexibility that makes systems concepts so useful to business in general and information systems design in particular.

Business Information Systems

Information systems are like any other system in an organization in that they have purposes and interact with other components of the enterprise. The purposes of information systems are to process input, maintain files of data about the organization, and produce information, reports, and other output.

Information systems consist of subsystems, including hardware, software, and data storage for files and data bases. Specific procedures describe systems used. The particular set of subsystems, that is, the specific equipment, programs, files, and procedures, comprise an information systems *application*. Therefore information systems can have purchasing, accounting, or sales applications.

Since information systems support other organization systems, analysts must first study the organization system as a whole and then its information systems details. Often people use organization charts (Figure 1.5) to describe the relations of the organization's components, such as

Figure 1.5. Organization charts leave many systems questions unanswered.

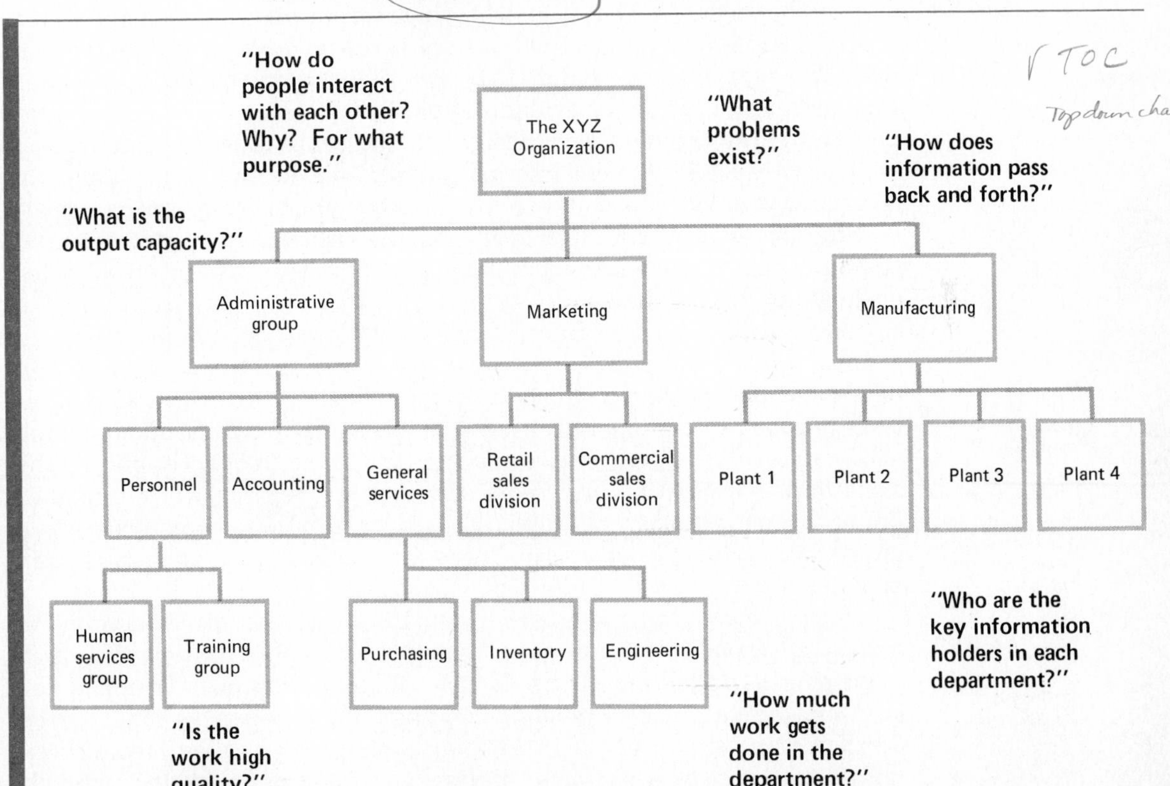

divisions, departments, offices, and people. Although the charts may show the formal relations between the components accurately, they do not tell how the business system operates since many important details cannot be described in the boxes on the chart. Examples of other details about the system that are important to systems analysts include:

1 Informal channels. What interactions between people and departments exist but do not show on the organization chart or in prescribed operation procedures?
2 Interdependencies. On which other departments and components in the organization is a particular one dependent?
3 Key people and functions. Which individuals and elements in the system are most important for successful existence?
4 Critical communication links. How do information and instructions pass back and forth between organization components; how do areas interface with one another?

This is not an exhaustive set of questions. But it does emphasize the importance of investigating and analyzing the way organizations operate.

During design, in contrast, analysts are responsible for identifying the important features needed in new systems. They specify how the system and its subsystems will operate, the input that will be required, and the output that will be produced. They also state which work uses computers and which is done manually. Systems analysts are involved with control systems in two ways. On the one hand, they describe control elements, such as standards and methods of evaluating performances against standards for the information systems they design. At the same time, the information systems they specify provide information to managers and users so they can determine whether the business systems they manage are operating properly. Building in feedback mechanisms for the organizations is an essential step in design to sustain the activities of both systems. Neither will last if adequate control is absent.

Analysts develop two different types of information systems in organizations. *Transaction processing systems* are aimed at improving the day-to-day business activities on which the organizations depend. Typical applications include processing accounting data, preparing payrolls, and handling sales orders. The activities are routine, occurring frequently and in the same form. Transaction processing systems typically substitute computer processing for manual procedures. The emphasis of automated transaction processing systems is efficiency, speed, and accuracy in processing high volumes of data.

Management decision systems are aimed at the direct support of managers responsible for decision making in the organization. Although management decision systems do not tell managers *how* to make the decision, they assist by providing important information as input to the decision process. *Management reporting systems* (also called *management information systems)*, one class of management decision system, provide information in report form on a regular basis to assist managers with decisions that recur and can be anticipated. They are therefore highly structured, and the reports are in a format predefined by the systems developer. *Decision support systems,* the other type of management decision system, in contrast, assist in decision making that is less structured and nonroutine, that is, in those decisions where part of the decision process is deciding what information is needed, as well as how to use it. Report formats are defined by the manager during the actual decision process. Therefore, they cannot be developed ahead of time. Often managers work interactively with the system through a terminal. The role of systems developers involved with decision support systems is to design systems with the needed flexibility to support the special analyses and unanticipated inquiries of management.

The steps of systems analysis and design that we will use throughout this book are based on the general systems concept discussed in this chapter. The methods to be described can be used for both transaction processing and management decision systems.

SYSTEMS DEVELOPMENT LIFE CYCLE

Systems development is a process consisting of the two major steps of systems analysis and design. It starts when management or sometimes systems development personnel realize that a particular business system needs improvement.

The systems development life cycle (Figure 1.6) is the set of activities analysts, designers, and users carry out to develop and implement an information system. This section examines each of the seven activities that make up the systems development life cycle. You should be aware that in

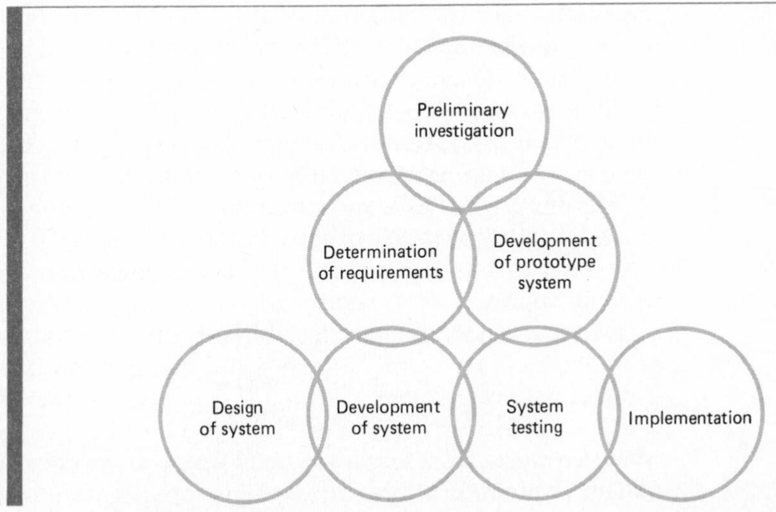

Figure 1.6. The system development life cycle: an integrated set of activities.

most business situations the activities are all highly related, usually inseparable. Many times even the order of the steps will be difficult to determine. Different parts of a project can be in varying phases at the same time. Some components may be undergoing analysis, while others are at advanced design stages.

The systems development life cycle consists of the following activities:

1 Preliminary investigation
2 Determination of requirements
3 Development of prototype system
4 Design of system
5 Development of software
6 Systems testing
7 Implementation

The remainder of this section overviews each activity. The chapters that follow are organized around this set of activities.

Preliminary Investigation

How many times have you been in situations where you have wondered if there was not a better way to do something? (The long lines you stand in for course registration or tuition payment might make you think that "there has to be a better way!") Or perhaps you can recall an instance where you knew a certain event was going to occur and the way a job was being performed would change: Opening an additional retail store creates a need for new billing procedures when a high percentage of customers use their company charge account and shop at all the stores. Doubling the number of customers, due to expanded facilities and the addition of many new products, may bring about new checkout requirements. A change in department managers may lead to new ways of recording sales, with implications for the computer-based order entry system. A growing company, such as the one described in the case at the end of this chapter, may look to computer information systems as a way of making continued growth possible, without having difficulties in processing customer orders. Or a request may be initiated for many other reasons. But the point is that someone—a manager, an employee, or a systems specialist—initiates a request to receive assistance from information systems. When that request is made, the first systems activity, the *preliminary investigation,* begins. This activity has three parts: request clarification, feasibility study, and request approval. The result will be to approve the request for further attention or reject it as not feasible for further development.

REQUEST CLARIFICATION

Many requests from employees and users in organizations are not clearly stated. Therefore, before any systems investigation can be considered, the project request must be examined to determine precisely what the originator wants. A simple telephone call may suffice if the requester has a clear idea but does not know how to state it. On the other hand, the requester may merely be asking for help without knowing what is wrong or why there is a problem. Problem clarification in this case is much more difficult. In either case, before any further steps can be taken, the project request must be clearly stated.

FEASIBILITY STUDY

An important outcome of the preliminary investigation is the determination that the system requested is feasible. There are three aspects in the feasibility study portion of the preliminary investigation:

1 Technical feasibility. Can the work for the project be done with current equipment, software technology, and available personnel? If new technology is required, what is the likelihood that it can be developed?
2 Economic feasibility. Are there sufficient benefits in creating the system to make the costs acceptable? Or, inversely, are the costs of *not* creating the system so great that the project must be undertaken?
3 Operational feasibility. Will the system be used if it is developed and implemented: Will there be resistance from users that will undermine the possible application benefits?

The feasibility study is carried out by a small group of people (sometimes even one or two), who are familiar with information systems techniques, understand the part of the business or organization that will be involved or affected by the project, and are skilled in the systems-analysis and design process. Typically people responsible for feasibility assessments are experienced, not new, analysts or managers.

REQUEST APPROVAL

Not all requested projects are desirable or feasible. (In fact, some organizations receive so many project requests from employees that only a few of them can be pursued.) However, those that are both feasible and desirable should be put into a schedule. In some cases, development can start immediately. But in most cases, systems staff members are busy on other ongoing projects. When this happens, management decides which projects are most important and schedules them. Many business organizations develop information systems plans as carefully as they plan for new products, new manufacturing programs, or plant expansion. After a project request is approved, its cost, priority, completion time, and personnel requirements are estimated and used to determine where to add it on any existing project list.

Later on, when other preceding projects are completed, the proposed application development can be launched. At this time, the collection of data and determination of requirements begin.

Determination of Requirements

The heart of systems analysis is aimed at acquiring a detailed understanding of all important facets of the business area that is under investigation. (For this reason, this activity is often termed the *detailed investigation.*) Analysts, working closely with employees and managers, must study the business process to answer these key questions:

1 What is being done?
2 How is it being done?
3 How frequently does it occur?
4 How great is the volume of transactions or decisions?
5 How well is the task being performed?
6 Does a problem exist?
7 If a problem exists, how serious is it?
8 If a problem exists, what is the underlying cause?

To answer these questions, systems analysts will talk to a variety of persons to gather details about the business process and their opinions of why things happen as they do and ideas about change. Questionnaires are used to collect this information from large groups of people who cannot be interviewed individually. Detailed investigations also require the study of manuals and reports, actual observation of work activities, and sometimes collection of samples of forms and documents to fully understand the process.

As the details are gathered, the analysts study the requirements data to identify features the new system should have, including both the information the system should produce and such operational features as processing controls, response times, and input and output methods.

Development of Prototype System

In some cases, it may not be possible to decide about all the features of the system in advance. Unique situations, about which developers have neither information nor experience, are often selected for prototyping. High-cost or high-risk situations, where the proposed design is new and untested, are also evaluated through prototypes. For example, the feasibility of having salespersons submit orders to the firm's computer system from the field, through portable terminals that are briefly linked to pay telephones, is still untested in many firms. Managers and systems developers may choose to build a small-scale version of the software, purchase a limited quantity of terminals, and have a selected group of salespersons test the concept by submitting orders from their scattered sales territories. The prototype will provide preliminary information about the workability of the concept. They may find, for example, that salespersons all try to call in their orders at a time of day when the computer is not available to receive sales orders.

You can see that the prototype is actually a pilot or test. It is expected that the prototype will be changed through several iterations. That is, the design will evolve as additional design information is learned through use. If use of the sales prototype system reveals that entering customers' names and addresses through a portable terminal creates too many errors, designers may modify the system so that only customers' names are necessary; the addresses can automatically be retrieved from files stored in the system.

The prototype is a working system. However, it is designed to be easily changed. Information gained through its use is applied to a modified design. The modified version may again be used as a prototype to reveal still more valuable design information. The process is repeated as many times as necessary to reveal essential design requirements.

Prototype development often coincides with systems design.

Design of System

The design of an information system produces the details that state how a system will meet the requirements identified during systems analysis. Often systems specialists refer to this stage as *logical design,* in contrast to developing program software, which is referred to as *physical design.*

Systems analysts start by identifying reports and other outputs the system will produce. Then the specific data on each is pinpointed, including its exact location on the paper, display screen, or other medium. Usually designers sketch the form or display as they expect it to appear when the system is completed.

The systems design also describes the data to be input, calculated, or stored. Individual data items and calculation procedures are written in detail. Designers select file structures and storage devices, such as magnetic disk, magnetic tape, or even paper files. The procedures they write tell how to process the data and produce the output.

The documents containing the design specifications use many different ways to portray the design—charts, tables, and special symbols—some of which you may have used and others that may be totally new to you. (We will see how all of these are used later in this book.) The detailed design information is passed on to the programming staff so that software development can begin.

Designers are responsible for providing programmers with complete and clearly outlined specifications that state what the software should do. As programming starts, designers are available to answer questions, clarify fuzzy areas, and handle problems that confront the programmers when using the design specifications.

Development of Software

Software developers may install or modify and then install purchased commercial software, or they may write new, custom-designed programs. The decision about which to do depends on the cost of each option, time available to write software, and availability of programmers. Typically in larger organizations, computer programmers (or combination analyst-programmers) are part of the permanent professional staff. In smaller firms, where permanent programmers have not been hired, outside programming services may be retained on a contract basis. As we will see in later chapters, there are several approaches to developing the software.

Programmers are also responsible for documenting the program, including comments that explain both how and why a certain procedure was coded in a specific way. Documentation is essential to test the program and carry on maintenance once the application has been installed.

Systems Testing

During testing, the system is used experimentally to ensure that the software does not fail, i.e., that it will run according to its specifications and in the way users expect it to. Special test data is input for processing, and the results are examined to locate unexpected results. A limited number of users may also be allowed to use the system so analysts can see whether they try to use it in unexpected ways. It is preferable to find these surprises before the organization implements the system and depends on it.

In many organizations, testing is performed by persons other than those who wrote the original programs. Using persons who do not know how certain parts were designed or programmed ensures more complete and unbiased testing and more reliable software.

Implementation

When systems personnel check out and put new equipment into use, train user personnel, install the new application, and construct any files of data needed to use it, we say it is *implemented.*

Depending on the size of the organization that will be involved in using the application and the risk associated with its use, systems developers may choose only to pilot (test) the operation in one area of the firm, say in one department or with just one or two persons. Sometimes they will run both the old and new systems together to compare the results of both. In still other situations, developers will stop use of the old system one day and begin use of the new one the next. As we will be seeing, each implementation strategy has its merits, depending on the business situation in which it is considered. Regardless of the implementation strategy used, developers strive to ensure that the system's initial use is trouble-free.

Once installed, applications are often used for many years. However, both the organization and the users will change. And the environment will be different over weeks and months too. Therefore, the application will undoubtedly be *maintained.* That is, modifications and changes will be made to the software, files, or procedures to meet emerging user requirements. Organization systems and the business environment are in continual change. The information systems should keep pace. In this sense, implementation is an ongoing process.

SUMMARY

Systems analysis and design for business is the process of studying a business situation to see how it operates and whether improvement is needed. The persons who carry out these tasks are called systems analysts. Before any project can be pursued, a systems study is conducted to learn details of the current business situation. Information gathered through the study forms the basis for creating alternative design strategies. Management selects the strategy to pursue.

Virtually all organizations are systems. They interact with their environment through receiving inputs and producing outputs. Systems, which may consist of other smaller systems, called subsystems, operate to accomplish specific purposes. However, the purposes, or goals, are only achieved when control is maintained. In open systems, meaning those that interact with the environment around them, performances are evaluated against standards. The results are fed back for use in adjusting systems activities to improve performances.

Information systems serve business systems through transaction processing and supporting decision makers. Transaction systems assist routine operations, while management reporting systems and decision support systems aid management decision makers. The components of these systems include hardware, software, and data stored in files and data bases. Information systems applications are specific procedures, programs, files, and equipment—all carefully integrated to accomplish specific purposes.

Analysts are responsible for developing information systems so that they are useful to management and employees in business systems. The systems development life cycle is the set of activities analysts and designers carry out to develop and implement an information system. It includes the preliminary investigation, collection of data and determination of requirements, development of prototypes, design of system, development of software, systems testing, and implementation. You should be aware that several of these activities may be going on concurrently. That is, different parts of the system may vary in their degree of completion.

The activities that comprise the systems development life cycle form the basis for the remainder of this book.

CASE STUDY FOR CHAPTER 1
DEVELOPING AN INFORMATION SYSTEM

To give you a good idea of what a full-scale systems development effort looks like, we will examine a sample analysis and design case. This project is typical of many that you will encounter in businesses and organizations. As you read through the description that follows, ask yourself whether you would have anticipated each of the steps described if you were responsible for managing the development. This will improve your understanding of the project.

ORGANIZATION OVERVIEW

The General Supply Company is a distributor of industrial maintenance and cleaning products (soaps, paper goods, mops and brooms, and floor-care machines). Its sales exceed $20 million yearly. The company was established 15 years ago by Bill Green. His hard work and competitive pricing strategies quickly built the firm into a highly successful and profitable business, with customers spanning five states.

The success of General Supply Company is attributed to good management and effective customer service. Bill Green and his key organization officials keep close watch on the prices of the products they sell to be sure to meet or beat competition, while providing reliable merchandise and better service to customers. They also monitor their costs closely and actively pursue suppliers to receive all appropriate discounts and quantity purchase price reductions.

In addition to Bill Green, both Harry Conklin, vice president (and responsible for inventory management), and Jim Venzelo, vice president for sales, have extensive sales experience so that they know what customers want and expect from their suppliers. Bob Wright, controller, has over 15 years experience in accounting. He worked for 8 years in a national public accounting firm, and the remainder of his experience is as controller in private businesses.

The Order Section, consisting of 3 persons, works closely with the 20 salespersons to handle all orders from customers. Two individuals are responsible for maintaining the inventory records and interacting with the warehouse staff of 18 persons. John Jenson is supervisor of the warehouse. The relation of these people to the company organization is summarized in Figure C1.1.

The firm currently uses a minicomputer to process accounts payable and accounts receivable. It also maintains a general ledger system on the system and processes payroll by computer. A separate information systems depart-

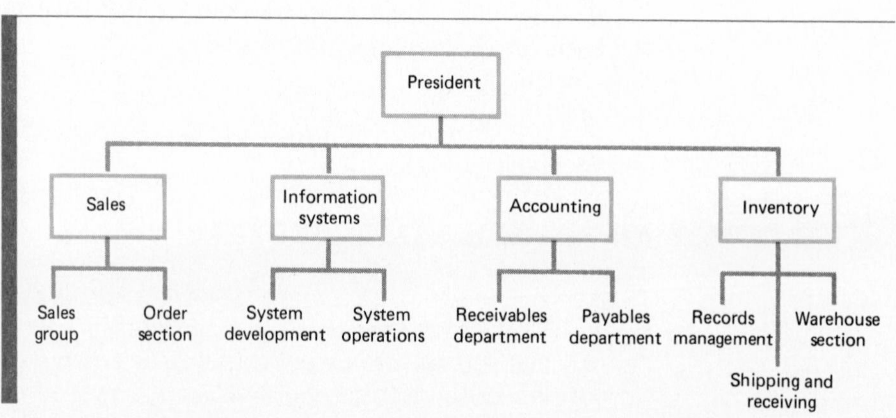

Figure C1.1. Organization chart of general supply company.

ment is responsible for the development of all new applications. The operating group in the department actually runs the computer to process data.

PRELIMINARY INVESTIGATION

Although General Supply Company is a very successful company, a continual problem arises in using correct merchandise prices. When fewer product lines were carried by the firm, many of the salespersons, as well as individuals in the order processing department, knew item prices so well they did not have to look them up in their price book when taking a customer order. Even when suppliers changed the costs to the company, salespersons were able to learn the new prices quickly so that it was unnecessary to use the price book.

As General Supply Company grew, so did the price book, the number of vendors who provide merchandise to the company, and the number of price changes. Sales personnel began to make mistakes in quoting customer prices, as did persons working at the order desk who quoted sales prices to customers placing orders over the telephone. In addition, the size of the price book itself became excessive: it took up nearly 3 feet of shelf space (Figure C1.2). Not only did wrong prices become embarrassing when pointed out by customers, but the company also lost money on some sales. In some cases, prices were too low, and the normal profit margin was not achieved. In other cases, high price quotations lost entire sales; customers bought from a cheaper supplier.

Harry Conklin and Bob Wright decided that the situation had to improve and thought that it was a case where the development of a more streamlined, easy-to-use pricing system was the key. They discussed the matter with company president Bill Green. All decided that a careful investigation should

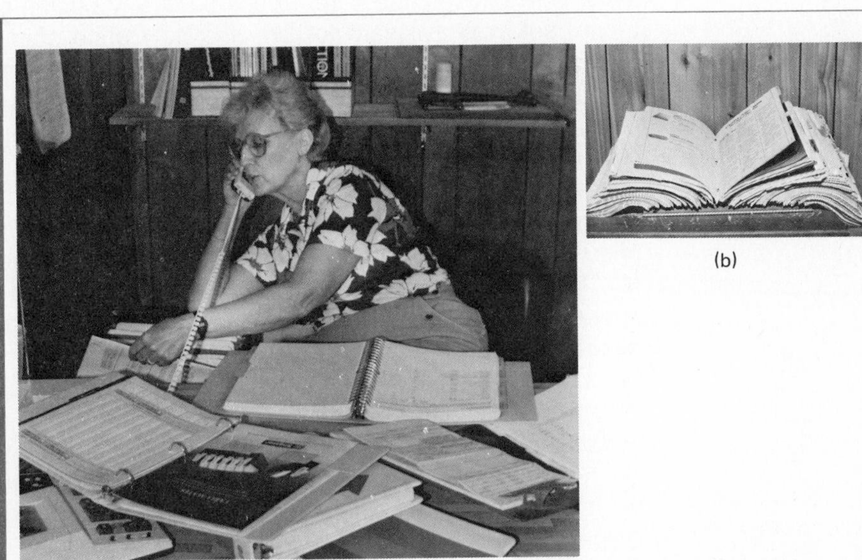

(a) (b)

Figure C1.2. General supply company and price book. (Craig Callan) be made. They contacted the head of the systems department to ask for an investigation of the apparent problems.

After receiving a written request from Bob Wright, John Peterson, manager of the information systems department, assigned an analyst to conduct a preliminary investigation of the current pricing system. The analyst interviewed order desk personnel and several salespersons. The apparent problem was also discussed with Bob Wright and Harry Conklin.

A report, prepared by the investigator and presented jointly to Green, Conklin, and Wright, confirmed that an excessive number of wrong prices were being quoted by staff members. The report also indicated that the pricing mistakes were hurting both sales and profits and suggested that more efficient pricing methods could be developed. A recommendation was made to conduct a more detailed investigation.

The written report was reviewed by management, which raised important questions about the possible approaches for improving the situation. After consideration of the feasibility of developing cost-effective and workable solutions to this serious situation, management approved a detailed investigation and determination of requirements of the pricing process.

DETERMINATION OF REQUIREMENTS

The manager of the information systems department received a written confirmation of the study approval and assigned several systems analysts to the project. Working as a project team, the analysts interviewed key company personnel, including Green, Conklin, Wright, Venzelo, and employees who staffed the order desk. Approximately 10 salespersons were also interviewed. Every member of the sales, order entry, and accounting departments was asked to complete a questionnaire that was developed to acquire facts about sales activities, pricing methods, and order writing. The questionnaire also asked for opinions about the existence of any pricing problems, whether the price book was awkward to use, and how price changes were handled. In addition, the questionnaire solicited suggestions for improvement.

Study team members thought it important to receive firsthand information about pricing activities also. They pulled copies of actual orders from the sales files and studied them for accuracy. In addition, they studied the order handling department to determine if prices were verified before processing the orders and how the price book was used. Samples were taken to compare price changes received from suppliers with those in the price book.

These data collection efforts revealed a great deal about the current operation. Analysts learned that orders arrive in three ways: over the telephone from the customer, through the mail in writing from the salesperson, and over the sales counter at General Supply. Current sales activities result in over 100,000 orders per year, with each order averaging four to five individual items. The company itself handles 6000 different items.

Salespersons have their own price books but, because of size of the price book, do not carry all parts of their price books with them. Some persons even prepare written notes about prices of items sold most frequently, so they can reduce the number of price sheets they carry.

The number of price changes varies. In some periods there are few changes. Other times of the year or when the economy and business environment is changing, prices change frequently. During these times it is not unusual for the company to receive 30 to 40 pages of price changes from individual suppliers in a week. The prices must be changed in each copy of the price book, but, when business is good, delays can result. Even when the price sheets are distributed to the sales staff, in person, or through the mail, there is no guarantee that they will make the changes in their books. At any time, it is conceivable that three salespersons can be pricing the identical product at three different levels.

Being competitive is important to the success of the company. Therefore, all salespersons are authorized to give quantity discounts to customers buying large quantities of items. Management gives guidelines about quantity pricing but leaves the actual quotations to the salespersons. However, Wright indicated that management felt this practice should be treated more uniformly and quantity prices established by the company.

Observing order desk activities revealed that frequently a call from a potential customer caused employees to scramble haphazardly through the price book to find the correct item. Price sheets are organized by supplier, not by product. In addition, each supplier has its own product numbering scheme. This gives anything but uniformity to the situation. There is currently no way to see all the prices on, for example, waxes or floor cleaners. Each item can only be found by searching through the section of the supplier, assuming either customer or employee knows who the supplier is.

The analysts learned that plans were in process to develop an automated inventory system to replace the inventory card system now in use. Although they limited the scope of their study to avoid the inventory area, they did see the importance of developing a uniform product identification system that would serve both pricing and inventory control.

The project team members concluded that a more effective pricing system was needed and discussed several options. One option called for a manual pricing system to be supervised by a pricing supervisor, a new position that would be staffed by hiring another employee. The responsibility of this person would be to post price changes and verify quotes given on all orders. However, because this option would not eliminate cases where salespersons did not carry their price books with them and the number of orders being processed prohibited one individual from verifying each order, it was discarded.

A report was presented to management, recommending that an automated pricing system, using a small computer system that would be dedicated to price handling, be developed. This system would later be integrated with the inventory system so that, when orders were received, inventory would be decreased. However, since a much larger study was necessary to develop the inventory system, which would probably require the acquisition of a large computer system, the analysts felt it inappropriate to postpone the price system until after the inventory application was developed. That could take over 2 years.

The small computer, costing approximately $10,000, could be acquired quickly and installed easily, with no special facilities necessary. In addition, it was estimated that the necessary pricing software could be developed by current systems staff members in 6 weeks. An additional 4 weeks appeared necessary to prepare for implementation, including training the employees who would use the system. No new employees would be hired to operate the revised pricing system.

Management approved and endorsed the recommendations of the project team. The next phase, the design phase, started 1 week later.

DESIGN OF SYSTEM

The systems design activities started by identifying the outputs that would be needed in the new pricing system. Next input requirements, and then file and processing specification were identified.

DESIGN OF OUTPUT

It was quickly evident that two different outputs were necessary. One, a price report, would list all the items sold by General Supply Company and give a description of the product, costs, small-quantity prices, and quantity discount prices. It was determined that the report should be presented in three ways: in order by category of item (such as waxes, floor-care machines, and cleaning supplies), alphabetically by product description, and numerically by identifying product number. Figure C1.3 contains the report specification.

The requirements at the order desk led to the design of a display format that enabled employees to request and retrieve information about a specific product, group of products, or category of products. It was decided that this interaction would be through the computer systems display device; so, rather than a printed report, a display screen was designed to present the output to the user. Figure C1.4 contains the display screen and the instructions to the user that are normally part of the output display.

At several points during output design, the analysts again interviewed sales and order-processing employees to get additional information about systems requirements and usage needs. They also observed order processing several additional times to verify details they had learned about earlier. It is quite common during the design of information systems to do additional data collection and determination of systems requirements. Information systems are not developed in a continual sequence; iterations of activities, such as those described here, are typical.

DESIGN OF INPUT

After output designs were formulated, the project team members turned their attention to the design of the input. It was decided that all the input of data and inquiries use the computer display. Therefore, the development of the input display screens resulted in input screens for instructing the system whether to produce output, accept data input, or permit editing of stored records. Display screens were also designed to input or edit data about individual items (Figure C1.5). In each case, information was included on the display screens to instruct the user how to use the system and enter or receive the necessary pricing and product data.

At several points during the input design stage, sample display screens

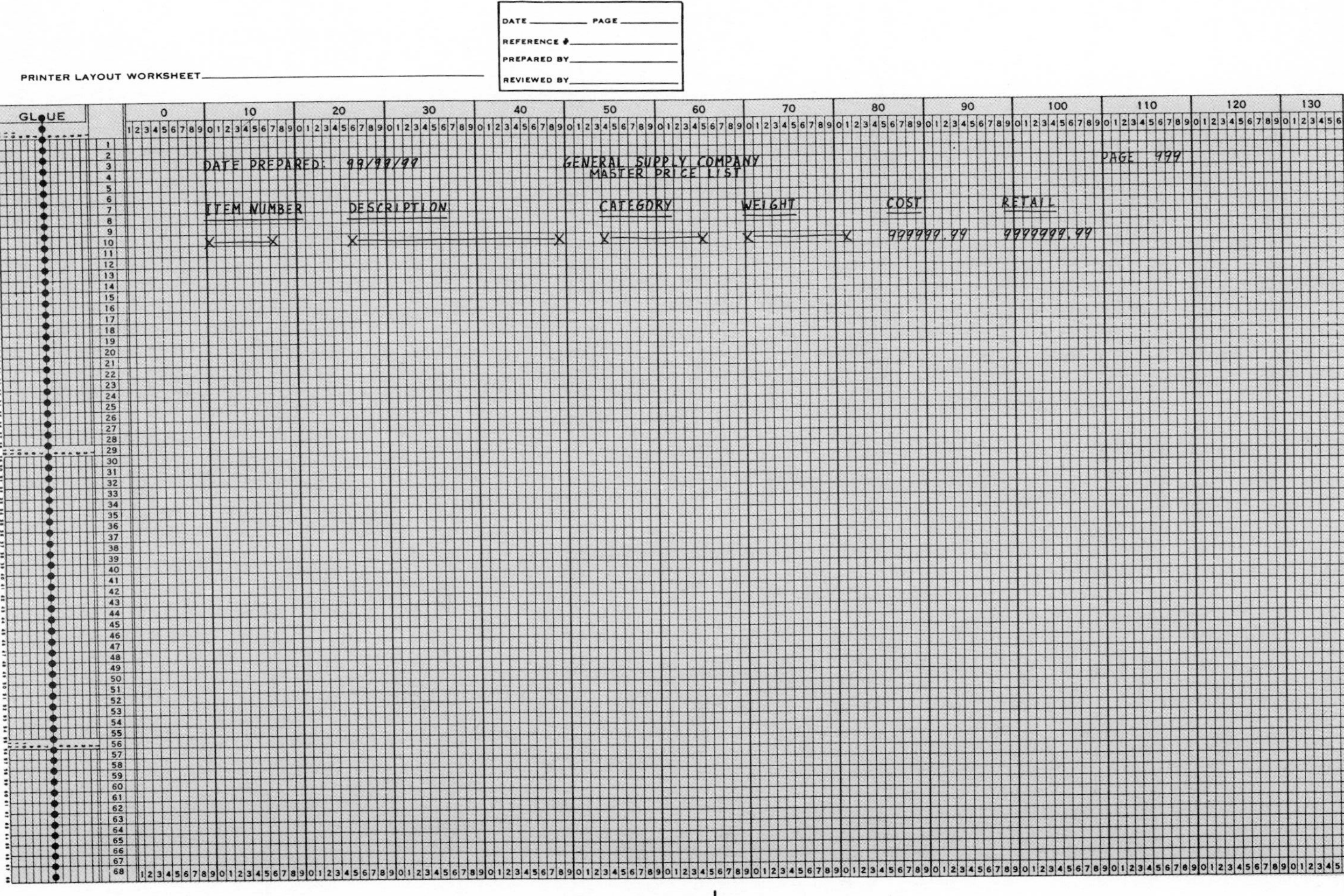

Figure C1.3. Report layout form for pricing report.

```
                                              DATE: JAN 1, 19XX
                  GENERAL SUPPLY COMPANY PRICE SYSTEM
                              MAIN MENU

              1   PRICE LOOK-UP BY ITEM NUMBER
              2   PRICE LOOK-UP BY ITEM DESCRIPTION
              3   PRICE LOOK-UP BY ITEM CATEGORY
              4   DISPLAY LIST OF AVAILABLE REPORTS
              5   ADD NEW ITEM TO FILE
              6   CHANGE PRICES OR ITEM DETAILS (EDIT)
              9   END SESSION

   *** DEPRESS NUMBER KEY CORRESPONDING TO FUNCTION WANTED ***
```

Figure C1.4. Sample display screen listing system capabilities.

were tested by having salespersons and order entry employees use them. The input prototypes produced suggestions about ways to assist the user more effectively and prevent errors from occurring.

DESIGN OF FILES AND FILE PROCESSING

Two files were specified in this design. One, the master file, contains prices, descriptions, and other identifying information on all products handled by the

```
                                              DATE:  JAN 1, 19XX
ITEM NUMBER          ..........
ITEM DESCRIPTION     .......................
CATEGORY             ..........
WEIGHT               ..........
RETAIL PRICE       $ ..........
QUANTITY BREAKS      ......    ......    ......    ......    ......
QUANTITY PRICE     $ ..........  ..........  ..........  ..........  ..........

[S] STORE INFORMATION     [C] CORRECT INFORMATION     [R] RETURN TO MENU
[N] RETRIEVE NEXT ITEM    [P] RETRIEVE PREVIOUS ITEM
```

Figure C1.5. Sample data entry and edit screen.

company. The other, a transaction file, is used to receive price change data entered by employees. It also temporarily holds data about new products, to be entered into the master file. Periodically, the transaction file is processed and its contents used to bring the master file up to date.

An important step in file design involved the development of a new product number system to identify all the items sold by the company. Using the vastly differing identification numbers that vendors assigned to their products was confusing. And, since the planned inventory system required the development of a new number for identification purposes, it was appropriate to carry out such development now.

The analysts, through continual interaction with sales personnel, learned that there were approximately 20 natural groupings of products. Both salespersons and order-processing employees used these group names to describe products. It was evident to the analysts that the groupings should be the basis for the product numbering system. They assigned an identification number to each category and grouped items within each category so that several extra digits could be assigned to make up the entire unique product number. A selected group of salespersons used the product numbers on a test basis. They made some suggestions for change, but largely approved of the product-number design. The newly designed number became the basis for ordering the records in the master file and for handling input and output processing when using the master file.

APPROVAL OF DESIGN

The systems design details were documented to describe what the new pricing application would do. Documentation, describing output, input, files, and processing, was presented to management and users. Having the continual involvement of management and employees throughout the analysis and design activities provided many useful details. However, important questions were still raised when the design was presented. One of the most important addressed the speed of the system for input and retrieval of data. Another concerned cost, and still other questions centered on the ease of use for the system. The analysts not only described their design, but demonstrated how the system would be used, through sample display screens and report samples. The feedback they had gathered, by having people try parts of the design in their normal work, was also important in answering management's questions.

Management approved the design, as well as the time and cost estimates that the project team supplied for the remaining development activities.

DEVELOPMENT OF SOFTWARE

The details of the design were given to programmers who translated the specifications into software. In addition to specifying the programming language, members of the design team provided file descriptions (Figure C1.6), processing procedures, and logic. The input and output layouts further guided the programmers as they turned the logical design into a physically working system.

Estimates of time requirements were developed by the project team and

MASTER FILE SPECIFICATION

APPLICATION NAME: General Supply Company Price Lookup System

DATE ITEM NAME	SIZE	TYPE
ITEM NUMBER	8	Alphanumeric
ITEM DESCRIPTION	24	Alphanumeric
CATEGORY	12	Alphanumeric
WEIGHT	12	Alphanumeric
RETAIL PRICE	9	Numeric, 2 decimals
COST	9	Numeric, 2 decimals
QUANTITY BREAK 1	4	Numeric
QUANTITY BREAK 2	4	Numeric
QUANTITY BREAK 3	4	Numeric
QUANTITY BREAK 4	4	Numeric
QUANTITY PRICE 1	9	Numeric, 2 decimals
QUANTITY PRICE 2	9	Numeric, 2 decimals
QUANTITY PRICE 3	9	Numeric, 2 decimals
QUANTITY PRICE 4	9	Numeric, 2 decimals
	186	

Figure C1.6. Price master file specification.

supplied to the programming manager. During a design review meeting, involving both analysts and programmers, many questions about the design and its translation into software were raised and answered. Some adjustments to the design details were made because of programmer suggestions.

SYSTEMS TESTING

Programmers test portions of the software as they write it. However, before a system is implemented, all the components are tested together to ensure that the entire system, and not just individual components, operates as expected. Each test activity was carefully planned and scheduled, with time allowed to make any necessary corrections.

Systems testing revealed cases where the system would be used in ways the programmers had not expected. It also uncovered certain features that were more error prone than desirable. Before the system was implemented, adjustments were made to the design so that these difficulties were corrected.

IMPLEMENTATION

An implementation date was scheduled and plans made to begin using the new system. Employees of the order-processing department received training on the use of the new system, including providing data, editing data, and running reports. Sales personnel participated in several lively discussions about the new reports and how to use them. Because many were aware of the development and in fact had reviewed some of the system's features during the design stage, there were no surprises during implementation.

Entering the data to build the master files was scheduled over 6 days. Test reports were also run and verified to ensure that no detail was overlooked at any point during the development. Questions from some users resulted in modifications to operating procedures to smooth systems use.

The new pricing was implemented with the full support of all persons involved in its use.

SUMMARY

The pricing system demonstrates the activities involved in bringing a system from the point where management or employees point to a possible need to actual implementation. The activities, although clearly identifiable, overlap. There are iterations of different activities as the need for more details arises. Furthermore, the project team members not only plan their own design but also learn about other planned applications that have a relation to the one they develop.

The activities described in developing the pricing system are typical of those associated with any well-conceived information systems analysis and design. This overview sets the stage to discuss development in greater detail.

KEYWORDS

Administrative user
Application programmer
Closed system
Control
Decision support system
Detailed investigation
Direct user
Feasibility study
Feedback
Implementation
Logical systems design
Management decision system
Management reporting system
Open system
Physical design
Preliminary investigation
Subsystem
System
Systems analysis
Systems analyst
Systems study
Systems testing
Transaction processing system

REVIEW QUESTIONS

1 What is systems analysis? Systems design?
2 What is the purpose of a systems study? Who should it involve? What outcome is expected?
3 How does the work of systems analysts vary from organization to organization? Why does this difference exist?
4 Describe common misconceptions about the intention of systems analysts.
5 Discuss the need for systems analysts to know how to write computer programs.
6 How has the work of systems analysts in business changed? Why is this so?
7 What are information systems? Describe the different types of information systems.
8 Compare the types of information systems users.
9 Describe the concept of systems. Why is this concept so important in organizations? In information systems?
10 What elements of control are important in systems? What is the benefit of knowing about control concepts for the systems analyst?
11 What is the systems development life cycle? Briefly describe the activities that are included.

APPLICATION PROBLEMS FOR CHAPTER 1

1 New England Maintenance Supply Company is a wholesale and retail distributor of commercial cleaning products. It buys supplies in large quantities and sells them to its customers in smaller lots ranging from individual items to multiple cases, depending on the type of item. The firm is well managed, profitable, and has been in business in its current location for 20 years.

The firm's owner is considering developing a computer-based system for managing the inventory that is on hand in the warehouse and for keeping track of the items that are on order. The owner also wants to develop an automated system for processing customer orders when they are received at the order desk by telephone or mail, or through the company salespersons.

The owner does not have any plans for expanding the company's building or its sales territory, which now covers much of the New England area. However, current plans do call for increasing sales in the area the firm now serves, with little change in the product lines carried.

You have been contacted by the company owner and have arranged a meeting to discuss the desired system. You have been given only the information listed above and must prepare for your first meeting with the owner. What questions will you ask to find out about the company, its customers, and the current inventory and order processing procedures? Your purpose is to find out relevant background information to determine whether a detailed systems study should be undertaken.

2 A systems analyst has developed a new system for managing the company's investments in the stocks and bonds markets. The firm regularly has $100 million invested in stocks and bonds and employs several persons whose sole responsibility is management of these funds. They are allowed to buy, sell, and trade stocks as they feel is appropriate to improve the value of the investment or to avoid losses when business conditions change.

The firm's investment managers subscribe to several newsletters and stock market services that provide information on current business trends as well as investment information on many specific securities. However, most of the information the managers use in deciding how to manage their investments is developed through personal contacts or by careful thought and detailed investigations on their part. The investors take pride in their work and are proud of the record of profits they have achieved. Although they acknowledge the pressure of their work and the many arithmetic calculations they must make to decide about a specific investment, they truly love their work.

An automated system has been developed to assist them in their investment activities. It is generally agreed by the systems analysts and the investment brokers that the new system will enable them to improve their performance. However, the brokers feel that it will be difficult to use, as it does not fit their normal pattern of thinking and analysis. Furthermore, the method used by the new computerized system will require quantification of specific stocks or bonds, and this departs from the normal form of analysis based upon the investor's intuition and experience.

a What factors should you consider in formulating a recommendation about whether to implement the new system? The new system will improve performance if it is used, but it will be awkward for the securities analyst to use. They were not involved in the development of the system.

b What is your recommendation? Why?

3 What importance do the following general systems concepts have for the systems analyst who is working on development of a computer-based information system? Give examples of each as they apply to information systems.

a system boundary.

b system environment.

c feedback.

d open system.
e closed system.
f subsystem.
g interface.
h performance standard.

4 Systems analysts are responsible for providing users in organizations with the information systems support they need. In many development situations, the analyst can formulate several different alternatives for meeting user requirements. The alternatives usually will vary in costs, benefits, and level of sophistication. In addition, the way in which computer facilities are integrated into a new system will differ.

Systems analysts must constantly wrestle with one question, that is, which of several system alternatives should they propose to management? Should the analysts always recommend the best system alternative, regardless of cost? Explain your thinking. Be sure to define what "best system" means.

5 A frequent question in university and college computer and information systems programs concerns the level of computer programming expertise that a future systems analyst should develop. Many students who are interested in a career in systems analysis, but who do not like computer programming, state that they do not see the need for developing computer programming expertise. They state that their job as a systems analyst will not require them to write computer programs and they do not therefore need a programming ability.

Other students register for as many computer programming courses as they can. They feel that an effective systems analyst must be proficient in computer programming. Not understanding programming, to them, means limiting their capabilities as a systems analyst.

Discuss these opposing views. Which view do you feel is correct? Explain your reasoning.

CHAPTER 2 GETTING THE PROJECT STARTED

QUESTIONS TO GUIDE YOU THROUGH THE CHAPTER

- For what reasons do users request information systems development?
- Who initiates systems projects? Who decides whether to approve a project request?
- What role do systems analysts play in the approval of information systems projects?
- What role do systems analysts play in the approval of user information systems projects? How does this role vary between organizations?
- What is the purpose of a preliminary investigation and what steps are involved in carrying out the investigation?
- Are there specific tests of a project's feasibility?

The systems study discussed in the preceding chapter described the activities leading to the development and installation of an information system. This chapter looks at one part of the study—how a project begins. Systems analysts do not work on just any project they desire but rather on those requested by managers, employees, even other systems personnel. You will see that, when projects are formally requested, the analysts, under management's direction, conduct a preliminary investigation to learn the reason for the request and gather enough information to respond to the request properly. Some projects are feasible, while others, for various reasons, are not.

When you complete this chapter, you will have a good idea of how new information systems projects get started and the kind of scrutinizing they deserve before management gives a go-ahead.

HOW SYSTEMS PROJECTS ARE BEGUN

Information systems applications originate from virtually all areas of firms and pertain to vastly different business problems. This section discusses the reasons requests are made for systems assistance and the origin of application proposals.

Reasons for Project Initiation

Users request information systems projects for different reasons. Sometimes it is to solve a problem, such as reducing the costs of doing certain tasks or getting better control over how the work is done. Other times it is to improve the efficiency of the work done in their departments. In most cases users have several reasons for requesting information systems help. This section discusses those reasons (Table 2.1).

GREATER PROCESSING SPEED

Since computers process data very quickly, their inherent speed is one reason why people seek the development of systems projects. Computer-based systems can help people by freeing them from many tedious calculations or comparing different items with each other. For example, when you go to the grocery store, you select the items you wish to purchase and take

TABLE 2.1

COMMON REASONS FOR INITIATING INFORMATION SYSTEMS PROJECTS

REASON	EXPLANATION
GREATER PROCESSING SPEED	Using the computer's inherent ability to calculate, sort, and retrieve data and information when greater speed than that of people doing the same tasks is desired.
BETTER ACCURACY AND IMPROVED CONSISTENCY	Carrying out computing steps, including arithmetic, correctly and in the same way each time.
FASTER INFORMATION RETRIEVAL	Locating and retrieving information from storage. Conducting complex searches.
INTEGRATION OF BUSINESS AREAS	Coordinating business activities taking place in separated areas of an organization, through capture and distribution of information.
REDUCED COST	Using computing capability to process data at a lower cost than possible with other methods, while maintaining accuracy and performance levels.
BETTER SECURITY	Safeguarding sensitive and important data in a form that is accessible only to those persons having authorization.

them to the checkout counters. The clerk rings up the price of each item on the cash register or terminal installed at the counter. Imagine how tedious the job would be if the register were missing and how long you would stand in line to pay for your purchase. Neither you nor the store employee would be happy about it.

Today stores are helping the clerks even more, improving speed by installing even better terminals, called point-of-sale systems. They are actually small computers that calculate and store purchase information with amazing speed. They also retrieve price information from memory, such as for products that are sold at special prices. These systems retrieve price details much more quickly than the employee. And, each individual is glad to turn that task over to the computer-aided terminal.

If fast processing is needed, an automated system may be helpful. However, it must be properly designed and used in an effective way—two concerns analysts have in examining user project requests.

BETTER ACCURACY AND IMPROVED CONSISTENCY

Sometimes information systems projects are requested to improve the accuracy of processing data or ensure that a procedure prescribing how to do a specific task is always followed.

The common business practice of processing invoices for payment will demonstrate this reason for project requests (Figure 2.1). Standard procedure calls for accumulating invoices into groups of 50. Before submission for processing, the order takers calculate the total of all invoices in the batch and send this information with the batch. Bookkeepers check each invoice in the group for arithmetic accuracy, retotal the costs, and add shipping costs and sales tax. The total of all invoices is accumulated to generate an overall total for the batch. It in turn is compared with the manual batch total, prepared by the order taker ahead of time. Any differences between the manual batch total and the new total signal that there is an error (such as an arithmetic mistake, unprocessed invoice, or lost invoice).

This example describes a common transaction processing case. The procedure outlined above is not difficult. However, if the procedure of recomputing each invoice and accumulating the running batch total is embedded in a computer program, the bookkeeper can be guided through each step so that nothing is overlooked. Steps will be completed consistently and accurately. Moreover, *all* steps will be carried out for each batch of transactions. Unlike a human, the system will not be distracted by telephone interruptions, lose its place in the batch, or tend to skip the tougher invoices. Management will benefit from the system's consistency. (And the person responsible for processing the invoices may be very glad to have the assistance.)

FASTER INFORMATION RETRIEVAL

Organizations store large amounts of data about their operations, employees, customers, suppliers, and finances. Two concerns are constant: where to store the data and how to retrieve it when it is needed. Data storage becomes more complex if users want to retrieve data in varying ways under different circumstances. Let us consider an example.

Figure 2.1.
Improving accuracy and efficiency of invoice processing using batch control procedures.

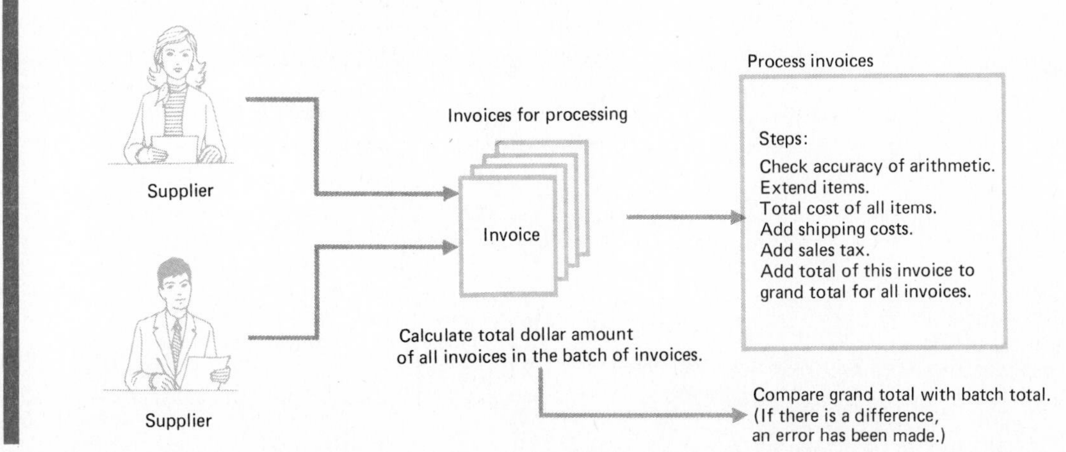

Information about supply and usage of raw materials is vitally important to manufacturing companies. Each part used in manufacturing a typewriter, for example, has a unique identifying part number and item description. In addition, each item is supplied by specific vendors and used in one or more different products. There are many users of the data, such as the production supervisor who manages manufacturing, the buyer who purchases raw materials, or the engineer who determines the set of parts needed to manufacture each product (Figure 2.2). Users need to be able to retrieve information to answer the following representative questions:

1. What materials are supplied by General Steelworks, Inc?
2. Who is the supplier of the 1 horsepower low-noise motor?
3. In what models of typewriters is an automatic tab stop used?
4. How many brand-name identification plates are in stock?
5. What product includes item number X234?

The answers to any of these questions can be found in a business setting that does not use computers, either by having the records manager go through every record in the file for each question or through the relevant file, if several files are kept, each organized to answer a different question. For example, if the file is stored in order of part identification number, to answer question 1 above, the order records clerk must look at every record to see if the supplier is General Steelworks, Inc. (unless a second file, in which records are stored by supplier, is kept). The costs of either option in time and storage space could be so prohibitive that management would

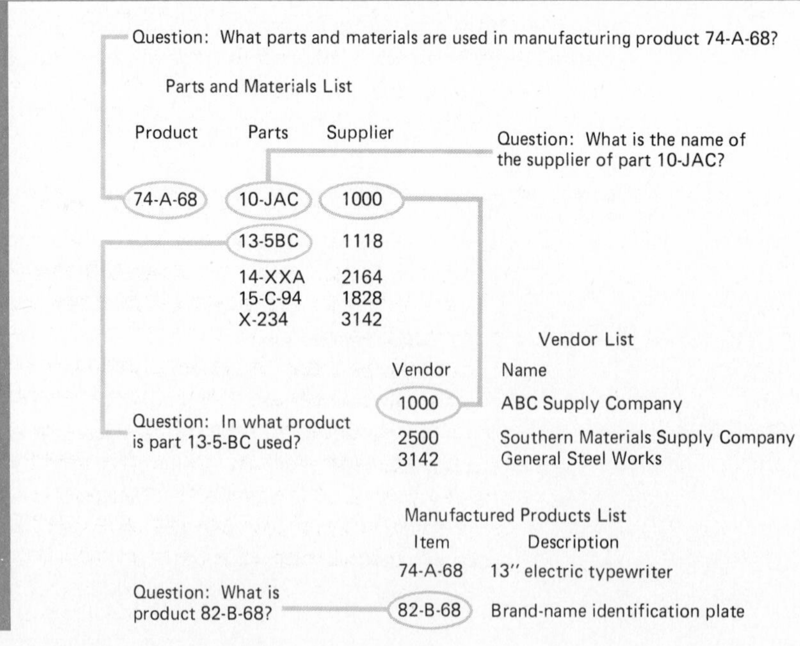

Figure 2.2. Information retrieval requirements in a manufacturing environment.

settle for less information than needed to operate effectively. However, by properly developing a computer-based system, management can ensure it is able to retrieve the answers to any of the above questions quickly.

INTEGRATION OF BUSINESS AREAS

Information systems are used to integrate activities that span several areas of the organization. In many businesses, work done in one area overlaps that taking place in another. Manufacturing, for instance, is dependent on materials ordered by the buyers. To coordinate the tasks better, management often distributes reports about both purchasing and manufacturing to both departments. To take another example, consider the job of coordinating the design and manufacture of a large passenger aircraft (Figure 2.3). One group of designers works on the wings, another on the cabin, another on the tail section, and so on. Still other groups, such as those who design electric, communication, and air supply systems, must know about the other designs before they can complete their tasks. For each task, different materials with varying costs are used. Tremendous coordination is needed to ensure that

Figure 2.3. Information requirements to coordinate aircraft design and manufacture.

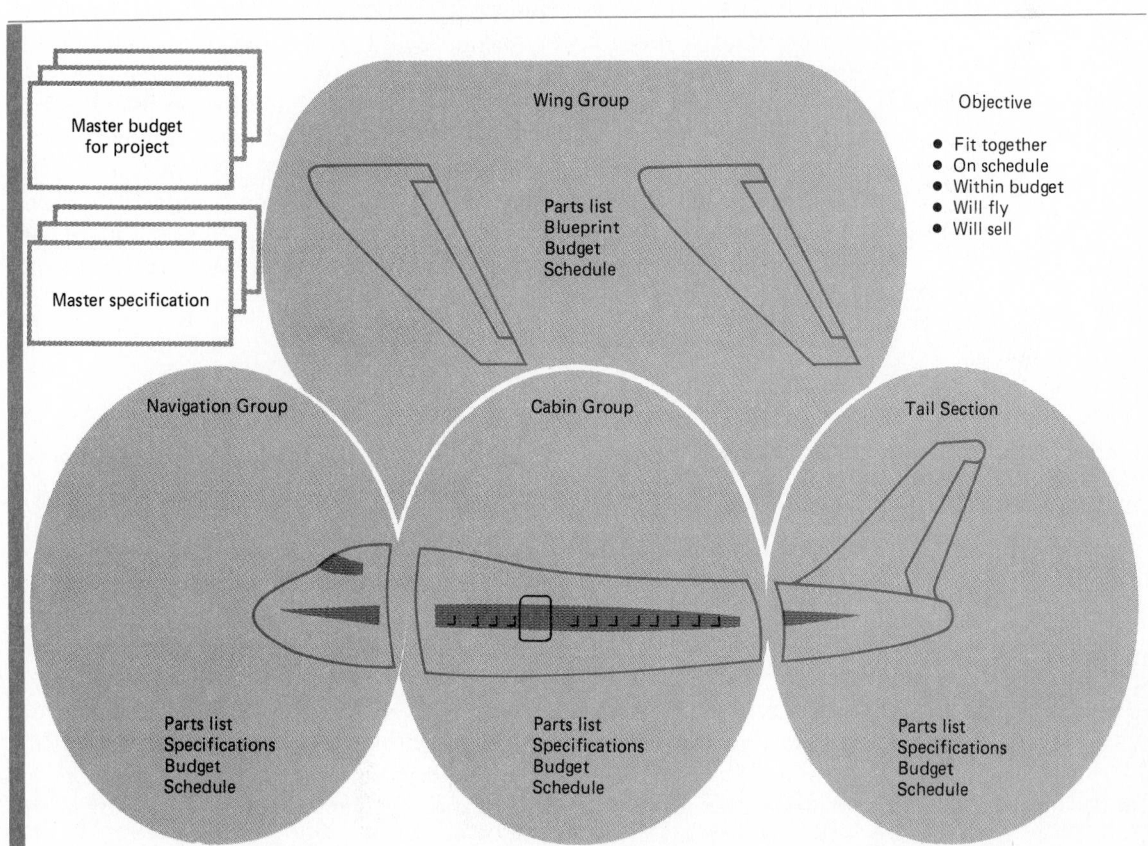

the components will fit together, the project will be completed on schedule, and costs will be in line with expectations. Coordination is made more complex because of the number of days and months it takes to complete the aircraft. Time in this example is a problem because months may pass between some tasks, even though they depend on each other in order for the aircraft to eventually fly. People also join and leave the project. Imagine the information needed to oversee and coordinate this work.

In this case, information systems are helpful to communicate design details between different groups, to maintain essential specifications in an easily accessible location, and to calculate such needed factors as stress and cost levels, from details provided by other groups.

REDUCED COST

Some systems designs will permit the same amount of work to be done at lower costs. Taking advantage of the automatic calculation and retrieval capabilities that can be included in a computer program streamlines procedures. Some of the tasks are taken over by the computer program, and fewer manual tasks remain.

Saving money is attractive to managers. In the past, many people thought that by developing information systems applications, especially highly automated ones, fewer people would be needed. While automated business procedures do change the nature of work—less attractive work can be turned over to computer-based systems—the need for people does not usually lessen. Users should be wary of expecting new applications to reduce personnel requirements. That frequently does not happen. On the other hand, people who are concerned about their jobs, when automated applications are developed, should feel reassured. They seldom are displaced, and in fact their work may become more interesting if the tedious tasks are automated.

BETTER SECURITY

Sometimes the fact that data can be stored in a machine-readable form provides security that would be difficult to achieve in a noncomputer environment. One manufacturing company that produces soaps and cleaners completely automated its manufacturing formulas, as shown in Figure 2.4. Prior to automation, a book of formulas was given to the workers who made the products. The book contained, for each product manufactured, the name and quantity of every ingredient used, along with its cost. Whoever had the book, therefore, had all the scientific knowledge that the company used in its business.

To provide better security, management developed an automated formula information system. All product formulas and costs were stored within the system. Access to this sensitive information was controlled through an intricate password system: one had to know the password to use any of the

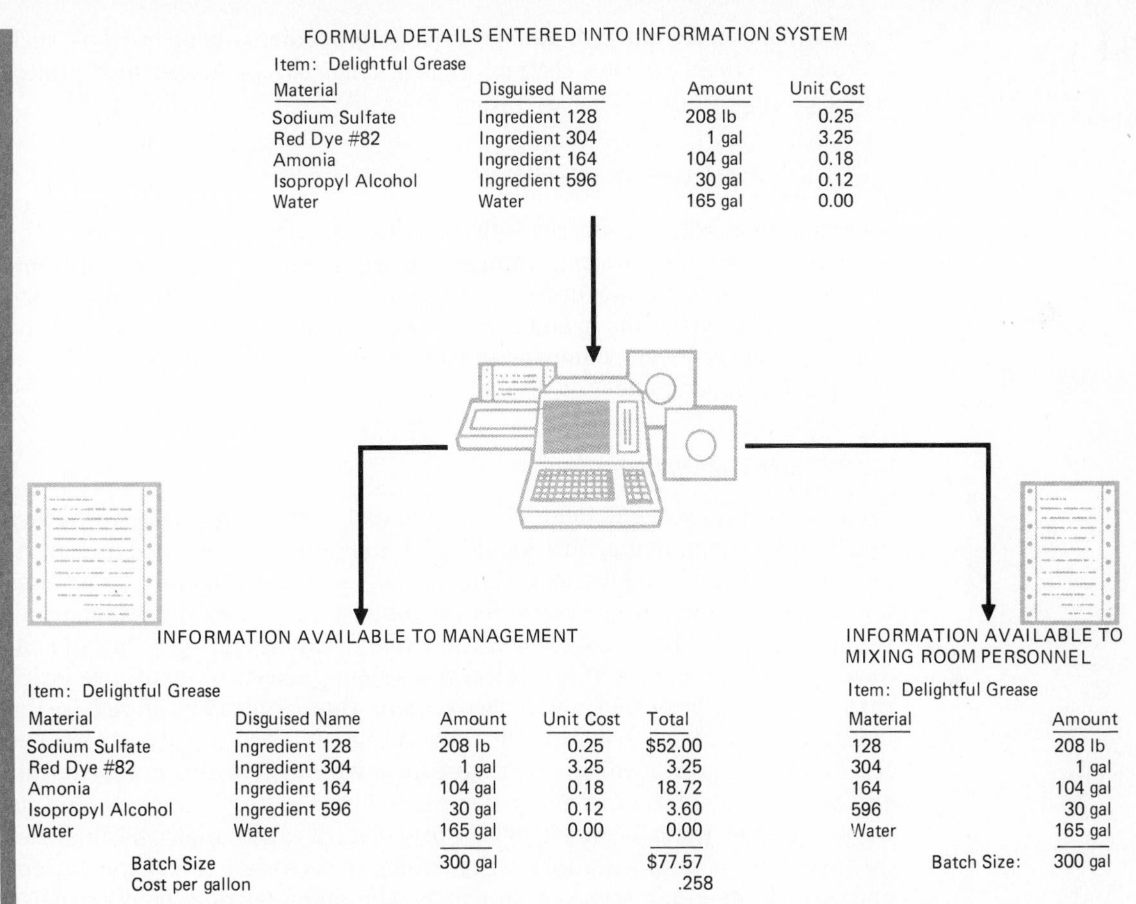

FORMULA DETAILS ENTERED INTO INFORMATION SYSTEM
Item: Delightful Grease
Material | Disguised Name | Amount | Unit Cost
Sodium Sulfate | Ingredient 128 | 208 lb | 0.25
Red Dye #82 | Ingredient 304 | 1 gal | 3.25
Amonia | Ingredient 164 | 104 gal | 0.18
Isopropyl Alcohol | Ingredient 596 | 30 gal | 0.12
Water | Water | 165 gal | 0.00
INFORMATION AVAILABLE TO MANAGEMENT
Item: Delightful Grease
Material | Disguised Name | Amount | Unit Cost | Total
Sodium Sulfate | Ingredient 128 | 208 lb | 0.25 | $52.00
Red Dye #82 | Ingredient 304 | 1 gal | 3.25 | 3.25
Amonia | Ingredient 164 | 104 gal | 0.18 | 18.72
Isopropyl Alcohol | Ingredient 596 | 30 gal | 0.12 | 3.60
Water | Water | 165 gal | 0.00 | 0.00
Batch Size | 300 gal | $77.57
Cost per gallon | .258
INFORMATION AVAILABLE TO MIXING ROOM PERSONNEL
Item: Delightful Grease
Material | Amount
128 | 208 lb
304 | 1 gal
164 | 104 gal
596 | 30 gal
Water | 165 gal
Batch Size: | 300 gal

Figure 2.4. Better security through computer storage and conversion of manufacturing formulas.

information. The printed formula sheets used on the manufacturing floor were changed by the computer to use simple letters in place of complex chemical names. (Barrels of ingredients in the warehouse were relabeled to coincide with the new ingredient letters.) Now the workers do not have the formulas; all information is concealed. The real ingredient names are maintained by the computer. At the same time, fewer errors occur since workers are not confused by the ingredient names. An extra advantage was built in: whenever the cost of an ingredient changes, a list of all products using that ingredient can be quickly retrieved and information about the cost to manufacture those products can be recomputed automatically.

As we indicated earlier, project requests are often submitted for more than one reason. Those listed here demonstrate areas where proposals are most justifiable. Wanting to develop a project to *appear* more advanced or more productive by having an automated system is not adequate justification to invest in computer-based systems. Improvements in operations, such as those outlined in this section, should form the basis for any project request.

Sources of Project Requests

There are four primary sources of project requests. The requestors inside the organization are department managers, senior executives, and systems analysts. In addition, government agencies outside the organization may also request information systems projects. Depending on the origin and the reason for the request, requestors may seek completely new applications or changes in existing ones.

DEPARTMENT MANAGERS

Frequently, persons who deal with day-to-day business activities, whether employees or managers, are looking for assistance *within* their departments. For example, a business manager in a large medical clinic supervises the preparation of patient claim forms submitted to insurance companies, which reimburse the clinic for medical care. The manager sees the tremendous amount of time spent by bookkeepers typing identical insurance forms that ask for information about the patient that is already stored in the individual's medical records. Or they recognize that a patient, who is receiving continual medical treatment for a period of weeks, even months, will require completion of many insurance forms so that the clinic and its physicians get paid for the services provided. Even though the business manager knows preparing insurance claims is necessary to aid the patient and ensure the clinic receives its money, the manager may be dissatisfied with the amount of time the staff devotes to the task, especially when so many of the insurance details (such as patient name, address, age, attending physician, and so on) are already in the patient's records. The bookkeepers also point out the duplication of work and express their wish to be free of the clerical part of insurance handling tasks.

After discussing the insurance problem with administrators in other clinics, the business manager asks the clinic's management committee to approve the development of a computer-based system for preparing insurance forms and maintaining patient records about insurance payments.

The clinic example is typical of cases where managers ask for systems projects. An ongoing activity needs improvement, either to solve a problem (for example, too many errors, excessive costs, or inconsistent work) or to improve the efficiency of a job (preparing insurance claim forms). The manager's request focuses on a specific issue, as the medical example demonstrates.

The department manager requesting a systems project may not consider the interaction between departments, even though the potential for such interaction can be high (Figure 2.5). For example, the manager who requests an inventory forecasting system for ordering materials and sup-

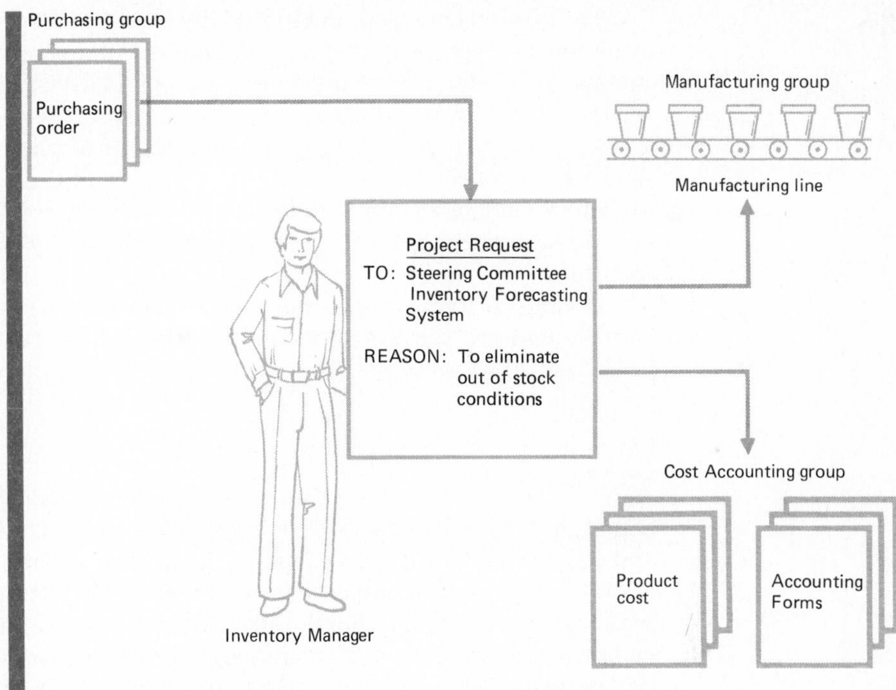

Figure 2.5. Single project requests often affect other areas of the organization.

plies may be looking primarily at ways to eliminate out-of-stock conditions. The request may not discuss the implications in other areas: fewer production problems due to material shortages, lower carrying costs for materials stored, or better prices through quantity purchasing. Yet on an organizationwide basis, the latter may be even more important reasons to consider the project. The point here is that project requests submitted by department managers, although often seeking specific operating assistance, may actually have wider implications that can benefit other departments.

SENIOR EXECUTIVES

Senior executives, such as presidents, board chairpersons, and vice presidents, usually have information about the organization not available to department managers. That information, coupled with the broader responsibilities they assume (they manage entire organizations rather than individual departments), influences the systems project requests they make. For example, the vice president for manufacturing who knows that an additional production plant will be built within 2 years in another city may want to launch a systems project to develop a centralized production planning system—one that will enable management to plan manufacturing at both plants at the same time. This project spans several departments (including manufacturing, inventory control, and purchasing) at two locations and involves many other managers.

The project requests submitted by senior executives are broader in scope than those prepared by department managers. As an additional example, consider how many departments and divisions of an organization are included within the scope of a systems request to design and implement a new corporatewide budget system or a financial planning model. You can see how these projects tend to cut across more of the organization than an inventory control system. Senior executives have more information available to tell them when broad applications, like those listed here, are required.

Because of their scope, multidepartment projects are more difficult to manage and control. Departmental projects, in contrast, are more likely to be successful, especially if the actual users take an active role early in the project.

SYSTEMS ANALYSTS

Sometimes systems analysts see areas where projects should be developed and either write a systems proposal themselves or encourage a manager to allow the writing of a proposal on their behalf. For instance, an analyst, who sees that a university course-registration procedure is slow, error-prone, and generally inefficient, may prepare a project proposal for a new registration system. The request prescribes the development of a system that takes advantage of new easy-to-use data entry terminals to speed registration.

Normally proposals for operating systems, like those for course registration, are prepared by department managers. However, in this case, the analyst has information about new equipment and technology that makes a more efficient registration system possible. The department manager, who is not responsible for being aware of computer technology, may not take the initiative for developing a systems proposal to manage registration better.

Do not forget that systems analysts and developers can also be users themselves. Project management systems, file monitoring packages, or programming library projects are typical of the application projects that systems developers might request.

OUTSIDE GROUPS

Developments outside the organization also lead to project requests. For example, government contractors are required to use special cost accounting systems, having government-stipulated features. (Otherwise they may not be able to receive government business.) You are also probably aware that the Internal Revenue Service requires organizations to keep careful payroll records, accounting for employee income tax withheld. The Internal Revenue Service specifies the format for many of the tax documents that must be prepared; the employer has no choice in the matter.

Quite often new demands from external groups bring about project requests, either for new systems or changes in current ones. Projects originating from this source are just as important as those from within the organization. In some cases, such as when there are strict deadlines imposed by the outside agency, these projects take on a higher priority than ones from, say, department managers.

MANAGING PROJECT REVIEW AND SELECTION

Many more requests for systems development are generated than most firms want or are able to pursue. Some requests are worthwhile; others are not. Before any actual work is done on these requests, someone must decide which ones to pursue and which to reject (perhaps to be solved by other means). The decision to accept or reject a request can be made in a number of different ways and by various members of the organization. The systems analysts are not the final arbiters.

One of the more common methods of reviewing and selecting projects for development is by committee. There are various kinds of committees that select projects. Let us look at three types: the steering committee, information systems committee, and user-group committee.

Steering-Committee Method

In many organizations, *steering committees* (also called operating committees, operating councils, or project selection boards) supervise the review of project proposals. The steering committee typically consists of key managers from various departments of the organization, as well as members of the information systems group. However, the committee is not dominated by systems specialists. In a typical 7- to 10-person committee, membership would consist of the following types of persons:

1 Upper-management members:
Executive vice president
Vice president for manufacturing

2 Departmental management:
Manager of retail marketing
Credit manager

3 Technical managers:
Manager of research and development
Quality control coordinator

4 Information systems group:
Data processing manager
Senior systems analyst

The committee receives proposals and evaluates them. The major responsibility of the committee is to make a decision, but, to do so, it often requires more information than the proposal provides. Therefore, a preliminary investigation is often requested to gather those details. The next section discusses the preliminary investigation.

The steering-committee method brings high respectability and visibility to the review of project proposals. The committee consists of important managers, who have both the responsibility and authority to decide which projects are in the best interest of the entire firm. Because several levels of management are included on the committee, members can have informed discussions on matters relating to day-to-day operations (treating patients, ordering materials, or hiring staff members) and long-range plans (new facilities, new programs) that may have a bearing on the project request. The managers have information and insight about each because they are involved in the work. Systems specialists on the committee provide technical and developmental information, useful in deciding about project management.

This approach is also favored because systems projects are business investments. Management, not systems analysts, or designers, selects projects for development. The decisions therefore are made on the basis of the cost of the project, its benefit to the organization, and the feasibility of accomplishing the development within the limits of information systems technology in the organization.

Information Systems–Committee Method

In some organizations, the responsibility for reviewing project requests is assigned to a committee of managers and analysts in the information systems department. Under this method, all requests for service and development are submitted directly to a review committee within the information systems department. The information systems committee approves or disapproves projects and sets priorities, indicating which projects are most important and should receive early attention.

This method can be used when many requests are for routine services or maintenance on existing applications. For these projects, systems persons have good insight into project requirements. In addition, through work with other projects (and if the organization has a business planning committee that includes the information systems manager), systems developers have access to information about where the firm is moving overall—important for effective project selection.

Sometimes, such as when major equipment decisions must be made or long-term development commitments are needed to undertake a project, the decision authority is shared with senior executives; the executives determine whether a project should proceed. However, sharing project decision authority may confuse users, who want to know how the committee will make the decision about a request. In addition, if top managers and systems-committee members disagree about the merit or priority of a request, the potential conflict is disruptive for handling future project proposals. In still other cases, users may attempt to submit a request directly to senior executives, after it has been disapproved by the information systems committee. If upper management approves the request, it undermines the authority of the information systems committee.

User-Group–Committee Method

In some organizations, the responsibility for project decisions is distributed to the users themselves. Individual departments or divisions hire their own analysts and designers, who handle project selection and carry out development. In effect, departments form their own selection committees, controlling what is developed and when it is implemented.

Although it does take some of the burden from the systems development group, the practice of user committees both choosing and developing systems can have disadvantages for the users. For example, a number of small departments could work independently toward the same goal and unknowingly waste resources and miss the opportunity to coordinate their efforts to plan a shared and integrated information system that could benefit the entire firm. A company's computer facilities can be unduly strained if the systems development team is not made aware of future demands on it that are being planned throughout the firm. Some user groups may find themselves with defective or poorly designed systems that require time and effort to correct, not to mention the time and effort that must be spent undoing any damage caused by the misinformation that such a system could generate. Although user groups may find the decisions of steering committees and information systems committees disappointing at times, the success rate for users taking on the development job is not very encouraging.

Under each of these committee formats, membership often rotates. Individuals serve for, say, 6- or 12-month periods. Membership changes are staggered so that new members are added at different times. The entire membership does not change at one time. The chairperson of each committee should be someone who has previously worked as a committee member. This will ensure experience in reviewing systems proposals and making decisions about project requests.

Other Methods

Other approaches are also tried from time to time, although usually with much less success. Some organizations have management planning committees that propose new projects, which are in turn evaluated by the systems department staff members. This method suffers from lack of user involvement, as well as limited insight into technology.

In still other cases, department managers are able to bypass the organizations' information systems departments to contract with independent systems companies, which will handle all analysis and design work for projects. In this approach it is possible for a department to sponsor the development of a system, while it is completely unknown to the information systems group or upper management that a project is in the making.

The Project Request

The project proposal, submitted by the users or analysts to the project selection committee, is a critical element in launching the systems study. Although the form of such a request varies from firm to firm, there is general agreement on the kind of information that should be provided. Figure 2.6 shows one example of a project request form.

In the proposal the requestor identifies the situation where assistance is needed and gives details. A statement describing the significance of the problem or situation is also useful to the committee members, who want to know why the requestor thinks the project is important.

The committee wants to know whether the project request was triggered by a single event or recurring situation. For example, knowing that there is a continual control problem in processing vendor checks, that costs the company several thousand dollars each year, tells the committee members that the situation is much more important than one where a single check worth $100 was lost. In contrast, a committee reviewing a patient information systems proposal will want to know that a mismarked patient hospital chart nearly resulted in the administration of the wrong drug to a patient. You can see that frequency and significance are both important details in this situation. Although the medical problem only occurred once, it may recur with dangerous results.

There is seldom a clear and simple solution to the problem or situation. Since a preliminary investigation will be conducted to learn more, it is

WHAT IS THE PROBLEM?
Inventory records are frequently inaccurate causing shortages at manufacturing time and variances with cost of goods sold.

DETAILS OF PROBLEM
Quantity on hand and actual physical count records do not always agree—no pattern appears evident. Sometimes quantity on record is high and other times it is low. The quantity should always agree if material requisitions are posted properly. The two buyers usually ensure that enough material has been ordered and delivered on time.

HOW SIGNIFICANT IS THE PROBLEM?
The shortage causes major problems. Sometimes we even have to shut down lines until emergency reorder occurs.
Controller becomes very upset when costs get excessive at end of month. Inventory manager fumes when books are out of agreement with his on-hand actuals.

WHAT DOES USER FEEL IS THE SOLUTION?
We need to automate receiving, withdrawal, inventory records, and posting to eliminate arithmetic errors.

HOW INFORMATION SYSTEMS WILL HELP
Cut down on arithmetic errors; also quicker information.

WHO ELSE KNOWS ABOUT THIS, COULD BE CONTACTED?
Controller
Buyers
Manager of Inventory

Signed by Mfg. Manager

Figure 2.6. Sample information system project request.

helpful if the requestor also provides the names of other people to contact for more information.

PRELIMINARY INVESTIGATION

Proposals submitted to the selection committee are reviewed to identify those projects most beneficial to the organization. The preliminary investigation is carried out by systems analysts, working under the direction of the selection committee. This section discusses the scope of, and the activities composing, the preliminary investigation.

Scope of Study

The purpose of the preliminary investigation is to evaluate project requests. It is *not* a design study, nor does it include the collection of details to describe completely the business system. Rather, the analysts collect information that permits committee members to evaluate the merits of the project request and make an informed judgment about the feasibility of the proposed project.

Analysts working on the preliminary investigation should:

1 Clarify and understand the project request. What is being done? What is required? Why? Is there an underlying cause different from the reason the requestor identifies?
Example: The user justifies a request for developing an accounts receivable system on the basis of wanting faster processing. However, the preliminary investigation may reveal that gaining better control of cash handling outweighs the need for speed. Lost checks, not speed of processing, is the real problem, but the requestor did not describe the need clearly.

2 Determine the size of the project.
Example: Is the request for a course-registration project for new development or modification of the existing system? The investigation to answer this question will also gather details useful in estimating the amount of time and number of people required to develop the project. Since many enhancements are costly, they are treated in the same way as new projects by the project selection committee.

3 Assess costs and benefits of alternative approaches.
Example: What are the estimated costs for developing a patient information system, as requested by the hospital's chief of staff? What expenses will be incurred to train medical and nursing personnel and install the system? Will the proposed system reduce operating costs? Is it likely that the cost of errors will decrease?

4 Determine the technical and operational feasibility of alternative approaches.
Example: Does the necessary technology to link office word processing systems to the main computer exist or can it be acquired? How workable is the request to enable administrative assistants to retrieve sales information

from the main system and insert it directly into typewritten reports prepared on a word processor?

5 Report the findings to management, with recommendations outlining the acceptance or rejection of the proposal.
Example: A proposal for the installation of an order entry system should be modified to allow salespersons to submit orders through ordinary telephone connections directly into the computer. The modification will improve the usefulness of the system and increase the financial benefits to the organization.

Conducting the Investigation

The data that the analysts collect during preliminary investigations is gathered through two primary methods: the review of documents and interview of selected company personnel.

REVIEWING ORGANIZATION DOCUMENTS

The analysts conducting the investigation first learn about the section of the organization involved in, or affected by, the project. For example, to review an inventory systems proposal, it is best to know first how the inventory department operates and who the managers and supervisors are. Analysts can usually learn these details by examining organization charts (see Chapter 1) and studying written operating procedures. The procedures describe how the inventory process should operate and identify the most important steps involved in receiving, managing, and dispensing stock.

CONDUCTING INTERVIEWS

Written documents tell the analysts how the systems should operate, but they may not include enough detail to decide about the merits of a systems proposal. Nor do they present user views about current operations. To learn these details, analysts use interviews.

In interviews, analysts discuss systems features to learn more facts about the nature of the project request and the reason for submitting it. Therefore, they must be sure to emphasize the request and the problem it addresses in their interviews. In other words, they should collect details that further explain the nature of the project request and show whether assistance is merited economically, operationally, and technically. This is not the time to be working out a solution to the situation, that comes later during the detailed investigation.

Usually preliminary investigation interviews involve only management and supervisory personnel.

Testing Project Feasibility

The data collection that occurs during preliminary investigations examines project *feasibility,* the likelihood the system will be beneficial to the organization. Three tests of feasibility are studied: operational, technical, and financial. All are equally important.

OPERATIONAL FEASIBILITY

Proposed projects are of course beneficial only if they can be turned into information systems that will meet the organization's operating requirements. Simply stated, this test of feasibility asks if the system will work when developed and installed? Are there major barriers to implementation? Here are questions that will help test the operational feasibility of a project:

- Is there sufficient support for the project from management? From users? If the current system is well liked and used to the extent that persons will not see reasons for a change, there may be resistance.
- Are current business methods acceptable to the users? If they are not, users may welcome a change that will bring about a more operational and useful system.
- Have the users been involved in the planning and development of the project? Early involvement reduces the chances of resistance to the system and change in general and increases the likelihood of successful projects.
- Will the proposed system cause harm:
  Will the system produce poorer results in any respect or area?
  Will loss of control result in any area?
  Will accessibility of information be lost?
  Will individual performance be poorer after implementation than before?
  Will customers be affected in an undesirable way?
  Will it slow performance in any areas?

Issues that are relatively small and seem just minor irritants in the beginning have ways of growing into major problems after implementation. Therefore, all operational aspects must be considered carefully.

TECHNICAL FEASIBILITY

The technical issues usually raised during the feasibility stage of the investigation are:

1. Does the necessary technology exist (can it be acquired) to do what is suggested?
2. Does the proposed equipment have the technical capacity to hold the data required to use the new system?
3. Will the proposed system and components provide adequate responses to inquiries, regardless of the number or location of users?
4. Can the system be expanded if developed?

5 Are there technical guarantees of accuracy, reliability, ease of access, and data security?

For example, if the proposal includes a printer that prints at the rate of 15,000 lines per minute, a brief search shows that this is technically feasible. (Whether it should be included in the configuration because of its cost is an economic decision.) On the other hand, if a user is requesting audio input to write, read, and change stored data, the proposal may not be technically feasible.

FINANCIAL AND ECONOMIC FEASIBILITY

A system that can be developed technically and will be used if installed must still be a good investment for the organization. That is, financial benefits must equal or exceed the financial costs. The economic and financial questions raised by analysts during the preliminary investigation seek estimates of:

1 The cost to conduct a full systems investigation
2 The cost of hardware and software for the class of application being considered
3 The benefits in the form of reduced costs or fewer costly errors
4 The cost if nothing changes (the system is not developed)

To be judged feasible, a project proposal must pass all these tests. Otherwise, it is not a feasible project. For example, a personnel record system that is financially feasible and operationally attractive is not feasible if the necessary technology does not exist. Or a medical system which can be developed at reasonable costs but which nurses will avoid using cannot be judged operationally feasible.

Handling Infeasible Projects

Not all projects submitted for evaluation and review are judged acceptable. What happens to them?

Requests not passing feasibility tests are not pursued further, unless the originators rework them and resubmit them as new proposals. In some cases, only part of the project is actually unworkable. In these instances, the selection committee may decide to combine the workable part of the project with another feasible proposal.

In still other cases, the committee may return the project with the suggestion that certain manual procedures used in the department be modified to improve operations. Sometimes preliminary investigations produce enough new information to suggest that improvements in management and supervision are really the solutions to reported problems, not the development of information systems.

SUMMARY

Information systems projects originate for many reasons: to achieve greater speed in processing data, better accuracy and improved consistency, faster information retrieval, integration of business areas, reduced cost, and better security. The sources vary. Project proposals originate with department managers, senior executives, and systems analysts. Sometimes the real origin is an outside source, such as a government agency, which stipulates a systems requirement the organization must meet.

Since the users may submit many project requests, organizations must have ways of evaluating the requests and selecting the best proposals for development. Three committee formats are in widespread use: the steering committee (a management committee with limited membership from the systems department), information systems committee (membership from within the systems department), and user-group committee (user-selected personnel who work independently of the systems department).

The project requests, which describe the organization systems involved and the reasons for wanting the development projects, are reviewed by the selection committee. To evaluate a request properly, the committee asks analysts to conduct a preliminary investigation that clarifies the request and gathers additional details about the business system. The preliminary investigation is aimed at clarifying the technical, operational, and economic feasibility of the request. While analysts gather the details, the decision whether to proceed lies with the selection committee. Unless this committee approves, analysts do not undertake the development.

CASE STUDY FOR CHAPTER 2
VALLEY INDUSTRIES

Valley Industries is a manufacturing firm specializing in the design and production of small electric components and parts. From its world headquarters in upstate New York, Valley ships to locations around the globe.

The company was started 7 years ago by a group of business persons who saw an unfilled niche in the electronics market. Working with guidance from various manufacturers in such markets as the automotive, aircraft, sound, and electronic test-equipment industries, these investors launched Valley from a 10,000-square-foot rented building. Today the firm operates a modern 50,000-square-foot manufacturing facility and is considering opening an additional one within 100 miles.

VALLEY MANAGEMENT

Valley Industries was founded by John Severski, who serves as its president and chairman of the operating committee. He is a businessman of wide interests, who has come to know electronics manufacturing from the bottom up. Starting as a manufacturing worker while still in high school, Severski worked with several different national firms while still in his twenties. His experience soon enabled him to see opportunities that were not being pursued by his employers. He decided to set up his own firm and arranged the necessary financial backing to launch Valley Industries. Today he presides over a firm with approximately $10 million in annual sales. Severski is the majority owner and the only one who is actually active in the day-to-day operations of the firm. Figure C2.1 describes current organization and staffing.

The director of operations is Harry Jacobson. He has been with the firm for the past 5 years. His background is in marketing and manufacturing. During the 30 years of his experience, Jacobson has worked with firms in electronics and hydraulics industries. He is actually the person who has control of the business. All relationships with the manufacturer's representatives who distribute Valley's product line, are established and monitored by Jacobson. He has line responsibility for all cost and profit centers of the firm.

The chief engineer, Jim Olson, directly oversees the manufacturing operation. He reports to Jacobson. All decisions about production scheduling, materials purchasing, and shipping are handled by Olson and his two assistants.

In addition to supervising manufacturing, Olson is also responsible for the design of the products manufactured by the firm. Of the 1000 different items produced, approximately 75 percent were designed by Jacobson. He thus

Figure C2.1. Organization chart for Valley Industries.

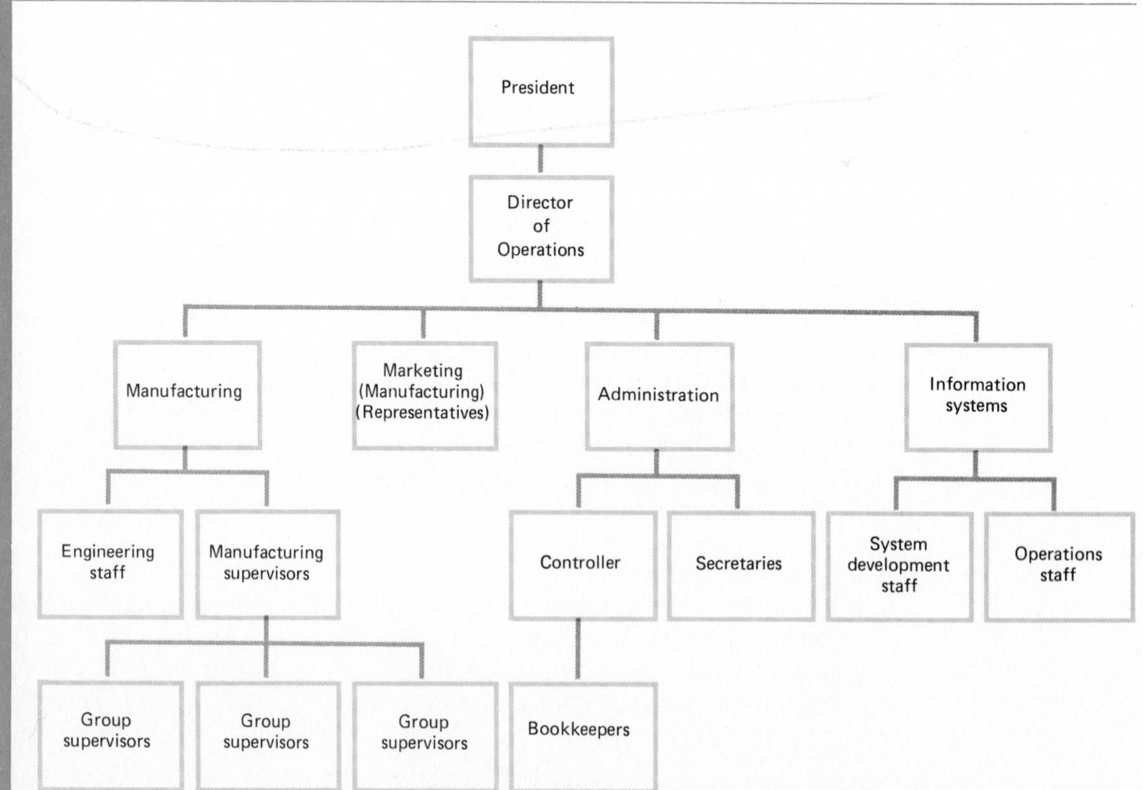

knows the product line very well. Customers and marketing representatives regularly call Olson for technical information about products. This may include details of operating tolerances, capacities, failure rates, or design specifications. Information about possible modifications is also directed to Olson.

The manufacturing force consists of 100 persons. The work force is broken into several production groups, each with a supervisor and assistant supervisor. They have direct responsibility for assigning hourly manufacturing personnel to specific machines and production orders. Each shop works a 5-day week, although overtime is common as large backlogs do develop from time to time. The firm is growing at a rate of about 40 percent per year. Hence hiring may not always keep pace with expanded orders.

All sales of the company's products are made by manufacturer's representatives. Eight firms sell the products throughout North America and Europe. They receive a commission for each sale, but no income if no sales are made. Because of its successful use of manufacturer's representatives, Valley does not have a permanent paid marketing staff.

The office staff consists of the controller, Marjorie Carbo, and three bookkeepers who handle all payables, receivables, and cash receipts. Ms. Carbo reports officially to Mr. Jacobson but also works closely with Jim Olson. In addition, two secretaries handle all correspondence and office responsibilities for Mr. Severski and Mr. Jacobson.

ORDER ENTRY AND INVOICING

The rapid growth of Valley Industries has brought about a need to examine the current order entry and invoicing processes used by the firm. The high volume of orders, coupled with the need for meeting definite shipping dates, is a matter of great importance to both Jacobson and Olson. Both are worried that, as business expands, they will lose control of orders and receivables. They have computer-based systems for accounts payable, accounts receivable, and employee payroll processing and are highly dependent on these sytems. The manufacturing and inventory records are maintained by an effective and efficient manual system.

Jim Olson requested a study of the firm's order entry and invoicing operations to determine the suitability for automating the processing of sales orders. He thinks that such an investment is justifiable, but wants to have a feasibility assessment conducted to determine the best way to develop the system. But, at the same time, Jacobson believes the current system is probably working relatively well. Most problems that occur are usually because of the high volume or increased growth that the firm is encountering.

FINANCES AND REVENUES

Current sales are approximately $10 million. Current capacity of the firm will enable it to attain approximately $20 million, with a single shift at each plant. Additional shifts could increase this capacity two- or three-fold.

Current interest rates make prediction difficult. The fluctuation of bank interest rates at high levels is unprecedented. Although it is expected that growth projections will be sustained, at least for the upcoming 2 years or so, it is possible that new government tax and investment policies could cause abrupt changes.

Materials and labor costs comprise the majority of expenses for the products produced. Administrative overhead is about 10 percent. The management team is a lean group that does not add excessively to overhead. Executive salaries are between $35,000 and $75,000. Administrative staff salaries average $17,000 (plus fringe benefits). Two full-time persons handle all order entry and receivables.

CONCERN OVER ORDER PROCESSING

Order processing is important. It must be carried out in a timely accurate fashion. Currently, orders are being lost ("Always seems to be at the wrong time too," according to Severski.) Backlogs build up for the two persons who process orders. The order system must permit capturing all relevant details about orders as they arrive at the facility. This should be done quickly and efficiently. At the same time, it should make it possible to track orders in process.

Management knows that customers complain when orders are lost or delayed. Fortunately, they feel, the loss rate is not excessive, but, when losses do occur, they must be dealt with quickly.

Employees who handle orders and invoicing do not like the backlog that builds up. Usually overtime is not necessary to reduce the backlog. Sometimes other work is delayed in order to catch up on "book work."

Valley officials have not placed any specific constraints on a study of ways to improve the order entry and invoicing system. They have indicated that anything that seems reasonable will be considered. Certainly a $2000 or $3000 study is feasible. However, $40,000 or $50,000 for a feasibility study or systems investigation would probably be considered excessive.

DATA PROCESSING AT VALLEY

Although it does use automation, Valley does not have a highly automated processing system for handling orders or business processing. The clerical staff is effective and reliable. Because of the relatively small size of the firm when it was formed, computer information systems did not seem justifiable. However, as it grew, it acquired an IBM System/34 for accounting operations. The system is currently in use.

Along with Valley's growth, there has been tremendous innovation in the computer industry, particularly at the microcomputer level. Microcomputers, small enough to fit on a desk top but powerful enough to process large volumes of data, have become available for costs ranging from $10,000 to $20,000. Personal computers of mass market appeal are even available for entry-level costs of less than $2000.

With the advent of microcomputers, Valley acquired its small computer, a TRS-80 Model II business computer. Largely with the strong support of Jim Olson, the system was installed to help in basic engineering functions (such as power and electrical calculations). It was not long before Olson was considering other uses for the system, including an order entry operation.

Soon a second system was purchased for use by Harry Jacobson. This system has been used primarily for word processing and correspondence handling. Jacobson does much of his own correspondence with customers and manufacturer's representatives alike.

Even the president, John Severski, purchased his own microcomputer, an Osborne I.

The information systems department is headed by Joyce Randal, who has a strong background in this field as well as business experience. Her experience, after graduation from college, first as an application programmer

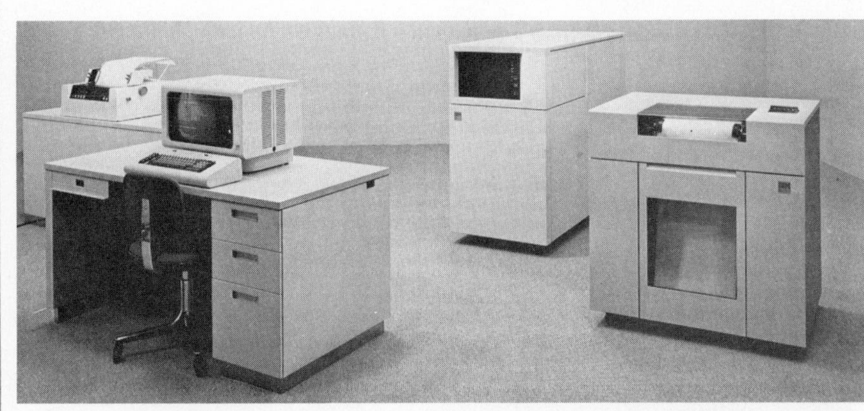

(a)

(b)

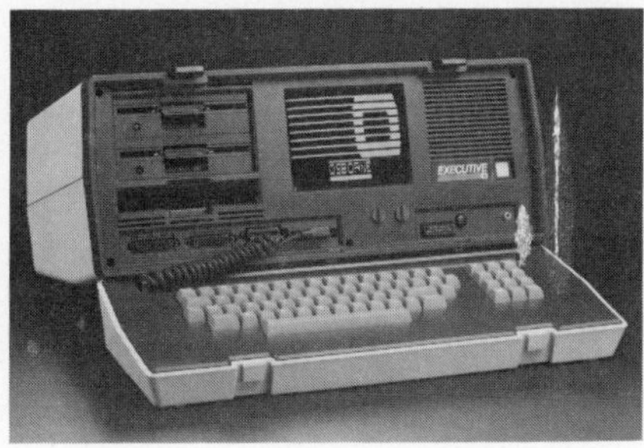

(c)

Figure C2.2. Computer equipment in use by Valley Industries; (*a*) IBM System 34 (Courtesy of International Business Machines Corporation), (*b*) TRS-80 Model 12 (Courtesy of Radio Shack, A Division of Tandy Corporation), (*c*) Osborne 1 Executive, Portable Computer (Courtesy of Osborne Computer, Corporation).

IBM System/34
- 64K Memory
- 2 double-density double-sided diskettes of 1.2M bytes capacity each (8 inch)
- 3 5251 CRT Displays
- 1 400 line per minute printer

TRS 80 Business Microcomputer
- 64K main memory with built-in disk drive of 600K capacity (8 inch)
- 3 Auxiliary Disk Drives; 600K capacity each
- 1 120 CPS dot matrix printer

TRS 80 Business Microcomputer
- 64K main memory with built-in disk drive of 600K capacity (8 inch)
- 1 Auxiliary disk drive; 600K capacity
- 1 55 CPS letter quality character printer

Osborne Portable Microcomputer
- 64K main memory
- 2 built-in disk drives of 90K capacity each (5 1/4 inch)

VALLEY INDUSTRIES
1200 Main Street
Binghamton, New York 13901

DATE: November 10, 198X

TO: Mr. Jim Olson, Chief Engineer

FROM: Mr. John Severski, President

SUBJECT: Order Entry and Invoicing System Study

I have received your memo and request outlining the need for a study of our order processing and invoicing system. Your concern in light of our rapid growth and dependence on reliable, accurate, and rapid order handling is shared by many of us. While I think there are some distinct advantages to be gained by automation and use of computing in this process, I do not wish to prejudge this.

I am asking Joyce Randal to conduct a preliminary investigation, studying the efficiency of our current system in light of planned operation and expansion. Based on the findings of this study, we will make a determination of whether a new system is feasible and should be pursued. The decision will be made by the management group here at Valley with substantial involvement of Ms. Randal and her senior analyst.

JS:jb

cc: Joyce Randal, Director of Information Systems
Harry Jacobson, Director of Operations

Figure C2.3. Memorandum to chief enginner.

VALLEY INDUSTRIES
1200 Main Street
Binghamton, New York 13901

DATE: November 10, 198X

TO: Mr. John Severski, President

FROM: Mr. Jim Olson, Chief Engineer

SUBJECT: Review of Order Entry/Invoicing System

I am concerned about the order processing system we now use to handle orders received from our customers and marketing representatives. As you know, we have ongoing backlog problems and from time to time will be unable to track a specific order through processing. I suspect a large part of the reason is due to our increased volume of business and therefore more orders to handle. It does not appear to be a staff or personnel problem.

Since we are fully dependent on our order processing system as it operates from the time an order is received until the invoice is processed by our accounts receivable group, it merits investigation. I am asking specifically for authorization of a study to determine if and how we should improve this system to meet our future demand. The possibility of opening the additional manufacturing facility in the near future is an additional factor to consider.

I would like to see the study conducted as soon as possible.

JO:jb

Figure C2.4. Memorandum to president.

and then as a systems analyst, gives her a good perspective not only on system development as a whole but also on user needs. Prior to college, she was a marketing representative for a major garment manufacturer for nearly 5 years.

Randal's staff of two analysts, two programmers, and three systems operators is always busy, but seems to be able to meet current demands. Like many information systems groups, the analysts and programmers devote a substantial amount of time to the maintenance and modification of existing systems. Valley management works closely with Randal to assess project priorities and select applications for development.

Computer data processing has been an interesting, if not major, development at Valley. Figure C2.2 lists the computer equipment presently used by the firm. Jim Olson has taken full responsibility for all programming and software development. Some software has been purchased, but most has been developed by Jorgenson. Recently he hired Mary Williams to handle the data entry work. Olson would like to automate more of the record keeping of Valley. His memo to Severski, outlining the need for the undertaking of a thorough computer study, is attached in Figure C2.3. Severski's approval of a study is attached in Figure C2.4.

KEYWORDS

Economic feasibility
Feasibility test
Information systems committee
Operational feasibility
Preliminary investigation
Project request
Steering committee
Technical feasibility
User-group committee

REVIEW QUESTIONS

1 For what reasons are information systems projects begun? Who are the initiators?
2 For each reason listed in question 1, describe *how* automation will improve the activity or deal with the problem identified.
3 Discuss the distinctions between projects submitted by managers, senior executives, and systems personnel. Why do these differences occur?
4 How much should groups outside the organization influence systems projects? Explain.
5 Distinguish between committee formats for project selection. What advantages and disadvantages does each offer? What is the responsibility of each?
6 What is the purpose of a preliminary investigation? What outcome is expected? Who carries out this investigation? On what basis is it initiated?
7 What steps are taken by investigators doing the preliminary investigation? For what purpose are they taken?
8 Projects may be deemed feasible after passing what tests? Briefly describe the meaning and purpose of each one.
9 What is the least-common reason for finding a project infeasible? Why do you suppose this is the case?
10 What is an infeasible project? How are infeasible projects handled?

APPLICATION PROBLEMS FOR CHAPTER 2

1 Management of Tate industries has recently established a steering committee to guide the firm in its continued development of information systems applications. The committee consists of representatives from each of the major departments of the firm (e.g., shipping, sales, and accounting), a member from the executive (top management) committee, the manager of information systems, and two systems analysts/designers. It is the responsibility of the committee to either approve or disapprove requests for information systems applications development and to set development priorities for approved project requests. All approved projects are supposed to be in line with the operating policies and growth objectives of the firm.

The company has a policy of charging user departments with the costs to develop any information systems projects. That is, users must pay for all applications developments out of their budgets. This includes the time analysts and designers spend on the project along with computer time and supplies expense. (They do not, however, assume the expenses of its running and of its application after it is developed and implemented.) All department managers have agreed to this policy.

However, in the course of establishing the responsibilities and authority of the steering committee, the users have disagreed with upper level management about whether the committee should be able to approve or disapprove development of applications projects. Many users feel that if they are willing to pay for the development of an application and are able to do so out of their budget, they should be allowed to have the application developed. They acknowledge the authority of the committee to arrange projects into an order for development based on priority, but they question the authority of the committee to disapprove any project that is technically and operationally feasible.

The users also feel that even though systems development group members need to be on the committee to advise other committee members about technical problems, other projects under development, and general information systems issues, they should not be allowed to vote on approval of project requests that are technically feasible. The users rationalize that since the information systems persons on the committee neither have to pay for the project nor will be using the system if it is developed, they should not be able to sway the decision by their vote on whether a project is a technically feasible one.

a Should all applications that are technically and operationally feasible be developed if the users are willing to pay the price? In other words, since the cost of developing the project is always to be paid by the users requesting its development, should the steering committee have the authority to disapprove projects? Why or why not? Explain.

b Discuss the issue of members of the information systems group having a vote on whether to approve a technically and operationally feasible project for development? Since development costs will be paid by the users, should systems group members be full-fledged members of the committee or only advisors to the management representatives who make up the remainder of the committee?

2 For each of the following situations indicate whether each is a candidate for assistance through computer-based information systems and what the most likely reason is:

a Managing the schedule and use of materials and labor required for development of a large metropolitan skyscraper

b Formulating the price quotation on a large landscaping project that will involve hundreds of trees and shrubs and a work crew of six persons who will require one calendar week to complete the project

c A system that will provide the capability to look up the price for any of over 10,000 different items sold in a food store d Using a portable computer at an automobile racing track to calculate tire wear and fuel usage, both dependent on track conditions, weather and temperature, and racing speed

e Maintaining your personal checkbook balance where the number of deposits per month is less than six and the checks written are less than 20

f Managing airline reservations for each specific flight where space is controlled and ticket prices are determined by seat location and date of purchase

3 The steering committee for the information systems function in a firm is evaluating a proposal for an on-line order entry system. The current computer system has sufficient memory space and processing availability to handle the new application without purchasing additional capacity. However, special terminals would have to be acquired to support the order entry process. These terminals would cost approximately $2500 each. It is anticipated that eight such terminals would be required. They are in sufficient supply from vendors so that delivery of the terminals in a reasonable time would be no problem.

The computer on which the order entry system is to be run if developed, already has a communications processing package. But, the proposed system would require an upgraded version of this package, available at a cost of approximately $100 per month.

Personnel to develop the application software for the proposed project will be drawn from the current staff. It is estimated that six persons, working for a 9-month period, would be needed to develop the system. The average salary for the system developers who would be selected to work on the proposed project is $24,000 per year (the benefit package for these employees costs the firm an additional 25 percent per person per year).

The firm is a leader in its industry for its use of information systems at the management level. Many sophisticated systems have been developed and implemented by the information systems staff. The group has received many favorable reviews by the management of the organization. In addition, representatives from other businesses in the industry have visited the firm to examine some of its management systems.

The order entry operation has been done manually for many years. Orders are prepared on handwritten sales forms by order writers. When completed, the order forms are reviewed for errors, extended, and totaled. The staff doing these jobs is very effective. However, a 3 percent error rate is still common. When errors occur, they are usually either wrong order quantities or wrong prices. On some occasions, items requested by customers are missed completely, although this is rare. When it does happen, the customers notify the firm of the problem and it is immediately rectified.

The order writers are proud of the job they do and have said that even though errors do sometimes occur, they cannot be avoided. Thus, they do not feel that there is any problem and that management should not be concerned. The order writers are not aware that an automated system has been proposed.

Management of the firm is expecting a significant increase in sales and orders from customers due to a combination of more aggressive marketing plans and a line of new products. Thus, it feels that the present order writing staff would have to be expanded by approximately 30 percent to meet order entry demands. However, if an automated system is developed, the current staff of eight would be able to handle the increased workload; no new order writers would have to be hired. (Note, these staff members cost the firm an average of $14,000 per year for salaries and benefits.)

a Based on the information provided, analyze and discuss the proposal in terms of its feasibility. Using only the information provided, decide whether the system should be pursued.

b What other specific information would you need to do a more extensive feasibility study for this proposal? For each item of information you identify, also indicate who should provide the information.

c Suppose that the final results of the feasibility study indicate that the proposed system is technically and economically feasible. However, the order writers are not supportive of the proposal and have given the impression that they would avoid or resist using it when it is developed and implemented. Using the information provided in the discussion above, what would your recommendation be for the feasibility of the system? Explain your reasoning.

4 General Product Company recently completed gathering data for a feasibility study about a proposed information system project. The project is aimed at automating a portion of the materials requisition and ordering process for the company's manufacturing division. When product orders come in now, it is necessary to order the materials to produce these items, and at the same time, to schedule the items for manufacturing. Each individual item is made up of many different parts, components, and assemblies. The particular set and quantity of parts is maintained on a paper sheet called a "Bill of Materials." There is a separate bill of materials for each manufactured product. These bills must be maintained constantly so that any engineering change is reflected in the bill of materials used by the manufacturing division. Recently, the company has been encountering difficulties maintaining the files. Both the number of products manufactured is increasing and the volume of changes to the bills is expanding. It is anticipated that two more persons will have to be hired merely to allow the company to keep this file up to date. Since the firm is growing, it is expected that further additions will be made to the file in the future.

There have been problems in getting the material needed for production ordered quickly. Often, apparently because the process is done by hand, errors are made. Items are not ordered, in which case production must be rescheduled since the final product cannot be assembled. This causes confusion and ill feelings on the part of the manufacturing managers.

There are occasions when too much material is ordered, in which case it builds up in inventory and is unused for long periods of time. Excessive inventory incurs unnecessary carrying costs for storage and handling (carrying costs currently average 30 percent per year). In general, the overall rate is about 1 1/2 percent on material requisitions of $25 million annually (Errors are equally distributed between the two problem types.)

An automated system has been proposed to aid the requisition and ordering process. In this system, the bill of materials file will be automated and stored on magnetic disk. This will necessitate the acquisition of an extra set of disk drives (consisting of two separate drives mounted in a single cabinet). The monthly lease for the drive set is $1800 plus a maintenance contract of $190 per month. Of course this file will have to be maintained on a regular basis, but it is anticipated that the current staff in the systems department will be able to handle these. No new help will be hired.

The main advantage will be a more systematic ordering of materials. Overages and underages will be reduced. Furthermore, it is expected that the organization as a whole will benefit from this project. The actual users will be involved in the development of this project if it proves feasible, although they have not been contacted about it yet.

Developing the system is estimated to require about 60 person-months of effort and will require some 300 hours of computer time. Analysts and programmers charge an average rate of $25/hour. Computer time is at the rate of $275/hour.

a What information should the committee have to determine feasibility other than that provided above? Indicate which aspect of feasibility the information you request will be used to evaluate.

b Based only on the information provided for costs and benefits, does the project appear economically feasible? Technically feasible? Operationally feasible? Explain each answer.

c Should a formal, extensive systems investigation be initiated? Why or why not?

CHAPTER 3 DETERMINING SYSTEMS REQUIREMENTS

QUESTIONS TO GUIDE YOU THROUGH THE CHAPTER

- What are information systems requirements? How are they determined?
- In what ways do requirements for transaction systems and decision systems vary?
- What methods do systems analysts use to investigate information systems requirements?
- What specific questions guide analysts in conducting systems investigations?
- Who is responsible for ensuring that essential systems requirements are identified?
- What factors determine when specific fact-finding techniques should be used?
- Is one method of gathering details about information systems requirements superior to all the others?

Systems analysis is understanding situations, not solving problems. Effective analysts, therefore, emphasize investigation and questioning to learn how a system currently operates and to identify the requirements users have for a new or modified one. Only after analysts fully understand the system are they able to analyze it and assemble recommendations for systems design.

This chapter is the first of four that discuss systems analysis and the determination of systems requirements. In the sections that follow, the meaning of requirements determination and the questions it includes are discussed. Then the methods for collecting data about requirements, called fact-finding techniques, are examined in detail. This chapter shows how to start a detailed systems study and what methods to use. Chapters 4, 5, and 6 explore strategies for organizing the details collected during an investigation and ways to analyze them.

WHAT IS REQUIREMENTS DETERMINATION?

Requirements determination means studying the current business system to find out how it works and where improvements should be made. Systems studies result in an evaluation of how current methods are working and whether adjustments are necessary or possible. They consider questions about both manual and computer methods, as we shall see; they are not just computer studies.

A *requirement* is a feature that must be included in a new system and may include a way of capturing or processing data, producing information, controlling a business activity, or supporting management. The determination of requirements thus means studying the existing system and collecting details about it to find out what these requirements are.

Since systems analysts do not work as managers or employees in user departments (such as marketing, purchasing, manufacturing, or accounting), they do not have the same base of facts and details as the managers and users in those areas. Therefore, an early step in the investigation is to understand the situation. There are certain types of requirements that are so fundamental they are common across all situations. By developing answers to a specific group of questions, which we discuss in this section, you will understand these basic requirements. There are also special kinds of requirements that arise, depending on whether the system is transaction- or decision-oriented and whether the system cuts across several departments.

We will raise the questions to address in studying an unfamiliar system. The following section of this chapter discusses how to find the answers in an investigation.

Basic Requirements

Analysts structure their investigation by seeking answers to these four major questions:

What is the basic business process?

What data is used or produced during that process?

What are the limits imposed by time and the volume of work?

What performance controls are used?

UNDERSTAND THE PROCESS

Begin with the basics. Raise those questions that will, when answered, provide a background of fundamental details and descriptions of the system. The following questions will help you acquire the necessary understanding:

What is the purpose of this business activity?

What steps are performed?

Where are they performed?

Who performs them?

How long does this take?

How often is it done?

Who uses the resulting information?

Suppose you are investigating an inventory reordering system, something about which you know very little. Where should you begin? Listed below are brief answers to the basic questions for the inventory reordering system. These are the kinds of answers you would have to seek for any system you were studying.

What is the purpose of inventory reordering?

To ensure that adequate quantities of stock and materials are on hand and available for use without carrying an excessive, and therefore costly, quantity.

What steps are performed?
  Verifying stock on hand. Determining future requirements and ideal time to place orders. Determining quantities to order. Placing the order.
Where are they performed?
  The purchasing department, using information provided by manufacturing, sales, and inventory staff members, as well as by its own records, handles ordering and lead-time projection.
Who performs them?
  Purchasing managers approve all orders. Stock managers assemble buying instructions and write orders.
How long does this take?
  The process may take a few minutes for simple and routine orders or it may require hours, for orders involving a new or high-priced item or other special circumstances.
How often is it done?
  This is a continuous process. Different items are always being ordered.
Who uses the resulting information?
  Information produced as a by-product of this process is used to manage inventory, schedule services and manufacturing, monitor purchasing, and pay suppliers, as well as meet unexpected requirements for purchasing and inventory reorder information.

Notice how quickly answers to these questions provide a broad understanding of what inventory reordering is all about and show that its objective is more than just buying stock. But the analyst cannot stop here. There simply is not enough information yet to understand inventory reordering fully. Instead the background acquired enables the analyst to raise more detailed questions.

IDENTIFY DATA USED AND INFORMATION PRODUCED

The analyst next needs to find out what data is used to perform each activity (Figure 3.1). For example, to reorder inventory, the buyer might require data describing the quantity of an item on hand, expected demand for the item, supplier name, and item cost. To know when to place an order, the buyer would also consider the necessary lead time (how far in advance the item should be ordered to be on hand when needed).

Most business transactions also produce information that is useful to managers when they evaluate employee, business, and systems performance and that may be useful in another context to both manager and analyst. An inquiring analyst will find out, for example, that data about inventory reordering and stocking also provides information about warehouse demands, purchasing practices, sales, and cash flow.

DETERMINE PROCESS TIMING AND VOLUME

The frequency of business activities varies greatly. For example, some activities, such as paying taxes, happen only a few times a year, whereas,

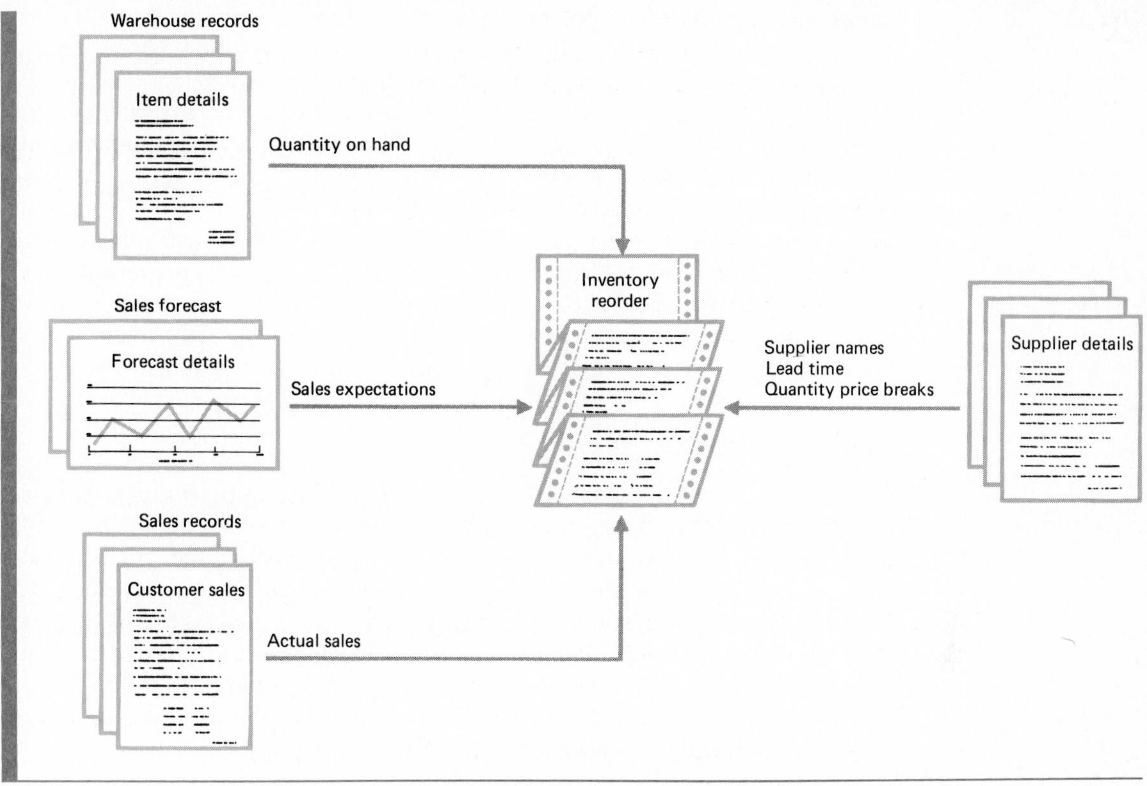

Figure 3.1. Information flow for inventory reorder process.

paying employees is a weekly activity. Therefore, the analyst should learn *how often* the activity is repeated. Knowing whether an activity occurs frequently may lead the analyst to raise many additional and important questions to determine the reason for the frequency and its effect on business activities.

Many times the easiest way to get this information is to identify the reason for the activity: *What causes* the activity to be performed? Analysts sometimes refer to the direct cause as the *trigger function*. (It *triggers* the activity.) Activities may be triggered by customers (through orders, telephone calls, or letters), by events (the completion of an application to open a new bank, charge, or credit account), and by the passage of time (for example, the end of the day, week, or month). Unless analysts know what triggers an activity, they may misunderstand the reason for the activity and give it more or less importance in the system than it merits.

Some activities, such as completing a purchase requisition, take only a few seconds. Others, such as deciding whether to accept a merger offer, occur infrequently but require a great deal of time when they do. Timing alone does not determine the importance of an activity, but it does affect the way analysts evaluate certain steps in carrying out the performance. For example, making a telephone call to obtain stock price information during a merger decision is quite acceptable since a merger is an infrequent occurrence. But making a telephone call to obtain information every time a purchase requisition is processed is another matter.

The *volume* of items to be handled may increase the amount of time needed to complete the activity. Savings banks prepare consumer account statements (summaries of deposits, withdrawals, interest accumulations, and balances) only four times a year. Therefore the frequency is very low. But, when the calendar triggers this event at the end of each quarter, the volume of work is very high, sometimes running into tens of thousands of statements to be prepared. The sheer quantity of items making up an activity may produce special problems for the analyst to study, even though the activity occurs infrequently.

IDENTIFY CONTROLS

In business situations that are well controlled either by management or process monitoring, determining whether an activity has been performed properly may be no problem. But, during the analysis stage, the analysts must examine control methods: Are there specific performance standards? Who compares performance against standards? How are mistakes caught? How are errors handled? Are the errors excessive? Weak or missing controls are an important discovery in any systems investigation.

The next two sections show how the basic fact-finding questions are used to understand transaction and decision systems.

User Transaction Requirements

Chapter 1 pointed out distinctions between transaction processing and decision-oriented systems that we will be using throughout the book. Figure 3.2 summarizes the differences between these systems.

TRANSACTION PROCESSING ACTIVITIES:	DECISION MAKING ACTIVITIES:
Are well structured.	Are structured by the individual.
Follow clear-cut routines.	Lack routines.
Recur frequently.	Occur irregularly.
Are highly predictable.	Are unpredictable.
Change infrequently.	Change continually.
Have highly structured data needs.	Have data needs determined by the individual.
Focus on current events.	Focus on past, present, and future.
Capture and process data.	Use existing and new data.
Emphasize details.	Require broad perspective using summary of details.

Figure 3.2. Distinctions between transaction processing and decision support activities.

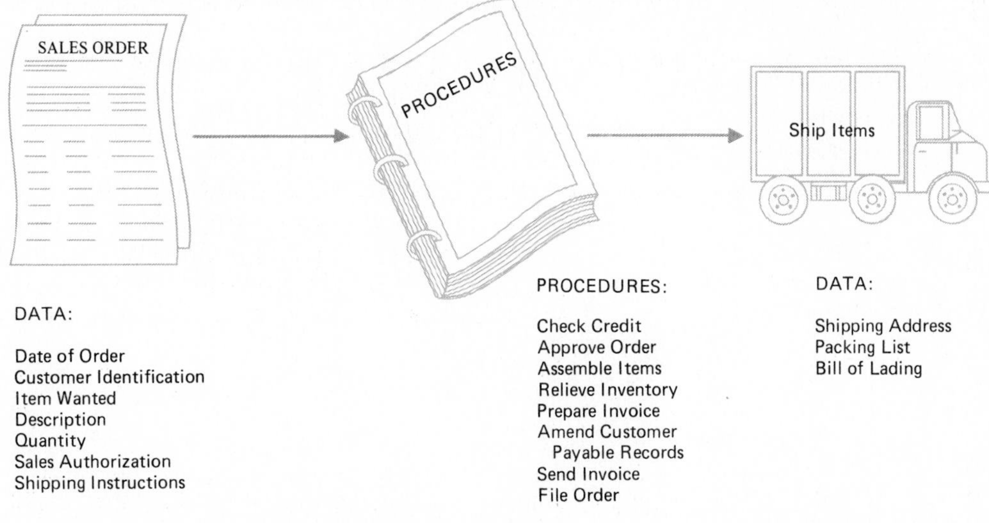

Figure 3.3. Activities in order processing stream.

Transaction-level systems capture, process, and store data for a reason. In an order entry system, for example, sales orders from customers are processed so that specified items can be shipped. This simple procedure applies to every order that is received (Figure 3.3).

Analysts assigned to work on an order entry system will want to know more about how these transactions are processed. They would undoubtedly ask questions like the following:

What makes up the transaction being processed?

What initiates the transaction?

Who actually initiates the order? For what purpose?

How often do orders occur?

What volume is associated with each?

Are there different conditions that can affect how orders are processed?

What details are needed to process the transaction?

What information is generated? What data is stored?

Table 3.1 lists the questions analysts ask to profile a system properly.

User Decision Requirements

Decisions, unlike transaction activities, may not follow a specific procedure. Routines are not as clear-cut, and controls may be very vague. Decisions are made by integrating information in such a way that managers can know what actions to take. Decision systems may focus on the past, the present, or

TABLE 3.1

QUESTIONS TO ANSWER IN DEVELOPING A SYSTEM PROFILE

The analyst should answer the following questions to develop a full profile of the system under investigation:

VOLUME	• What volume of activity occurs?
	• How frequently does the activity occur?
	• Does the activity occur according to any cycle?
CONTROL	• What areas need specific control?
	• What control methods are currently used?
	• What yardsticks are used to measure and assess performance?
	• What methods of detecting lapses in control are used?
	• Are specific security precautions taken to safeguard against improper activity?
	• Are there methods of avoiding the system? Why do they occur?
PROCESSES	• What separate processes, steps, or functions make up the activity?
	• What triggers the activity?
	• How long does each activity take? What factors govern the amount of time taken?
	• What delays (can) occur?
	• How does interaction with ouside elements occur?
	• What is the cost of system operation?
	• Are there specific management objectives to be satisfied?
DATA	• What data enters the system and what is its origin?
	• In what form is the system data received? Stored?
	• Which data items are stored in the system or as part of the activities of the system?
	• Who uses the information produced by the system? What is it used for? What is not used (extraneous parts)?
	• What data is often missing?
	• Is any data developed or used on an *ad hoc* basis?
	• What reference tables, charts, or other data are used?
	• How are data or activities coded or abbreviated?
OTHER	• Who are the key persons in the system? Why are they important?
	• What obstacles or political influences affect system efficiency?

the future. Some may support recurring decisions (like merchandise pricing), while others are unique and do not recur (like the merger example used earlier). They may use data that originates inside the firm, such as through transaction processing, or outside, for example from trade associations or commercial sources (such as marketing research firms who sell information to organizations). In some cases, transaction data is processed to provide new information for decision making. For instance, summarized sales transaction data will tell managers which products sell frequently and which do not.

The analyst investigating decision support systems should raise the same questions about timing and frequency discussed above. But other questions should also be posed:

1 What information is used to make the decision?
2 What is the source of the information?
Which transaction systems produce the data used in the decision process?

Which data is required but does not result from processing transactions? Which data originates from sources outside the organization?

3 How should data be processed to produce the necessary information?

4 How should the information be presented?

These questions also point out the relationship between transaction and decision systems. If transaction systems do not capture and store the data needed for decisions, important information will be unavailable. Inventory systems capture details about ongoing ordering, receipt, sale, and shipment of items. The data they store are further processed to produce information periodically to analyze sales, determine pricing policy, or decide on marketing plans for product lines.

This means that (1) an analyst investigating decision systems must be aware of supporting transaction systems and (2) effective decision systems require that suitable transaction processing procedures be in place first.

Organizationwide Requirements

In business, departments depend on each other to provide services, manufacture products, and satisfy customers. Therefore, the work that one department does affects other departments. When analysts study systems for one department, they also assess the implications for other departments that interact with the system being investigated. Sometimes systems involve work that takes place across several departments. In other instances, systems that operate separately depend on data provided from other departments. It is the analysts' responsibility to identify dependencies between departments and determine how a systems project may affect them.

The order entry example shows how important it is to consider the ramifications of one type of activity on the rest of the organization. When the sales group takes an order, it sets off a series of activities that affect other areas. An order may eventually involve the credit department, manufacturing, inventory control, purchasing (if materials should be ordered to fill the customer order), shipping, and accounts payable (for invoicing and annotation of the amount of the sale in the records). The analysts who are concerned about the order entry process probably will not be working on an invoicing system at the same time. However, they should be aware of any requirements elsewhere in the organization that depend on the order entry process. For example, how would material be shipped or invoices mailed if the order entry process did not call for the capture of the customers' shipping or billing addresses? You can see how important it is to be aware of other organization requirements.

FACT-FINDING TECHNIQUES

Analysts use a variety of methods to gather facts about an existing situation—interview, questionnaire, record inspection (on-site review), and observation. Each has particular advantages and disadvantages. Generally, two or three are used to complement each other and help ensure a thorough investigation. Let us look at each.

Interview

Interviews are used to collect information verbally through questions posed by the analyst. Respondents may be managers or employees who are current users of the existing system or potential users of the proposed system or who will provide data for, or be affected by, the proposed application. The analyst can interview people one at a time or in groups. Some analysts favor this method over the other techniques we will discuss. However, interviews may not always be the best sources of application data.

COLLECTING DATA BY INTERVIEW

Interviewing is a form of conversation, not interrogation! By discussing systems characteristics with respondents carefully selected for their knowledge of the system, analysts may learn of details that are not available through any other means.

In systems investigations, both qualitative and quantitative forms of information are important. Qualitative information deals with opinions, policies, and narrative descriptions of activities or problems, while quantitative descriptions deal with numbers, frequencies, or quantities. Interviews are often the best source of *qualitative* information; the other methods tend to be more useful in collecting quantitative data.

If it is important to find out about upcoming plans for new products, changes in customer relations policies, construction projects, or planned growth in sales, interviews may be the best way to capture that information. Opinions, comments, ideas, or suggestions about how work is or could be done are valuable. Interviewing is sometimes the best way to learn about them.

Many people who are not able to express themselves well in writing can discuss their ideas in detail verbally. As a result, interviews can quickly uncover misunderstandings, false expectations, or even potential resistance to applications under development. Furthermore, it is often easier to schedule an interview with upper managers than to have them complete questionnaires.

DETERMINING THE TYPE OF INTERVIEW

The amount of structure in interviews varies. If the intent of the interview is to acquire general information, *unstructured* questioning, with a free question and answer session, is suitable. The open and free-flowing atmosphere of this format provides greater opportunity to learn about the feelings, ideas, and beliefs of the respondent. However, when analysts need to acquire specific application details or wish to ensure high reliability of answers to questions posed to all interviewees, structured interviews are better.

Structured interviews use standardized questions. The response format for the questions can be open or closed. *Open-response questions* allow the interviewees to provide whatever answers seem appropriate. They can answer fully in their own words. With *closed-response questions* the user is given a set of answers from which to select. All respondents select from the same set of possible answers (Figure 3.4).

Reliability is only one consideration in selecting an interview method. Analysts must also choose between spending time developing interview questions and spending it analyzing answers. Unstructured interviews require less time to set up because the precise wording of the questions is not needed in advance. However, analyzing responses after the interviews are completed takes more time than for structured interviews. Overall the greatest cost is typically in the preparation, administration, and analysis of closed-question structured interviews.

Table 3.2 summarizes the advantages and disadvantages of each approach.

SELECTING INTERVIEWEES

Conducting interviews takes time. Thus it is not possible to use this method to gather all the information needed in an investigation. Moreover, the analyst should verify the data gathered by using one of the other data collection methods.

Since a limited number of persons will be selected for interviewing, analysts should be careful to include those people who have information that will not be collected through some other method. During the early stages of a systems study, when analysts are determining project feasibility, interviews are often limited to management or supervisory personnel. However, during the detailed investigation, where the intention is to

OPEN QUESTION FORM

Example: Obtain information about critical design features for employees

"Some employees have suggested that the best way to improve order processing is to install a computer system that will handle all calculations that staff members now do with calculators so they can focus more on other processing steps.
Under what circumstances would you encourage development of such a system?"

CLOSED QUESTION FORM

Example: Obtain insight into system likes and dislikes

"Your experience has given you a good deal of insight into the way this organization handles sales orders. Think about the way orders are received, processed, and disposed of. I would like you to answer some specific questions about this:

—What steps work well? What steps do not?
—What parts of order processing do employees dislike most?
—Where do most problems occur?
—Where are there fewest problems?
—What can be done to increase speed?
—What will reduce errors still further?
—When a backlog develops, how is it handled?"

Figure 3.4. Open and closed form structured interview questions.

TABLE 3.2

COMPARISION OF STRUCTURED AND UNSTRUCTURED INTERVIEW METHODS

	STRUCTURED INTERVIEW	UNSTRUCTURED INTERVIEW
ADVANTAGES	Ensures uniform wording of questions for all respondents.	Interviewer has greater flexibility in wording questions to suit respondent.
	Easy to administer and evaluate.	Interviewer can pursue areas that arise spontaneously during interview.
	More objective evaluation of both respondents and answers to questions.	May produce information about areas that were overlooked or not thought to be important.
	Limited interviewer training needed.	
	Results in shorter interviews.	
DISADVANTAGES	Cost of preparation is high.	May be inefficient use of both respondent and interviewer time.
	Respondents may not accept high level of structure and mechanical posing of questions.	Interviewers may introduce their biases in questions or reporting results.
	High level of structure may not be suitable for all situations.	Extraneous information may be gathered.
	High level of structure reduces respondent spontaneity and ability of interviewer to follow up on comments of interviewee.	Analysis and interpretation of results may be lengthy.
		Takes extra time to collect essential facts.

uncover specific facts and opinions and learn how operations are actually performed, interviews are used at all management and employee levels, depending on who can provide the most useful information for the study. Therefore, analysts studying inventory management may interview shipping and receiving workers, warehouse personnel, and shift supervisors—those persons who are actually doing the warehouse work. They will also interview the appropriate managers.

CONDUCTING THE INTERVIEW

The skill of the interviewer is vital to the success of fact finding through the interview. Good interviews depend on preparation, on the analyst's knowing both the objective of a specific interview and the questions to ask a specific respondent. Figure 3.5, contains guidelines for managing the interview process for best results.

Tact, impartiality, and even appropriate dress help ensure a successful interview. Lack of them may undermine any chance of success. For example, an analyst, working on an application aimed at reducing errors seen by upper-level management, probably would not be successful if the analyst entered a middle manager's office with the wrong lead-in: "Hi. I was sent to find a way to improve performance and reduce the errors around here." The introduction, "we're here to solve your problem," is equally bad. You can imagine how quickly a respondent becomes irritated and annoyed with such an approach by an analyst.

Respondents may also create difficult situations. Figure 3.6 summarizes

HOW TO CONDUCT A SUCCESSFUL INTERVIEW

Interviewing is an art as well as a skill that comes through practice and knowledge of the system under investigation. Those who are successful and effective in using interviewing methods during system studies agree on the steps analysts should follow.

To ensure the interview is useful, the analyst should follow these guidelines:

1. Make an appointment with the interviewees in advance. Interviews are successful only if carefully planned and arranged in advance. Dropping in on a senior executive without advance notice would be a mistake. Advise the interviewees of the nature of the interview. Plan to hold the typical interview for no longer than one hour.
2. Prepare for the interviews in advance by learning about the individuals to be interviewed. Become familiar with the topic of the interviews and prepare an appropriate set of questions that should be answered during the planned conversations.
3. During the interview:
   a. Begin by introducing yourself, outlining the topic of the interview and stating the nature of the project on which you are working.
   b. Begin with general questions that will establish the framework in which the rest of the interview will be conducted.
   c. Follow up on topics and issues raised by the respondents. Be sure to find out why the respondents felt the topic important enough to bring up as well as the facts of the topic.
   d. Limit your notetaking to avoid distracting the respondents.
   e. When all of the topics brought up by the interviewees have been discussed, bring up other specific questions you feel should be discussed.
   f. At the end of the interview, summarize the information gathered during the interview. If appropriate, indicate that a written summary of the interview will be prepared for the respondents' examination. Consider the possibility of follow-up interviews later.

Figure 3.5. How to conduct a successful interview.

RESPONDENT BEHAVIOR	INTERVIEWER ACTION
1. Appears to guess at answers rather than admit ignorance.	1. After the interview, cross-check answers that are suspect.
2. Attempts to tell the interviewer what he presumably wants to hear instead of the correct facts.	2. Avoid putting questions in a form that implies the answers. Cross-check answers that are suspect.
3. Gives the interviewer a great deal of irrelevent information or tells stories.	3. In friendly but persistent fashion, bring the discussion back into the desired channel.
4. Stops talking if the interviewer begins to take notes.	4. Put the notebook away and confine questions to those which are most important. If necessary, come back later for details.
5. Attempts to rush through the interview.	5. Suggest coming back later.
6. Express satisfaction with the way things are done now and wants no change.	6. Encourage him to elaborate on present situation and its virtues. Take careful notes and ask questions about details.
7. Shows obvious resentment of the interviewer, answers questions guardedly, or appears to be withholding data.	7. Try to get him talking about something that interests him.
8. Sabotages the interview by noncooperation. In effect, refuses to give information.	8. Ask him, "If I get this information from someone else, would you mind checking it for me?" Then proceed on that plan.
9. Gripes about his job, his pay, his associates, his supervisors, the unfair treatment he receives.	9. Listen sympathetically and note anything that might be a real clue. Don't interrupt until he has poured out his gripes. Then make friendly but noncommittal statements, such as "You sure have plenty of troubles. Perhaps the study can help with some of them." This approach should bridge the gap to asking about the desired facts. Later, make enough of a check on his gripes to determine whether there is any foundation for them. In this way, you neither pass over a good lead nor leave yourself open to being unduly influenced by groundless talk or personal prejudice.
10. Acts as eager beaver, is enthusiastic about new ideas, gadgets, techniques.	10. Listen for desired facts and valuable leads. Don't become emotionally involved or enlist in his campaign.

Figure 3.6. Difficulties that can occur during interviews.

many potential problems and suggests ways to deal with them. Analysts should be alert for attempts to undermine the research effort with misleading or incomplete answers. (Verification through other data collection methods is important!) Some employees use expected or approved responses, even though these may not express their true feelings. Analysts must also watch for attempts to shift the blame for problems to other areas or persons. An untrained interviewer can easily be mislead by a clever employee.

Throughout the interview analysts should ask themselves the following questions:

1 *What* is this person telling me?
2 *Why* is this person telling it to me?
3 What is being *left out?*
4 Are *facts* being presented (rather than hunches or opinions)?
5 *What* does this person expect *me* to do?

If each element of information is considered against these questions, analysts will have a much better understanding not only of the information acquired but also of its significance.

Questionnaire

Questionnaires provide a useful alternative to interviews. However, there are certain features that make them appropriate in some situations and inappropriate in others. Like interviews, they should be designed carefully for maximum effectiveness.

COLLECTING DATA BY QUESTIONNAIRE

Questionnaires may be the only feasible way for the analyst to contact a large number of persons about various aspects of the system. When large, multidepartment studies are being conducted, questionnaires can be distributed to all appropriate persons to collect facts about the system. Of course, it is not possible to watch the expressions or reactions of the respondents to the questionnaires. (If this is important, interviews may be necessary.) In most cases, the analyst will not even see the respondents. However, it is an advantage too, because wide distribution helps ensure the respondent has greater anonymity and may lead to more honest answers (and fewer pat or expected responses). Standardized questions can also yield more reliable data.

There are disadvantages to questionnaires also. Even though distribution may be made to a large number of individuals, full response is very rare. Follow-up questionnaires may be needed to encourage individuals to respond, but, even then, overall response rates of only 25 to 35 percent are not uncommon. Many people take their time in completing questionnaires too; the questionnaires they receive about the system study may not be their top priorities. When large groups can be gathered together for the sole purpose of completing a questionnaire, response rates may improve (but seldom will everyone show up).

SELECTING QUESTIONNAIRE FORMS

Development and distribution of questionnaires is expensive. Therefore, time invested in developing a questionnaire—and it will take time—should be used wisely. The format and content of the questions is all-important in collecting meaningful facts.

There are two ways to collect questionnaire data with open-ended and with closed questionnaires, depending on whether the analysts know all the possible responses to the questions in advance and can include them. Often both forms are used in systems studies.

Open-Ended Questionnaire

Like interviews, questionnaires can be open-ended. Open-ended forms are good for finding out about feelings, opinions, and general experiences. They are also useful for exploring a process or problem. For example, an analyst, using questionnaires to study credit verification methods in a retail sales environment would probably collect the most useful information from an open question such as: "How could the process of verifying credit for customers be simplified and improved?"

The open format provides ample opportunity for the respondents to describe the reasons for their ideas. Some people, however, find it easier to check one of a set of prepared responses than to think for themselves.

Closed-Questionnaire

The closed-questionnaire method limits the possible responses of the recipient. Through careful wording of the question, the analyst can control the frame of reference. This format is the best method for eliciting factual information. It also forces individuals to take a stand or form an opinion about important issues. Figure 3.7 includes examples of the most common forms of closed-questionnaire responses: yes/no, agree/disagree, scaled, point selection, range, and limited response selection. The examples ask respondents about sales-form coding errors.

CLOSED QUESTIONNAIRE RESPONSES

YES/NO

"Do you feel that too many errors are made in coding account numbers from sales forms?"

[] YES
[] NO

AGREE/DISAGREE

"Too many errors are made in coding account numbers from sales forms."

[] AGREE
[] DISAGREE

SCALED

"Too many errors are made in coding account numbers from sales forms."

[] STRONGLY AGREE
[] AGREE
[] NOT SURE
[] DISAGREE
[] STRONGLY DISAGREE

NUMBER

"Out of every 100 sales forms that are processed by the department, how many do you feel contain errors?"

____
enter number

RANGE

"Out of every 100 sales forms that are processed by the department, how many do you feel contain errors?"

[] 0 to 5
[] 6 to 10
[] 11 to 15
[] 16 to 20
[] 21 to 25
[] 26 to 30
[] 31 to 40
[] 41 to 50
[] MORE THAN 50

LIMITED RESPONSE SELECTION

"When errors occur in coding account numbers from sales forms, what is the most frequent cause? (Enter the number of the appropriate response)"

(Also 2d most common reason and least common reason)

1 . . . . .
2 . . . . .
3 . . . . .

Figure 3.7. Closed questionnaire response forms.

STEPS IN QUESTIONNAIRE DEVELOPMENT

Good questionnaires are not developed quickly. They take time and hard work. The first consideration is to determine the objective of the questionnaire. What details is the analyst attempting to learn through its use? The analyst determines how to use questionnaires to gather the facts by considering the structure that will be most useful to the study and most easily understandable to the recipients.

Good questions take time to develop, and they should always be tested and modified, if necessary, before a finalized form is printed and distributed. Figure 3.8 discusses guidelines for the effective collection of systems facts, using questionnaires.

SELECTING QUESTIONNAIRE RECIPIENTS

Recipients of questionnaires should be selected for the information they can provide. The mere fact that a questionnaire has been written and printed

HOW TO DEVELOP A QUESTIONNAIRE

Good questionnaires are not just written, they are designed. Careful thought coupled with pretesting of both the format and the questions are the basis of meaningful data collection through questionnaires.

Here are guidelines to assist in the formulation of a questionnaire:

1. Determine what facts need to be collected and which persons are best qualified to provide them. If other groups may provide varying data and insight, identify them also.
2. Select the type of questionnaire to be used (open or closed). Recognize that some questionnaires can be more useful if they contain a section with closed response questions and another with open response questions.
3. Develop a pool of questions to be included in the questionnaire. Extra questions that are intentionally redundant can be helpful in ensuring consistent responses from the respondent.
4. Examine the questionnaire for flaws and defects; such as:
   a. Unnecessary questions—the same thing has been asked in another question, and there is no need for intentional reverification.
   b. Questions that can be misinterpreted because of focus or wording.
   c. Questions that the subject cannot possibly answer because he or she does not know.
   d. Questions that are written in such a way that a preferred response will be elicited.
   e. Questions that will be interpreted differently because of the frame of reference of each respondent.
   f. Questions that do not provide adequate response choices.
   g. Improper ordering of questions or responses.
5. Pretest the questionnaire on a small group of people to uncover other possible problems. Doing this not only uncovers problems in wording, spacing, spelling, and methods of recording answers but also provides an indication of the kind of responses that will be gathered from the larger group. If there are many unexpected responses, they will be revealed during pretesting rather than during actual data collection. Be sure the pretest sample is comparable to the larger group that will receive the sample.
6. Analyze the responses of the pretest sample to ensure that the intended data analysis can be carried out with the type of data collected. If the pretest data does not reveal something that the analysts did not already know and did not need to verify, the questionnaire may not be necessary in its current form.
7. Make final editing changes, typing corrections, and adjustments to the form. Then have the questionnaire printed in a neat, easily readible type.
8. Distribute the questionnaire. When possible, address each person by name. You start on the wrong foot with names and addresses such as "occupant," "Manufacturing Hourly Employee," or "Mail Stop 34A."

Figure 3.8. How to develop a questionnaire.

does not mean it can be widely distributed without forethought. Unqualified persons may respond (and, if the questionnaire is anonymous, it may not be possible to remove their responses from the sample). The practice is also wasteful and expensive.

Before distributing the questionnaire, ensure that the recipients will have the information necessary to answer the questions. Verify that their backgrounds and experiences qualify them to respond. For example, if an analyst is studying inventory control and food storage procedures in a restaurant, asking front-office accounts about high food costs, attributable to storage methods, would probably be inappropriate. On the other hand, the analyst would surely want to include cooks and food preparers, waiters and waitresses, and kitchen and dining-room management. These people are called upon to use the storage lockers regularly, and their backgrounds may provide insight into weaknesses in the current procedures. In the same situation, the controller should receive a questionnaire aimed at finding more effective ways of tracking food costs through invoices submitted to the accounting department. The controller would have the necessary facts about this process; waiters and waitresses seldom would. You can see how the selection of respondents can increase or decrease the reliability of the data captured during the fact-finding process.

Record Review

Information is often already available in many organizations to tell analysts about organization units or operations with which they are not familiar. Many types of records and reports are available if the analysts know where to look. In record reviews, the analysts examine details and descriptions, that are already recorded or written, about the system and the user departments. This form of fact finding can be an introduction for the analysts, if it is done at the beginning of the study, or a basis for comparing what is happening in the department with what the records say should be happening.

COLLECTING DATA BY RECORD INSPECTION

The term "records" refers to the written policy manuals, regulations, and standard operating procedures that most organizations maintain as a guide for managers and employees. Manuals that document or describe operations for existing data processing or information systems falling within the area of investigation also provide insight into how business should be conducted. They usually show the requirements and constraints of the system (such as volume of transactions or data storage capability) and design features (controls and checks on processing).

Records enable analysts to become familiar with some operations that must be supported, offices in the organization, and formal relations. They do *not* show how activities actually occur, where the real power lies in decisions, or how tasks are actually carried out. The other fact-finding methods discussed in this section are better able to provide the analyst with that information.

SELECTING RECORDS TO REVIEW

Manuals and standard operating procedures in most organizations are continually falling out of date; they often are not kept current enough to reflect existing procedures. Organization charts show how different units *should* relate to one another, but may not reflect actual operations.

Documents and forms that are used through the system, even blank ones, can fill gaps in the analysts' understanding of the system. Comparing blank forms with procedure and operations manuals tells the analysts how they should be filled in. Then collecting and comparing completed forms and reports permits the assessment of any variance between the actual and prescribed use of the documents. Often there are differences. Some spots on the forms are left blank. Others are completed with data different from what is requested. Still others are distributed to different offices from those prescribed (or are not distributed at all). In some investigations that are undertaken to find the cause of a particular operations problem, analysts are able to trace causes back to discrepancies between intended and actual procedures.

It may be quite revealing actually to sample some of the documents or forms used in the process. Analysts can pull copies and look at them to see what is present and what is missing. Sampling a set of copies at random and examining each allows the development of error rates and statistics that more fully describe a situation.

Some analysts catalog the actual documents themselves to determine which ones are used and when and which ones are not used after they are filled in. While this extra effort can be difficult and time-consuming if there are many documents, establishing such a repository may be useful in trying to relate all the tasks to each other. Of course, analysts sometimes miss documents too, so cross-checking document use through the other data collection methods is necessary.

Analysts should watch for *bootleg* forms and documents—ones that individuals make up for their own use but that are not part of the prescribed procedures. They can be signs of weaknesses in standard methods or causes of problems.

Reports of previous studies, consultant briefs, and management reports should not be overlooked either. They can provide a history explaining the rationale behind some of the things the analysts see during the study. And they may provide insight into points of past resistance too.

Observation

Seeing is believing! Observing operations gives the analysts facts they could not get any other way.

COLLECTING DATA BY OBSERVATION

Reading about a business activity gives the analyst one dimension of system activities. Interviewing persons, either directly or through questionnaire, tells something else. Neither gives complete information, just as reading about jet travel does not duplicate the feeling of flight at 30,000 feet.

Observation provides firsthand information about how activities are carried out. Questions about the use of documents, the way tasks are completed, and whether specific steps occur as prescribed can readily be answered by observing operations. An analyst, who wants to find out what a senior-level manager does when deciding whether to pursue a merger offer received in the morning, observes the kind of information requested, how soon it arrives, and where it comes from. Also important is whether the information is used. Every question the analyst has will not get answered this way (more will probably be raised!), but information can be obtained that would not be available by any other means.

WHEN TO OBSERVE

Observation is most useful when the analyst needs to see firsthand how documents are handled, how processes are carried out, and whether specified steps actually occur. Observation is an art in itself. Knowing what to look for and how to assess its significance also requires experience. Skilled observers watch who uses documents and whether they encounter difficulties. They also are alert for documents or records that are not used. For example, if a salesperson does not use a price book in completing a large customer order, does that mean the salesperson is certain of the correct price for that particular item (even though there are over 10,000 different items in the book)? Many times memory can be faulty, as we all know. Relying on memory may be one of the causes for a problem the analysts are investigating. (And even if the salesperson remembers the last price correctly, a price change may have occurred.)

Analysts should also watch for other unusual steps. Is a telephone call made for every sales order processed? Why? What information is missing in the office? Can the call be avoided through a better systems design? Is an extra photocopy of the order made for every transaction? Is that necessary? Or perhaps a copy of a multipart order is always torn off and thrown in the wastebasket. Who should really be receiving that copy? Or, should the form be redesigned?

Tasks that are troublesome, so that individuals make frequent errors completing them, as well as those that tend to slow up processing should always be identified. *Bottlenecks* are places in a processing system where backlogs of work build up because the work cannot be performed as quickly as it arrives. They are not only an operations problem; bottlenecks also occur at upper management levels (such as where signatures or formal approval are required). Observation may help detect the causes and reveal whether the bottleneck is broken from time to time (and how) or whether it continues to build.

POTENTIAL PROBLEMS

Observing business operations, whether at the transaction level or in decision-making situations, has its pitfalls. The mere fact that someone is watching can change the way work is done. This is normal, but, if it happens, analysts will develop a distorted view about whether prescribed procedures are being followed. Trained analysts must know when to overlook these temporary adjustments and understand how daily work is normally done. Picking the wrong time and viewing an unusual volume of work (very high or very low) may totally distort the analysis.

Sometimes the nature of the job is such that analysts cannot fully learn what is going on or understand how to perform a job without doing it. In *participant observation,* the analysts become part of the situation and do the work themselves. In an order entry application, they might answer the telephones at the order desk and complete sales forms for a period of time. Or, in designing a hotel system, they might spend time registering guests and checking them into their rooms at the beginning of the week and out at the end. Participation will give a firsthand feel for the day-to-day work of the front-desk personnel. It will be informative, so long as analysts can step back afterwards and be objective about what they have experienced.

When they are finished, the analysts should have captured additional information not available through any other data collection method we have discussed (see Figure 3.9).

The fact-finding techniques discussed in this section represent one aspect of systems analysis. The next chapter discusses data flow analysis, a method that assists analysts in organizing the details collected, while at the

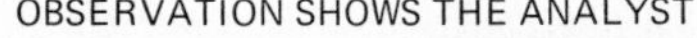
OBSERVATION SHOWS THE ANALYST

What should happen . . .	What actually occurs . . .
Standard operating procedures	Delay in doing work
Controls and checks for accuracy and completeness	Information recalled from memory (incorrectly)
Properly completed documents	Skipped steps
Efficient and timely, completion of work.	Extra photocopy needed
	New controls needed
	Information not in file — telephone calls needed
	Documents not completed as required
	Employees not aware of prescribed procedures

Figure 3.9. Observation provides firsthand information about how work is done.

same time pointing out where additional facts are needed to understand a system.

SUMMARY

Analysts are often at a disadvantage when they first undertake a systems investigation. The area for which they will be making important recommendations later may be one about which they initially know very little. Therefore, it is essential for them to acquire important facts about systems requirements in a rapid and accurate fashion. The fact-finding methods of interview, questionnaire, on-site record review, and observation assist the analysts if used properly. Each has particular advantages and disadvantages; none are adequate by themselves. Cross-checking the systems facts is very important.

When initiating a study, analysts want to know why and how certain activities are performed and what data is used in the work. Timing, frequency, and volume of activities are also important facts to collect. Studying systems controls enables analysts to see how business functions can be maintained in an acceptable manner. These requirements are basic, apply to both transaction and decision systems, and are normally part of the organizationwide needs.

CASE STUDY FOR CHAPTER 3
PRELIMINARY INVESTIGATION

Interviews conducted during the feasibility study stage are aimed at determining the reason for a project request and collecting enough information to decide whether a detailed investigation should be conducted. The following information was obtained through interviews with Olson, Jacobson, Carbo, and Severski, with attention on the nature of the problem and how it occurs. (i.e., What is the problem? Who is involved with it? When does it occur? Why does it appear to arise? How often? What is the effect? How significant is it?)

INTERVIEW WITH OLSON

"We seem to have trouble keeping track of all of our orders. Orders get lost, although I am not sure why. Perhaps it is simply because we are growing so fast that we cannot keep up with demand. It's kind of a nice problem to have, I suppose, but that does not take away from the difficulty when an order is lost. Unfortunately, we do not find out about it until the customer calls and complains.

"Our receivables are high, I am told, but I do not know much about that. My concern is that, when an item is shipped, the invoice is prepared by the staff in the accounting department. That is my most important responsibility, outside of manufacturing and product design.

"It is awfully important that, when orders arrive here, I am told about it. The production work form is only as good as the information that goes on it. We are fairly good in this area, but even losing track of 1 out of 100 orders is too many when you get right down to it.

"Probably automation is a key to improving the situation. A computer of some size in here, with a system properly designed and implemented, would be just the thing to handle the volume of paper we push in running this shop. If we open remote plants, they will need administrative help to be successful too."

INTERVIEW WITH JACOBSON

"Our main problem seems to be that we do not get the information we need about our customers or their orders quickly. Too often, when we want to know the status of work for the month, we have to go through the production records by hand. We are held up by batch time too often. It takes a long time to go through active orders and summarize them by part number *and* to generate an alphabetical listing by customer.

"Accounting for receivables is a big job also. We ship from 100 to 200 lots each week. While that is not a lot per se, if it is not done correctly, it can be a real headache. I don't think we are in trouble with our receivables, but then again, I am not sure. Sometimes I wake up at night trying to figure out whether our records are fully reliable."

INTERVIEW WITH CARBO

"We are really growing in this company. You have probably heard that our growth rate is in the neighborhood of 40 percent. However, that means that our work rate here in accounting is growing too.

"Our facility has two full-time persons (salary $12,000, plus fringe benefits) employed doing these jobs (order entry and receivables). With the volume of business we handle, they are more than busy. Sometimes orders get lost or invoices are missed. That does not happen too often, although accounting always gets the blame when it does occur.

"Our main problem is the amount of work. We never work overtime. That is our policy. Thus, when orders or receivables get behind, we drop everything else and work on that. We need more people to eliminate that difficulty.

"I heard someone talking about computerization. That is getting pretty common in accounting shops. Some of our neighbor firms have recently installed new automated systems. I am not sure just what they are using them for. But, they tell of some interesting experiences. One of the systems seems to be working pretty well, I guess. We would not be that lucky unless it is carefully planned and not rushed. Chances are an automated system would be difficult to develop here, but I certainly think we should consider it and make an informed decision. The IBM system in use for inventory and manufacturing seems quite effective. If an accounting system can be similarly developed, we should consider it."

INTERVIEW WITH SEVERSKI

"We are in a period of continued growth and will be for the next several years. As a matter of fact—you may have heard this—we are anticipating opening satellite facilities in the surrounding communities. Since there is growth, there are bound to be growing pains. The project request deserves careful attention. An important question has been raised, and we need to find the answer.

"At the same time, I do not want this request to get out of hand. Let's get the facts. Sales are high, growth is good, and those are the main things today. Tomorrow depends on more efficient support systems. I don't want to rock the boat if the shops are generally under control and orders and receivables are being handled in an acceptable manner. But I don't know that. This is why I am supporting the feasibility study. Your findings and recommendations will be very important to me."

FINDINGS

The investigation indicated that management did not have the information to answer basic operating questions. Enough instances were found to indicate that improvement in order processing and the maintenance of accounts receivable was needed. The number of lost orders was not specifically determined. However, it was clear that the frequency was greater than the normal industry average of 1 to 2 percent of all orders placed.

Management accepted the findings of the preliminary investigation and instructed the systems department to begin immediately on a detailed investigation to identify systems requirements. It expects a formal proposal outlining strategies to improve Valley Industries' order entry and accounts receivable systems.

REQUIREMENTS ANALYSIS PLANS AND INFORMATION REQUESTS

The analysis of requirements was conducted by a project team appointed within the systems department. This section outlines the strategies followed in organizing the investigation. The questions raised during interviews with selected managers and employees of Valley Industries are also presented.

OVERALL STRATEGY

In order to understand the current processes for order entry and maintenance of accounts receivable, the following strategy for determining information requirements was developed:

1. Interview:
   John Severski, president
   Henry Jacobson, director of operations
   Jim Olson, chief engineer, and his two assistants
   Marjorie Carbo, controller, and the accounting clerks
2. Sample all documents and records of information used by personnel for order entry, invoicing, and receivables. Sample all reports, currently prepared for management or staff, pertaining to order processing and accounts receivable.
3. Observe actual procedures followed for processing incoming orders, preparing customer invoices, and managing accounts receivable.
4. Study any existing standard operating procedures and manuals and

investigate current standards for processing incoming orders, preparing customer invoices, and managing accounts receivable.

The following general objectives guide this investigation:

1 Describe all order and account processing activities, including formal and informal communication requirements, as well as actual procedures followed to process orders and accounts receivable.
2 Identify and describe all critical data elements used to accept and maintain customer orders, to prepare and mail invoices when orders are shipped to customers, and to maintain and notify customers of account balances.
3 Assess current and future order, record, and production volume.
4 Determine current strategies for record retention, access control, security procedures, and measures for maintaining data integrity.

INTERVIEWS

According to the plans developed and described in the preceding sections, interviews were conducted with all individuals as planned. For each individual, the interview objectives and questions asked are provided.

The interviews go into increasing detail. Those persons who are interviewed first are asked the most general questions, while those later are asked much more specific and probing questions, both because of their involvement in daily operations and because of the details already gathered by the analysts. In some cases, the analysts have planned questions that anticipate certain responses. These questions will not be used if the expected response is not received. Instead an alternate form will be asked by the interviewer. Information and details gathered through the interviews are summarized in the next section.

INTERVIEW WITH JOHN SEVERSKI

The objectives of this interview are to elicit goals and objectives for Valley Industries, plans for the next 5-year planning period, and the performance needed from order entry and accounts receivable processing to achieve these goals. It is also expected that during the interview, we will assess Severski's support for the systems concept underlying the current investigation.

QUESTIONS

1 What is your plan for Valley Industries for the next 5 years? Your vision?
2 What are your goals and objectives for Valley for the next 5 years? Has the board of directors developed a different set? If so, what is the reason? How do those you present differ from those of the board?
3 How are you achieving these goals?
4 How does the current order entry system fit into your plans? How do you rate its effectiveness? What is the reason for the level of effectiveness you describe?
5 Can you be more specific about the level of performance needed in order

entry processing, invoicing, and managing accounts receivable? Do you have specific standards? Do any standards currently exist? Who do you feel has the best insight into current order and account processing? Do you know whether the current status is because of any particular person or persons?

6 What difficulties do you foresee in meeting future growth and operating expectations under the current systems? Do you have suggestions for handling the anticipated difficulties you outline? What is your feeling about the cost and benefits of implementing these suggestions? Have you developed a cost projection in your thinking?

INTERVIEW WITH HARRY JACOBSON

The objectives of this interview are to determine the goals and objectives for Valley Industries, as well as to assess current problems in the use of the existing systems. In addition, it will assess Jacobson's requirements to deliver the same or better service during the expected growth period.

QUESTIONS

1–6 Same questions as for Severski.

7 What details and information that you receive about order processing and account management are most vital? What are they used for? How often do you receive them? Is this adequate?

8 What excess or unnecessary information are you receiving that you do not find helpful? Do you know why you receive it? Would you rather not receive it?

9 Have you identified information that, although you do not now receive it, you feel is so useful it should be produced by any new or modified systems that emerge from this investigation? If preparation of this information is costly, do you still think it should be prepared? How will you evaluate its cost effectiveness?

10 What bottlenecks or problems do you have with needed information? Where do they occur? Why? What suggestions do you think will improve this?

11 Who do you suggest we talk to to find out about how these systems function?

12 Do you feel your staff is adequate to meet the increased demand? What problems could originate from current staff if changes are made in processing orders, invoices, and accounts receivable? Do you have specific suggestions or cautions that we should be aware of when discussing these matters with your staff?

13 Describe the manner in which your sales representatives interact with the order entry system. Do you or the staff feel this is an efficient method? Should it be improved? What alternatives have been considered?

14 How are telephone orders handled? Who receives incoming telephone orders? What is the rate of mail orders? How are they processed? By whom? What is produced from the initial order beside the production request?

15 It is important for us to have you describe, in an overview fashion, how the current order, invoicing, and accounts receivable systems operate. What is the path a work order follows from its receipt through to the billing stage?

16 How are orders filed when they are active? After they are filled? Who receives copies of open invoices? How are they stored and retrieved? How do invoices enter accounts receivable? Under what organization are customer accounts filed? When are they maintained and what is the process used? How often are customer statements prepared? How often are account summaries and reports prepared for management use? We would like to observe the processing of orders and preparation of receivable accounts. Do we have your approval? Would you inform staff members in each of these areas that we will be contacting them to arrange a time for this?

17 Often order and accounting systems are viewed as staff functions that contribute excess expenses to operating the business. Do you feel that this perception is held by many persons in Valley Industries? Are there areas of excess cost? Can you suggest improvements within the current system and procedures that could avoid these costs, improve service, or increase revenue?

18 Specifically, would up-to-date information on the status of work orders or customer accounts, as requested, be useful? Would it help to cut costs?

19 Is your perception that the age of receivables is increasing, decreasing, or staying the same? How do you keep track of these accounts?

20 What decision-making processes could best be supported by an automated system? What support would be most useful to you?

INTERVIEW WITH JIM OLSON AND ASSISTANTS

The objectives of these interviews are not only to determine company goals and objectives and Olson and his assistants' knowledge of them, but also to determine Olson's problems with the current system and what he needs in order to deliver the same or better service during the planned growth.

QUESTIONS

1–9 Same questions as for Harry Jacobson.

10 How do you keep track of the product line? What records or specifications do you have now? What files and filing procedures do you presently use?

11 How are you made aware of an order?

12 What information, records, or forms do you use for production schedul-

ing? Do you see a need to keep better track of orders? Why? What are your suggestions for accomplishing this?

13 How do you notify Carbo that it is time to prepare an invoice for an order ready for shipment? Should this method be changed? Why? What suggestions do you have for this system?

14 What roles do your assistants play in this area? Do they have specific responsibilities? Please describe them.

15 What tasks in your department are most time-consuming, repetitious, and tedious? Which tasks are liked the most? The least?

16 Please describe or trace the steps in processing an order from receipt to completion so that we see the role your department plays in the processing.

17 How do you determine whether an incoming order can be filled? Please relate this to order timing and plant capacity.

18 Which decisions about handling orders are the most complex to formulate? Which are the least complex decisions to make?

19 What decision-making processes are highest in volume and very routine? (This is one test we use when considering whether computer assistance is useful for a task area.)

20 You indicated that order loss is one of your concerns. How often do orders get lost? How do you find out about it? How long does it take the customer to complain? Why do orders get lost? How is the loss resolved? What costs arise from losing an order? From resolving the loss?

21 What information is included with a shipment and where does the document originate? How do accounting, production, and shipping interact? May we have copies of blank and completed orders and order processing reports?

22 Please explain shipping and receiving operations for production and the flow of information to and from that area.

23 What are typical daily and weekly volumes? What are low and high levels? Do you make any specific adjustments in processing when the volume reaches a high level for a period of time? Please describe them if you do.

24 Are a large percentage of orders for a small number of products, or are orders fairly evenly distributed over the product line?

25 Would it be feasible to establish an inventory for certain products, would this streamline ordering and reduce backlogs, or is it more efficient to continue production to order?

INTERVIEW WITH MARJORIE CARBO

The objectives of this interview are, first, to determine the goals and objectives for her department and to learn what she needs to deliver the same or better service during this growth period; second, to get a description of all processing activities and procedures involved in order entry, invoicing, and receivables operations; third, to get a description of stored data and uses, and relations between the data and the files; fourth, to get a statement about the size and characteristics of reports, files, frequency of access, retention and

VAL SYR

GMM SEP 6 1109
847692 KAYEN G

09.06.8_ 1827/AN

ATTENTION SALES.

PLEASE ACCEPT ORDER NO 58165/4000 FOR:-

JOB NO. 2587
JOB NO. 2588

6 OFF E705/2512R @ 13.00
55 OFF E613/E0003 @ 4.20

REQUIRED EXTREMELY URGENTLY.
PLEASE ADVISE PRICE BY RETURN OF THIS AND PREVIOUS ORDER.

REGARDS

L. AHLSTROM
847692 KAYEN G
VAL SYR

REPLY TO THIS TELEX VIA GMM

Figure C3.1. TELEX order annotated to indicate order number for manufacturing.

Production is FIFO (first in–first out, the first order received is the first order produced), except where unusual customer demands require that an order be rescheduled or expedited. This happens only occasionally. The order in fact becomes the production order.

When work is completed, the production manager writes down (on a regular sheet of paper) who the part is for and how many are ready for shipping. This information is given to one of the staff, who types the invoice and packing slip (Figure C3.6). The packing slip is the last copy of the invoice.

The parts are moved to the shipping area where they are packaged; the packing slip is enclosed in the shipping carton.

One copy of the invoice goes to the bookkeeper who files it in the customer's accounts receivable file. An additional copy is placed in a master invoice file. This file is for reference only; it is not an active file but merely a duplicate backup file.

Invoices are numbered and logged on an invoice log sheet (Figure C3.7).

VALLEY INDUSTRIES
OPEN PART/JOB REPORT

September 6, 1985 Page 6

Customer Name	VALLEY Part Number	Qty Due	VALLEY Job Number	Due Date	Date Promised	Date Booked
Westinghouse	V515-220ct	100	2274	10/18/85	10/20/85	08/22/85
Worth Wire Inc	V1612-2.030S	50	1697	10/15/85		04/21/85
Xerox	V924-.45100V9	180	2191	09/11/85		08/10/85

Figure C3.2. Details contained on order log.

CUSTOMER Smith Robbins
CUSTOMER NO.
BILL TO: 2500 Snetana Drive
Santa Monica, CA 90406
SHIP TO: 2502 Snetana Drive
BUYER: Bob Bardow
PHONE NO.: 213-453-8765
ACCEPTED BY: AK DATE: 10/12/85
REP: Stockleman REP. NO: C84
ADDITIONAL REMARKS:

CUSTOMER PART NO:
OUR PART NO.: V509-2.5300
E.C. LEVEL
P. O. NO. S 48746
QUANTITY 18
PRICE 37.90 ea
ENG. CHARGE
TOOLING:
DELIVERY REQ.
DELIVERY PROM.
UPS Blue
JOB NO. 2508

CUSTOMER General Milling & Mfg
CUSTOMER NO.
BILL TO: 3055 32nd Ave. South
Minneapolis, Minnesota 55455
SHIP TO: Same
BUYER: Lewis Ahlstrom
PHONE NO.: 602-373-6423
ACCEPTED BY: JO DATE: 9/6/85
REP: Jerold Adv. Mdsing. REP. NO:
ADDITIONAL REMARKS:

CUSTOMER PART NO:
OUR PART NO.: E705/2512R
E.C. LEVEL
P. O. NO. TX 9.06.8-1827
QUANTITY 6
PRICE 13.00
ENG. CHARGE
TOOLING:
DELIVERY REQ.
DELIVERY PROM. UPS
JOB NO. 2587

Figure C3.3. Order card.

			Shipping Quantity								1800
Special Instructions	Rep	Date	Packing Slip	Shipped	How		Date		Shipped	How	
	ADV. MOSING.						8/15				
							8/15	5614	125	6152237 FED. EXPRESS	1638.87
							8/29	5750	100	UPS BLUE	1312.87
							9/6	5816	48	"	637.87
							9/6	5817	48	"	637.87
							10/6	5927	48	"	637.87
							10/8	5973	6	UPS BLUE	90.87
BILL TO:											
GENERAL MILLING & MANUFACTURING											
3055 32ND. AVENUE SOUTH											
MINNEAPOLIS, MINNESOTA	55855										
612-373-6423											
ATTENTION: LEWIS AHLSTROM											
DO NOT INVENTORY -											
MAKE TO CUSTOMER'S											
TELEX ORDER											

Date	Qty.	Bal.	Date	Qty.	Bal.	Date	Qty.	Bal.	Date	Qty.	Bal.	Date	Qty.	Bal.	Date	Qty.	Bal.	Date	Qty.	Bal.	Date	Qty.	Bal.	Date	Qty	Bal.		

Ship To: GENERAL MILLING AND MANUFACTURING	Customer Job # EACH REQUEST SUBMITTED	Price 13.00	Customer GENERAL MILLING & MANUFACTURING
3055 32ND AVENUE SOUTH	Order Date SEPARATELY BY TELEX	Eng. Chg.	P. O. No. ———
MINNEAPOLIS, MINNESOTA 55455	How Ship UPS	Job No.	Customer Part No.
			Valley Part No.

Figure C3.4. Customer order card.

GENERAL MILLING AND MANUFACTURING
3055 32nd Avenue South
Minneapolis, MN 55455
612-373-6423

CONTACT: Lewis Ahlstrom

SALES REP: Advance Merchandising

Figure C3.5. Customer information on rolodex card.

Figure C3.6. Invoice

VALLEY INDUSTRIES
1300 Main Street
Binghamton, New York 13901

DATE	NUMBER
10/8	5973

SOLD TO

GENERAL MILLING AND MANUFACTURING
3055 32nd Avenue South
Minneapolis, Minnesota 55455

SHIP TO

SAME

SALESPERSON: Jerold; Advance Merchandising SHIP: UPS AUTH: Telex 9.06.8 1827

QUANTITY	STOCK NO	DESCRIPTION	UNIT	EXTENSION
6 OFF	E705/2512R	12 Volt connection assemblies	13.00	78.00
		Shipping & Freight		12.87
		TOTAL AMOUNT THIS INVOICE		90.87

VAL JOB NOS: 2587

PAYMENT AND CREDIT CYCLE

When a payment is received from a customer, the bookkeeper pulls a copy of the original invoice and posts the payment against the manual accounts receivable record. The customer's account balance is adjusted to show the current balance. In all cases, a balance forward method is used. (That is, account balances, rather than individual invoice numbers, are maintained in the accounting system.)

Credits are handled as negative orders. They are approved and then forwarded to the bookkeeper, who adjusts the account balances.

Interest charges are added to any balances that are more than 30 days old. The interest is at the rate of 1½ percent per month on any unpaid balance. Valley has found that it can collect this additional amount from all firms that are regular Valley customers. Those that are only submitting one-time orders may ignore the finance charge when they settle their account.

Terms of payment are net amount due within 30 days of invoice date. In the past, Valley experimented with net 10 days, but the customers did not take the time period seriously.

Each month an accounts receivable report is prepared manually. Customer and total accounts receivable are determined by adding the balances of all unpaid invoices. If necessary, accounting will also report balances by the 30-day periods in which they were incurred (i.e., this month, last month, and over 60 days old).

PRODUCT IDENTIFICATION

Each product manufactured by Valley Industries has its own distinctive number, assigned by the engineering department. For example, a typical part number is V912-2.530S. The "912" is the series number and indicates the part uses 12 volts of power. This part produces 250 volts output (represented by "2.5") at 30 milliamps (the "30") with single output (S). The part number defines the price, but only the chief engineer can read a part number and know what the price is.

Valley also uses other part numbers. For example, 1583-A is a part that is manufactured only for one customer. It is a special item, manufactured under Valley's standard design. However, Valley uses the *customer's* part number since it is a one-customer item.

Valley Industries considered developing a part number system that would define prices and identify items. Currently, since the part number does define the price and accurately defines the *unit* or *part* itself, it is not possible to change the part number. The chief engineer pointed out to the interviewer that this problem is common throughout the electronics industry and not unique to Valley.

PRODUCT PRICING

The prices for products are established on a per unit basis. However, quantity discounts are given at the levels of 250, 500, 1,000, 2,500, 5,000, and 10,000,

SHIPPING/INVOICE LIST

Week Ending 10/23/85

DATE	INVOICE	COMPANY	PART #	PIECES	TOTAL	SHIPPING CHARGE	TOTAL INVOICE	JOB NO.
10/8	5969	Buick	V724-2.512R	600	2142.00		2142.00	1739
	5970	Honeywell	PS12-430	25	182.75	4.32	187.07	2579
10/8	5971	Sunspots Inc	1583-A	283	1635.74		1635.74	2354
	5972	Tex Instru.	V1212-2.530S	2	105.80	2.38	108.18	2572
10/8	5973	Gen Mill & Mfg	E705/2512R	6	78.00	12.87	90.87	2587

Figure C3.7. Details contained on invoice log sheet.

according to a complex algorithm supplied to the interviewer. The algorithm is used regularly to determine the amount of discount for each customer order. It appears to work well.

ORDER TRACKING

Each part goes into approximately eight manufacturing operations. Management discussed developing a status code to indicate the status of an order, but one has not yet been developed. Currently there is no way of getting feedback or updated reports and worksheets on order status.

Jacobson and Olson are concerned about a better method for tracking orders and the progress of orders through the system. Carbo feels this is also an important control issue.

Problems are associated with approximately 5 percent of the orders received. When a problem arises, it is called to the attention of the production people who reschedule the order on a rush basis. Orders are not really lost revenue but delayed income, since customers seldom cancel the order even if it is delayed.

BUSINESS CYCLES

There is some seasonality to this business. Orders drop at the end of the calendar year, as customers reduce stock prior to physically counting inventories. However, it picks up again in January, as these same customers realize a strong need to rebuild their stock. In addition, late spring results in a drop, due to line slippage in the automotive industry, an industry that provides nearly half of Valley's orders. The automotive industry picks up again in July and August, as it starts production of next year's models.

TRANSACTION VOLUME

Examining the order and accounting records confirmed the statistics received from operating personnel during interviews. The following transaction volumes and information were noted:

Number of open orders:	Average 300 to 400 Peak in past 700 to 800
Number of orders shipped per day:	Average 25 to 30 per day Peak in past 75 per day
Number of invoices per day:	Same as number of shipments
Number of lines per invoice:	Typical 1 or 2 lines Maximum 10 (when there are extra charges)
Payments per day:	Average 25
Credit and debit memos	Approximately 10 per week
Statement production:	Monthly
Pricing errors:	$10,000 annually
Average accounts renewable balance: (overdue amount):	$1.1 million ($250,000)

Current report frequency is acceptable to all individuals, although the need for the production manager to hold on to orders and verify them against the open order report on Monday is not well-liked by anyone. Other reports seem to be getting the job done.

EMPLOYEE BENEFITS
Fringe benefits are approximately 30 percent above the employee's salary. Salary increases are planned to average 10 percent per annum.

KEYWORDS

Bottleneck
Closed questionnaire
Closed-response question
Decision requirements
Fact finding
Interview
Observation
Open-ended questionnaire
Open-response question
Participant observation
Questionnaire
Record review
Requirement
Requirement determination
Transaction requirement
Trigger function

REVIEW QUESTIONS

1 What is a systems requirement? How are requirements determined?
2 Why are systems analysts often at a disadvantage, compared with managers of departments where systems investigations are being conducted? How is this disadvantage overcome?
3 Discuss the four major questions that analysts seek to answer during systems investigations. Are the questions applicable to any systems study? Explain.
4 What is a "trigger"? Why is it of concern to systems analysts? What role does it play in a systems study?
5 Distinguish between transaction sys-

tems and decision requirements. What relation exists between them? How do organizationwide requirements affect them?

6 What type of information is often best obtained through interview? Distinguish between the types of questions posed during interviews. What advantages and disadvantages does each type offer?

7 What problems should analysts watch for when conducting interviews? How should investigators evaluate the responses they receive to their questions?

8 When should analysts use open- and closed-form questionnaires? For what types of information is each form most useful?

9 Discuss the steps that should always be taken to develop and administer questionnaires.

10 When is record review an effective data collection method? What is the purpose of this method? Are there disadvantages to its use?

11 What role does observation play in systems investigations? Should the analyst ever become directly involved in the system under investigation? Explain the reason for your answer.

12 What is a bottleneck? A bootleg form?

APPLICATION PROBLEMS FOR CHAPTER 3

1 Goodwrecks Auto Rental Agency is in the process of redesigning its on-line reservation system. The current system uses a CRT with a standard typewriter keyboard and a dot matrix printer on which all rental contracts and reports are printed. All interaction with the system is through the CRT and all printed output is through the printer. Responses to inquiries may also be received on the CRT display if printed output is not wanted or needed.

Goodwrecks management wants to upgrade the capabilities of the system to make it easier to use for operators and to overcome some problems with the way reservation clerks use it. Most of these problems, management feels, stem from the way operators use the system. It is believed that carelessness causes nearly all of the problems encountered.

The system is located in St. Louis, Missouri, but terminals are located throughout North America at Goodwrecks's offices in major airports and hotels. The data communication portion of the system is working well. No changes are planned in the near future. Furthermore, the proposed redesign will not affect the data communication process.

Major corporate users receive discounts on auto rentals. To determine the appropriate discount, the reservation clerk, using the corporate name, must look up the discount rate in a master record book. Frequently personnel try to remember discount rates for specific firms or take the rate the customer suggests as the correct one. In both cases, too many errors are made. Audit problems result when the amount of revenue actually in the cash drawer at the end of the day or shift does not match the amount the systems control report says should be on hand.

An additional problem contributing to the revenue audit discrepancy is credits and payouts. Whenever either of these events occurs, for whatever reason, a paidout slip is to be completed by the agent handling the transaction. This is not always done.

Payments by customers may be in the form of cash, check, or major credit card. Cash is no problem. For check payments, operators must key into the terminal the individual's driver's license number and state of registration. In some cases, one or both numbers may be omitted. In other cases, the license number may be entered erroneously.

Credit card transactions are usually handled properly. When problems do occur, they are often in the form of wrong or incomplete card numbers being used, the wrong card name indicated, or the amount of the transaction not entered.

In some cases, automobiles are given to customers and returned several days later. But at the time of return, no paperwork or contracts are found in the files or in the computer-based files. This happens with all types of customers, both corporate and private.

The computer system maintains an inventory file of cars at the different agency locations (i.e., airports and hotels). In this file is such data as car description, serial number, license number, location, status (rented, in repair, awaiting rental, reserved), date of purchase, date due for sale, etc. When specific cars are rented, this file is updated to show the name of the renter, driver's license number, date rented, date due back, and rental rate. The system also prints out a contract which the renter signs.

When the system goes down, whatever the reason, reservation agents write up the contracts by hand. Later, when the computer system is available again, they try to enter as much of the data as possible into the system to update the files.

Design a data collection study to acquire all data and information you feel you need to begin logical design of an improved system. Indicate the *specific* facts, opinions, and information you wish to collect. Also indicate which data collection method you would use for each item you specify. Be sure to indicate the source of the data too (e.g., what person(s), files, records, documents, etc.).

2 Which fact-finding techniques are the most effective ones for requirements determination in each of the following situations?

a Whether an organization is planning new store sites.

b How patient health insurance forms are actually completed.

c Whether the steps in an auditing procedure are followed properly.

d The opinion of the majority of employees about using automation to improve quality control and how it will affect them.

e How stock market quotes are received and used in the formulation of buy/sell decisions for an investment portfolio.

f What system or control problems related to the current investigation have arisen in the recent past and how they were dealt with.

g The number of airline tickets purchased every month over a year's time.

h Whether specific managers believe a proposed system is a good idea.

i Whether there are enough personnel processing accounts payable records to avoid a bottleneck.

j Opinions about unauthorized use of computer facilities from a group of 25 persons.

3 A view about systems investigations often expressed by some persons is that the best way to find out about the users' most important requirements is to ask them what they are. The rationale behind this belief is that, if the users cannot identify the information they need or clearly state their requirements to systems analysts, it is unlikely the analysts will be able to develop the right system. This is also the reason that users must be closely involved in systems development activities.

Discuss this idea, indicating whether you feel effective information systems can be developed even if the users cannot express their requirements. Explain why your position is correct. Give examples to support your position.

4 The manager of a Broadway theatrical agency in New York City is interested in conducting a systems study to determine the feasibility of establishing a North American network for the sale of theater tickets to the performances of touring companies. The manager envisions a network in which an agent in each city that a particular touring group will visit accepts reservations for performances or cash payment for the tickets themselves. The sales may be made well in advance of the theater company's arrival.

A tour group is always booked for a minimum number of performances in every city it visits since it must reserve the theater for the performance day(s) and allow enough time to set up the stage and light and sound systems. However, if there is sufficient demand, extra performances can also be scheduled on the day(s) the theater is reserved.

Advanced sale information will also assist the producer in knowing whether extra advertising is needed to boost ticket sales. And, it will aid in the control of revenue by ensuring that neither tickets nor money are lost.

a Assume you know only the details provided in the description above and must conduct a systems study to determine the feasibility of such a system. What information should you seek to develop a profile of the theater system, the tour, and the proposed system?

b How will you collect the information?
(*Note:* Do not be concerned with the computer issues. Focus on the theatrical activities described above.)

5 The city is considering the development of an automated traffic control system that will regulate the traffic lights in the downtown metropolitan area. The system, which will run 24 hours a day and 7 days a week, will sense the number of motor vehicles moving on the city streets and the number waiting for traffic signals to change. The data will be processed continually to determine how long the electric signals should stop traffic from one direction and allow movement in other directions. It will also control right and left turn signals.

Because the regulation of one traffic signal in the downtown area affects the movement of vehicles for many blocks in all directions, the system must control a large number of signals for all the intersections. A large computer system will be dedicated to the task of sensing and processing the data.

One step in the systems investigation for this project is to send questionnaires to all traffic police who have been assigned to regulation of vehicles and traffic in the downtown area (say for the last 24 months). They will have important information and suggestions about which electric signals should be regulated to smooth vehicle movement.

Assume you know only what has been described above and are familiar with driving in a metropolitan area, as a typical motorist would. What facts and opinions do you want to learn as part of your systems study? That is, what information do you seek and what questions do you want to raise to acquire that information? (Assume that the system has already been identified as a feasible project that will be undertaken and you are now beginning the detailed investigation.)

6 The staff of over 30 administrative assistants for a large law firm has requested the development and acquisition of a centralized word processing system. The word processing would use computer processing logic to improve the efficiency with which all written materials the staff lawyers and attorneys use are prepared. The administrative assistants have indicated that there is a large amount of repetition in many of the documents they prepare or that a single document, even if unique, is revised many times before it is in final form. At the current time, each document or revision is retyped completely each time. The use of word processing equipment would eliminate much of the manual retyping, they feel.

The features of the word processing system, if adopted, include:

a Entry of data (such as manuscripts, legal documents, and memoranda) through a terminal keyboard that also displays the details visually as they are entered. Corrections and changes are made as the text is entered. The operator can see the text as it is typed.

b Storage of text data in a form that permits later retrieval. The text can be stored temporarily in the system itself or, for long periods of time, on magnetic media that can be removed from the system. However, the user can retrieve the data whenever it is needed.

c Editing of text data after it has been stored. Entire manuscripts can be retrieved or parts of different documents can be retrieved and linked together with newly entered data to produce a new document. In addition, sentences, paragraphs, and entire sections of documents can be moved around to meet legal requirements. For example, a general format for a real estate lease can be stored on the system and retrieved when needed. Then modifications can be made quickly to meet the requirements for current use. Later the same format can be retrieved and edited to suit a different use.

d Printing of the document after all changes are made and editing is complete. The document can be printed in the same format as that produced by an ordinary office typewriter, but in a fraction of the time. Multiple copies can be made with ease.

Design a data collection study to determine whether a word processing system is needed in this office and how it would be used. Be sure to gather details that will enable you to determine whether efficiency will improve. You need not be concerned with evaluating the technical feasibility of automated word processing.

PART TWO

INFORMATION REQUIREMENTS ANALYSIS MODULE

CHAPTER 4 STRATEGIES FOR DETERMINING SYSTEMS REQUIREMENTS

QUESTIONS TO GUIDE YOU THROUGH THE CHAPTER

- Are there different strategies for assessing information systems requirements?
- What is data flow analysis? What benefits does it offer?
- How do data flow methods differ from other methods of describing systems?
- How are data flow diagrams drawn? What do they contain?
- In what ways are descriptions of the data developed and stored?
- What do data dictionaries contain? How are they developed?
- Are data dictionaries useful once analysts understand a system's requirements?

Computer information systems often consist of many components. In most cases, it is difficult for analysts to understand all these components at one time. Investigators therefore have to start with general questions about the purpose of a system, its inputs and outputs, and the processes involved. Gradually, studying major sections of the system independently of others, analysts learn more details. In large systems projects, several analysts conducting an investigation partition the investigation among themselves so that each can work independently, while communicating important information and details to the others.

This chapter is about strategies for determining systems requirements when it is necessary to study components separately and in increasing detail. First two general strategies for studying a system to determine information requirements are introduced. The remainder of this chapter discusses one of those strategies, data flow analysis, how it is useful to analysts, and how it is developed. The last section of the chapter discusses how data dictionaries are used to store descriptions of both data and processes in a system.

Each of the strategies relies on the ability of analysts to use the fact-finding techniques of the last chapter to gather details about the system. There is an interplay between the strategies that indicate where information and facts are missing and the techniques (interview, questionnaire, observation, and record review) that investigators use to collect those facts. This will be pointed out throughout the chapter.

DETERMINING SYSTEMS REQUIREMENTS

There are two widely used strategies for determining information requirements. This section introduces both: the data flow and decision-analysis strategies for understanding information systems.

Data Flow Strategy

Analysts want to know the answers to four specific questions: What processes make up a system? What data is used in each process? What data is stored? And, what data enters and leaves the system? The emphasis is clearly on *data analysis.*

Data drives business activities. It can trigger events (for example, new sales order data) and it can be processed to provide information useful to personnel wanting to know, for example, how well events have been handled (by measuring work quality and rate, profitability, etc.). Systems analysis recognizes the central role of business data in organizations. Following its flow through business processes, which is the purpose of *data flow analysis,* tells analysts a great deal about how organization objectives are accomplished. In the course of handling transactions and completing tasks, data is input, processed, stored, retrieved, used, changed, and output. Data flow analysis studies the use of data in each activity. It documents these findings in *data flow diagrams,* that graphically show the relation between processes and data, and in *data dictionaries,* that formally describe the systems data and where it is used.

Decision-Analysis Strategy

The *decision-analysis* strategy for determining information systems requirements complements data flow analysis. This strategy emphasizes studying the objectives of an operation and the decisions that must be made to meet those objectives and carry on business. The decisions occur both at operating and senior managerial levels. The decision-analysis strategy addresses these questions: What conditions can arise that will affect a decision? What are the alternative actions available to the decision maker? Which conditions are most important in making a decision of what action to take? This strategy reveals the data and information needs for persons who have to make specific decisions.

Decision analysis is also often used in understanding upper-management decision making. The choice managers responsible for the decision make to select a pricing strategy from a set of alternatives is handled differently than the choice a department supervisor makes to

STEPS IN DATA FLOW ANALYSIS STRATEGY

1. Study operations and ongoing processes.
2. Identify how data is processed in handling transactions and completing tasks.
3. Follow flow of data: input
   processing
   storage
   retrieval
   output
4. Gradually add details at lower levels.

STEPS IN DECISION ANALYSIS STRATEGY

1. Study objectives and necessary decisions.
2. Develop a model of the decision process.
3. Test model with sample data.
4. Identify processing requirements for data.

Figure 4.1. Strategies for requirements determination.

accept or reject orders. In the first, analysts must learn about the pricing question by identifying management objectives and decisions that have to be made. Next, a model of the decision process is developed. Then data needed to formulate the decision is identified, and the model is tested using sample data (Figure 4.1).

The order rejection decision generally occurs more frequently; so the conditions and actions are usually known. Studying the decision may not require the development and testing of new models, but determining how to make the decision remains an important question.

Analysts summarize the results of decision analysis graphically, in tables or in highly structured statements of the relations between conditions and decisions.

The methods for decision analysis are discussed in detail in Chapter 5. The remainder of this chapter explores data analysis, using data flow concepts.

DATA FLOW CONCEPTS

Data flow analysis examines the use of data to carry out specific business processes within the scope of a systems investigation. Data flow diagrams *show* the use of data in the system *pictorally.* They show all the essential components in the system and how they fit together. It can be difficult to fully understand a business process through a verbal description alone; data flow diagrams help by illustrating the essential components of a process and the way they interact.

This section discusses the notation used in data flow diagrams, as well as the objectives in drawing them during an investigation. It shows what to include in the diagram and how to use it for analysis.

Notation

Logical data flow diagrams can be completed using only four simple notations:

1 *Data Flow*. Data moves in a specific direction from an origin to a destination in the form of a document, letter, telephone call, or virtually any other medium. The data flow is a "packet" of data.

2 *Processes*. People, procedures, or devices use or produce (transform) data. The physical component is not identified.

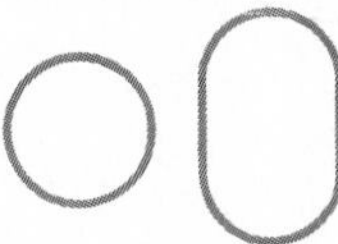

3 *Source or Destination of Data*. External sources or destinations of data, which may be people, programs, organizations, or other entities, interact with the system but are outside its boundary.

4 *Data Store*. Here data is stored or referenced by a process in the system. It may represent computer or noncomputer devices.

Each component in a data flow diagram is labeled with a descriptive name. Process names are further identified with a number that will be used for identification purposes. The number assigned to a specific process does not represent the sequence of processes. It is strictly for identification and will take on added value when we study the components that make up a specific process. Figure 4.2 shows the notation in a simple data flow diagram consisting of five data flows, two processes, a data store, a source, and a sink. In actual use, each label will be replaced with one that fits the situation being studied.

Parallel Activities

Notice in Figure 4.2 that several data flows can be going on simultaneously. Data flows 1 and 2 may occur in *parallel*. This feature of data flow diagrams, to show parallel activities, is an additional benefit. Other charting methods, such as flowcharts, show *serial* processes—activities that only occur in a specific order, one after the other. Yet organizations have many activities occurring at the same time with concurrent data flows. Data flow diagrams enable the analyst to represent activities more accurately by showing simultaneous activities when they are occurring.

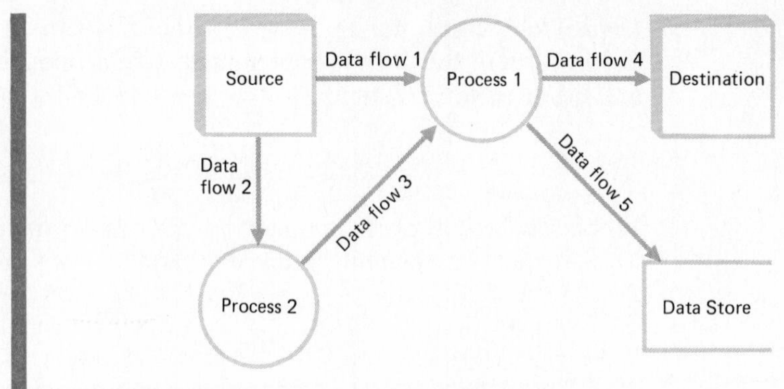

Figure 4.2.
Data flow diagram

As the name suggests, data flow diagrams concentrate on the *data* moving through the system, not devices or equipment. Throughout the process of understanding the application area, the analysts identify and describe the data moving through the system, why it is being input or output, and what processing is done. It is just as important to determine when data enters the application area as when it leaves. Sometimes data is stored for later use or retrieved from previous storage. Data flow diagrams also show this.

Advantages of the Method

These simple notations are easily understood by users and business persons who are part of the process being studied. Therefore, analysts can work with the users and actually involve them in the study of data flow diagrams. Users can make suggestions for modifications of the diagrams to more accurately describe the business activity. Users can examine the charts and spot problems quickly so that they can be corrected before other design work

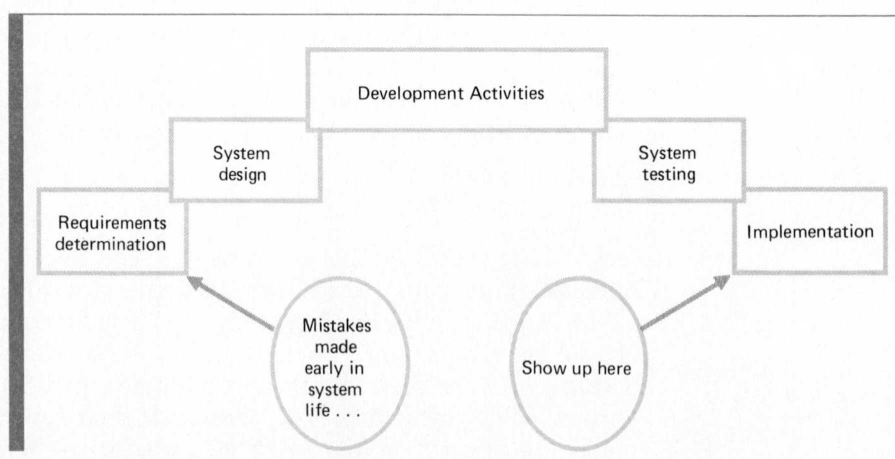

Figure 4.3.
Effect of errors during requirements determination.

begins. If problems are not found early in the development process, they will be very difficult to correct later, when they are noticed (Figure 4.3). Avoiding mistakes early may even prevent system failure.

Data flow analysis permits analysts to isolate areas of interest in the organization and study them by examining the data that enters the process and seeing how it is changed when it leaves the process. As analysts gather facts and details, their increased understanding of the process leads them to ask questions about specific parts of the process, which lead to still additional investigation. Figure 4.4 shows this practice in general, as the area of investigation is broken into successively lower-level details until the analysts understand all the essential components and their interrelations.

A comprehensive systems investigation produces sets of many data flow diagrams, some providing overviews of major processes and others going into great detail to show data elements, data stores, and processing steps for specific components of a larger system. If analysts want to review the

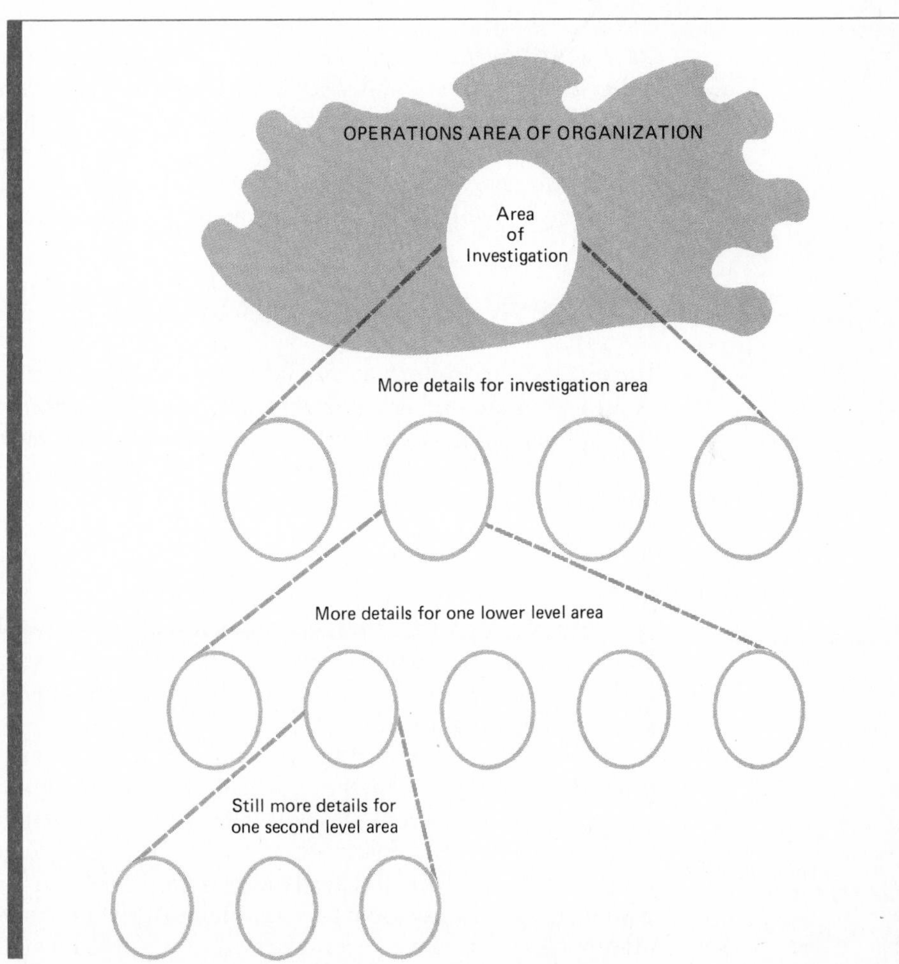

Figure 4.4. System details are acquired one level at a time.

overall system later, they use the overview diagrams. However, if they are interested in studying one particular process, they use the data flow diagram for that lower-level process.

The levels of data flow diagrams can be compared to highway and street maps, used when traveling in an unfamiliar area (see Figure 4.5). On a long trip, you first use a national map, showing major highways and cities. As you near the city you are visiting, you need a more detailed map, showing the major parts of the city and how to enter them. After you reach the area of the city you want, a detailed street map, that even shows important landmarks like bridges and buildings, is especially helpful. This much detail is essential then to find the right street address. But it is not useful when you are first starting on the trip and still having trouble getting the lay of the land.

Data flow diagrams are used the same way. They are developed and used progressively from the general to the specific for the system of interest.

Logical Systems View

Data flow diagrams show the *logical* features of applications. That is, they tell *what* is occurring and *when* it takes place. They do not state how events occur. In other words, such *physical* details as storage methods, input devices, or computer components are not primary concerns for analysts during the early part of analysis. Only after the logical components are understood, should physical components be addressed.

DEVELOPING DATA FLOW DIAGRAMS

To be useful and informative, data flow diagrams must be drawn properly. This section shows how to draw them: where to start, how to add detail to descriptions, when to add control information, and how to be consistent in naming items included on the diagrams. The discussion also points out common mistakes that should be avoided.

Work from the Top Down

The first steps in requirements determination, as we have indicated, are aimed at learning about the general characteristics of the business process under investigation. The top layer of details, so to speak, is studied. As analysts better understand those details, they dig deeper to collect more specific and detailed information. Specific questions are pursued in increasingly greater detail. This process is called *top-down* analysis.

A continuing example will show the development of a data flow diagram. One step is described in each of the following sections.

Suppose you are an analyst starting work on an accounts payable system. You are interested in learning about what the system works on (the inputs) and what it produces (the outputs). And you surely would ask about

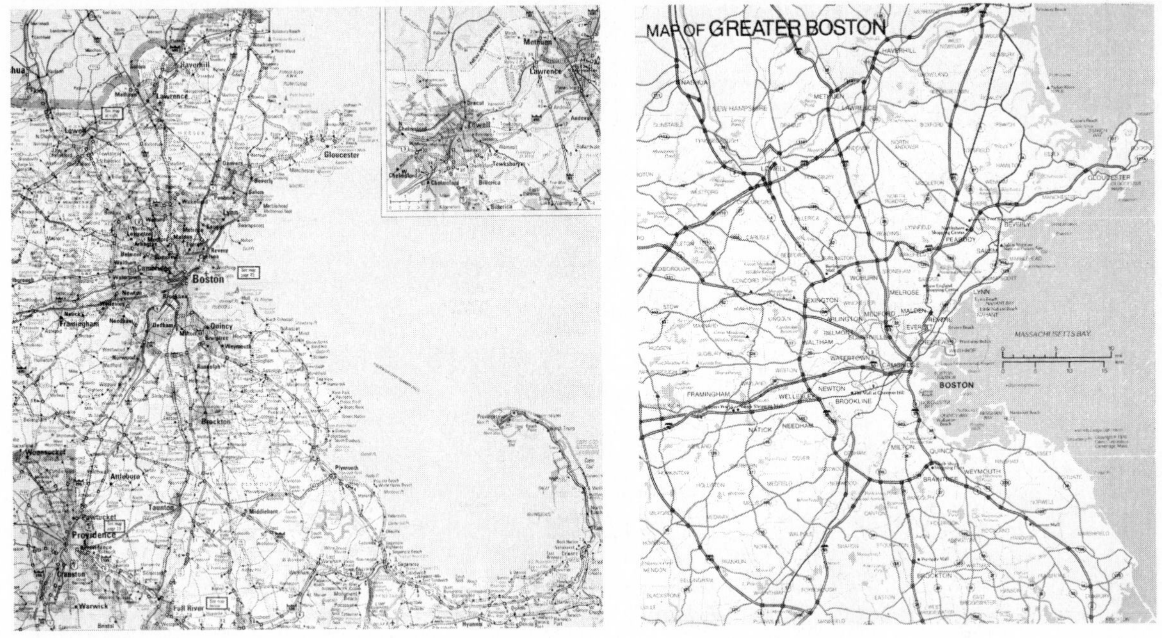

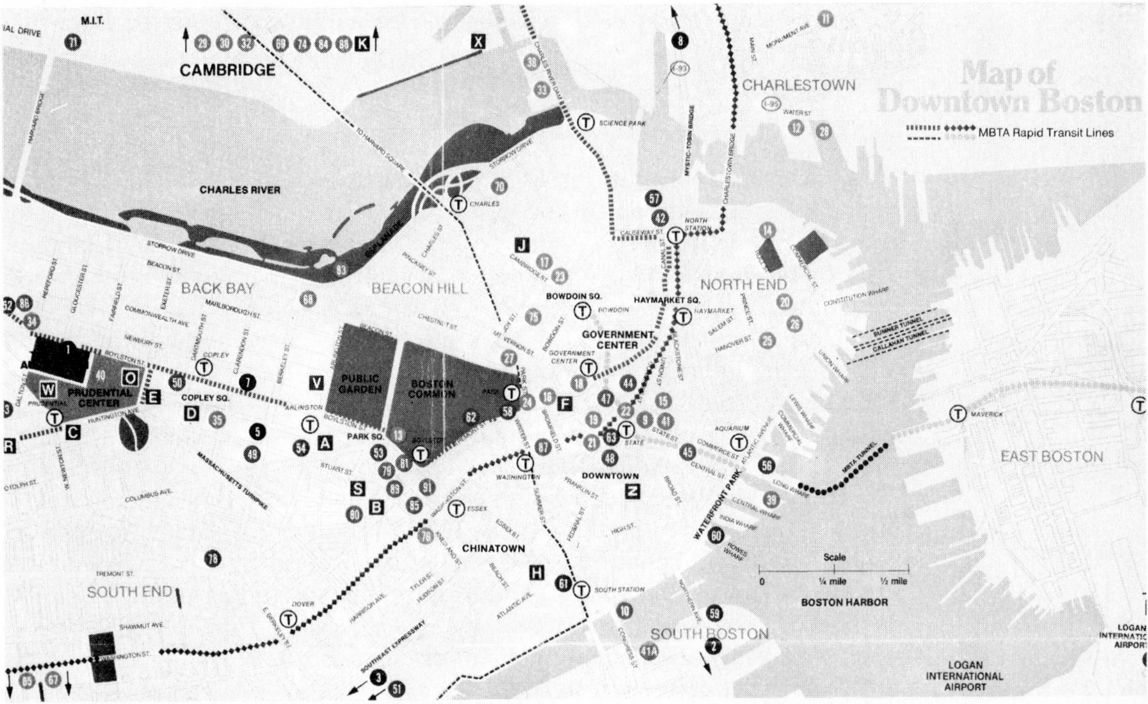

Figure 4.5. Geographic example of Top-down analysis. (3 parts)

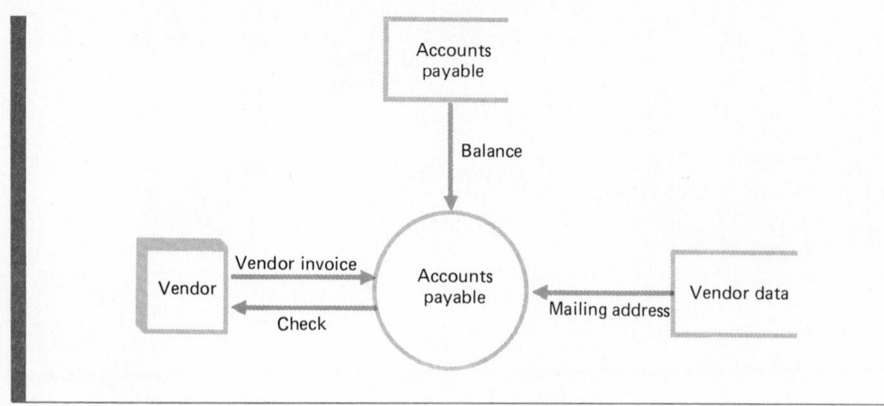

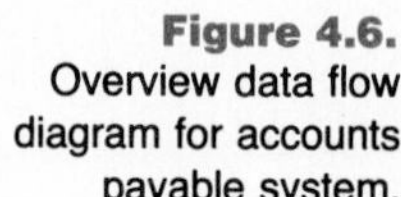

Figure 4.6. Overview data flow diagram for accounts payable system.

data referenced in processing accounts payable claims from vendors and suppliers to whom your firm owes money for merchandise or services provided.

The data flow diagram in Figure 4.6 describes accounts payable processing at a very general (top) level. This diagram shows that vendors submit invoices and receive checks from the organization. This accounts payable process itself requires accounts payable and vendor data. Notice that each arrow, representing data flow, is labeled to show what data is being used. Balance data is retrieved from the accounts payable data store for each vendor being paid, and the vendor address is retrieved from the vendor data store.

Explode Processes for More Detail

The information contained in Figure 4.6 is inadequate to really understand systems requirements, as you probably realize. The next step in this investigation is to describe accounts payable processing in more detail. Figure 4.7 has "exploded" accounts payable processing into three subprocesses: INVOICE APPROVAL, REVISE BALANCE DUE, and WRITE CHECKS. Each is part of the accounts payable process identified in the higher-level diagram shown in Figure 4.6.

The numbers 1.0, 2.0, and 3.0 are also used to identify processes. Processes can be referenced by their numbers (such as 1.0) or their names (such as INVOICE APPROVAL).

This step of top-down description is repeated many times in a systems investigation: Understanding at one level of detail is exploded into greater detail at the next level. Figure 4.7 shows the original process exploded into three subprocesses, which add detail to the understanding of the accounts payable process. In large systems, a single process can be exploded many times over until an adequate amount of detail is described for analysts to understand the process fully.

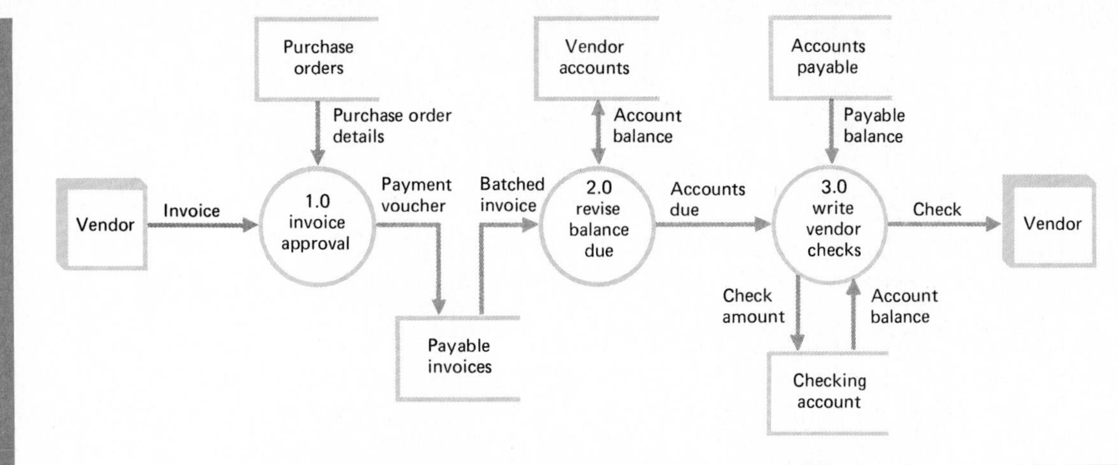

Figure 4.7. First level data flow diagram for accounts payable processing.

Data flow diagrams will not be helpful if they are drawn improperly or are awkward to handle. Each lower level is defined using from three to seven processes to explode a higher-level process. Using more than seven makes the diagram difficult to manage. Data flow diagrams are easiest to read if the description of a process at one level can be drawn on a single sheet of paper. The guideline of using three to seven processes to explode the higher-level process should confine the description to a single sheet. If more details are needed, the next level can be exploded.

The flow of data between processes is like an envelope or package that contains one or more pieces of data. The envelope contains all the data that flows together between two processes each time. However, if different data moves about at different times, there are two separate data flows. The data flow PAYMENT VOUCHER in Figure 4.7 includes the invoice data submitted by the vendor and the internal purchase authorization data: they always go together and so are included in the PAYMENT VOUCHER envelope. It would be incorrect to show *two* data flows from the process 1.0 INVOICE APPROVAL (one for invoice and another for purchase authorization) in this example.

Maintain Consistency between Processes

Notice in Figure 4.7 that the first process has the same input (vendor invoice) as Figure 4.6. The output from the check-writing process also matches the output from Figure 4.6. Thus the explosion is consistent; no new inputs or outputs to the overall process, that were not identified in the higher-level diagrams, are introduced at the lower level. However, within the process, new data flows and data stores are identified. Notice, for example, that data flows for "invoice," "batched invoice," and "accounts due" were identified in exploding the accounts payable processing. This is

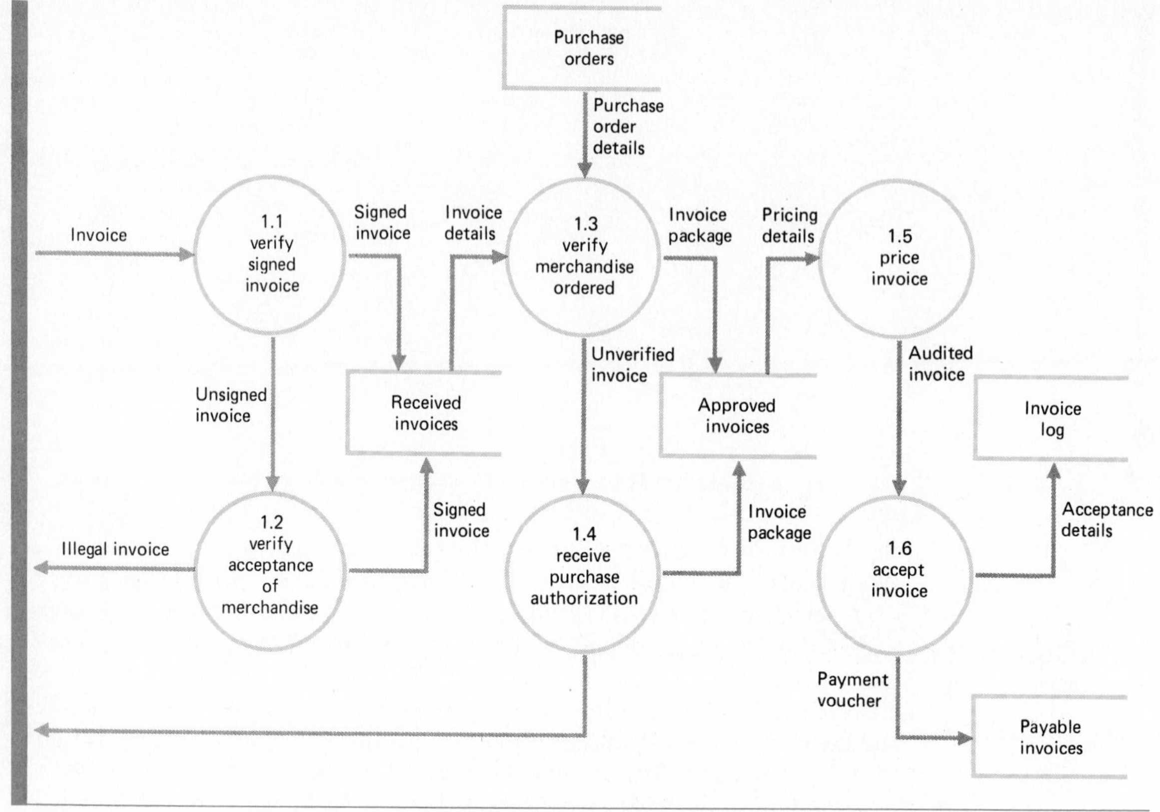

Figure 4.8. Second level data flow diagram for invoice approval process.

precisely the point of lower-level explosion—to find out more about internal processes.

Add Control on Lower-Level Diagrams Only

The diagrams developed to this point do not include control information. No mention has been made of how to handle errors or exceptions, such as processing incoming invoices that are incomplete. Although this information is necessary in the final analysis, it should not be a concern while identifying the overall data flow. The secondary diagrams (below the second or third level) show error and exception handling in the process being exploded.

Figure 4.8 is the secondary data flow diagram for the process "invoice approval" from Figure 4.7. The earlier figure did not take into account such exceptions as unsigned invoices or invoices without authorized purchase orders. Yet these conditions are important in correct invoice processing. They are specific details of invoice processing and therefore are added to the explosion of that process.

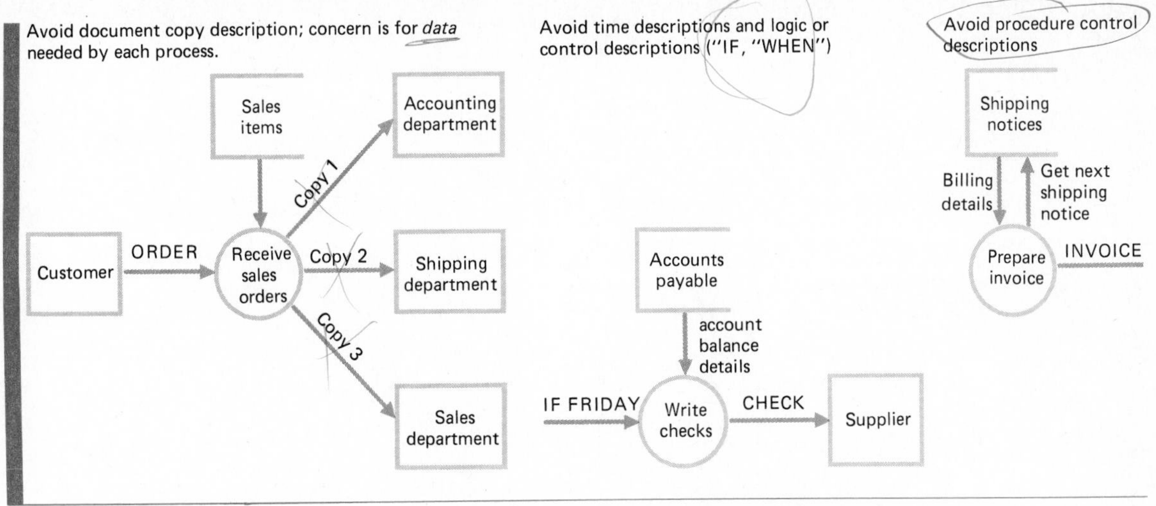

Figure 4.9. Common mistakes in drawing data flow diagrams.

Some physical control information is not necessary at all. Figure 4.9 includes samples of common mistakes made by including physical controls in data flow diagrams. Copy numbers or annotations for documents (for example, Copy 1, Copy 2, Shipping Copy, or Accounting Copy), procedural orders (Find the record. Review the record. Annotate the record.), or day-of-week triggers (Do on Monday. Do on last day of month.) do not belong with the logical and data aspects of requirements determination. The important elements for understanding a process during data flow analysis are not document copy numbers but descriptions of the data needed to perform the process.

Assign Meaningful Labels

The descriptions assigned to data flows and processes should tell the reader what is going on. All data flows should be named to reflect their content accurately.

DATA FLOW NAMING

The names assigned to data flows should reflect the data of interest to the analysts, not the document on which it resides. Some systems, such as those using computers to do on-line processing, may avoid paper entirely. For example, an invoice contains many different elements of information. Analysts are concerned with the contents of the invoice that are important for a particular process. It may be the invoice number and date of issue or the signature or authorization associated with the invoice. It is not the sheet of paper itself. (If the analysts later design a paperless system, the sheet will be omitted, but the important data will still be used in the system.)

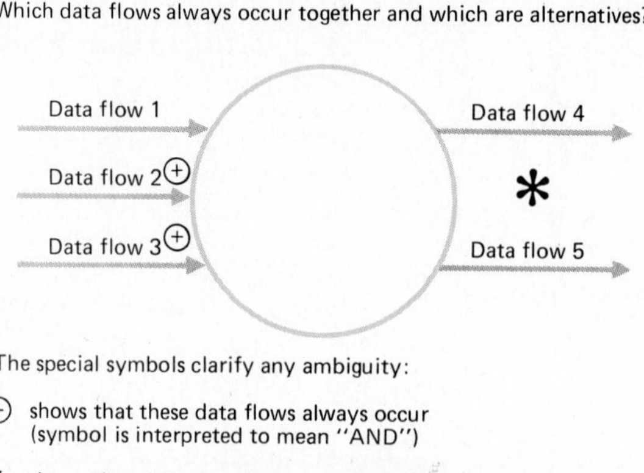

Figure 4.10. Symbols for clarifying data flow questions.

Data flowing into a process undergoes change. Therefore, the outbound data flow is named differently from the inbound one. (If no change is made to the data flow, what would be the purpose of the process?)

In almost all cases, the data flow names should clarify the relationship between multiple data flows, entering and leaving processes. Some analysts use additional notation to clarify cases where there are multiple data flows, as shown in Figure 4.10. The ⊕ (representing AND) indicates that both data flows occur, while the * (representing OR) shows that one of several data flows takes place.

PROCESS NAMING

All processes should be assigned names that tell the reader something specific about the nature of the activities in the process. The names INVENTORY CONTROL, PURCHASING, and SALE are much too general to be useful. It is much better to say specifically that the process is ADJUST QUANTITY ON HAND, PREPARE PURCHASE ORDER, or EDIT SALES ORDER to describe the process.

The numbering system introduced earlier further identifies processes, especially between levels of detail. The highest-level diagram, that defines the overall system under study, need not be numbered. All lower-level diagrams should be given an identification number. For example, five processes might be identified with numbers 1, 2, 3, 4, and 5. Lower-level explosions of these processes are assigned a decimal to indicate that they are further explanations of a higher-level process. For example, identify four lower-level explosions of process 3 as 3.1, 3.2, 3.3, and 3.4. Successive explosions add additional decimal digits: 3.1.1, 3.1.1.1, 3.1.1.1.1., etc.

Figures 4.11 and 4.12 use this convention to explain the invoice approval and vendor payment processes within accounts payable processing. Notice how the number identifies the higher-level process which it

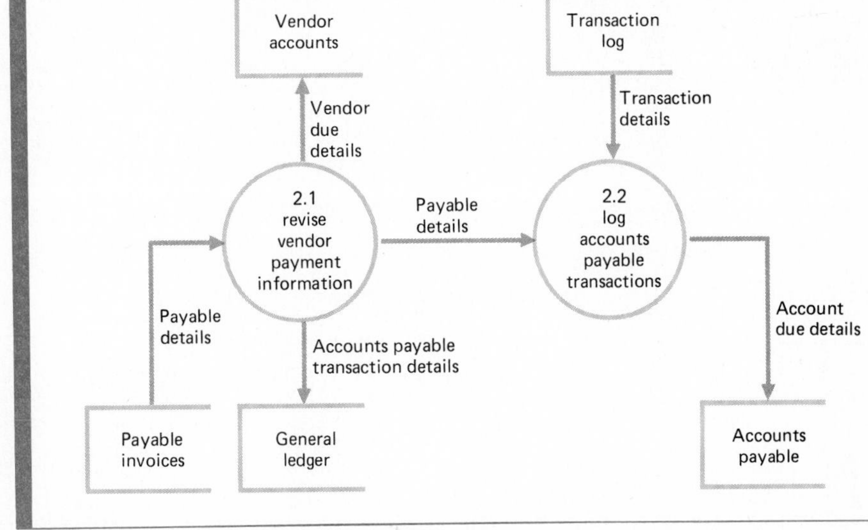

Figure 4.11. Second level data flow diagram for maintaining vendor balances.

explains. When you pick up a single diagram, you know the name of the process and the level of explosion you are seeing.

Figure 4.13 combines all of the data flow diagrams we have drawn in the accounts payable example.

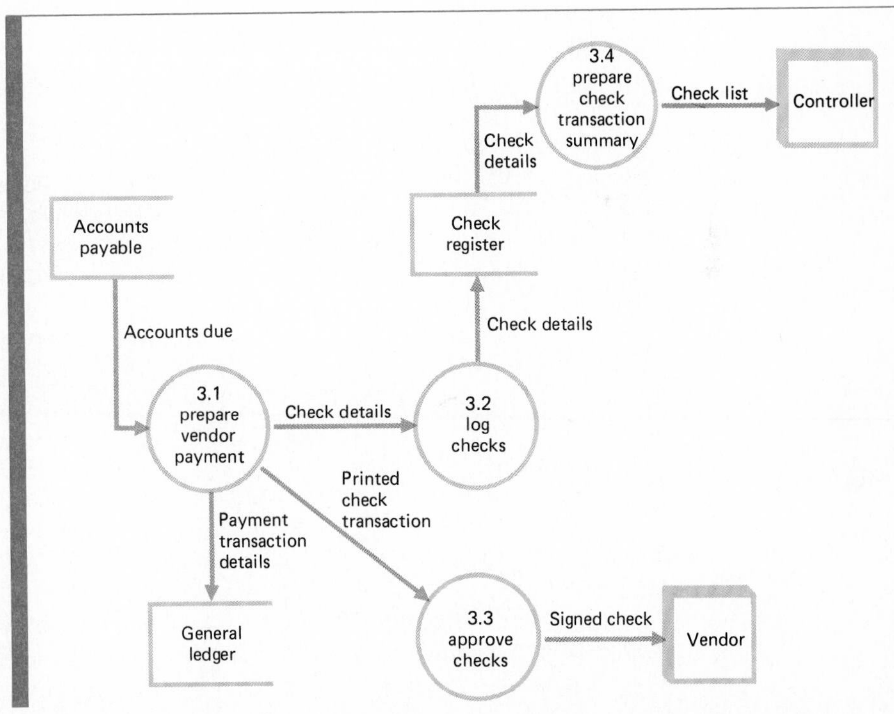

Figure 4.12. Second level data flow diagram for vendor payment processing.

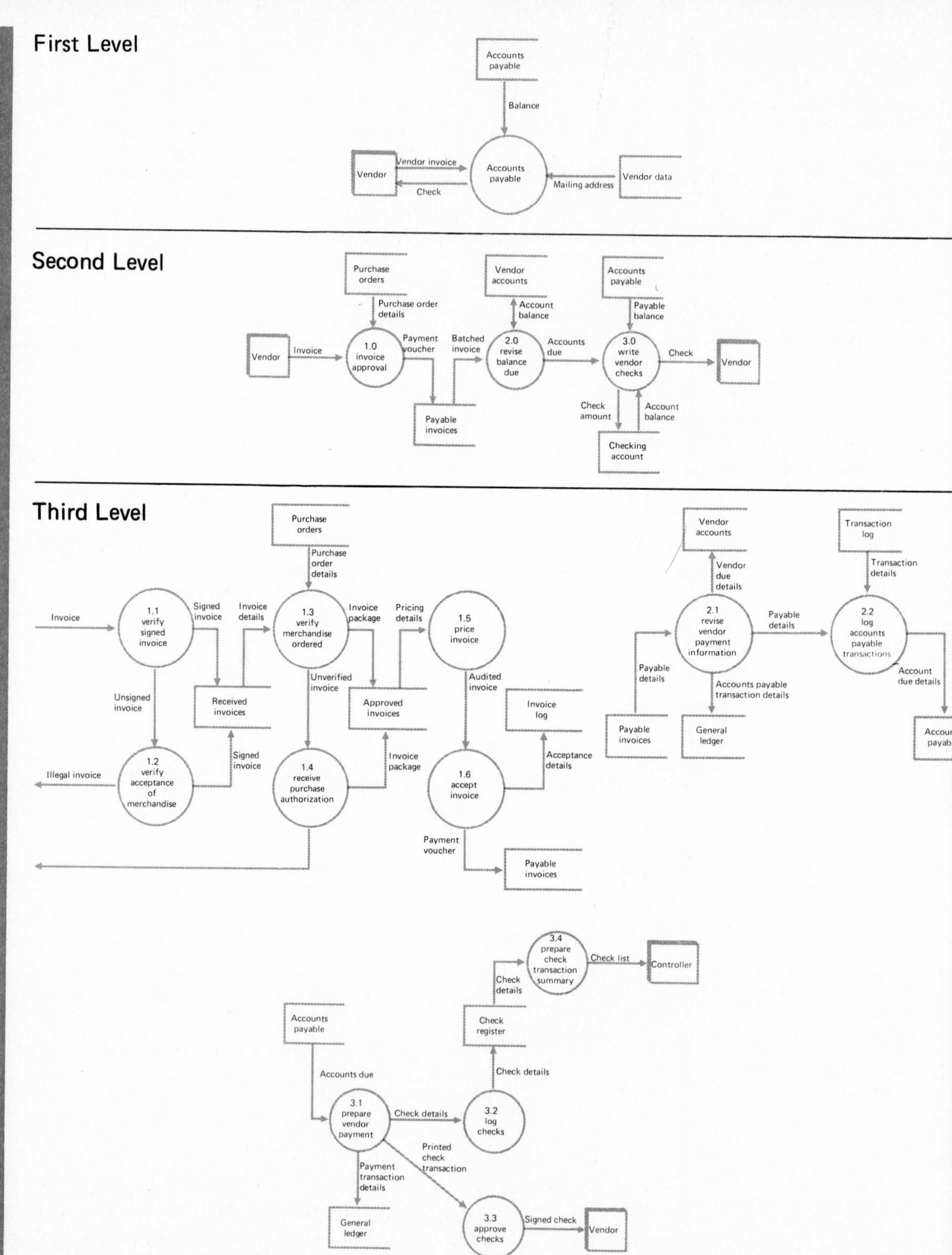

Figure 4.13. Accounts payable example showing three levels of data flow analysis.

DATA DICTIONARY

Data dictionaries are the second component of data flow analysis. Data flow diagrams by themselves do not fully describe the subject of the investigation. The data dictionary provides additional information about the system. This section discusses what a data dictionary is, why it is needed in data flow analysis, and how to develop it. The accounting systems example will be used to describe data dictionaries.

What Is a Data Dictionary?

A *data dictionary* is a list of all the elements included in a set of data flow diagrams, describing a system. The major elements in a system, discussed in the preceding sections, are data flow, data stores, and processes. The data dictionary stores details and descriptions of these elements.

If analysts want to know how many characters are in a data item, by what other names it is referenced in the system, or where it is used in the system, they should be able to find the answers in a properly developed data dictionary.

The data dictionary is developed during data flow analysis and assists the analysts involved in determining systems requirements. However, as we will see later in the book, the contents of the data dictionary are used during systems design as well.

Need for a Data Dictionary

As you examined the sample data flow diagrams in the previous section, you probably had little trouble understanding what such data as invoice and check represent. They are common terms in business, and most people know what they mean. But, is your understanding the same as someone else's? Does "invoice" mean the amount owed to a supplier? Does the amount include tax and shipping costs? How is one specific invoice identified among others? Getting the answers to these questions or verifying assumptions made about what the answers mean will further clarify and define systems requirements by more completely describing the data used or produced in the system. Data dictionaries record additional details about the data flow in a system, so that all involved can quickly look up the description of data flows, data stores, or processes.

All data in a system consists of data elements. Data elements are grouped together to make up a data structure.

DATA ELEMENT

The most fundamental data level is the *data element*. (You may have heard this called by other names: field, data item, or elementary item.) No smaller unit has meaning to the system's users. For example, invoice number,

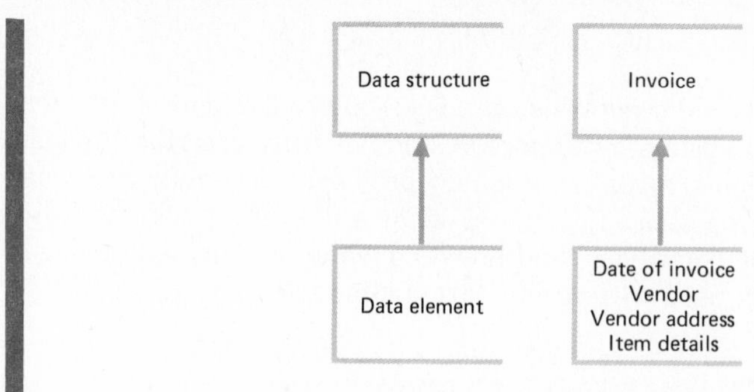

Figure 4.14. Relation of components in data flow diagrams.

invoice date, and amount due are data elements included in the invoice data flow.

Data elements are building blocks for all other data in the system. By themselves they do not convey enough meaning to any user. For example, the meaning of the data item DATE on an invoice may be well understood: it means the date the invoice was issued. However, out of this context, it is meaningless. It might pertain to a pay date, graduation date, starting date, or invoice date.

DATA STRUCTURE

A *data structure* is a set of data items that are related to one another and collectively describe a component in the system. For example, the data structure INVOICE is defined to consist of data items including the date of the invoice, vendor, vendor address, and item details (Figure 4.14).

Both data flows and data stores are data structures. They consist of relevent elements that describe the activity or entity being studied.

Figure 4.15 defines "payment voucher." This structure clearly shows the major components of invoice package and payment approval data. These data structures are broken down to their lowest-level data items. For example, vendor details, invoice number, date of invoice, purchase order reference, item details, and amount due are data items of the data structure invoice details.

Describing Data in the Dictionary

Each entry in the data dictionary consists of a set of details that describe the data used or produced in the system. Each item is identified by a data name, description, alias, and length and has specific values that are permissible for it in the system being studied.

DATA NAME

To distinguish one data item from another, analysts assign meaningful names. The names are used to refer to each element throughout the entire

PAYMENT VOUCHER

INVOICE PACKAGE
Vendor Details
Vendor name
Vendor address
Vendor telephone . . . . area optional if local phone
Invoice Number . . . . optional
Date of Invoice
Purchase Order Reference . . . . optional
Item Details . . . . repeated for each item
Amount Due. . . . . when verified called "Audited Invoice"

Receiving Acknowledgement
Date of receipt
Receiver. . . . . when present called "Signed Invoice"
Purchasing Authorization. . . . . may be added after invoice arrives if special order

Purchase order number
Department prefix
Date of purchase order
PAYMENT APPROVAL. . . . . when present called "Approved Invoice"
Audit Approval
Voucher Details
Voucher number
Date of voucher
General ledger account . . . . may be multiple accounts
Total payable amount

Figure 4.15. Annotated description of selected data used in accounts payable processing.

systems development process. Therefore, care must be taken to select meaningful and understandable data names. For example, the invoice date is more meaningful if it is named DATE OF INVOICE rather than ABCXXX.

Some organizations prescribe standards for developing data names (often patterned after the computer programming languages they are using at the time). A common standard specifies that data names should not exceed 30 characters (capital letters A through Z, numbers 0 through 9, and the hyphen) and should contain no blanks. Date might then be written as DATE-OF-INVOICE.

DATA DESCRIPTION

The data description briefly states what the data item represents in the system. For example, the description for DATE-OF-INVOICE indicates that it is the date on which the statement was prepared (to distinguish it from the date on which it was mailed or received).

Data descriptions should be written assuming that the person who will be reading the description does not know anything about the system. Jargon or special terms should be avoided; all words should be understandable to the reader.

ALIAS

Often the same data item can be referred to by different names, depending on who is using the data. The additional names are called *aliases*. For example, INVOICE may be called STATEMENT, BILL, or PRICE DOCUMENT in other areas of the organization or among suppliers. Or, the name may be amended as the data is augmented through processing: INVOICE becomes APPROVED INVOICE, which in turn becomes AUDITED INVOICE. Yet these names all refer to the same data, and we would say they are aliases for INVOICE.

The use of aliases should avoid confusion for all. A meaningful data dictionary will include all aliases.

LENGTH

When systems design features are developed later in the systems development process (See Chapters 6 through 10), it will be important to know the amount of space needed for each data item. Analysts can capture these details when developing data flow diagrams. Length identifies the number of spaces (for letters, numbers, or symbols) that are required but without concern for how they are stored. In other words, if a customer name can be up to 30 characters long when written on a sales form, the data dictionary entry should show a length of 30.

DATA VALUES

In some processes, only specific data values are permissible. For example, purchase order numbers in many organizations are often given a one-letter prefix to indicate the department of origin. This detail belongs in the data dictionary description of department numbers. The following table shows the purchase order number prefixes for one company:

PREFIX	DEPARTMENT
A	Accounting Department
B	Purchasing Department
M	Manufacturing Division
P	Personnel Section
S	Sales Department
T	Transportation

The system may later be designed so that the above prefixes are the only ones that are acceptable input.

If data values are restricted to a specific range, that information belongs in the data dictionary entry for the data item as well. Financial (dollar-and-cents) fields often have limited values. For example, if no product sold by a firm exceeds $25, that annotation belongs in the data dictionary. Similarly, the fact that all purchase order numbers should have five-digit identification numbers should also be stated. These details will be helpful to the analysts later, when they design systems controls. They will want to be sure the system treats a four-digit purchase order number as an error.

Recording Data Descriptions

Since data descriptions will be used repeatedly throughout an investigation and later during design, an easy-to-use format, that simplifies recording and retrieving details when needed, is suggested. The notation and several sample formats are presented in this section.

NOTATION

To limit the amount of narrative needed to describe relationships between data items and at the same time to show the relationships clearly, analysts often use special symbols. Figure 4.16 shows these symbols and their use.

Aliases are easily represented with an equals (=) sign linking the data items. For example, INVOICE and PAYMENT REQUEST are aliases; they both refer to the same data. Similarly AUDIT APPROVAL and AUDITED INVOICE are aliases, as described in Figure 4.16.

Invoice = Payment request *May be unlabeled from some*

Payment Voucher = Invoice package + payment approval

Invoice Receipt = signed invoice

Audit Approval = audited invoice

purchase Authorization = [purchase order number / Manager approval] + authorization date

Item Details = Item number + item description + item cost + item extension

Amount of Invoice = {item extension} + shipping amount (+ sales tax)

Vendor Balance = beginning balance + {purchases} + {payments} + {credits}

Beginning Balance = vendor balance *sets up next month cycle*

Symbols:

=	is equivalent to
+	and
[ ]	either/or
{ }	iterations of
( )	optional
*	encloses annotation

Figure 4.16. Data descriptions and notation.

Data structures are described by connecting individual data items with a plus (+) sign. We see that ITEM DETAILS consists of ITEM NUMBER, ITEM DESCRIPTION, ITEM COST, and ITEM EXTENSION. The value of an invoice, AMOUNT OF INVOICE, consists of ITEM EXTENSION + SHIPPING COST + SALES TAX.

The definition of AMOUNT OF INVOICE includes braces ({}) around the data item ITEM EXTENSION. Often invoices carry details about more than one item. In that case, the total amount of the invoice is calculated by summing the price of each item. This is called *iteration:* the individual items are added together until there are no more (then the shipping cost and sales taxes are added on). The definition of VENDOR BALANCE shows how multiple invoices for a supplier are accounted for in calculating a balance due amount. Payments and credits, for which there may by 0, 1, or more during the period, are also explained. The iteration symbol, that is the brackets, should always be interpreted to mean 0, 1, or more occurrences.

Sometimes there are optional occurrences. For example, a telephone number may have an extension, but it is not essential in all cases. Optional data items are shown in parentheses.

If an item must be present, but the value can be one of several, we refer to it as an *either/or* situation. Square brackets ([ ]) show this case in a data dictionary. For example, PURCHASE AUTHORIZATION can be *either* PURCHASE ORDER NUMBER *or* MANAGER APPROVAL. The fact that Figure 4.16 shows both data items in brackets means that one or the other should be present.

DEFINING DATA FLOWS AND STORES

A complete explanation of all elements in the data flow diagram includes a description of each data flow, data structure, and process. Figure 4.17 shows a sample form for recording these details. The data flow INVOICE PACK-

DATA FLOW NAME: Invoice package

DESCRIPTION: Signed billing details from vendor and internal purchasing authorization - unaudited for correct total and tax

FROM PROCESSES: 1.3 verify merchandise ordered
1.4 receive purchasing authorization

TO PROCESSES: 1.5 price invoice (batched through approved invoices delay)

DATA STRUCTURES: Invoice package
- invoice details
- receiving acknowledgement
- purchasing authorization

Figure 4.17. Sample data flow dictionary entry.

AGE, shown earlier in Figure 4.8, originates from processes 1.3 and 1.4 and becomes an input to process 1.5, PRICE INVOICE. This example demonstrates a complex data flow and emphasizes data flow, not document movement. An invoice is not officially approved until it has been verified against an authorized purchase order. If a purchase order does not exist when the merchandise arrives, authorization must take place as a separate step before further processing is possible. Therefore, the invoice package data can arrive in two different streams. As Figure 4.8 shows, there is a delay in processing verified invoices: they are batched (represented by the data store) until the next step in processing starts.

All these details are captured in the sample data flow form. As you see, each data flow is named and briefly described. The names and identification of processes associated with this data flow are also included. The volume (amount) of data flow (Figure 4.18) tells how busy this portion of the system is. To complete the definition of this data flow, the appropriate data structures are also listed. (It is not necessary to define the contents of the data structures; that is handled elsewhere in the data dictionary.)

The same information is collected for each data store. Figure 4.18 explains the APPROVED INVOICES data store. The access entry indicates how the data store is retrieved for the next stage of processing.

DEFINING DATA STRUCTURES

Figure 4.19 contains one entry in the dictionary. It describes the data structure for PAYMENT VOUCHER. This structure consists of all payment

DATA STORE: Approved invoices

DESCRIPTION: Vendor requests for payments submitted for processing. Itemizes merchandise received, cost of each, and contains signature of employee receiving merchandise

INBOUND DATA FLOWS: 1.1 signed invoice
1.2 signed invoice - when signature needed

OUTBOUND DATA FLOWS: Item details - batched invoice details

DATA DESCRIPTION:

Vendor Details	Item Details
Invoice Number	Amount Due
Invoice Date	
Purchase Order Reference	

VOLUME: 200 daily; growing 10% annually; heaviest at beginning of month

ACCESS: Delayed for batching, then accessed together; sequentially processed from within batch.

Figure 4.18. Sample data store dictionary entry.

DATA STRUCTURE: Payment voucher

DESCRIPTION: Invoice and internal approvals and audits of invoice and purchasing authorization; indicates payment can be made for merchandise or services

CONTENTS: Invoice Package
  invoice details
  vendor name
  (invoice number)
  invoice date
  (purchase order reference)
  {item details}
  Amount Due

  receiving acknowledgement
  purchase authorization
Payment Approval
  audit approval
  voucher details

VOLUME: 200 daily

Figure 4.19. Sample data structure dictionary entry.

details and authorizations. The notation indicates that multiple items can be included on the invoice (shown by the braces, representing iteration).

Separate data item definitions are used to describe permissible values for items. Figure 4.20 shows the acceptable values for the data item PURCHASE ORDER NUMBER.

DESCRIBING PROCESSES

A separate definition is also given for each process in the system. The sample in Figure 4.21 identifies and describes the VERIFY MERCHANDISE ORDERED process. This process uses INVOICE DETAILS and PURCHASE ORDER DETAILS and produces two outputs: INVOICE PACKAGE and UNVERIFIED INVOICE. The purpose of the process is to associate a purchasing authorization with every received invoice. The processing logic is summarized. If a purchase order cannot be found, a separate authorization step must be completed before the invoice is approved.

Using the Data Dictionary Details

It is very valuable to have a concise set of definitions for all the entities in the business process being studied. Often the data dictionary is the only common source of definitions for users and investigators alike. It is used as the single source of answers to all questions regarding the format and content of the data sets used in the system.

DATA ELEMENT: Purchase order number

DESCRIPTION: Identification and authorization for each order given to an outside supplier

TYPE ©AN N

LENGTH: 7

ALIASES: PO, Requisition

RANGE OF VALUES: TO

TYPICAL VALUE increasing from 10000

LIST OF SPECIFIC VALUES (IF ANY)

Valid Prefixes	Meaning
AC	Accounting
AD	Advertising
EX	Executive Office
PE	Personnel
PU	Purchasing
RD	Research and Development
SA	Sales

OTHER EDITING DETAILS Purchase order number includes 5 digit number and department prefix

Figure 4.20. Sample form for describing data elements.

PROCESS: Verify merchandise ordered

DESCRIPTION: Matches every incoming invoice with a valid purchase order number or authorization

INPUT: Invoice Details
Purchase Order Details

OUTPUT: Invoice Package
Unverified Package

LOGIC SUMMARY: Match received invoice with valid purchase authorization. Attach purchase order information to complete invoice package.

If there is no valid purchase order, have manager approve.

If approved by manager, note approval on invoice and complete invoice package.

If not approved by manager, return invoice to originator noting that it is not approved for payment.

Figure 4.21. Sample process dictionary entry.

The process of developing the data dictionary itself forces analysts to clarify their understanding of the data in the system. Finding out about missing data flows, detecting duplicate definitions, or uncovering data that is not used by any process during the investigation will avoid later problems in requirements determination and system design.

In addition, the data dictionary itself can be processed to reveal additional information:

1 *Data element/data structure listing.* A complete set of all data used in the system under investigation, including name, description, length, and alternate names (aliases).
2 *Process listing.* A complete set of all processes that take place in the system, together with a description of the activities associated with each. Includes the identification of data used and data flows involved.
3 *Cross-reference checking.* Determination of where data is used in the system; i.e., which processes use the same data? Which data is unused?
4 *Error detection.* Finding inconsistencies in the area under investigation, such as data needed by a process that is never entered into the system, processes that are not supplied with an inbound data flow or do not produce data flow as output, or multiple processes that duplicate each other's purpose.

The examples in this chapter use simple paper forms to capture data definitions. Manual systems such as these work very well. However, some organizations use automated data dictionary systems. Although their purpose and function is the same as we have been describing, they may be more convenient in large systems. Automated data dictionary systems will produce glossaries of data, cross listings, and error reports on demand and save a great deal of time, compared with manual systems. However, their cost can be quite high, ranging from approximately \$3,000 to over \$20,000.

Regardless of the form, data dictionaries are an essential aspect of data flow analysis and requirements determination. They should be used in conjunction with logic and process definitions, the topic of the next chapter.

SUMMARY

Two widely used strategies for determining information requirements are data analysis and decision analysis. This chapter discusses data analysis, the examination of how data is used and changed by business processes and activities. Its primary tools are data flow diagrams and data dictionaries.

A data flow diagram is a graphic description of a system or portion of a system. It consists of data flows, processes, sources, destinations, and stores—all described through the use of easily understood symbols. An entire system can be described from the viewpoint of the data it processes with only four symbols. At the same time, data flow diagrams are powerful enough to show parallel activities.

Data flow diagrams present a logical, rather than physical, view of the system. That is, they show what takes place, rather than how an activity is accomplished. They also support a top-down approach to systems analysis, whereby analysts begin by developing a general understanding of the system and gradually exploding components in greater detail. As details are added, information about control can also be included, although upper-level general diagrams are drawn without showing specific control issues to ensure focuses on data and processes.

The data dictionary stores descriptions of data items and structures, as well as systems processes. It is intended to be used to understand the system by analysts, who retrieve the details and descriptions it stores, and during systems design, when information about such concerns as data length, alternate names, and data use in specific processes must be available. The data dictionary also stores validation information to guide the analysts in specifying controls for the system's acceptance of data.

Data dictionaries can be developed manually or by using automated procedures.

The next chapter examines the decision-analysis strategy for determining information systems requirements.

CASE STUDY FOR CHAPTER 4
DATA FLOW ANALYSIS FOR VALLEY INDUSTRIES

The data flow analysis for Valley Industries consists of data flow diagrams, describing processes and data movement in the system, and data dictionary components, defining systems elements. Both provide useful information for determining information systems requirements.

DATA FLOW DIAGRAMS

The data flow analysis for Valley Industries revealed five major processes: entering the order, processing the order, producing the invoice, posting payments and adjustments to customer accounts, and maintaining accounts receivable records. The overall system, consisting of these processes, is shown in Figure C4.1. This data flow analysis also shows that the system currently uses three primary data stores: accounts receivable, which are records of customer account balances; the order log, which is a record of every order entering processing; and the parts inventory, which is the source of price data. The latter data store is the most questionable one because it combines several different types of data. In a new design, the set of data contained in this data store merits better organization.

The system interacts with three entities outside the system itself: the customer, Valley management, and the production department within the company. The production department is definitely outside of the order processing system, even though it depends on the interaction it maintains with the order entry process. The orders initiate production, but they are not themselves part of the production process.

The system is explained in detail through the four lower-level subsystems diagrams, developed to understand the activities associated with the current system.

Four of the five processes are exploded downward, as shown in Figures C4.2 through C4.5. The order entry process consists of the activities of verifying price and customer account status, approving the order for processing, and eventually the manufacturing department supplying the requested items. In the current system, order data is sent out of the system for approval by management, after which the customer is informed of the action and the approved orders are sent on for further processing. Figure C4.2 is consistent with the systems-level data flow diagram in Figure C4.1 since it shows the same inputs and outputs, and includes no activities that contradict the overall systems definition.

The downward explosion of the process order process maintains the numbering scheme introduced at the systems level (that is, the first-level details of process 2 are shown as 2.1, 2.2, 2.3, and 2.4 in Figure C4.3). A new data store, open order list, is shown in this diagram. It is the result of preparing the order card and is used to provide open order information to the persons responsible for monitoring customer account balances and total accounts receivable.

A related data store is shown in the explosion of the invoice preparation

Figure C4.1. Valley Industries order entry and receivables system.

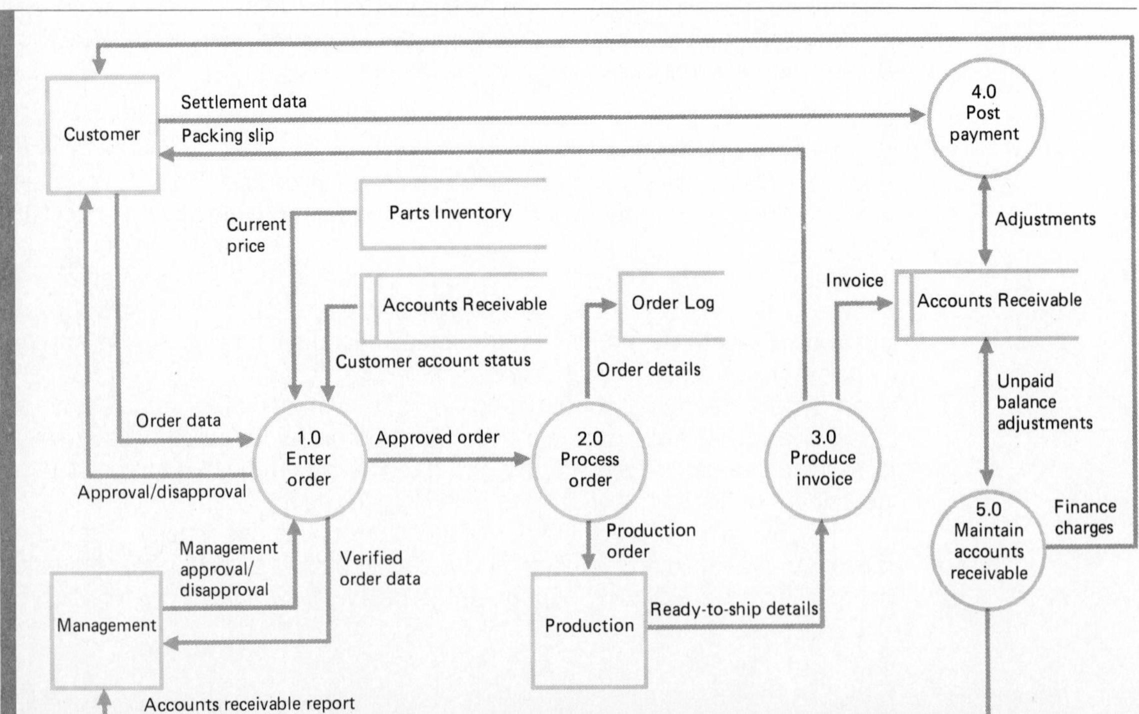

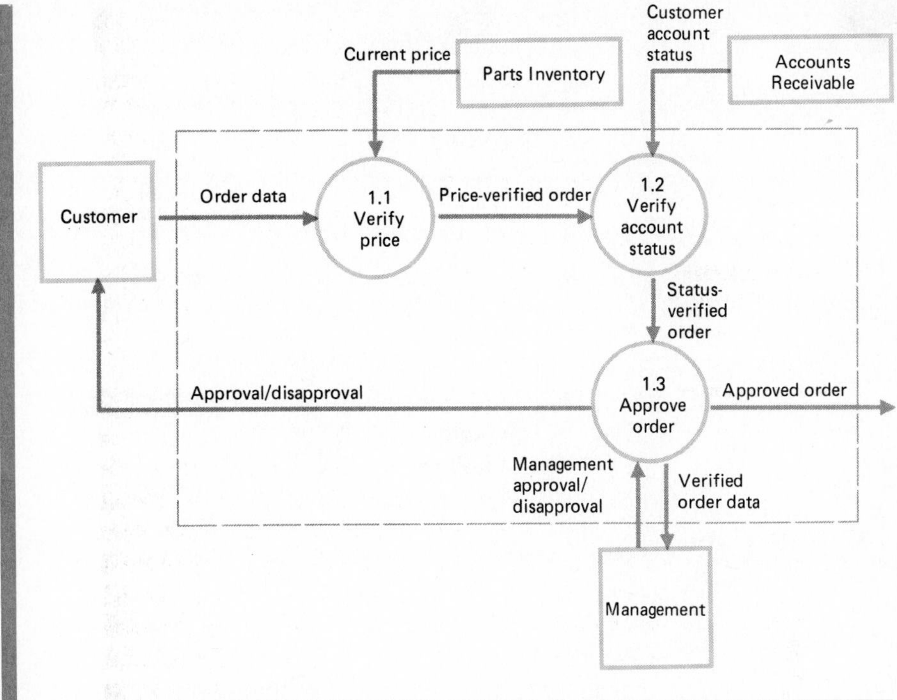

Figure C4.2.
1.0 Enter order.

Order Log
Order details
Job number
Approved order
2.1 Log order
Logged order
2.2 Assign job number
Numbered order
2.3 Prepare order card
Order card
Open Order List
Open orders
2.4 Prepare open order report
Open order report
Production order
Production
Ready-to-ship details

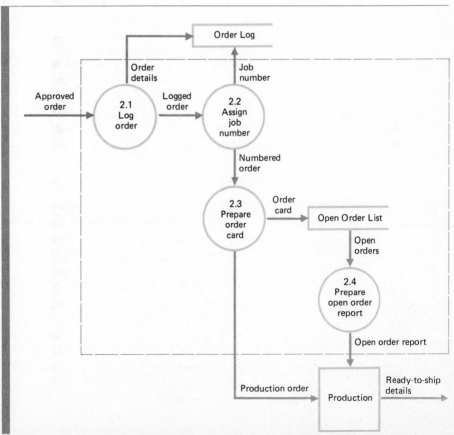

Figure C4.3.
2.0 Process order.

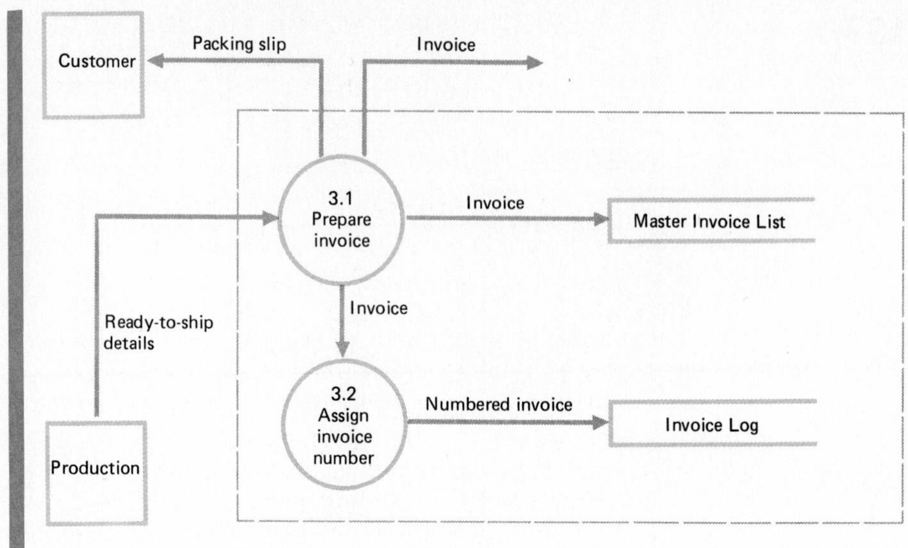

Figure C4.4.
3.0 Produce invoice.

process (Figure C4.4). A master list of open invoices, those not yet paid, is maintained as a by-product of the system. However, analysis of the data flow diagram raises questions about the numbering of invoices. Currently this is done after the invoices are prepared rather than by using prenumbered invoices. Furthermore, as the data flow diagram shows, the master invoice list is prepared before invoice numbers are assigned.

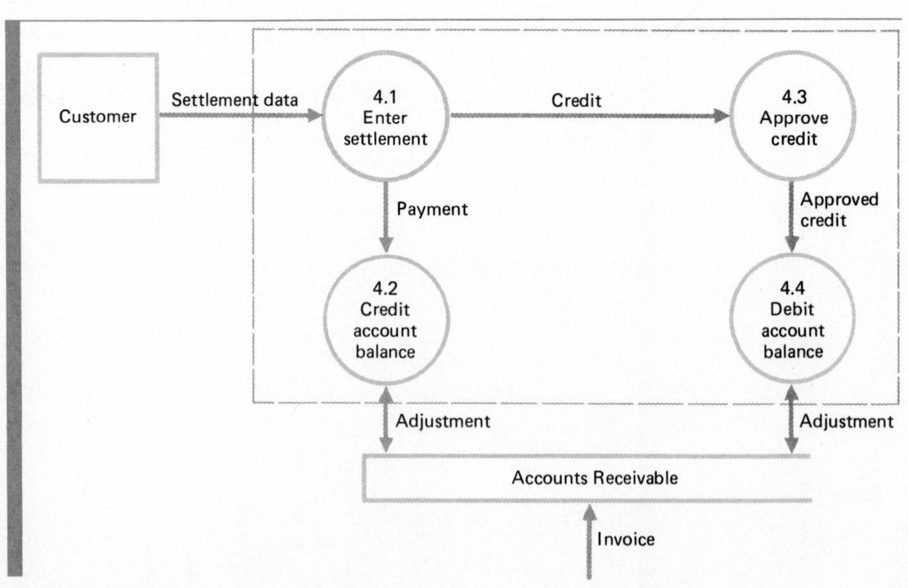

Figure C4.5.
4.0 Post payment.

Figure C4.5 shows the details of processing to maintain accounts receivable. The basis for all payments and adjustments is from the customer submissions. It appears that a better-controlled procedure must be established for credit and debit adjustments, including those that Valley personnel may want to make.

DATA DICTIONARY

The data dictionary elements developed for the current system used by Valley Industries consists of process, data flow, and data structure details. Figure C4.6 identifies each of the processes included in the systems-level data flow diagram. Each process is briefly described to clarify its purpose. The inbound and outbound data flows for each of the five processes are also shown.

Figure C4.7 defines 29 data flows that are included in the system. Each data flow is briefly described so that anyone examining the data gathered during the analysis can quickly see what each data flow does. The processes that data flows originate from and go into are also identified by number and name. Some data flows go out of the system rather than to other processes. Others do not originate from a process. These considerations are shown in the data flow entries in the data dictionary.

Each data flow is also described by the data structures it contains. The data structures that are part of this system are described in list form in Figure C4.8. There are 14 data structures defined for this system. In some cases, the definitions show iterations or alternatives, using the notation described in the chapter. Aliases are also marked to indicate where data structures are called by different names in various systems processes. Marking aliases will assist the systems analysts in identifying when the same data is being used repeatedly throughout the system, even if the users apply different names.

Some data structures are used much more than others. For example, order details, customer details, and customer account details are part of many data flows. This information will emphasize to the analysts that they must organize the data storage and retrieval structures in a manner that will support all uses of the data, across each process, efficiently.

More analysis of the data flow diagrams will reveal additional concerns. We will return to these in the next chapter.

DATA DICTIONARY

DATA STORES:

ACCUMULATED-PRODUCTION-ORDERS
  ORDER-CARD *(1−)

BACKLOG
  APPROVED-ORDER *(1−)

CUSTOMER-ACCOUNTS-RECEIVABLE
  CUSTOMER-NAME
  CUSTOMER-BILLING-ADDRESS
  DATE-BILLED
  AMOUNT-BILLED
  INTEREST-CHARGES
  CURRENT-BALANCE

(*Continues on page 147*)

PROCESS NAME: 1.0 Enter Order

DESCRIPTION: Customer order is received and is approved or disapproved for further processing

INBOUND DATA FLOWS: Order Data; Customer Account Status; Current Price; Management Approval/disapproval

OUTBOUND DATA FLOWS: Approval/disapproval; Verified Order List; Approved Order

PROCESS NAME: 2.0 Process Order

DESCRIPTION: Accepted customer order is logged to provide a record of all received orders.

INBOUND DATA FLOWS: Approved order

OUTBOUND DATA FLOWS: Order Details; Production Order

PROCESS NAME: 3.0 Produce Invoice

DESCRIPTION: When the production department informs the invoicing group that an order is ready to ship, an invoice is prepared and copies are sent to the customer and the accounting department

INBOUND DATA FLOWS: Ready-to-ship details

OUTBOUND DATA FLOWS: Packing slip; Invoice

PROCESS NAME: 4.0 Post Payment

DESCRIPTION: Payments are received from customer and account adjustments are used to change the accounts receivable record

INBOUND DATA FLOWS: Settlement data; Adjustments

OUTBOUND DATA FLOWS: Adjustments

Figure C4.6. First level process descriptions.

DATA FLOW NAME: Order data

DESCRIPTION: Order details received from customer

FROM PROCESSES:

TO PROCESSES: 1.0 Enter order

DATA STRUCTURES: Order details

DATA FLOW NAME: Approval/disapproval

DESCRIPTION: Acknowledgement of customer's order refelecting approval or disapproval of the order

FROM PROCESSES: 1.0 Enter order

TO PROCESSES:

DATA STRUCTURES: Order details
Management approval/disapproval

DATA FLOW NAME: Current price

DESCRIPTION: The company's current price for the part ordered by the customer

FROM PROCESSES:

TO PROCESSES: 1.0 Enter order

DATA STRUCTURES: Item details
Item price

DATA FLOW NAME: Customer account status

DESCRIPTION: Indication of whether customer has an overdue account or poor payment history

FROM PROCESSES:

TO PROCESSES: 1.0 Enter order

DATA STRUCTURES: Customer account details
Customer account status

DATA FLOW NAME: Management approval/disapproval

DESCRIPTION: Management approval or disapproval of the verified order data

FROM PROCESSES:

TO PROCESSES: 1.0 Enter order

DATA STRUCTURES:

DATA FLOW NAME: Verified order data

DESCRIPTION: Customer's order after price and account status have been checked against file data

FROM PROCESSES: 1.0 Enter order

TO PROCESSES:

DATA STRUCTURES: Order details
Approval details
  Price verification
  Status verification

Figure C4.7. Data dictionary entries for data flows.

DATA FLOW NAME: Approved order
DESCRIPTION: Customer's order after it has been verified and received management approval

FROM PROCESSES: 1.0 Enter order

TO PROCESSES: 2.0 Process order

DATA STRUCTURES: Order
    Order details
    Approval details

DATA FLOW NAME: Order details
DESCRIPTION: Details from approved customer order which are recorded by the company in a log

FROM PROCESSES: 2.0 Process order

TO PROCESSES:

DATA STRUCTURES:

DATA FLOW NAME: Production order
DESCRIPTION: Copy of the customer order given to production manager

FROM PROCESSES: 2.0 Process order

TO PROCESSES:

DATA STRUCTURES: Job number
Order details
Order number

DATA FLOW NAME: Ready-to-ship details
DESCRIPTION: Details from production concerning a part or parts ready to be shipped to customer

FROM PROCESSES:

TO PROCESSES: 3.0 Produce invoice

DATA STRUCTURES: Production order
Completion status

DATA FLOW NAME: Invoice
DESCRIPTION: Details of the filled order, specifically, the total amount of payment due

FROM PROCESSES: 3.0 Produce invoice

TO PROCESSES:

DATA STRUCTURES: Invoice details
Customer details

DATA FLOW NAME: Adjustments
DESCRIPTION: Adjustments to he customer's account balance reflecting payments, credits, interest charges, etc.

FROM PROCESSES:

TO PROCESSES: 4.0 Post payment

DATA STRUCTURES: Payment or
Credit

Figure C4.7. (*Continued*)

DATA FLOW NAME: Unpaid balance adjustments

DESCRIPTION: Customer account balances reflecting the addition of interest charges

FROM PROCESSES: 5.0 Maintain accounts receivable

TO PROCESSES: 5.0 Maintain accounts receivable

DATA STRUCTURES:

DATA FLOW NAME: Statement

DESCRIPTION: Statement sent to customer reflecting the addition of interest charges

FROM PROCESSES: 5.0 Maintain accounts receivable

TO PROCESSES:

DATA STRUCTURES: Customer details
Customer account details
Invoice details

DATA FLOW NAME: Settlement data

DESCRIPTION: Payment or credit from the customer to settle his account or adjust the balance

FROM PROCESSES:

TO PROCESSES: 4.0 Post payment

DATA STRUCTURES: Payment or
Credit

DATA FLOW NAME: Packing slip

DESCRIPTION: Last copy of the invoice which is enclosed in the shipping carton

FROM PROCESSES: 3.0 Produce invoice

TO PROCESSES:

DATA STRUCTURES: Invoice
  Invoice details
  Customer details

DATA FLOW NAME: Accounts receivable

DESCRIPTION: Total balance of all customer's unpaid invoices

FROM PROCESSES: 5.0 Maintain accounts receivable

TO PROCESSES:

DATA STRUCTURES: Customer details
Customer account details

DATA FLOW NAME: Customer Account Status

DESCRIPTION: Status of customer account in terms of account balance and eligibility for further credit transactions

FROM PROCESSES:

TO PROCESSES: 1.2 Verify account status

DATA STRUCTURES: Customer details
Customer account details
  Account status

DATA FLOW NAME: Logged order
DESCRIPTION: An order that has been accepted, acknowledged, and assigned an internal order number

FROM PROCESSES: 2.1 Log order

TO PROCESSES: 2.2 Assign job number

DATA STRUCTURES: Order
   Order details

DATA FLOW NAME: Numbered order
DESCRIPTION: An internal order that has been given an official job number

FROM PROCESSES: 2.2 Assign job number

TO PROCESSES: 2.3 Prepare order card

DATA STRUCTURES:

DATA FLOW NAME: Order Card
DESCRIPTION: A production order that is stored as an open order

FROM PROCESSES: 2.3 Prepare order card

TO PROCESSES:

DATA STRUCTURES: Production order
   Job number
   Order details
   Order number

DATA FLOW NAME: Open order
DESCRIPTION: An internal order that has been assigned an order number and is in production

FROM PROCESSES:

TO PROCESSES: 2.4 Prepare open order report

DATA STRUCTURES: Job number
Order details
Job status

DATA FLOW NAME: Price Verified Order
DESCRIPTION: An internal order that has been verified for correct price

FROM PROCESSES: 1.1 Price verified order

TO PROCESSES: 1.2 Verify account status

DATA STRUCTURES: Order details
Approval details
   Price verification

DATA FLOW NAME: Status Verified Order
DESCRIPTION: An internal order that has been verified for acceptable account status

FROM PROCESSES: 1.2 Verify account status

TO PROCESSES: 1.3 Approve order

DATA STRUCTURES: Order details
Approval details
   Status verification

Figure C4.7. (*Continued*)

DATA FLOW NAME: Packing slip

DESCRIPTION: A by-product of the invoicing process, this information identifies the customer's order and its cost. It is enclosed with the order when it is shipped.

FROM PROCESSES: 3.1 Prepare invoice

TO PROCESSES:

DATA STRUCTURES: Invoice
  Invoice details
  Customer details

DATA FLOW NAME: Invoice

DESCRIPTION: A specification of the order authorization, details of the order, and the cost for which the customer is billed

FROM PROCESSES: 3.1 Prepare invoice

TO PROCESSES: 3.2 Assign invoice number

DATA STRUCTURES: Invoice details
Customer details

DATA FLOW NAME: Payment

DESCRIPTION: Money or checks that are received from customers to reduce their account balance

FROM PROCESSES: 4.1 Enter settlement

TO PROCESSES: 4.2 Credit account balance

DATA STRUCTURES: Settlement data
  Payment

DATA FLOW NAME: Approved credit

DESCRIPTION: Credit action that has been received and approved for adjustment of the customer's account

FROM PROCESSES: 4.3 Approve credit

TO PROCESSES: 4.4 Debit account balance

DATA STRUCTURES:

DATA FLOW NAME: Ready-to-ship details

DESCRIPTION: The notice from the production department that an order has been manufactured and is ready for shipping.

FROM PROCESSES:

TO PROCESSES: 3.1 Prepare invoice

DATA STRUCTURES: Production order
  Completion status

DATA FLOW NAME: Credit

DESCRIPTION: Credit action received but not yet approved for adjustment of customer's account

FROM PROCESSES: 4.1 Enter settlement

TO PROCESSES: 4.3 Approve credit

DATA STRUCTURES: Settlement data
  Credit

DATA FLOW NAME:	Adjustment
DESCRIPTION:	Payments or approved credits that are subtracted from a customer account to lower the account balance
FROM PROCESSES:	4.2 Credit account balance 4.4 Debit account balance
TO PROCESSES:	4.2 Credit account balance 4.4 Debit account balance
DATA STRUCTURES:	Settlement data Payment Credit

PROCESS NAME:	5.0 Maintain accounts receivable
DESCRIPTION:	Accounts receivable records are examined to produce account statements and a list of open balance accounts
INBOUND DATA FLOWS:	Unpaid-balance-adjustments
OUTBOUND DATA FLOWS:	Statement Accounts receivable

Figure C4.7. (*Concluded*)

```
ACCOUNTS RECEIVABLE
        CUSTOMER-DETAILS
        CUSTOMER-ACCOUNT-DETAILS........................for nonzero account balances

APPROVAL/DISAPPROVAL.................................. alias ACKNOWLEDGEMENT
        ORDER-DETAILS
        MANAGEMENT-APPROVAL/DISAPPROVAL

CUSTOMER ACCOUNT DETAILS
        CUSTOMER-NUMBER
        ACCOUNT-BALANCE
        CREDIT-LIMIT
        ACCOUNT-STATUS

CUSTOMER-DETAILS
        CUSTOMER-NAME
        BILL-TO-ADDRESS
        SHIP-TO-ADDRESS
        TAX-CODE

INVOICE .......................................one copy sent to customer as packing list
        INVOICE-DETAILS
             ORDER-NUMBER
             VALLEY-JOB-NUMBER
             INVOICE-NUMBER
             INVOICE-DATE
             SPECIAL-CHARGES
             ITEM-DETAILS
             SHIPPING-CHARGE
             AMOUNT
             TAX
             CASH-DISCOUNT-ALLOWED
             TOTAL-INVOICE-AMOUNT
        CUSTOMER-DETAILS

ITEM DETAILS
        ITEM-NUMBER
        DESCRIPTION
        ORDER-QUANTITY
        ITEM-PRICE ............................................alias CURRENT-PRICE
        ITEM-COST-EXTENSION
        ITEM-QUANTITY-SHIPPED
```

Figure C4.8. Data dictionary for order entry/accounts receivable processing.

```
NUMBERED-INVOICE
      INVOICE-NUMBER
      INVOICE-DETAILS

OPEN-ORDER
      JOB-NUMBER
      ORDER-DETAILS
      JOB-STATUS

ORDER
      ORDER-DETAILS
          ORDER-NUMBER.........................when present called LOGGED-ORDER
          ORDER-DATE
          CUSTOMER-DETAILS
          ITEM-DETAILS
          REQUIRED-DATE
          TERMS
      ORDER-MAKEUP
          E-C-CHARGE
          ENG-CHARGE
          TOOLING
          ADDITIONAL-REMARKS
      APPROVAL-DETAILS                                              }  when present
          PRICE-VERIFICATION................alias VERIFIED-ORDER     }  called
          STATUS-VERIFICATION..........alias STATUS VERIFICATION    }  APPROVED-
          MANAGEMENT-APPROVAL                                       }  ORDER
      ORDER-NUMBER

ORDER CARD
      PRODUCTION-ORDER

PRODUCTION-ORDER............................when present called NUMBERED-ORDER
      VALLEY-JOB-NUMBER
      ORDER-DETAILS
      ORDER-NUMBER

READY-TO-SHIP-DETAILS
      PRODUCTION-ORDER
      COMPLETION-STATUS ......................................alias JOB-STATUS

SETTLEMENT DATA
      PAYMENT
          ACCOUNT-NUMBER
          PAYMENT-AMOUNT ...................................alias ADJUSTMENT
      or
      CREDIT .................................. if approved, called CREDIT-APPROVAL
          ACCOUNT-NUMBER
          CREDIT-AMOUNT .....................................alias ADJUSTMENT
          APPROVAL

STATEMENT
      CUSTOMER-DETAILS
      CUSTOMER-ACCOUNT DETAILS
      INVOICE-DETAILS
```

Figure C4.8. *(Concluded)*

(Continued from page 139)

```
CUSTOMER-ORDER-JACKET
   INDIVIDUAL-CUSTOMER-INFORMATION
   CURRENT-ITEMS-ON-ORDER
   RUNNING-ACCOUNT-BALANCE

INVOICE-LOG-SHEET
   WEEK-ENDING-DATE
   DATE
   INVOICE-NUMBER
   CUSTOMER-NAME
   VALLEY-PART-NUMBER
   QUANTITY
   TOTAL-CHARGE
   SHIPPING-CHARGE
   TOTAL-INVOICE-CHARGE
   VALLEY-JOB-NUMBER
```

MASTER-INVOICE-FILE
  INVOICE *(1–)

OPEN-ORDER-LIST
  ORDER-CARD *(1–)

ORIGINAL-INVOICE-FILE
  INVOICE *(1–)

PRICE-LIST
VALLEY-PART-NUMBER
  UNIT-CHARGE

DATA FLOWS:

ACKNOWLEDGED-ORDER
  DATE-BOOKED
  ACKNOWLEGED-BY
  P-O-NUMBER
  QUANTITY
  VALLEY-PART-NUMBER

ACKNOWLEDGMENT
  CUSTOMER-NAME
  CUSTOMER-BILLING-ADDRESS
  ORDER-ACKNOWLEDGMENT

ACCOUNTS-RECEIVABLE-REPORT
  CUSTOMER-ACCOUNTS-
  RECEIVABLE *(1–)

APPROVED-CREDIT
  CUSTOMER-NAME
  CUSTOMER-BILLING-ADDRESS
  AMOUNT-CREDIT
  MANAGEMENT-APPROVAL

APPROVED-ORDER
  ORDER-AND-PRICE
  MANAGEMENT-APPROVAL

APPROVED-ORDER-AND-JOB-NUMBER
  APPROVED-ORDER
  VALLEY-JOB-NUMBER

CREDIT
  CUSTOMER-NAME
  CUSTOMER-BILLING-ADDRESS
  AMOUNT-CREDIT

INVOICE
  CUSTOMER-NAME
  CUSTOMER-SHIPPING-ADDRESS
  DATE-BOOKED
  SHIPPING-METHOD
  VALLEY-JOB-NUMBER
  ASSEMBLY-NUMBER
  ORIGINATOR
  DATE-PROMISED
  ITEM
  QUANTITY
  UNIT
  DESCRIPTION
  UNIT-CHARGE
  TOTAL-CHARGE

INVOICE-DETAILS
  INVOICE

INVOICE-SUMMARY-REPORT
  INVOICE-DETAILS *(1–)

OPEN-ORDER-REPORT
  DATE-OF-REPORT
  CUSTOMER-NAME
  VALLEY-PART-NUMBER
  QUANTITY
  VALLEY-JOB-NUMBER
  DUE-DATE
  DATE-PROMISED
  DATE-BOOKED

ORDER
  CUSTOMER-NAME
  CUSTOMER-BILLING-ADDRESS
  CUSTOMER-SHIPPING-ADDRESS
  CUSTOMER-PART-NUMBER
  QUANTITY
  DELIVERY-REQ

ORDER-AND-PRICE
  ACKNOWLEDGED-ORDER
  PRICE

ORDER-CARD
  CUSTOMER-NAME
  CUSTOMER-NUMBER
  CUSTOMER-BILLING-ADDRESS
  CUSTOMER-SHIPPING-ADDRESS

BUYER-NAME
BUYER-PHONE-NUMBER
ACCEPTED-BY
DATE-ACCEPTED
REP
REP-NUMBER
CUSTOMER-PART-NUMBER
VALLEY-PART-NUMBER
E-C-LEVEL
P-O-NUMBER
QUANTITY
UNIT-CHARGE
ENG-CHARGE
TOOLING
DELIVERY-REQ
DELIVERY-PROM
VALLEY-JOB-NUMBER

ORDER-DETAILS
ORDER-CARD *(1–)

PACKING-SLIP
INVOICE

PAYMENT
CUSTOMER-NAME
AMOUNT-OF-PAYMENT

PRODUCTION-ORDER
ORDER-CARD

READY-TO-SHIP-INFORMATION
CUSTOMER-NAME
QUANTITY-READY-FOR-SHIPPING

STATEMENT
CUSTOMER-NAME
CUSTOMER-BILLING-ADDRESS
INTEREST-CHARGE
TOTAL-CHARGE

PROCESS LIST:

ENTER ORDER
ACKNOWLEDGE ORDER
VERIFY PRICE
APPROVE ORDER
LOG ORDER

PRODUCE ORDER CARD
PREPARE ORDER CARD
PREPARE WORK INFORMATION
CREATE OPEN ORDER LIST
PREPARE OPEN ORDER REPORT
VERIFY ACCUMULATED ORDERS

PRODUCE INVOICE
PREPARE INVOICE
LOG INVOICE
PREPARE INVOICE SUMMARY

APPLY PAYMENT TO INVOICE
POST INVOICE
POST PAYMENT
APPROVE CREDIT
ADJUST ACCOUNT BALANCE

PREPARE ACCOUNTS RECEIVABLE REPORT

AGE ACCOUNTS

KEYWORDS

Alias
Data dictionary
Data element
Data flow analysis
Data flow diagram
Data structure
Decision analysis
Iteration
Logical
Physical

REVIEW QUESTIONS

1 How do the data flow and decision-analysis methods differ? How are their purposes similar?
2 What is the advantage of showing data flow *graphically,* rather than using narrative description to study or explain a system?
3 What is a data flow? How does it differ from a document? What is its relation to a process? To a data store?
4 What advantages do data flow methods offer over other methods of data collection and systems charting?
5 Identify the symbols used in data flow diagrams and explain how each is used.
6 Distinguish between logical and physical views of the system. Which view is included in a data flow diagram? Why?
7 How and where do elements of processing control get incorporated into data flow diagrams. What guidelines govern their inclusion?
8 In what two ways are processes identified? Discuss guidelines for their use in data flow diagrams.
9 Summarize the procedures for developing data flow diagrams.
10 How are data and processes described in a data dictionary? Explain briefly.
11 What is the relation of data items and structures to data flows, processes, and data stores?
12 What notation is used to describe data dictionary entries? Is the notation necessary? Explain.
13 Are data flow diagrams useful without data dictionaries? Explain.

APPLICATION PROBLEMS FOR CHAPTER 4

1 Each semester, students register for courses offered by various departments and colleges within the university. Not all persons register on the same day, as there are too many students and too few staff members to handle registration en masse. Therefore, students are assigned specific registration dates and times. These details are communicated to registrants by a mailed registration permit. The permit, which is sent to the permanent address of the individual well in advance, contains the date and time of registration, as well as personal identification data (name, student number, academic standing, and matriculation status). Individuals must prove they have permission to register when they appear on a specific date and time at the registration hall. The permit itself need not be shown. They receive approval, and a record is made that they did appear at the appointed time. (This prevents others from appearing to impersonate an earlier registrant.)

In some cases students telephone in advance to learn of their assigned dates and times. Permits do not reach everyone, for various reasons.

During actual registration, students are allowed to sign up for any courses that are still accepting registration (i.e., that are not full and therefore closed) and for which they have met the prerequisites. (Students are responsible for ensuring they know about and have met the prerequisites.) When they register, their name, student identification number, and course credits are added to their registration record.

The last phase of registration is the payment of fees. Students pay tuition based on whether they are state residents, the numbers of credits they register for, and their academic standing. Tuition per credit varies by college within the university. Depending on whether students are in full- or part-time status (determined by the number of credits being carried), they may also be assessed a student activity fee.

All fees must be paid at the end of registration, before the individual leaves the registration hall. Payment may be made by cash, check, or credit card. (Credit card payments are authorized by telephone from the regional clearing hours of the credit card agency, which assigns a transaction approval number.)

a Develop a data flow diagram for the registration activities described above. Be sure to show all processes, data stores, sources, and destinations. Label all data flows.
Show the data flow diagram to at least three levels, including an overall context diagram. Use a meaningful numbering scheme to associate lower-level processes with higher-level ones.
Identify any missing details that you need to develop a more complete data flow diagram.

b Indicate all data flows that must involve paper or documents.

c Define all data structures in a data dictionary format that includes the name and description of the individual data elements.

2 Processes in data flows operate on data to transform the data in some manner. Therefore, no process should exist unless it accepts data as input and produces a changed set of data. Explain whether any of the following are acceptable descriptions of the data transformations a process can do. Give examples of each. Develop a segment of a data flow diagram that demonstrates your example.

a Processes transform the *structure* of the data (for example, by reformatting it).

b Processes transform the *information* contained in the data.

c Processes generate *new* information.

3 Describe any mistakes in the segments of data flow diagrams shown on page 152. (*Hint:* Only one of the data flow segments shown is acceptable.)

4 Develop the first- and second-level data flow diagrams for the narrative description that follows. Be sure to fully label the diagram to show all elements and the relations among them. Use only standard labeling methods.

The BIG-CHARGE credit card network is worldwide. When customers open a BIG-CHARGE account, they receive a plastic card containing their name, account number, and the account expiration date. The back side of the credit card also contains a space in which the customer signs the card. The signature is used by merchants for identification purposes.

The procedure for using BIG-CHARGE to make a purchase is as follows: When customers have selected the items they wish to purchase (e. g., clothing, airline tickets, or meals) the cashier tallies the amount of the purchase and completes a charge slip. Part of the charge slip is written by hand: the amount of the purchase, sales tax amount, and total of the purchase. (Other optional information includes a list of each individual item purchased and its cost.) The other part is completed using a roll-over machine as follows: The customer's plastic account card is placed in the roll-over machine and the charge slip is placed on top of it. The roller is then rolled over both, leaving an impression of the customer's name, account number, and card expiration date on the charge slip. The customer then signs the slip, acknowledging the amount of the charge and authorizing the merchant to charge his or her account in the amount of the purchase.

If the purchase is over a prespecified flow limit (e. g., $50), the merchant must telephone the BIG-CHARGE regional processing center to obtain authorization for the transaction. To obtain the authorization, merchants give their store identification number, the customer account number, card expiration date, and an authorization number. (If the card is invalid for any reason the regional center denies the purchase and refuses to provide a transaction number.) If the transaction is denied (regardless of the reason), the merchant cancels the customer transaction, destroys the charge slip, and retains the merchandise. If a consumable transaction has occurred (such as a meal that has been served), the merchant insists that the customer pay for the purchase in some other way.

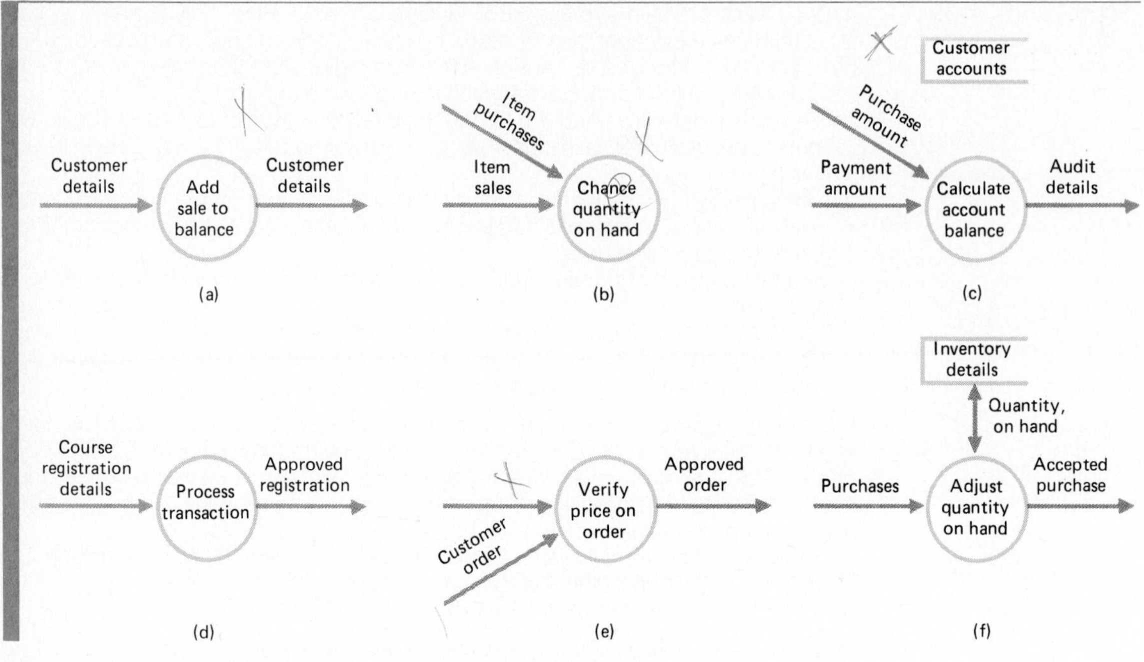

If the purchase is authorized and approved, the merchant gives a copy of the charge slip to the customer and places the remaining copies in the cash drawer for later processing.

5 Heartbreak Hotel is a 500-room convention hotel located in the southwest. The hotel includes adjacent restaurants and lounges, a nightclub, and a gambling casino. Sales for the hotel derive from guest room rentals (approximately $20 million yearly), banquets and special catered functions ($8 million yearly), and beverage and food sales from the lounge and bar areas and the dining rooms.

A major concern to general management is the operation of the front desk—the area of the hotel where arriving guests check in to their rooms, pay their bills upon departure, or order special services (laundry, room services, Gray Line tours, etc.). In addition, the front desk is responsible for processing billing and payment information for banquets and special catered functions taking place elsewhere in the hotel.

GUEST CHECK IN

All guest check in is at the front desk. Most guests arriving at the hotel have made reservations well in advance (or have had their travel agents make them on their behalf). Others are walk-ins, persons who show up unexpectedly (i.e., without a reservation) hoping to be able to acquire a room.

When a guest arrives, the front desk clerk asks whether the person has a reservation and what name it is under. The reservation list for the day is checked to find out what room has been reserved for the guest. Sometimes guests will say they have reservations when in fact they do not. When people arrive without reservations, the front desk clerk must check to see whether any rooms are available. If none are available, they are advised which other hotels in the area may have rooms available.

Each room has a specified rate group assigned to it, depending on the type of room. The exact rate within the group will vary depending on whether the room will be occupied by one, two, three, or more persons. When the guest completes the registration card, the front desk person writes the room rate in, taking into account the number of persons being registered.

When guests check in, the front desk clerk verifies the planned length of stay and method of payment. This information is noted on the registration card. Credit card information is also taken, unless the guest has made prior payment arrangements with the hotel's general manager.

If guests arrive early in the day, it is possible that their room will not yet be available. The front desk must determine whether the previous day's guests have checked out and the housekeeping department has cleaned the room and made it up for the next guests. Sometimes rooms are placed out of order at the last moment if housekeeping personnel find that previous guests have damaged the furniture or fixtures. When this happens, the front desk will have to change the guests' assigned room.

GUEST CHECKOUT

All guest checkouts are handled by the front desk. At checkout time, the individual's folio/record is closed out. The folio/record contains all rentals for the rooms plus any other charges that have been incurred at the hotel's various facilities as a result, for example, of telephone calls made or having laundry done up. The data and amount of each of these charges are posted to the folio/record. This is done on a day-by-day basis.

Guest payments are most often made by cash or credit card. Sometimes credit terms are allowed in which case the guests' checkouts add to the hotel's accounts receivable. (This does not affect the balancing process at the front desk at the end of the day. Regardless of the form of payment, the total receipts for the day must equal the total charges for that day for guests who have checked out.)

CATERING AND BANQUET RECEIPTS

Since the front desk operates 24 hours a day, it also assists in handling banquet and special-event billing. When parties, receptions, and catered special events are planned, an event slip is made up. The staff at the front desk receives a copy of this so it knows what events are going on. (This is also useful in answering incoming telephone calls when the caller is trying to get in touch with someone attending a specific function.) When an event is completed, the catering manager on duty informs the front desk of the charges for the event. If payment has been made, the catering manager also turns this over to the front desk. Otherwise, the amount is billed (which again affects the hotel's accounts receivable).

The following day, the accounting department audits the previous day's sales, paying particular attention to the total room revenue, miscellaneous revenues from guest rooms, and any revenue from special events. Any discrepancies between actual and expected revenues are investigated and appropriate adjustments are made. Accounts receivable, cash deposits, and credit card vouchers are processed. Bank deposits are made in the morning, and invoices are mailed in the afternoon. This is done the same way each day.

a Assume that the above description was given to you by the general manager. Having just returned from a workshop, conducted by the American Hotel and Motel Association, concerning automation of hotel management, the manager is interested in investigating better methods of managing guest services. But, in order to decide whether to proceed further, the manager needs to know what is feasible and what is not. The manager is well-aware that the technology in the computer area exists to improve guest service operations (check in, reservation, checkout, billing, cash handling, etc.).
   1 Identify the information you would need to have to determine whether it is feasible to pursue a full systems investigation concerning an automated and improved front desk operation. Focus *only* on the feasibility assessment.
   2 Identify the detailed operating information you would like to collect about front desk and billing operations, assuming your earlier feasibility study

resulted in a formal project launch. Indicate what specific information you want to obtain and how you would collect it.

b Using the information provided in the description of the hotel's front desk operation, develop a data flow diagram. Identify data flows, processes, data stores, sources, and sinks. Include a data dictionary. Incomplete information should be addressed in your data collection strategy.

6 Keeping track of manuscripts submitted for review and publication is a difficult task in the offices of major newspapers and magazines. Literally hundreds of manuscripts, ranging in length from 1 to 50 or 60 pages, arrive in editorial offices each day. It is important for these businesses to have an orderly system for keeping track of incoming items, their status, and their eventual dispositions. Not only is it a good business practice, but doing so is also important from a public relations standpoint.

We wish to examine the system used by one magazine publisher. The firm is considering redevelopment of its system, which consists of both manual and automated processes.

SUBMISSION CYCLE

Manuscripts to the company are submitted directly by the authors (or agents acting for authors) and arrive either by mail, courier, or are delivered in person. All incoming articles are delivered to the editorial department, where they are reviewed for acceptance or rejection. There is a high rejection rate. Even those articles that are eventually accepted must often undergo editing before they are finally in a usable form that can be forwarded to the copy department for actual publication.

All manuscripts are logged when they arrive in the editorial department, regardless of how they are delivered. Once logged, they are evaluated for suitability and usability on the basis of various criteria, including general interest for the subject matter of the article. Various members of the department review manuscripts, depending on their areas of interest and expertise. In all cases, the reviewers make an acceptance or rejection decision and return the manuscript to the control clerk who originally forwarded it to them. Two persons handle all the logging and control work. However, once an item is accepted, it is worked on by others, but the control clerks still maintain the log.

Accepted manuscripts are forwarded by the control persons to the editing staff responsible for the primary edit of the written material. When this edit is completed. the manuscript is forwarded to a staff that does a secondary edit for final style and phrasing. In essence this is the final edit of the manuscript.

Finished manuscripts are logged out of the editorial department's control system. They are then sent to the copy department, where they are prepared for publication in the magazine.

Between primary and secondary editing, it is often necessary to redraw figures and line art for some of the manuscripts. After this is completed, the articles are sent to those staff members who do the secondary editing work.

The editorial department maintains both an author file and an article file. When a new article is logged in, a record is added to the article file. This record is updated when the same manuscript is logged out of the editorial department at the end of editing.

The author file contains the names of all authors who have previously written manuscripts for the magazine. When a manuscript is first logged in, the control clerk updates the author's record in the author file (or enters a new one if it is a first-time author). The file is used again when the accepted manuscript has been edited to update the status of the manuscript (i.e., ready for publication).

Not all manuscripts submitted for review are actually accepted. After being logged in, the manuscript is carefully evaluated. Some are accepted, and some are rejected. Rejected manuscripts are returned to the author with an accompanying rejection letter. Acceptance letters are generated for the other manuscripts and are accompanied by a royalty check. Curiously enough, some authors neglect to include a name or address with their manuscript. These manuscripts are logged, like the others, after which they are removed from the editorial department.

Once sent there, all accepted and edited manuscripts become the responsibility of the copy department.

a Develop the main level for the magazine acceptance and review process.

b Develop a detailed data flow diagram for the editorial department. Indicate all processes, data flows, and data stores. Include data inflows and outflows.

CHAPTER 5 STRATEGIES FOR DECISION ANALYSIS

QUESTIONS TO GUIDE YOU THROUGH THE CHAPTER

- What components are analyzed in making a decision or formulating a decision strategy?
- How do analysts study decision processes in situations they are not familiar with?
- What methods are used to describe and understand decisions which require that conditions be identified in a particular sequence?
- Are different methods used when describing quantitative or qualitative conditions?
- Which decision-analysis strategies use graphic methods rather than English statements?
- How are errors in decision analysis caught and corrected?

Decision making is an integral part of business. In fact, managing itself is essentially decision making. Some decisions, such as whether to accept merger offers, affect entire organizations. Others, like deciding when to reorder supplies, are less complex and involve fewer people. Both however are important to systems analysts when they are within the business system under investigation. (Developing an inventory reorder system, for example, without examining the decision about how much of an item to put on order, could be a disaster.)

This chapter looks at decision-analysis strategies—methods for studying decision-making steps and documenting them for study. The strategies help analysts collect additional information to supplement the systems requirement details that they learned through data flow analysis.

The chapter first discusses features common to all decision situations. The remainder of the chapter examines three methods for decision analysis: decision trees, decision tables, and structured English. Each method is in widespread use. When you finish this chapter, you should have learned how to examine a decision and describe the necessary steps to make it. It is essential for the analyst to understand that decisions will involve information or activities associated with the information system.

DECISION CONCEPTS

When analyzing decisions, start by identifying conditions and actions—concepts common to all decisions.

Conditions and Decision Variables

If, when looking at a system, you ask the question, "What are the possibilities?" or "What can happen?", you are asking about *conditions,* the possible states of an entity (person, place, thing, or event). You have undoubtedly described automobiles, furniture, and even people by their good or bad condition. "Good" and "bad" are two specific alternative conditions that are applied to each of the above entities. Conditions vary,

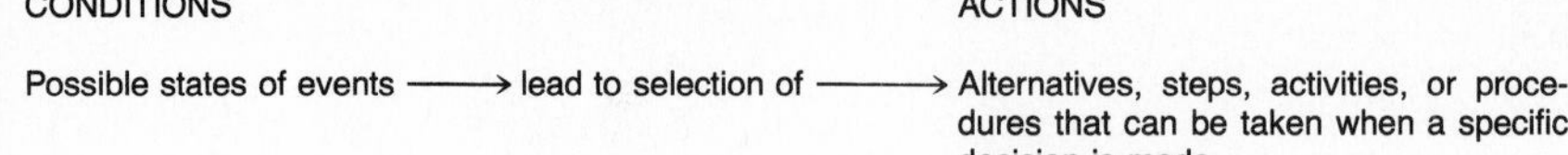

CONDITIONS
ACTIONS
Possible states of events → lead to selection of → Alternatives, steps, activities, or procedures that can be taken when a specific decision is made.

Figure 5.1. Important decision concepts.

which is why analysts may refer to them as *decision variables*. In the order processing example of the last chapter, the invoice condition is a decision variable. The two alternatives for invoices received by an organization are: signed or unsigned. The same invoice could also be described by other alternate conditions: authorized or unauthorized, correctly priced or incorrectly priced.

In decision analysis, the investigator must identify both the relevant conditions that can occur in a situation, and the permissible ones. Only those conditions relevant to the study should be included. The fact that the invoice is signed or unsigned is a relevant decision variable. However, the size of the sheet of paper on which it is printed probably is not.

Actions

When all possible conditions are known, the analyst next determines what to do when certain conditions occur. *Actions* are alternatives—the steps, activities, or procedures that an individual may decide to take when confronted with a set of conditions (Figure 5.1). The actions can be quite simple in some cases and extensive in others, as will be seen.

The order processing example that has been used calls for specific actions, depending among other things on whether the invoice is signed or unsigned (the conditions). If signed, the invoice is moved to order verification processing. If it is unsigned, then acceptance of the merchandise must be verified. In this example the relevant actions are: (1) begin order verification processing and (2) begin merchandise acceptance processing (Figure 5.2).

Actions can also be related to quantitative conditions. For example, businesses often give discounts on purchased merchandise, depending on the size of the order. One might base discount amounts on three different values for the condition SIZE OF ORDER: over $10,000, $5,000 to $10,000, and less than $5,000. Three actions apply: take 3% discount, take 2% discount, and pay full invoice amount (Figure 5.3).

In many decisions, analysts must consider combinations of conditions

Figure 5.2. Relation of conditions and actions for order processing example.

CONDITION	ACTION
Order is signed	Begin order verification process.
Order is unsigned	Begin merchandise acceptance processing.

Figure 5.3. Condition-action example with multiple values.

CONDITION		ACTION
Size of order:	Over $10,000	Take 3% discount from invoice total.
	$5,000 to $10,000	Take 2% discount from invoice total.
	Less than $5,000	Pay full invoice amount.

and actions. To assist them in understanding and matching combinations, they use decision trees, decision tables, and structured English. These tools are examined next.

DECISION TREES

As you know well, people say the same things differently. For example, the discount conditions discussed in the last example can also be stated in the following ways:

1 Greater than $10,000, greater than or equal to $5,000, less than or equal to $10,000, and below $5,000
2 Not less than $10,000, not more than $10,000 but at least $5,000, not $5,000 or more

Since different ways of saying the same thing can create difficulties in communication during systems studies (analyst and manager may misunderstand each others' comments or forget to discuss all the details), analysts want to prevent misunderstandings. They also need to organize information collected about decision making.

Decision trees are one of three methods for describing decisions, while avoiding difficulties in communication.

Decision-Tree Characteristics

A *decision tree* is a diagram that presents conditions and actions sequentially and thus shows which conditions to consider first, which second, and so on. It is also a method of showing the relationship of each condition and its permissible actions. The diagram looks like branches on a tree, hence the name decision tree.

The root of the tree, on the left of the diagram, is the starting point of the decision sequence. The particular branch to be followed depends on the conditions that exist and the decision to be made (Figure 5.4). You progress from left to right along a particular branch by making a series of decisions. Following each decision point is the next set of decisions to be considered. The nodes of the tree thus represent conditions and indicate that a determination must be made about which condition exists before the next path can be chosen. The right side of the tree lists the actions to be taken, depending on the sequence of conditions that is followed.

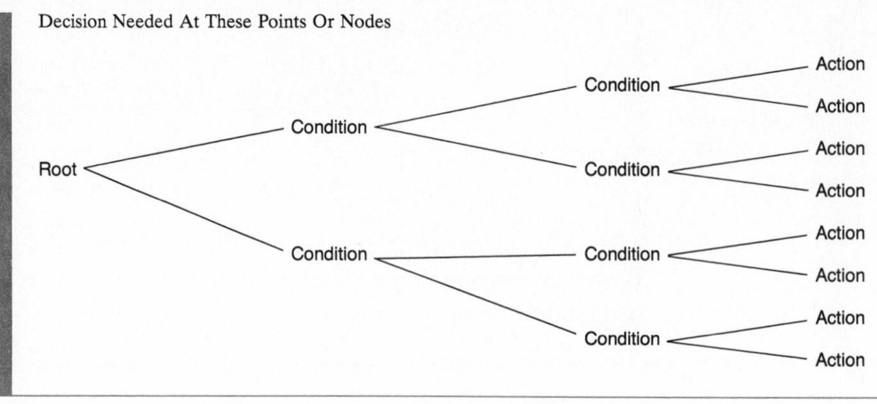

Figure 5.4. Decision tree sequence of decisions is from left to right.

Using Decision Trees

Developing decision trees is beneficial to analysts in two ways. First of all, the need to describe conditions and actions formally forces analysts to identify the actual decisions that must be made. It becomes difficult for them to overlook an integral step in the decision process, whether it depends on quantitative or nonquantitative variables.

It is possible, for instance, to show how to take certain actions that depend on the number of dollars spent by customers. When an organization opens accounts with dealers and suppliers, it formalizes an agreement for taking discounts from the full invoice price. Two conditions are specified in this agreement: First, the invoice must always be paid within 10 days of its receipt, and, second, the size of the discount will depend on the value of the invoice. It is agreed that under some conditions the organization can take the action of deducting a 3 percent discount; under others, a 2 percent discount; and under all other conditions, no discount is allowed.

Decision trees also force analysts to consider the sequence of decisions. Consider the sequence of decisions in this example (Figure 5.5). You should quickly determine that one condition, the size of the invoice in terms of dollars, does not matter unless the other condition is met and the invoice is paid within the time established by the supplier, 10 days. The other conditions are relevant only if that condition is true. Therefore the decision tree identifies the time condition first and shows two values (within 10 days and longer than 10 days). The discount condition is described next, but only for the branch of the tree for WITHIN 10 DAYS. The LONGER THAN 10 DAYS branch has no other relevant conditions and so shows the resulting action (unconditionally). This tree shows that the action PAY FULL INVOICE AMOUNT applies under two different conditions. It also implicitly says that there is no reason to pay invoices of less than $5000 within 10 days since there is no available discount.

The decision tree in Figure 5.6 shows the nonquantitative conditions for processing accounts payable: signed invoice, authorized purchase, and

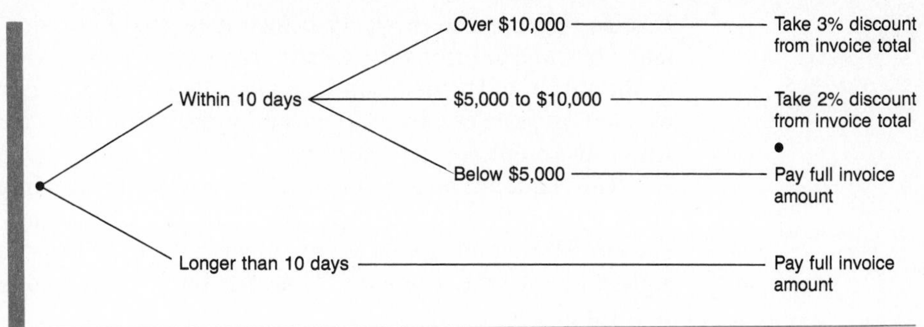

Figure 5.5.
Decision tree for discount authorization.

correct pricing. Depending on the set of conditions that exist, one of two actions can be taken: payment can be authorized or the submitted invoice can be rejected. Notice how clearly each alternative is shown in the decision tree. Sometimes in more complex business situations, the specific action most appropriate under several conditions is not readily apparent without formal analysis of this nature.

Analysts will find that it is necessary in accounts payable processing to determine whether a purchase order is available and valid and whether the

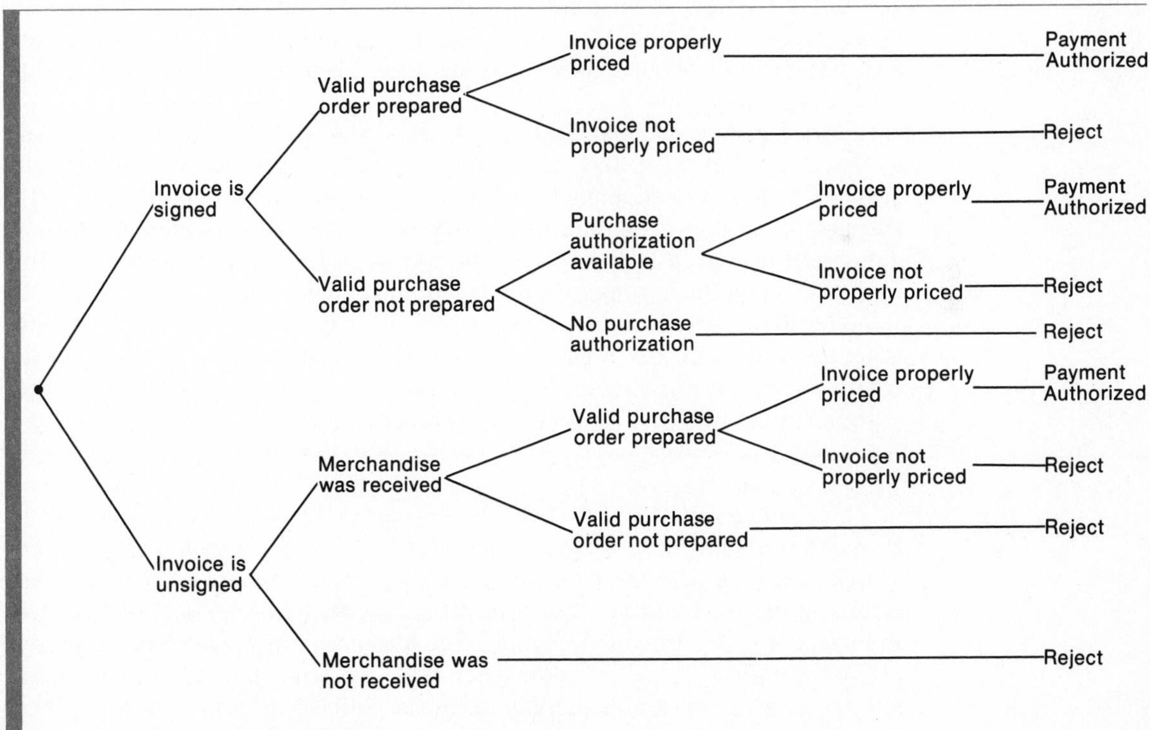

Figure 5.6.
Decision tree for invoice processing example.

invoice is processed properly before it is actually paid. In turn, they must learn of the conditions for proper invoice processing. Full development and examination of the decision tree also shows clearly that there are only two ways an invoice can be authorized for payment, but many conditions under which payment can be rejected.

The sequence of decisions is easy to see in this example. The condition of having a valid purchase order does not matter *unless the invoice has been signed*. The signature is more important since the condition of having a signed invoice must be met. Then the analysts can consider the authorization condition.

Identifying Data Requirements

We have already pointed out the use of decision trees to formally highlight the sequential nature of many business decisions. And we have shown that decision trees are effective when describing business problems of more than one dimension or condition. However, they also identify critical data requirements surrounding the decision process, because they indicate the sets of data the manager requires to formulate decisions or select actions. The data in the payment example are explicitly payment data, amount of invoice, and discount allowance percentage. Implicitly there are other important data elements, such as invoice details (number, supplier name and address), new invoice amount payable, and adjustment to "discount taken" account. The analyst must identify and list all the data used in the decision process, even though the decision tree does not show all the individual data items.

If decision trees are assembled after the completion of data flow analysis, critical data may already be defined in the data dictionary. If decision trees are used alone (they seldom are), analysts must be certain to accurately identify each data element needed to make a decision. The data dictionary format, discussed in Chapter 4, is useful for listing and describing data elements as they are identified and understood.

The data requirements discussed for decision trees also apply to the other decision-analysis methods that are discussed below. Analysts will need to describe and define all data used in decision making, so that the system can be designed to produce it properly.

Avoiding Problems with Decision Trees

Decision trees may not always be the best tools for decision analysis. If the system itself is so complex that there are many sequences of steps and combinations of conditions, the analyst should avoid decision trees because their size will become unwieldy. A large number of branches and too many paths through them will cloud rather than aid analysis. The analyst may not be able to determine which business policies or practices guide the formulation of specific decisions. Where these problems arise, decision tables should be considered.

Figure 5.7. General form for decision table.

CONDITION	DECISION RULES
Condition statements	Condition entries
Action statements	Action entries

DECISION TABLES

A *decision table* is a matrix of rows and columns, rather than a tree, that shows conditions and actions. Decision rules, also included in the table, state what procedure to follow when certain conditions exist. This method has been used since the mid-1950s, when it was developed at General Electric for the analysis of business functions like inventory control, sales analysis, credit analysis, and transportation control and routing.

Decision-Table Characteristics

The decision table is made up of four sections, displaying condition statements, condition entries, action statements, and action entries (Figure 5.7). The *condition statement section* identifies the relevant conditions. *Condition entries* tell which value, if any, applies for a particular condition. *Action statements* list the set of all steps that can be taken when a certain condition occurs. *Action entries* show what specific actions in the set to take when selected conditions or combinations of conditions are true. Sometimes notes are added below the table to indicate when to use the table or to distinguish it from other decision tables.

The columns on the right side of the table, linking conditions and actions, form decision rules. A *decision rule* states the conditions that must be satisfied for a particular set of actions to be taken. Notice that we have dropped the ordering sequence in which conditions are examined, that was necessary with decision trees. The decision rule incorporates *all* the conditions that must be true, not just one condition at a time.

Figure 5.8 contains a decision table, describing the actions taken in

Figure 5.8. Sample decision table for payment of health services.

	CONDITIONS	DECISION RULES			
		1	2	3	4
C1	Patient has basic health insurance	Y	N	Y	N
C2	Patient has social health insurance	N	Y	Y	N
A1	Pay amount of office call	X			
A2	Pay nothing		X	X	
A3	Pay full amount for services				X

CONDITIONS	DECISION RULES					
	1	2	3	4	5	6
Time	Within 10 days	Within 10 days	Within 10 days	Not within 10 days	Not within 10 days	Not within 10 days
Business volume	Over $10,000	$5,000 to $10,000	Below $5,000	Over $10,000	$5,000 to $10,000	Below $5,000
Take 3% discount	X					
Take 2% discount		X				
Pay full invoice amount			X	X	X	X

Figure 5.9. Decision table for payment discount example.

handling payments from patients in a medical clinic, depending on whether the patient has medical insurance and, if so, which type. Two types of insurance coverage are identified: basic health insurance (condition 1) and national health insurance (condition 2). That the first condition (the patient has basic health insurance) may or may not exist is represented by Y and N (which stand for yes and no) in the condition entries portion of the table. Four rules relate the combinations of conditions 1 and 2 to three different actions: the patient must pay the cost of the office call, but no other charges; the patient pays none of the charges; or the patient pays the full cost of treatment (office call and other charges). Reading this table, it is clear that, when C1 and C2 are Yes and No, respectively, the rule states that action A1 should be applied: the patient must pay only for the cost of the office call. When the values for condition C1 and C2 are reversed (C1 is No and C2 is Yes), rule 2 indicates that action A2 should apply: the patient need not pay for any of the charges. Rule 3 says to use action A2 again, this time because both C1 and C2 are Yes. If rules 2 and 3 are compared, it can be concluded that the value for condition C1 is not relevant to invoking action A2: as long as the patient has national health insurance coverage, regardless of other insurance, no payment is required. Finally rule 4 says that, if both C1 and C2 are No, meaning that the patient has no insurance, staff members must follow action A3: the full charges for visiting the clinic must be paid.

The payment discount case, described earlier in Figure 5.5, is a more concrete example. It is shown in decision-table form in Figure 5.9. Rules 1 and 2 properly reflect that discounts are taken only when payments are made within the 10-day limit and sales are either high (more than $10,000) or medium (from $5,000 to 10,000). In all other cases, no discount is taken. Rules 3, 4, 5, and 6 guide selection of this action. (The table itself has 12 conditions: 2 decision variables times 6 values for each variable.)

The decision table is shown in Figure 5.10 in a Y-N format. Y and N are used in the condition entries section, but actual values for each of the conditions are shown in the condition statement section. Whether the

CONDITIONS	DECISION RULES					
Within 10 days	Y	Y	Y	N	N	N
Over $10,000	Y	N	N	Y	N	N
$5,000 to $10,000	N	Y	N	N	Y	N
Below $5,000	N	N	Y	N	N	Y
Take 3% discount	X					
Take 2% discount		X				
Pay full invoice amount			X	X	X	X

Figure 5.10. Decision table using Yes/No format for payment discount example.

analyst uses this format or one of the others discussed in a moment is a matter of personal preference. The format does not change the usefulness of decision tables.

Building Decision Tables

To develop decision tables, analysts should use the following steps:

1 Determine the most relevant factors to be considered in making a decision. This identifies the *conditions* in the decision. Each condition selected should be able to either occur or not occur; half occurrence is not possible.

2 Determine the most feasible steps or activities under varying conditions (not just current conditions). This identifies the *actions*.

3 Study the combinations of conditions that are possible. For every number N of conditions, there are 2^N combinations to be considered. For example, for 3 conditions, there are 8 possible combinations; $2^3 = 8$. For 4, $2^4 = 16$ combinations are possible and can be included in the table.

4 Fill in the table with decision rules. There are two ways to fill in the table.

The first and longer method is to fill in condition rows with a yes or no value for each possible combination of conditions. That is, fill in the first half of the row with Y and the second half with N. The next row should be filled alternately with Y and N at 25 percent of the row: i.e., 25% Y, 25% N, 25% Y and 25% N. Repeat this process: fill in each remaining row alternately with Y and N dividing by increasing powers of 2. (That is, $2^2 = 4$ for the second row, 2^3 for the third row, until 2^N for the last row N, where N is the number of conditions).

The other method of completing the table deals with one condition at a time and adds to the table for each additional condition but does not add duplicate combinations of conditions and actions, as discussed below and shown in Figure 5.11:

a State the first condition and permissible actions.

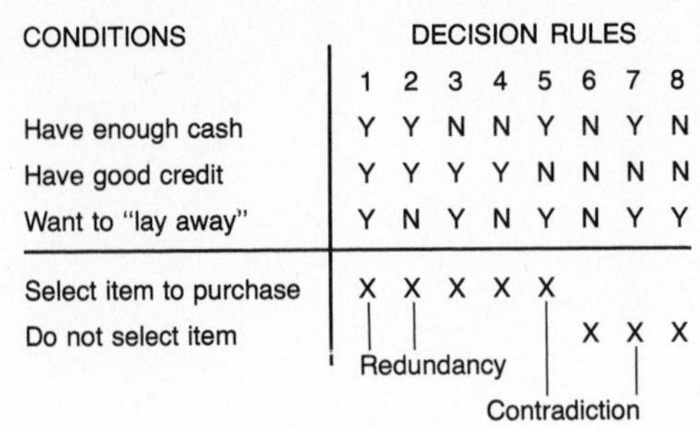

CONDITIONS	DECISION RULES							
	1	2	3	4	5	6	7	8
Have enough cash	Y	Y	N	N	Y	N	Y	N
Have good credit	Y	Y	Y	Y	N	N	N	N
Want to "lay away"	Y	N	Y	N	Y	N	Y	Y
Select item to purchase	X	X	X	X	X			
Do not select item						X	X	X

Figure 5.11. Common discrepancies in decision tables.

 b Add the second condition by duplicating the first half of the matrix and filling in the different Y and N values from the new condition in both halves of the expanded matrix.

 c Repeat step b for each additional condition.

5 Fill in action entries with X to signal action(s) to take and leave cells blank or mark with "-" to show that no action applies to that row. Figure 5.10 shows the result of using this approach to develop the decision table for the example introduced earlier.

6 Examine the table for redundant rules or contradictions between rules (discussed below).

These simple guidelines will not only save time in building a decision table from information collected during an investigation but will aid in pointing out where information is missing, conditions do not matter in a process, or where there are important relations or results that others were not aware of or not considering. In other words, using decision tables can produce more complete and accurate analysis.

Checking Decision Tables

After constructing each table, the analysts verify it for correctness and completeness to ensure that the table includes all the conditions along with the decision rules that relate them to the actions. The analysts should also examine the table for redundancy and contradictions.

ELIMINATING REDUNDANCY

Decision tables can become large and unwieldy if allowed to grow in an uncontrolled fashion. Removing redundant entries will help manage table size. *Redundancy* occurs when *both* of the following are true: (1) two decision rules are identical except for one condition row, and (2) the actions for the two rules are identical.

Figure 5.11 contains redundant decision rules: decision rules 1 and 2. For both, the action "Select item to purchase" is suggested by the X in the action entries section, corresponding to columns 1 and 2. A closer look at the

CONDITIONS	DECISION RULES 1	2	3	4	5
Have enough cash	Y	—	Y	N	N
Have good credit	Y	Y	N	N	N
Want to "lay away"	—	N	Y	Y	N
Select item to purchase	X	X	X	X	
Do not select item					X

Figure 5.12. Decision table with discrepancies removed.

condition rows reveals that the decision rules for conditions 1 and 2 are identical, but opposite for condition 3. This indicates that actions do not depend on the value for condition 3: regardless of the value, the actions are the same. Since this is true, the decision rules are redundant and can be combined into one rule. Replace the condition row where they differ by a blank or a "-" to show that the condition does not matter. Figure 5.12 shows the results of removing this redundancy from our sample table.

REMOVING CONTRADICTIONS

Decision rules *contradict* each other when two or more rules have the same set of conditions and the actions are *different.* (Remember, if they are the same, then it is a redundancy.)

Contradictions mean that either the analyst's information is incorrect or there is an error in the construction of the table. Many times, however, contradiction is a result of the analyst's receiving discrepant information from different individuals about how they make decisions. A specific decision may be made using different rules. Finding out about that can be very useful to an analyst trying to improve a decision situation.

There is a contradiction between decision rules 5 and 7 in Figure 5.11. Both have the same values for conditions 1, 2, and 3 (Y, N, and Y), but rule 5 says to follow action strategy A1, while rule 7 indicates A2. Verifying which is the proper action and eliminating the inconsistency will resolve the contradiction. Figure 5.12 shows the correction to remove the contradiction.

Types of Table Entries

LIMITED-ENTRY FORM

The basic table structure used in the previous examples, consisting only of Y, N, and "-" entries, is called the *limited-entry* form. It is one of the most commonly used formats. Two other forms are also widely used.

EXTENDED-ENTRY FORM

The extended-entry form replaces Y and N with action entries telling the reader how to decide. In this format, the condition and action statements

CONDITIONS	DECISION RULES					
	1	2	3	4	5	6
Time	Within 10 days	Within 10 days	Within 10 days	Not within 10 days	Not within 10 days	Not within 10 days
Business volume	Over $10,000	$5,000 to $10,000	Below $5,000	Over $10,000	$5,000 to $10,000	Below $10,000
Action	Take 3% discount	Take 2% discount	Pay full invoice amount	Pay full invoice amount	Pay full invoice amount	Pay full invoice amount

Figure 5.13. Extended entry format for decision tables.

themselves are not complete, which is why the entries contain more details than Y and N.

Figure 5.13 demonstrates the extended-entry method, applied to the discount example introduced earlier. The limited-entry table lists three conditions in the action statement section. The X in the action entry section signals the correct action. However, the extended-entry form has only one action statement, ACTION. For each rule, a short phrase is entered in the action statement section: TAKE 3% DISCOUNT, TAKE 2% DISCOUNT, or PAY FULL INVOICE AMOUNT.

Many persons favor this format over the limited-entry method because of its more explicit signaling of actions.

MIXED-ENTRY FORM

Analysts may prefer to combine features of both the limited- and extended-entry forms in the same table. Generally only one form should be used in each section of the table, but between the condition and action sections either form can be used. The mixed-entry example in Figure 5.9 combines a limited-entry format for the action entries and an extended-entry format for condition entries.

ELSE FORM

Still another variation in decision tables is aimed at omitting repetitious rules through ELSE rules. To build an ELSE-form decision table, specify the rules with condition entries to cover all sets of actions except for one which will be the rule to follow when none of the other explicit conditions is true. This rule is in the final column on the right, the ELSE column. If none of the other conditions hold, then the ELSE decision rule is followed. The ELSE rule eliminates the need to repeat conditions that lead to the same actions.

The payment discount decision table in Figure 5.14 uses an ELSE form. As you can see, the ELSE decision rule has replaced four separate decision rules, all calling for the same action.

CONDITIONS	DECISION RULES 1	2	ELSE
Time	Within 10 days	Within 10 days	
Business volume	Over $10,000	$5,000 to $10,000	
Take 3% discount	X		
Take 2% discount		X	
Pay full invoice amount			X

Figure 5.14. ELSE form for selecting proper action.

Multiple Tables

Large decision tables can become unwieldy, and analysts must therefore control table size. The ELSE form is one way of managing size. A second way is by using multiple decision tables linked together. Depending on the actions selected on the first table, additional actions are explained by one or more additional tables; each additional table provides greater details about the actions to take. Multiple tables also enable the analysts to state repetitive actions that should occur after some decisions have been made and will continue until a certain condition has been reached.

To use this method, the analysts construct separate decision tables that meet all of the normal requirements and deal with a specific decision. They are linked together in a hierarchical fashion: a top-level table contains the major conditions which, when selected, determine what additional actions and table to reference for further details. A transfer statement, such as GO TO or PERFORM, in the action section of the controlling (upper-level) table directs the routing to lower tables. There are two types of transfer: direct and temporary.

DIRECT TRANSFER

Direct transfer uses a one-time transfer: the referenced table does not refer back to the original table. The action statement "GO TO table name" indicates which table to examine next. Figure 5.15 outlines a direct-transfer table. The statement "GO TO Table 2" tells the reader to examine another decision table, identified as Table 2. The conditions, decisions, and actions specified in Table 2 are examined and appropriate ones selected to complete the work.

TEMPORARY TRANSFER

In contrast, Figure 5.16 links Table 1 to Table 2 through the statement "PERFORM Table 2." At the end of Table 2 a RETURN statement sends control back to the statement following the GO TO in Table 1.

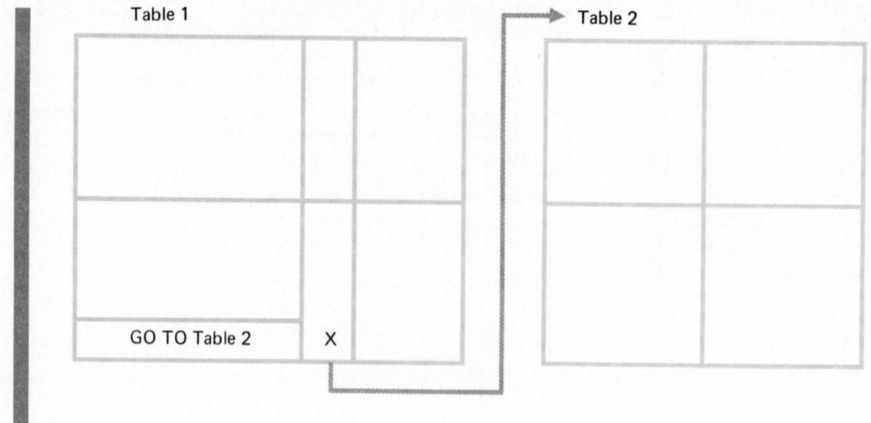

Figure 5.15. Multiple table linkage using "GO TO" form.

Decision-Table Processors

Decision tables have been partially automated. Table processors are computer programs that handle actual table formulations on the basis of input provided by the analyst. They also do all the checking for redundancy and consistency. Some turn the set of decisions and conditions into actual computer program instructions (Figure 5.17).

The usefulness of decision-table processors is in saving programming time and checking for errors. Decision-table processors were widely publicised during the 1960s and early 1970s.

STRUCTURED ENGLISH

Structured English is an additional method to overcome problems of ambiguous language in stating conditions and actions in decisions and procedures. This method does not use trees or tables, but rather narrative statements, to describe a procedure. It does not *show* decision rules: it *states* them.

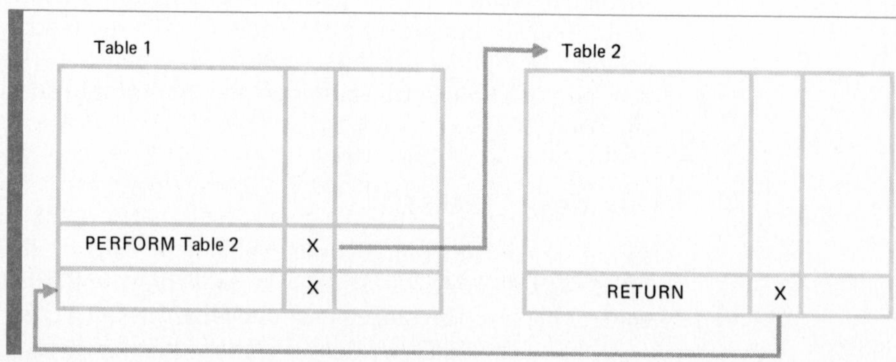

Figure 5.16. Multiple table linkage using "PERFORM" form.

```
100010  DETAB     CHECK-TAX                    07 13  08  X
100011  N NOTE THIS TABLE CHECKS TAX LOGIC.
100020  RH                                      01020304050607EL$
100030  C CARD-READ EQUAL TO 0                   Y N N N N N N
100040  C ITEMIZED GREATER THAN 100                Y N N N N N
100050  C TENPERCENT-DED GR 1000                     Y N N N N
100060  C TWO-HUNDRED-PLUS-DED GR 1000                 Y N N N
100070  C ITEMIZED GR TENPERCENT-DED                     Y N -
100080  C ITEMIZED GR TWO-HUNDRED-PLUS-DED               Y - N
100090  C TENPERCENT-DED GR TWO-HUNDRED-PLS-DED            Y N
100100  A MOVE 1 TO CARD-READ.                   X
100110  A PERFFFORM TAX-INFO-READ.               X
100120  A PERFORM TWO-HUNDRED-PLUS.              X
100130  A PERFORM TEN-PERCENT.                   X
100140  A GO TO CHECK-TAX-LOGIC.                 X
100150  A MOVE ADJ-GROSS-INC TO TAXABLE-INC.       X X X X X X
100160  A PERFORM DED-2-ITEMIZED.                  X     X
100170  A PERFORM DED-1-1000.                        X X
100180  A PERFORM DED-3-TWO-HUNDRED-PLUS.                    X
100190  A PERFORM DED-4-TENPERCENT.                        X
100200  A MOVE TAXABLE-INC TO TAXABLE-INC-OUT.     X X X X X X
100210  A GO TO CALC-OF-TAX-LOGIC.                 X X X X X X
100220  A GO TO TABLE-1-ERROR.                                 X
        ENDTB

                            TABLE DIAGNOSTICS
NO DIAGNOSTICS
101010  DETAB    CALC-OF-TAX                   08   13  10  X
101019  N NOTE THIS TABLE CALCULATES TAX
101020  RH                                      010203040506070809EL$
101030  C TAXABLE-INC GR 16000                   Y N N N N N N N N
101040  C TAXABLE-INC LESS THAN 0                N Y N N N N N N N
101050  C TAXABLE-INC GR 1000                    Y N N Y Y Y Y Y Y
101060  C TAXABLE-INC GR 2000                    Y N N N Y Y Y Y Y
101070  C TAXABLE-INC GR 3000                    Y N N N N Y Y Y Y
101080  C TAXABLE-INC GR 4000                    Y N N N N N Y Y Y
101090  C TAXABLE-INC GR 8000                    Y N N N N N N Y Y
101100  C TAXABLE-INC GR 12000                   Y N N N N N N N Y
101110  A PERFORM ERROR-TOO-BIG.                 X
101120  A MOVE 0 TO TAXABLE-INC.                   X
101130  A PERFORM TAX-CALC-14.                       X
101140  A PERFORM TAX-CALC-15.                         X
101150  A PERFORM TAX-CALC-16.                           X
101160  A PERFORM TAX-CALC-17.                             X
101170  A PERFORM TAX-CALC-19.                               X
101180  A PERFORM TAX-CALC-22.                                 X
101190  A PERFORM TAX-CALC-25.                                   X
101200  A PERFORM TAX-OUTPUT.                    X X X X X X X X X
101210  A MOVE 0 TO CARD-READ.                   X X X X X X X X X
101220  A GO TO CHECK-TAX-LOGIC.                 X X X X X X X X X
101230  A GO TO TABLE-2-ERROR.                                     X
101240  ENDTB
```

Figure 5.17. Decision table processor operations.

Structured-English specifications still require analysts to identify the conditions that occur in a process, decisions that must be made when they occur, and alternative actions to take. However, this method also allows the analysts to list steps in the order in which they must be taken, as examples in this section will show. No special symbols or formats are used, a feature some dislike about decision trees and tables. Furthermore, entire procedures can be stated quickly since only English-like statements are used.

The terminology used in the structured description of an application

```
000010 IDENTIFICATION DIVISION.
000020 PROGRAM-ID. INCOME-TAXES.
000030 AUTHOR.
000040 DATE-WRITTEN.
000050 REMARKS.
000060
000070           AN INTRODUCTION TO THE USE OF DECISION TABLES.
000080      DETAB/65MODIFIED, A DECISION TABLE PRE-PROCESSOR FOR
000090      LIMITED ENTRY DECISION TABLES WRITTEN USING COBOL , WAS
000100      USED TO CHANGE THE STUDENT PROGRAMS CONTAINING DECISION
000110      TABLE FORMAT SOURCE INPUT ALONG WITH STANDARD COBOL FORMAT
000120      INTO STANDARD COBOL SOURCE ACCEPTABLE TO THE COBOL COMPILER.
000130      THE PROBLEM THAT FOLLOWS IS A SIMPLIFIED TAX CALCULATION
000140       USING THE STANDARD TAX TABLES FOR 1968.  THREE METHODS OF
000150       CALCULATING THE TAXPAYERS DEDUCTIONS WERE ANALYZED TO
000160      PRODUCE THE SMALLEST TAX PAYMENT FOR THE INPUT VALUES
000170       PROVIDED ON THE INPUT CARD OF EACH TAXPAYER.
000180 ENVIRONMENT DIVISION.
000190 CONFIGURATION SECTION.
000200 SOURCE-COMPUTER. 6600.
000210 OBJECT-COMPUTER. 6600.
000220 SPECIAL-NAMES.
000230      OUTPUT IS PRINT-ER.
000240 INPUT-OUTPUT SECTION.
000250 FILE-CONTROL.
000260      SELECT TAX-INFO ASSIGN TO INPUT.
000270      SELECT TAX-OUTPUT-DATA ASSIGN TO OUTPUT.
000280 DATA DIVISION.
000290 FILE SECTION.
000300 FD   TAX-INFO
000310      LABEL RECORD IS OMITTED
000320      DATA RECORD IS TAX-INFO-REC.
000330 01   TAX-INFO-REC.
000340      02  NAMES          PICTURE X(15).
000350      02  FILLER         PICTURE X(5).
000360      02  EXEMPTIONS     PICTURE 999.
000370      02  ADJ-GROSS-INC   PICTURE 99999V99.
000380      02  ITEMIZED       PICTURE 99999V99.
000390      02  FILLER         PICTURE X(43).
000400 FD   TAX-OUTPUT-DATA
000410      LABEL RECORD IS OMITTED
000420      DATA RECORD IS TX-OUTPUT-DTA.
000430 01   TX-OUTPUT-DTA.
000440      02  SPACER         PICTURE X.
000450      02  DATA-OUT       PICTURE X(135).
000460 WORKING-STORAGE SECTION.
000470 01   LINE-SPACE-1        PICTURE X VALUE ≠-≠.
000480 01   TWO-HUNDRED-PLUS-DED    PICTURE 99999V99.
000490 01   TENPERCENT-DED          PICTURE 99999V99.
000500 01   LINE-DATA-OUT.
000510      02  SKIP-CONTROL    PICTURE X     VALUE ≠≠.
000520      02  FILLER         PICTURE X(4)  VALUE SPACES.
000530      02  ID-NAME         PICTURE X(20)  VALUE SPACES.
000540      02  FILLER         PICTURE  X(3)   VALUE SPACES.
000540      02  ADJGRINC-OUT      PICTURE  $ZZZZ9.99.
```

Figure 5.17. (*Continued*)

consists largely of data names for elements that are defined in the data dictionary developed for the project.

Developing Structured Statements

Structured English uses three basic types of statements to describe a process. They work well for decision analysis and can be carried over into programming and software development, as will be shown in the software

COBOL

```
PROCEDURE DIVISION.
START.
     OPEN INPUT TAX-INFO.
     OPEN OUTPUT TAX-OUTPUT-DATA.
     MOVE 0 TO CARD-READ.
TITLE-HEADINGS.
     MOVE LINE-SPACE-START TO SPACER.
     MOVE SPACES TO DATA-OUT.
     WRITE TX-OUTPUT-DTA.
      MOVE LINE-TITLE TO TX-OUTPUT-DTA.
     WRITE TX-OUTPUT-DTA.
     MOVE LINE-EXCEPTION TO TX-OUTPUT-DTA.
     MOVE LINE-SPACE-1 TO SPACER.
     WRITE TX-OUTPUT-DTA.
     MOVE LINE-HDG-1 TO TX-OUTPUT-DTA.
     MOVE LINE-SPACE-2 TO SPACER.
     WRITE TX-OUTPUT-DTA.
     MOVE LINE-HDG-2 TO TX-OUTPUT-DTA.
     WRITE TX-OUTPUT-DTA.
     MOVE LINE-HDG-3 TO TX-OUTPUT-DTA.
     WRITE TX-OUTPUT-DTA.
     MOVE ALL ≠*≠ TO DATA-OUT.
      WRITE TX-OUTPUT-DTA.
     MOVE LINE-SPACE-1 TO SPACER.
     MOVE SPACES TO DATA-OUT.
     WRITE TX-OUTPUT-DTA.
     MOVE SPACES  TO SPACER.
PROCESS-INPUTS.
     GO TO CHECK-TAX-LOGIC.
TAX-OUTPUT.
     MOVE NAMES TO ID-NAME.
     MOVE EXEMPTIONS TO EXEMPT-OUT.
     MOVE ITEMIZED TO ITEMIZED-OUT.
     MOVE ADJ-GROSS-INC TO ADJGRINC-OUT.
     MOVE TAXABLE-INC TO INC-TAX-OUT.
     MOVE LINE-DATA-OUT TO TX-OUTPUT-DTA.
     WRITE TX-OUTPUT-DTA.
TAX-END-BEGIN.
     DISPLAY ≠ EOJ≠ UPON PRINT-ER.
     CLOSE TAX-INFO.
     CLOSE TAX-OUTPUT-DATA.
     STOP RUN.
TAX-INFO-READ.
     READ TAX-INFO AT END GO TO TAX-END-BEGIN.
TWO-HUNDRED-PLUS.
     MULTIPLY 100 BY EXEMPTIONS GIVING TWO-HUNDRED-PLUS-DED.
     ADD 200 TO TWO-HUNDRED-PLUS-DED.
TEN-PERCENT.
     MULTIPLY ADJ-GROSS-INC BY 0.10 GIVING TENPERCENT-DED.
DED-1-1000.
     MULTIPLY 600 BY EXEMPTIONS GIVING TEMPORARY-1.
     SUBTRACT 1000, TEMPORARY-1 FROM TAXABLE-INC.
     MOVE ≠DEDUCT 1000≠ TO METH-OUT.
DED-2-ITEMIZED.
     MULTIPLY 600 BY EXEMPTIONS GIVING TEMPORARY-1.
     SUBTRACT TEMPORARY-1, ITEMIZED FROM TAXABLE-INC.
```

Figure 5.17. (*Continued*)

design chapters later in this book. The three are sequence structures, decision structures, and iteration structures.

SEQUENCE STRUCTURES

A *sequence structure* is a single step or action included in a process. It does not depend on the existence of any condition, and, when encountered, it is always taken. Typically, several sequence instructions are used together to describe a process.

For example, to purchase a book in a bookstore, you would probably follow a procedure similar to the one below:

1 Pick out a desirable book.
2 Take the desirable book to the checkout counter.
3 Pay for the book.
4 Get a receipt.
5 Leave the store.

This simple example shows a sequence of five steps. None of the steps contains a decision or any conditions that determine whether the steps are taken. Furthermore, they are taken in the order listed. In the book purchase example, for instance, it would make little sense to pay for the book before picking one out. Therefore, the procedure is described to point out the correct order of actions.

In the accounts payable processing example, the sequence of steps would be as shown in Figure 5.18. As written, the five sequence steps are always carried out, one after the other and without any decision about order or exceptions.

DECISION STRUCTURES

Structured English is another way of showing decision analysis. Therefore, the action sequences described are often included within decision structures that identify conditions. Decision structures thus occur when two or more actions can be taken, depending on the value for a specific condition. One must assess the condition and then make the decision to take the stated actions or sets of actions for that condition. Once the determination of the condition is made, the actions are unconditional, as mentioned above.

Let us expand the bookstore example to show the decision structure. If you go into a bookstore, you may not find a book you wish to purchase. Therefore, you can show actions for each condition: finding a desirable book and *not* finding a desirable book:

IF desirable books are found THEN
    Take the books to the checkout counter.
    Pay for the books.

Figure 5.18. SEQUENCE statements in structured English.

ACCOUNTS PAYABLE PROCESSING

Accept invoice for processing
Prepare payment voucher using invoice
Revise account balance due using payment voucher
Write vendor check for account balance and adjust checking balance by amount of check
Mail check to vendor

ACCOUNTS PAYABLE PROCESSING

```
If invoice is signed
  Else
    If merchandise was not accepted
    Reject invoice
    End if
  If valid purchase order was prepared
    Else
      If authorization not received
      Reject invoice
      End if
    If invoice is properly priced
      Else
      Reject invoice
      End if
    Then
    Log invoice
    Prepare payment voucher
End if
End do
```

Figure 5.19. IF-THEN-ELSE progression in structured-English specification.

Be sure to get a receipt.
Leave the store.
OTHERWISE
Do not take anything.
Leave the store.

This decision structure, through use of IF/THEN/OTHERWISE phrases, points out alternatives in the decision process quite clearly. Two conditions and two actions are indicated. Notice how sequences were contained within each condition. The IF portion contains four separate sequence statements, while the OTHERWISE portion contains two. This also is very common. In structured English, you can embed individual structures within other structures. Writing the details in an indented format also helps group the conditions and actions that go together. The extra clarity gained through this convention becomes even more helpful when dealing with large or complicated decision situations.

Figure 5.19 demonstrates structured English to describe how invoices are approved in the example accounts payable system. Compare this structured presentation with the data flow diagram (Figure 4.8) for the same process. The data flows themselves are not explicit with structured-English descriptions. However, the decisions and nesting of sequences are much clearer. Both, however, relate back to data definitions in the data dictionary.

Decision structures are not limited to two condition-action combinations. There can be many conditions. Figure 5.20 diagrams the nesting of multiple levels of conditions and actions for each decision point. Notice (in Figure 5.21) that the phrase IF/THEN/ELSE is used in place of IF/THEN/OTHERWISE. Either is acceptable, although computer specialists prefer ELSE.

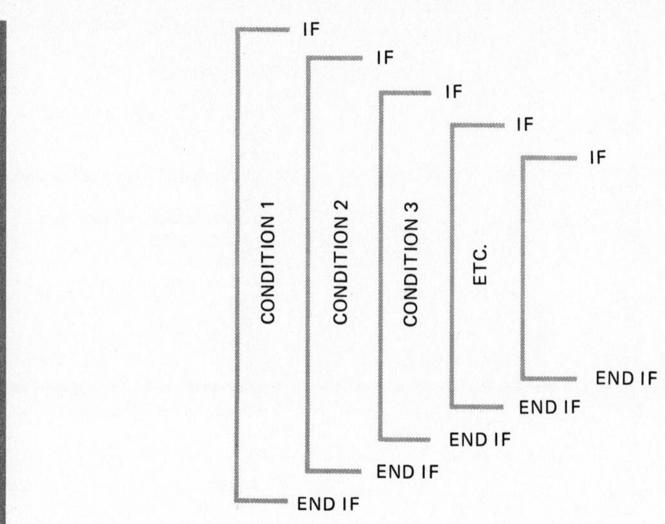

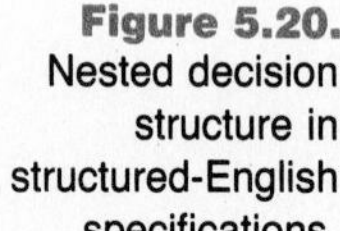

Figure 5.20. Nested decision structure in structured-English specifications.

ITERATION STRUCTURES

In routine operating activities, it is common to find that certain activities are repeated *while* a certain condition exists or *until* a condition occurs. *Iteration* instructions permit analysts to describe these cases.

In searching for a book in a bookstore, you might repeat these steps:

```
DO WHILE still examining more books
    Read the title of the book
    IF the title sounds interesting
        THEN pick up the book and thumb through it.
        Look at the price.
```

ACCOUNTS PAYABLE PROCESSING

```
Do until all invoices are processed
If invoice is signed
    Else
        If merchandise was not accepted
        Reject invoice
        End if
    If valid purchase order was prepared
        Else
            If authorization not received
            Reject invoice
            End if
        If invoice is properly priced
            Else
            Reject invoice
            End if
        Then
        Log invoice
        Prepare payment voucher
End if
End do
```

Figure 5.21. DO UNTIL progression in structured-English specification.

```
        IF you decide you want the book
          Put it in the DESIRABLE BOOK stack.
          ELSE put it back on the shelf.
        END IF
        ELSE continue
END DO
IF desirable books are found THEN
    Take the books to the checkout counter.
    Pay for the books.
    Be sure to get a receipt.
    Leave the store.
ELSE
    Do not take anything.
    Leave the store.
END IF
```

In this example, we see that 0, 1, or more iterations of the search for desirable books are described. Additional steps are nested within the iteration loop. They give instructions on what to do when the title sounds interesting and when a desirable book is found. The repetition continues as long as the condition of still examining more books exists. Then the procedure shows the steps to be taken if any desirable books have been found.

The iteration structure in Figure 5.21 shows how invoices are processed. Since many invoices can be received for payment, the process is repeated 0, 1, or more times, depending on how many invoices are received. Notice that the structure uses a DO UNTIL form of repetition. In otherwords, the process is repeated UNTIL all invoices have been processed.

Benefits of Structured English

You can see how structured English can be useful to describe conditions and actions clearly. When examining a business setting, analysts may use structured English to state decision rules as they are being applied. If they cannot state what action to take when a decision is made, it means they need to acquire more information to describe it. On the other hand, after activities have been described in this structured fashion, analysts can have other persons review the narrative and quickly determine whether mistakes or omissions have been made in stating the decision processes.

We have been discussing structured English as an analysis tool. Later we will see that it is also effective in systems design.

SUMMARY

Decision making, an integral part of any organization, requires the identification of conditions and actions. It also means that it is necessary to have information available to suggest actions to take when specific combinations of conditions arise. The purpose of decision analysis, which is an alternative but complimentary strategy to data flow analysis, is to structure decisions by determining the conditions under which alternative actions are taken. The three decision-analysis strategies are decision trees, decision tables, and structured English.

Decision trees are presentations of decision variables that are graphic and sequential, showing which conditions to consider first, which second, and so on. The root of a decision tree is the starting point for analyzing a specific situation. As you follow along the branches of the tree, you select the occurring condition and follow further along that branch. At the end of the branch, after having decided on the accuracy of each condition, the proper action to take is identified.

Constructing decision trees forces analysts to consider the sequence in which decisions must be made and permits the inclusion of both quantitative and nonquantitative information. However, in complex problems, the size of the decision tree may become unmanageable.

An alternative strategy, decision tables, relates conditions and actions through decision rules. A decision rule states the conditions that must be satisfied for a particular set of actions to be taken. The decision rule incorporates all the conditions that must be true, not just one condition at a time.

There are four forms of decision tables: limited-entry, extended-entry, mixed-entry, and ELSE forms. Multiple tables are also used in large decision cases or where it is desirable to set up separate procedures to be followed when a particular condition occurs. All forms, however, should be developed without redundancy and contradiction.

Structured English is used to state decision rules with the three types of statements termed sequence structures, decision structures, and iteration structures. These statements show unconditional actions, repetitive actions, and actions that occur only when and while certain conditions occur.

Structured English is a concise way of summarizing a procedure, where decisions must be made and actions taken. It can be reviewed by other persons quite easily so that misunderstandings and mistakes can be detected and corrected. Mistakes left in an analysis after a systems investigation will show up during design and implementation, when it is much more costly to correct them.

CASE STUDY FOR CHAPTER 5
DECISION ANALYSIS OF VALLEY INDUSTRIES ORDER ENTRY PROCEDURE

To further understand the steps involved in receiving and processing orders and the decisions made each step of the way, decision tools were developed. We show the results in this section and the questions raised in the process of developing them.

ORDER ENTRY PROCEDURE

The order entry procedure includes all activities that occur from the receipt of an order from a customer until it is accepted by the firm. All the details captured during the various interviews and examination of records enable analysts to understand the activities and decisions that comprise the order entry procedure.

Five distinct conditions are shown in the decision table in Figure C5.1. They include the manner in which the order is received, the correctness of the order, and the customer status. Depending on the combination of conditions, acknowledgements are sent, orders are entered, or disapprovals are given.

During the process of developing this decision table, analysts raised questions concerning information they did not have as a result of their investigation. In each case, it was necessary to return to Valley officials and records to answer them. The questions included the following:

Are order acknowledgments sent when there is an order request or only after the order has reached approved status?

Are all orders logged, regardless of whether they are approved? If so, is there a separate step to dispose of disapproved orders and show they were rejected and returned to the originator?

Do any customers submit cash with their orders? If so, how are the cash and the order processed?

Must all customers use numbered purchase orders? If not, how does the firm distinguish between multiple orders from customers?

The decision table in Figure C5.1 references other decision tables. Details of some of the procedures are too extensive to include in a single table.

The sequence of decisions quickly points out which conditions have the

ORDER ENTRY PROCEDURE

CONDITIONS	DECISION RULES							
Order received by Telex	N	N	N	Y	Y	—	—	—
Order correctly priced	Y	Y	Y	Y	Y	Y	Y	N
Customer account overdue	N	N	Y	N	N	N	Y	—
Customer slow paying account	N	N	—	N	N	—	N	—
New customer	Y	N	N	N	Y	N	N	—
Send acknowledgment	X	X						
Telex acknowledgment				X	X			
Log order	X	X		X	X			
Write up proper order	X	X		X	X			
Assign internal job number	X	X		X	X			
Perform new customer procedure	X				X			
Perform order acceptance procedure	X	X			X			
Disapprove order			X			X	X	X

Figure C5.1. Decision table for order entry procedure.

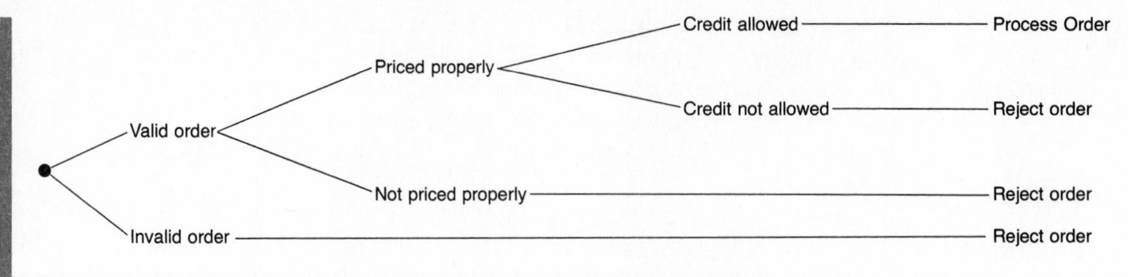

Figure C5.2. Decision tree for order acceptance decisions.

control over order rejection. A decision tree for order acceptance, shown in Figure C5.2, indicates that only a valid, properly priced order for a customer who has sufficient credit will be accepted and processed. All others are rejected.

NEW-CUSTOMER PROCEDURE

Valley Industries, a growing company, is acquiring new customers as a result of its expansion. At the same time, demographic information about current customers (such as name, address, telephone, ownership, or credit status) changes. Both cases must be dealt with in an order entry system of the nature needed at Valley. A decision table summarizing the decisions made in the new-customer procedure is shown in Figure C5.3.

In examining the procedure for adding or changing customer information, the analysts determined they needed additional details about how authorization for credit is determined (what information is needed and what rules guide the decision) and whether all customers use, and therefore must be approved for, credit. These details had not been reported during their investigation, even though it was clear credit approval was a necessary step in order processing.

NEW CUSTOMER PROCEDURE

CONDITIONS	DECISION RULES				
New Customer	N	N	Y	Y	Y
Customer information form	N	Y	Y	Y	N
Customer wants credit	—	—	Y	N	—
Customer change request	—	Y	N	N	—
Acquire customer information		X			X
Change customer record			X	X	
Prepare rolodex card		X	X		
Receive credit authorization			X		
Exit procedure	X				X

Figure C5.3. Decision table for new customer procedure.

ORDER ACCEPTANCE PROCEDURE

CONDITIONS	DECISION RULES				
Approved order	N	Y	Y	Y	Y
Order details complete	—	Y	Y	N	N
Sufficient copies received	—	N	Y	Y	N
Assign internal job number		X	X	X	X
Prepare order card		X	X	X	X
Update customer information		X	X	X	X
Update "on order" information		X	X	X	X
Send order copy to production		X	X	X	X
Make extra order copies		X			X
Acquire missing information				X	X
Return order to order desk	X				

Figure C5.4. Decision table for order acceptance procedure.

ORDER ACCEPTANCE PROCEDURE

The order acceptance procedure consists of three distinct conditions: whether the order is approved, whether the information supplied is complete, and whether a sufficient number of copies of the information are provided. As shown in Figure C5.4, there are eight separate actions to take, depending on the decision about order conditions.

Additional questions were raised in developing the decision table:

How many copies of the order form are needed and who uses them?

Is the copy to the production manager photocopied or is it automatically supplied in the order form set?

In what sequence do staff members carry out the proper order processing tasks?

Where is the order copy filed?

The usefulness of the decision table development process for pointing these questions out will be important to the completeness of eventual systems design.

PAYMENT AND CREDIT CYCLE

The payment and credit cycle for Valley Industries is summarized in Figure C5.5. This procedure is based on the existence of three conditions. Each in turn triggers either one or two of five possible actions.

A related procedure consists of details about determining how order discounts are calculated. Figure C5.6 shows this procedure in a concise fashion using structured English. What it does not show is when the decision is made and whether the records at the time of order entry show the gross or net value of the order. The analysts did not think about these questions until developing the procedure. They must find the answers.

PAYMENT AND CREDIT CYCLE

CONDITIONS	DECISION RULES			
Payment notice received	Y	Y	N	N
Credit notice received	N	N	Y	N
Copy of original invoice available	N	Y	N	—
Search for invoice	X		X	
Adjust customer account balance	X	X	X	
Annotate invoice is paid		X		
Record transaction in questions file	X		X	
Return copies to control desk				X

Figure C5.5. Decision table for payment and credit cycle.

```
DO FOR EACH ORDER

  IF CUSTOMER AND MERCHANDISE QUALIFIES FOR DISCOUNT
    IF QUANTITY IS FROM 250 TO 499 UNITS
      THEN
      USE DISCOUNT RATE 1
    ELSE
    IF QUANTITY IS FROM 500 TO 999 UNITS
      THEN
      USE DISCOUNT RATE 2
    ELSE
    IF QUANTITY IS FROM 1000 TO 2499 UNITS
      THEN
      USE DISCOUNT RATE 3
    ELSE
    IF QUANTITY IS FROM 2500 TO 4999 UNITS
      THEN
      USE DISCOUNT RATE 4
    ELSE
    IF QUANTITY IS GREATER THAN 4999 UNITS
      THEN
      USE DISCOUNT RATE 5
    ELSE
      CUSTOMER IS NOT ENTITLED TO DISCOUNT
ENDDO
      PROCEDURE FOR DISCOUNT PERCENTAGE
```

Figure C5.6. Procedure for discount percentage.

KEYWORDS

Action
Action statement
Condition
Condition statement
Contradiction
Decision analysis
Decision rule
Decision structure
Decision table
Decision tree
Decision variable
ELSE form
Extended-entry form
Iteration structure
Limited-entry form
Mixed-entry form
Redundancy
Sequence structure
Structured English

REVIEW QUESTIONS

1 What is decision-analysis strategy? How does it differ from data flow analysis? How does it complement data flow analysis?
2 What are conditions and actions? What roles do they play in decision analysis?
3 In what way do decision trees assist in decision analysis? Explain how analysts should develop a decision tree?
4 "It does not matter how a decision tree is organized as long as it identifies the proper actions and when to take them." Do you agree or disagree with this statement?
5 What disadvantages do decision trees present for analysts?
6 How does the purpose of decision tables differ from that of decision trees? What components comprise a decision table?
7 How do analysts develop a decision table?
8 What is a decision rule? How is it stated in decision tables?
9 What forms of decision tables are used?
10 What benefits do multiple decision tables offer? How are multiple tables used?
11 How are redundancies and contradictions in a decision table found? How are they removed?
12 How does structured English differ from the decision tree and decision table? What advantages does it offer over the other decision-analysis methods?
13 Briefly describe each of the structures used in structured English.
14 "Structured English is a programming tool, not a decision-analysis tool." Discuss this statement, indicating where you agree and disagree with it.

APPLICATION PROBLEMS FOR CHAPTER 5

1 A major produce supplier has a distinct set of criteria for preparing the bills it gives to customers when they purchase produce. The firm sells to both retail and wholesale customers.

When the customer places the order, one of the sales staff prepares the order and writes the bill. If there is not a sufficient quantity of an item on hand, the items available are shipped and a bill is prepared for those items. A backorder is set up for the other items. The customer receives the back-ordered items and the bill for them when they are delivered.

Quantity purchases over a specified limit are sold at discounted prices. However, this only applies to wholesale customers. Retail customers do not receive the discount even if they purchase more than the minimum quantity level.

All retail customers pay sales taxes on their orders. Wholesale customers do not pay taxes, provided they have a state tax exemption form on file (otherwise they also must pay sales taxes on their orders).

All bills are mailed to the customers unless they pay for the order when they receive the merchandise.

a List the conditions and actions included in the above description.
b How many possible decision rules are there for the above situation? Show how you derived this number.
c Develop a complete decision table, showing all conditions and actions together with appropriate decision rules. Be sure that there are no redundant decision rules or contradictions in the decision table.

2 When customers arrive at the Natural Wonder Resort for check in, the front desk clerk must determine whether they have a reservation. Most guests make advance reservations since they expect the resort to be very busy and want to be assured of accommodations. However, some guests just arrive without advance notice and hope to find housing. The resort is not always able to help them. This depends on the number of available rooms remaining in the room pool.

When guests are assigned to a room, whether they have advance reservations or not, the room they occupy must be removed from the room pool so that it continues to reflect accurately the remaining space in the resort.

Some guests guarantee their reservations, meaning they assure the resort they will pay for them even if they do not arrive. In return, the resort promises not to give their accommodations to anyone else regardless of how late it is in the evening. On occasion, the resort will accidentally overbook. If the resort is overbooked and a guest who has a guaranteed reservation arrives late in the evening, management locates the guest at another nearby resort for the evening and assumes all expenses.

During the check in process, the front desk manager must receive from the guest either a credit card number or a cash deposit for the accommodations. A registration card must also be completed so that important descriptive information is available about the guest. This card is filed in the in-house guest file, where it remains until the guest checks out. At that time it is removed from the file.

All guests settle their charges and bill before leaving. This is the policy of the hotel. The front desk manager prepares a statement indicating all charges. One copy is given to the guest when the bill is paid. The registration card is attached to the other copy and both are filed.

a Develop a decision table describing the processes and decisions involved in handling guest check in and -out.
b Identify the missing information (if any) you need to complete the decision table.
c Are there any contradictions in the rules described or in your decision table? If so, explain.

3 Develop a decision tree that describes the decisions the town dog catcher must make.

When dogs are running lose, unleashed and without their owner in sight, they can be picked up by the dog catcher and taken to the city animal shelter. However, if the dog catcher's truck is already full or the owner of the dog is in sight, unleashed dogs may be ignored.

At the dog shelter, the dog catcher calls the dog owner. This is only possible if the dog is currently licensed and the owner's name or telephone number is written on the filed application form. If the dog catcher cannot determine or reach the owner, the dog must remain at the shelter until it is claimed.

4 Develop a statement of the following decision process using structured English.

A retail store check cashing policy clearly states under what conditions and how checks from customers should be handled. This policy is in effect only for customers who are making purchases. The store does not cash checks if the individual is not completing a purchase.

Customers are allowed to use checks when paying for the exact amount of their purchase provided they have valid identifications such as drivers' licenses or photo identification cards issued by government or law enforcement agencies. However, if they wish to cash checks for more than the amount of their purchases, they must provide second identifications, specifically valid credit cards. In this case, they are allowed to write the checks for up to $50 over the purchase amounts. If the customers wish to exceed this limit, they must have special approvals from management.

In all cases, the checks must be verified by the recipients to ensure that they are complete and correct.

5 The following description of course registration is a common one across university and college campuses:

Students who have preregistered for courses do not have to go through formal course registration. However they must pay tuition and fees and receive receipts or they will be unable to attend the first day of classes.

For a student who has not preregistered, a list of courses and times desired must first be prepared, using the published course schedule. The student's advisor must approve the course selection and sign the registration form. Next the student must go to the registration area for each independent department within the university and pick up a course registration card. The student's name is written on a separate class list by the department assistant.

When the student has officially registered for all courses, he or she goes to the payment table, where the assistant follows a procedure to determine the amount of tuition and fees. To do so, state of residency, class standing, and college in which the student is officially enrolled must be determined. This information enables the assistant to calculate tuition. An activity fee of $20 is automatically added to the tuition to arrive at the total amount the student must pay. The student may make payment then and receive a receipt or the student may simply leave.

a Develop a structured English statement for the description. Indicate, if necessary, any areas where you do not have sufficient information to complete the statement fully.

b Develop a multitable decision table representing the registration process. What are the advantages and disadvantages of the decision table form for this example in contrast to the structured English statement?

CHAPTER 6 DEVELOPING THE SYSTEMS PROPOSAL

QUESTIONS TO GUIDE YOU THROUGH THE CHAPTER

- How are systems requirements data analyzed?
- What is the purpose of a systems proposal? What does it consist of?
- How is the systems proposal developed?
- Do systems proposals vary depending on whether they are for automated or manual systems?
- How are systems proposals presented to management?
- How do cost/benefit types vary?
- Which components in cost/benefit analysis are most difficult to identify and assess? Why is this so?
- Are there alternate methods for comparing systems costs and benefits?

Systems analysts collect details about the study area that define the work performed and the quality and productiveness of the business area. However, gathering the details is only one part of systems analysis. The systems analysts also examine the details, assess the situation, and recommend ways to meet those requirements that led to the systems study in the first place (such as the need to process more transactions, install data communication facilities, or provide managers with information not previously produced). The costs and benefits of each alternative are assessed.

This chapter discusses strategies for developing design recommendations for management. First data is assembled about the requirements to assess the needs of the users of the information system. Each strategy will have both costs and benefits that analysts must recognize and consider before advising management to select one approach over several others. Both costs and benefits have multiple components to relate into an overall systems cost/benefit picture. When you finish this chapter, you will be able to examine data about systems requirements and identify alternatives for improving the business process. You will also know how to formulate estimates of design costs and systems benefits and present all this to management.

ANALYZING SYSTEMS DATA

After gathering sufficient data to understand how a current system operates, you should study the data to evaluate how well current operations are performed. This section discusses ways to assess the findings and identify strategies for improving the system you have studied. It also examines the steps to take when preparing recommendations for management that outline systems development alternatives.

Assess Current Findings

Systems analysis is fact finding followed by analysis of the facts. You might say that first you define and document—then analyze (Figure 6.1).

Certain facts, like the purpose of work steps, personalities of workers, or number of copies made of certain documents, may at first seem like background details that, although describing a system, are not critical to your work. Later during analysis they often turn out to be of central importance. For example, soaring labor costs or dropping sales levels may actually be caused by personality clashes that affect the rate at which people work and lead to the hiring of more people. The number of copies made of a document may be a clue that steps are being skipped if one of the copies is always discarded, unused. There is also a relation between whether persons know the reason for specific steps in a work stream and how well they perform the steps.

These isolated cases are only a few of those that may result when you begin your analysis of systems details. But they illustrate the kind of information you should seek. Analyze the details to learn what works well, what is ineffective or inefficient, and where adjustments are needed to accommodate future growth.

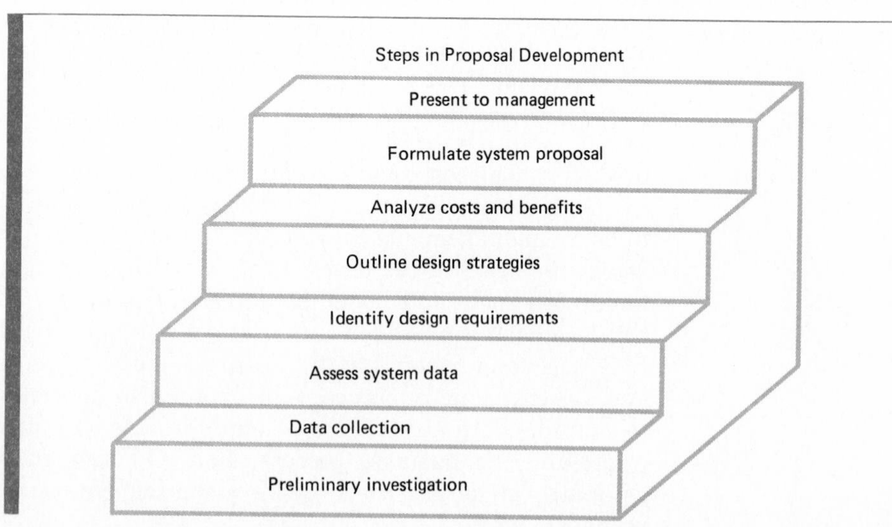

Figure 6.1. Steps in system proposal development.

ASSEMBLE DETAILS FROM INVESTIGATION

The details of the system learned by the analyst during the investigation tell *what* is happening, *how* it is done, *when* it is carried out, *where,* and *with what.* The details are assembled in order to study them and evaluate the current system.

This phase of systems analysis focuses on how efficiently certain steps are performed and how they contribute to the intended outcome. The analyst must also determine the results of *not* completing a specific step. For example, studying an accounts payable system may reveal that, when an invoice is received for merchandise that has not been delivered, no one detects the discrepancy so that the vendor is paid even though payment is not required.

To demonstrate the transition from the collection of systems details to their analysis, a sample analysis is discussed. From this example, a set of guidelines for evaluating a system and suggesting improvements is developed.

SAMPLE ANALYSIS

After examining the data collected about the system, the analyst develops a profile of each application area (or subsystem within the area). For example, in an accounts payable activity, a thorough fact-finding effort produces a profile of the system described in Table 6.1. The systems profile consists of details describing the operating characteristics of the system, such as frequency of occurrence, volume of work, or rate of error.

These details are the results of the analysis and show the facts collected using the questions raised earlier. The details are studied by the analyst to evaluate the effectiveness of the situation. It is clear, for example, that, in daily invoice processing and payment voucher preparation, two persons handle 200 items on an average day, for a total of 8000 individual transactions per 20-working-day month for the two processes.

The analyst must determine whether excessive errors or mistakes are being made, how often they occur, why they occur, and what they cost the organization. Usually a specific period, such as a day, week, month, or year, is chosen as a vehicle to quantify the error rate.

Each of the three major activities, i.e., approving invoices, revising balances due, and writing checks, suffer from error. Unsigned invoices occur about 10 percent of the time and require that extra steps be taken to correct the problem. Missing purchase orders occur in about 19 percent of the cases and again require an extra step to correct the problem. The analysis also uncovered incorrect sales-tax payments, caused in part by varying tax schedules in the state's counties. Using the wrong rate adds an additional $6000 in costs to the firm over the span of a year.

Each transaction requires a certain amount of time to handle and complete. Determining the average and range of times for each transaction will indicate the volume of work that can be handled in a period of time.

TABLE 6.1

REPRESENTATIVE SYSTEM FACTS FOR ACCOUNTS PAYABLE EXAMPLE

Major Processes	Invoice approval Revise balance due in accounts Check writing
Personnel	Two persons handle all invoice and payment processes Overtime not wanted by either person (overtime charged at 1½ times normal wage)
Processing Details	Some 200 invoices processed daily; 1000 per week Growing annually by 10 percent Heaviest at beginning of month Delay in processing—batches processed in sequence Some 200 payment vouchers prepared daily Continual arrival of transactions Number of items per invoice—average of 6 product sales price under $25
Assessment of Processing	Error processing for unsigned invoices is 10 percent of all invoices Error processing for missing purchase orders is 19 percent of all invoices Invoices and packing lists sometimes sent separately—frequent duplicate payment of invoice—costs $10,000 annually Tax varies by county—not properly handled—costs $6,000 annually Time to process invoice or voucher (without problems)—5 minutes

This information also helps the analyst decide whether workers are keeping up with incoming work or falling behind.

In the example, invoices arrive continually, but employees batch them before processing. This causes delay. Yet when analyzed, the facts point to a more significant and growing problem. Each day, 200 items are received for processing. A single one can be handled in approximately 5 minutes, depending on the number of items on each invoice. During the 7 hours the individual works with the invoices daily, it is generally possible to handle only 140 of them. This statistic also applies to the rate for payment vouchers. Overtime, at 1½ the normal wage rate, is worked to catch up when a backlog accumulates. However, employees want neither the overtime work nor the processing backlog. The rush is even responsible for paying some invoices twice. Conservative estimates are that this one problem costs the firm approximately $20,000 yearly.

The analysis of the details collected during the systems investigation indicates that there are serious gaps in control and a bottleneck exists for processing claims.

Identify Design Requirements

The example in the preceding section demonstrates only one very specific situation. But the analysis it represents is typical of that performed during any systems investigation. Table 6.2 summarizes the questions that are asked during an in-depth analysis of systems data.

From the analysis, design requirements are formulated. The requirements for the new system are those features or details that must be incorporated to produce the improvements or changes the analyst determined were needed. In other words, they are the activities or improvements that the new system must provide. They are determined by comparing current performance with the objectives for acceptable systems performance.

Typical systems requirements, summarized in Table 6.2, include operational improvements, such as improving the volume of work that can be handled or the timeliness of information retrieval. There are economic benefits through reduced cost of processing or fewer errors. Integrating data or sections of organizations are also common systems requirements.

In the example above, the requirements for the new system include the following:

- Greater speed of processing for input and processing
- More reliable and consistent procedures to eliminate errors in invoice handling and paying, as well as in calculating taxes
- The ability to interact with purchasing information to avoid extra steps and needless delays
- Lower-order processing costs and fewer and less costly mistakes through better processing controls.
- Ability of the system to handle the expected growth

Outline Design Strategies

Analysis of the study data typically suggests several alternatives that will lead to the change or improvement wanted. There is seldom only one

TABLE 6.2

QUESTIONS GUIDING SYSTEM PROPOSAL DEVELOPMENT

FACT-FINDING	ANALYSIS	OBJECTIVES
WHAT . . . is done?	HOW WELL controlled?	GREATER processing speed
HOW . . . is it done?	HOW OFTEN omitted?	BETTER accuracy
HOW OFTEN . . . is it done?	HOW QUICKLY performed?	IMPROVED consistency
WHEN . . . is it done?	ANY MISSING steps?	FASTER information retrieval
WHO . . . does it?	ANY EXTRA steps?	INTEGRATION of business areas
WHERE . . . is it done?	ANY FORMAL procedures?	INTEGRATION of data
WITH WHAT . . . is it done?	ANY EXCESSIVE formal handling?	REDUCED cost
WHAT IF . . . not done?	IS DATA duplicated?	GREATER capacity
	ANY STEPS without purpose?	
	ANY POORLY DESIGNED procedures?	
	ANY POORLY DESIGNED forms?	
	IS STAFFING sufficient?	
	IS COMMUNICATION adequate?	
	ARE FACILITIES adequate?	

solution. Therefore the analyst tries to identify those that are the most feasible technically, economically, and operationally. The options thus identified are *design strategies.*

Design strategies may consist of such items as changes in operating procedures, new working methods, personnel changes, addition of controls, introduction of automated transaction processing or decision support methods, or a combination of several of these steps.

One strategy of the analyst is to improve a business situation by developing better operating procedures. Revising procedures to eliminate unnecessary forms and documents or duplicate steps simplifies and speeds work. It may also reduce the potential for errors.

The analyst often suggests input, process, reporting, and control procedures to guide operations or decision making. The procedures may be manual or automated, usually some of each. The point is that the analyst is responsible for suggesting where new or revised operating procedures seem useful. Management will decide whether to accept and use them.

The role of the computer in a design centers around its capabilities for calculation, storage and retrieval of data, summarization, sorting, classification, and communication of data. The analyst must decide when, for example, the speed and storage capacity of a computer is an essential ingredient in meeting systems requirements or when developing on-line rather than batch processing is needed. The analyst does this by matching a knowledge of computer capabilities with an understanding of the systems requirements.

A new system might, for example, call for the automation of invoice handling to classify an invoice quickly as it is received and to insure it is properly totaled. All these steps can take place by the simple action of entering the invoice number, purchase order number, and vendor identification through a terminal (Figure 6.2). The computer in turn can be substituted for human processing. These processes could occur rapidly, and retrieving information from appropriate files for purchasing approval and accounting balances can be incorporated into the procedure. The results of a day's work can be totaled and communicated to supervisors, whether they are in the same building or miles away.

The point is that the analyst must decide where the processing components should be used to improve situations learned about during data collection and understood during analysis. Later, decisions will be made about the extent of automation and processing mode required. The processing method, such as automated or manual procedures and batch or interactive mode, will eventually shape the overall design (see chapters 7 through 9). The analyst will also make recommendations about the tasks that should be handled by people and those, if any, that should be developed so they involve computers.

As you can imagine, each strategy has certain advantages and disadvantages, depending on the particular business situation. Therefore, the analyst selects those alternatives most workable and studies them further.

In the invoicing example, one design strategy includes the capability to interact with an on-line invoice system through a terminal. The operator,

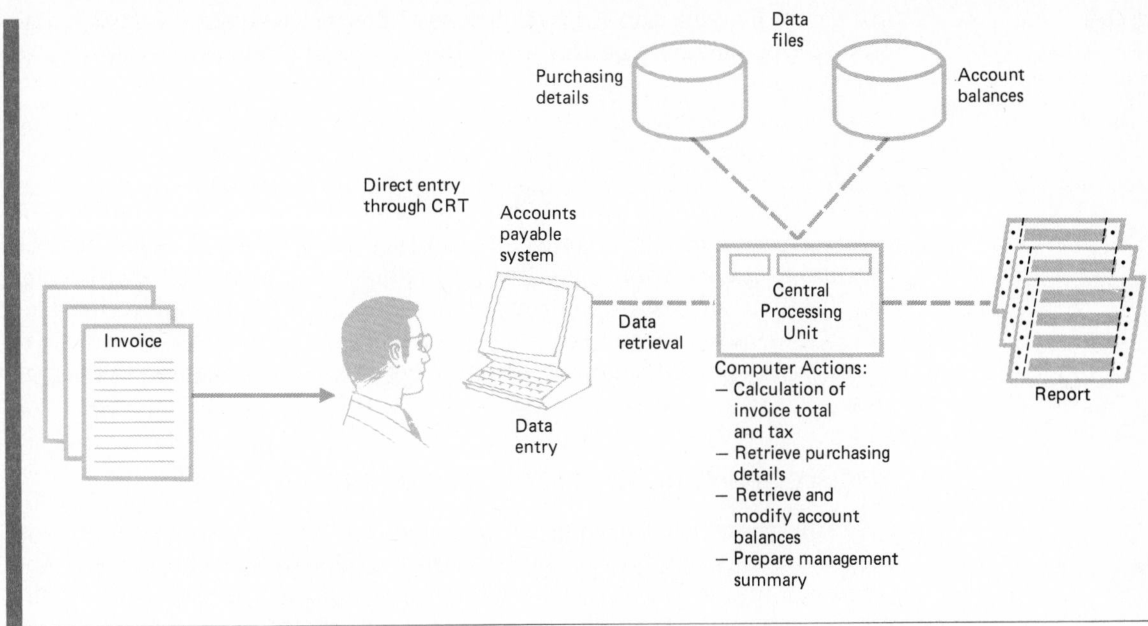

Figure 6.2.
Proposed accounts payable processing activity.

using unique invoice numbers, enters and retrieves invoices. Each invoice is associated with a vendor and stored in the system as it is received for payment. When each invoice is entered, the computer automatically will recalculate the item costs, sales tax, and total amount due and signal the operator when errors are detected.

When the operator wishes to pay a specific vendor, all invoices for that vendor can be retrieved so the operator, using the invoice numbers, can select those to be paid. When each is paid, the system notes the date of payment and check number used. It also automatically reduces the total amount owed to the vendor by the amount of the payment. Duplicate payment is impossible, because the system keeps track of whether an invoice has or has not been paid.

This is one way of meeting the previously identified requirements. You can probably identify others that use batch processing or do not involve the computer at all. Each may be a viable design strategy.

The costs and benefits of each strategy guide the selection of one alternative over the others. Since this aspect of analysis is so important, it will be looked at in detail in the next section.

ANALYZING SYSTEMS COSTS AND BENEFITS

Since cost is one of the things that determine whether a new system is accepted, the analyst ensures all costs are identified and estimated properly.

Costs vary by type and consist of several distinct elements. Benefits also vary by type and are classified according to the advantages they provide to management.

Types of Costs and Benefits

The *costs* associated with a business system are the expenses, outlays, or losses arising from developing and using a system. The *benefits* are the advantages gained from installing and using the system. The three major classifications of costs and benefits are tangible or intangible, fixed or variable, and direct or indirect. These categories are not mutually exclusive. Thus a cost or benefit item may fall into more than one category at the same time.

TANGIBLE OR INTANGIBLE COSTS AND BENEFITS

The term "costs" is often equated with money or finances. However, outlays of cash are only one type of costs, which we refer to as *tangible costs*. The expense of a specific piece of equipment, the salary of an employee, or the cost of electricity is tangible, meaning that it is known and can be estimated quite accurately. For example, an analyst can learn the purchase cost of a piece of equipment by contacting the appropriate supplier.

Some costs, such as the value of a lost customer or a lowered company image, are known to exist, but their financial amount cannot be accurately determined. They are *intangible costs*. The estimate is only an approximation; it is not feasible to fix exact intangible costs. Most costs are tangible and can be identified by analysts.

Benefits, also classified as tangible or intangible, are often more difficult to specify accurately than costs. Suppliers can quote the cost of purchasing a terminal, but they are unable to cite specific financial advantages for using it in a system. The value of the benefit is the advantage that will be gained by using the system. Tangible benefits, such as reduced expenses or lower error rates are quantifiable. Intangible benefits, like the value of improved customer service, faster response to customer inquiries, or better working conditions, often cannot be quantified. Systems projects should not be developed on the basis of intangible benefits alone.

FIXED OR VARIABLE COSTS AND BENEFITS

Some systems costs and benefits are constant and do not change, regardless of how much or little an information system is used. They are *fixed*. For example, if a firm purchases and pays for computer equipment, the cost is fixed. It will not vary, whether the equipment is used a great deal or very little. This type of cost is also referred to as a *sunk cost;* once encountered, it is not controllable nor will it reoccur.

In contrast, *variable costs* are those that are incurred in proportion to activity or time. Computer supply costs vary in proportion to the amount of processing performed. Printing more pages increases paper cost. Paper cost, therefore, varies as a result of print volume. However, it is eliminated if the preparation of reports ceases.

Fixed and variable costs and benefits can also be called nonrecurring and recurring costs, respectively. The cost of developing and installing a new system is nonrecurring: once encountered it cannot be changed or recovered. Using the system, however, produces recurring costs, that continue every month the application is used. Similarly, the benefit of personnel savings may recur every month, and the benefits of quicker information retrieval will depend on how often the system is used.

DIRECT OR INDIRECT COSTS AND BENEFITS

If costs and benefits are specifically attributable to a business system, information system, or work activity, they are termed *direct*. In other words, using the system or doing the work directly produces costs or benefits. Reducing the cost of mistakes is a direct benefit, as is handling 20 percent more transactions in a time period with the new system, compared with the old system.

Indirect costs are support or overhead expenses that, while real and sometimes substantial, are not specifically associated with the information system. They are the result of operating other systems or performing necessary activities in the organization, that support the system under investigation. For example, heating, air conditioning, insurance, and cost of space are real and tangible costs. However, it is very difficult, if not impossible, to determine the exact proportion of these costs that are created by producing one specific report one time. Often management divides, or *allocates,* indirect costs among all users as an approximation of the actual costs.

Indirect benefits are achieved as a by-product of another system. For example, a system that tracks sales calls on customers provides an indirect marketing benefit if it provides additional information about competition. In this case, competitive information becomes an indirect advantage, even though it is difficult to place a value on its worth.

Cost Categories

Developing cost estimates for a system requires the identification of the elements that make up the overall cost, whether tangible, direct, or fixed. There are five major cost elements.

EQUIPMENT COSTS

Equipment costs result from acquiring or using all the devices associated with the work. The actual components in the computer system are an important element. However, when purchasing storage cabinets, alarm systems, or tables and desks, the analyst should also include their costs in the estimate of equipment expenses.

Equipment costs are more difficult to estimate if several systems will share the items. In these cases, it may be desirable to divide the total cost and assign specific shares of the total to each application. When a large system is shared by many users, it may be more manageable to treat the expenses as an operating cost.

OPERATING COSTS

Operating costs, the expenses incurred to run the system, are variable, depending on the amount of use required for a system component. For example, many information systems centers charge users only for the amount of processing they ask of the system, using such cost items as:

Calculation (central processing unit) time

Number of punched cards read into the system

Number of output lines printed by the system

Amount of disk space used

Table 6.3 illustrates a charging method that identifies a variety of very detailed cost items.

PERSONNEL COSTS

Personnel costs include the salary or wages of all individuals who develop or operate the system. The salaries and wages of systems analysts, application programmers, consultants, training staff, data entry personnel, and computer-operator salaries and fees are personnel costs. In some cases, they are on a per hour basis, while in others their entire salary (if they work full time on a project) is included for the duration of the project.

When estimating salary costs, the cost of employee fringe benefits, such as health insurance, vacation time, and retirement fund contributions, must be added. These costs generally average an additional 15 to 30 percent of salaries or hourly wages. As you can see, they can be substantial and are therefore a significant cost element.

Depending on the organization and specific application, personnel costs may be one-time costs during development or recurring costs after installation. Management must decide whether individuals' salaries and wages that are incurred after a new system is installed are treated as direct expenses or overhead.

SUPPLY AND EXPENSE COSTS

Supplies will be consumed both during development and after installation. Paper, ribbons, and replacement of magnetic storage media are ongoing

TABLE 6.3

SAMPLE CHARGING SCHEDULE FOR COMPUTER PROCESSING ACTIVITIES

RESOURCE MEASURES	MACHINE UNITS
Each batch hour	.250
Each processor hour	670.000
Each 1000 writes to disk	.400
Each 1000 writes to tape	.750
Each 1000 lines printed	.800
Each 1000 punched cards read	.800
Each 1000 cards punched	5.000
Each 1000 remote job transmissions	.200
Each on-line connect hour	1.375

COST FACTORS

Machine units indicate relative utilization of a computer's components. Each machine unit is charged at the rate of $1.20.

To determine the cost of an activity, multiply the machine units for that activity by the machine unit charge (Example: 1 hour of central processor usage costs 670.000 × $1.20, i.e., $804.00).

Priority service can be requested. The following multipliers are used to adjust the charge rate depending on the processing priority desired:

PRIORITY	MULTIPLIER
Urgent	3.00
High	1.50
Normal	1.00
Low	.75
Wait	.50

[Example: one hour central processor usage at high priority is determined as (670.000 × 1.20) × 3.00 = $2,412.]

costs. Other expenses, such as purchasing training and systems manuals or traveling, will also be incurred. They should be estimated and included in the overall systems cost.

FACILITY COSTS

Facility costs are those expenditures necessary to prepare the site where the new system or application will be used. The organization first acquiring a computer system, for example, may need to prepare a special location for the equipment, including arranging wiring, flooring, and air conditioning in some cases. Even when there is already a large computer site, analysts may request that new cables be connected to link additional terminals or printers into the system to handle new tasks. Sometimes, remodeling rooms or moving walls is required to provide the proper working environment.

Since these costs are all associated with the system and require cash expenditures, it is essential that they be incorporated into the overall cost estimates.

Benefit Categories

Benefit analysis means first identifying the beneficial effects and then assigning a monetary value to each one. You should show specific operating benefits when recommending a system, as well as all intangible benefits. Tangible benefits have financial value that are compared with actual costs to determine whether to proceed with the development of a system. Benefits fall into the categories of improved performance and cost avoidance. Performance and cost-avoidance benefits are equally important and common. Information systems often produce both when installed.

PERFORMANCE BENEFITS

Often a system is developed to improve the quality of work or to permit new activities to be undertaken. The improvements and advantages gained are *performance benefits*. A specific financial gain can be attributed to systems that produce performance benefits.

Common performance benefits include error reduction, increased speed of activity, and access to information that previously was not stored or could not be retrieved and that produces a direct tangible benefit. Systems may also increase their flexibility by permitting users to handle a greater variety of situations in a specific manner.

COST-AVOIDANCE BENEFITS

Frequently information systems are developed to achieve cost-avoidance benefits. If clerical errors are high, costing the organization $10,000 annually, and will be avoided when the new system is installed, we say the new application produces a cost-avoidance benefit. The $10,000 cost will be avoided.

On the other hand, a new system may mean that, say, the firm will not have to hire two additional employees to keep up with growing workloads. The amount of their salaries is a cost-avoidance benefit. If staying with the old system means two people would be hired at a cost of $20,000 each annually, *not* hiring them because of a new system means the system has a cost-avoidance benefit of $40,000 annually.

Performance and cost-avoidance benefits are equally important and common. Information systems often produce both when installed.

STRATEGIES FOR COST/BENEFIT COMPARISON

Systems costs and benefits are compared in financial terms to determine whether to proceed with a particular design alternative. Different strategies are used, depending on the preferences of management, to compare cost and benefits on the basis of time, cash expenditure, or project life costs. Each of the four strategies examined below presumes tangible cost and benefit data have been determined and development time and system life have been estimated. A full cost/benefit comparison will often use all the methods.

Break-even Analysis

Break-even analysis is frequently used in business activities of all types, including information systems project analysis. This method compares the cost of using the current system with that of using the new one. The *break-even point* is the time at which the cost of the new system equals the cost of the current one. New systems usually have initial costs, due to development expense, that are higher than the cost of running current systems. The break-even point is reached when they are equal, and the costs of the current system are the same as the costs of the new system.

During the months of use after the break-even point, the new system typically shows greater benefits than the old one. The period before the break-even point is reached is called the *investment period,* while the time after is the *return period.* Figure 6.3 shows in graphic form the break-even point for the sample accounts payable system.

Payback Analysis

The payback method relates accumulated costs and benefits for a new system by determining the *payback period,* the amount of time that must pass before benefits equal costs. Table 6.4 shows the predicted accumulation

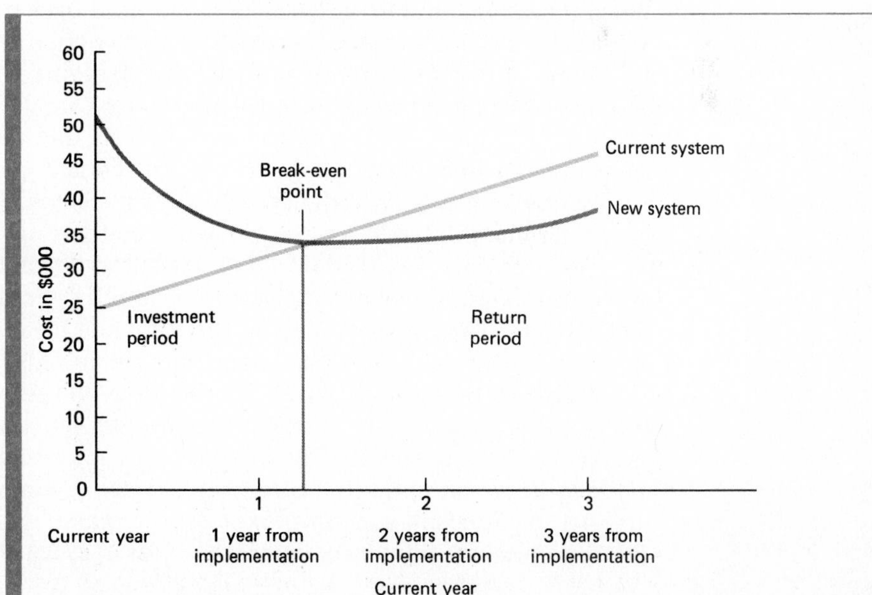

Figure 6.3. Break-even analysis for accounts payable example.

TABLE 6.4

PAYBACK ANALYSIS FOR ACCOUNTS PAYABLE SYSTEM

	NEW SYSTEM COST	NEW SYSTEM BENEFITS	NET DIFFERENCE
Year 1	$50,350*	$27,740	$−22,610
Year 2	31,800	51,000	− 3,410
Year 3	38,000	58,800	17,390
Year 4	43,000	55,000	29,390
Year 5	48,000	49,000	30,390

*Includes development costs during first year

of costs and benefits for the accounts payable system. Costs exceed benefits by $22,610 at the end of the first year and by $3,410 during the second. However, during the third year, benefits exceed costs. This indicates that the costs have been paid back.

The payback period is therefore slightly over 2 years. The policy of the individual organization must be considered to determine whether the proposed project is acceptable. If the organization's policy is that all projects must pay for themselves within 2 years of their initiation, a very conservative policy, this project is not acceptable. On the other hand, this project meets the criterion of a 3-year payback period.

Notice the difference between the break-even and payback methods. Break-even analysis compares the *costs* of current and proposed systems. The payback method compares *costs and benefits* of the *proposed* system. Both methods are useful in evaluating systems alternatives.

Present-Value Analysis

Since a systems project is developed and used over a period of time that stretches into the future, it is often difficult to compare costs today with the full value of benefits tomorrow. Inflation, changing costs, and fluctuating interest rates alter the value of the investment funds.

An additional concern of systems analysts and managers alike is the comparison of projects that have varying benefit periods. The *duration period,* the length of time the system will be used, may be months or years longer for one project in comparison with another.

The present-value method of cost/benefit analysis allows individuals to overcome both of the above difficulties. It applies equally well to both costs and benefits. Through this method the costs and benefits of the system are calculated in terms of the value of the investment today and then compared.

A critical factor in this kind of analysis is the selection of the *discount rate,* a percentage factor similar to the interest rate for loans or the cost of capital to an organization. The discount rate may be set equivalent to the *opportunity cost* of funds, the percent return the organization could earn if it invested the funds in another project. (If, for example, the money needed for the system could be invested in another project to earn a 15 percent return, *not* investing it would mean losing the opportunity to earn the 15 percent. Hence the opportunity cost of this project, 15 percent, is used as the discount rate.)

Let us assume a 20 percent discount rate for the accounts payable project (Table 6.5). To calculate the net present value of costs, a decimal number that represents 20 percent is determined either through calculation or, more frequently, from an accountant's present-value table (see Table 6.6). A decimal number is determined for each year of the project. The decimal varies from year to year to reflect the amount of time into the future.

The number for each year is multiplied by the costs and benefits for each year, as shown in Table 6.5. Summing the costs and benefits enables you to compare them as if they were being paid in today's funds. If the benefits exceed the costs, the investment is usually considered a good one, although organization policy may require that benefits exceed costs by a specified minimum percentage.

As shown, the benefits of the accounts payable project significantly exceed the costs. Furthermore, the present-value method permits comparing them in terms of dollar values today, rather than several years ahead, when inflation and other factors may have reduced the actual value of the project.

Cash Flow Analysis

Some projects produce revenues through the sale of information systems services. The *cash flow* analysis method shows the accumulation of costs and revenues on a period-by-period basis. It also combines the benefits of the break-even and payback methods.

In the cash flow method, projected revenues and costs are identified and totaled. The difference between incoming revenues and outgoing expenses is the *cash flow*. Adding the cash flow values for several months produces the accumulated cash flow.

Table 6.7 shows the cash flow analysis for a project expected to produce increasing revenues over its life through the sale of information processing

TABLE 6.5

PRESENT VALUE ANALYSIS USING 20% INTEREST RATE

YEAR	SYSTEM COSTS		PRESENT VALUE FACTOR FOR 20%		PRESENT VALUE	SYSTEM BENEFITS		PRESENT VALUE FACTOR FOR 20%		PRESENT VALUE
1	$50,350	×	0.833	=	41,942	$27,740	×	0.833	=	23,107
2	31,800		0.694		22,069	51,000		0.694		35,394
3	38,000		0.579		22,002	58,800		0.579		34,045
4	43,000		0.482		20,726	55,000		0.482		26,510
5	48,000		0.402		19,296	49,000		0.402		19,698
	Present value of costs				$126,035	Present value of benefits				$138,754

TABLE 6.6

PRESENT VALUE OF 1 (AT COMPOUND INTEREST) $\frac{1}{(1+i)^n}$

Where i = interest rate and n = number of periods.

Periods	2½%	3%	4%	5%	6%
1	0.975 610	0.970 874	0.961 538	0.952 381	0.943 396
2	0.951 814	0.942 596	0.924 556	0.907 029	0.889 996
3	0.928 599	0.915 142	0.888 996	0.863 838	0.839 619
4	0.905 951	0.888 487	0.854 804	0.822 702	0.792 094
5	0.883 854	0.862 609	0.821 927	0.783 526	0.747 258
6	0.862 297	0.837 484	0.790 315	0.746 215	0.704 961
7	0.841 265	0.813 092	0.759 918	0.710 681	0.665 057
8	0.820 747	0.789 409	0.730 690	0.676 839	0.627 412
9	0.800 728	0.766 417	0.702 587	0.644 609	0.591 898
10	0.781 198	0.744 094	0.675 564	0.613 913	0.558 395
11	0.762 145	0.722 421	0.649.581	0.584 679	0.526 788
12	0.743 556	0.701 380	0.624 597	0.556 837	0.496 969
13	0.725 420	0.680 951	0.600 574	0.530 321	0.468 839
14	0.707 727	0.661 118	0.577 475	0.505 068	0.442 301
15	0.690 466	0.641 862	0.555 265	0.481 017	0.417 265
16	0.673 625	0.623 167	0.533 908	0.458 112	0.393 646
17	0.657 195	0.605 016	0.513 373	0.436 297	0.371 364
18	0.641 166	0.587 395	0.493 628	0.415 521	0.350 344
19	0.625 528	0.570 286	0.474 642	0.395 734	0.330 513
20	0.610 271	0.553 676	0.456 387	0.376 889	0.311 805
21	0.595 386	0.537 549	0.438 834	0.358 942	0.294 155
22	0.580 865	0.521 893	0.421 955	0.341 850	0.277 505
23	0.566 697	0.506 692	0.405 726	0.325 571	0.261 797
24	0.552 875	0.491 934	0.390 121	0.310 628	0.246 979
25	0.539 391	0.477 606	0.375 117	0.295 303	0.232 999
26	0.526 234	0.463 695	0.360 689	0.281 241	0.219 810
27	0.513 400	0.450 189	0.346 817	0.267 848	0.207 368
28	0.500 878	0.437 077	0.333 477	0.255 094	0.195 630
29	0.488 661	0.424 346	0.320 651	0.242 946	0.184 557
30	0.476 743	0.411 987	0.308 319	0.231 377	0.174 110
31	0.465 115	0.399 987	0.296 460	0.220 359	0.164 255
32	0.453 770	0.388 337	0.285 058	0.209 866	0.154 957
33	0.442 703	0.377 026	0.274 094	0.199 873	0.146 186
34	0.431 905	0.366 045	0.263 552	0.190 355	0.137 912
35	0.421 371	0.355 383	0.253 415	0.181 290	0.130 105
36	0.411 094	0.345 032	0.243 669	0.172 657	0.122 741
37	0.401 067	0.334 983	0.234 297	0.164 436	0.115 793
38	0.391 285	0.325 226	0.225 285	0.156 605	0.109 239
39	0.381 741	0.315 754	0.216 621	0.149 148	0.103 056
40	0.372 431	0.306 557	0.208 289	0.142 046	0.097 222

8%	10%	12%	14%	16%	18%	20%
0.926	0.909	0.893	0.877	0.862	0.847	0.833
0.857	0.826	0.797	0.769	0.743	0.718	0.694
0.794	0.751	0.712	0.675	0.641	0.609	0.579
0.735	0.683	0.636	0.592	0.552	0.516	0.482
0.681	0.621	0.567	0.519	0.476	0.437	0.402
0.630	0.564	0.507	0.456	0.410	0.370	0.335
0.583	0.513	0.452	0.400	0.354	0.314	0.279
0.540	0.467	0.404	0.351	0.305	0.266	0.233
0.500	0.424	0.361	0.308	0.263	0.225	0.194
0.463	0.386	0.322	0.270	0.227	0.191	0.162
0.429	0.350	0.287	0.237	0.195	0.162	0.135
0.397	0.319	0.257	0.208	0.168	0.137	0.112
0.368	0.290	0.229	0.182	0.145	0.116	0.093
0.340	0.263	0.205	0.160	0.125	0.099	0.078
0.315	0.239	0.183	0.140	0.108	0.084	0.065
0.292	0.218	0.163	0.123	0.093	0.071	0.054
0.270	0.198	0.146	0.108	0.080	0.060	0.045
0.250	0.180	0.130	0.095	0.069	0.051	0.038
0.232	0.164	0.116	0.083	0.060	0.043	0.031
0.215	0.149	0.104	0.073	0.051	0.037	0.026
0.199	0.135	0.093	0.064	0.044	0.031	0.022
0.184	0.123	0.083	0.056	0.038	0.026	0.018
0.170	0.112	0.074	0.049	0.033	0.022	0.015
0.158	0.102	0.066	0.043	0.028	0.019	0.013
0.146	0.092	0.059	0.038	0.024	0.016	0.010
0.135	0.084	0.053	0.033	0.021	0.014	0.009
0.125	0.076	0.047	0.029	0.018	0.011	0.007
0.116	0.069	0.042	0.026	0.016	0.010	0.006
0.107	0.063	0.037	0.022	0.014	0.008	0.005
0.099	0.057	0.033	0.020	0.012	0.007	0.004
0.092	0.052	0.030	0.017	0.010	0.006	0.004
0.085	0.047	0.027	0.015	0.009	0.005	0.003
0.079	0.043	0.024	0.013	0.007	0.004	0.002
0.073	0.039	0.021	0.012	0.006	0.004	0.002
0.068	0.036	0.019	0.010	0.006	0.003	0.002
0.063	0.032	0.017	0.009	0.005	0.003	0.001
0.058	0.029	0.015	0.008	0.004	0.002	0.001
0.054	0.027	0.013	0.007	0.004	0.002	0.001
0.050	0.024	0.012	0.006	0.003	0.002	0.001
0.046	0.022	0.011	0.005	0.003	0.001	0.001

TABLE 6.7

DETAILED CASH FLOW ANALYSIS FOR PROPOSED INFORMATION SYSTEM

	MONTH 1	MONTH 2	MONTH 3
REVENUE			
from sale of information processing services	$ 4,700	7,050	8,930
EXPENSES			
Facility Preparation and Startup Costs	$20,000	20,000	10,000
Equipment Lease	8,400	8,400	8,400
Hardware Maint Fees	758	758	758
Software Maint Fees	425	425	425
Security Box Deposit	150		
Personnel Costs	4,250	4,250	4,250
Forms and Supplies	15,000	15,000	5,000
Postage and Supplies	3,675	2,175	500
Insurance	125	125	125
Professional Fees	3,000	2,000	
Travel	800	100	100
Recruitment and Education	2,000	2,000	2,000
Miscellaneous	500	500	500
TOTAL EXPENSES	59,083	55,733	32,058
CASH FLOW (revenue − expenses)	(54,383)	(48,683)	(23,128)
ACCUMULATED CASH FLOW			

services. The revenues begin at $4,700 and grow to $21,177 in the ninth month. The expenses of acquiring hardware and software, travel, consultants, and other items are the highest in the first 3 months. Comparing revenues and expenses results in a negative cash flow, that is, a net expenditure of money, of over $50,000 during the first month. A break-even point for monthly revenues and costs occurs during the seventh month. At the end of 9 months, when the cash flow levels off at approximately $3,054, the accumulated cash flow is -$133,364. If the monthly cash flow stays at the $3,000 level, achieved in month 8, an additional 43 months will pass before the accumulated cash flow reaches a payback point. This appears to be an unusually long payback period, which may not be acceptable to management.

It is not possible to say that one method is better than the others. Organizations vary in the cost/benefit analyses they use.

THE SYSTEMS PROPOSAL

The systems analyst selects only the most beneficial and feasible strategies for the organization. Usually one is specifically recommended to management in a formal systems proposal. The analysts recommend, but management actually decides whether to proceed and which strategy to follow.

MONTH 4	MONTH 5	MONTH 6	MONTH 7	MONTH 8	MONTH 9
10,810	13,097	15,117	19,157	21,177	21,177
8,400	8,400	8,400	8,400	8,400	8,400
758	758	758	833	858	858
425	425	425	635	740	740
4,250	4,500	4,500	4,500	4,450	4,500
3,000	2,100	2,100	2,100	2,100	2,100
500	500	500	600	600	600
125	125	125	125	125	125
100	100	100	100	100	100
200	200	200	200	200	200
500	500	500	500	500	500
18,250	17,608	17,608	17,993	18,123	18,123
(7,440)	(4,511)	(2,491)	1,164	3,054	3,054
					(133,364)

The *systems proposal* is a detailed summary of the investigation that has been conducted. It outlines the study itself, summarizes findings, and highlights major problems or opportunities. The proposal also outlines the options developed by the analysts and presents their recommendations. This written report is the most important tool used by management to determine whether to proceed with the new or modified system.

Effective proposals are planned carefully and follow a format that management can understand easily and use. Typically a verbal presentation to management is also made, with ample time allowed for questions and discussion.

Cover Memorandum

A memorandum (or letter) accompanies the systems proposal and introduces the report. It should be addressed to the steering committee or its chairperson and summarize the objective of the study and the nature of the report.

Summary of Recommendations

The first portion of the report previews the recommendations to management, so the readers know the specific points that will be made before all the details are presented. In addition, if managers only have time to skim part of the report, they will still see the essence of the recommendations.

Table of Contents

If the report is long, a table of contents, showing section headings and page numbers, will guide management through the report. The report is intended to be a working tool that will be scrutinized carefully as the project decision is made. It is likely that some sections will be read and reread repeatedly and in varying order. A numbered table of contents will speed the location of important sections.

Overview of Systems Study

This section of the proposal outlines the study that was conducted. It lists the methods used to collect the requirements data, including persons interviewed or surveyed by questionnaire. Some analysts also attach tables, identifying documents and reports studied, so that management is assured that all of the important items were given adequate attention. The purpose is to show that a thorough study was made and the findings that follow are accurate and reliable.

Detailed Findings

This section consists largely of the conclusions reached about the system and any facts that support them. Details, such as volumes of work, growth rates, and error rates, demonstrate conclusions about missing controls, inadequate staffing, out-of-date methods, or rising costs (such as those shown in Table 6.1). The findings may also project the costs that will be incurred if the current system is retained.

Optional Solutions

The most acceptable systems alternatives are presented to management. Typically no more than three or four alternatives are listed. Each option should be described, and the specific actions management should take (such as hiring two people, purchasing a special computer program, acquiring a computer system, or developing new software with in-house staff) should be listed. The results that each strategy will produce should be so the reader understands exactly what is expected to occur if the option is selected. If it will reduce errors and speed work, but will not reduce personnel needs, for example, it should be stated. Both advantages and disadvantages should be presented objectively.

Costs and benefits should be listed for each alternative. As the previous section of the chapter discusses, costs include both development *and* operating costs. The expenses to use a new system after it is installed (such as supply costs, telecommunication expenses, or personnel salaries) should be included in the listing.

Recommendations

This section suggests to management the strategy the analysts feel is most beneficial and manageable. It should be consistent with the study conclusions, the advantages and disadvantages outlined, and the cost/benefit estimates presented. The reasons for the recommendations should be listed in a clear and concise manner, free of technical language and jargon.

Verbal Presentation

It is common for analysts to present their findings and recommendations in person before the steering committee. The written proposal outlined above is still prepared and submitted. However, the presentation is an additional opportunity for management to hear the analysts' views and ask about them.

During the presentation, the analysts sell both their recommendations and themselves. They must be confident of their facts. Summarizing them, using visual aids (flip charts, overhead transparencies, video tape, slides, or sample documents), and allowing management to *see* suggestions as well as hear them, increases management's understanding of them. Questions should be anticipated and direct and specific answers prepared, using facts from the study.

Analysts should expect to be asked their opinions. However, they must be sure to separate fact from opinion. For example, they may be asked whether they feel that the major weaknesses in the current system are controls or personnel. They must be prepared to give their opinions on such questions, but they should also explain the reasons underlying those opinions. Management looks to analysts as experts in their area of systems development and wants to know what they think and *why* they think it.

Prior to the presentation, analysts should outline the presentation content, prepare visuals, identify possible questions, and organize responses to the possible questions. They should go through their presentations several times to be sure of all details and how they will be presented. The time required to make the presentation should be watched, so that it does not become excessive. Most of all, analysts must remember to sell their ideas and recommendations orally and visually, as well as in writing. Their appearance and a smooth, understandable delivery can aid in convincing management.

SUMMARY

The fact-finding activities in a systems study produce details that describe current operations and point to areas where improvement is needed or possible. Systems analysts are responsible for examining the facts, assessing existing systems and procedures, and formulating design recommendations. Each design recommendation outlines operating requirements, procedures, and processing components included in the proposed system.

The recommendations of the systems analysts are presented to management in a written proposal. This document summarizes the study and its findings and states the most feasible systems alternatives. Each alternative is briefly described, together with its advantages and disadvantages and its costs and benefits. Often a verbal presentation is made to management in addition to the written proposal. During the presentation, management asks questions about the study, recommendations, and analysts' opinions about systems features.

Both the written and verbal systems proposals discuss systems costs and benefits. Whether they are tangible or intangible, fixed or variable, or direct or indirect, it is necessary to know what the investments and benefits for a new system will be if it is developed. Costs are easier to estimate than benefits, yet the benefits are the reason for developing a system and so must be well understood. Basing an investment on intangible benefits is a mistake. There must be tangible benefits too, or it may be impossible to justify financial investment in the project.

To compare costs and benefits, analysts use one of four strategies: break-even, payback, present-value, or cash flow analysis. Each method focuses on a specific feature, ranging from a comparison of current and proposed systems costs to the actual inflow or outflow of money. A full cost/benefit study will often use all the methods.

CASE STUDY FOR CHAPTER 6
RECOMMENDATIONS FOR ORDER ENTRY AND ACCOUNTS RECEIVABLE SYSTEM

VALLEY INDUSTRIES
1200 Main Street
Binghamton, New York 13901
607-798-2000

TO: John Severski, President
FROM: Joyce Randal, Director of Information Systems
SUBJECT: Recommendations for Order Entry and Accounts Receivable System

In response to an internal request from John Olson, the systems department conducted an in-depth study of the procedures currently utilized for entering orders from customers and sales representatives and for monitoring their statuses until manufactured items are shipped to the customer. The study team also examined accounts receivable management and reporting activities. Both areas were analyzed to evaluate their effectiveness and efficiency in light of current operations and projected growth and expansion of Valley Industries.

Discussions were held with all key users of order and accounts receivable information. In addition, business activities were observed and records were studied to evaluate operations.

The results of the systems study are included in the attached report. The report is organized into four sections. An overview of the current system is presented both to summarize its key features and to indicate the understanding that served as the basis for the evaluation, remarks, and suggestions in the remainder of the report. The systems study methods and findings are presented in the next section and serve as the basis for the remainder of this report. Part 3 of the report outlines the features of a proposed new system to meet current and planned operating requirements and expected company growth. The final part of the report presents development costs, system benefits, and a development time estimate.

SUMMARY OF RECOMMENDATIONS AND FINDINGS

The efficiency and accuracy of current order processing and accounts receivable systems can be improved through the design and development of a new system. Growth to date in the number of orders handled has exceeded current personnel capacity. Planned growth and expansion will increase order entry and billing demands in a manner that cannot be met through the hiring of additional personnel. A new system is proposed that will pay for itself within slightly over 1 year, while providing better control over orders and revenues and better management information in a timely manner.

A PROPOSAL FOR A COMPUTER-BASED ORDER ENTRY AND ACCOUNTS RECEIVABLE SYSTEM

This report outlines a study conducted to examine the current order entry and accounts receivable system in use at Valley Industries. The study was conducted by staff members of the Information Systems Department to determine whether improvements in operating effectiveness and efficiency were possible and to assess the ability of current operating methods to meet planned growth and expansion. This report first summarizes current systems features and operating characteristics. The nature of the study that was conducted is also described. The recommendations for a new system and a cost/benefit analysis are also presented.

CHARACTERISTICS OF CURRENT SYSTEM

The current manual system for processing orders and maintaining accounts receivable records is highly paper-oriented and labor-intensive. It is centered around proper concerns for the credit worthiness of the customer placing an order, whether through our sales representatives or directly by mail, telephone, or telex. The procedure that calls for credit verification followed by approval of order prices is an important one for ensuring that a specific order should be accepted and prices should be accurate.

Similarly, integration with the production department, where manufacturing of the order occurs, is an essential element of the system. The link between manufacturing, invoicing, and maintenance of accounts receivable records is also a necessary one. The reliability of this link directly affects revenue since orders that are shipped but not correctly invoiced or posted to a customer account will result in lower sales recorded than actually occur.

The firm is growing quickly, at a rate of 40 percent annually. Therefore, management is looking toward more efficient ways for processing orders, monitoring the progress of orders through production, and managing accounts receivable. Expansion to additional production locations, also an expected development in the near future, will further increase management's concerns for managing customer orders from reception to final payment.

If the current system for order entry and accounts management is retained, additional personnel will be required to handle the volume of work. Currently, additional time is required just to keep up with the volume of business Valley Industries is receiving. Because overtime hours are not worked, the extra time is taken away from other office activities and they are put behind schedule. Therefore additional office help is already needed. The growth in orders, coupled with additional production sites, will dramatically increase the number of employee hours needed just to keep pace. Improving the control of orders and increasing the management information needed to monitor sales, production, and accounts receivable will only amplify personnel requirements.

The remainder of this report outlines the findings produced in our systems study. It also presents recommendations for a revised system for order entry, invoicing, and accounts receivable. The proposed automated system will provide the needed ability to support future growth and expansion and ensure the capability to determine the status of any order at any time. It will also integrate order activities with accounts receivable management.

OVERVIEW OF SYSTEMS STUDY

The systems study conducted to examine order entry and billing activities involved interviews with all personnel involved in either of the activities. The current system was discussed at length with J. Severski, M. Carbo, J. Olson, and H. Jacobson. In addition, the supervisors in the production department were interviewed to learn their suggestions about improving order control during manufacturing activities. Staff analysts also observed the receipt of orders by mail, telephone, and telex and discussed order processing activities with accounting staff members.

The systems study additionally focused on the documents used to receive, process, and track orders from their arrival at Valley through to completion and the creation and posting of invoices. We examined actual documents and forms used to process each order. And we followed orders from receipt to shipment, including their approval, posting to records, creation of invoices and accounting transactions, and eventual collection of revenue from customers.

SUMMARY OF ORDER PROCESSING STATISTICS

The following statistics summarize the current order processing system:

1. Approximately 35 orders are received on the average day; current high volume is 65 orders on a single day.
2. Most orders are not processed on the day they are received. A delay of 2 to 4 days is typical, although as much as a calendar week may go by before the order is sent to the production department if the order department is busy or short-staffed.
3. The office receives approximately 25 payments on account daily. They are typically processed on the same day or the following morning.
4. Currently, at least 350 orders are in process at any given time, although in excess of 700 have been awaiting settlement during peak business periods. The number of open orders is increasing continually and the volume is expected to increase at a greater rate in the future.
5. The current number of customers is 1000. This number will increase if the company maintains its current product line. Additions to the product line or to sales campaigns will raise the level of increase management can expect.
6. Problems in order processing include:
   a. Item prices are incorrect; this costs the firm an estimated $10,000 annually.
   b. Errors occur on approximately 5 percent of all orders. The average order is valued at $1500. We estimate that errors are made in orders valued at $500,000. The reason is a combination of increasing workload and inefficient procedures, as a result of more business.
   c. Overdue accounts receivable average $250,000. The majority of this amount is a normal business fact. However, better collection and credit verification procedures could reduce this amount from $20,000 to $50,000 annually.
   d. A complex quantity discount procedure is error prone, although we were not able to estimate the cost of errors annually.
   e. Orders are lost, although no data is available on the number or frequency of lost orders. They are generally not known to be lost until a customer inquires about the status of an order.

FINDINGS AND RECOMMENDATIONS

The systems study reveals a distinct need for an updated order processing and accounts receivable system to sustain current growth expectations and to ensure that future expansion goals will not be hindered by these systems. The benefits of the improvements suggested in this report quickly exceed both development and operating costs. In addition, personnel almost uniformly realize a need for replacing the current order processing system with a more efficient one. They do not want to be forced to exert unacceptable extra efforts to reinforce an outgrown system.

It is recommended that an automated system be developed using current computer equipment now in place at Valley Industries, with supplemental equipment acquired to meet the design requirements specified in this report. Two existing computer systems meet many of the design requirements:

1 TRS-80 business microcomputer
2 IBM System/34 business system

The IBM System/34 is recommended because of its processing speed and expandable memory capacity. Although both systems can be configured to provide data entry and inquiry capabilities from multiple locations within the current building, the System/34 is better designed to support data communication activities. The potential for developing other manufacturing locations is high. The System/34 will allow the addition of more remote terminals and will enable more efficient communication using telephone lines because of the transmission methods it uses.

The TRS-80 alternative would meet many current requirements but would not provide sufficient processing speed or computing power to meet peak demand. In addition, it would not be able to meet all future demands. In contrast, the System/34 alternative will cost more (in cash outlay) for development and implementation, although the payback for the investment is better than average. Industry experts believe that a replacement for the System/34 will be announced by the manufacturer within the next few months. However, shipments will begin several months after that and it will be some time before all early customer orders would be filled. The same industry experts believe that any new system will be compatible with our current equipment. Thus, if it is appropriate to move to a newer, compatible system in, say, 2 years, such a move can be made using the proposed design. In this sense, then, the design provides appropriate upgrade capability.

FEATURES OF ORDER ENTRY PORTION

The proposed system has two distinct, but integrated aspects. The order entry/invoicing portion will be designed to include the following features:

1 Customer credit status and account verification
2 Item price verification
3 Automatic order logging
4 Computer preparation of order acknowledgments
5 Interactive inquiry capability to respond to credit, customer, and order status information requests
6 Integration of order processing with production processing
7 Computer preparation of reports to describe the status of all orders received or in process during a period

It should be noted that this system will not include production scheduling or supervision of manufacturing activities. However, manufacturing supervisors will be expected to enter data describing the starting and completion dates of manufacturing activities for an order. This information is essential to monitor order activities and respond to customer and management inquiries.

FEATURES OF ACCOUNTS RECEIVABLE PORTION

The accounts receivable portion of the system will provide computer processing for:

1 Automatic preparation of customer invoices, including adding all charges for an order to the proper customer account
2 Interactive inquiry capability to respond to customer account status information
3 Calculation of finance charges and aging of customer balances
4 Computer preparation of invoices
5 Computer preparation of monthly account statements, showing all charges, payments, and adjustments processed during the preceding month
6 Automatic preparation of management reports to show account balances along with sales and payment activities

In addition to the above, the proposed system will include appropriate auditing controls to ensure that order and revenue activities are correctly handled. The ability to link multiple locations into the system in the future will be of paramount importance.

COSTS AND BENEFITS

The costs of developing the proposed system, using the recommended System/34 computer system, are summarized in Appendix A. Development costs, including the costs already incurred for the systems study on which this report is based, will be approximately $48,500. In addition, it will be necessary to purchase several new computer display terminals and to install them in locations prepared for their use. Total new systems costs are estimated at $64,500, including the new equipment. In addition, the first year operating costs, for paper and supplies and maintenance, are estimated at $10,000, with projected increments coincidental with inflation and the age of the system.

There are distinct benefits to the new system. They are described in three categories. By developing the new system, the accounting department will avoid the need to hire additional staff members to meet order processing needs this year and in future years. However, the new system will not reduce current staff requirements either. Instead, the same staff will be more efficient in meeting current and future order handling requirements. The savings from not needing additional personnel will be compounded over the life of the system.

Owing to the new controls and improved procedures that will be installed along with the new system, errors and revenue loss will be reduced. A very conservative estimate indicates that this amount will total at least $5000 the first year. Future savings should increase, but, for comparison, a fixed savings is used. Accounts receivable will decrease by at least $20,000 annually as well.

The system will produce benefits that are classified as intangible. Although they are both important and noticeable, it is difficult to place a dollar value on them. They are listed in Appendix A, but they are not used in the cost/benefit comparison.

The new system has an anticipated life of 5 years, although in the later years the cost of using and the maintaining the system will increase. This is a normal expectation.

Using the reported costs and estimated benefits over the 5-year life, the system will pay for itself in 18 months. Industry experts normally consider a system a good investment if it pays for itself in under 30 months. Hence, the payback period for the proposed system is much better than average. A present-value comparison that uses current cost of funds to analyze system costs and benefits is also shown in Appendix B. Both analyses indicate that the proposed system is a cost-effective investment.

If Valley management wishes to initiate the development effort, it is estimated that design, programming, training of personnel, and implementation of the system will require 4 calendar months. Two systems analysts or programmers will be assigned to work full time on the project.

APPENDIX A

COST/BENEFIT ANALYSIS FOR PROPOSED ORDER ENTRY AND ACCOUNTS RECEIVABLE SYSTEM (IBM System/34)

SYSTEMS START-UP COSTS	
Development	
Systems analysis and requirements determination	
2 weeks (320 hours)	$12,000
Systems Design	
3 weeks (240 hours)	18,000
Development and implementation	
6 weeks (480 hours)	18,000
Indirect costs for staff personnel	2,500
Equipment Purchase	
Three display terminals @ $2,000	6,000
Computer furniture	2,500
Installation	
Site preparation	1,000
Training	3,750
Systems generation (by IBM)	750
Total start-up costs	$64,500
SYSTEMS OPERATING COSTS	
Supplies	
Additional equipment maintenance	
Program maintenance	
Total operating costs (first year)	$10,000
SYSTEMS BENEFITS	
Savings on additional personnel not needed	$22,100
Operating savings	
Elimination of pricing errors (minimum)	5,000
Reduced accounts receivable balances (minimum)	20,000
Intangible Benefits	
Better planning information	
Better customer relations	
More satisfied employees	
Necessary to grow	
Ability to add communication and avoid courier costs (if expansion occurs)	
Total tangible systems benefits (first year)	$47,100

COST/BENEFIT ANALYSIS

5-YEAR SYSTEMS LIFE

Year	Systems Costs	Systems Benefits	Net Cumulative Difference
1	$ 74,500	$ 47,100	$ (27,400)
2	11,000	24,300	10,900
3	12,500	26,750	50,150
4	15,000	29,400	89,550
5	17,000	32,300	$129,850
	$130,000	$259,850	

Payback occurs between 17 and 18 months after start of project.

PRESENT-VALUE ANALYSIS (@ 18% INTEREST)

Year	Systems Costs	Systems Benefits
1	$74,500 × 0.847 = $63,101	$47,100 × 0.847 = $ 39,894
2	11,000 0.718 = 7,898	24,300 0.718 = 35,397
3	12,500 0.609 = 7,612	26,750 0.609 = 31,516
4	15,000 0.516 = 7,740	29,400 0.516 = 28,070
5	17,000 0.437 = 7,473	32,300 0.437 = 25,040
	$93,824	$159,917

Systems benefits exceed costs by 70% over 5-year life.

KEYWORDS

Break-even analysis
Cash flow analysis
Cost-avoidance benefit
Direct cost, direct benefit
Discount rate
Fixed cost, fixed benefit
Indirect cost, indirect benefit
Intangible cost, intangible benefit
Investment period
Opportunity cost
Payback analysis
Performance benefit
Present-value analysis
Return period
Systems proposal
Tangible cost, tangible benefit
Variable cost, variable benefit

REVIEW QUESTIONS

1 What are the two major components of systems analysis? How are they related?
2 What are design strategies? What do they consist of?
3 Discuss the purpose of a systems proposal. What are its contents? Who uses it?
4 Identify the questions analysts use to guide their study of a process or

system after collecting information requirements data. Discuss the analysis process for this data in general.

5 What is the purpose of a verbal systems proposal? How does it differ from the written project report prepared by the analysts?

6 Discuss the major types of systems costs and benefits. Give examples of each.

7 It is more difficult to identify systems benefits than costs. Why is this true?

8 What elements comprise systems costs? What are the different categories of systems benefits?

9 What is the purpose of break-even analysis? How is this analysis made? What time periods comprise a break-even schedule?

10 How do payback and break-even methods of analysis differ? Is one type more useful than the other? Explain.

11 Define the following terms: investment period, period of return, duration period, sunk cost, opportunity cost, and cash flow.

12 How do cash flow and payback methods differ?

13 What is the purpose of present-value analysis? What additional information does it provide that the other analysis methods omit?

14 If the services provided by an information system are to be sold, either to departments within an organization or outside firms, do all the cost/benefit methods discussed in this chapter still apply? Explain.

APPLICATION PROBLEMS FOR CHAPTER 6

1 The controller of a medium-sized organization is responsible for assembling an advanced budget and projection of sales, labor costs, supplies costs, and operating expenses. Budgets are prepared on a weekly basis, 3 weeks in advance of the week to which they pertain. They are distributed to the manager of each department, who in turn schedules employees to meet expected sales but to stay within budgeted labor and expense guidelines.

First the sales forecast is prepared. Then labor and materials costs are determined, using a fixed percentage of the expected sales level. Similarly, a predetermined portion of the budgeted sales are allocated for overhead costs. Unfortunately, the controller makes many errors in the calculation.

After the week the budget pertains to is completed, the controller enters the actual sales and expenses on the pencil form, beside the forecast amounts. From time to time, special reports are prepared to accumulate forecasts and actual sales and expenses over 13-, 26-, and 52-week periods.

The entire process is done manually with the aid of a calculator. Even the annual summaries are prepared by hand.

The controller has asked to purchase a desktop computer and to develop special software to perform the budget and analysis calculations and to store budgeted and actual sales and expense information week by week. The system will also have the capability to be used as a terminal, linked to the company's mainframe system where account records are stored. This capability will improve the controller's access to information that currently loses some usefulness because it arrives late.

a Based on the details described above, should the system be developed? Why or why not? (You need not consider actual costs and benefits for your analysis.)

b If the system will cost \$15,000 to implement, what factors will you consider to determine whether benefits exceed costs? Will the factors examined change if the cost of the proposed system is \$30,000?

c What features of the desktop computer should be examined to decide whether it has sufficient capabilities to meet processing requirements?

2 The Costume Center provides the arts community with valuable assistance in performances through its vast supply of costumes for rent by theaters, opera companies, and other performing arts organizations. The center owns and rents over 25,000 different costume pieces (such as coats, dresses, gowns, ties, and shoes). The rental charges for each item vary depending on the item's cost, age, uniqueness, and condition. For example, one type of men's formal wear rents for $25 daily, $110 weekly, and $350 monthly.

The stock and rental manager wishes to improve the Center's ability to manage inventory. The manager feels that costs must be better controlled and improved management information on rentals and expenses available. The manager wants to know more quickly when specific items are due back from rental and how often they are rented. The manager also wants to monitor items by category to know which categories are in greater demand than others. Finally, the manager wants information about which customers use the greatest number of items.

a Based on the above, what are the most essential systems requirements?
b For which requirements is computer assistance most beneficial? Identify the computer attribute(s) that are most meaningful and useful for each one you identify.
c What factors will you examine in forming a cost/benefit analysis?

3 The data processing department of a large commercial bank has experienced excessive problems with delays in processing checks through the department, and the rate of error has been excessive. Each day thousands of checks pass through the department. Every check must be examined for correctness and completeness, and the amount of the check subtracted from the proper customer account. Automatic equipment is used to assist in processing the checks, but a large portion of the responsibility for the proper handling of each check lies with the person who actually handles the check.

The quantity of checks to be processed is constantly increasing and more persons are continually hired to meet demand. However, the quantity of checks processed does not increase in proportion to the persons on the staff, even after new employees have completed training and been on the job several weeks. The check processing group does not use a quota system to guide the productivity of each employee, and management does not know the quantity of work each person produces on a regular basis.

Errors do occur in check processing. Often checks will be processed for the wrong amount or they will be deducted from the wrong account, although management does not monitor error levels. In fact, most errors are not detected until a customer complains that their account balance is incorrect or that they have been charged for a check that is not theirs.

Management is considering the installation of a new system that will improve the speed with which checks can be processed. The system will cost approximately $25,000 more a month compared to the present system. However, management feels that this sum will be repaid through faster check processing.

a Using the information provided above, identify the questionable areas where you want more information to determine systems requirements.
b What information do you want to have in order to develop a cost/benefit analysis for the proposed change?
c Why will the automation proposal improve or fail to improve the situation described above? Explain your answer.

4 A point-of-sale system will be installed in a busy restaurant to assist the waitresses. The system costs $32,000 to purchase and will require the acquisition of an additional parts and labor maintenance contract at a cost of $1,800 per year. Included in the system are five terminals, two printers, and a small central

processor. The terminals will be used for two purposes: They will precheck an order for food, when the waiter or waitress enters an order for food and beverage using the terminal keyboard. The order will be printed in the kitchen or at the beverage station and thus indicate what item should be prepared. During the precheck, the system will also preprice each item, using data contained in memory. This precheck feature avoids the need for the preparation of food before it is actually needed and speeds the preparation when it is needed; servers do not have to go back into the kitchen to verbally ask for an order. It also prevents errors in pricing food, a problem that currently costs this busy restaurant at least $20,000 per year.

The terminals will also total patrons' food and beverage purchases when they are ready to pay their bills. The amount of each check is tallied by the system throughout the day. The total tells management how much sales are for the day. The system also tallies the sales by the categories of food and beverage, by each menu item sold, and by each waiter or waitress.

This information is used by management to evaluate the salability of each menu item. It also permits the assessment of each server's sales and is used to determine how much money a server should turn in each night. In the past, cash shortages have averaged approximately $300 per week.

The system will produce some expenses for supplies of paper and ink ribbons needed to print the reports and customer checks. The customer checks will be different from those now in use, but their cost will stay approximately the same.

The system will require approximately 2 hours per day of accounting time to audit it and compare cash received from servers versus the amount tallied. The annual salary of a member of the accounting staff is $20,000.

To install the system, the restaurant will have to expend approximately $5000 for electrical wiring and carpentry work.

a Identify the different costs and indicate the type or category of cost they represent. If there are none in a particular category, indicate that.
b Assuming a 20 percent cost of money, is the system a wise investment if costs and benefits are compared under the net present-value method?
c How long before the system will reach the break-even point if it is developed? What is the payback period?

5 A manager is considering the development of a decision support system using a desktop computer. The system will use specially designed software that will provide enough flexibility for the manager to formulate special analyses of data for unique business situations that arise. Using the proposed system, this person will be able to enter the details of the situation and pose different sales and expense levels to determine the effect on profits and market strength. However, it is impossible to anticipate the situations that will arise or the specific questions that will be addressed in using the system.

The manager is interested in developing the system but is not certain the investment is a good one. Even though the cost of the system can be estimated very accurately, no one has been able to quantify the benefits. Therefore, the manager does not know whether the system should be pursued.

a Can a cost/benefit analysis be developed for decision support systems such as the one described above? If so, explain how. If not, describe how analysts can determine whether development of a decision support system is a wise investment.
b Explain why you would or would not proceed with the proposed system.

6 A systems project proposed to management will take an estimated 15 months to develop. The work on the system will be evenly divided across the 15 months. When implemented, it is expected that the system will have a useful life of 4 years before major modifications will be needed. The development costs are estimated to be $50,000. Benefits will average at least $25,000 during the life of the system. The cost of operating and maintaining the system once it is implemented will average $7500 per year.

a Assuming the cost of money is 18 percent, examine the costs and benefits of the proposed system using a cost/benefit analysis. Should the system be developed? Explain the reason for your answer.

b How long before the costs will be paid back by the benefits of using the new system if it is developed? Using this element, should the system be developed? Explain.

c Can a break-even point be determined for the proposed system? Why or why not?

PART THREE SYSTEMS DESIGN

CHAPTER 7 DESIGN OF OUTPUT

QUESTIONS TO GUIDE YOU THROUGH THE CHAPTER

- How are logical and physical designs different?
- What is the purpose of output design?
- What role do users play in the design of output?
- How do analysts communicate output designs to others?
- Which methods should be considered for presenting output? How do analysts choose one?
- What guidelines should analysts follow in the design of output?
- How do designs for printed and displayed output differ?
- In what ways can analysts design output to reduce details but increase the communication of information?
- How do analysts use color and graphics to enhance information presentation?

The systems objectives outlined during requirements analysis serve as the basis from which to structure an information systems design. This chapter and those that follow examine all facets of designing an information system. The first section of this chapter previews the process of design, both logical and physical. The remainder of the chapter discusses the design of output—the concerns and options of the analyst responsible for specifying what information the system produces and the form in which it is presented.

Many output options are available in the systems most organizations work with. This chapter looks at ways to select those options most useful for a given project. It also examines the many output methods available in computer-based information systems, stresses ways to use them, and shows how to structure an effective output design. Finally it examines when and how to use color and graphics in computer output.

When you complete this chapter you will know how to select output methods and use them in a manner that meets user requirements.

PROCESS OF DESIGN

The design is a solution—the translation of requirements into ways of meeting them. The features of a new system are stated at the two levels of logical and physical design. This section describes the purpose of each level, the relation to requirements analysis, and how other persons are involved in this aspect of system development.

Levels of Design

Systems design proceeds through the two phases of logical design and physical design. When analysts formulate a *logical design,* they write the detailed specifications for the new system. That is, they describe its features: the outputs, inputs, files and data bases, and procedures—all in a manner that meets project requirements.

The logical design of an information system is like the engineering blueprint of an automobile: it shows the major features (like the engine, transmission, and passenger area) and how they are related to one another (where components interconnect or how far apart the doors will be).

The reports and output of the analyst are the engineer's components. Data and procedures link each together to produce a working system.

In designing an inventory system, for example, the systems specifications include reports and output-screen definitions describing stock on hand, stock additions and withdrawals, and summarizing transactions that occur throughout, say, a month of operation. The logical design also specifies input forms and screen layouts for all transactions, and files for maintaining stock data, transaction details, and supplier data. Procedure specifications describe methods to enter data, run reports, copy files, and detect problems, should they occur (Figure 7.1).

Physical design, the activity following logical design, produces program software, files, and a working system. Design specifications instruct programmers about what the system should do. The programmers in turn write the programs that accept input from users, process data, produce the reports, and store data in the files.

The physical design for the sample inventory system introduced above consists of program steps, written in a programming language, that change quantities on hand by using transaction data, print the reports, and store the data. The analyst *specifies* the algorithms that say how to change the

Figure 7.1. Design of system consists of logical and physical design.

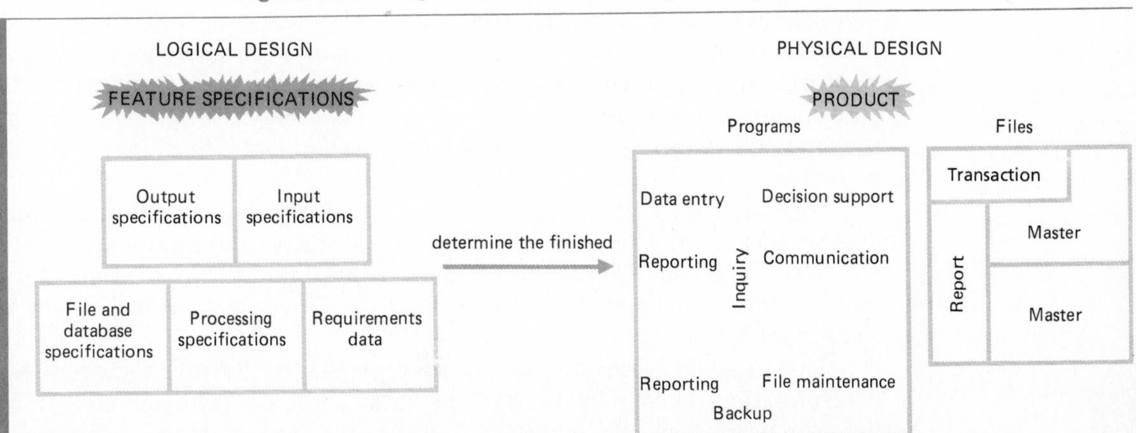

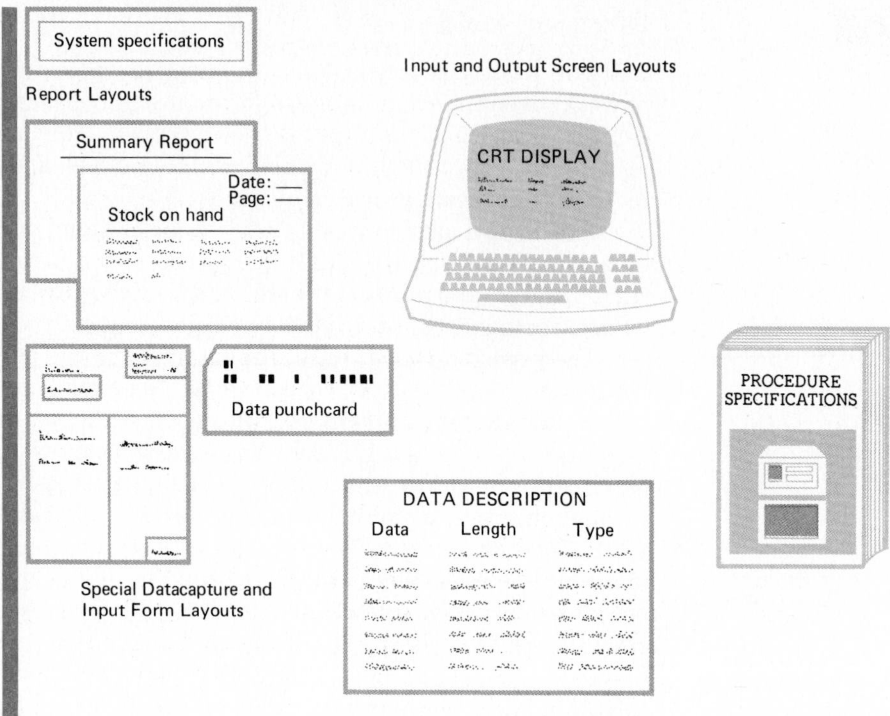

Figure 7.2. Logical design produces documents containing system specifications.

stock quantities. During physical design, programmers *write* the program instructions to compute the changes and produce the results (Figure 7.2).

Use of Requirements Data

The scope of the systems design is guided by the framework for the new system developed during analysis. For example, the earliest data flow diagrams define the boundary of the systems study. That boundary remains a guideline for design purposes. Requirements data, gathered during the investigation, shape the activities and components of the system. The analysts formulate a logical design that supports the processes and decisions within the system they studied and that provides ways to interact with persons and entities outside of the system. Therefore, the contents of the system may change as a result of the new design. Data flow diagrams may be redrawn to reflect the proposed changes.

Logical design proceeds from the top down, just as requirements determination did. General features, such as reports and inputs are identified first. Then each is studied individually and in more detail: Describing the data items used and their locations defines the contents of each report or each input form.

The analysts continue to use data collected during requirements determination. The descriptions in the data dictionary state not only which data are used in specific processes, but also the type (numeric or alphanumeric) and length of each data element. In output design, for example, analysts must know the length of a specific data item in order to decide how much space to allow for it in the report, visual display, or file.

As part of the design, the analysts may decide to simplify or combine processes learned about during the systems study. Or they may decide that input forms and worksheets must be changed. Even new controls may be specified during logical design. However, the requirements data is the basis for making these design decisions. In other words, the requirements data describes what a new or modified system must do, the logical design says how to do it, and the physical design actually carries it out.

Throughout design, data flow diagrams are redrawn and data dictionary descriptions amended to reflect changes in the procedures analysts are establishing. Documentation therefore remains current and information is automatically collected for use in writing the descriptions of procedures, a later activity.

Involvement of Users

The managers and users of the system also play an important role in design of the system; it is not solely the analyst's project. During design some are asked to review mock-ups of reports, review input formats, and assist in writing procedures to tell other individuals how to use the system properly.

User involvement gives the analysts important feedback as the design proceeds, but it also ensures that users have a nontechnical understanding of what the new system will and will not do. They know which functions are manual and which are computer-assisted.

Involvement also paves the way for a smoother introduction of the project when it is completed. It assists in gaining full acceptance by other persons affected by it.

This overview of systems design outlines the design issues that will be examined in the next few chapters. The remainder of this chapter discusses the design of systems output.

SYSTEMS PROTOTYPING

In the best of situations, systems requirements and design specifications are clearly stated and well understood, and the analysts have the experience to turn the requirements into an efficient and well-working system. Of course, this does not always occur. In these cases, systems prototypes may be developed to provide the necessary information to produce a suitable system. This section discusses the rationale behind prototype systems, methods for developing prototypes, and how prototypes are used once developed.

Reasons for Systems Prototyping

In spite of the best efforts of systems analysts, information requirements are not always well-stated. This may occur for two reasons. The users may only know that they need improvement in certain business areas or that they must change existing procedures. Or they may know that they need better information for managing certain activities, but they themselves are not sure what that information is. The technology to support the user may be well understood by the analysts, but the requirements they must meet are too vague to even begin formulating a design.

In other cases, a well-managed system investigation may produce a comprehensive and well-stated set of systems requirements. But the knowledge about how to build a system that will meet those requirements may not exist. The analysts have not built such a system before, and the knowledge about how to design and program the system may not exist elsewhere either. The requirements of the system may require development of new technology. For example, working with users, the analysts may devise a complete, precise, and well-articulated specification for computer graphics for use by management for long-range planning, executive briefings, and sales presentations. However, if they have not built a comprehensive graphics system before, and the knowledge does not exist among information systems experts to use graphics in the way specified, the means to achieving the end are unknown. How then should the systems analysts proceed?

In both of these cases, analysts may consider prototyping to provide the needed information to formulate the design or develop the system. A *prototype* is a working system that is developed quickly to test ideas and understandings about the new system. In other words, it is not just a design on paper but software that runs and produces printed or displayed information.

A Prototyping Example

When prototypes are used to clarify user requirements, the main aspects are the output or reportability of the system and the method by which the user interacts with the system, such as visual display screens. The steps in prototyping consist of identification of basic system requirements, development of a working prototype, use of the prototype system, and refinement of the prototype system until the system's features meet user needs.

For example, the prototype for a management reporting system aimed at providing senior managers with a daily report that summarizes the preceding day's sales, costs, and profitability of performance may take many forms. To determine the most suitable form, management and the systems analysts may agree to develop a prototype that presents the information in printed form. This system is developed very quickly, in approximately one week, and the report spans three pages. It includes summaries of sales, labor costs, material costs, and overhead expenses for every department in the organization. The report also indicates cash receipts from sales and from payments on accounts that arrived by mail the preceding day. It indicates changes in accounts receivable from new sales and payments on credit account balances. It also includes information about the estimated value of inventory on hand.

Two senior managers use the report and work closely with the systems analyst to make the necessary modifications to the prototype until they are satisfied that the report meets their needs. During a four-week period the prototype is changed and the following adjustments are made:

1 Management asks to have the report reduced in length from three pages to one.
2 Comparison of sales with budgeted levels is added.
3 Because sales budget information is so useful, daily budget data is also added for labor and materials costs as well as overall contribution to profits.
4 Week-to-date sales and cost data is reported along with daily sales and expense information.
5 Because some departments are very constant in sales and expenses, management decides that it only wants to receive information on those reports on a weekly basis. Two versions of the one-page report are developed. The daily version focuses only on a selection of departments with high variability. The weekly version includes information on all departments and includes totals for all sales and expense categories by department and for the organization as a whole.
6 The ability to accumulate historical data is developed, along with a facility to receive reports for whatever period of time management requests. Data for up to one year can be included in a single report.
7 A section is added to the one-page report, for both the daily and weekly versions, to show sales, credits given, bad debt writeoffs, and miscellaneous income, and to compare them to changes in accounts receivable and bank deposits (for auditing purposes).
8 A graphic version of the report is developed, enabling presentation of any of the above data in bar graph and line graph form for any specified period of time. It is the first graphics project for the team of analysts.

Throughout the entire series of events described above, the system is used by the managers to monitor their business operations. Thus, both the information and the system itself are real. As each version of the report is changed, system adjustments, ranging from contents of master files, to the display screens used to enter data, to data capture and input procedures, to processing methods, are altered, often significantly. In some instances, when information is not input for processing properly, handwritten corrections are made on the report so that the output remains correct and reliable.

When the prototype was finished, management was extremely pleased with the results, even though it was their first experience with development of and reliance on an automated system. Two years after the report format was agreed on, it was still in use and had been altered only slightly (once).

Using Prototypes

As indicated above, the prototype is an actual working system, not just an idea on paper. Through use, the design and the information produced by the system is evaluated by users. This can only be effectively done if the data is real and the situations live.

As the above example demonstrates, prototyping is an iterative process. It may begin with only a few functions and be expanded to include others that are identified later. Or it may start with what both analyst and user believe is a complete set of functions. The set may expand or contract through use and experience.

Methods for Prototype Development

A prototype system is created quickly, often within a matter of a few days or weeks. Usually it is also relatively inexpensive to build compared with the cost of a conventional system. It may also not be as efficient as a system developed over a period of months.

Prototype systems may be developed using conventional programming languages and methods. However, the system does not contain all the features and final touches normally included in a completed system. For instance, headings, titles, and page numbers on reports may be missing. File organizations may be temporary and record structures left incomplete. Processing and input controls may be missing and documentation of the system is usually avoided entirely. The emphasis is on trying out ideas and providing assumptions about requirements, not on system efficiency or completeness.

In some cases, segments of programs will be taken from other systems or from libraries of reusable program code. For example, on-line system input and editing routines often have similarities in processing structure even though the details of the application themselves will vary. During prototyping, analysts may link sections of reusable code together with sections they write themselves to get a system up and running for evaluation.

The computer industry is actively pursuing *application generators,* programs that generate other programs, to support prototyping efforts. Often also called *program generators,* these tools allow analysts to define the structure of visual displays, input records, and report formats which in turn are processed by the application generators to produce working computer programs. Because this can be accomplished very quickly, usually in a matter of hours, generators are receiving increased use in prototyping.

In some cases, such as when the system will be used only infrequently, the prototype may in fact become the final working system. However, the prototype itself is usually considered a temporary system. Once requirements are agreed on or designs formulated, the system may be reprogrammed to run more quickly or to have all the desired features that were initially ignored.

DESIGN OF SYSTEMS OUTPUT

Often the most important feature of an information system for users is the output it produces. Without quality output, they may even feel the entire system is so unnecessary they avoid using it and thus possibly cause the system to fail.

As this section points out, there are many types of output, all of which can be either highly useful or detrimental to the organization, depending on the manner and degree to which they are used. Key questions help analysts make the proper design decisions about form and content and suggest various presentation methods.

Logical Output Design

The term "output" is applied to any information produced by a system, whether printed, displayed, or spoken. When analysts design output, they *select* methods for presenting information, and *create* documents, reports, or other formats that contain information produced by the system.

The methods of output vary across systems. For some, such as an inventory report of the quantity of merchandise, the computer system, under program control, simply retrieves the data on hand from storage (usually in secondary storage) and assembles it into a presentable form. Little if any calculation is needed since the data already exists and therefore only needs to be retrieved. Other output may require substantial processing before it is available for use. For example, to produce output on the cost to manufacture a product, the system first locates descriptions of all the parts used in the final product and necessary quantity of each one, used in the final product. Next, the cost of each is determined. Finally, the costs and quantities for all the parts are multiplied and totaled to produce the output sought. The processing steps in this example are much more extensive than in the inventory example, yet both sets of information may be equally important to inventory report users.

Key Output Questions

Five questions, answered fully and properly, tell analysts a great deal about what the output of a newly designed system should be like.

The questions are:

1 *Who will receive the output?*
Is the user inside or outside the organization? External users may have specific requirements governing content, format, and medium requirements that are unchangeable. Organizations may decide to package the same information differently when it is received by internal and external users.
2 *What is its planned use?*
Does the output present information (quantity sales report), ask for a

response (renewal of driver's license), or trigger an action (an overdue payment notice)? Usage determines content, form, and media.

3 *How much detail is needed?*
Only a few items of data are needed to tell someone to renew a driver's license (name, address, renewal date, and renewal fee plus the fact that it is a motor-vehicle renewal notice). However, the quarterly report on sales contains many details in varying formats that help get the message (of what happened, how it happened, and what the outcome is) across to users. High and low amounts of data also suggest whether print or display methods should be used.

4 *When and how often is the output needed?*
Timing and timliness guide specific designs. Some output will be produced infrequently and only when certain conditions arise: the license notice every 4 years when it is due for renewal or the payment notice when an account is overdue. However, the organization may require output every month for license renewals coming up in the next month or every week for customer accounts with new overdue balances for the week.

5 *By what method?*
Should the output be printed, displayed, or spoken? The previous examples demonstrate output for which printed methods are used frequently. However, if your system responds to simple yes/no inquiries ("Is there a seat available today on Flight 130?"), a simple display response is often appropriate. The electronic switching systems used by many telephone companies in the United States use audio output to provide new or changed telephone numbers. However, you would not want to examine a long list of inventory quantities using audio output.

The above questions are raised to assist in determining output methods. The analysts must decide whether to print, display, or audibly present output. Printed output may use blank paper or preprinted forms. Visual output may use single or multiple screens to display information. The next section outlines each option and suggests guidelines to assist the analysts.

Selecting Output Methods

Information systems, whether on small desktop systems or large mainframe systems, use three primary methods for output that we will look at in detail. Each of these output types—print, display, and audio—demand specific devices to produce the output. We will indicate these in the discussion that follows.

PRINTED OUTPUT

Many people associate computer information systems with the production of large volumes of printed reports. However, the decision to use printed output should not be automatic. There should be a reason for it (such as the need to mail a document to a customer or supplier, to have a printed record of data, or to circulate a large volume of information to several persons simultaneously). The attention of the analysts should also be on reducing, not increasing, the number of printed reports moving through the organization. One well-designed report may replace several poorly designed ones. And of course providing unnecessary detail does not assist anyone, so analysts should be alert to avoid producing extraneous data simply because it is easy to print it.

The most common printed output options in organizations are paper and film reports, special forms, and mailers.

Printed Reports

As organizations conduct their business, they produce many transactions and make decisions about various business activities. Reports to management are natural parts of business. Printed reports summarize transactions, point out problems or exceptions that are occurring, and present historical details.

Printed reports can be designed in virtually any size, although analysts often use the standard sizes of 9½ by 11 inches, 11 by 14⅞ inches, and 8 by 14⅞ inches. These sizes assume that continuous forms (see Figure 7.3) are being used. *Continuous forms* (sometimes called *pin-fed* or *fan-fold forms)* is the name given to connected sheets of paper that feed into printers one after the other. A light perforation keeps the sheets continuous so they do not tear or separate when printing. However, they tear apart quickly when this is wanted. (Separating a large set of continuous forms is called *bursting.)*

Each side of the paper has tear strips, ½ inch wide. The holes in these strips, which can be torn off after the form is printed, are used by pins on the printer to move the sheets through printing quickly and evenly. Thus a 9½-inch-wide sheet—the size specified when ordering paper—is really 8½ inches wide after removing the strips.

Printing Methods

All printing methods (see Figure 7.4) use a computer printer to place output information on the report paper. Two methods, impact and nonimpact

(a)

(b)

Figure 7.3. Continuous forms for computer printing. (Courtesy Control Data Corporation)

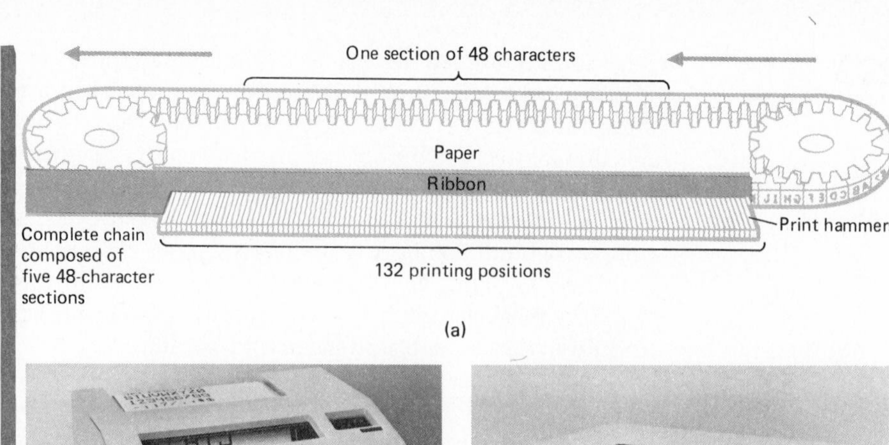

(a)

(b)

(c)

Figure 7.4. Printing process for computer printing. [(*b*) *Left*, photo courtesy of Hewlett-Packard Company; *right*, photo courtesy of International Business Machines Corporation; (*c*) courtesy of Dataproducts Corporation]

printing, dominate. In *impact printing,* contact is made between the print element and the paper. The two impact printer types are:

1 *Computer line printer.*
The printer prints a full line of up to 144 characters per line (depending on the specific manufacturer) at one time. That is, it prints the full line all at once. The paper is pressed against the type slugs on the print chain or drum. Table 7.1 summarizes the speeds of all printers.
2 *Character printer.*
Character printing takes place one character at a time. To print a line of 132 characters, the print element strikes the paper 132 separate times. Character printers (Figure 7.5) are much slower than any other impact printer.

Nonimpact printers use other methods that do not require striking the paper. The need for increased speed in printing, achieved by reducing the relatively slow mechanical movements in printing, led to their development.

1 *Page printer.*
Some printers are so fast they print full pages, rather than lines or characters. Imagine the volume of printed output needed for customer utility bills (gas, electric, or communication services). Printers using laser or electronic methods achieve speeds of 20,000 lines per minute (Figure 7.6). Ink jet printers, which *spray* dots of ink to produce the data on the report form, produce nearly 50,000 lines per minute. Because they both work so fast, they fill a page at a time, hence the name page printers.
2 *Thermal printer.*
Thermal image printers (Figure 7.7) print using heat sensitive paper and metal rods. To print, the heated rods touch the paper leaving an image of the letters and numbers on the special paper.

TABLE 7.1

PERFORMANCE OF COMMON PRINTER CLASSES

TYPE OF PRINTER	APPROXIMATE OPERATING SPEED
IMPACT	
Low-Speed Line Printer	600 lines/minute
High-Speed Line Printer	
Dot Matrix Character Printer	100–350 characters/second
Solid Font Character Printer	10–75 characters/second
NONIMPACT	
Ink/jet Printer	45,000 lines/minute
Laser/Electronic Page Printer	20,000 lines/minute

(a)

(b)

Figure 7.5. (*a*) Character printer (courtesy of Hewlett-Packard Company) and (*b*) daisy wheel print element (courtesy of Dataproducts Corporation).

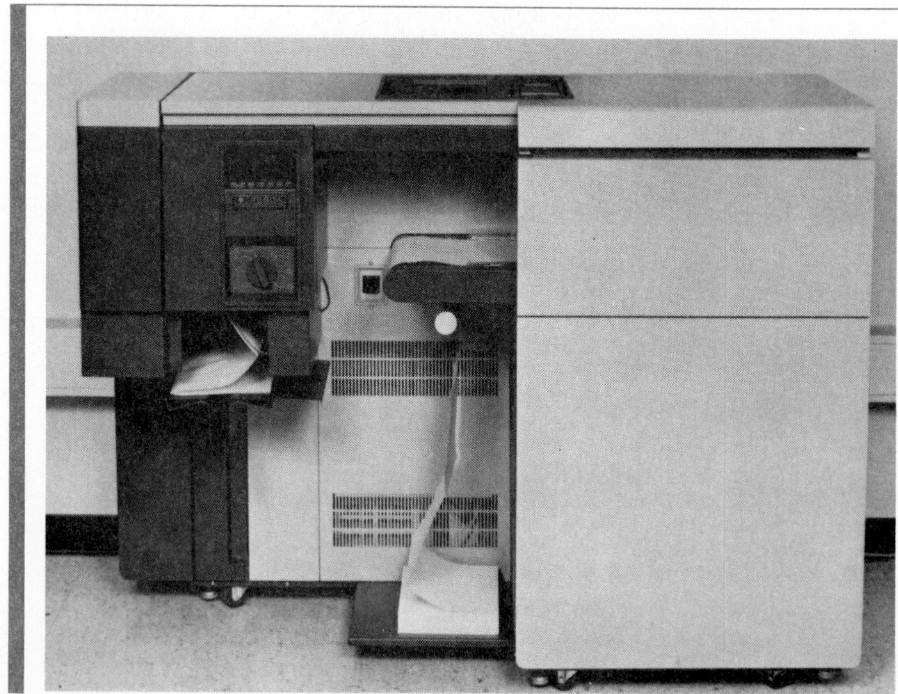

Figure 7.6. Electronic page printer. (Photo courtesy of Hewlett-Packard Company)

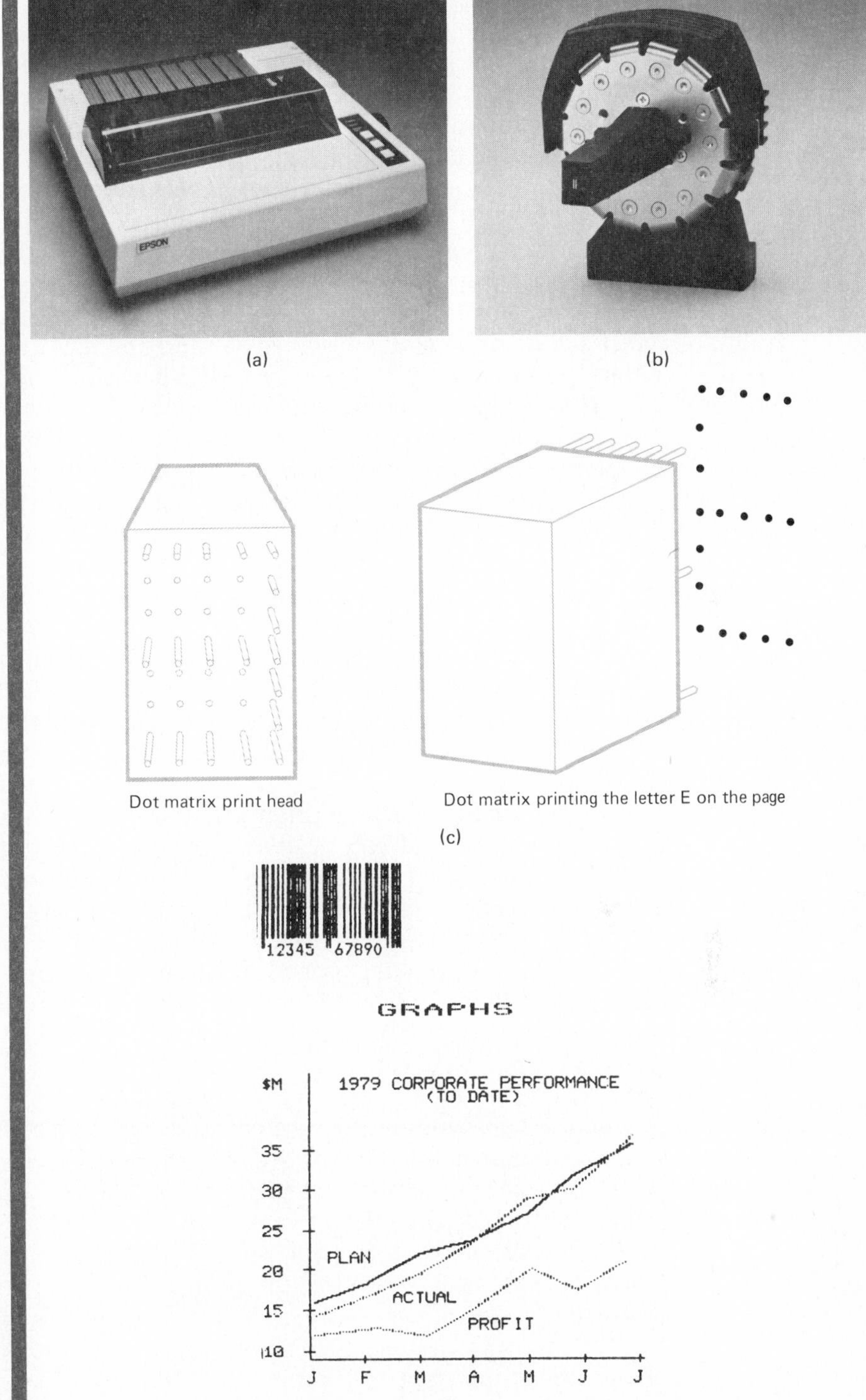

Figure 7.7. (*a*) Dot matrix printer (courtesy Epson America, Inc.), (*b*) print head (courtesy Dataproducts Corporation), and (*d*) print pattern (courtesy Datasouth Computer Corporation).

There is really no limitation on the equipment to which these printers can be connected. For example, micro and minicomputers will operate high-speed line printers. Character printers are often also used on mainframe systems. You can see that the decision is not technical, but operational and economic: the speed and cost of equipment are the deciding factors when selecting printers.

Some printers use solid font type. The printers make letters and characters that are continuous, like those made by an ordinary office typewriter. Others use dot matrix printing patterns (Figure 7.7). In impact printers, the dots are formed from a select set of wires in a matrix pushing against ribbon and paper to produce the desired character printer. Nonimpact *ink jet printers* are designed so that tiny holes in the print head (the "dots") spray a dot pattern to print the character.

Film output (Figure 7.8) should also be considered when printed information is desirable. All the features of printed output are available in microfilm and microfiche, the two film output methods. Microfilm consists of strips of film that store data as pages along the length of the film. Microfiche is a film card that stores many pages of output in rows and columns on the card. Output data is stored as small characters—so small that special readers are needed to view them—at a cost approximately one-third lower than that of paper output having the same data.

The film (Figure 7.9), after developing in the microfiche machine, can be stored and retrieved when needed. For reference data used only sporadically, such as private savings account balances that change infrequently and have interest posted every three months, microfilm could be a useful output option.

The microfilm machine (Figure 7.10) converts pages of written characters into a form that can be stored on film. Each page of output is very small—so small that 1 square inch of film can store several pages of paper report. A simple 3-by-5-inch card stores hundreds, even thousands, of pages.

The time it takes to locate the film reel or card containing the information wanted—the user must maintain an index to it—and to load it into a microfilm or microfiche reader so that the information can be viewed is a disadvantage.

Special Forms

Computer-based information systems can also produce special forms. One of the most common is the *preprinted form,* a customized form that is designed to include special symbols and trademarks for the organization and have color printing, depending on the requirements established by the analyst or user. The special custom print work is placed on blank paper stock by a forms maker, who does all of the print work with regular (noncomputer) printing presses. When they are delivered, all details that will not be added by the information system's printer are already on the forms (Figure 7.12) hence the name *pre*printed form.

Some forms used by organizations have a traditional format that

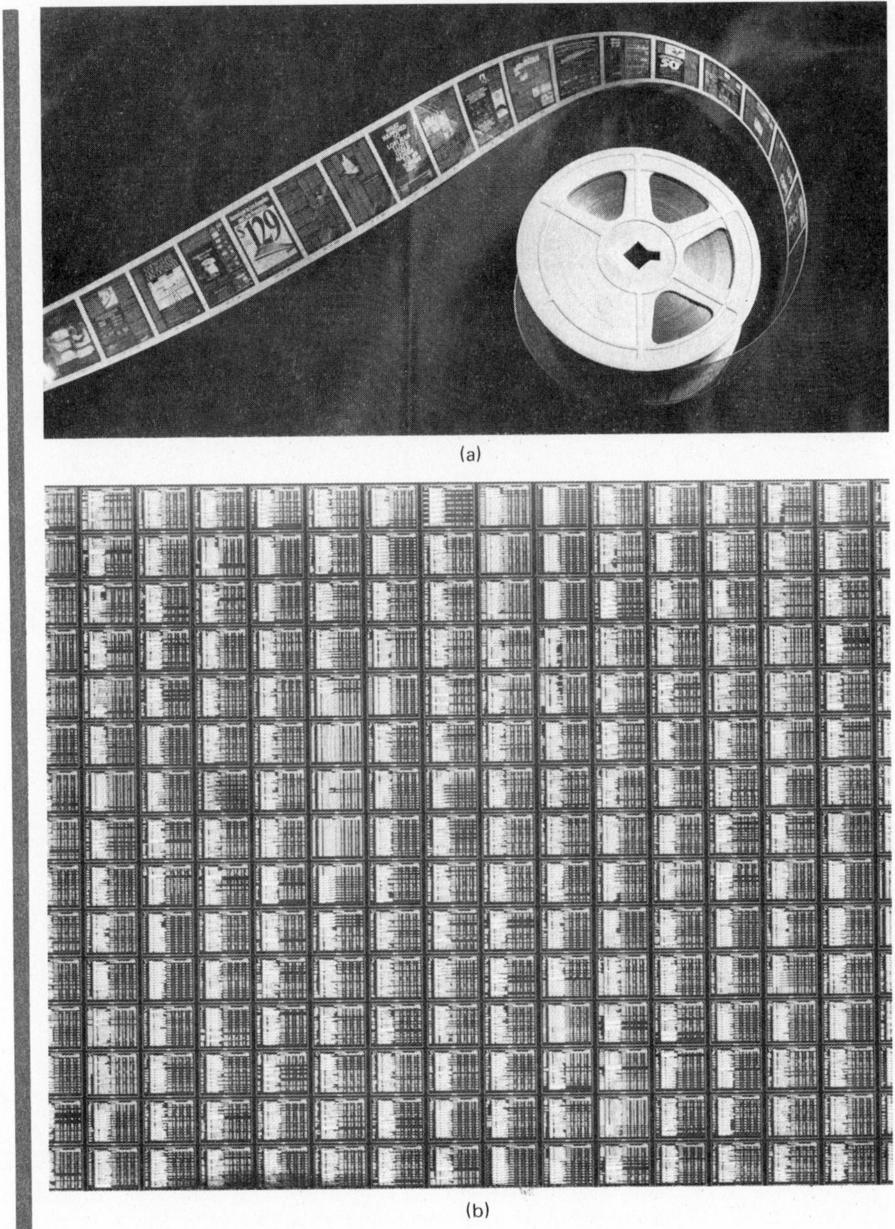

(a)

(b)

Figure 7.8. Both microfilm and microfiche cards replace printer paper output. (Photo by Brian P. Griffin; microfiche: McGraw-Hill Book Company)

remains unaltered even when computer systems are introduced. These forms are preprinted to retain standard features. For example, the account statement in Figure 7.11 is widely used by many companies. So is the accompanying bank check. On these, all constant, unchanging details, like

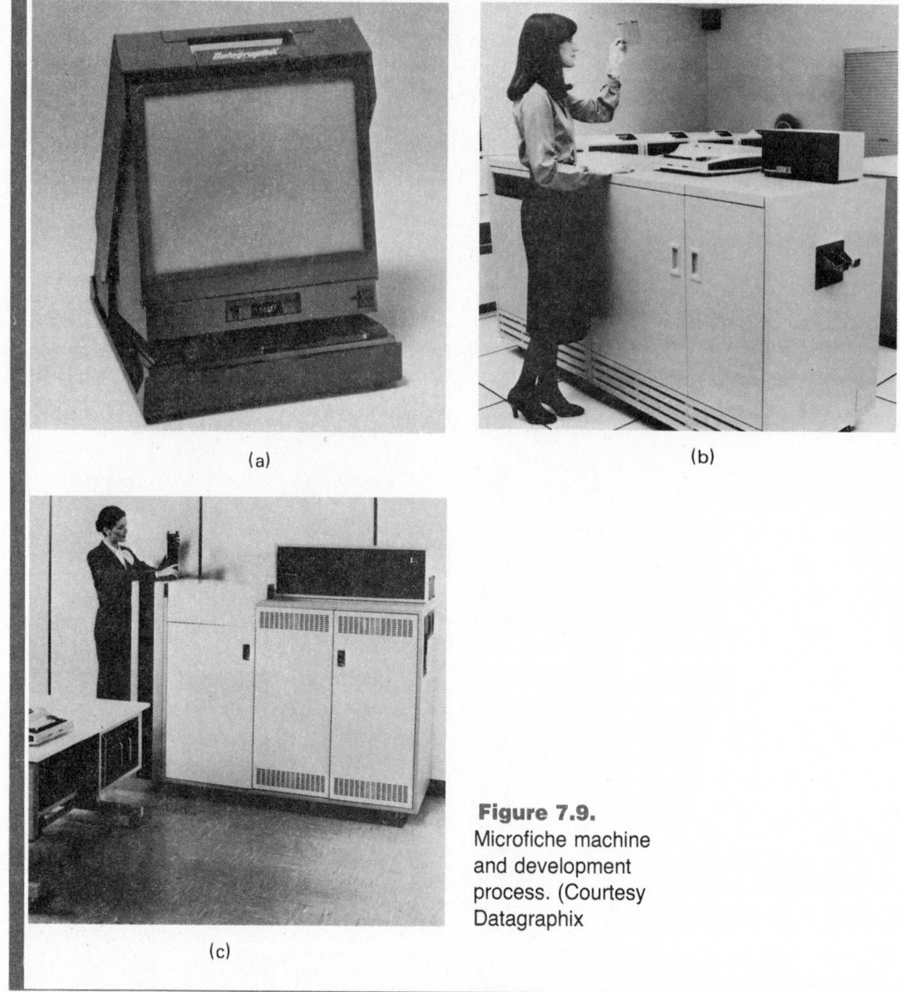

(a) (b) (c)

Figure 7.9. Microfiche machine and development process. (Courtesy Datagraphix

headings, notes, and names, are preprinted. Details that change, including dollar amounts, dates, and names of persons are not. In a computer-based system, they are entered by the computer printer.

The use of preprinted forms adds to paper costs dramatically, sometimes doubling them. Therefore the analysts must have good reasons for recommending their use. In some cases there is no choice. For example, government W-2 withholding tax summary forms are prepared for employees at the end of every tax year to summarize the amount of income tax withheld for each employee during that year. Analysts designing a payroll system have no choice but to specify preprinted W-2 summary forms (Figure 7.12). The federal government specifies the size of, and location of information on the form in great detail for everyone. It also specifies what information must be preprinted and what can be computer printed or simply typewritten.

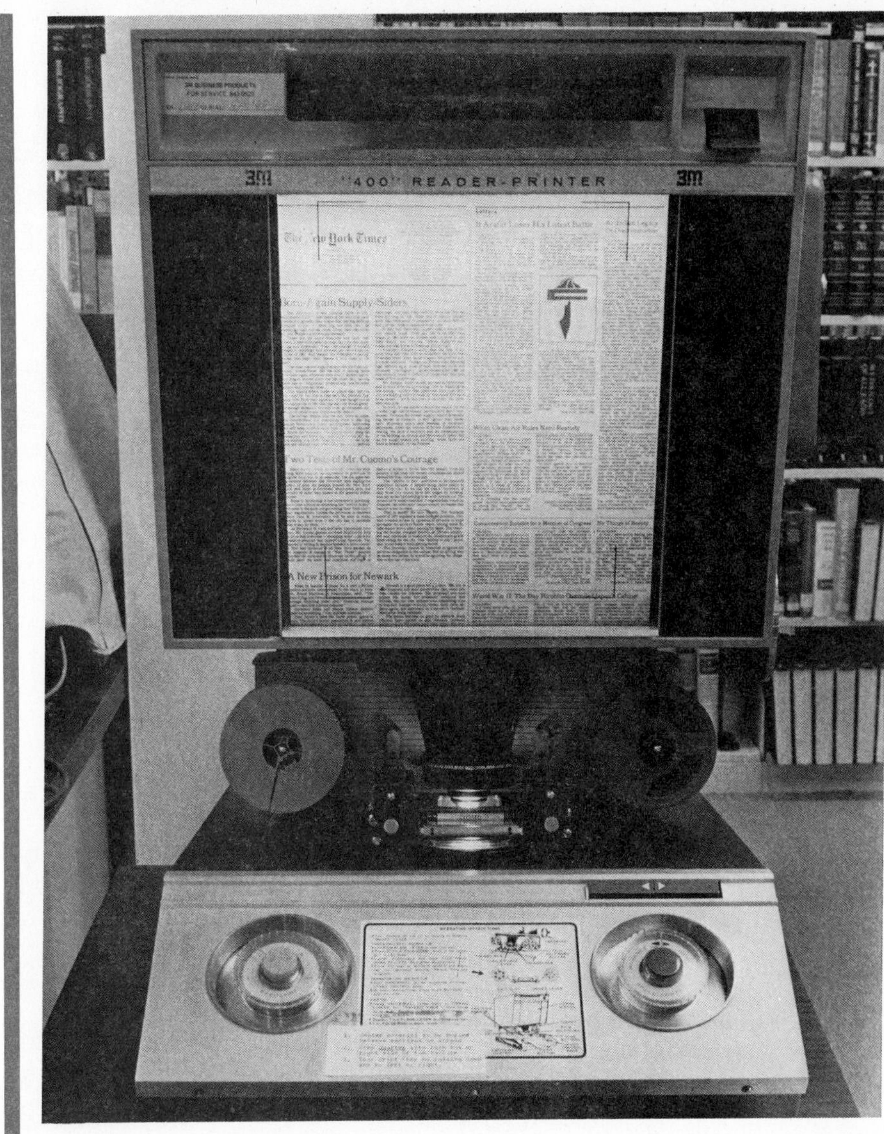

Figure 7.10.
Microfilm machine.
(Brian P. Griffin)

Many other situations are not so specifically controlled. However, when a report will be sent outside the company or when the appearance of a report is important, preprinting may be specified. The extra type sizes and styles plus the use of colored ink and special symbols associated with the firm enhance the appearance of the report and the message it sends to readers.

The analysts are responsible for specifying the preprinted and computer-generated parts when developing the output design. At the same time, they are responsible for knowing or finding out where preprinted forms *must* be used (such as for income tax reporting).

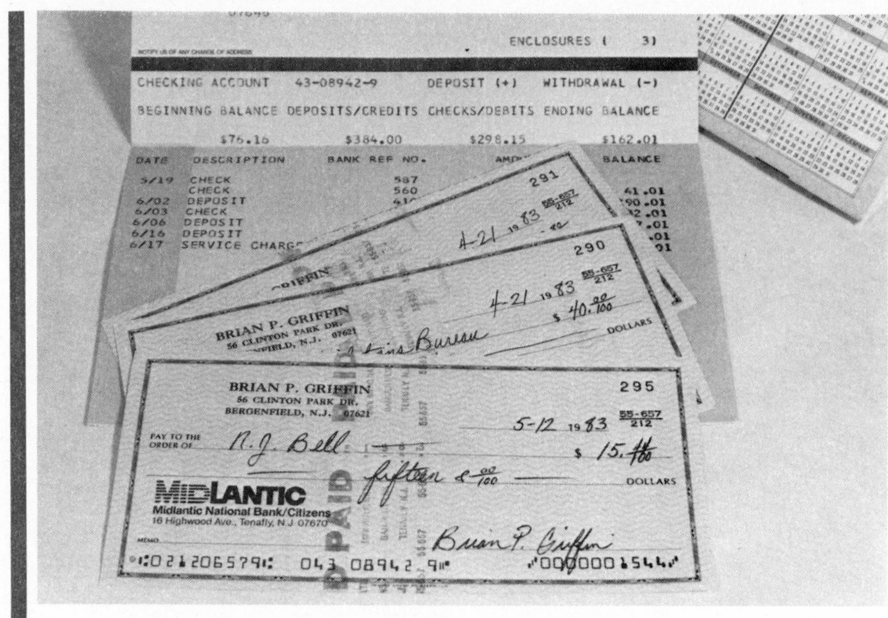

Figure 7.11.
Magnetic ink character.
(Brian P. Griffin)

Multiple Copies of Output

Organizations often need more than one copy of a report or document prepared by the computer. There are several ways to do this, such as repeated printing of the report or the use of an office photocopier. However, the most common and cost-effective way to produce a report needed in, say, two to six copies is to specify *multipart forms.* They automatically produce

1 Control number	22222	OMB No. 1545-0008	
2 Employer's name, address, and ZIP code		3 Employer's identification number	4 Employer's State number
		5 Stat. employee ☐ Deceased ☐ Pension plan ☐ Legal rep. ☐ 942 emp. ☐ Subtotal ☐ Correction ☐ Void ☐	
		6	7 Advance EIC payment
8 Employee's social security number	9 Federal income tax withheld	10 Wages, tips, other compensation	11 FICA tax withheld
12 Employee's name, address, and ZIP code		13 FICA wages	14 FICA tips
		16 Employer's use	
		17 State income tax / 18 State wages, tips, etc.	19 Name of State
		20 Local income tax / 21 Local wages, tips, etc.	22 Name of locality

Form **W-2 Wage and Tax Statement 1982** **Copy B To be filed with employee's FEDERAL tax return** This information is being furnished to the Internal Revenue Service. Department of the Treasury Internal Revenue Service

Figure 7.12.
Preprinted form for printing tax information.
(Brian P. Griffin)

duplicates of the top (original) copy. A three-part form, for example, includes the original and two copies.

There are two types of multipart forms:

1 *Interleaved carbon copies.*
Carbon paper suitable for one time use is interleaved between each sheet of paper (Figure 7.13).

2 *Carbonless copies.*
Multiple copies using carbonless paper are possible because of a special chemical coating on the back side of each copy except the last. Writing or printing on the first copy carries through to the next copy. The coating causes the image to appear on the underneath copy.

Carbonless forms are more expensive than those with interleaved carbon. However, they have the advantage of not requiring extra time or equipment (a bursting machine) to remove the carbon paper from continuous forms. Both kinds of multipart forms work well for up to approximately six copies, depending on the weight of the paper. (Thinner paper makes better copies.)

These copy methods rely on impressions to produce the copies. Therefore they work well for impact printers, but are not appropriate for ink jet printers, that spray rather than press the data onto the form. With ink jet printers, printing two and three side-by-side forms, called two-up or three-up forms (Figure 7.14), may be a better alternative for multiple copies.

Figure 7.13. Interleaved carbon forms for computer output. (Courtesy National Business Forms Association, photo by Brian P. Griffin)

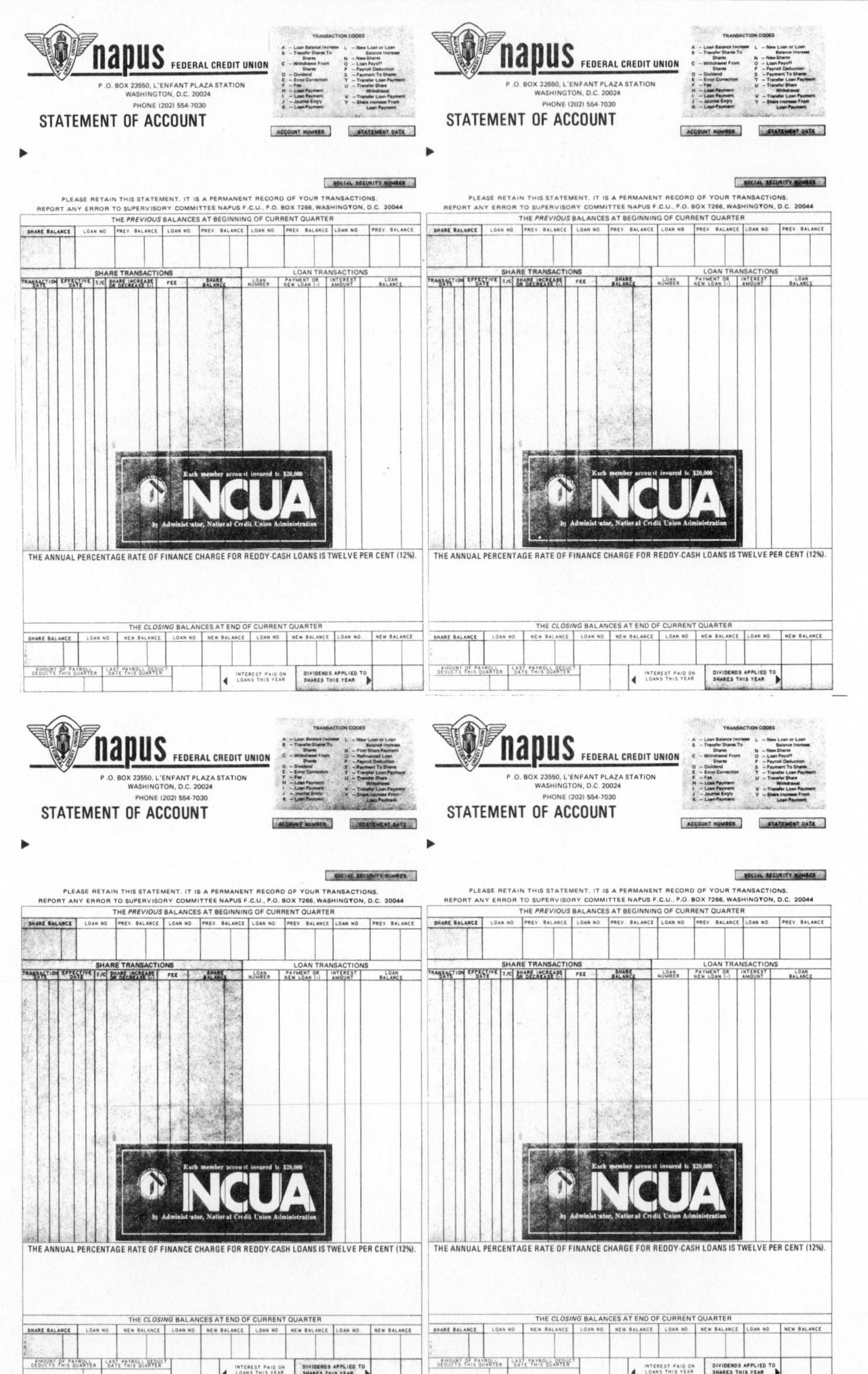

napus FEDERAL CREDIT UNION

P.O. BOX 23550, L'ENFANT PLAZA STATION
WASHINGTON, D.C. 20024
PHONE (202) 554-7030

STATEMENT OF ACCOUNT

TRANSACTION CODES

A – Loan Balance Increase
B – Transfer Shares To Shares
C – Withdrawal From Shares
D – Dividend
E – Error Correction
F – Fee
H – Loan Payment
I – Loan Payment
J – Journal Entry
K – Loan Payment
L – New Loan or Loan Balance Increase
N – New Shares
O – Loan Payoff
P – Payroll Deduction
S – Payment To Shares
T – Transfer Loan Payment
U – Transfer Share Withdrawal
V – Transfer Loan Payment
Y – Share Increase From Loan Payment

ACCOUNT NUMBER | STATEMENT DATE

SOCIAL SECURITY NUMBER

PLEASE RETAIN THIS STATEMENT. IT IS A PERMANENT RECORD OF YOUR TRANSACTIONS.
REPORT ANY ERROR TO SUPERVISORY COMMITTEE NAPUS F.C.U., P.O. BOX 7266, WASHINGTON, D.C. 20044

THE *PREVIOUS* BALANCES AT BEGINNING OF CURRENT QUARTER

SHARE BALANCE	LOAN NO	PREV. BALANCE	LOAN NO	PREV. BALANCE	LOAN NO	PREV. BALANCE	LOAN NO	PREV. BALANCE

SHARE TRANSACTIONS						LOAN TRANSACTIONS			
TRANSACTION DATE	EFFECTIVE DATE	T/C	SHARE INCREASE OR DECREASE (-)	FEE	SHARE BALANCE	LOAN NUMBER	PAYMENT OR NEW LOAN (-)	INTEREST AMOUNT	LOAN BALANCE

Each member account insured to $20,000
NCUA
by Administrator, National Credit Union Administration

THE ANNUAL PERCENTAGE RATE OF FINANCE CHARGE FOR REDDY-CASH LOANS IS TWELVE PER CENT (12%).

THE *CLOSING* BALANCES AT END OF CURRENT QUARTER

SHARE BALANCE	LOAN NO	NEW BALANCE	LOAN NO	NEW BALANCE	LOAN NO	NEW BALANCE	LOAN NO	NEW BALANCE

AMOUNT OF PAYROLL DEDUCTS THIS QUARTER	LAST PAYROLL DEDUCT DATE THIS QUARTER		INTEREST PAID ON LOANS THIS YEAR	DIVIDENDS APPLIED TO SHARES THIS YEAR	

napus FEDERAL CREDIT UNION
P.O. BOX 23550, L'ENFANT PLAZA STATION
WASHINGTON, D.C. 20024
PHONE (202) 554-7030
STATEMENT OF ACCOUNT
(same form repeated three more times: TRANSACTION CODES, ACCOUNT NUMBER, STATEMENT DATE, SOCIAL SECURITY NUMBER, PLEASE RETAIN THIS STATEMENT. IT IS A PERMANENT RECORD OF YOUR TRANSACTIONS. REPORT ANY ERROR TO SUPERVISORY COMMITTEE NAPUS F.C.U., P.O. BOX 7266, WASHINGTON, D.C. 20044, THE PREVIOUS BALANCES AT BEGINNING OF CURRENT QUARTER, SHARE TRANSACTIONS, LOAN TRANSACTIONS, NCUA, THE ANNUAL PERCENTAGE RATE OF FINANCE CHARGE FOR REDDY-CASH LOANS IS TWELVE PER CENT (12%)., THE CLOSING BALANCES AT END OF CURRENT QUARTER)

Figure 7.14. Example of a two-up computer output form. (Courtesy National Business Forms Association)

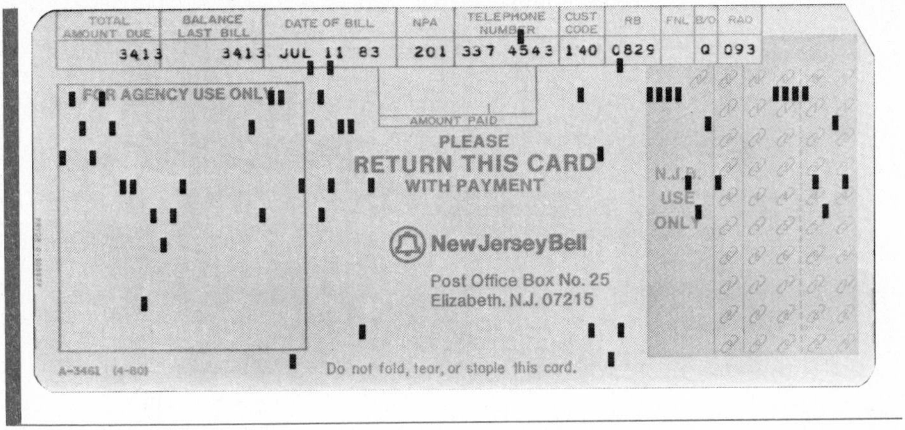

Figure 7.15.
Punch card produced as computer output. (Brian P. Griffin)

Punched Cards

Often punched card output is specified, particularly when the output will be used as a turnaround document. A *turnaround document* is output at one point and later comes back as an input document. The cards themselves are usually preprinted: company names and unchanging details are printed on the card, but the computer punches variable information into the card. The holes represent the data that the program encoded. Interpretations of the data are listed along the top of the card by the system card punch under control of the central processing unit (CPU).

Utility companies provide a common example of the use of punched card output as turnaround documents (Figure 7.15). Each month when the utility company prepares its statements, it first calculates the amount due from the customer. The statement is prepared for the customer in the form of a punched card and mailed to the customer (a printed report of all customer amounts owed for the month is also prepared for management). When paying the bill, the customer returns the punched card with the payment. The turnaround document, which contains all details about the customer, account number, and amount due, can be fed into the computer system, eliminating input preparation steps that would otherwise be needed (such as keying or entering the name, address, and account number). See Figure 7.16.

Optical-Scan Forms

If the firm uses special optical scanners (discussed in Chapter 8) capable of reading printed or handwritten forms, then a paper statement or other form can be prepared by the system and used as a turnaround document in place of the punched card. For instance, a utility bill, printed on ordinary paper, may be used as a turnaround document if part of the statement is designed to be returned (with a payment) and optically scanned to read the account number and amount due.

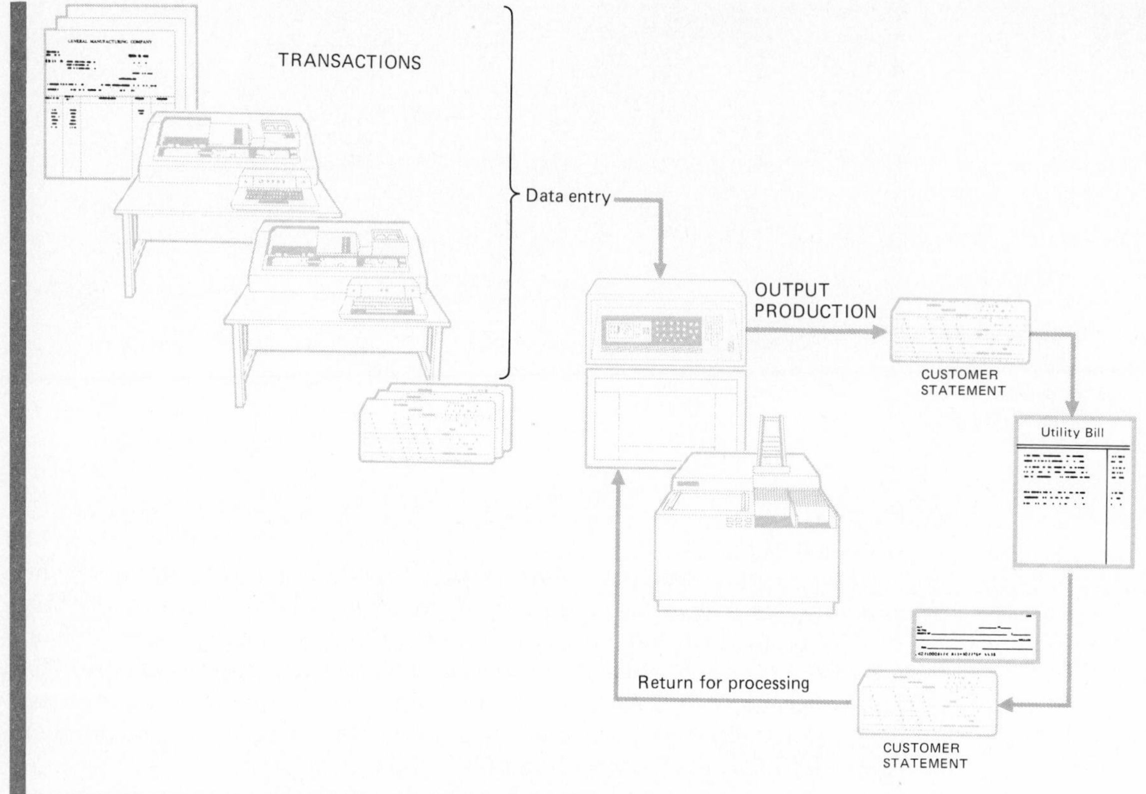

Figure 7.16. Production and use of turnaround document.

BADGES AND PLASTIC CARDS

Have you ever wondered how charge cards, credit cards, and, in some states, plastic driver's licenses and identification cards are produced? All these are computer output forms (Figure 7.17). Computer-driven badge printers punch data into plastic cards, leaving a raised impression.

There are advantages in using computer facilities to print plastic cards besides speed. There is also control, which is very important in bank card operations where it is necessary to ensure that only authorized cards are prepared; there is an automatic record of every card, and the details on the card are the same as those in the organization files.

DISPLAY OUTPUT

Computer output is frequently displayed, rather than printed or punched. The use of displays is growing rapidly because of the dropping cost of display equipment, the increase in the number of on-line systems, and the convenience display output offers to users. Many micro- and minicomputers rely

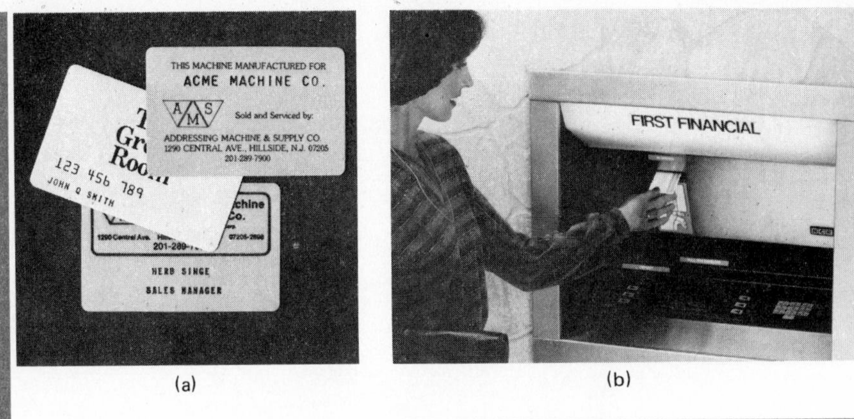

Figure 7.17. (*a*) Computer badges. (Brian P. Griffin) (*b*) Badge reader. (Courtesy of NCR Corporation)

almost exclusively on displayed information and use printed output only a small portion of the time.

The most common display medium is a *cathode-ray tube (CRT),* consisting of a display screen and a keyboard. In some applications, the output is displayed on a *monitor,* a high-resolution screen that can show details with extra clarity. Many business microcomputers use separate detachable monitors (Figure 7.18), whereas the screens on CRTs are integral parts of the devices.

All output data appearing on the screen of the display is produced by the computer itself. The size of the letters is fixed (although that can sometimes be modified if special programs are written), as is the capacity of the screen.

Display-screen capacities are measured by the number of rows and columns of letters that can be displayed. Most display screens have 80 columns of characters and either 24 or 25 rows. An 80-by-24 display screen can present 1920 characters at a time, if every position on the screen is used. (Usually the analyst tries to avoid this for greater readability.)

Some older CRTs, as well as a few home computers, use monitors displaying only 40 columns per row and 16 rows per screen. Analysts working with these systems have far less flexibility in output design.

AUDIO OUTPUT

Although still very new and the subject of much research, audio output methods are appearing in business applications. These output methods rely on stored digital patterns that produce sounds, not letters, over computer-controlled speakers. (Speakers have been part of large computer mainframe systems since the 1950s, and they are now appearing on the smallest personal computers as well). When a sound is wanted, such as a number or a phonic that is part of a word, the program sends a code to the audio system and the sound is produced. A word is actually a combination of computer-

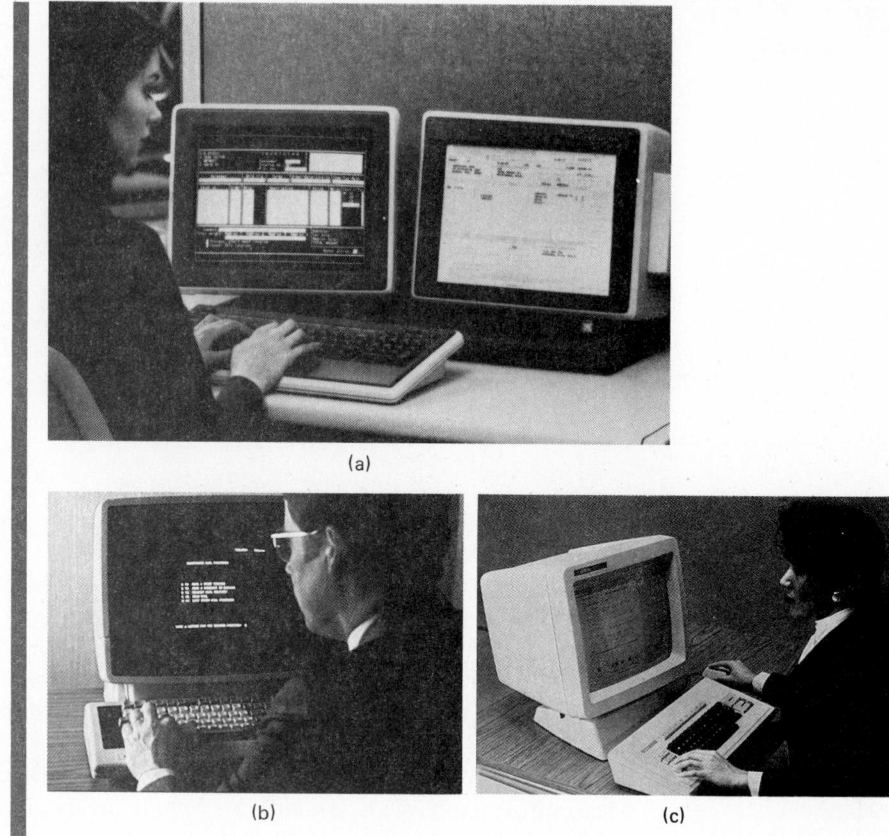

(a) (b) (c)

Figure 7.18. Computer visual displays [(*a*) Courtesy Burrough Corporation, (*b*) John Blaustein: photo courtesy of Four-Phase Systems, and (*c*) courtesy Xerox Corporation]

generated sounds, and therefore a combination of outputs, that, when played one after the other, is heard as a common word. (If we did not have the particular word in our vocabulary, we would not recognize the combinations of sounds.)

Depending on the industry you are or will be working in, you may design systems with audio output. The telephone communication industry in the United States already uses audio output as part of its customer directory service. Military forces are using voice output to aid pilots and navigators, and educational agencies and entertainment firms are beginning to use these methods.

Even if the analysts design audio output systems, the key questions introduced earlier in this section still apply. The purpose of output design does not change; only the medium is different.

OUTPUT LAYOUT DESIGN

Using the proper output medium and being sure that the output is calculated correctly does not guarantee that the reports, documents, or displays will be useful. The layout does this. This section discusses the processes to consider when developing an output layout design. It also discusses the differences between printed and displayed output designs.

Designing the Layout

An output *layout* is the arrangement of items on the printed output or the visual display. When analysts design an output layout, they are building a mock-up of the actual report, as it will appear after the system is in operation. The purpose of the layout is to show the location and position of every detail of the intended output. Both preprinted and computer-produced details are shown on the layout.

The layout will be reviewed by analysts, users, and programmers repeatedly during logical and physical design. It is, as we discussed earlier, the blueprint that will guide the construction of programs to produce live output later on.

For efficiency, special forms that show space allowances and print positions available are used. As we will see in the examples we develop in this section, the layout form tells the analysts precisely where data will be printed, how far away it is from other details, and whether there is enough space to include all the essential details without a cluttered appearance.

The notation to use in designing an output layout includes:

1 *Variable information.*
X to denote that the computer will print an alphabetic character or special character (for example, A–Z, a–z, *, /, $, and so on)
9 to denote that the computer will print or display a number (0–9)
2 *Constant information.*
The information written on the form as it should appear when printed

Designing Printed Output

Begin the design of a report layout by determining what items will be included in the report. The requirements analysis provides this information, and the data dictionary contains the necessary descriptive information: data-item type and length. Table 7.2 lists 18 data items for an inventory-on-hand report.

HEADINGS

All output produced from an information system should have a title. Table 7.2 indicates that the report we are designing is the inventory-on-hand report. Enter the report title and headings on the layout sheet, using the specific columns in which you wish the information to appear. Center the title. Note that the sample layout in Figure 7.19 also includes a page number and date. Include this information on every page to tell the users not only what report they are working with, but also the date on which it

TABLE 7.2

DATA DICTIONARY FOR INVENTORY-ON-HAND REPORT

DATA ITEM	TYPE	LENGTH
1. ITEM NUMBER	9	8
2. ITEM DESCRIPTION	X	20
3. UNIT	X	4
4. STOCK CLASS	X	2
5. MINIMUM BALANCE	9	6
6. STOCK ON HAND	9	6
7. STOCK ALLOCATED	9	6
8. STOCK ON ORDER	9	6
9. STOCK ON BACKORDER	9	6
10. UNIT COST	9	9(3),9(3)·9(2)
11. VALUE ON HAND	9	9(3),9(3)
12. VALUE ALLOCATED	9	9(3),9(3)
13. VALUE ON ORDER	9	9(3),9(3)
14. VALUE ON BACKORDER	9	9(3),9(3)
15. TOTAL VALUE ON HAND	9	9,9(3),9(3)
16. TOTAL VALUE ALLOCATED	9	9,9(3),9(3)
17. TOTAL VALUE ON ORDER	9	9,9(3),9(3)
18. TOTAL VALUE ON BACKORDER	9	9,9(3),9(3)

was prepared. The page number provides a quick reference for the users who work with data found at various locations throughout the report.

After the headings, turn your attention to the actual contents of the report, the inventory data. Since the amount of space for each is listed, you can quickly determine that the total space needed for data on each line is 74 print positions. If you want to have 3 unused spaces between each of the 10 data items, 101 spaces of the 130 available are accounted for. As the report layout shows, this report will begin in column 13 and be centered on the page.

Before actually marking in the data fields, write the column headings you wish printed on each page of the report. It is a good practice to use an underline, dash, or some other symbol to separate the column headings from the start of the data. Every column should have a heading that describes its contents. Spell out names and words, avoiding abbreviations.

DATA AND DETAILS

Enter the description of the data below the column headings, using the X and 9 conventions for alphabetic and numeric data. If decimal points, currency symbols, or other special symbols will be used, mark them in accordingly. Some organizations use the approach taken here for item description: they mark the first and last character of the field with the proper data symbol (an X in this case for alphabetic data) and connect them with a line to show the complete field. Other organizations require 20 X's to be marked to show that the field is 20 characters long. Either form is acceptable.

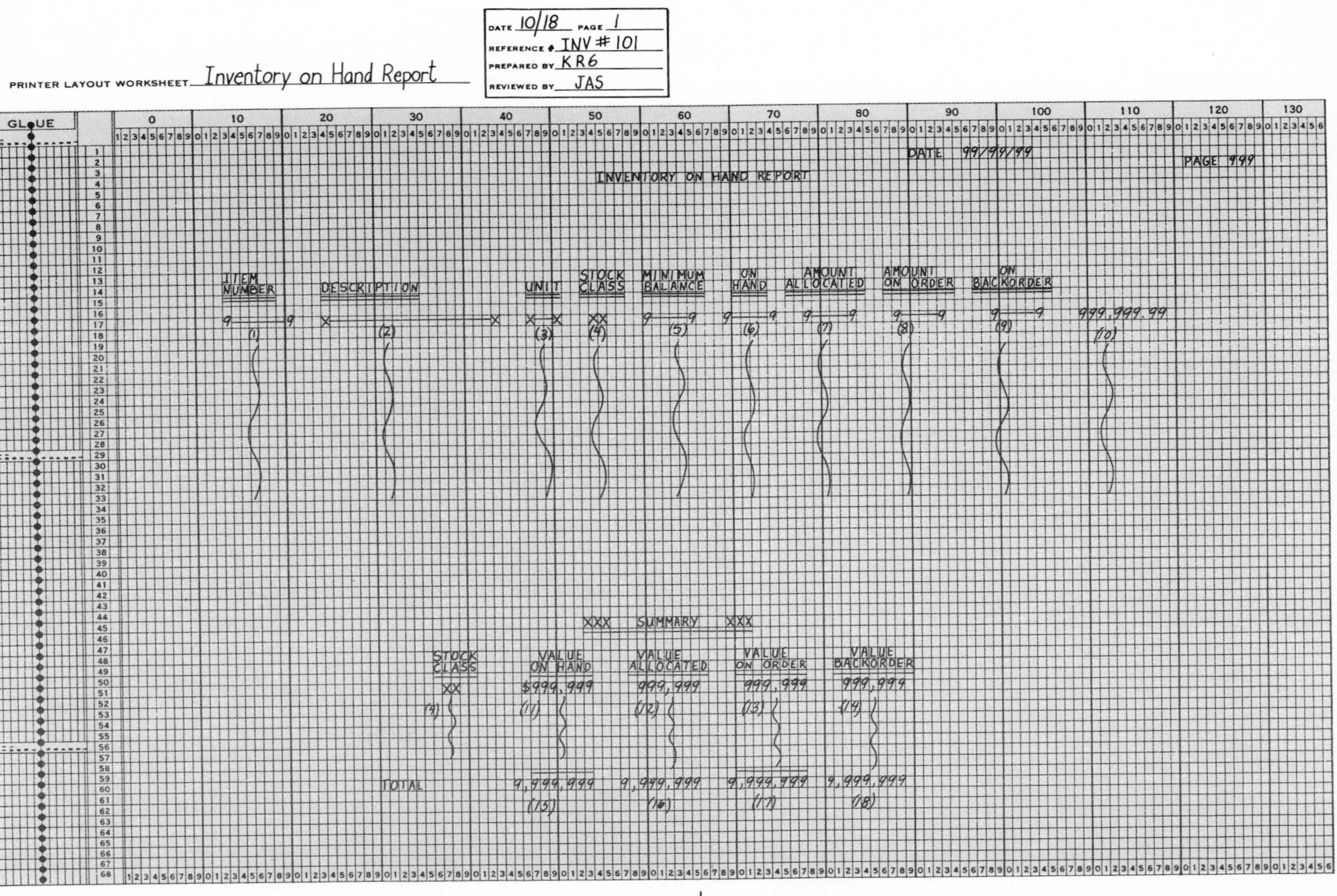

Figure 7.19. Report layout for inventory on hand report.

Although reports may continue for pages, you need to define the detail line (containing the inventory details in this example) only once. The wavy line descending from each data item indicates that it is repeated as many times as necessary on each page of the report.

SUMMARIES

Some report designs specify summary information, column totals, or subtotals. They are marked on the layout form in the manner just described. The inventory report contains a summary of all the items by stock class. For each class monetary values are presented along with a grand total for all the stock classes. The principle for showing them remains the same: label all titles and headings as you wish them to appear; denote variable data by X or 9 specifications, according to field type; and indicate the maximum length of the field.

Notice the link between the data item specification on the report layout and the data element listings. Rather than the name of each item, the number assigned to that item on the data element listing is entered on the layout form. Hence the (1) on the layout refers to the 1. ITEM NUMBER, on the data element list, (2) represents ITEM DESCRIPTION, and so on.

None of the steps just taken are unique to inventory systems or, for that matter, to reports. They are used in the design of all output. Figure 7.20 shows the layout for a preprinted accounting statement. However, the principles for indicating field length, subtotals, and other data are unchanged.

GUIDELINES

There are many guidelines that will make the analysts' job easier and, more important, will ensure the users of receiving an understandable report. We have used several, which are summarized here:

1 Reports and documents should be designed to read from left to right and top to bottom.
2 The most important items should be the easiest to find. (Item Number is the most important item in the inventory example since it identified one item from all others. It is placed on the left margin.)
3 All pages should have a title and page number. Use dates to show when the output was prepared.
4 All columns should be labeled to identify their contents.
5 Avoid abbreviations.

It is easy to put many details on a report and cause overcrowding. In fact one of the most frequent complaints of users is *too many details; too little information*. Your first concern should be to ensure that unnecessary details are avoided. However, there are other features you should select to further enhance readability. Figure 7.21 shows a report designed to tell the user

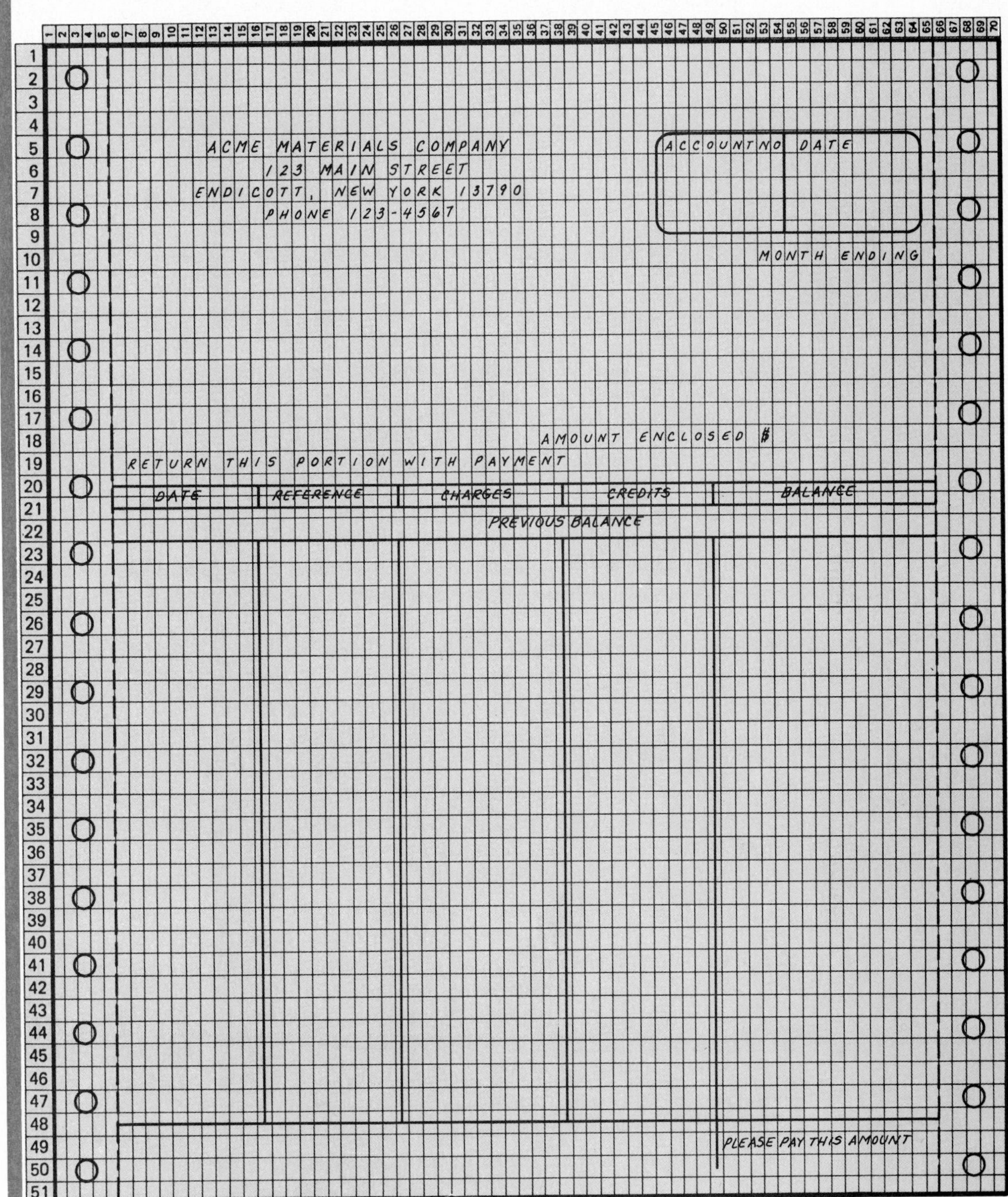

Figure 7.20. Account statement layout form.

				MARCH 1, 1985	
	CUSTOMER OPEN ORDER LISTING				
CUSTOMER	WORK ORDER	PO NUMBER	DUE DATE	AMOUNT	TYPE
ARBOGAST MATERIALS	15678	248-D	10-12-82	41,345.98	STOCK
ARBOGAST MATERIALS	26645	835-L	10-23-82	98,746.77	CUSTOM
ARBOGAST MATERIALS	29840	899-L	10-31-82	15,976.36	STOCK
ARBOGAST MATERIALS	49876	1065-S	11-15-82	9,764,46	STOCK
ARBOGAST MATERIALS	62345	2075-L	12-02-82	76,345.98	CUSTOM
BORGUST CONSTRUCTION CO	9865	78-D-9873	9-15-82	9,677.65	CUSTOM
BORGUST CONSTRUCTION CO	10453	78-D-0032	10-12-82	11,674.23	STOCK
BORGUST CONSTRUCTION CO	11064	78-A-1827	11-15-82	45,848.90	STOCK
BORGUST CONSTRUCTION CO	14087	79-L-8765	1-15-83	23,857.90	STOCK
CARLTON SUPPLY CORP	28239	12287X	9-23-82	78,857.64	CUSTOM
CARLTON SUPPLY CORP	59646	41258S	9-30-82	65,958.89	STOCK
CARLTON SUPPLY CORP	78579	32980X	2-15-83	9,756.89	CUSTOM
DENTON DISTRIBUTING	28576	11582JS	8-30-82	3,856.89	STOCK
DENTON DISTRIBUTING	31459	21382MN	10-01-82	14,644.56	STOCK
***TOTALS				506,333.10	

Figure 7.21. Overcrowded open order report layout with sample data.

about outstanding customer orders. Notice how the designer has limited the number of items on the page, labeled all columns, and added totals. To make it easier to locate customer orders, the details are presented in alphabetical order.

We can further improve this report. Since the customer name repeats, it only needs to be stated when there is a change. For example, print Arbogast Materials for the first order and do not repeat it until the customer name changes (in this example, to Borgust Construction Co.).

The dotted lines between the column headings and the first-order details add emphasis to the heading.

Adding subtotals for each customer and sorting individual details within a customer's orders tells the user more about the orders in a simple manner.

Subtotals printed when the entries for one customer end are called *control breaks*. Control breaks communicate information and add emphasis, both useful to the reader. An additional space between groups is a small price to pay for readability.

When data is unchanging, there is no reason to print it; it does not tell the reader anything new. This principle is used in the right-hand column, TYPE OF ORDER. In order processing, stock orders are routine, while customer orders require special attention. They are treated as exceptions. Therefore, eliminate STOCK. Only CUSTOM is printed when it applies.

Compare the revisions in Figure 7.22 with the earlier report to see the difference in readability and usefulness these changes make.

Designing Display Output

Many of the principles discussed above also apply to designing output that is displayed on CRTs. Keep in mind, however, that you have less space to work

					MARCH 1, 1985
	CUSTOMER OPEN ORDER LISTING				
CUSTOMER	WORK ORDER	PO NUMBER	DUE DATE	AMOUNT	TYPE
ARBOGAST MATERIALS	15678	248-D	10-12-84	41,345.98	
	26645	835-L	10-23-84	98,746.77	CUSTOM
	29840	899-L	10-31-84	15,976.36	
				156,069.11	
	49876	1065-S	11-15-84	9,764,46	
	62345	2075-L	12-02-84	76,345.98	CUSTOM
	*******			242,179.55	
BORGUST CONSTRUCTION CO	9865	78-D-9873	9-15-84	9,677.65	CUSTOM
	10453	78-D-0032	10-12-84	11,674.23	
	11064	78-A-1827	11-15-84	45,848.90	
	14087	79-L-8765	1-15-85	23,857.90	
	*******			91,058.68	
CARLTON SUPPLY CORP	28239	12287X	9-23-84	78,857.64	CUSTOM
	59646	41258S	9-30-84	65,958.89	
				144,816.53	
	78579	32980X	2-15-85	9,756.89	CUSTOM
	*******			154,573.42	
DENTON DISTRIBUTING	28576	11582JS	8-30-84	3,856.89	
	31459	21382MN	10-01-84	14,644.56	
	*******			18,521.45	

Figure 7.22. Modified open order report layout.

with compared with most print pages. You will also have to give instructions to the user about how to use the display. With a printed output, people know how to search through a report, how to turn to the next page, and what steps to take when finished with the report. You cannot make any of these assumptions in designing displays.

SCREEN DESIGN

A layout form for displays guides your design (Figure 7.23). Each display page is commonly called a *screen*. Proper design of the screen includes a title and column headings (for example, Price Retrieval System, item number, package, category, and units). The data items for each column are shown as discussed above for printed output.

Information instructing the users how to proceed is generally shown at the bottom of the screen. You should tell them how to retrieve the next screen of information ("PRESS THE N . . .") and how to leave the system ("PRESS X TO EXIT"). Your design should also tell the programmer to write the software in such a way that, if the user presses another key and

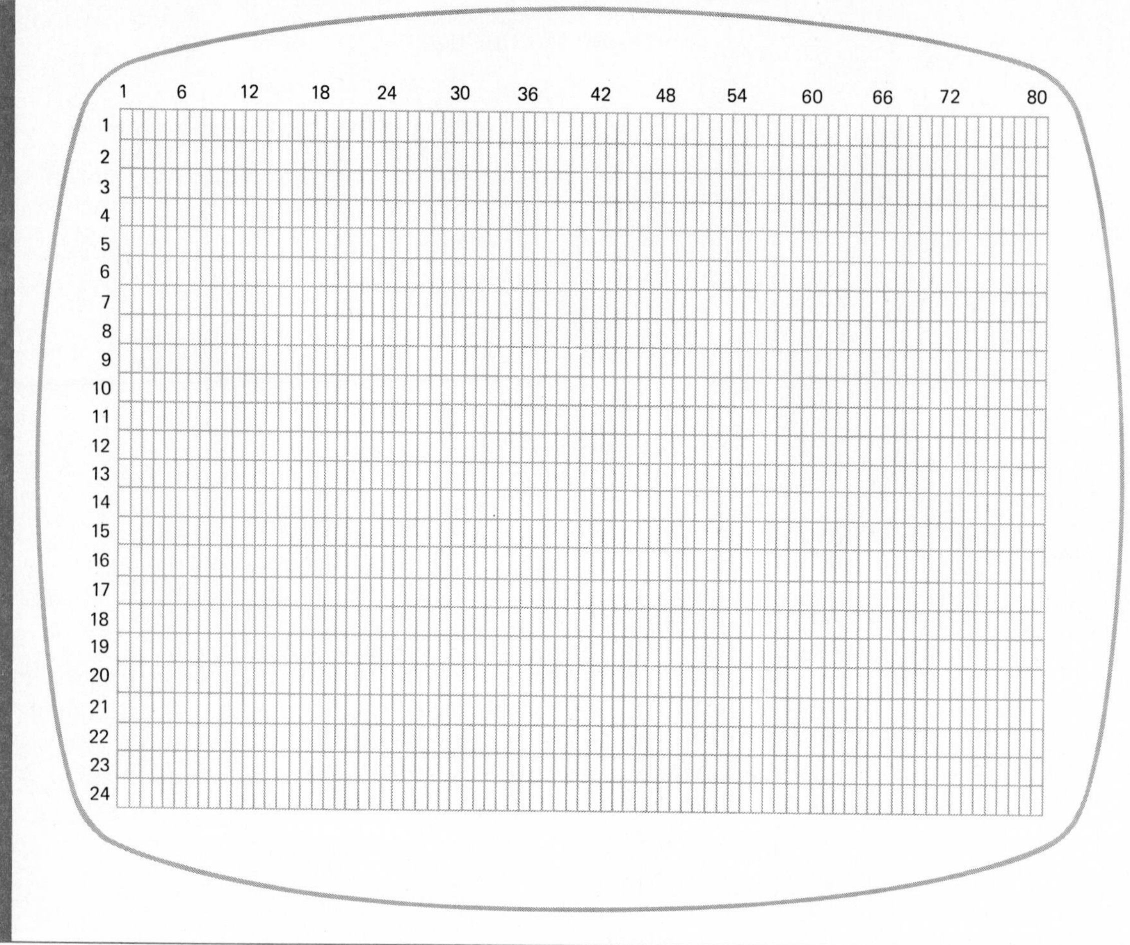

Figure 7.23. Layout form for display screen.

could cause an error, the software will catch the entry and prevent the error. For example, if the operator depresses a Q (or for that matter, any key other than N or X in this specific design), the program should detect that and refuse to take any action or do any processing until a correct key is depressed. (The chapter on input design examines these concerns in detail.)

MULTIPLE SCREEN DESIGN

Frequently designers use multiple screens to give users the information they need. The first screen gives general information. By depressing a specified key, the user retrieves a second screen containing the details. Figure 7.24 presents such a two-screen sequence. The first shows data about many different products—one is briefly described on each detail line of the display. The user scans the list and selects one requiring more explanation.

PRICE RETRIEVAL SYSTEM 12/15/8X

ITEM NUMBER	DESCRIPTION	PACKAGE	CATEGORY	UNITS
10-0305	ENDUST	QT	WAX	EACH
10-0354	VISTA	QT	WAX	EACH
10-0578	FINAL TOUCH	GAL	LAUNDRY	4/CASE
10-0580	FINAL TOUCH	5 GAL	LAUNDRY	EACH
10-0612	COLD WATER ALL	30 GAL	LAUNDRY	DRUM
10-0625	LP-RINSE-AID	GAL	DISHWASH	4/CASE
10-0628	LP-RINSE-AID	5 GAL	DISHWASH	EACH
10-0630	LP-RINSE-AID	30 GAL	DISHWASH	EACH
10-7501	LSI STAIN REMOVER	5 GAL	DISHWASH	EACH
10-7503	LSI STAIN REMOVER BLEACH	5 GAL	DISHWASH	EACH
10-7505	LSI ALKALI	5 GAL	DISHWASH	EACH
10-7507	LSI FABRIC SOFTENER	5 GAL	DISHWASH	EACH
10-7510	LSI SOUR	5 GAL	DISHWASH	EACH

PRESS D FOR DETAIL

Figure 7.24A. General information screen for pricing system.

Figure 24*a* shows the *cursor,* a bar of light serving as a pointer to tell the system and user where to look on the display, at item 10-7503. When the user depressed the D key (meaning "find details for this item"), the screen in Figure 7.24*b* is displayed and much more detail is presented.

The above technique is common in designs for CRT displays. It allows

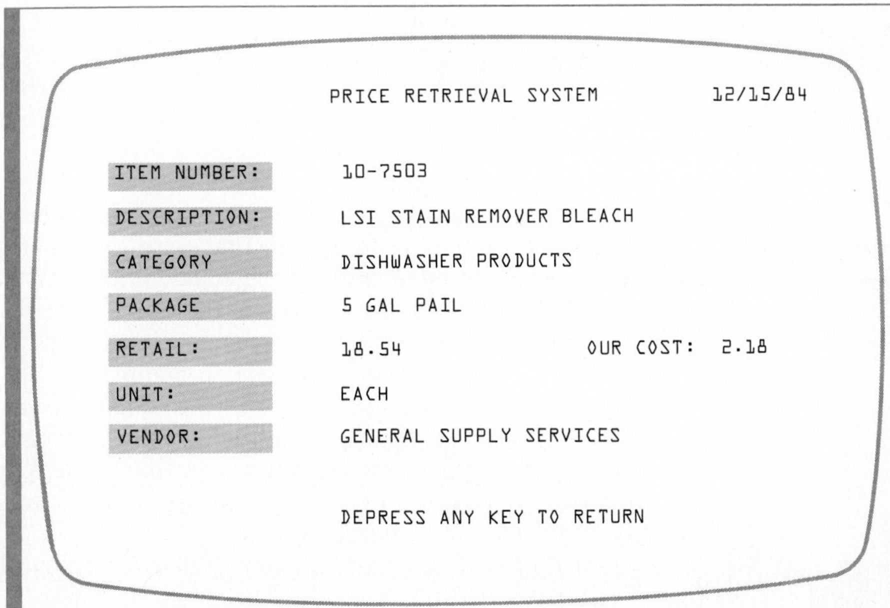

Figure 7.24B. Detail screen for pricing system.

users to browse through the data quickly and identify each item about which more detail is needed. At the same time, the "explosion" into detail for one specific item on a second (or even third) screen maintains the readability of the first screen by requiring display of only enough detail to identify the item wanted.

As we move into greater detail on design in our discussions, we will be looking at additional features for design of display screens.

Enhanced Business Presentations

Analysts are increasingly supplementing tabular and narrative information with color and graphic enhancements. Hardware and software capabilities for such enhancements are increasing in availability, while the costs of components are dropping. Systems ranging in size from very small microcomputers to the largest mainframe systems can selectively be enhanced with easy-to-use software packages that print and display in color and with graphic shapes.

BUSINESS GRAPHICS

Business graphics is not itself a new area. Management presentations have been enhanced by graphics and visual aids for a long time. However, the ability to produce satisfactory low-cost graphics by computer is relatively recent. This capability has mixed blessings for users. While graphics can enhance information presentation, there is the chance that many presentations will suffer because the graphics will be poorly used. At the same time, few managers are willing to accept computer-generated graphics as a replacement for traditional reports. Business information will continue to be based on numeric data, although supplements will be encouraged.

Business graphics consist of five types of charts: pie, curve, step, bar, and map charts. *Pie charts* describe portions of a whole associated with a particular development or activity. For example, a firm wishing to describe the percentage of expenditures allocated to manufacturing applications can show how it compares with other categories through a pie chart. *Curve charts* show change in performance along a scale over multiple time periods. A horizontal scale indicates time (days, months, years) and a vertical scale measures the units of interest (such as dollars, percentages, or number of units). Several items overlaid on the same chart enable the reader to compare the change in one item compared to others. For example, comparing the increase in expenditures for manufacturing systems, marketing systems, and personnel applications on the same curve chart emphasizes the overall trend in expenditures, while it indicates which category of expense had the greatest change. No more than three to five lines should be shown on a single chart. If different line widths are used to convey information, a maximum of three different widths is suggested.

Step and *bar charts* also show changes in categories. However, rather than connecting each individual data point (such as the manufacturing system expense during one specific year), they measure each data point from the horizontal scale up to the proper level on a vertical scale. Individual periods may be discrete, as in the bar chart, or they may be shown side by side, as the step chart does. Several different items are often overlaid to compare categories from year to year.

Maps offer an effective way to show how performance varies across geographic areas. You see weather maps used frequently to show differences in temperature, precipitation, or sunshine. A quick glance tells you which areas of the country are having warm or cold, wet or dry weather. Computer-generated maps are equally effective to show sales or market penetration.

The charts should be annotated to indicate the scale used, the meaning of each line or shape, and what the chart represents. Business graphics supplement other information; they do not replace it. Therefore, few additional words are needed. Business graphics are like road signs: they must make their point quickly or the reader will lose interest. Therefore, they should contain few words and a lot of graphic information.

A familiar format is also essential to communicate a message through graphics. The five forms of charts discussed above are universal in use. The reader does not need to spend time understanding how to use the chart, but can focus attention on its content. This is ideal.

Business graphics may not save decision-maker time or reduce the volume of information produced by the system. That depends on the individual users and other design features of the information system, such as how well nongraphic information is prepared. However, if properly designed, they are excellent supplements for tables and narrative reports. They may communicate information to some people who would otherwise overlook important details.

COLOR PRESENTATION

Color facilities are also increasing on both large and small computer systems. However, like graphics, improper use can hinder rather than help users and management productivity. Color should enhance, not replace, good output design. In fact, a good practice for analysts is to first design the output in the best form possible. Only after that is completed should the use of color be considered.

In general, four or less colors on a screen or report are suggested. The more colors used, the greater the sizes of the data or shapes must be to communicate information. If information is displayed visually, less information can be shown clearly when four colors are used than when only two are included in the design.

The analyst must take care to maintain consistent color usage across output and reports. For example, the color red is excellent for highlighting exceptions (such as in management exception reporting) and problems.

Green and blue, in contrast, are best for representing normal situations. If the analysts specify these color usages on one report in a system, they should be used consistently for all reporting in the system.

The brightest colors emphasize the most important information on a display screen. Bright colors include white, turquoise, and pink. Dark colors include magenta, red, green, and blue.

As indicated above, neither color nor use of graphics will enhance or replace a poor design. However, they may improve the results managers and users achieve when working with system output.

SUMMARY

The design of systems includes two levels of activity that are called logical and physical design. During logical design, analysts develop the specifications (the blueprint) for the new system, including the details of output, input, files, and procedures. These specifications are used by programmers, who translate them into the physical design—the programs and files that do the required work. Throughout the design, user requirement data is used, including the data dictionary, to decide about features to include in the new system.

To the user, the output is one of the most important features—sometimes the only reason for sponsoring the project. Therefore the analyst must select output methods that communicate information effectively.

Output may be produced using a variety of devices, including printers, film recorders, punches, and badge printers. Impact printing has an additional advantage because it can be used in carbon or carbonless processes to produce multiple copies of output. Display and audio output are also effective if properly used, although the latter has as yet only limited applications.

To specify the logical design, analysts make a layout, a mock-up showing the location of information. Both constant and variable details are marked and summaries, totals, and control breaks are indicated to emphasize specific points of information. When designing screens for CRT display, analysts may find they need to use multiple screens to present information in a form that is easy to read. Readability must be a guiding objective when designing systems output.

CASE STUDY FOR CHAPTER 7
SUMMARY OF REPORTS AND DOCUMENTS

The systems analysts responsible for the output design of the new order entry/receivables system of Valley Industries have specified 14 specific printed output items. In addition, display screens to show responses to specific user inquiries have also been designed.

For each of the output designs included in this section, information is presented to indicate who the user or recipient of the output is. The frequency with which each individual output report or document will be generated is also identified.

EXTERNAL OUTPUT

There are five separate output or report items (Figures C7.1 through C7.5) intended for distibution outside of Valley Industries:

1 Order acknowledgement
2 Invoice
3 Bill of lading
4 Monthly statement
5 Delinquency notice

The bill of lading is the shipping information prepared when an order is transferred to the shipper or transporter. In this design, a delinquency field has been added to assist Valley management in collecting amounts owed them and to aid in reducing the perpetual accounts receivable balance.

Each of the five documents listed above are preprinted forms. The document layouts specify Valley's name, address, and company logo, as well as column headings. The information is preprinted on the form. The remainder of the variable information will be generated by the computer system preparing each document. To indicate data item sizes, the analysts have marked in length and type information using the symbols X, to indicate alphanumeric data, and 9, to show numeric data. These details are shown on the first three documents only. We omitted the length specifications on the remainder of the documents in reproducing them here. Normally, length and type specifications are included on all documents before they are turned over to the programmers.

INTERNAL OUTPUT

Nine different output items (Figures C7.6 to C7.14) have been designed for internal company use. Registers, reports, and special documents are specified.

The three registers used in the new system are:

1 Batch update register
2 Invoice/accounts receivable register
3 Cash receipts and adjustments register

The registers are intended to assist in auditing and controlling system activities and will aid management in ensuring that transactions enter the system properly and in monitoring any changes and adjustments made to customer and accounting records. The specific controls included in this design are discussed in greater detail in the input portion of the design.

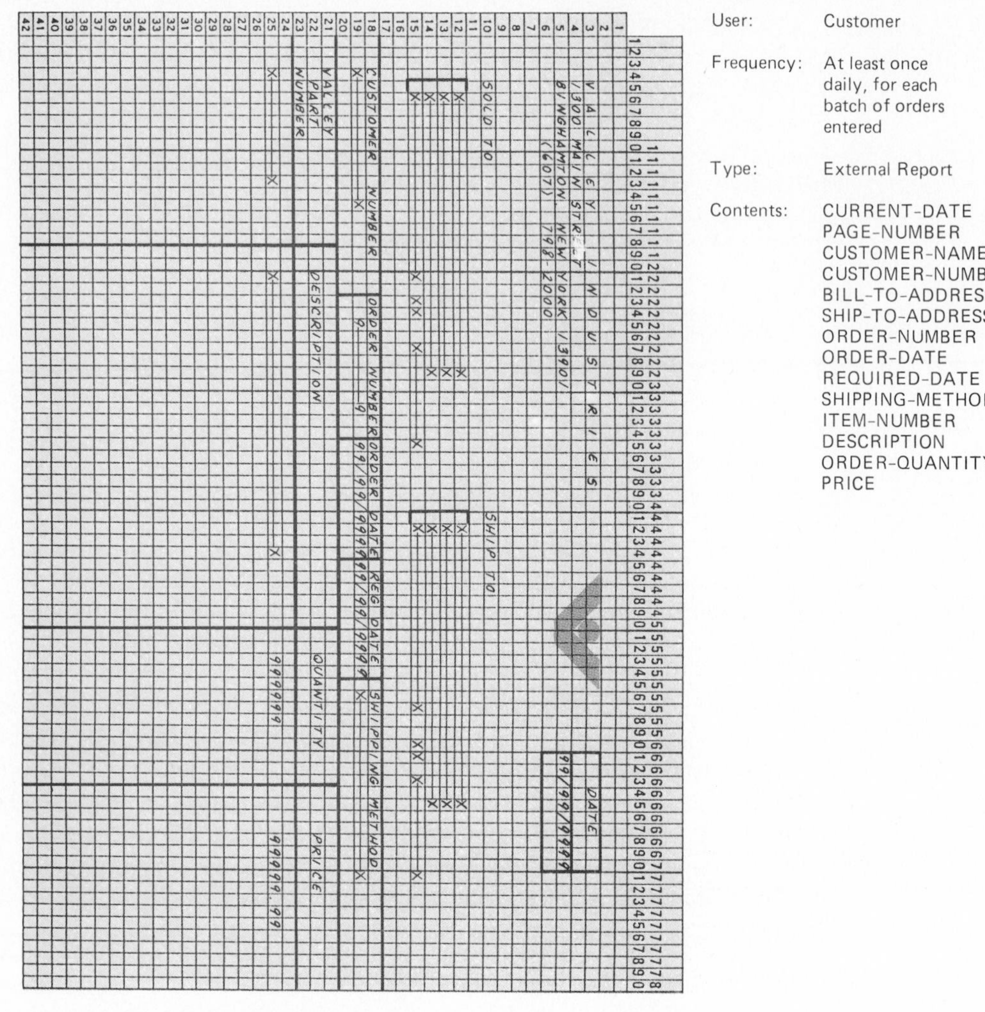

User: Customer

Frequency: At least once daily, for each batch of orders entered

Type: External Report

Contents: CURRENT-DATE
PAGE-NUMBER
CUSTOMER-NAME
CUSTOMER-NUMBER
BILL-TO-ADDRESS
SHIP-TO-ADDRESS
ORDER-NUMBER
ORDER-DATE
REQUIRED-DATE
SHIPPING-METHOD
ITEM-NUMBER
DESCRIPTION
ORDER-QUANTITY
PRICE

Figure C7.1. Invoice.

The other internal output items include:

1 Order card
2 Ready-to-ship notice
3 Open order report
4 Invoice summary
5 Apply invoices to master files
6 Aged trial balance

These documents reflect the interactive nature of the system by the replacement of manual document preparation with automatic generation

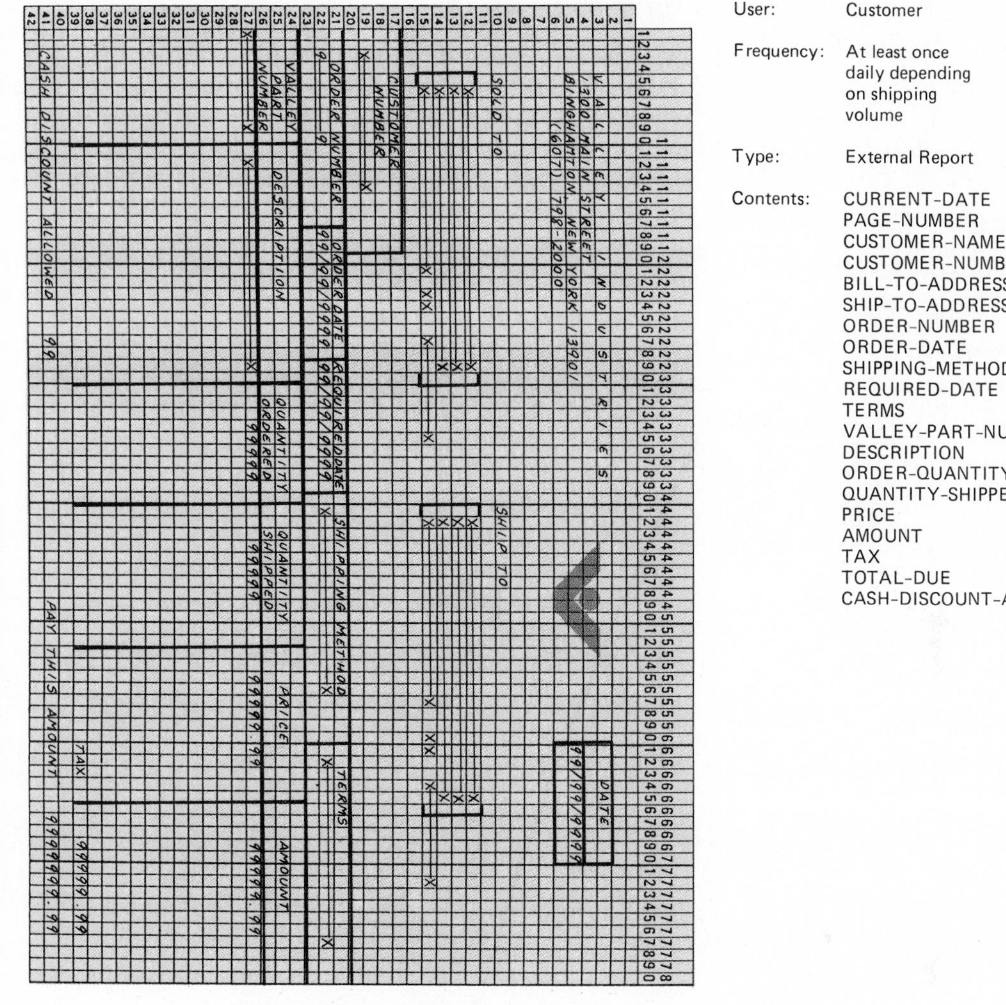

User:	Customer
Frequency:	At least once daily depending on shipping volume
Type:	External Report
Contents:	CURRENT-DATE PAGE-NUMBER CUSTOMER-NAME CUSTOMER-NUMBER BILL-TO-ADDRESS SHIP-TO-ADDRESS ORDER-NUMBER ORDER-DATE SHIPPING-METHOD REQUIRED-DATE TERMS VALLEY-PART-NUMBER DESCRIPTION ORDER-QUANTITY QUANTITY-SHIPPED PRICE AMOUNT TAX TOTAL-DUE CASH-DISCOUNT-ALLOWED

Figure C7.2. Order acknowledgement.

through the system. Order cards and ready-to-ship notices will be produced by the system.

The audit and control emphasis built into this system is also evident by the invoice processing report and the aged trial balance. Through these reports, the users can monitor systems activities and determine that account activities and balances are correct.

DISPLAY SCREENS

The systems design includes display screens that enable users to enter inquiries about customer activities and to receive information in response to their inquiries on a video display. Three output display screens have been designed:

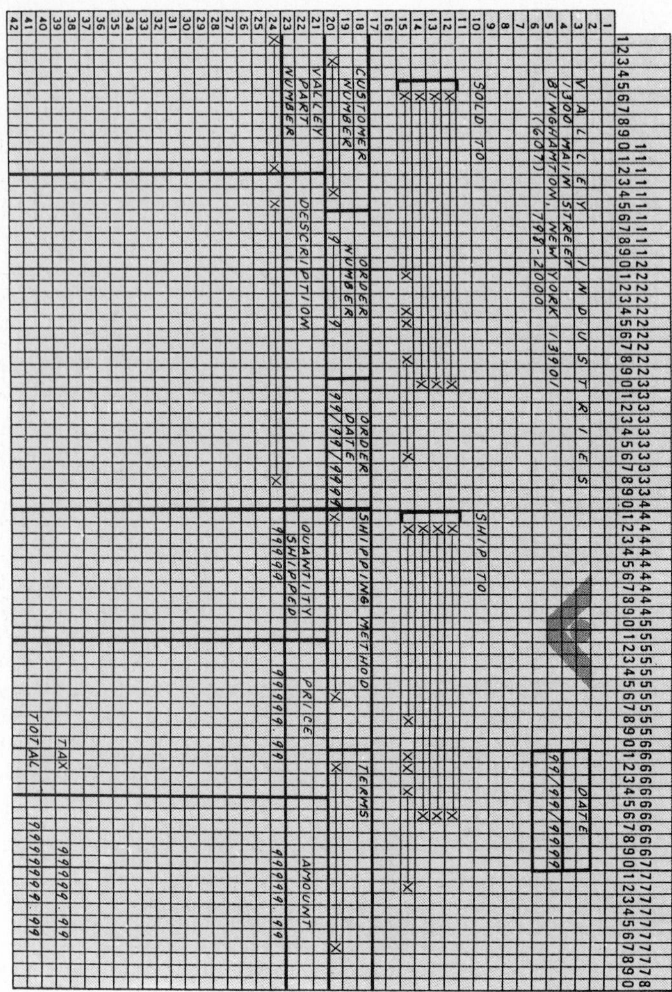

User: Invoice Clerk

Frequency: At least once daily, whenever invoices are prepared

Type: External Report

Contants: CURRENT-DATE
PAGE-NUMBER
CUSTOMER-NAME
CUSTOMER-NUMBER
BILL-TO-ADDRESS
SHIP-TO-ADDRESS
ORDER-NUMBER
ORDER-DATE
SHIPPING-METHOD
TERMS
ITEM-NUMBER
DESCRIPTION
QUANTITY-SHIPPED
PRICE
AMOUNT

Figure C7.3. Bill of lading.

1 Customer orders inquiry screen
2 Customer status inquiry screen
3 Accounts receivable open item inquiry screen

These display screens, listed above, will also be included with the input screens discussed in the next chapter. The required entry of data to invoke the displays will be examined at that time.

DATA DICTIONARY

The data included on each output is shown with the output layout. The data item names listed for each output are identical to those in the data dictionary.

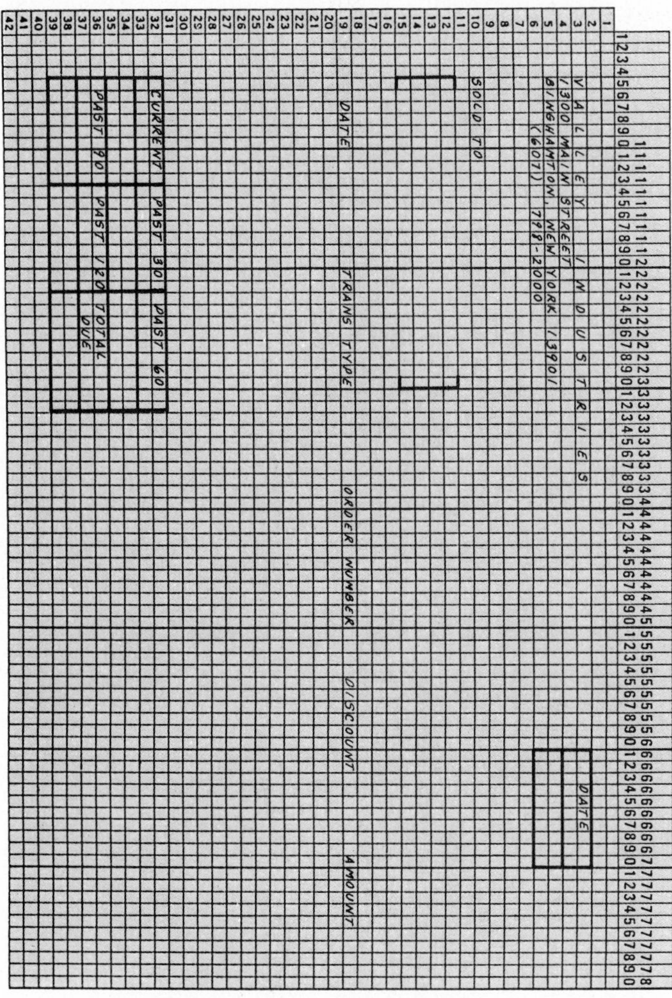

User: Customer

Frequency: At period closing

Type: External Report

Contents: CURRENT-DATE
PAGE-NUMBER
CUSTOMER-NAME
BILL-TO-ADDRESS
DATE-TRANS
TRANS-TYPE
DISCOUNT
AMOUNT
ORDER-NUMBER
CURRENT-DUE
PAST 30
PAST 60
PAST 90
PAST 120
ACCOUNT-BALANCE

Figure C7.4. Statement.

You may have noticed that we have added some details that were not found in the original analysis. For example, the user requirements clearly indicated that better information about customer activities and account balances were needed. Therefore, the analysts included aging information to show current, 30-, 60-, 90-, and 120-day account balances. The data dictionary was expanded to include those data elements.

The data dictionary developed during the design also includes other data used to produce the report. For example, data elements needed to develop the proper audit and control totals have been added.

As you examine the report layouts, you will see how requirements have been translated into design features.

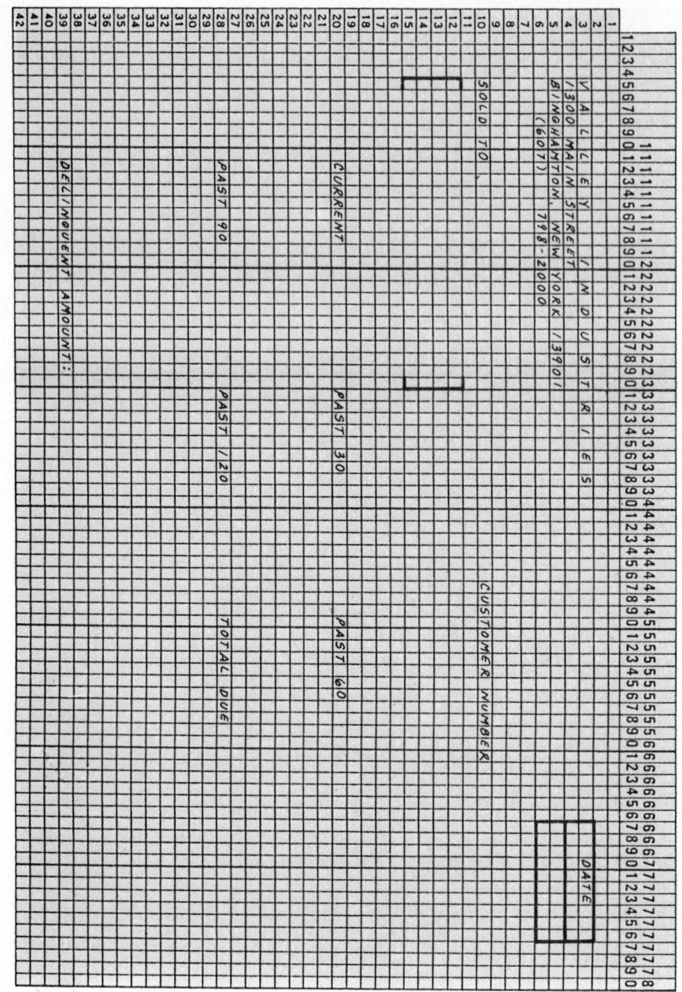

User:	Customer
Frequency:	At period closing
Type:	External Report
Content:	CURRENT-DATE CUSTOMER-NAME BILL-TO-ADDRESS CUSTOMER-NUMBER CURRENT-DUE PAST 30 PAST 60 PAST 90 PAST 120 DELINQUENT-AMOUNT ACCOUNT-BALANCE

Figure C7.5. Delinquency notice.

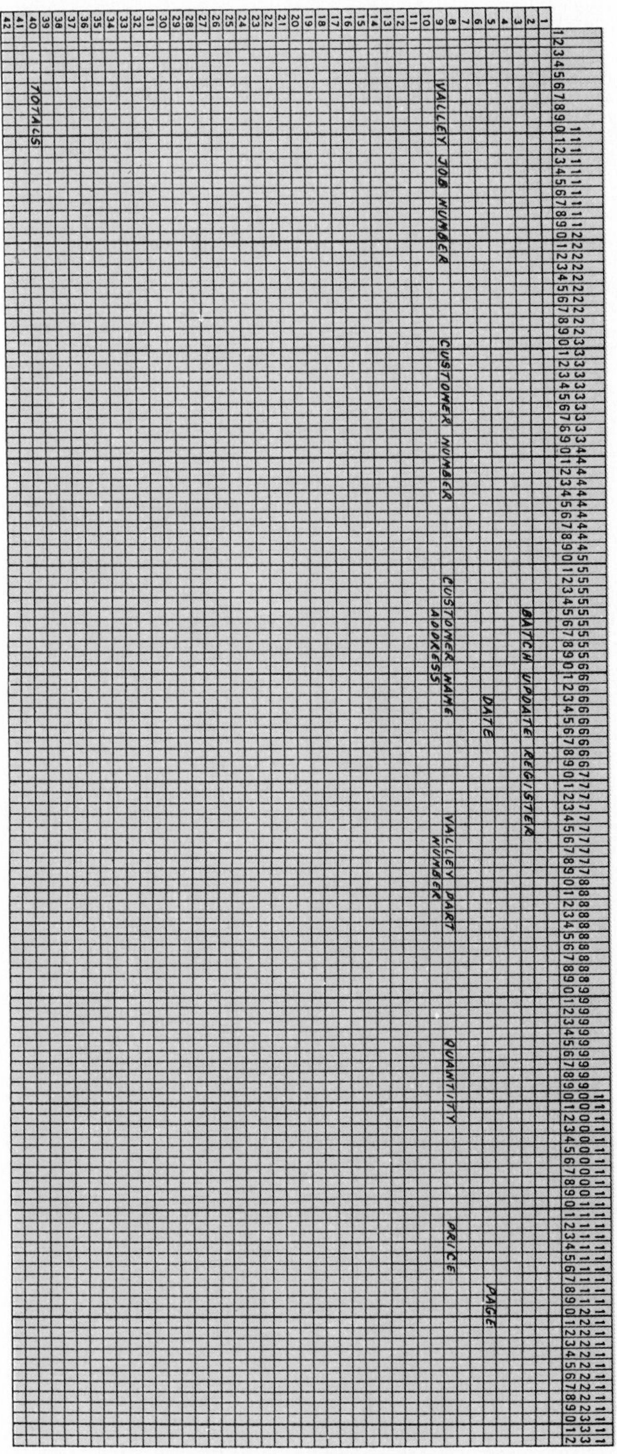

Figure C7.6. Batch update register.

User:	Carbo Production Mgr.
Frequency:	At least once daily
Type:	User Report
Contents:	CURRENT-DATE PAGE-NUMBER REGISTER-TITLE VALLEY-JOB-NUMBER ORDER-NUMBER CUSTOMER-NAME BILL-TO-ADDRESS VALLEY-PART-NUMBER ORDER-QUANTITY PRICE TOTAL-NUMBER-ORDERS TOTAL-$-AMOUNT

User:	Carbo Production Mgr.
Frequency:	At least once daily, depending on volume of invoices
Type:	User Report
Contents:	CURRENT-DATE PAGE-NUMBER INVOICE-DATE INVOICE-NUMBER CUSTOMER-NUMBER CUSTOMER-NAME INVOICE-AMOUNT SPECIAL-CHARGES SHIPPING CHARGE DISCOUNT TAX INVOICE-TOTAL TOTAL-SALES TOTAL-SPECIAL-CHGS TOTAL-FREIGHT TOTAL-DISCOUNT TOTAL-TAXES TOTAL-INVOICES

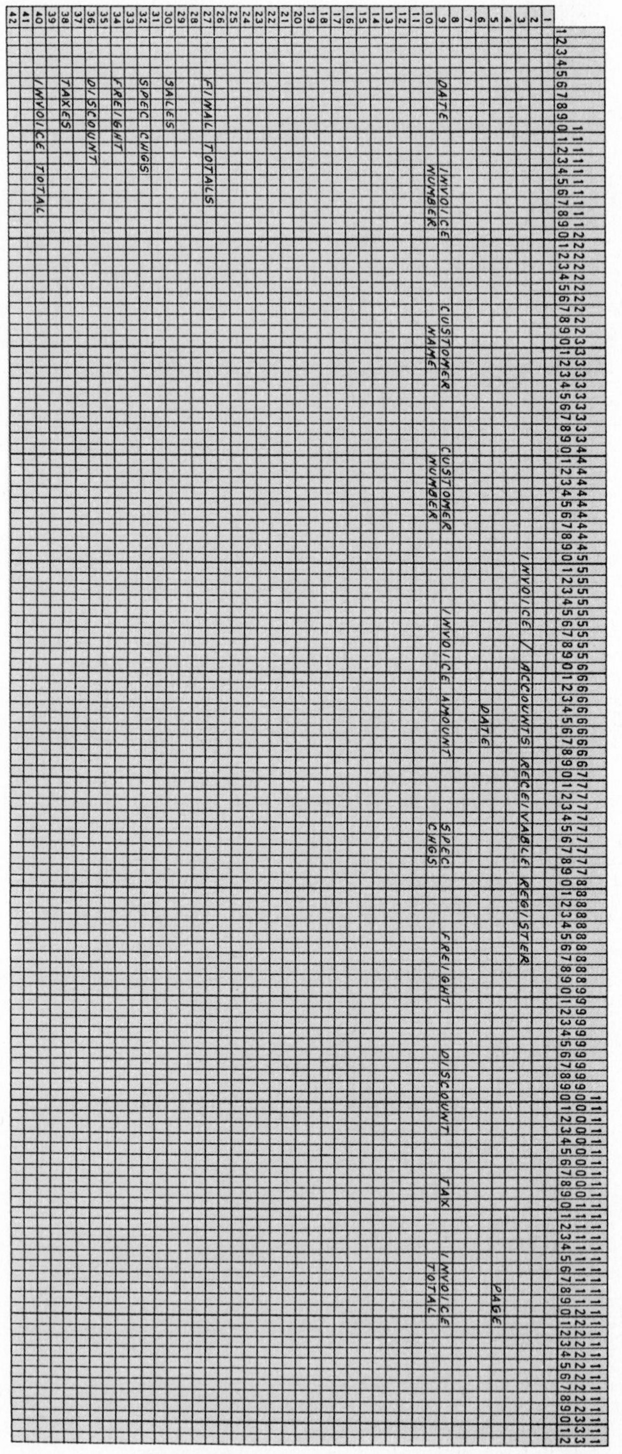

Figure C7.7. Invoice/accounts receivable register.

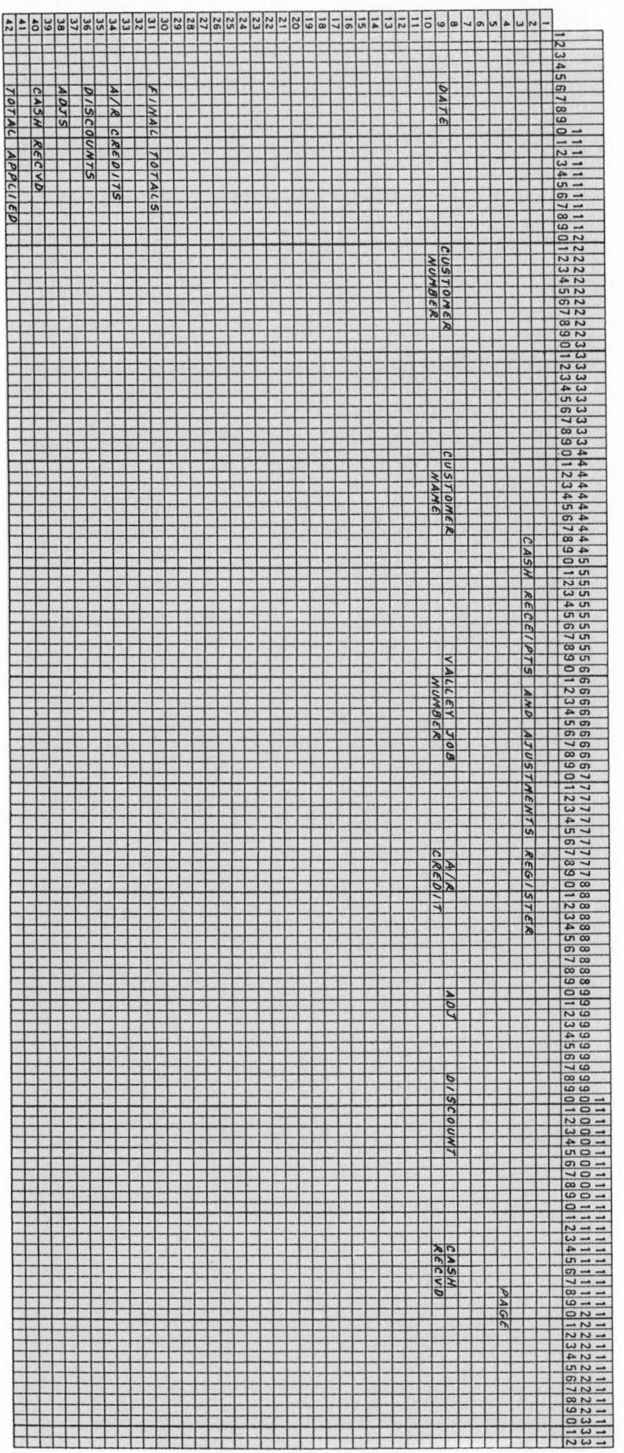

User:	Carbo Production Mgr.
Frequency:	Daily
Type:	User Report
Contents:	CURRENT-DATE PAGE-NUMBER A/R-DATE CUSTOMER-NUMBER CUSTOMER-NAME VALLEY-JOB-NUMBER A/R-CREDITS DISCOUNT ADJUSTMENTS CASH-RECEIVED TOTAL-A/R-CREDITS TOTAL-DISCOUNTS TOTAL-ADJUSTMENTS TOTAL-CASH-RECEIVED TOTAL-APPLIED

Figure C7.8. Cash and receipts adjustments register.

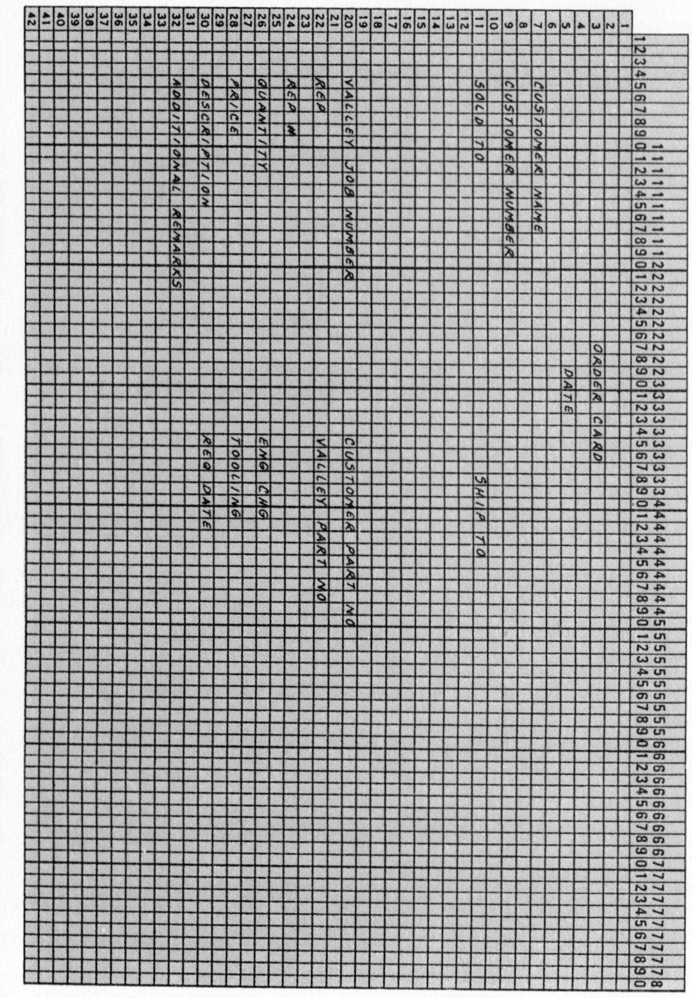

User:	Carbo Production Mgr.
Frequency:	At least once daily, for each batch of orders entered
Type:	User Report
Contents:	CURRENT-DATE PAGE-NUMBER CUSTOMER-NAME CUSTOMER-NUMBER BILL-TO-ADDRESS SHIP-TO-ADDRESS VALLEY-JOB-NUMBER REP-NAME REP-NUMBER QUANTITY PRICE DESCRIPTION CUSTOMER-PART-NUMBER VALLEY-PART-NUMBER ENG-CHARGE TOOLING REQ-DATE ADDITIONAL-REMARKS

Figure C7.9. Order card.

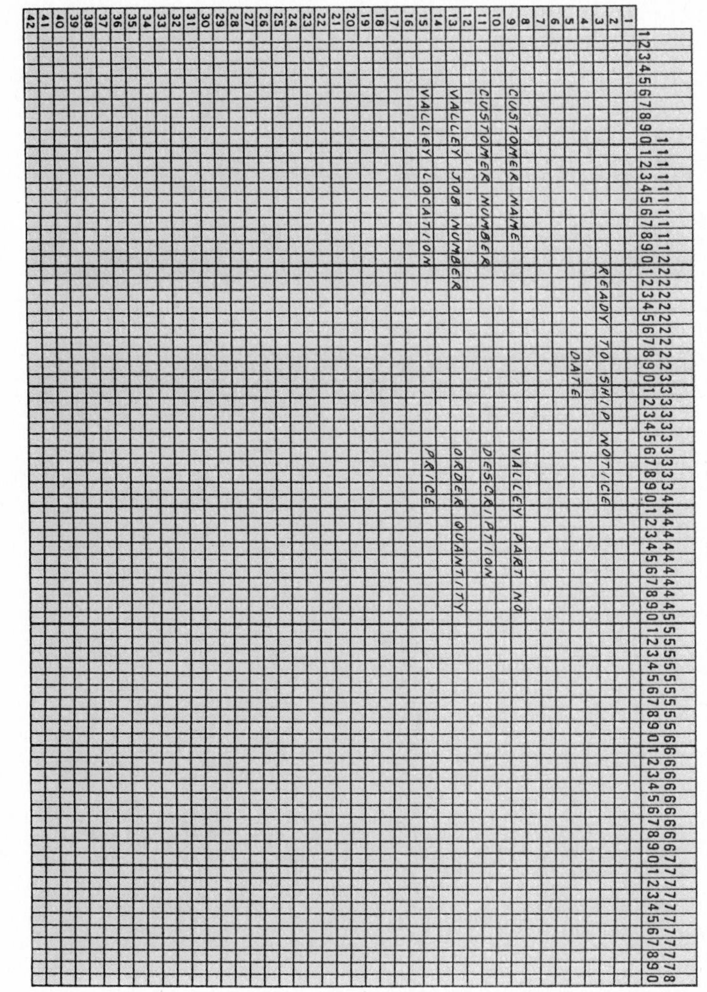

User:	Invoicing Clerk
Frequency:	At least once daily, depending on production volume
Type:	User Report
Contents:	CURRENT-DATE CUSTOMER-NAME CUSTOMER-NUMBER PRODUCTION-LOCATION VALLEY-PART-NUMBER DESCRIPTION ORDER-QUANTITY PRICE VALLEY-JOB-NUMBER

Figure C7.10. Ready-to-ship-notice.

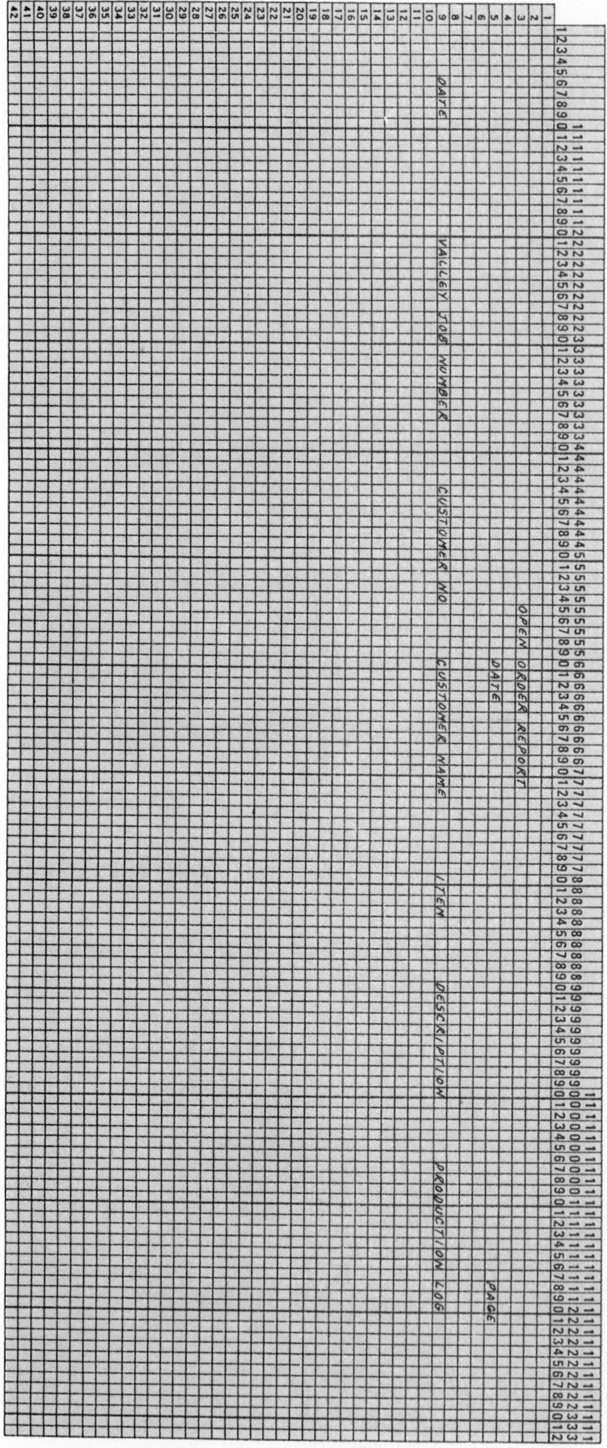

Figure C7.11. Open order report.

User:	Carbo Production Mgr.
Frequency:	Run as required, at least once weekly
Type:	User Report
Contents:	CURRENT-DATE PAGE-NUMBER DATE VALLEY-JOB-NUMBER CUSTOMER-NUMBER CUSTOMER-NAME ITEM DESCRIPTION PRODUCTION-LOCATION

*User selects sorting by one of the following:

- Date
- Valley-job-number
- Customer-number
- Item

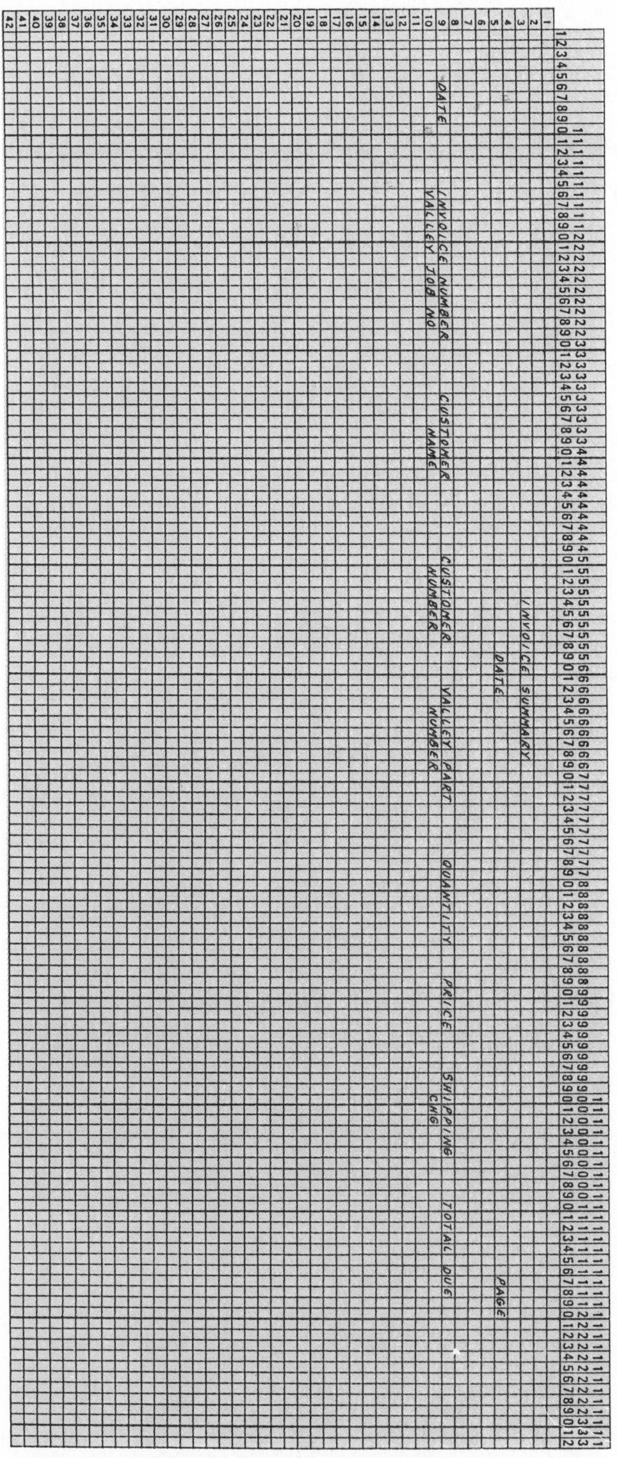

User: Olson
Jacobson

Frequency: Weekly

Type: User Report

Contents: CURRENT-DATE
PAGE-NUMBER
DATE
INVOICE-NUMBER
CUSTOMER-NAME
CUSTOMER-NUMBER
VALLEY-PART-NUMBER
ORDER-QUANTITY
PRICE
SHIPPING-CHARGE
TOTAL-DUE
VALLEY-JOB-NUMBER

Figure C7.12. Invoice summary.

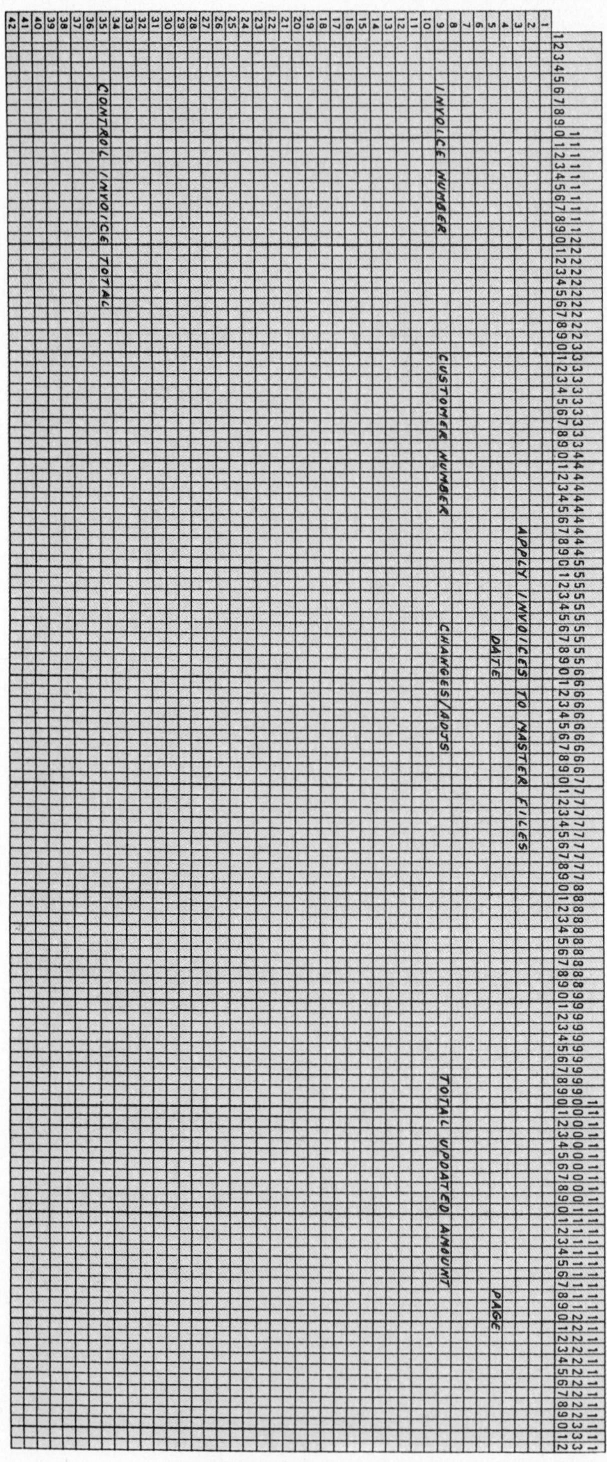

User:	Carbo Production Mgr. (for audit purposes)
Frequency:	At least once daily, for each batch of invoices
Type:	User Report
Contents:	CURRENT-DATE PAGE-NUMBER INVOICE-NUMBER CUSTOMER-NUMBER TOTAL-UPDATED-AMT CONTROL-INVOICE-TOTAL CHANGES/ADJS

Figure C7.13. Apply invoices to master files.

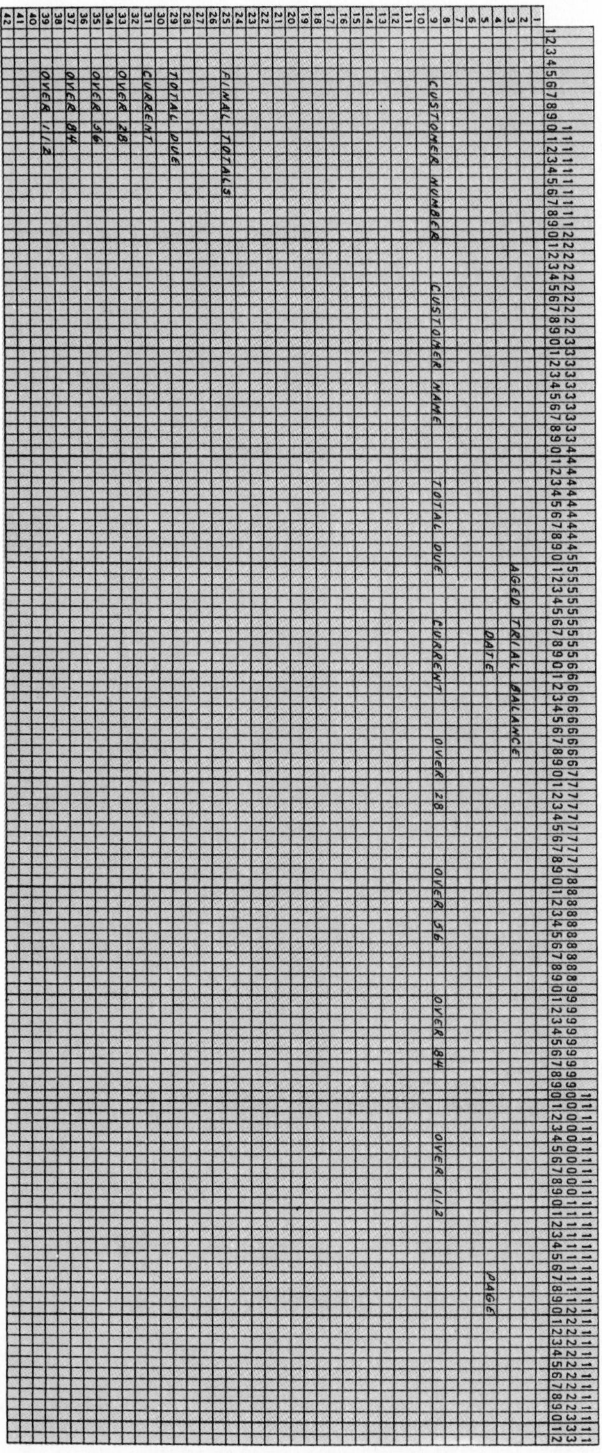

Figure C7.14. Aged trial balance.

User:	Carbo Production Mgr. Olson Jacobson
Frequency:	At period closing
Type:	User Report
Contents:	CURRENT-DATE PAGE-NUMBER CUSTOMER-NUMBER CUSTOMER-NAME TOTAL-DUE CURRENT-DUE PAST 30 PAST 60 PAST 90 PAST 120 TOTAL-TOTAL-DUE TOTAL-CURRENT-DUE TOTAL-PAST-30 TOTAL-PAST-60 TOTAL-PAST-90 TOTAL-PAST-120

	TYPE	LENGTH
ACCOUNTS RECEIVABLE		
CUSTOMER-DETAILS		
CUSTOMER-ACCOUNT-DETAILS		
APPROVAL-DISAPPROPAL		
ORDER-DETAILS		
MANAGEMENT-APPROVAL-DISAPPROVAL	X	1
BATCH-CONTROL-DETAILS		
BATCH-NUMBER	N	5
WORKSTATION-IDENTIFICATION	N	3
BATCH-DATE	N	6
BATCH-RECORD-NUMBER	N	5
BILL-TO-ADDRESS		
BILL-TO-STREET	C	24
BILL-TO-CITY	C	16
BILL-TO-STATE	C	2
BILL-TO-POSTAL-CODE	C	9
CHANGES/ADJS	C	8
CONTROL/ADJS	C	8
CURRENT-DATE	N	6
CUSTOMER ACCOUNT DETAILS		
CUSTOMER-NUMBER	C	12
ACCOUNT-BALANCE	N	8.2
CREDIT-LIMIT	N	8.2
ACCOUNT-STATUS	C	1
CURRENT-DUE	N	8.2
DELINQUENT-AMOUNT	N	8.2
PAST-30	N	8.2
PAST-60	N	8.2
PAST-90	N	9.2
PAST-120	N	8.2
OPEN-ORDER-COUNT	N	3
CUSTOMER-DETAILS		
CUSTOMER-NUMBER	C	12
CUSTOMER-NAME	C	24
BILL-TO-ADDRESS		
SHIP-TO-ADDRESS		
TAX-CODE	N	2
TELEPHONE	N	10
INVOICE		
INVOICE-DETAILS		
ORDER-NUMBER	N	8
VALLEY-JOB-NUMBER	N	8
INVOICE-NUMBER	N	8
INVOICE-DATE	N	6
SPECIAL-CHARGES	N	5.2
SPECIAL-CHARGE-DESCRIPTION	N	16
ITEM-DETAILS		
SHIPPING-CHARGE	N	5.2
AMOUNT	N	5.2
TAX DETAILS		
CASH-DISCOUNT-ALLOWED	N	2
TOTAL-INVOICE-AMOUNT	N	8.2
CUSTOMER-DETAILS		
INVOICE-SUMMARY		
TOTAL-SALES	N	8.2
TOTAL-SPECIAL-CHGS	N	8.2
TOTAL-FREIGHT	N	8.2
TOTAL-DISCOUNT	N	8.2
TOTAL-TAXES	N	8.2
TOTAL-INVOICE	N	8.2

Figure C7.15. Data dictionary for new order processing and accounts receivable system

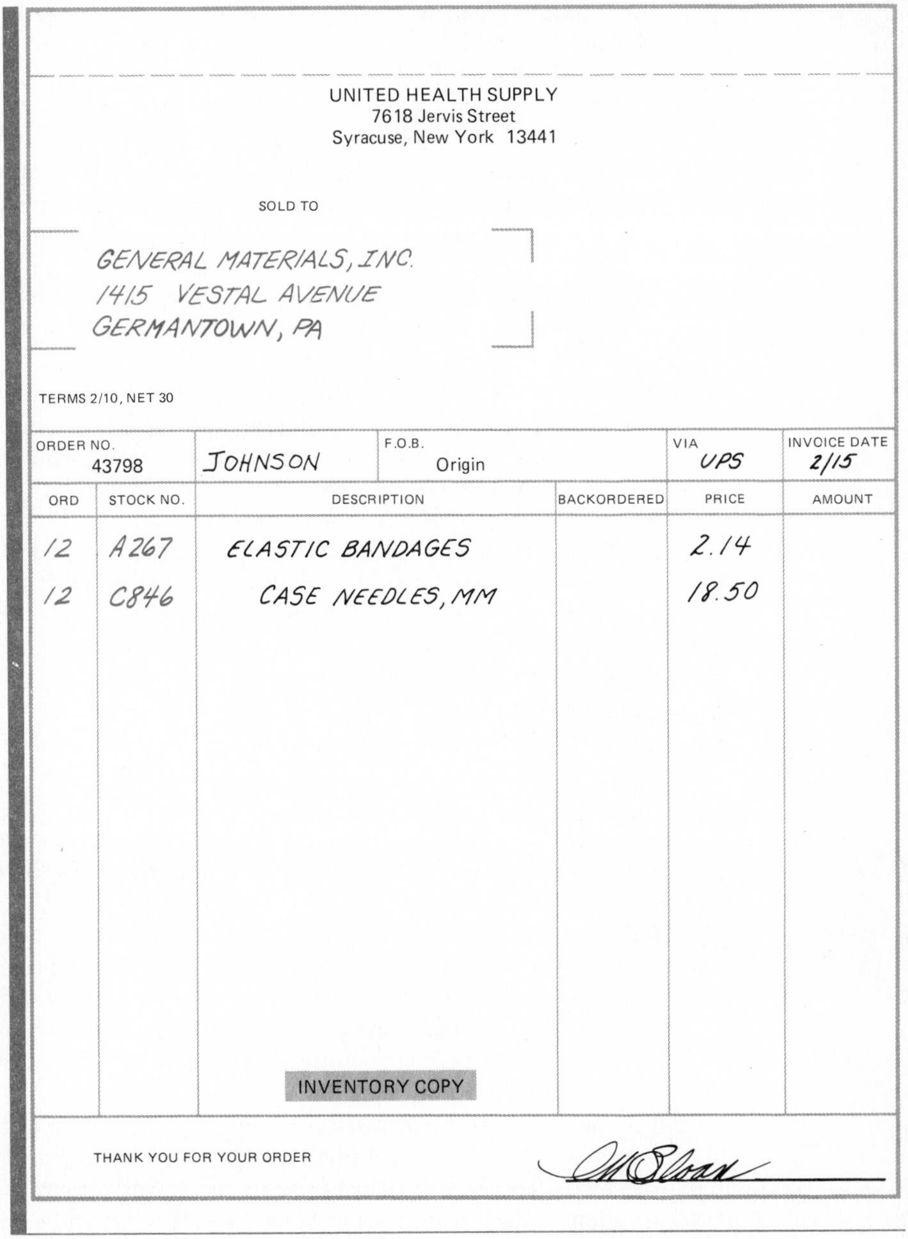

UNITED HEALTH SUPPLY
7618 Jervis Street
Syracuse, New York 13441

SOLD TO

GENERAL MATERIALS, INC.
1415 VESTAL AVENUE
GERMANTOWN, PA

TERMS 2/10, NET 30

ORDER NO.			F.O.B.		VIA	INVOICE DATE
43798		JOHNSON	Origin		UPS	2/15
ORD	STOCK NO.	DESCRIPTION		BACKORDERED	PRICE	AMOUNT
12	A267	ELASTIC BANDAGES			2.14	
12	C846	CASE NEEDLES, MM			18.50	

INVENTORY COPY

THANK YOU FOR YOUR ORDER

Figure 8.3. Inventory copy of sales slip.

sales tax, and draw a grand total. The data entry to do all this is quite simple.

Figure 8.3 contains an inventory withdrawal form, designed for use in either a batch or on-line environment. The items the operator should supply are in color. Those the system best retrieves or calculates are in black. The data items DESCRIPTION, UNIT PRICE, and DATE are included for the benefit of the customers who may wish to have these details listed for their records. However, when data is entered into the system, only quantity and item number are necessary if the other details are stored in secondary storage.

Design of Source Document

The *source document* is the form on which data is initially captured, i.e., recorded. For example, the inventory withdrawal form used in Figure 8.3 is the source document for recording transaction data that will enter the information system. To decide how source documents should be designed to capture data that will enter the system, the analyst asks the following questions:

1 Is the data in a form that is usable and readable by the system?
2 What method is best for entering data while still minimizing the amount of input, the number of errors in the data, and the time required to prepare and enter the data?

To design the source document, the analyst must first decide what data must be captured, using the guidelines outlined in the last section. Then a layout of the document will be developed showing what items are to be included and where they will be placed. The document includes not only a place for data, but also captions and information telling the user how to complete the form and what information to provide.

LAYOUT

The layout organizes the document by placing important information in locations where it is most noticeable and instructs the user how to proceed by establishing a sequence of items. Most people fill in documents from the left to right and top to bottom, so the source document layout should be designed for use in the same way. It should be possible for the user to provide information by following a logical sequence rather than having to skip to different locations on the document (Figure 8.4).

The design of a well-planned form goes unnoticed, even as it makes the form easy to use and to follow.

Be aware of form zones, the large information groupings on a source document. Headings and identifying information are provided at the top of the form. Totals and results are in the lower zones (Figure 8.5). The most frequently used information belongs at the top and on the left side. Within the zone, ask for data in the expected order. For instance, users expect to be asked for name followed by address, followed by city, state, and postal code. If this order is changed, there is a good chance information will be given incorrectly. A well-designed form will ask for each item of data only once; there are very few occasions when the user should have to provide the same information more than one time.

Forms that do not allow enough space to provide the information requested will not be completed correctly by users. Typesetters often use a 5-character-to-an-inch guideline to allow ample space. This is also a useful guideline for the analyst. For example, if an 11-character item of data, such

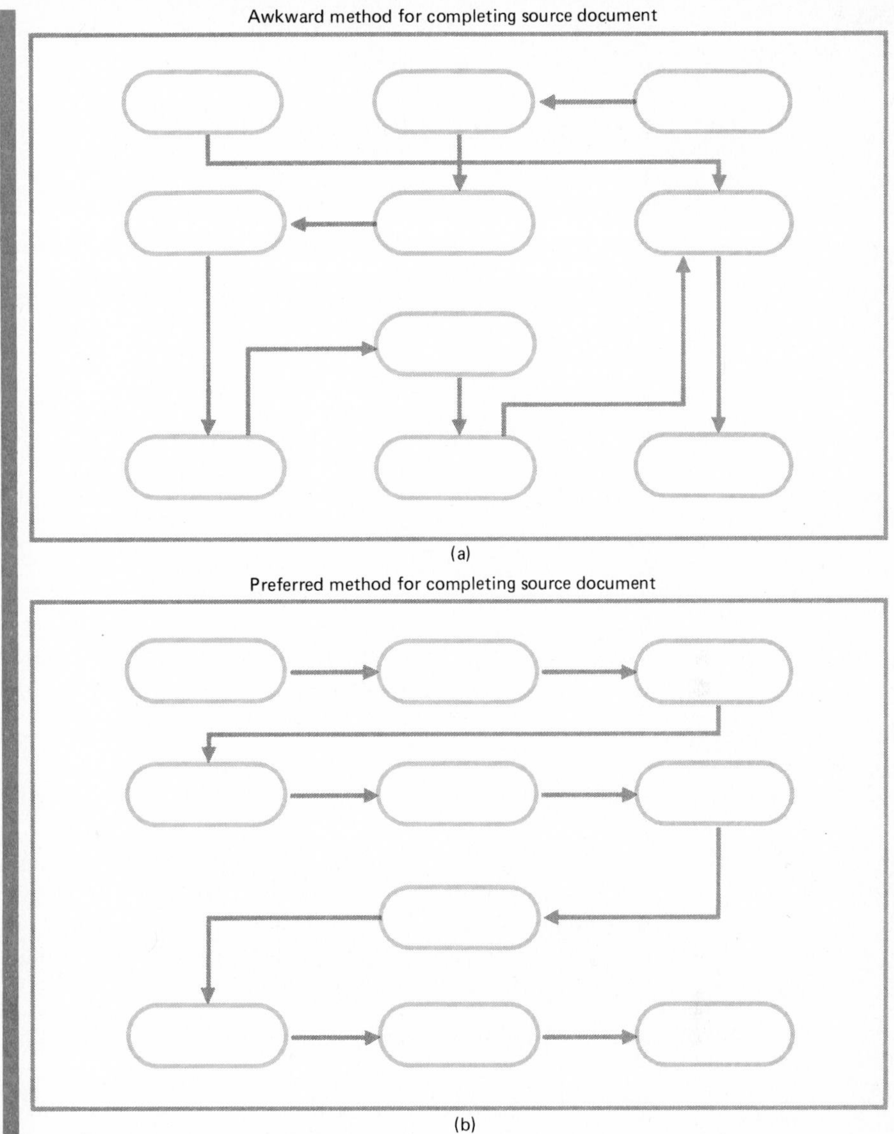

Figure 8.4.
Document layouts determine ease of completion.

as a social security number, will be handwritten on a form, a space approximately 2¼ inches should be allowed.

The analyst must consider how the form will be completed. Will it be handwritten or typewritten in most cases? The space between lines will vary accordingly. If the form will be completed by typewriter, allocating space at the rate of six typewritten lines to a vertical inch is recommended, unless the analyst expects double-spaced responses which means three lines per inch.

The actual document layout shows the location of each item of data and all headings and instructions to users. The names of data items, drawn from

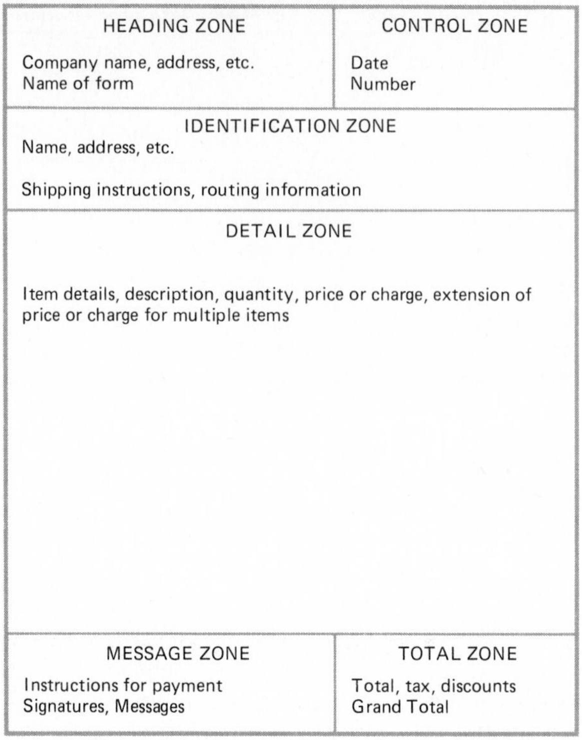

HEADING ZONE	CONTROL ZONE
Company name, address, etc. Name of form	Date Number
IDENTIFICATION ZONE Name, address, etc. Shipping instructions, routing information	
DETAIL ZONE Item details, description, quantity, price or charge, extension of price or charge for multiple items	
MESSAGE ZONE Instructions for payment Signatures, Messages	TOTAL ZONE Total, tax, discounts Grand Total

Figure 8.5.
Zones guide layout of source document.

the data dictionary developed throughout the systems development process, identify each item, so there is no mistake when software and file construction begin. The convention, used in output design, of placing a numeric identifier in the data field is also used for input layouts (Figure 8.6).

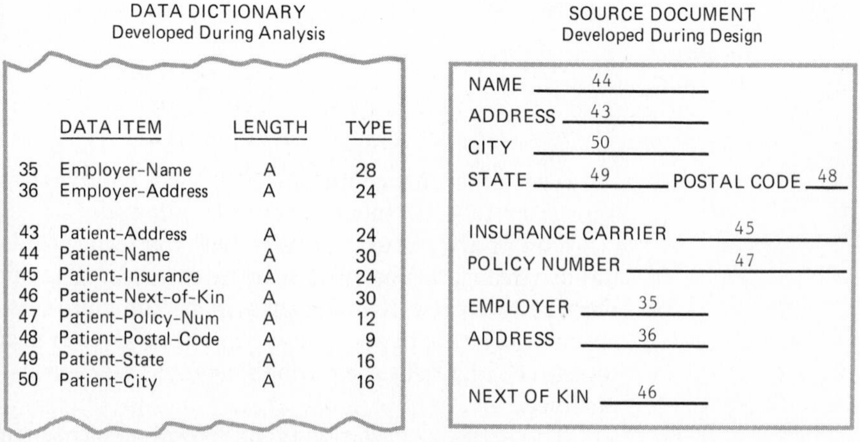

DATA DICTIONARY
Developed During Analysis

	DATA ITEM	LENGTH	TYPE
35	Employer-Name	A	28
36	Employer-Address	A	24
43	Patient-Address	A	24
44	Patient-Name	A	30
45	Patient-Insurance	A	24
46	Patient-Next-of-Kin	A	30
47	Patient-Policy-Num	A	12
48	Patient-Postal-Code	A	9
49	Patient-State	A	16
50	Patient-City	A	16

SOURCE DOCUMENT
Developed During Design

NAME 44
ADDRESS 43
CITY 50
STATE 49 POSTAL CODE 48
INSURANCE CARRIER 45
POLICY NUMBER 47
EMPLOYER 35
ADDRESS 36
NEXT OF KIN 46

Figure 8.6.
Link between source document and data dictionary.

CAPTIONS AND DATA CAPTURE

Captions on source documents tell the user what data to provide and where it should be entered. They should be brief but easily understood. Use standard terms that all persons using the form will know. Avoid abbreviations. Including a simple example will help eliminate respondent's questions about what information to provide. For example, in asking for date of birth, the form might specify how the date should be provided (such as "MONTH, DATE, YEAR" or "MM/DD/YY" or "MM/DD/19YY"). It is easy to overlook the fact that persons using this form may be from countries or from cultures where such simple items as dates are provided in different orders than expected. Thus an example is a small price to pay for correctly supplied details.

Figure 8.7 shows a sample of caption forms. The space each one uses varies. Some captions also tell the user where to write the data better than others.

A well-designed source document is easily completed, and the process of actually recording the data should be rapid. Figure 8.7 includes eight commonly used methods for data capture. Notice how easy it is to understand the question and provide the data. When checkmarks and boxes will be sufficient, the respondent should not be asked to write longer responses, otherwise they may not respond at all.

The last example in Figure 8.8 shows a two-part form. On the original copy the respondent marks the correct response to the question. However, the second page contains codes for the responses. In other words, the respondent is automatically providing coded answers while working with names and terms that are familiar to them. The next section discusses coding methods in detail.

CODING METHODS

Since information systems projects are designed with space, time, and cost savings in mind, *coding systems* in which conditions, words, ideas, or relationships are expressed by a code are developed to reduce input, control errors, and speed the entire process. A *code* is a brief number, title, or symbol used instead of more lengthy or ambiguous descriptions. When an event occurs, the details of the event are often summarized by the code. Fewer details are necessary in input, but no loss of information results. The six types of coding methods discussed in this section are classification, function, card, sequence, significant digit, and mnemonic codes.

Classification Code

Classification codes place separate entities, like events, people, or objects, into distinct groups, called classes. A code is used to identify one class from another. The code is recorded on the source document by the user or in an on-line system it may be keyed directly into the system through a terminal. The user (who either has learned the codes or looks them up) classifies the event into one of several possible categories and records the code.

COMMON CAPTION FORMS

LINE CAPTIONS

Before line — Name______ ID Num. ______ Department ______

After line — ______ Name; ______ ID Number; ______ Department

Above line — Name / ______; ID Number / ______; Department / ______

Below line — ______ / Name; ______ / ID Number; ______ / Department

BOXED CAPTIONS

Inside box — [Name]; [ID Number]; [Department]

Below box — [ ] Name; [ ] ID Number; [ ] Department

BALLOT BOX

Personnel Status
[ ] Active Officer
[ ] Active Enlisted
[ ] Retired
[ ] Civilian

Figure 8.7.
Common caption forms

For example, the New York State Thruway, like all public toll roads, counts the numbers of each type of vehicle traveling the highway to determine who use the roads. In addition, tolls themselves are based on the type of vehicle. There are many, many types of vehicles traveling the roads, and it is difficult to describe each one if you use the common attribute of size,

YES/NO CHECKOFF

	YES	NO
1. Are you under medical treatment now?	[ ]	[ ]
2. Have you had any major operations?	[ ]	[ ]
3. Have you ever had a serious head injury?	[ ]	[ ]
4. Are you taking any drugs or medications?	[ ]	[ ]

VERTICAL CHECKOFF

Please indicate any illnesses you have had.
[ ] Allergies
[ ] Rheumatic fever
[ ] Infectious hepatitis
[ ] Tuberculosis
[ ] Diabetes

HORIZONTAL CHECKOFF

Health	Excel.	Good	Fair	Poor

COMMON DATA CAPTURE METHODS

CODING FORM

Last name

ID Number

SCANABLE FORM

2 DEPT. NAME & NO.

COURSE CODE

SECTION(S): DISCUSSION, LAB, LECTURE

CR HRS.

ACTION: ADD, CHG, DROP

GRADE OPTION: NORMAL, PASS NO CR OR PASS FAIL, AUDIT

APPROVAL

TO INVALIDATE THIS COURSE BLOCK, MARK THIS RESPONSE POSITION

Figure 8.7.
(Continued)

weight, state of origin, etc. Therefore, most states establish vehicle classes such as those shown in Figure 8.9. A passenger car traveling the thruway is categorized as a class 1 vehicle and charged the lowest rate. However, a passenger car towing a two-wheel trailer is coded as class 2 and, if towing a four-wheel trailer (two axles on the trailer), class 3.

DATA CAPTURE USING AUTOMATIC ENCODING
TWO-PART FORM

ORIGINAL COPY	DUPLICATE COPY
Pilot	181
CoPilot	181
Aircraft Commander	078
Navigator	216
Elec Warfare Officer	334
Circle the correct title for your position.	Keypunch columns 3-5

Figure 8.8.
Data capture using automatic coding.

Classification codes vastly simplify the input process because only a single-digit code is required. The need for writing lengthy descriptions or making judgments is eliminated. In a word, it is simpler.

Function Codes

Function codes state the activities or work to be performed without spelling out all of the details in narrative statements. Analysts use this type of code frequently in transaction data to tell the system how to process the data. For example, the design for file processing may specify the addition of records in one transaction by means of an A or a 1 or any other coding scheme the analyst selects. For deletions of records, the function code might be D or 2. And, for changing or updating stored data, the analyst may specify use of the code C, U, or 3.

The particular function code may determine the contents of the input record (Figure 8.10). For instance, in order for the system to add a record, all the data elements for the record must be included in the input data. On the other hand, to delete a record, only the delete code and the identification numbers or key of the record to be deleted must be specified. If a field in the record is to change, the input should include the code for change, an indication of which field to change, and the new data for that field.

Card Codes

Punched cards are still used by many organizations who batch process. Since the cards contain 80 data columns (with a few exceptions that are unique to particular vendor's equipment), you may often work with projects where data will span several punched cards (Figure 8.11). Card codes allow the program to distinguish between the type of card and to determine whether the contents of a specific card are correct.

The analyst designing a bibliography system, such as the one researchers keep for referencing journal and magazine articles or books, may decide to separate author, title, publisher, and descriptive information across four

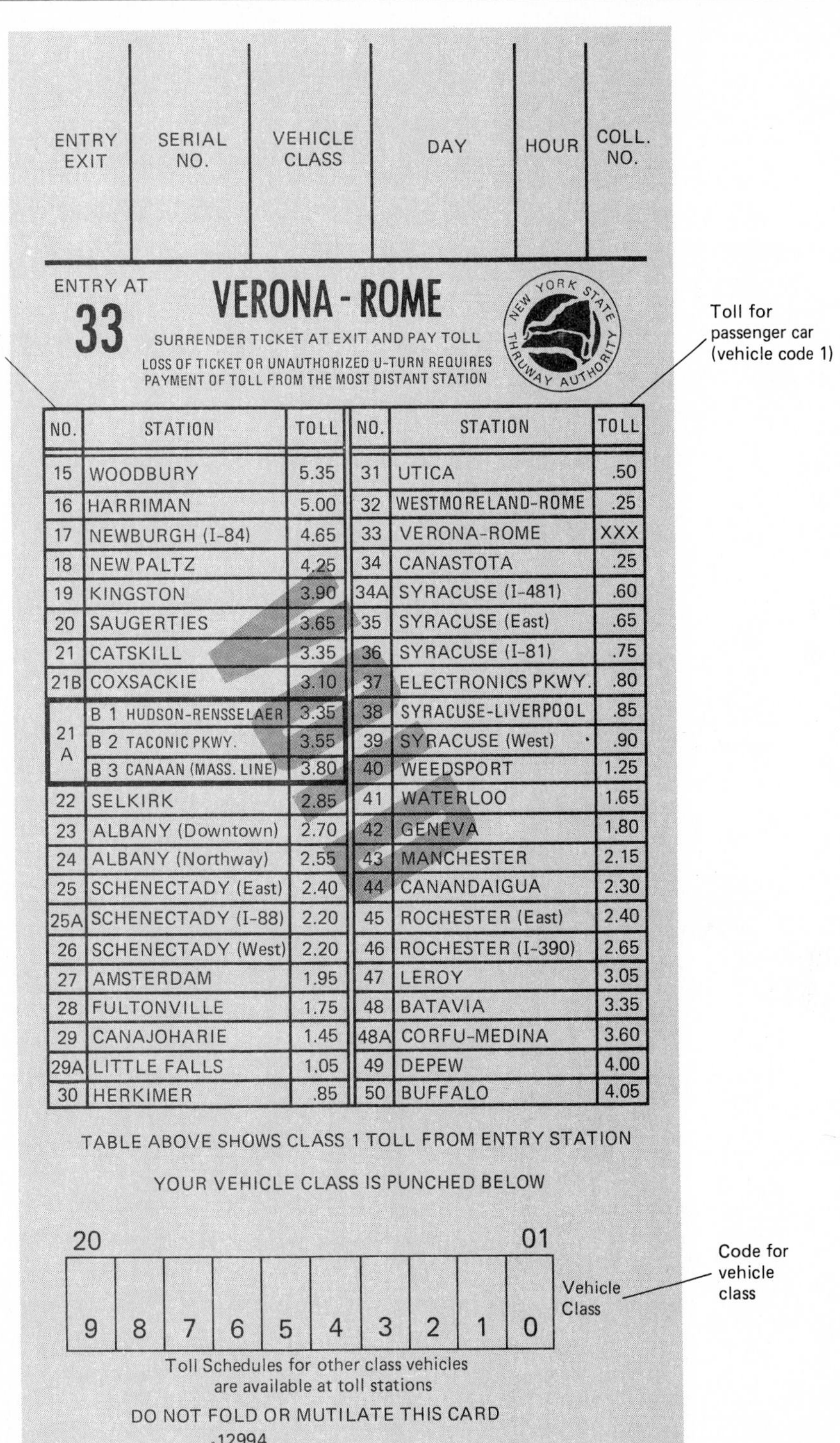

ENTRY EXIT	SERIAL NO.	VEHICLE CLASS	DAY	HOUR	COLL. NO.

ENTRY AT

33

VERONA - ROME

NEW YORK STATE THRUWAY AUTHORITY

SURRENDER TICKET AT EXIT AND PAY TOLL

LOSS OF TICKET OR UNAUTHORIZED U-TURN REQUIRES PAYMENT OF TOLL FROM THE MOST DISTANT STATION

NO.	STATION	TOLL	NO.	STATION	TOLL
15	WOODBURY	5.35	31	UTICA	.50
16	HARRIMAN	5.00	32	WESTMORELAND-ROME	.25
17	NEWBURGH (I-84)	4.65	33	VERONA-ROME	XXX
18	NEW PALTZ	4.25	34	CANASTOTA	.25
19	KINGSTON	3.90	34A	SYRACUSE (I-481)	.60
20	SAUGERTIES	3.65	35	SYRACUSE (East)	.65
21	CATSKILL	3.35	36	SYRACUSE (I-81)	.75
21B	COXSACKIE	3.10	37	ELECTRONICS PKWY.	.80
21 A	B 1 HUDSON-RENSSELAER	3.35	38	SYRACUSE-LIVERPOOL	.85
	B 2 TACONIC PKWY.	3.55	39	SYRACUSE (West)	.90
	B 3 CANAAN (MASS. LINE)	3.80	40	WEEDSPORT	1.25
22	SELKIRK	2.85	41	WATERLOO	1.65
23	ALBANY (Downtown)	2.70	42	GENEVA	1.80
24	ALBANY (Northway)	2.55	43	MANCHESTER	2.15
25	SCHENECTADY (East)	2.40	44	CANANDAIGUA	2.30
25A	SCHENECTADY (I-88)	2.20	45	ROCHESTER (East)	2.40
26	SCHENECTADY (West)	2.20	46	ROCHESTER (I-390)	2.65
27	AMSTERDAM	1.95	47	LEROY	3.05
28	FULTONVILLE	1.75	48	BATAVIA	3.35
29	CANAJOHARIE	1.45	48A	CORFU-MEDINA	3.60
29A	LITTLE FALLS	1.05	49	DEPEW	4.00
30	HERKIMER	.85	50	BUFFALO	4.05

TABLE ABOVE SHOWS CLASS 1 TOLL FROM ENTRY STATION

YOUR VEHICLE CLASS IS PUNCHED BELOW

20 01

9	8	7	6	5	4	3	2	1	0

Vehicle Class

Toll Schedules for other class vehicles are available at toll stations

DO NOT FOLD OR MUTILATE THIS CARD

-12994

Figure 8.9. Data coding for toll charges on New York State Thruway.

MULTIPLE-CARD LAYOUT FORM

Application________________

Card								
Add new item code 1	Code	Item number	Description	Retail price	Unit cost	Weight	Package	Order quantity
Delete item code 2	Code	Item number						
Change price code 3	Code	Item number		Retail price				
Cost change cost code 4	Code	Item number			Unit cost			
Change weight code 5	Code	Item number				Weight		
Change package code 6	Code	Item number					Package	
Change order quantity code 7	Code	Item number						Order quantity

Figure 8.10. Function codes control content of input records.

separate cards for input purposes. The card codes used to identify the *intrarecord* data in our example are 1, 2, 3, and 4 with the restriction that there should only be one of each type of card for a single bibliographic citation. The card layout form in Figure 8.12 describes the name, location, size, and type of each data element for the bibliography system.

A new analyst will quickly learn that, despite the best work, the cards will invariably arrive for processing at times in a jumbled fashion, not the desired 1-2-3-4 sequence. The card code can be checked by the program to determine what type of card it is and therefore what the contents should be.

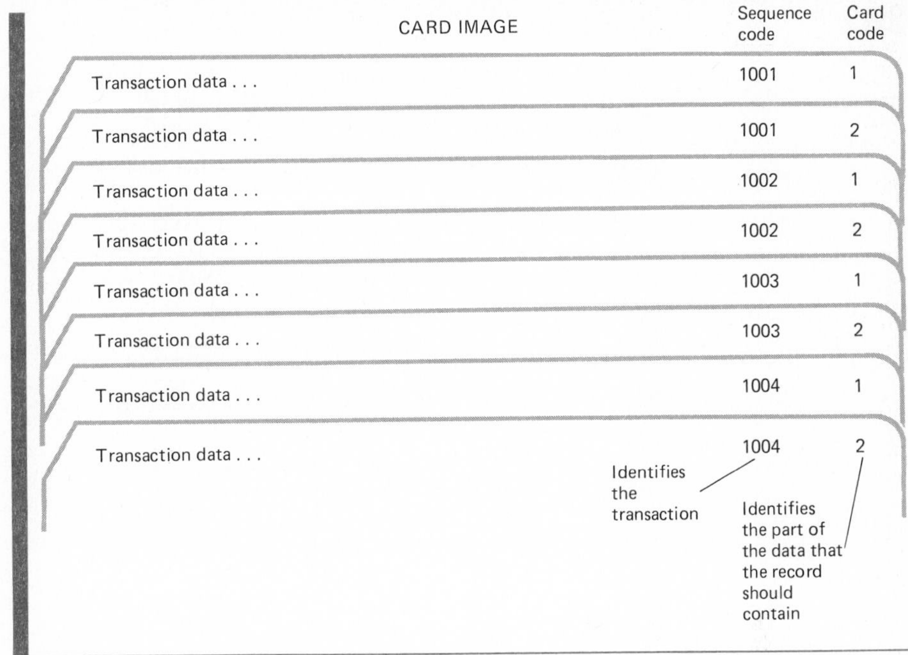

Figure 8.11. Multicard coding methods.

For example, if the card code is "1," the system will know that it should contain author data.

Sequence Codes

Sequence codes are numbers or letters assigned in series. They tell the order in which events have occurred. For example, a banking system must be able to keep track of the order of transactions, so it is clear which transactions to process first, which second, and so on. Therefore, a sequence number should be specified in the design to order the transactions.

Sequence codes are also used for identification purposes but are assigned in the order in which customers enter the system. For example, Figure 8.13 shows a pool of four-digit customer numbers being assigned to customers in the order they arrive.

Carelessly assigned sequence numbers do not allow the insertion of new members between existing ones. Thus, if we wish to add customer Burger after Burgan, we do not have an easy way to do so. Therefore analysts often specify assignment of sequence codes in intervals of 10 or 20 or some other range to allow later expansion.

Significant-Digit Subset Codes

A well-conceived coding scheme, using subcodes within larger codes or numbers, can provide a wealth of information to users. Suppose item numbers will be assigned to the different materials and products a firm

DATE ________ PAGE ________
REFERENCE # ________
PREPARED BY ________
REVIEWED BY ________

PUNCHED CARD LAYOUT Bibliography Data Cards

1. Author Card

First Author (X)	Initial-1 (X)	Second Author (X)	Initial-2 (X)	Third Author (X)	Initial-3 (X)	Blank	Sequence Number (9)	Card Code (9)

2. Title Card

Publication Title (X)	Sequence Number (9)	Card Code (9)

3. Publication Card

Publishing Details (X)	Series (X)	Year (9)	Sequence Number (9)	Card Code (9)

4. Description Card

First Keyword (X)	Second Keyword (X)	Third Keyword (X)	Fourth Keyword (X)	Blank	Sequence Number (9)	Card Code (9)

Figure 8.12. Identification and arrangement of data on multiple punched cards.

stocks or sells. One way is to assign numbers in sequence, starting with the first and going through to the last one. Or a prefix can be added to the identification numbers to further describe the type of item: steel has an S prefix, plastic a P, and so on.

The codes can be divided into subsets or subcodes, characters that are

Customer number	Customer name	
1101	James J. Aldrich	Want to add record for Burger
1102	Edgar Burgan	←
1103	Alvin Chalmers	
1104	Shirley Demske	
1105	Randy Krimsnatch	

Dense sequence means no room for additions without losing the sequence.

Customer number	Customer name	
1110	James J. Aldrich	Add record for Burger, #1121
1120	Edgar Burgan	←
1130	Alvin Chalmers	
1140	Shirley Demske	
1150	Randy Krimsnatch	

Spaced sequence allows for additions while preserving the alphabetic sequence.

Figure 8.13. Sequence codes used for identification purposes.

part of the identification number that have special meaning. The subcodes tell the user additional information about the item. In the inventory example, the most important information to know is the class of product, the item within that class, and the supplier. Therefore, the analyst develops an identification number carrying this information through significant digits in several subsets of the overall item number:

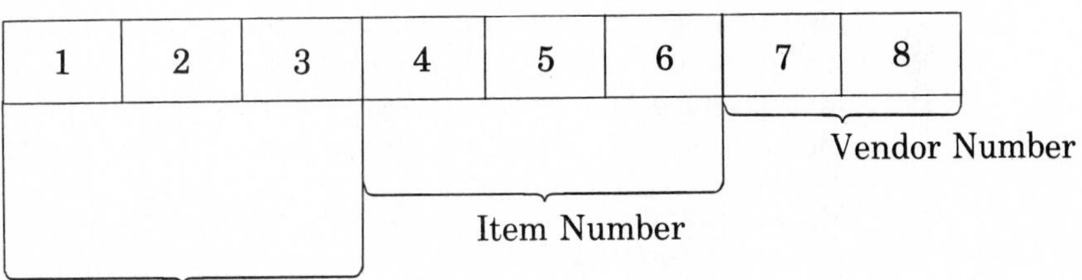

If management wants to know how sales are in the waterwheel line, #323, the data can be sorted on that subset and a report produced. Similarly, if information is wanted about all products supplied by vendor 28, a quick examination of this subset of products will provide the information.

Utilizing digits in an identification number to convey additional information does not add to the length of the data or to processing time. However, the extra information subcodes provide may be invaluable to management.

Mnemonic Codes

Mnemonic codes use letters and symbols from the product to describe it in a way that communicates *visually*. For example, to describe a 21-inch color television set, a useful code is TV-CL-21 (black and white is TV-BW-21). It is difficult to confuse the mneumonic *TV* with that of other products. Universities use mnemonics to code students all the time: MBA for Master of Business Administration or CS for computer science major.

The data and transaction coding reduces the volume of data for input and simplifies the process so that the likelihood of errors is reduced. Selection of one code over another will of course depend on the data and the objective of the analyst. Card codes are useful if data spans several punched cards, sequence codes should be used when transaction order is important, etc. But several codes may be used within the same transaction. For instance, the bibliography example may use card codes to identify the type of card and the data it contains, function codes to instruct the system how to process the data, and sequence codes to show the position of a record in a batch of records.

METHOD OF DATA CAPTURE

The method in which the data is captured from transactions markedly affects the analyst's ability to meet the objectives we have been discussing. There are four different methods to consider, each using specific data preparation and input equipment. They are source document capture using keypunching, key-to-storage devices, optical character recognition, or direct entry through intelligent terminals.

Source Document Capture with Keypunching

The best-known and historically most widely used method for data entry employs both a source document and a punched card. The source document is completed by the employee while the transaction is taking place: relevant details, such as quantity and names of items sold, date of event, and perhaps buyer and seller names, are recorded. After the transaction has been completed, usually the next day or even later, the data is prepared for processing.

Preparing data includes coding the transaction data into a form that coincides with the design of the computer program that will process it and, in some cases, copying it onto a coding form. Then the data is punched into cards (Figure 8.14). Because business needs accurate and valid data, many organizations require a separate verification process in which data is *re*keyed into a verifier, that compares the newly punched data with that already in the cards. Cards in error are notched or otherwise marked for correction.

After data preparation and correction, the data is read into the card reader (Figure 8.15) of the computer for processing. The first step in handling a transaction in the computer is making an additional validation check to ensure that data is not missing, that the data values are reasonable, and that no errors have occurred during preparation and submission for processing. (This step is called computer *input validation,* a topic discussed in detail later in this chapter.)

To summarize, the input steps required when data is captured on a source document used for keypunching are:

1. Write the data on the source document.
2. If necessary, code the data from the source document into a form acceptable for computer processing.
3. Keypunch the data into cards.

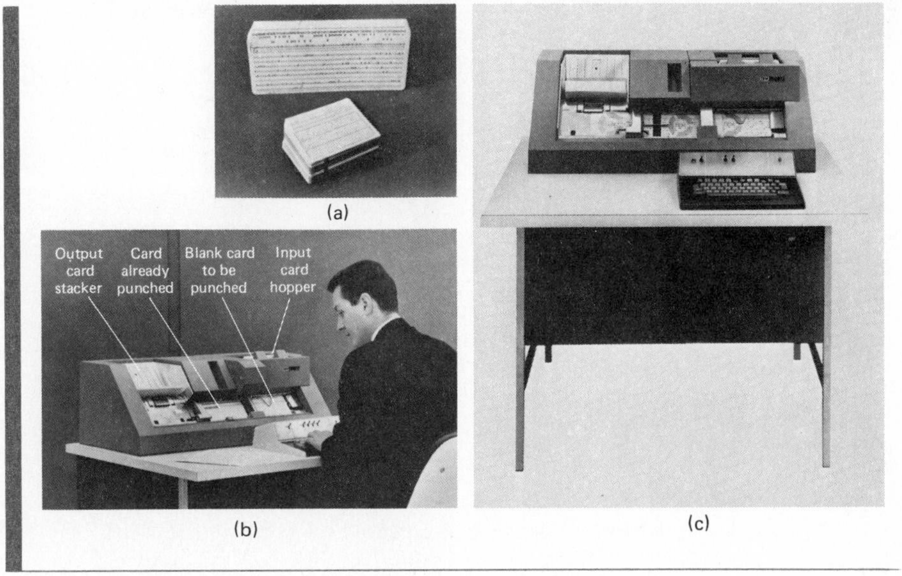

Figure 8.14. Punched cards keypunch, and key verification machines. (Courtesy of International Business Machines Corporation)

4 Verify the punched cards by rekeying the data on a verifying machine that compares previously punched data with repunched details.
5 Batch the cards together and read them into the computer for processing.
6 Validate the data as it is read into the computer for processing.
7 Process the data.

Source Data Capture with Key to Storage

Source documents are also used in environments where data are not entered through punched cards. With the key-to-storage devices (that include key-to-magnetic tape and key-to-magnetic disk), data entry personnel work from the same type of source document just described. The data is entered through a *work station,* consisting of a typewriterlike keyboard for keying the data and a visual display. As details are entered, the work station checks the data for misspellings, incorrect product numbers, or unacceptable data. (For example, it might refuse a social security number with embedded dashes or blanks if it has been so instructed.) Other aids include special tabs, lights, and a display screen that enables the operator to see the data as it is entered. (Figure 8.16). The data is recorded on magnetic storage media.

Key-to-storage devices improve the data entry process compared to keypunched cards in several other ways. They are over 30 percent faster and thus allow the employees to enter data much more quickly. Because the data is stored in sequence on the magnetic tape or disk, records are automatically stored in sequence and stay in sequence (unlike a dropped deck of punched cards). Storage density is improved considerably; this means that much more data can be stored in a given amount of space compared with punched cards.

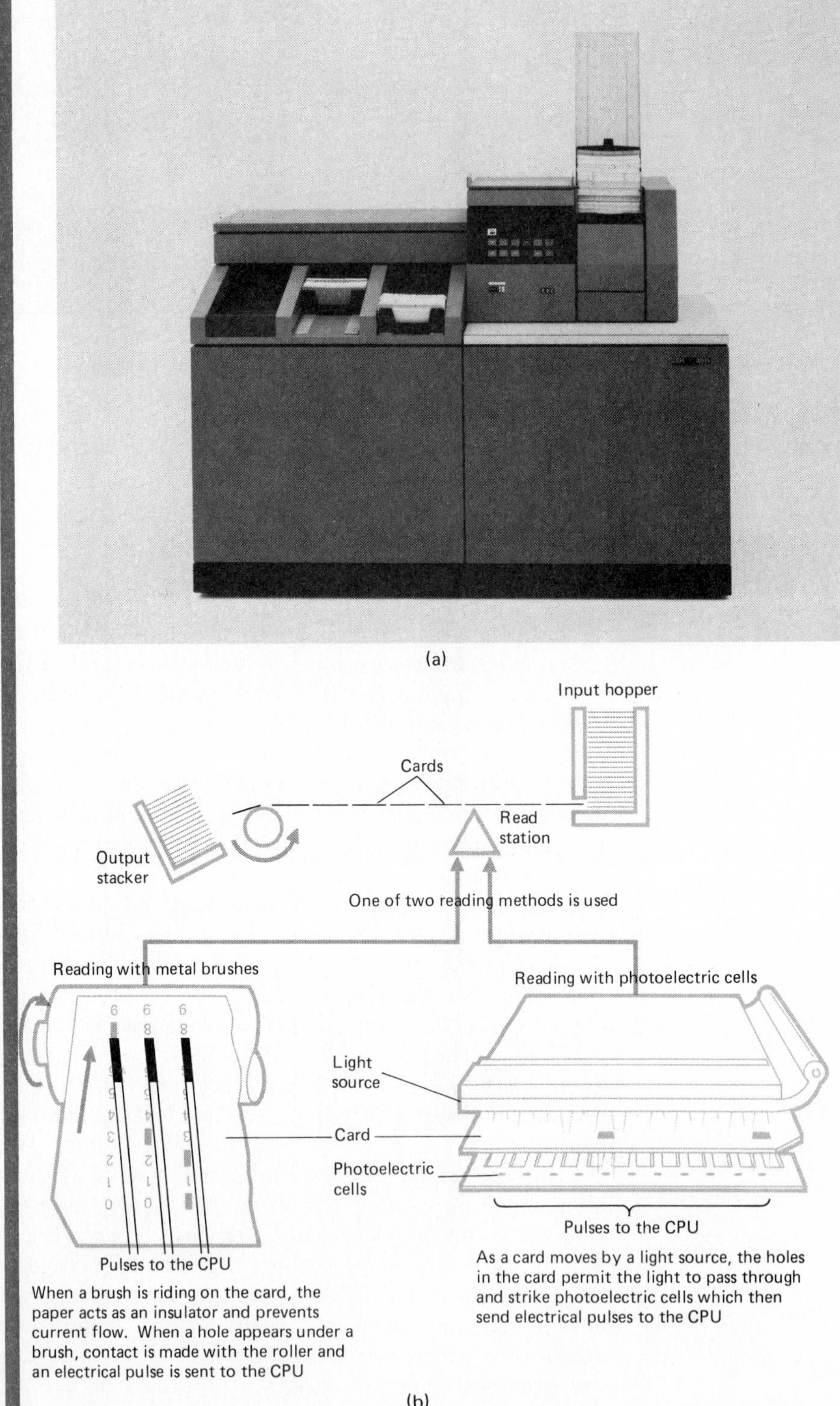
(a)
Input hopper
Cards
Read
station
Output
stacker
One of two reading methods is used
Reading with metal brushes
Reading with photoelectric cells
Light
source
Card
Photoelectric
cells
Pulses to the CPU
Pulses to the CPU
When a brush is riding on the card, the paper acts as an insulator and prevents current flow. When a hole appears under a brush, contact is made with the roller and an electrical pulse is sent to the CPU
As a card moves by a light source, the holes in the card permit the light to pass through and strike photoelectric cells which then send electrical pulses to the CPU
(b)

Figure 8.15. Card reader. (Courtesy of International Business Machines Corporation)

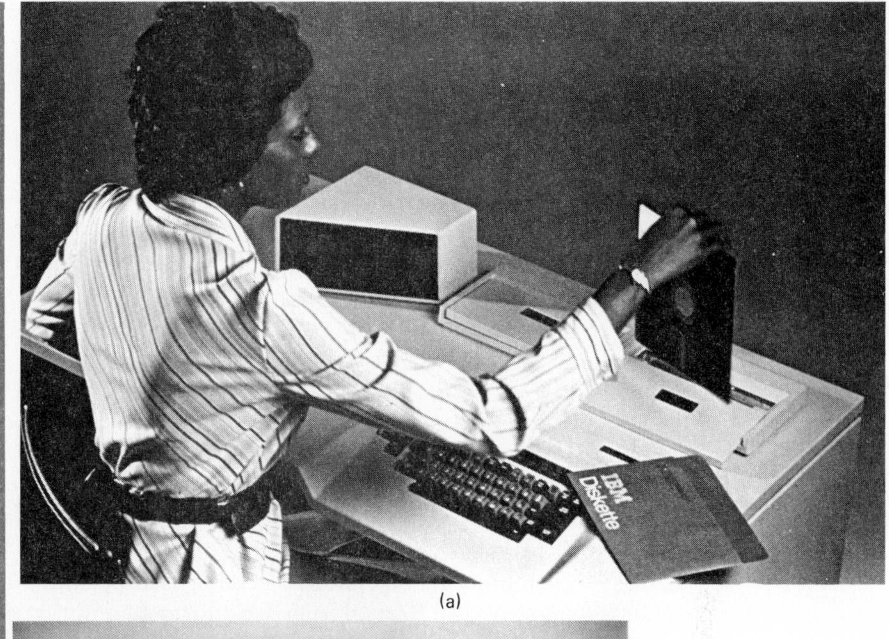

(a)

(b)

Figure 8.16. Keyboard of computer work station. [(*a*) Courtesy of International Business Machines; (*b*) photo courtesy of Digital Equipment Corporation]

To summarize, the input steps required when data is captured on a source document used in a key-to-storage environment are:

1. Write the data on the source document.
2. If necessary, code data from source document into a form acceptable for computer processing.
3. Process the tape or disk of data directly. No extra steps are needed to enter it into the computer.
4. Validate the data as it is read into the computer for processing. (Some validation takes place during key entry.)
5. Process the data.

Source Data Capture with OCR

Optical character processing of input data enables organizations to speed their input activities by 50 to 75 percent over traditional methods. A source document that can be directly used as an input document for scanning by the optical character reader (Figure 8.17) is required. When transactions occur, the data is written or marked on the scannable form, sometimes with ordinary hand printing and in other cases by marking special symbols or boxes to represent data. Notice the omission of many of the data preparation and coding steps we discussed above.

Optical character forms are directly read by the input device, the optical character reader (OCR). Validation of data is done as it enters the computer, and then processing begins. OCR Forms are generally batched for processing.

The input steps required when data is captured on a source document used in an OCR environment are:

1. Write the data on the source document.
2. Batch the source documents together and read them into the computer for processing.
3. Validate the data as it is read into the computer for processing. (Some validation takes place during data entry.)
4. Process the data.

Direct Entry through Intelligent Terminals

Intelligent terminals are similar to CRTs with built in processing capability (comparable to having a microprocessor stored inside). The point-of-sale devices used in supermarkets and retail stores are one type of intelligent terminal. Others are common in manufacturing, airline ticket sales, and stock market operations. If they are used for data capture, the need for source documents may even be eliminated, unless a paper record of the transaction is also required. That is, as an event is taking place, the operator can key the data directly into the system. The processor validates the data as it is entered to detect errors or to ask for verification of questionable data (such as a sale for $10,000 in a retail store).

Unlike the other methods, intelligent terminals may interact directly

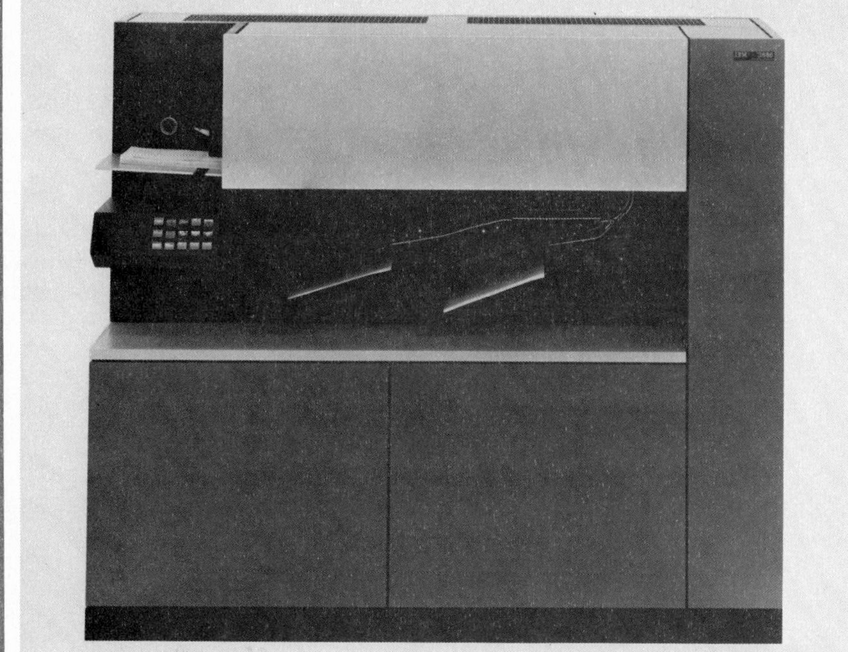

(a)

Shoe Place
Main Street
Goodtowne, N.Y.

Date

NO. 47302

ITEM NUMBER								DESCRIPTION	QUANTITY	AMOUNT
0	3	1	5	4	2	8	0	SHOES	1	$32.99
9	8	4	6	0	0	1	9	PURSE	1	$18.99

(b)

Figure 8.17. Optical character reader (Courtesy of International Business Machines Corporation) and recognition document.

with the computer in one of two ways. Complete interaction, called an *on-line system* means that the operator submits transactions and receives processing results quickly, while the customer is still present. The stream of events then is: submit data, verify data, process data, return results (output) to the terminal.

A variation on on-line processing combines certain batch features discussed above. With *deferred on-line* systems, data entry and validation occurs interactively, in an on-line mode. However, processing is deferred, meaning that the transactions are accumulated into a batch and processed later, off-line. If on-line data capture is needed, but processing can occur later, the cost savings in hardware and special software may lead the analyst to chose deferred on-line processing.

The input steps required when data is captured using terminals (on-line or deferred on-line) are:

1 Enter the data into the terminal.
2 Validate the data as it is entered through the terminal.
3 Process the data (if deferred, transactions are accumulated for later batch processing).

Figure 8.18 shows an optical reader which will save in data preparation and data entry work. Equipment costs vary, and so the economic side of any decision about data entry methods must be considered by the analyst. However, it is generally true that high labor costs can be reduced through better data entry methods, even though initial equipment costs may be incurred.

Figure 8.18.
Optical mark reader. (Courtesy of National Computer Systems)

INPUT VALIDATION

Input designs are aimed at reducing the chance of mistakes or errors. However, always assume that there is a chance errors will occur. They must be found during input and corrected prior to storing or processing the data. It is much more difficult to correct erroneous data after storage has taken place. In fact, erroneous data is frequently forgotten about until someone using a report based on that data questions its accuracy and validity.

The general term given to methods aimed at detecting errors in input is *input validation*. There are three main categories of methods, including checking the transaction, checking the transaction data, and changing the transaction data.

Checking the Transaction

First and foremost, it is essential to identify any transactions that are not valid, that is, ones that are not acceptable. Transactions may be invalid because they are incomplete, unauthorized, or even out of order.

BATCH CONTROLS

In batch environments, there are delays between the occurrence of a transaction and the time the data about them is processed. *Batch processing* means delaying processing by accumulating the transactions into batches or groups of records. (An important design question is knowing how much delay is acceptable to users.)

When transactions are accumulated and not processed as they are occurring, there is a good chance some will be misplaced, forgotten, or simply overlooked. Whether large or small, a lost transaction should always be a concern to the analyst.

One method of batch control uses fixed *batch size*. Transactions are accumulated into groups of, say, 50 transactions. That comprises one batch. During the course of a business period (a morning or afternoon, a shift, a day, or a week, for instance), more than one batch will undoubtedly accumulate. Therefore, management will want to be sure that all batches are processed and none are lost or overlooked. Knowing the number of batches accumulated and submitted for processing (the *batch count*) will ensure this. In fact, the analyst might even specify that a serial number be assigned to each batch in succession.

Still a third concern in batch processing is the assurance that all transactions in the batch get processed properly. *Batch totals* help provide this assurance. This method requires calculating the total for an element of data that is present in every record in the batch, such as the number of items ordered, regardless of what that item is. The total is determined before the batch is sent for processing. As the batch undergoes processing, the total is again accumulated either by the computer, if it is an automated process, or by a person other than the one who calculated the original batch

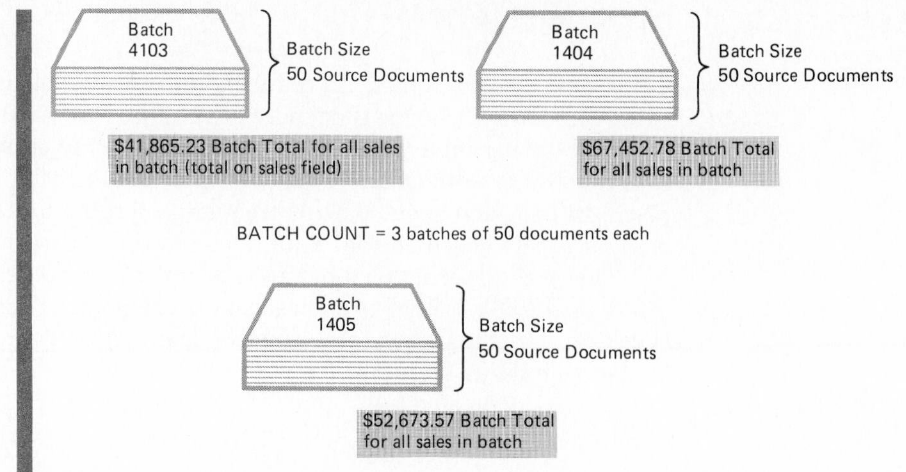

Figure 8.19.
Batch control methods.

total. If the totals are the same (Figure 8.19), management will know that all transactions in the batch have been processed accurately. If there is a discrepancy, management will know that and can investigate the cause.

We have identified three very important methods for checking batch transactions: *batch size* determines whether all transactions are in the batch; *batch count* indicates whether any batch was lost or overlooked; and the *batch total* tells you when all transactions in the batch are processed properly.

TRANSACTION VALIDATION

Inexperienced analysts sometimes assume that users will submit only valid transactions, that is, only those that are acceptable to the system and can be properly processed. Unfortunately, users often attempt to process data in unexpected ways, either accidentally or intentionally. It is the responsibility of the analyst to specify validation procedures that will test the acceptability of a transaction. Such validation has several parts (Figure 8.20).

The transaction itself must be acceptable to the system; then it can be processed. The steps the system takes to ensure the transaction is acceptable is called *transaction validation*. For example, a typical inventory system will be designed to expect inventory transactions to add items to inventory, delete items, or change the quantity on hand through withdrawal of stock. However, it is not acceptable to add a new item when there is already an item with the same name and identifying stock number. The latter is an invalid transaction and should be detected during processing, so that the data in the inventory system remains reliable.

Transactions having no relation to the purpose of the system can also be submitted for processing, usually inadvertently. For example, if someone attempts to submit a payroll transaction in an inventory system, even if it is accidental, the design specifications should provide for detecting this invalid input so that it does not enter processing.

The analyst must also ensure that the transaction validation process will detect the situation where acceptable input is submitted by an unauthorized user. In processing payroll, for instance, it is acceptable to raise salary and wage rates, but only by authorized individuals. Employees are not authorized to raise their own salary rate or adjust withholding tax allowances. Here we have a case of valid input being submitted by an unauthorized user. The combination makes the entire transaction invalid. The specifications in designing a payroll system should state those conditions that make a transaction valid. The programmer should be instructed to assume all other conditions are invalid.

SEQUENCE TEST

Sequence tests use codes in the data—serial numbers—to test for either of two different conditions, depending on the characteristics of the application. In some systems, the *order* of transactions is important. When processing bank checking deposits and withdrawals, it is important to ensure that each is processed in the order in which it arrived. If a series of withdrawals are mistakenly processed before a deposit that actually occurred first, the customer could be penalized for overdrawing the account when in fact that did not actually happen.

Sequence tests also point out *missing* items. Your checking account uses check numbers to identify every check. When you reconcile your account at the end of a month or quarter, you probably sort the checks into order based on the identifying number. If there is a jump in the numbers from, say 1140 to 1143, you immediately know that two checks, numbers 1141 and 1142 are missing. Without the numbers, it is difficult to determine whether all transactions are present.

Figure 8.20. Classes of input validation methods.

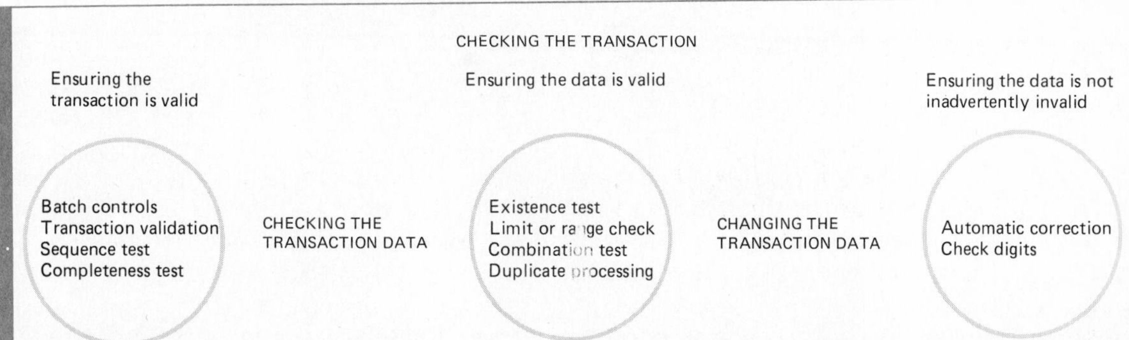

COMPLETENESS TEST

There is little point in accepting input that is missing some items of data, since that results in incomplete and erroneous information when stored. Therefore, input validation checks on each transaction should ensure that all essential data is included. For instance, in accepting deposits from a customer, banks must know the account number, amount of deposit, and date of transaction. They also want to know which teller processed the deposit. If any of these details are absent when the deposit information is input to the banking system, the transaction should be rejected as invalid.

Point-of-sale systems in retail centers are oriented to automatically performing completeness tests. In fact, many point-of-sale terminals use systems of lights that instruct the operators what to do next. The light under the key for transaction type lights up first (Figure 8.21). Until a valid transaction code (such as sale, void, or credit) is entered, nothing else can happen; the keyboard locks. Then step by step, the operator is guided through the transaction by lights coming on under the key to be depressed next. If the purchaser's credit card number is not entered for a charge transaction, for instance, the terminal will not allow completion of the transaction; it will wait indefinitely until the correct data is entered.

Completeness tests are one more way of validating the transaction to ensure it is accurate and acceptable before any data is accepted into the system for further processing or storage.

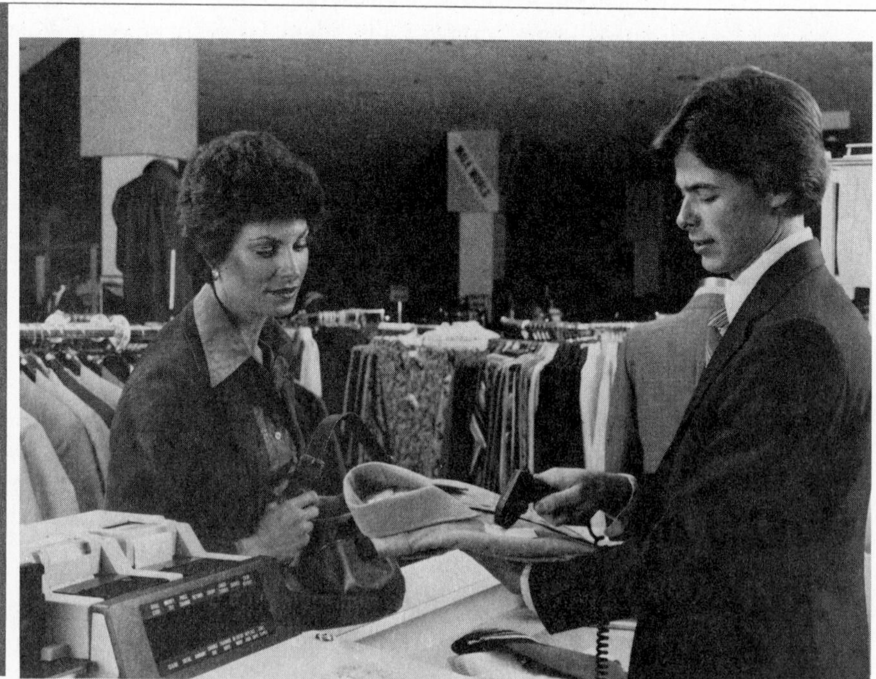

Figure 8.21. Point-of-sale terminals. (Courtesy of NCR Corporation)

Must not be greater than 12

Order #: Must not be blank   Date (M/D/Y): / /   Customer #: Must not be blank

Bill to: Ship to:

Address to: Address:

City: City:

State: Zip code: State: Zip code:

Retrieve from storage based on customer number   Retrieve from storage based on customer number

P.O. #: Must not be blank   Ship via: Fill in   Terms:

Quantity	Product	Description	Unit Cost	Total Cost
Reasonable value	Fill in	Retrieve from storage	Retrieve from storage	Calculate
Must not be blank	Fill in			

Tax Rate: Retrieve %   Sales Tax: Calculate   Total: Calculate test for reasonable amount

Figure 8.22. Data validation methods applied to sales transactions.

Checking the Transaction Data

Even valid transactions can contain invalid data. Therefore, analysts should be sure to specify methods for validating the data itself when developing input procedures. There are four data validation methods.

EXISTENCE TEST

Some data fields in transactions must not be left empty or blank. *Existence tests* examine those essential fields to determine that they contain data. For example, in processing inventory, it is incorrect to accept orders that do not specify the quantity of an item ordered. A blank in this field is unacceptable and therefore indicates an error (Figure 8.22).

Sometimes blank items are acceptable. For instance, customers placing small orders may not submit purchase orders or they may pay in advance. In these cases, there is no purchase order number that can be entered into the sales order record and it would be pointless for the system to demand one. Similarly, patients entering a hospital as a general rule will have health insurance. But not *all* patients must have it to be treated. Therefore, this item may not have to pass an existence test.

In developing a file maintenance processing program, for example, we know that some items (a key field, a data item in the record that uniquely discriminates that record from all other records in a file) should always exist, as should a code indicating the type of transaction (add, delete, or change). Only if the transaction is a deletion is it necessary to have preexisting data other than the record key. For a new record, all data items are needed. For a change, only those items being changed need exist in the transaction record (see Figure 8.10).

It is the task of the analysts, working with the users, to learn when data items must be present and when their absence is acceptable. This information in turn belongs in the design specifications and should be passed along to the programmers.

LIMIT OR RANGE TESTS

These tests verify the *reasonableness* of the transaction data. (They can also be used to verify the *result* of processing.) *Limit tests* validate either the minimum or maximum amount acceptable for an item. *Range tests* validate both minimum and maximum values.

In banking, many tellers must notify a bank officer before completing a cash transaction in excess of $10,000. That is, $10,000 is the limit they are authorized to accept without a second approval when actual cash changes hands. If checks or bank drafts are deposited, the $10,000 limit does not apply. Analysts working on the design of banking systems must build the $10,000 limit check for cash transactions into their specifications. When such transactions occur and a second approval is not input, an exception should be noted and the transaction rejected as invalid.

Sometimes both upper and lower limits are important. Universities registering students for courses will want to know about students wanting to take less than 1 credit, the lower limit, and more than, say, 22 credits (because extra tuition is required). Therefore, the analyst developing this system specifies a range of from 1 to 22 credits for validation purposes. Not meeting this criterion may be explainable, but, as far as the systems specifications are concerned, an exception should always be noted so the decision can be made by a responsible official, such as the university registrar.

COMBINATION TEST

Combination tests validate that several data items jointly have acceptable values. That is, the value for one element of data determines whether other data values are correct. Suppose an ordering system is being designed for the automotive industry. The analyst is responsible for identifying all combinations of conditions that require special attention. For example, a systems design should note that, if a customer orders an automobile with factory air conditioning, other parts must also be specified in the order: heavy-duty battery, heavy-duty shock absorbers, and an oversize radiator. All must be ordered in combination with each other. Therefore the validation requirement spans several different elements of data.

DUPLICATE PROCESSING

In especially sensitive areas, it may be necessary to process data more than once, either on different equipment or in different ways. The results are then compared for agreement and accuracy. In the United States space program, where computers are relied on heavily for course and direction control, multiple computers process the same data and compare the results. This ensures utmost accuracy. (If there is disagreement, there are also specific procedures used to resolve the difference.)

Modifying the Transaction Data

Still a third way of validating data involves modifying the data itself. Two methods are automatic correction of errors and self-checking digits on key fields.

AUTOMATIC CORRECTION

Sometimes analysts specify that programs be written to correct errors in the data. This input validation method is used to minimize the number of separate error correction steps or rejections of transactions during processing. This method simply requires the program to detect an error and make the correction automatically. For example, data entry personnel keying data into, say a six digit numeric field, may only enter three digits. Yet the entire field must contain numbers. (A blank is not a number.) Rather than have the program reject the transaction because of missing leading zeroes (zeroes in the unused positions at the beginning of a data field), it may be designed to insert them automatically. Only leading zeroes, not trailing ones, are inserted, however.

CHECK DIGITS

Two of the most common errors in handling data are made with data that is captured correctly but entered into processing incorrectly. *Transcription errors* occur if data is inadvertently copied incorrectly by the data entry person. For example, a customer number of 24589 is transcribed incorrectly if it is entered as 24587. (The operator mistakenly copied the last digit as a 7 rather than the correct digit 9.) With *transposition errors,* the other common error type, two or more digits are reversed so that their position in the data is incorrect. We would say a transposition error had occurred if the customer number was entered as 24598 instead of 24589.

Since the chance of these errors occurring is high, a special method was devised to help detect them during computer processing. This method, called the *check digit* method, adds an additional digit to a data element being used for identification purposes. The check digit is added to the original number *before* that number goes into use. In other words, to use check digits with customer numbers, the check digit is computed and added to the customer number, making it a 5 digit number, before it is assigned to any customer. As a matter of fact, users of the number need be aware a check digit is involved.

Suppose we have a system of four-digit customer numbers and want to assign check digits. The original customer number is 2458. We will use modular division to develop the check digit. In modular division, the information of interest is the remainder rather than the quotient, and we will use the remainder in developing the check digit. The divisor selected here is 11, a commonly used one for this method, hence the name *modulus 11* check digit method.

First we assign weights to each digit, starting from the low order (right) position in the data, using values 2 through 10 (starting over again with 2 if we run out of digits), and moving to the left. Figure 8.23 shows weights of 2, 3, 4, and 5 under each digit in the customer number, reading from right to left.

The next step is to multiply the weights by the numbers above them. As Figure 8.23 shows, this yields products of 10, 16, 15, and 16. Next the numbers are summed, giving a total of 57.

The sum is divided by the modulus number, 11, giving a result of 5 with a remainder 2. Now we subtract the remainder 2 from the modulus divisor and get the result 9. The number 9 is the check digit. It becomes a permanent part of the customer number when the number goes into everyday use.

How does the extra digit assist in detecting transcription or transposition errors? As you can see, the procedure for determining check digits is quite simple and always follows the same steps. Therefore, it can easily be included as part of a computer program, if the analyst desires this. Assume that a modulus 11 check digit procedure is part of a sales system that requires use of customer numbers. The data entry person keys in the customer number, but mistakenly enters it as 24539. Will the program find this error?

When the data is entered for processing (either in a batch or directly in an on-line system), the program reads the first four digits of the customer number, 2453. The modulus 11 process is carried out, as shown in Figure 8.23. The result of multiplying and adding the digits is 47. Dividing by 11

Customer number:	2 4 5 8
Weights:	5 4 3 2
Multiply numbers X weights:	10 16 15 16
Sum results:	10 + 16 + 15 + 16 = 57
Divide by modulus number:	57/11 = 5 with remainder of 2
Subtract remainder from modulus number:	11 − 2 = 9
Add check digit to original number: →	24589

Figure 8.23.
Modulus 11 check digit method.

produces a remainder of 3, which in turn is subtracted from 11 to produce a check digit of 8. When the program compares the value 8 just computed with the original check digit of 9, it will find that they do not match and can signal that an error has occurred.

While it is true that check digits add an additional number to the data, they improve the quality of data entering the system by helping to eliminate transposition and transcription errors.

The systems analyst should always assume that invalid data will be submitted for processing and develop methods for detecting them so that corrections can be made. As this section indicated, errors should be caught during input so that erroneous data will not be stored. Figure 8.20 summarizes the input validation methods discussed in this section.

INPUT DESIGN FOR ON-LINE SYSTEMS

On-line systems raise additional questions for the analyst and for the users. This section discusses input design for on-line systems where data is entered through CRTs (Chapter 10 examines on-line systems in detail).

CRT Input Screen Design

When a system will require the entry of data through CRT screens, the designer takes extra precautions to ensure that users know how to provide the data. Such concerns as length of data fields and paging from one form or page to another are almost nonexistent in batch environments, where data is recorded on source documents that show the number of characters permissible on a line or where page two is reached by turning page one over. However, the analyst can make no such presumptions if CRT input is expected.

As discussed for output design, all CRT screens should tell the user about the data presented. For instance, headings and titles should clearly indicate the purpose of the screen (such as entering data, editing data, or determining what step to take next). Information about how to move from one screen to another is also essential.

The system must tell the user where to enter data and how long each item can be. There are several approaches to doing this. One method uses a dot or other special character to indicate where data can be entered, as well as how many characters or numbers are permissible. The system can communicate the fact that a field is five characters long by marking the field with five dots or periods. As the operators enter data, they key right over the dots. Dashes or lines can also be used to instruct the users.

Another common alternative marks the beginning and end of the field with brackets, braces, colons, or other distinctive symbols. Users then key data in to fill the blank. The markings show the maximum length of the data that the system will accept rather than indicating that every character must be filled.

Figure 8.24. Computer CRT keyboard showing special function keys. (Courtesy of Honeywell Information Systems, Inc.)

Terminal keyboards have arrows and special keys that enable the user to move the cursor (the block of light that tells the user where the system is pointing) around the screen when entering data (Figure 8.24). Only a few minutes use is necessary to become very comfortable with cursor movement.

However, even when individuals are familiar with the CRT or terminal, they may still need instructions about how to enter data. For example, it is not uncommon for users to ask questions such as "How do I correct the mistake I just made?" or "How do I store the data in the system now that I have finished this transaction?" or "How do I tell the system that I am done and I want to get off the terminal?" These are important questions to the user and to the analyst. The analyst will want to anticipate them and tell the user what actions to take by putting simple messages on the screen. If the analyst does not, the user is liable to figure out an incorrect solution, such as turning off the terminal or depressing a key that produces unexpected actions, either of which could cause data to be lost.

Figure 8.25 shows a CRT screen for data entry. Notice how the brief messages at the bottom of the screen quickly tell the user how to store data, make corrections, go to the next page of data for the transaction, and exit from the system. The keys to depress are highlighted (they can also be underlined or blinking on some terminals), and the messages are very brief. Yet they are clear. Analysts' specifications to the programmer should also state that these actions are the only valid ones; any others should be

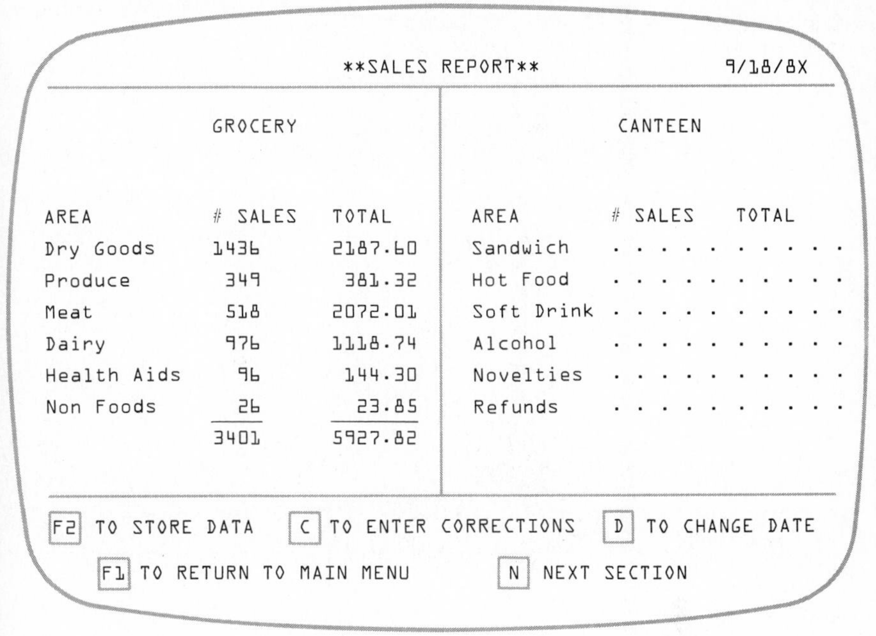

SALES REPORT 9/18/8X

GROCERY			CANTEEN		
AREA	# SALES	TOTAL	AREA	# SALES	TOTAL
Dry Goods	1436	2187.60	Sandwich	. . . . .	. . . . .
Produce	349	381.32	Hot Food	. . . . .	. . . . .
Meat	518	2072.01	Soft Drink	. . . . .	. . . . .
Dairy	976	1118.74	Alcohol	. . . . .	. . . . .
Health Aids	96	144.30	Novelties	. . . . .	. . . . .
Non Foods	26	23.85	Refunds	. . . . .	. . . . .
	3401	5927.82			

[F2] TO STORE DATA [C] TO ENTER CORRECTIONS [D] TO CHANGE DATE

[F1] TO RETURN TO MAIN MENU [N] NEXT SECTION

Figure 8.25. Data entry CRT screen for sales system.

considered unacceptable, and the software should be written to prohibit entry of any other instruction. This will prevent errors.

Editing in On-Line Systems

In batch systems, when corrections to data are necessary, a new transaction containing the corrections is created and submitted for processing, perhaps as part of a batch other than the one in which the error was made. However, in on-line systems, all changes are made through the CRT or terminal.

Editing refers to any changes made to records that are stored in the system or that have been submitted for processing but have not yet been stored. Editing also includes deletion of records.

To understand how editing occurs in an on-line system, you might consider *addition* of new records to be a special case of editing. In other words, when you enter data to create a new record to store in the system, you are going through many of the same steps as in editing, including keying in the data you want stored, making corrections for any keying mistakes, and telling the system to store the data. The data that is keyed in overwrites blanks, dots, dashes, or lines. But you *are* keying over *something*. Editing does the same thing: it allows you to key over something to change the current values. Instead of blanks or dashes, it is usually numbers or characters. If you think of on-line editing in this manner, it will turn out to be quite easy to understand.

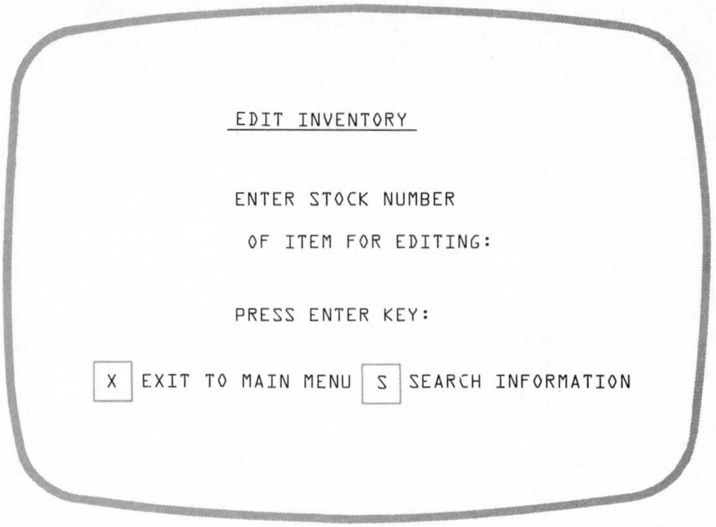

EDIT INVENTORY

ENTER STOCK NUMBER
OF ITEM FOR EDITING:

PRESS ENTER KEY:

X EXIT TO MAIN MENU S SEARCH INFORMATION

Figure 8.26. Instruction screen to enter data.

IDENTIFYING DATA FOR EDITING

To design an edit function, you must first provide a way for users to tell the system which record of data they wish to edit. Figure 8.26 shows a display screen instructing the users to enter the item number of the inventory part they wish to edit. Notice the instructions tell the user exactly what to do in brief, simple terms.

In Figure 8.27, using the data entered by the user, the computer retrieves from storage the data for product number BC-148A and displays it on the screen, along with instructions for making changes. By moving the cursor down to the price field and keying the data value 2.85, the user changes the price of item BC-148A from 2.50 to 2.85. The new data is keyed right over the old. The analyst may use an alternative design in which the changes are keyed alongside the current values (Figure 8.28) and replace the existing data only when the user depresses the enter key. Either format is acceptable and common.

After the changes are made through editing, they are stored.

DELETING RECORDS IN ON-LINE EDITING

Deleting records in on-line systems requires the analyst to provide a way for the users to indicate the proper record, as described above, as well as instructing the system that the transaction is a deletion.

Two ways are common. The first allows the user to depress a key that instructs the system to delete the current record on the screen. (Some analysts use a design that requires the user to change a record key to blanks

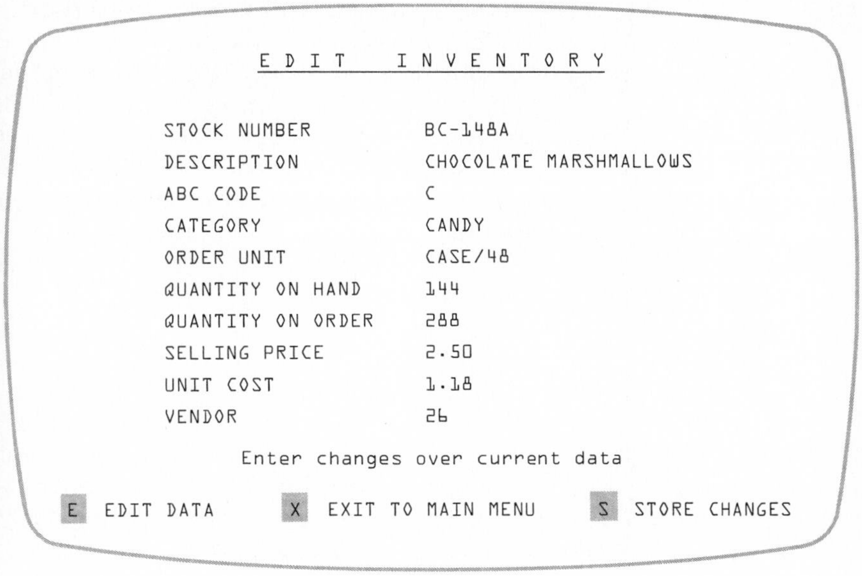

Figure 8.27. Sample edit screen for inventory system.

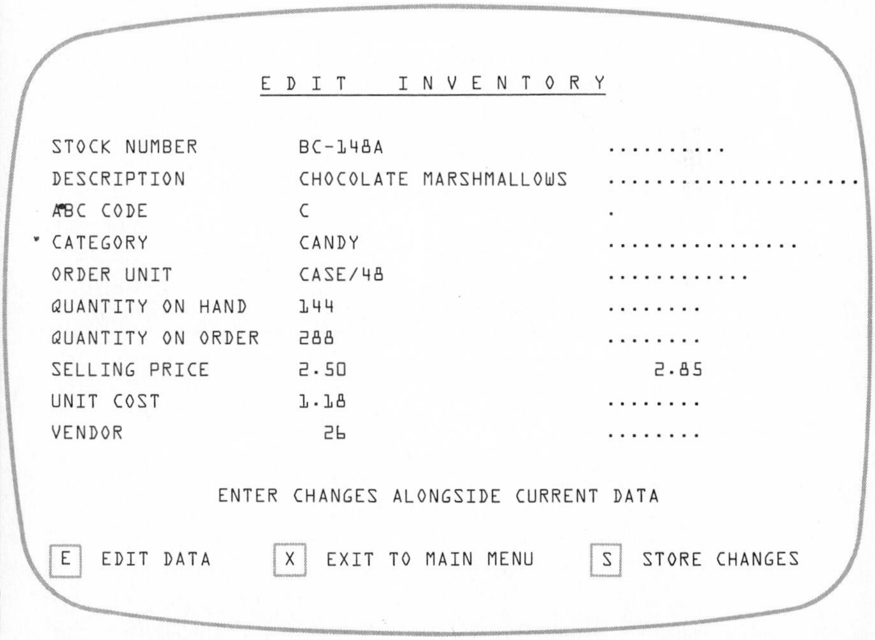

Figure 8.28. Sample edit screen showing "Key Alongside" format.

to delete records, although this is much less desirable since it is too easy for the user to forget to blank out the key field.) This method requires that the proper record first be retrieved and displayed on the screen.

The other way analysts build delete procedures asks the user to identify the proper record by entering the record key (such as item number) and then depressing a key telling the system to delete the record.

Both methods are common, although the first one is preferred since the user views the record before telling the system to delete the record.

Menu-Driven On-Line Systems

Since on-line systems provide several input and processing options to users, a method of showing the options the user can choose from is needed. Menus serve this purpose. A *menu* is a screen of information displayed on the CRT that shows the user what functions can be performed and how to select them. The menu in Figure 8.29 shows the options available to a user of a sales system. There are four options: entering budget data, entering sales information, editing data, and receiving reports. In addition, the user can leave the system (terminate the working session) if desired. These are the only options available.

Notice that each option is identified by a number. The designers of this system could also have used letters or special characters to identify each option. To invoke a particular option, the user depresses the key corresponding to the desired option. For instance, depressing "3" selects the editing function in the sales system.

Notice that option 3 is for an edit *menu*. This means that another menu will be shown. Figure 8.30 is a menu for editing data in the sales system. Like the main overall menu, the editing menu lists those editing options that are available in this design.

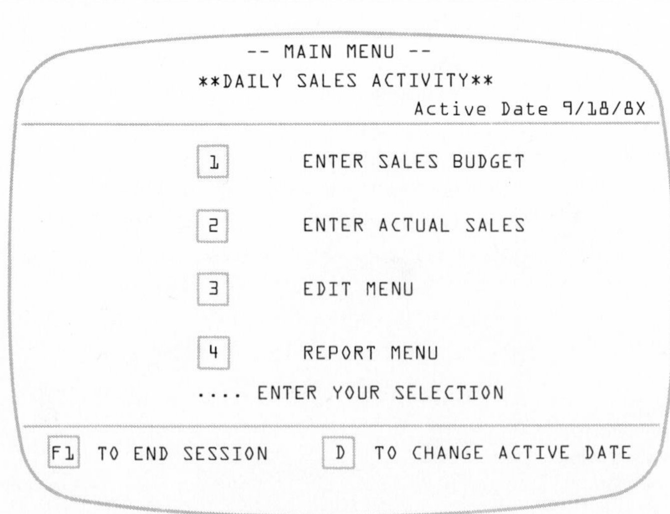

Figure 8.29. Main menu for sales system.

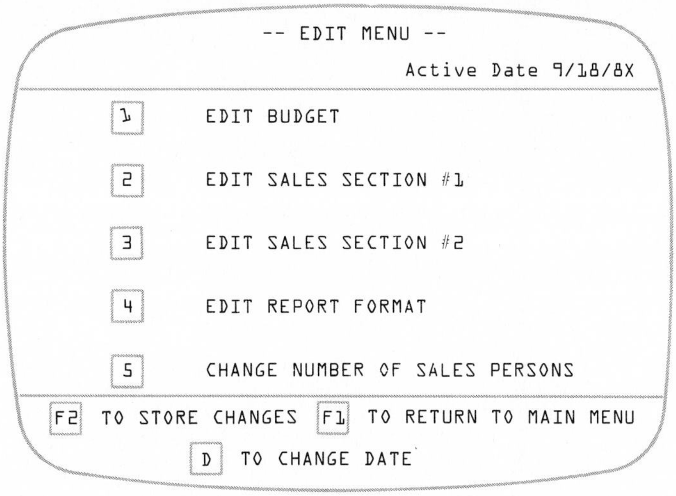

Figure 8.30. Edit menu for sales system.

Menus that provide selections to users in a top-down fashion (Figure 8.31) ensure that systems are easy to use, while making the choice of what to do next a simple procedure. The system leads the user through a series of decisions until the correct procedure is selected. For instance, a narrative dialogue to lead someone through the steps in editing sales budget data would probably sound something like this:

1 You are using the sales system. Which function do you wish to select? (The user depresses "3" for the EDIT MENU option shown on the main menu.)
2 You have selected the edit option from the main menu. Which of these editing options do you wish? (The user depresses "1" for the EDIT BUDGET option shown on the edit menu.)
3 You have selected the edit budget option from the edit menu. Enter the changes.

Menus accomplish the same thing with few words. This is why analysts and users alike prefer them to written instructions or the display of narrative information on the screen. And have you noticed the uncluttered look of the screen, even after all headings and options are displayed? It would be difficult to preserve the easy-to-read displays if the narrative above was shown instead of the menu option.

Emphasizing Information on Display Screens

Often the analyst will use features built into hardware and software to call information or messages to the attention of users. For example, error messages or reports of unacceptable actions (such as submitting invalid

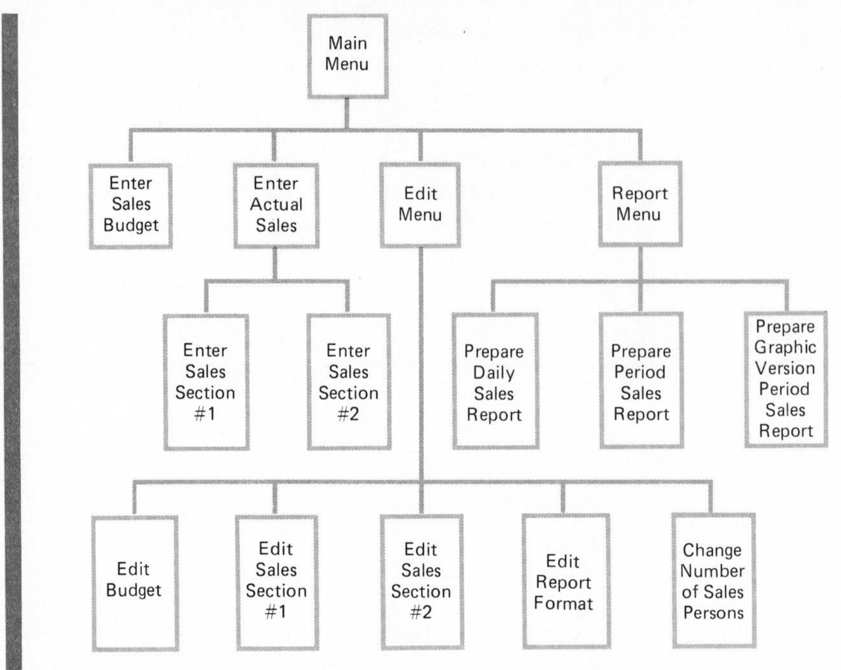

Figure 8.31. Top-down menu for sales system.

data or asking the system to perform a function now expected by the program) are best displayed by using one of the emphasis techniques listed below. Likewise, when the user enters data for processing, the analyst may display a message informing the user the data has been accepted and processing begun (for example, SORTING DATA, PREPARING REPORT, WRITING DATA TO DISK, or PROCESSING INQUIRY).

The methods of emphasis that many systems offer are:

1 Blinking
2 Underlining
3 Increased/reduced light intensity
4 Inverse video (black letters on light screen)

Advances in hardware and software will continue to produce other methods for emphasizing information for users.

COLOR USE IN SCREEN DESIGN

As color capability is added to more on-line systems, the analyst will add a new dimension to design. If properly used in the design, color will assist the user in understanding information on the screen, determining what steps are valid, and reducing errors.

Color has four primary uses: (1) identifying valid operations the user can carry out, (2) tying related data together, (3) highlighting information about organization performance, and (4) communicating messages about system performance. In many systems, only selected data fields presented on a display screen can be edited. For example, in a personnel file that retrieves a record by using the employee identification number as a record key, it is allowable to change the name, address, family, and work history information. However, changes should not be allowed in the employee number field because modifying the record key improperly will lose the employee record and because such a change is seldom valid in the first place. (Employee numbers in most organizations are assigned once when the individual is hired and do not ever change. Furthermore, the proper way to change a key field is by deleting the record entirely and recreating it.) The analyst may chose to indicate that a field may not be edited by coding it with a different color. The system may also be designed so that it the user cannot instruct the cursor to move into the employee number field, prohibiting editing. Color explains to the individual why the field cannot be changed.

When large amounts of information must be presented on a display screen, the analyst may use color to provide better structure and meaning to the information. Related items can be tied together by color so the user can spot them more quickly. For instance, a report showing sales, costs, and profits for various regions may be presented using colors to show each type of cost across departments.

The reporting of performance is commonly shown through use of specific colors. Poor performance that results in losses is usually shown in red. (You probably have heard the saying that "profits for the year were in the red.") Acceptable performance, in contrast, is represented through use of other colors, such as black or blue. The analyst should follow these standards when reporting performance information or users will either misread the meaning of information or spend extra time ensuring they are interpreting the displays properly.

COLOR SELECTION

Color meanings are lost if they are used improperly or if excessive color is used. The traditional colors of red, amber (yellow), and green have the common meanings of stop or danger, caution, and normal. Any color usage in display of information should follow these common meanings. No more than four colors can be quickly recognized by users. The most useful colors are red, green, yellow, and blue. Contrasts are most effectively presented through the color pairs of red and green, yellow and blue, or white and blue.

Color can be effective when there is a reason for its use, as indicated. However, if the analyst specifies color only for the sake of color, the impact of information may be lost through the distraction of color. Thus its utilization must be carefully planned.

Chapter 10 will discuss other aspects of on-line systems in greater detail.

SUMMARY

The input design specifies how data enter batch and on-line systems for processing. It also includes methods for capturing data and validating its correctness. The overall objectives of input design stress minimizing the quantity of data for input, while controlling errors and delay. An effective design will also avoid extra steps in input, while ensuring the entire process is as simple for the user and data entry personnel as possible. The data captured for input should include only those items that vary from transaction to transaction, including identification data (keys). Data that the system can either retrieve from storage or calculate should not be specified for input.

The source document plays an important role in the entire input process since it is used for the initial capture of the data. The careful selection of coding methods to identify classifications, functions, sequences, data subsets, or even cards further simplifies data preparation and input. Mnemonic codes enhance visual communication of data values.

There are several methods for capturing data, depending on the processing mode and use of a source document. With some methods, such as those involving keypunching, key to storage, or optical character readers, source documents are always used to collect the data that will later be input. However, if intelligent terminals will be used at the point of the transaction, direct entry of data may be specified.

Regardless of the processing mode or method of data entry, the input must be correct. Three categories of input validation methods are used. In checking the transaction, validation methods certify the correctness and completeness of the transaction itself. Batch controls may be used if groups of transactions are prepared for processing, to ensure data is not lost and every record is input properly. Sequence and completeness tests verify that the order is acceptable and data is not missing. The second group of methods, checks the actual data in each transaction to ensure that it is present, reasonable and within limits, and consistent between individual data items within the transaction. Still a third way of validating data uses automatic correction and the addition of self-checking digits on key fields. All methods are aimed at finding errors before the data is processed and stored.

Special considerations are needed for input designs in on-line environments. The analyst must design CRT screens that tell the user what to do and what steps to take next in a way that is brief, yet easy to understand. Menus are often used to present options to users and data fields are marked to show their length while telling the user where to enter the data. Data entry in on-line systems also includes the ability to edit data. In each of these cases, valid entries must be identified and communicated to programmers so they construct the software to accept correct entries and reject those that are invalid.

CASE STUDY FOR CHAPTER 8
INPUT DESIGN FOR ORDER ENTRY AND INVOICING

The input design for Valley Industries is intended to accommodate current business operations as well as future expansion, including remote site operations. The input features are discussed here. The communication aspects of data entry and retrieval will be discussed after Chapter 11.

DESIGN IN AN ON-LINE ENVIRONMENT

The input design for the new system includes the following display screens:

Screen # 1 Order Entry and Invoicing Main Menu
Screen # 2 Order Processing Menu
Screen # 3 Order Entry Screen - Customer Data
Screen # 4 Order Entry Screen - Customer Order Data
Screen # 5 Order Entry Screen - Customer Basic Item Entry
Screen # 6 Order Entry Screen - Customer Item Entry
Screen # 7 Invoicing Screen - Customer Item Selection
Screen # 8 Customer Orders Inquiry Screen
Screen # 9 Customer Requirements by Item Inquiry Screen
Screen #10 Customer Status Inquiry Screen
Screen #11 Accounts Receivable Main Menu
Screen #12 Transaction Processing Menu
Screen #13 Accounts Receivable Screen - Cash Receipt Entry
Screen #14 Accounts Receivable Screen - Cash Receipt Posting
Screen #15 Accounts Receivable Screen - Invoice Entry
Screen #16 Accounts Receivable Inquiry Screen - Open Items

Their use is discussed in the following sections, which describe order entry, invoicing, and accounts receivable activities. Input validation and verification methods are pointed out where appropriate. Additional validation and design features are included in the processing design (discussed at the end of Chapter 12).

ORDER ENTRY AND INVOICING

ENTERING ORDERS

Order entry and invoicing begins with the *Order Entry and Invoicing Main Menu* (screen #1), from which the *Order Processing* screen (screen #2) can be

```
                ORDER ENTRY AND INVOICING

                       MAIN MENU

                 1  ORDER PROCESSING
                 2  INQUIRY
                 3  REPORTS
                 4  MONTHLY CLOSE
                 5  FILE MAINTENANCE
                 6  FILE LISTINGS

                 X  EXIT FROM SYSTEM

ENTER NUMBER                              ACTIVE DATE
                                            99/99/99
```

Figure C8.1. Order entry and invoicing main menu.

called and Order Entry selected. To enter an order, the operator enters the customer number and purchase order number from the *Order Form* (input #1). The system responds with *Order Entry Screen - Customer Data* (screen #3). If this is a new customer, the operator can enter the basic customer information, which will then be posted to the file. If the customer is not new, the information

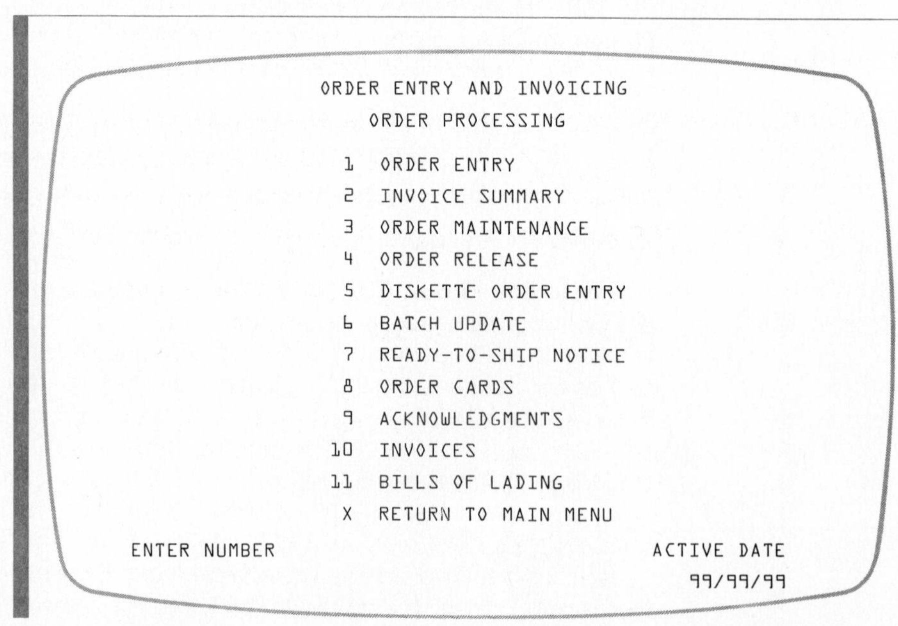

Figure C8.2. Order processing menu.

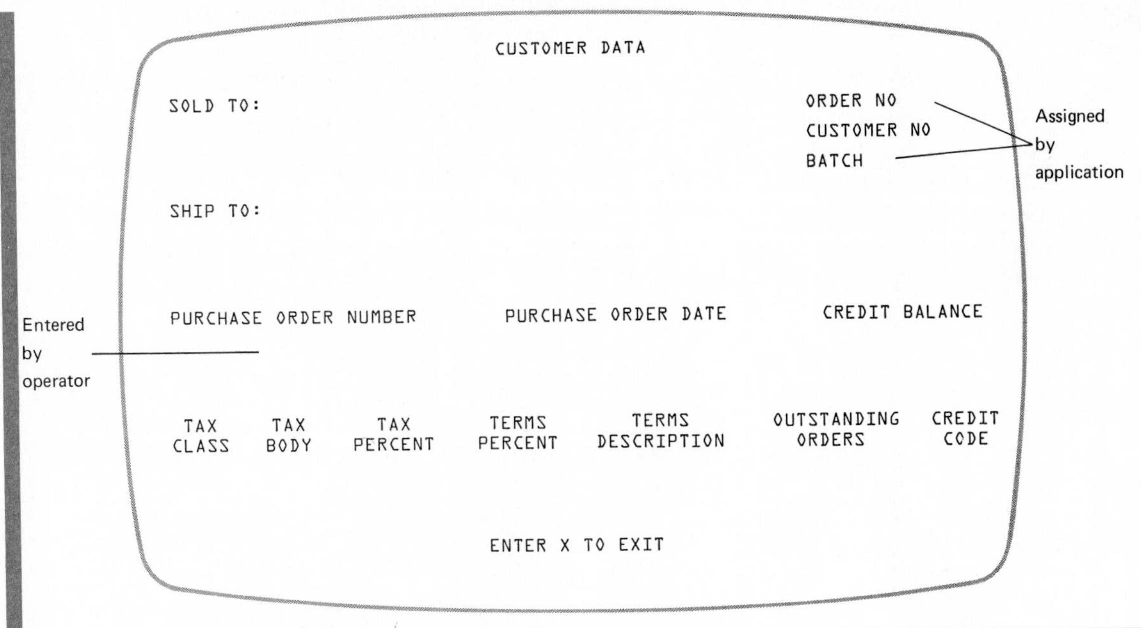

Figure C8.3. Order entry screen—customer data.

will be filled in and the operator will verify it before going on. If the information is accurate, the system then displays *Order Entry Screen - Customer Order Data* (screen #4). The operator enters and verifies the order data.

The operator can choose between two data entry methods. *Order Entry Screen - Customer Basic Item Entry* (screen #5) allows the entry of the item number and quantity only, and the system displays the description and price for the item entered.

The second method, *Order Entry Screen - Customer Item Entry* (screen #6), allows the operator to enter the basic information and also override information regarding this item for the specific order (for example, selling price, tax code, etc.). The system displays the description and price information.

As each order is entered, the operator can process the order immediately into the open order files (allowing for immediate printing of the order card) or can have the order held for batch processing.

INVOICING

The operator enters the Valley job number to be invoiced, and the system selects the customer and item information associated with this order. When the ordered items are displayed to the operator for verification on *Invoicing Screen - Customer Item Selection* (screen #7), changes to pricing information and quantity shipped information can be made.

Once the batch is completed, the operator can initiate the actual invoicing procedure or leave the batch for later invoicing.

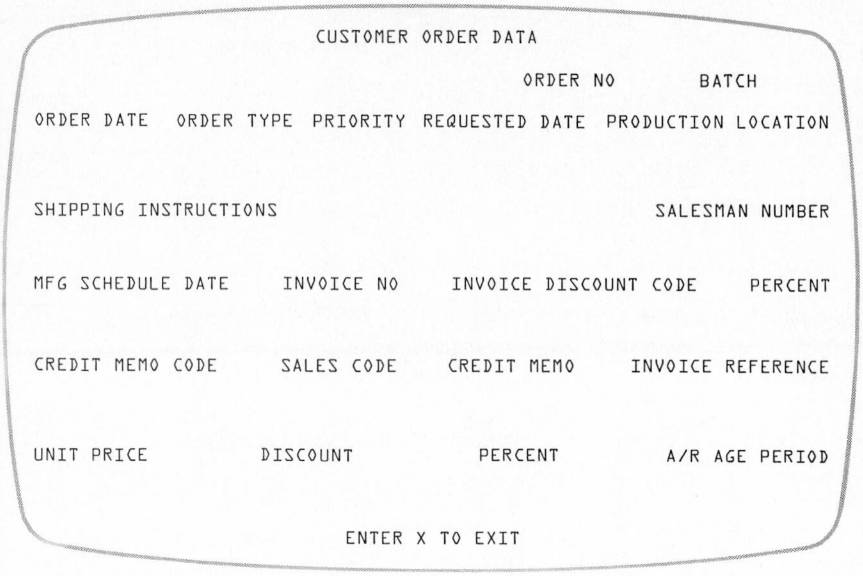

Figure C8.4. Order entry screen—customer order data.

INQUIRIES

The order entry and invoicing application has an inquiry capability which permits the operator to determine the status of any item or customer on file.

The customer requirements by item inquiry displays all of the current

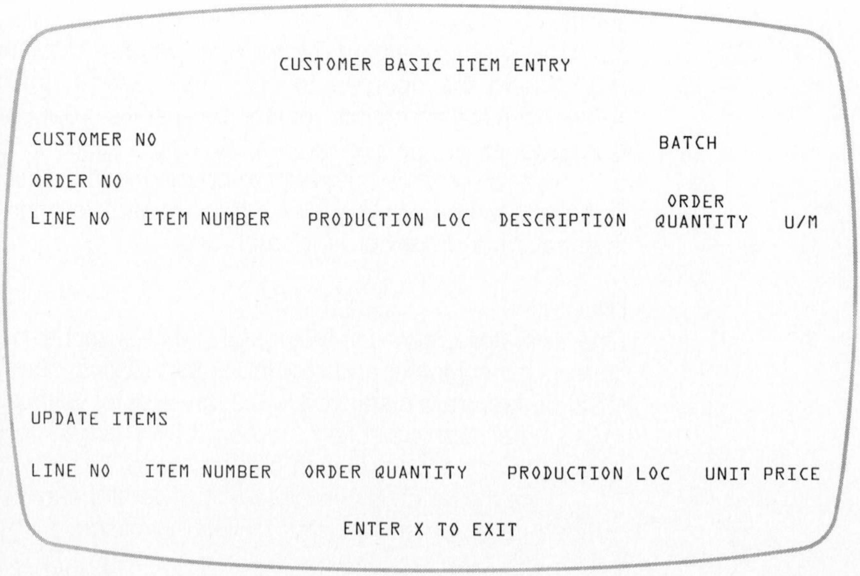

Figure C8.5. Order entry screen—customer basic item entry.

CUSTOMER ITEM ENTRY

CUSTOMER NO BATCH

ORDER NO

ITEM NUMBER QUANTITY ORDERED

UNIT PRICE | MARKUP PERCENT | QTY DISCOUNT PERCENT | CONTRACT PRICE | SELLING PRICE | NET SALES AMOUNT

CREDIT | TAX CODE | PRODUCTION LOC | UNIT WEIGHT | UNIT COST

DESCRIPTION | TYPE | CLASS | U/M

ENTER X TO EXIT

Figure C8.6. Order entry screen—customer item entry.

orders for a particular customer. Using the *Customer Orders Inquiry Screen* (screen #8), it shows each open order for the customer.

The customer requirements by item inquiry also displays all outstanding customer orders for any inventory item on the *Customer Requirements by Item Inquiry Screen* (screen #9).

The customer status inquiry displays basic information regarding a

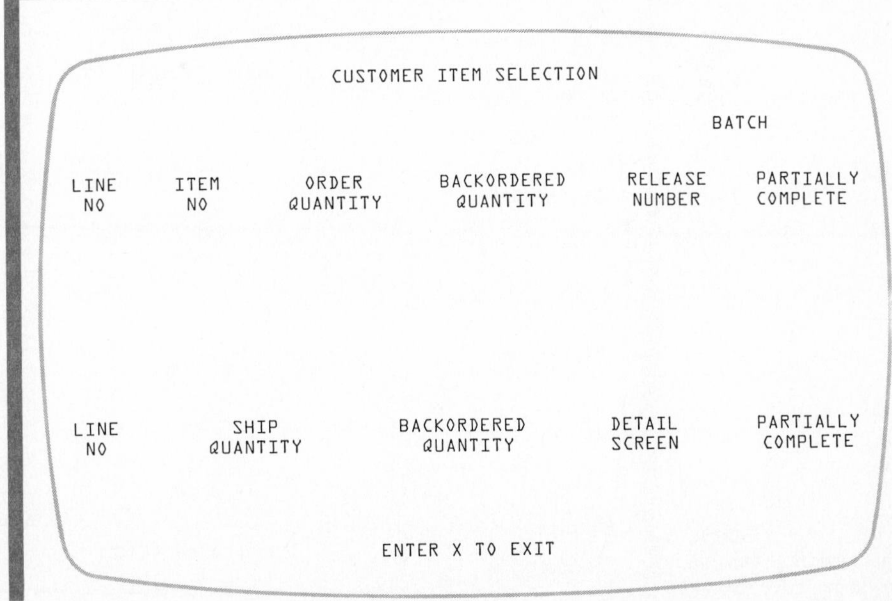

Figure C8.7. Invoicing screen—customer item selection.

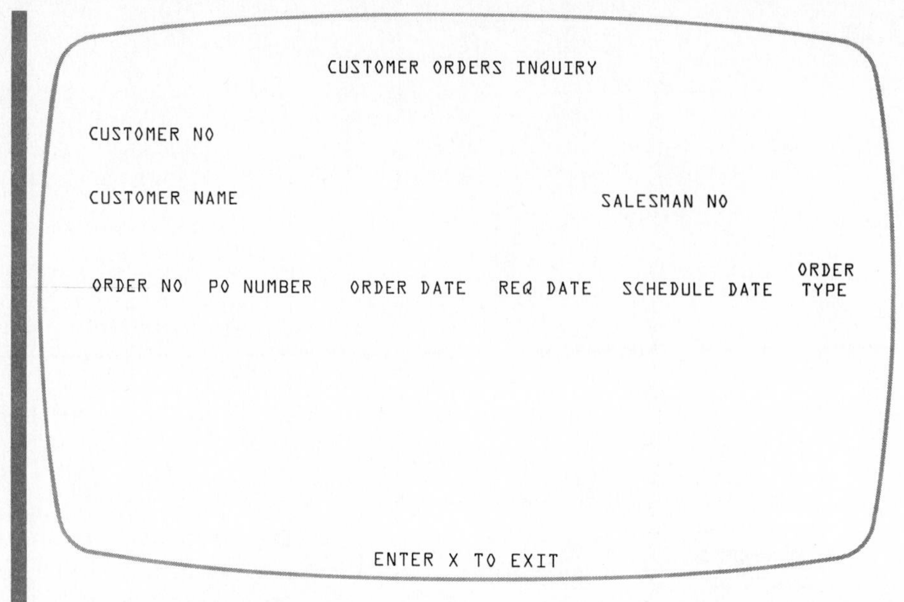

Figure C8.8. Customer orders inquiry screen.

customer. Accounts receivable balance is also included. The *Customer Status Inquiry Screen* (screen #10) is used.

ACCOUNTS RECEIVABLE

All operations for the accounts receivable application start with the *Accounts Receivable Main Menu* (screen #11). This menu provides flexibility in selecting the job to be performed.

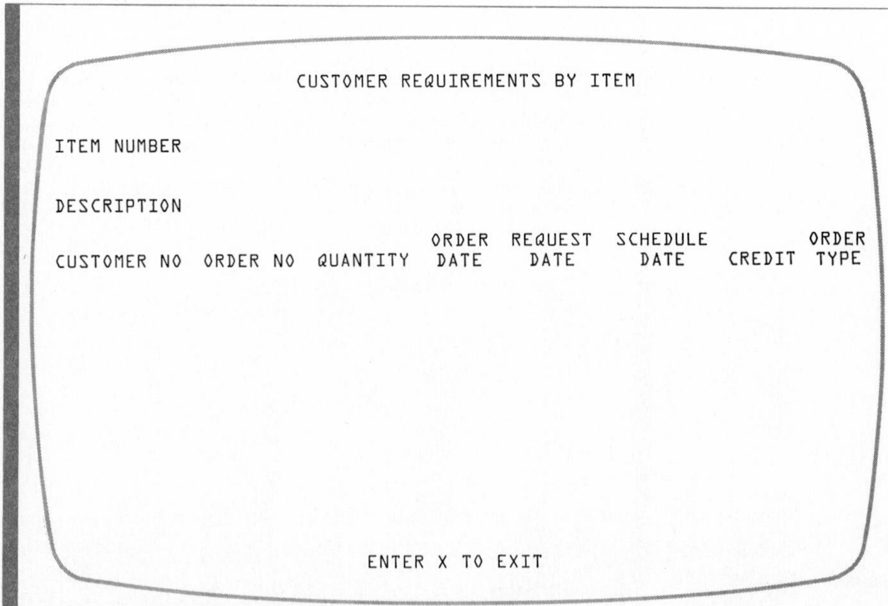

Figure C8.9. Customer requirements by item inquiry screen.

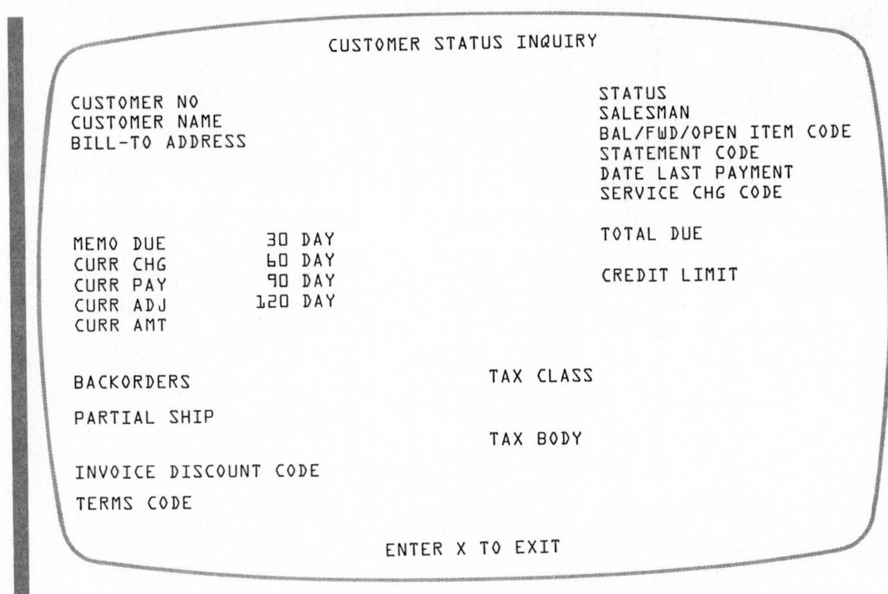

Figure C8.10. Customer status inquiry screen.

ENTERING CASH AND ADJUSTMENT TRANSACTIONS

The input document is *Customer Payment or Credit* (input #4). When cash and adjustments are processed, the operator first calls the *Transaction Processing* screen (screen #12) and selects the Receipts/Adjs Entry. When the operator enters the customer number, the system displays the *Accounts Receivable*

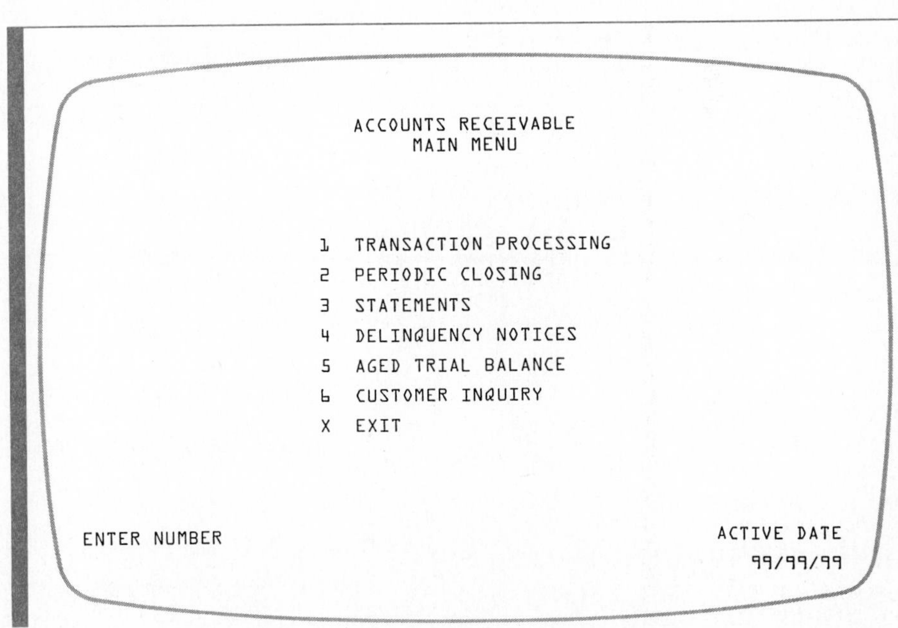

ACCOUNTS RECEIVABLE
MAIN MENU
1 TRANSACTION PROCESSING
2 PERIODIC CLOSING
3 STATEMENTS
4 DELINQUENCY NOTICES
5 AGED TRIAL BALANCE
6 CUSTOMER INQUIRY
X EXIT
ENTER NUMBER
ACTIVE DATE
99/99/99

Figure C8.11. Accounts receivable main menu.

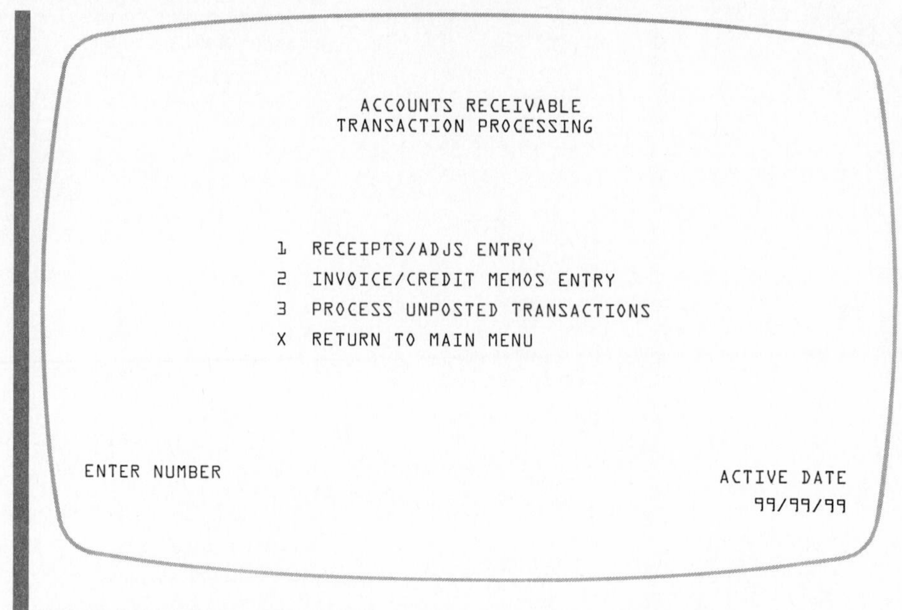

ACCOUNTS RECEIVABLE
TRANSACTION PROCESSING
1 RECEIPTS/ADJS ENTRY
2 INVOICE/CREDIT MEMOS ENTRY
3 PROCESS UNPOSTED TRANSACTIONS
X RETURN TO MAIN MENU
ENTER NUMBER
ACTIVE DATE
99/99/99

Figure C8.12. Transaction processing.

Screen - Cash Receipt Entry (screen #13). The operator can verify the customer name and address and then enter the cash receipt transaction.

The reference field (REF) determines the method of cash application for this particular receipt. Three entry methods are available based on information entered in the reference field:

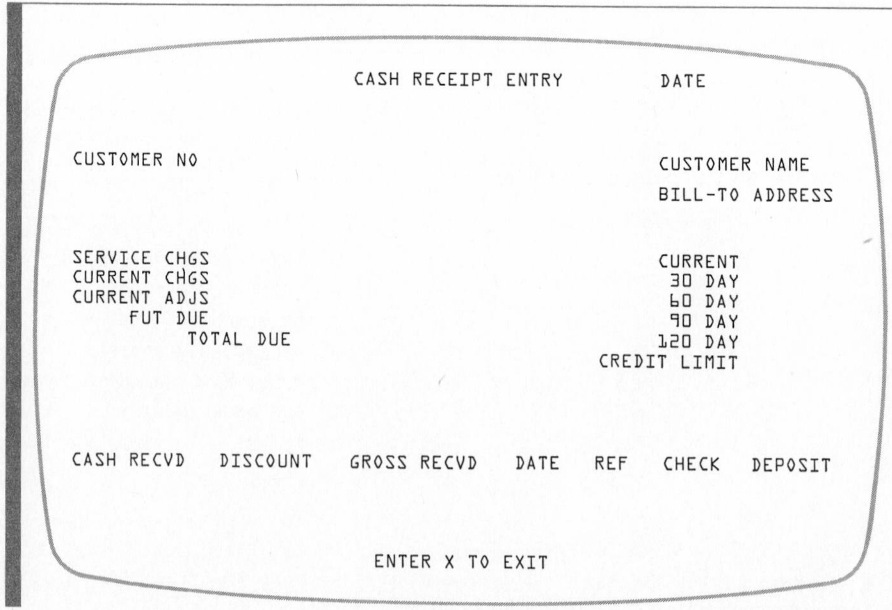

Figure C8.13. Accounts receivable screen—cash receipt entry.

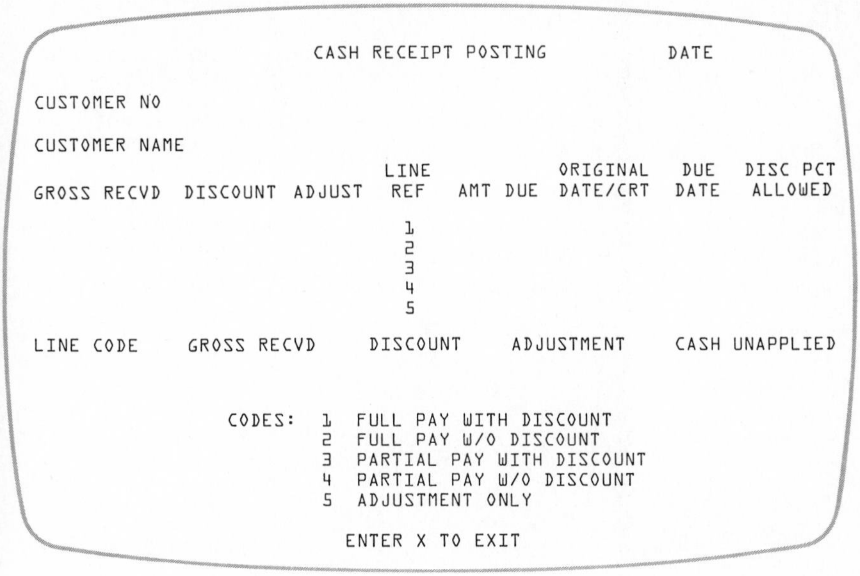

```
                        CASH RECEIPT POSTING          DATE

CUSTOMER NO

CUSTOMER NAME
                                   LINE              ORIGINAL   DUE   DISC PCT
GROSS RECVD  DISCOUNT  ADJUST      REF    AMT DUE    DATE/CRT   DATE  ALLOWED
                                    1
                                    2
                                    3
                                    4
                                    5

LINE CODE    GROSS RECVD    DISCOUNT    ADJUSTMENT    CASH UNAPPLIED


                 CODES:  1  FULL PAY WITH DISCOUNT
                         2  FULL PAY W/O DISCOUNT
                         3  PARTIAL PAY WITH DISCOUNT
                         4  PARTIAL PAY W/O DISCOUNT
                         5  ADJUSTMENT ONLY

                            ENTER X TO EXIT
```

Figure C8.14. Accounts receivable screen—cash receipt posting.

1 Operator enters ALL. The entire customer account is paid.
2 Operator enters a specific invoice number. The system searches for the referenced invoice and applies the cash to it.
3 Operator leaves the reference field blank. This method is used most often since a customer might pay several but not all invoices with one check. The

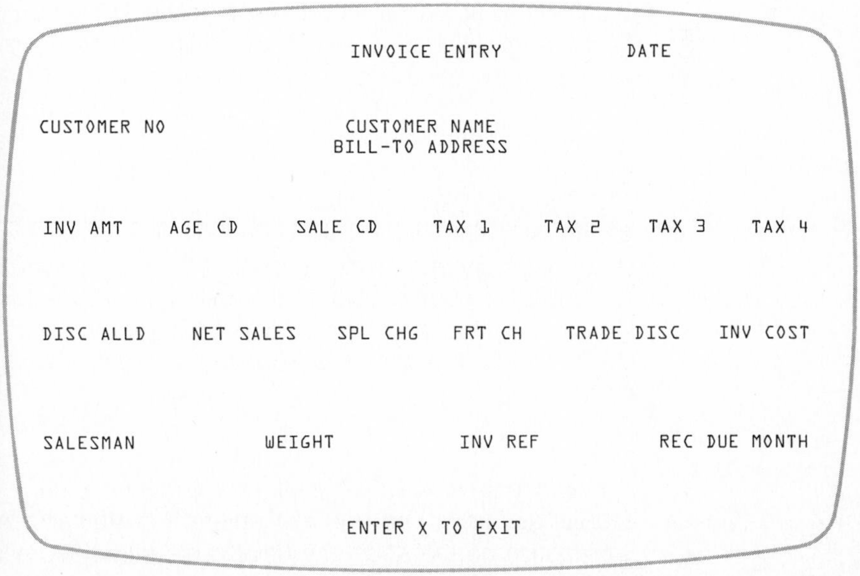

```
                          INVOICE ENTRY          DATE


CUSTOMER NO               CUSTOMER NAME
                         BILL-TO ADDRESS


INV AMT    AGE CD    SALE CD    TAX 1    TAX 2    TAX 3    TAX 4


DISC ALLD   NET SALES   SPL CHG   FRT CH   TRADE DISC   INV COST


SALESMAN          WEIGHT          INV REF          REC DUE MONTH


                          ENTER X TO EXIT
```

Figure C8.15. Accounts receivable screen—invoice entry.

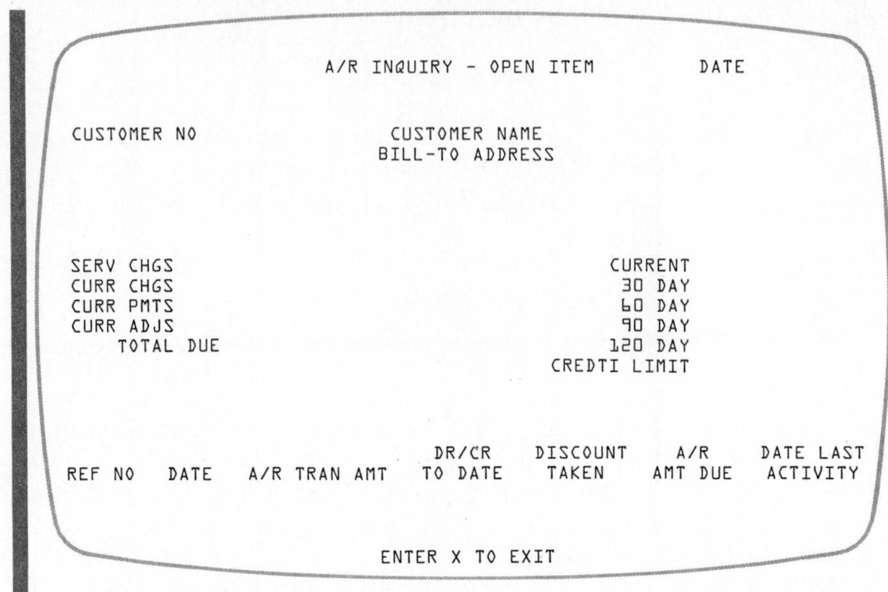

Figure C8.16. Accounts receivable inquity screen—open items.

system displays the outstanding items five at a time until the transaction is completed. *Accounts Receivable Screen - Cash Receipt Posting* (screen #14) is used. The operator enters the line numbers selected for payment. This method allows the operator to write off minor discrepancies in each invoice or to apply partial payments against an invoice.

The adjustment application feature allows the operator to process adjustment entries against the customer's account. The flow of processing is similar to the application of cash. As the entry is made, it is first verified and then applied to the referenced item in the detail file.

At the end of cash receipt and adjustment posting, a display shows the control totals for the data just entered.

ENTERING INVOICE SUMMARIES

Invoice summary records are required only for invoices not processed through the order entry and invoicing application. The invoice summary entry verifies the customer number prior to accepting the transaction. This entry allows the operator to enter a credit memo and apply it directly to a particular invoice for the customer. The *Accounts Receivable Screen - Invoice Entry* (screen #15) is used.

INQUIRY

The accounts receivable application provides inquiry into a customer's data files at any time. The operator enters a customer number and receives the information on the *Accounts Receivable Inquiry Screen - Open Item* (screen #16).

INPUT DOCUMENTS

ORDER FORM (INPUT #1)
Contents:
Customer-name
Bill-to-address (Validate to file # during screen process.)
Ship-to-address (Validate to file # during screen process.)
Order-date
Required-date
Purchase-order-number
Quantity (Validate by reasonableness test.)
Valley-part-number (Validate to file # during screen process. By use of a check digit, validate that the number is a valid Valley number.)
Salesperson
Added to original order:
Current-date (take transaction date from system.)
Customer-number (System assigns.)
Price (System assigns.)
Valley-job-number (Validate by sequence test.)

All orders will be written on the revised order form. Even though orders come into Valley in a number of different ways (telephone, telex, written, and directly from the salesperson), orders will not have to be on the new form. However, the order form information will still have to be supplied. The information necessary to log an order will be brought out in the training sessions.

The customer's credit status is validated during the on-line data entry process, using the file number. Exceptions are then brought to Ms. Carbo's attention. In order to validate that all orders received are properly posted to the system, the system will compile a total for the number of items ordered. This hash total will appear on the screen and on the batch update register the next day. After the data entry process, a manual tape of the orders will need to be run and compared against the screen. If they do not match, the batch update register will have to be retrieved and audited against the order forms and the necessary correction made.

In order to verify that all cash receipts were posted properly, a net change in accounts figure on the cash receipts and adjustments register will be compared to the daily bank deposit plus customer credits. If they do not compare, an audit of the receipts against the cash receipts and adjustments register will have to be made and the error corrected.

KEYWORDS

Batch count
Batch size
Batch total
Card code
Check digit
Combination test
Completion test
Constant data
Deferred on-line processing
Duplicate processing

Existence test
Function code
Key
Identification data
Limit/range check
Menu
Mnemonic code
Modulus 11
Sequence code
Sequence test
Significant-digit subset code
Transcription error
Transaction validation
Transposition error

REVIEW QUESTIONS

1 What objectives guide input design? Briefly describe each.
2 Describe the types of data that should always be part of systems input. Which types of data should *not* ordinarily be input?
3 "If a form is well-designed, you will not notice the form." Discuss the meaning of this statement. List each guideline analysts should use when designing source documents. What steps are taken to design source documents?
4 What spacings are suggested for information users will provide on handwritten or typewritten source documents?
5 What are coding systems? What purpose do they serve? Discuss the different types of coding methods.
6 Discuss the methods of capturing and entering input data. What are the advantages and disadvantages of each? Which are utilized with batch systems and which with on-line systems?
7 Why is it so important to validate data during input? What methods exist to do this? Briefly explain each method.
8 Distinguish between batch size, batch total, and batch count. What assurance does each provide to analysts and users who are concerned about having reliable input?
9 How do transaction validation and data validation differ? What methods exist for each type? Explain each one.
10 What are transcription errors? Transposition errors? What should analysts include in their input design to detect these errors? Explain how it will detect these errors.
11 What differences exist in the design of input for on-line systems and that of batch environments?
12 Discuss the ways of designing CRT input screens for the processing of editing data.
13 What is a menu? What purpose does it serve?
14 In what ways is the use of color most effective in on-line systems?
15 How is information emphasized and enhanced when presented on visual displays?

APPLICATION PROBLEMS FOR CHAPTER 8

1 A new on-line system for maintaining customer information and retail transaction details will consist of the major functions of entering and revising retail transactions, entering and revising customer information, printing detailed transaction lists, and closing out sales periods. As part of the customer information portion of the system, the user is able to enter information for new customers, edit details of existing customer records, delete customer records, and print customer information. Within the printing portion of the program, the user has the option of displaying the

information for a specific customer or listing information for all customers. If complete information is listed, the user has the option of printing the information in alphabetical, customer-number, or zip-code order.

The system is menu driven, and, from any point in the system, the user will be able to return to the previous menu or leave the system entirely.

a This system should be designed as a multimenu system. Develop the menus for the application described as they pertain to the customer portion of the system. Design the screens to include all relevant information as it should be shown to the user. (The screen is 24 lines by 80 columns.)

b For the editing portion of the system, describe the input processing required to add, delete, and change customer records. That is, describe the input the user should provide for each type of transaction and how it should be validated by the system.

c Indicate any use of visual emphasis in *a* and *b*.

2 A decision support system to assist managers in planning and forecasting will be designed for use on a desktop computer. The system will display the following details: sales estimates, labor estimates, cost-of-goods estimates, management overhead, facilities overhead, and miscellaneous expenses. The system will calculate facilities overhead and cost of goods estimates as a fixed percentage of sales. Management overhead is a fixed dollar amount. Labor estimates and miscellaneous expenses vary and must be input by the user.

Gross profits will be calculated automatically by the system as sales less all costs.

a Develop an input screen(s) for the above system. Be sure to use a design that is easy to look at and contains guides to assist the individual in entering and examining data.

b Design a screen for editing the data in the application described. Indicate any utilization of highlighting to aid the user.

c What changes, if any, would you make if the system allows color data presentation? Explain.

3 An on-line entertainment system makes it possible for a user to retrieve records by function date, function identification number, or position. Each item is stored in the system under the function number. However, the system maintains an internal record of the functions, so it knows which one follows in ascending sequence and in descending sequence.

The data displayed on the screen includes:

Function number	8 characters
Sponsor	24 characters
Event date	6 digits (MM/DD/YY)
Cost of event	10 digits, 2 decimal values
Downpayment	10 digits, 2 decimal values
Balance due	10 digits, 2 decimal values
Billing address	48 digits
Notes and comments	24 characters

a Develop an input screen for the entry of data describing the entertainment function. Indicate any data validation you want to have the system do. Also indicate any fields that the system should calculate automatically.

b Develop an input screen for data that has been stored in the system. On the screen show the user how to edit the data, how to retrieve records of specific events by date or function number, and how to step sequentially through the function records. The display screen has 24 lines, each 80 characters in length.

4 The invoice shown on page 342 will be produced automatically when a new on-line order processing system is installed. Currently it is typed manually. All customers have identification numbers if they are regular purchasers who have established credit with the company (do not have to pay for their orders in advance). All customers who have arranged credit are given terms of net 30 days.

All orders are shipped by United Parcel Service (UPS), unless the customer requests another means. In either case, the cost of shipping is added to the invoice. The amount is a predetermined cost that is based on the weight of the item.

No item the firm sells has a unit price in excess of $1000.

All invoices are numbered as they are prepared (the typist prints the number on the invoice form), and all have internal job orders and order dates. The FOB point (for shipping) is always the origin. Some customers provide their own purchase order numbers for reference. When supplied, they are always printed on the invoice.

Each order is prepared by using a billing and shipping address. Both addresses are included on the invoice, even if they are the same.

a Design a data entry screen for the invoicing system described. All details of the order must be displayed, although they may be displayed between multiple screens.

b Indicate all details that must be entered, those that will be calculated by the system, and those that will be retrieved from systems files. For items you indicate for retrieval, also state how the system will be told what to retrieve.

c Indicate any input data that should be validated in the proposed system. What validation method do you recommend for each?

d How do you propose handling invoices where the total number of items ordered cannot be printed in the space allowed on a single invoice form?

INVOICE

INVOICE NO.

CUSTOMER NO.

BILL TO: SHIP TO:

DATE	SHIP VIA	F.O.B.	TERMS

PURCHASE ORDER NUMBER	ORDER DATE	SALES PERSON	OUR ORDER NUMBER

QUANTITY			ITEM NUMBER	DESCRIPTION	UNIT PRICE	EXTENDED PRICE
ORDERED	SHIPPED	B.O.				

5 A medical records system will use batch processing to maintain information about patient name, address, and medical insurance coverage. Allergies and reactions to specific medicines and any identifying marks are also recorded in a special notes section of the patient record.

Each patient has a unique identification number that is used on all records. If the patient is a child or dependent spouse, the record also shows a second account number, that of the persons who are responsible for the patient.

Patients may have many different types of insurance coverage, including private insurance, medicare, medicaid, worker's compensation, and no-fault (automobile) insurance. For each patient the record must show either an insurance code for one of these types of coverage or a specific code indicating that the patient does not have any insurance coverage. (The current record also allows space to mark a second form of insurance coverage for those persons to whom it pertains.)

Whenever patients receive medical care, a transaction is created that will identify who was treated, what the treatment was, and the date care was provided. This information will be translated from handwritten notes, prepared by the nurse or physician, into a punched card. It is important that no transaction is lost since medical records must be accurate.

a Develop a punched card layout form, indicating data items you feel belong on the card (based on the information provided). Be sure to include any necessary control information. (Indicate the data item field lengths you assume.)

b Develop data coding methods, appropriate for the situation described. Indicate both the code and the meaning of the code. Explain why coding is recommended.

c Indicate where input validation is needed and the type of validation that should be used.

6 A firm is planning to use key-to-disk for entering data into its new system. The average operator speed is 7500 keystrokes per hour. The data to be prepared includes four different types of transactions:

Sales order activities: 15,000 transactions per week, average transaction length 90 characters

Customer file maintenance activities: 8000 transactions per week, average transaction length 40 characters

New customer file activities: 2500 transactions per week, average transaction length 600 characters

Inventory transactions: 45,000 transactions per week, average transaction length 125 characters

In a normal workday, approximately 6 hours are available for data entry activities.

a If a 25 percent excess capacity safety factor is wanted, how many key-to-disk stations should be purchased to meet current demand?

b If the average salary and benefit cost for a data entry operator is $7.50 per hour, what is the cost of data entry operations per week (not including equipment costs)?

7 A metropolitan bank is adding an on-line system to speed the processing of transactions. Terminals will be located at all points where there is sufficient banking activity. Two types of terminals will be used. One will be a special display terminal that will be operated by a bank teller. The teller will be able to enter deposits and withdrawals for customers who are at the teller's window.

The other type of terminal will be a point-of-sale device, which customers use to withdraw money from their account. To use this terminal, which will be located in shopping centers and downtown office buildings, the customer must insert a special bank card containing identification information recorded on a magnetic strip on the back of the card. The customer must also provide an identification number by keying it in using a calculatorlike keyboard on the front of the terminal. When the transaction is completed, the customer receives the cash requested and a receipt for the transaction.

You must develop the input specifications for the new system. What validation information will you require for each transaction? What information do you want stored for each transaction? Use examples to explain your answers.

CHAPTER 9 FILE AND DATABASE DEVELOPMENT

BASIC FILE TERMINOLOGY
- DATA ITEM
- RECORD
- RECORD KEY
- FILE

TYPES OF FILES
- MASTER FILE
- TRANSACTION FILE
- TABLE FILE
- REPORT FILE
- OTHER FILES

METHODS OF FILE ORGANIZATION
- SEQUENTIAL ORGANIZATION
  - Reading Sequential Files
  - Searching for Records
  - Evaluation of Sequential Files
- DIRECT-ACCESS ORGANIZATIONS
  - Direct Addressing
  - Hash Addressing
- INDEXED ORGANIZATION
  - Characteristics of an Index
  - Index Nonsequential Organization
  - Index Sequential Organization

SYSTEMS DEVELOPMENT INVOLVING DATABASES
- DATABASE CONCEPTS
  - Shared Data
  - Redundancy and Integrity
  - Data Retrieval

QUESTIONS TO GUIDE YOU THROUGH THE CHAPTER

- How is data organized for storage and retrieval in information systems?
- What types of files are used to store data?
- What roles do record keys play in the design and processing of files?
- Which file organization makes the most efficient use of storage space?
- How do file processing methods vary?
- Are design methods different when database systems are used in an information system?

Information systems are file-oriented. Data is accumulated in files that are processed or maintained by the system. The systems analyst is responsible for designing the files and selecting their contents, selecting from options available for organizing the data.

This chapter discusses files and how to process them in information systems. The different types of files and methods of accessing them are discussed first. The computer equipment used to store files of data is also examined. Three methods of using the files for input, output, and computation are discussed. Since the data in the system is valuable, analysts design methods for ensuring that copies always exist. Several backup strategies, as these methods are termed, are pointed out. Finally, the chapter considers how file design and processing change when shared databases are included in the information system.

When you are finished with this chapter, you should be able to select the best way to store and retrieve a set of data for a specific use. You should also know what file methods can be used with each type of storage device. And, you should know how files are processed when the system stores and retrieves data.

BASIC FILE TERMINOLOGY

Analysts use specific terms in file design. Some of these terms are common and have been used in preceding chapters. Others may be new to you. This

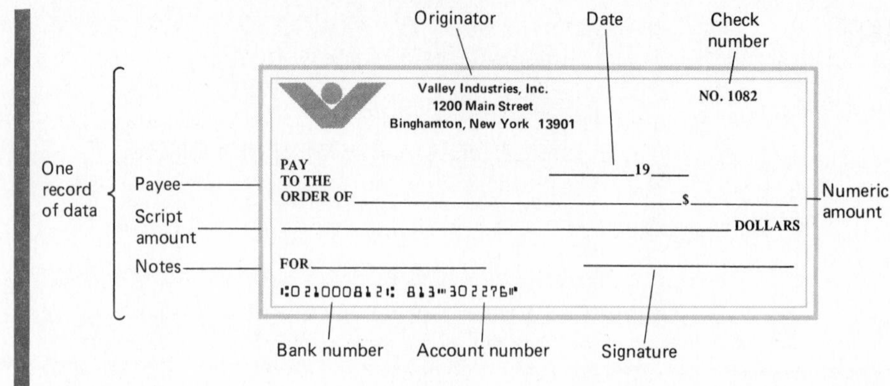

Figure 9.1. Bank check as a record of data with items noted.

section briefly discusses the commonly used terms: data item, record, file, and key.

Data Item

Individual elements of data are called data items. For example, a bank check (Figure 9.1) consists of the following data items: check originator, check number, date, payee, numerical amount, script amount, note, bank identification, account number, and signature.

Each data item has a specific value associated with it. For example, the number 1082 is a *data value* assigned to the data item called Check Number. A set of data for check 1082 that analysts will want to retain is:

DATA ITEM NAME	VALUE
Check Originator	Valley Industries 1200 Main Street Binghamton, New York 13901
Check Number	1082
Date	10/06/8X
Payee	S. Holmes Agency
Amount	300.58
Bank Number	023100460
Account Number	483479301

To summarize, each data item is identified by a name and is assigned a value. The association of a value with a field creates one *instance* of the data item. An alternative name for instance is *occurrence*.

Other synonyms for "data item" are "field" or simply "item."

Fields can be comprised of *subitems*. For example, date is often used as a single data item, consisting of the three subitems of month, day, and year. In the bank check example, the field Originator consists of these subfields:

originator name, address, city, state, and postal code. Whenever a field consisting of subfields is referenced by name, it automatically includes all the subfields. However, a reference to a subfield includes only that subfield and excludes all other subfields in a data item. Therefore the subfield day in the data item Date excludes month and year.

Record

The complete set of data pertaining to one entry, such as a bank check, is a *record.* The bank check treated as a single unit is therefore a record consisting of seven separate fields. Notice that all the data items are related to the payment transaction. Since this is a characteristic of records, a more complete definition of the term is *a set of related data items pertaining to an entity of interest.*

In the checking example, the number of data items is always the same. As was discussed in the sections on design of input and output, the analyst determines the length and type (alphabetic, alphanumeric, or numeric) of each item. A record description of the bank check contains:

RECORD NAME: BANK CHECK

DATA ITEM NAME	TYPE	LENGTH
Check Originator	C	90
Check Number	N	6
Date	C	8
Payee	C	24
Amount	N	8, 2 decimals
Bank Number	N	9
Account Number	N	9

When the number and size of data item in a record is constant for every record, it is called a *fixed-length record.*

The advantage of fixed-length records is that they are always the same size, so the system does not have to determine how long the record is or where one stops and the next one begins when stored. However, fixed-length records do not always make use of all allocated space. For instance, the Payee field in the bank check example is allocated 24 spaces. But, if the payee for a specific instance is S. Holmes Agency, requiring 16 characters, the remaining 8 are unnecessary. (They are filled with blanks.) In this example, the analyst decided to avoid the extra processing time requirement by using extra space (the unused 8 characters in the Payee field).

Variable-length records are less common in most business applications than fixed-length designs. Record size may vary because the individual data items vary in length or because the *number* of data items in a record changes from one occurrence to another. If, in the checking example, each data item is allocated only the needed space, the size of each record must vary (Figure 9.2).

Date	Check number	Payee	Check amount	Bank number	Account number	Space required for fixed length record 67 characters
99/99/99	999999	XXXXXXXXXXXXXXX	9999999.99	999999999	999999999	

Space required for variable length record

09/18/8x 1082 B.J.JONES 4.85 123456789 123456789 ← 43 characters
09/18/8x 1082 THOMAS BAKERY, INC. 348481.52 123456789 123456789 ← 58 characters
10/24/8x 1082 AMERICAN MANUFACTURING AND SUPPLY COMPANY, INC. 86.58 123456789 123456789 ← 80 characters
07/15/8x 1082 IBM 754000.00 123456789 123456789 ← 42 characters

Figure 9.2. Comparison of storage requirements for fixed and variable length records using checking example.

To demonstrate how the number of data items in a record can vary, consider how a record for an invoice might be designed. Certain elements of data, such as date, invoice number, and sold-to and ship-to name and address details are included on every invoice. Assume these items are fixed-length (Figure 9.3). For the remainder of the invoice, details are included to describe the items sold: quantity, item number, item description, unit cost, and extension (price times quantity). This information is required once for each item on the invoice. The invoice is designed so that it has enough space to hold up to 20 different items. At the bottom there is space for a subtotal, sales tax amount, and invoice total. The question for the analyst is how to design this record for storage. Assume that the heading information is fixed-length and that extensions, taxes, and totals will not be stored. (They can be computed when the record is used so that no unnecessary space is used.) Should the record be fixed-length, meaning that the design allows for the maximum of 20 items, or should it be variable-length, so that only the amount of space actually needed will be used? The design decision will depend on whether the typical invoice has few or many items (which determines the average amount of space needed) and the available amount of storage space. (We will see later in the chapter how to determine storage needs.)

Record Key

Often it is necessary to distinguish one specific record from another. Analysts select one data item in the record that is likely to be unique in all records of a file and use it for identification purposes. This item is called the *record key*. It is important to note that the record key, or simply *key*, is an item that is already part of the record rather than an additional piece of data added to the record just for identification purposes.

Common examples of record keys are the part number in an inventory

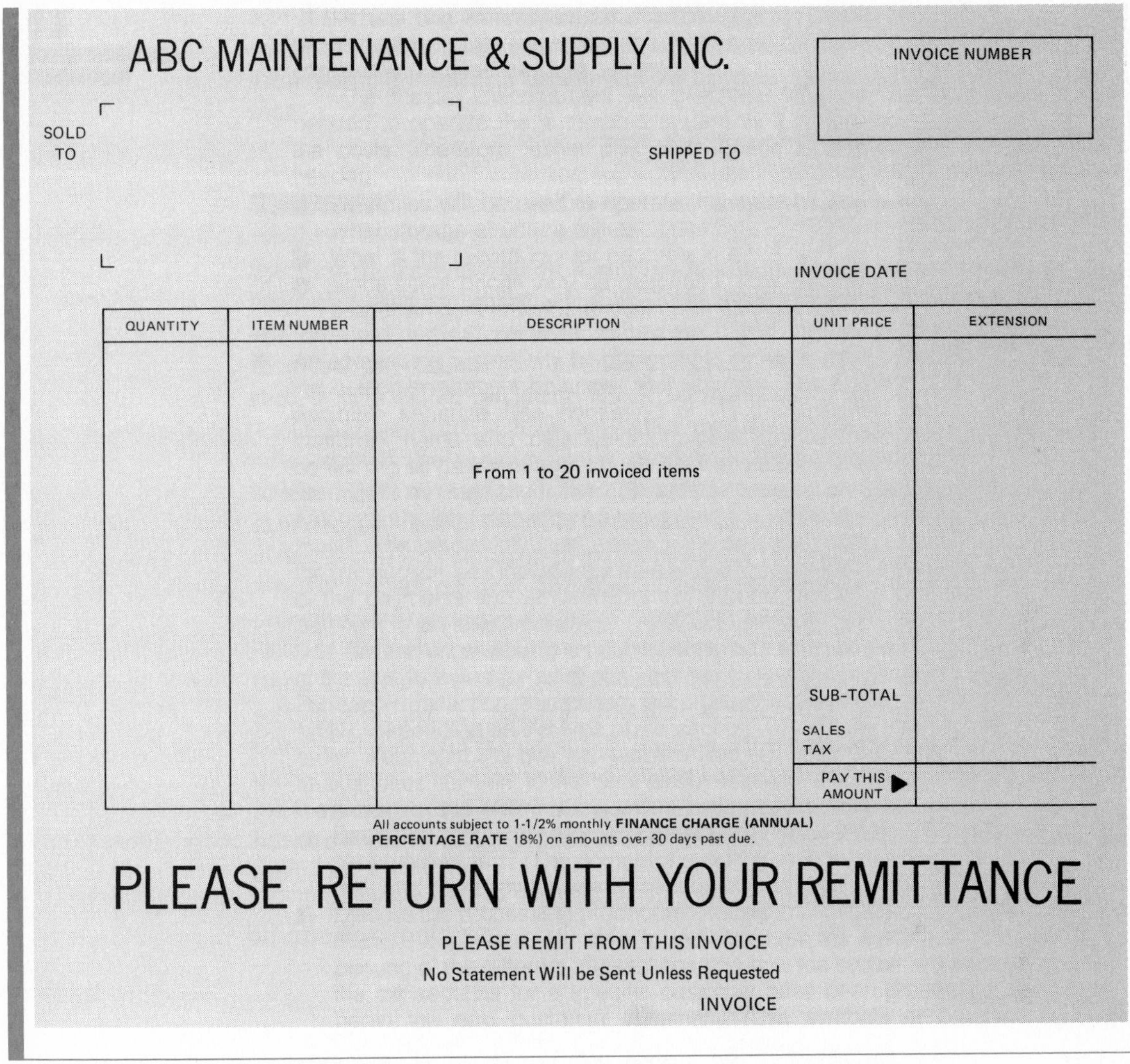

ABC MAINTENANCE & SUPPLY INC.

INVOICE NUMBER

SOLD TO

SHIPPED TO

INVOICE DATE

QUANTITY	ITEM NUMBER	DESCRIPTION	UNIT PRICE	EXTENSION
		From 1 to 20 invoiced items		
			SUB-TOTAL	
			SALES TAX	
			PAY THIS AMOUNT ▶	

All accounts subject to 1-1/2% monthly **FINANCE CHARGE (ANNUAL) PERCENTAGE RATE** 18%) on amounts over 30 days past due.

PLEASE RETURN WITH YOUR REMITTANCE

PLEASE REMIT FROM THIS INVOICE

No Statement Will be Sent Unless Requested

INVOICE

Figure 9.3. Invoice contents must be provided through proper file design.

record, the chart number in a patient medical record, the student number in a university transcript record, or the serial number of a manufactured product. Each has various uses in the organization or business setting but can also be used to identify one record from all others. This ability is essential in processing files in information systems.

File

A *file* is a collection of related records. Each record in a file is included because it pertains to the same entity. A file of checks, Figure 9.4 for example, consists only of checks. Inventory records and invoices do not belong in a check file as they pertain to different entities.

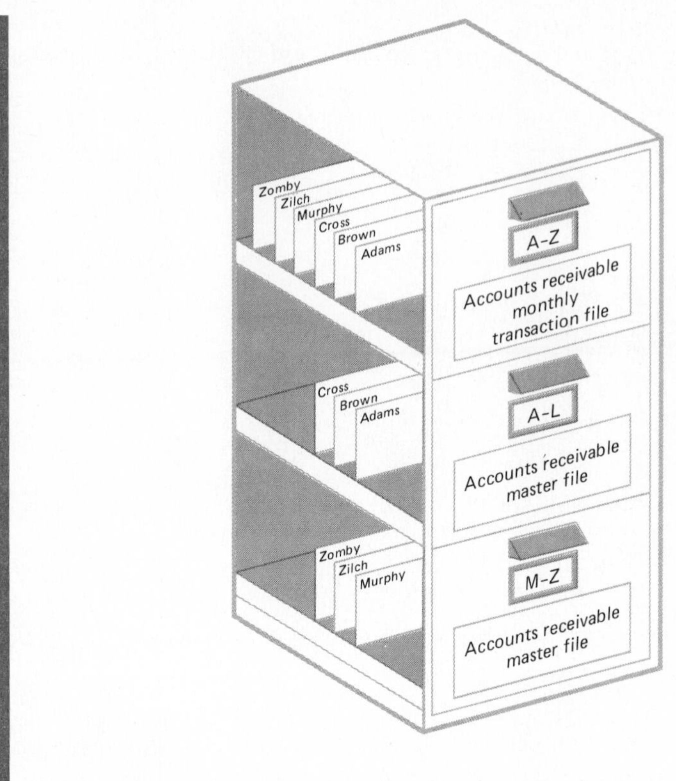

Figure 9.4.
File of bank checks.

The number of records in the file determines the file size. The example in Figure 9.4 shows 5 records. If each record is fixed-length and uses 200 characters of storage, the file uses 5 times 200 characters of storage.

TYPES OF FILES

Businesses and organizations, whether computerized or not, are file-oriented. Records are collected and maintained as files. The four main types of files are master, transaction, table, and report files.

Master File

Information systems are ongoing. They continue to exist and are used as long as they are meaningful to the organization. Therefore the files into which information about business activities are accumulated also continue to exist. A *master file* is a collection of records about an important aspect of the activities of the organization. It may contain data describing the current status of specific events or business indicators. For example, the master file in an accounts payable system shows the balance owed to every vendor or supplier from whom the organization purchases supplies or services. The balance owed to each supplier, as shown in Figure 9.5, reflects the current

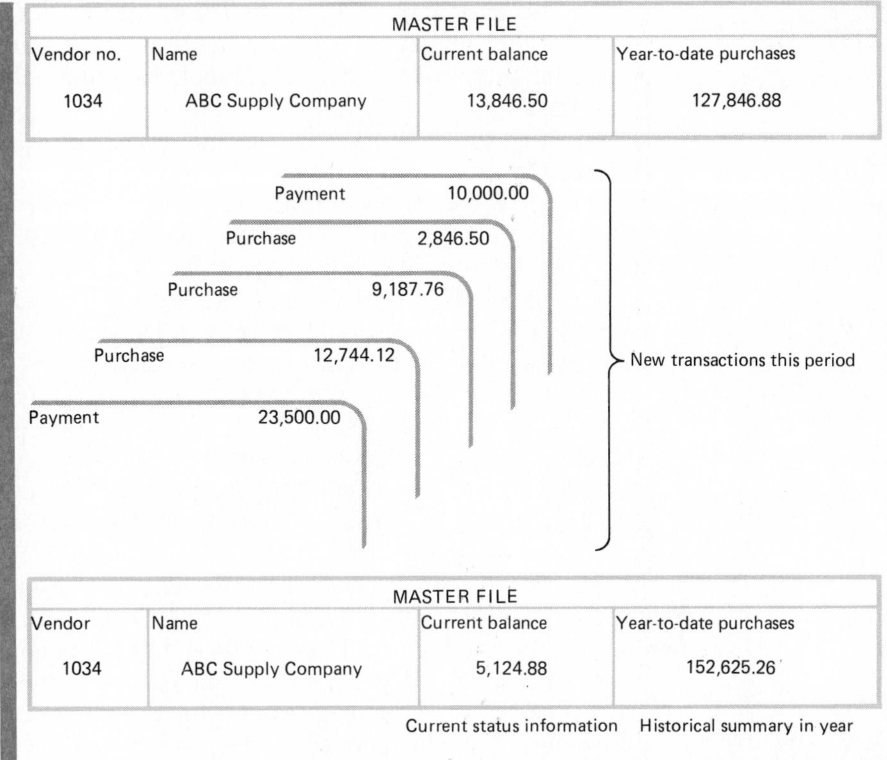

Figure 9.5. Master file record containing current status and historical information.

status of all accounts, that is, the result of all purchases, payments, and credits made between organization and supplier. This example shows one type of master file—that used to reflect the *current status* of entities (like vendor payable accounts).

A second type of master file reflects the *history of events* affecting a particular entity. For example, the sales history for commercial business is reflected in a master file containing a record of each sale made to a customer over a specified period of time (say 1 year). Each record in the file (see Figure 9.5) shows the date and amount of the sale.

In many applications, there are benefits to having both types of information available. Figure 9.5 shows this combination by reporting current account balances and historical data using year-to-date totals.

Master files are useful only so long as they are accurate and up to date. In other words, they must be maintained to reflect even the most recent events that change the file before the file can be used. Master files are kept up to date through the use of transaction files.

Transaction File

A *transaction file* is a temporary file that has the two purposes of accumulating data about events as they occur and updating master files to reflect the results of current transactions. The term *transaction* refers to any business event that affects the organization and about which data is captured. Examples of common transactions in organizations are making purchases, paying for purchases, hiring personnel, paying employees, and recording sales. Data important to the organization is collected about each event and accumulated into a file, the transaction file. A file is a collection of related records; the records in a transaction file are related to each other in the sense that they all pertain to the same entity. For example, records in an accounts payable transaction file are payments, credits, or purchases from suppliers. Employee hiring transactions or even payroll transactions, for example, do not belong in an accounts payable transaction file as they have no relation to suppliers. (However, each belongs in a different transaction file that pertains to those particular entities.)

Transaction files are processed against master files to bring the latter up to date. In Chapter 8, we discussed the design of a coding system to identify the purpose of a transaction input for processing (such as A for add, D for delete, or C for change). These codes guide the *update program,* the specific computer program that controls the processing of transactions against master file records.

Figure 9.6 shows the sequence of events that occur as transactions take place and data is captured and processed. Data capture occurs according to those guidelines discussed in the last chapter. The details are accumulated into the transaction file, a record at a time. The transaction and master files are read as input by the update program; this produces a revised master file that reflects the results of the processing. Two transactions pertain to the master file record of ABC Supply Company. Prior to processing, the account balance for this company was $189.50. After applying the purchase transaction of $279.36 and the payment transaction of $250.00, a new balance of $218.86 is calculated and shown on the master file record for ABC Supply Company. Through this example you can see how transaction files are used to maintain master file records.

Master files are permanent. They exist as long as the system exists. However, the contents of the file change through processing and updating. Transaction files on the other hand are temporary. At some point in time they are no longer needed and are erased or destroyed, depending on the method used for storing the data. Actually transaction files may be retained for months, sometimes even years, after they are created, depending on legal and organization requirements. Thus "temporary" does not mean "momentary." However, unlike master files, at some time after they are created, they will no longer be needed even though the system continues.

Table File

A special type of master file is included in many systems to meet special processing requirements where data must be referenced repeatedly. *Table files* are permanent files containing reference data used when processing transactions, updating master files, or producing output. As the name indicates, these files store tables of reference data.

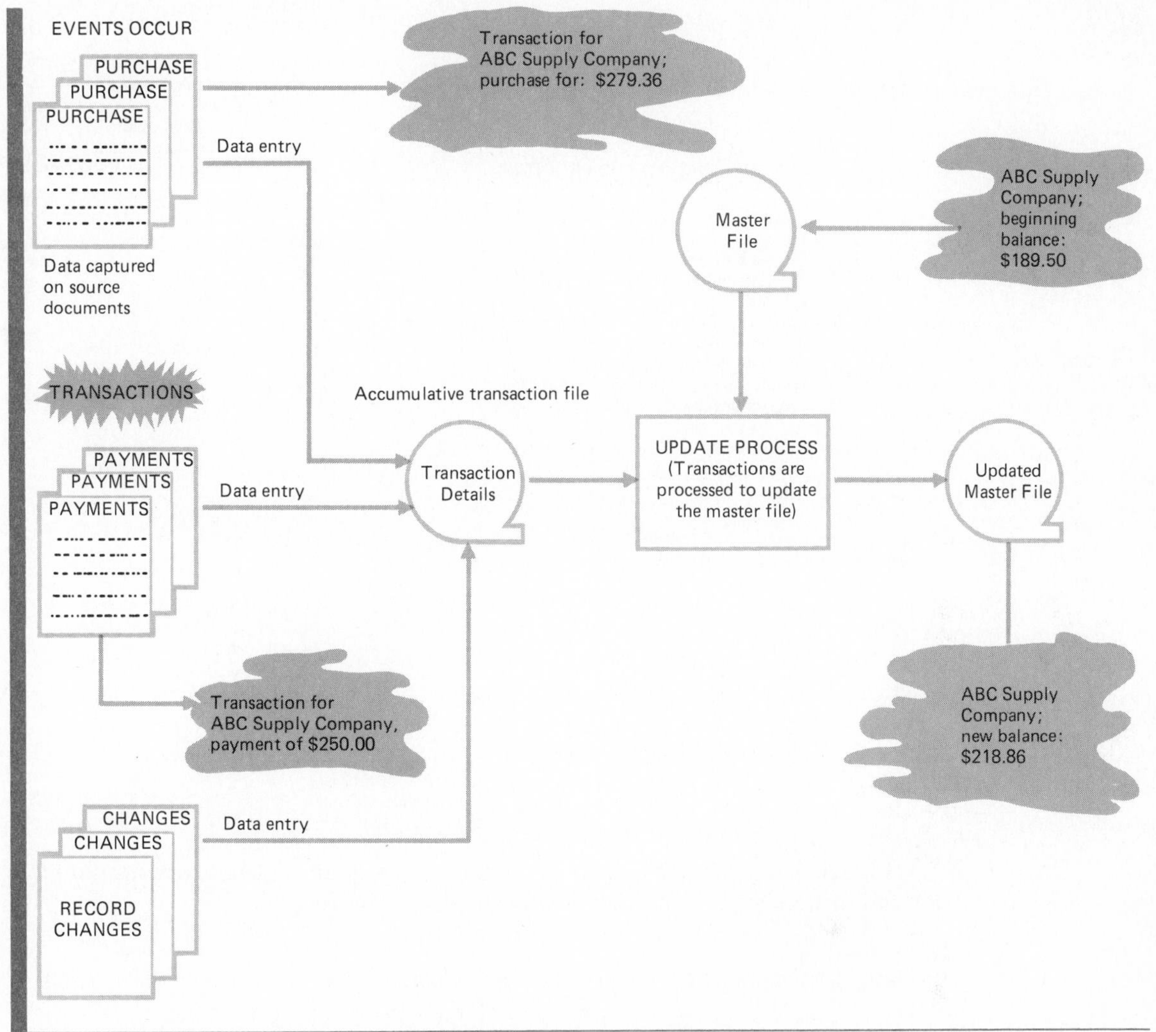

Figure 9.6. Transaction processing sequence.

Analysts often specify the use of table files to store data that otherwise would be included in master files or embedded in computer programs. Table files conserve storage space and ease program maintenance by storing data in a file, that otherwise would be included in programs or master file records.

In a computerized payroll processing system, it is necessary to calculate the amount of state and federal tax to be withheld from each employee's paycheck. Legal requirements for doing this are very specific, so much so that government tax agencies publish tables indicating the amount of money to withhold for each level of salaries earned or paid, depending on the number of exemptions (family, dependents) the employee claims. The withholding data is stored as a table file and referenced by the program

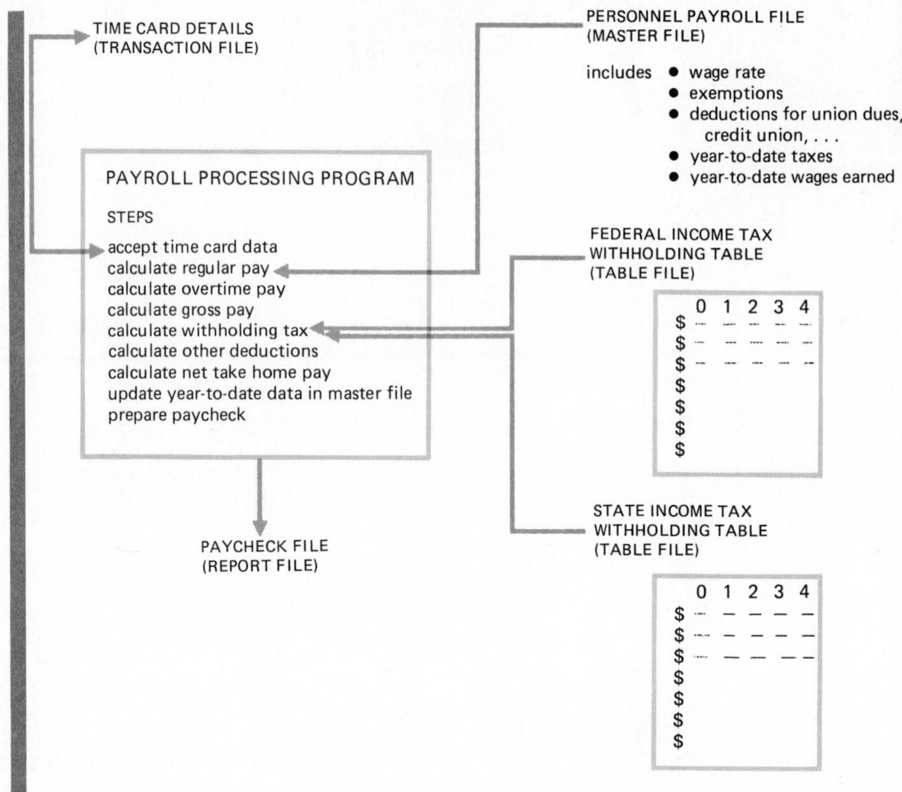

Figure 9.7. Files used in payroll processing system.

(Figure 9.7) when it needs to determine the amount of tax to accumulate for the income and exemption levels shown in the record.

Report File

Very often in information systems centers, operators find that the central processing unit of the computer produces much more data for output than the printer can possibly keep up with. Following the normal sequence of events then, the CPU is delayed while results are produced on the printer.

Since the CPU is the most powerful (and expensive) part of most computer systems, we want to get as much use out of it as possible. Therefore, many systems are designed to use overlapped processing and report files. *Overlapped processing* is the capability of a computer to simultaneously carry out input, processing, *and* output operations, rather than executing each step in sequence. The throughput (rate of processing) increases considerably.

Report files are the collected contents of individual output reports or documents produced by the system. They are created by the system where many reports are produced but printing time is not available. This situation frequently arises in overlapped processing. In this case the computer writes the report contents to a file on magnetic tape or disk, where it remains until

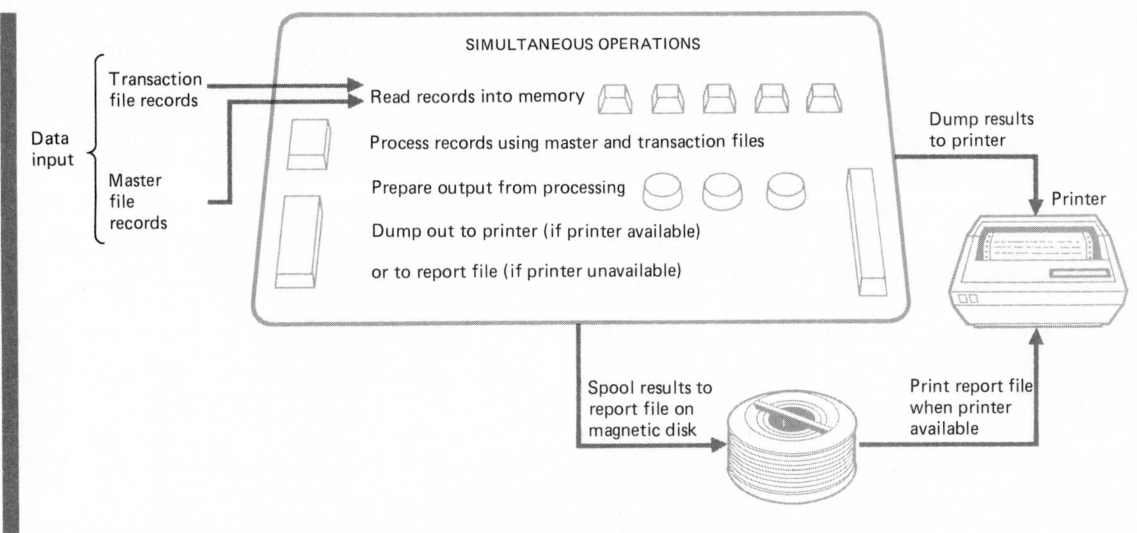

Figure 9.8. Spooled report files in system using overlapped processing.

it can be printed (Figure 9.8). The report file contains the unprinted output data. The process of creating it is known as *spooling;* i.e., output that cannot be printed when it is produced is spooled into a report file. Later, in a few minutes or hours, depending on the volume of work and speed of the printers, the system will be instructed to read the report file and print the output.

Report files may be used with many other output devices, such as graphic plotters, microfilm and microfiche units, or commercial typesetting systems. They are a part of the standard operating procedures of many information systems.

Other Files

Other files also play a role in information systems. In most cases, they are special uses of one of the file types discussed. For example, a *backup file* is a copy of a master, transaction, or table file that is made to ensure a copy is available if anything happens to the original. (We discuss backup copies in depth later in this chapter.)

Archival files are copies made for long-term storage of data that may be needed at a much later date. Usually archival files are stored away from the computer center so they cannot be quickly accessed or retrieved for use.

METHODS OF FILE ORGANIZATION

Records are stored in files using a file organization that determines how storage is used and how the records will be located and retrieved. This section discusses three common ways of storing and retrieving records in a file. Two of the methods, sequential and direct, are available on all computers. The third, indexed, is possible only if special software is acquired.

Sequential Organization

This is the simplest way to store and retrieve records in a file. In a sequential file, records are stored one after the other without concern for the actual value of the data in the records. The first record stored is placed at the beginning of the file. The second is stored right after the first (there are no unused positions), the third after the second, and so on. This fact never changes in a sequential file. (It will change with the other organizations to be discussed.)

It is a characteristic of sequential files that all records are stored by position: a record is the first record, the second record, and so on. There are no addresses or location assignments in sequential files.

READING SEQUENTIAL FILES

To read a sequential file, the system always starts at the beginning of the file. If the record sought is somewhere in the file, the system reads its way up to it, one record at a time. For example, if a particular record happens to

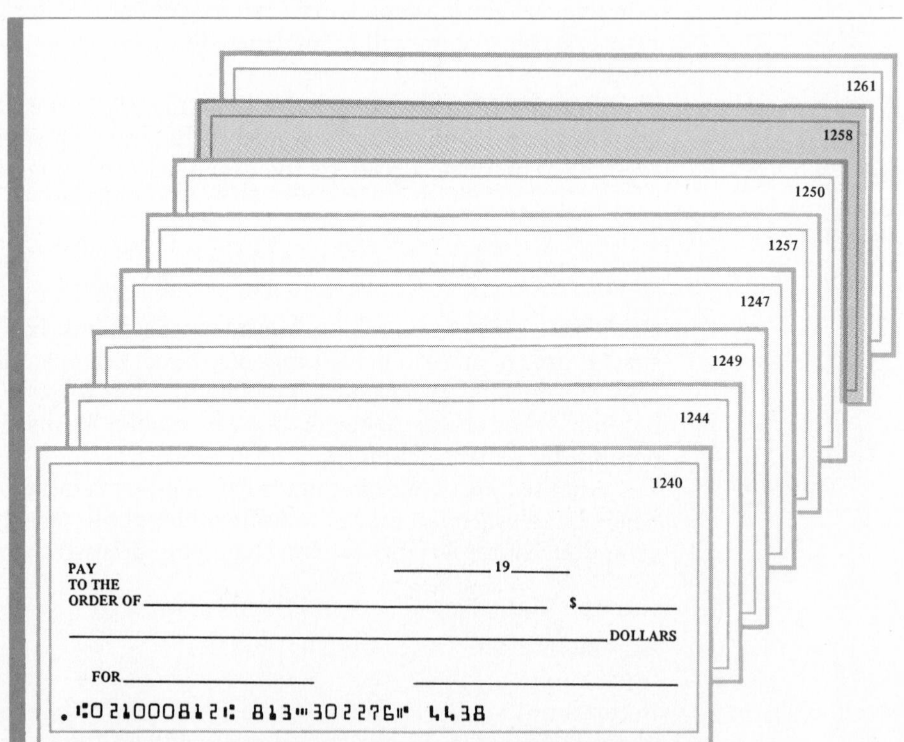

Figure 9.9. Sequential file: bank checks sequenced by order of processing.

be the tenth one in a file, the system starts at the first one and reads ahead one record at a time until the tenth one is reached. It cannot go directly to the tenth one in a sequential file without starting from the beginning. In fact, it does not know it is the tenth one. Depending on the nature of the system being designed, this feature may be advantageous or it may be a drawback, as will be shown later in the chapter.

The checking example introduced at the beginning of this chapter will illustrate sequential files. Checks are written in sequence, one at a time. You use the top (front) check from the book first, the second one next, and the third one after that. In a sense, the book of blank checks *is* a sequential file where the checks are in order based on check number (the record key).

Assume the checks are written and sent to the payee ("pay to" field) who cashes them at a bank. Later they are returned to you in a group that is in order, based on when your bank processed them. They are not in the same order as they were when you wrote them, but they are in a sequential order. The tenth check is still after the ninth one, etc.

Now there are two sequential files—the remaining original checks, in order by check number, and the processed check transaction file, in order by time processed. (If you prefer to have the processed checks in a different sequence, you must sort them into that order yourself.) In either case, the way to process the check file is to look through the checks, starting from the beginning (Figure 9.9).

SEARCHING FOR RECORDS

It was pointed out that the system does not care what data values are stored in the fields within a record. In fact, sequential files do not use physical record keys. (For this reason, analysts refer to sequential files as *nonkeyed* files.) How then does a system retrieve a specific record? In our example, how is check 1258 located and retrieved? We will call the check number, 1258, the *search key*—the data value being sought.

The program controls all the processing steps that follow. The first record is read and its check number is compared with the search key: 1240 versus 1258. Since they do not match, the process is repeated. The check number for the next record is 1244, and it also does not match the search key. Therefore, the process of reading and comparing records continues until the check number and the search key match. If the file does not contain a check numbered 1258, the read and compare process will continue until the end of the file is reached.

This method is the only way to process a sequential file. Could the program be written to compare the check number of the first record and the search key to calculate where the check is? The answer is no because, although the file is not in ascending sequential order, there is not an occurrence of every check number; some checks are missing. Check number 1258 − 1240 gives a result of 14. But the fourteenth check after number 1240 is 1269. (Even if the file was in ascending order, the system would not know this.)

EVALUATION OF SEQUENTIAL FILES

Is sequential organization an advantageous way to order and process files? The answer depends on how it will be used. The method is simple and easy to understand. You simply store records one right after the other or read them one after the other. To process the file, you start at the beginning and read each record one after the other.

Suppose it is necessary to do something with every record in the file for a particular system. In this case, a sequential file is a good organization. If you want to use on the average of about one-half of the records in the file, sequential organization is still acceptable since one out of two records retrieved will be used and the time to look at an adjacent record is brief.

On the other hand, in a very large file where the requirement is to find one particular record, sequential file organization is a disadvantage. The program must start at the beginning of the file and read past every record in the file until the correct one is found. This could be very time-consuming unless the record turned out to be one of the first ones.

Direct-Access Organizations

When the features of sequential files are a disadvantage for a proposed system, the alternative design uses a *direct-access organization.* This method requires the program to tell the system where a record is stored. Then it can access the record at that location. In contrast to sequential organization, processing a direct-access file does not require the program to start at the first record in the file.

Direct-access files are *keyed* files. They associate a record with a specific key value and a particular storage location. All records are stored by key at addresses rather than by position. In other words, if the program knows the record key, it can determine the location address of a record and retrieve it independently of every other record in the file.

In general, if fewer than 10 percent of the records in a file will be needed during a typical processing run, the file should not be established as a sequential file. On the other hand, if more than 40 percent of the records will be accessed, the analyst should select the sequential organization. (Between 10 and 40 percent the decision depends on the size the file, the frequency of use, and whether it will be updated frequently or just used for retrieval.)

DIRECT ADDRESSING

In the checking example, the direct access of records is demonstrated using a storage area that has a space reserved for every check from 1240 to 1300 (Figure 9.10). The system uses the check number as a *physical record key.* It knows the key exists and uses it (unlike the nonkeyed sequential file) to store data. Therefore check number 1248 is stored at address 1248, the location reserved for the check of that number. To retrieve that check from storage in a computer system, the program is told to use 1248 as the search

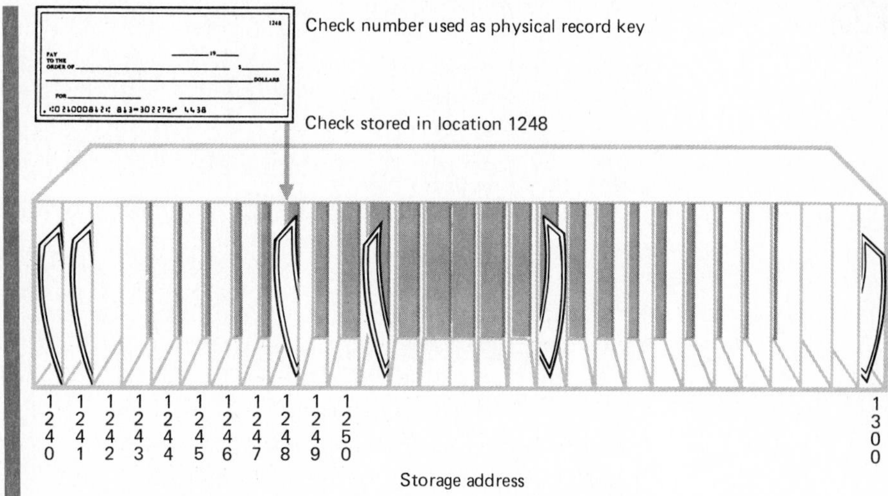

Figure 9.10. Direct addressing using physical record key.

key. It knows the key serves as the address and goes directly to the assigned location for the record with the key of 1248 and retrieves the record. This is the attractive feature of direct organization: records are retrieved much more quickly than when the file must be searched from the beginning.

Requirements for Direct Addressing

The type of direct access that uses the record key as the storage address is called *direct addressing*. When it can be used, it is simple and quick. However, the requirements of this method often prevent its use. Direct addressing should have a data set where:

1 The key set is in a dense, ascending order with few unused values—unused values mean wasted storage space. Therefore few open ranges of key values are wanted.
2 The record keys conform to the numbers of the storage addresses. In other words, there is a storage address for each actual or possible key value in the file and there are no duplicate key values.

In a dense keylist, for each key value there is a storage space with an address that is equivalent to the key. The key values are also in a close sequence; there are few skips in the sequence. This is important in file design since, when storage is assigned for the file, it starts at the lowest key value and extends to the highest key value. If, as Figure 9.11*b* shows, the range of keys includes skips in the range, it creates wasted storage space. Storage must be allocated even though it will go unused.

Another problem prohibiting use of direct addressing is the keys for the records not matching storage addresses. Even if the analyst wants to use direct addressing, it is impossible to do so since there is not an address of AB1CD.

(a) PART NUMBER		(b) ACCOUNT NUMBER	
01-0000	Dense key list with few skips in range of values.	103487	Range of keys contains many skips causing wasted storage under direct addressing.
01-0101		103541	
01-0102		103544	
01-0103		103547	
01-0104		103601	
01-0105		103648	
01-0106		103759	
01-0108		103892	
01-0109		114874	
01-0112		114875	
01-0114		114906	
01-0115		114981	

Figure 9.11. Key list variations.

HASH ADDRESSING

When direct *addressing* is not possible but direct *access* is necessary, the analyst specifies the alternative access method of hashing. *Hashing* (also called *key transformation* or *randomizing)* refers to the process of deriving a storage address from a record key. An algorithm, that is, an arithmetic procedure, is devised to change a key value into another value that serves as a storage address. (The data value in the record itself does not change.)

Types of Hashing Algorithms

There is virtually no limit to the number of algorithms that analysts may develop. For example, in storing records of information about people, analysts often select the social security number (or some other unique personal identification number) for use as a record key. However, since the social security number does not meet the earlier criteria for direct-address keys, the design must specify a hashing procedure that converts the social security number into a value corresponding to a storage address.

The social security number consists of three major sections, normally separated by dashes ("-") or blanks. (It is an input design decision whether dashes or blanks are entered during data preparation and entry.) A simple hashing algorithm for changing the social security number into a suitable storage address is as follows:

Step 1 Strip off the first three digits of the social security number. They are regional digits and likely to recur in many employees within one organization. 456821455 becomes 821455.

Step 2 Divide the new key by a prime number. A prime number is any number that is divisible evenly (without a remainder) only by itself or the number 1. The prime number 41 is used in this example; later we will see how to select appropriate prime numbers. 821455 is divided by 41.

Step 3 Modular division is used. This procedure specifies that the quotient is discarded and the storage location is signified by the remainder, 19 in this case. (Depending on the actual storage media, address 19 will mean something specific, a slot in a card rack or a block on a magnetic disk for instance.) The result is quotient 19,558, remainder 19.

Division by prime is one type of hashing algorithm. Actually analysts may develop many possible algorithms. Other common methods are:

1 *Folding* Split the key into pieces and process them further (add, subtract, divide, etc.).
E.g., 821
455
1276 storage location

2 *Extraction* Select specific digits from the key and process them with the remaining digits.
E.g., 814 (1st, 3rd, 4th digits)
−255 (2nd, 5th, 6th digits)
599 storage location

3 *Squaring* Multiply the number by itself and then apply other hashing methods.
E.g., 821,455 × 821,455 = 67,478,831
Fold first half with second half.
6747
8831
15,578
Extract 1st and 2nd to other digits.
578
15
593 storage location

There is virtually no limit to the number of hashing algorithms analysts may devise, although those that use division by prime are among the most common type.

Requirements for Hashing Algorithms

There are several important features we want these hashing algorithms to have:

Repeatable Be able to store a record under an algorithm and retrieve it using the same algorithm. In division by hashing, for example, a random number is not used since it changes each time. A record stored with one number in division will not be found if a different number is used since it produces a different address from the one where the record is stored.

Even Distribution Evenly distribute records throughout the allocated storage space. If a file will be stored in a space that will permit the storage of 10,000 records, we want to distribute the records throughout the space rather than bunch them all together. This distribution ensures more rapid retrieval of records and makes better use of the allocated space. (In division by prime, the divisor chosen is the one closest to, but usually less than, the number of storage areas.)

Minimize Synonyms There is no perfect hashing algorithm, although some are much better than others when it comes to minimizing synonyms. In practice, *synonyms* occur when the hashing procedure is applied on different keys and produces the same address in storage.

A simple example will show how this can happen. The procedure is dividing by 1000 and using the remainder as the result.

Key 1	10,485 Quotient 10 Remainder 485	*Key 2*	11,485 Quotient 11 Remainder 485

This is a very poor procedure because it frequently generates synonyms. The simple example procedure would never be used as a result. But the point is that the analysts must test the hashing algorithms they devise to minimize the chance of synonyms.

A separate place, called an *overflow area,* is set aside to provide for record storage when synonyms occur (Figure 9.12). When a record is stored, the hashing algorithm is performed and the address derived. The program accesses that storage area, and, if it is unused, the record is stored there. If there is already a record stored there, the new record is written in the overflow area.

When the system must retrieve a record, the hashing algorithm is performed and the storage address determined. Then the record in the storage area is checked. If it is not the correct one (meaning that a synonym occurred earlier), the system automatically goes to the overflow area and retrieves it for processing.

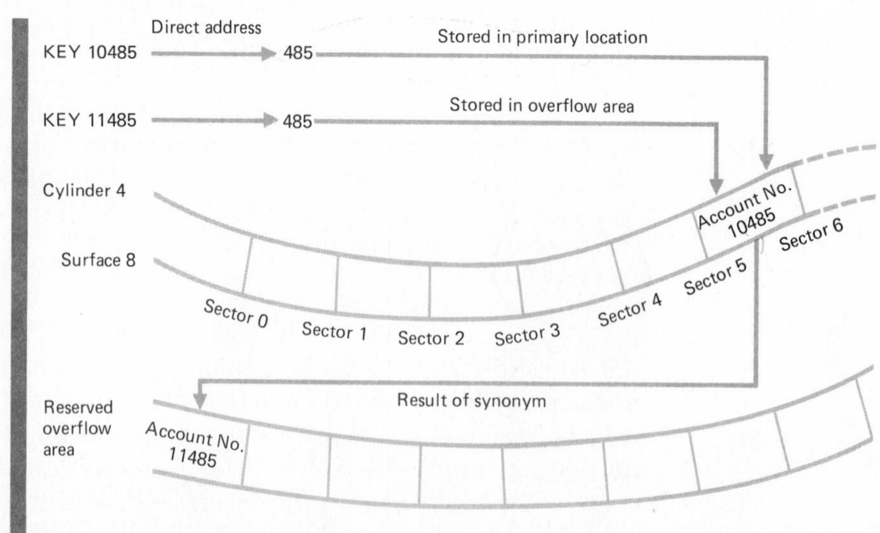

Figure 9.12. Using overflow areas to handle synonyms in key transformation.

INDEX

RECORD KEY	ADDRESS
AB	1021
AC	1022
AD	1018
BC	1014
BD	991
BF	1008
BL	997
CA	1020
CC	1012

MASTER FILE

	0	1	2	3	4	5	6	7	8
Cylinder 9 Surface 9	MN	BD	LM	CZ	XY	AA	BB	BL	
Cylinder 10 Surface 0	LX	AL	MC	BR	CB	SA	BD		BF
Cylinder 10 Surface 1	RS	UU	CC		BC	TT			AD
Cylinder 10 Surface 2	CA	AB	AC						

Figure 9.13. Index nonsequential organization.

Indexed Organization

A third way of accessing records stored in the system is through an index. The basic form of an index includes a record key and the storage address for a record. To find a record when the storage address is unknown (as with direct address and hashing structures), it is necessary to scan the records. However, if an index is used, the search will be faster since it takes less time to search an index than an entire file of data.

CHARACTERISTICS OF AN INDEX

An *index* is a separate file from the master file to which it pertains. (For this reason some analysts refer to it as a *detached index.)* Each record in the index contains only two data items: a record key and a storage address. (It does not duplicate each data item in the master file record.)

To find a specific record when the file is stored under an indexed organization, the *index* is searched first to find the key of the record wanted. When it is found, the corresponding storage address is noted and then the program accesses the record directly. This method uses a sequential scan of the index, followed by direct access to the appropriate record. The index helps speed the search compared with a sequential file, but it is slower than direct addressing.

INDEX NONSEQUENTIAL ORGANIZATION

The file of data in Figure 9.13 is stored using indexing. The index on the left contains record keys for each record in the master file (AB, AC, AD, BC, BD, etc.) and the storage location for the corresponding master file. Hence the index shows address 1021 for AB, 1022 for AC, etc. In the example in Figure 9.13, the master file is not in any specific order. This method of file organization is called *index nonsequential organization*. There is one entry in the index for every record in the master file.

INDEX SEQUENTIAL ORGANIZATION

Another type of indexed organization, the one that has been the most widely used in information systems, creates a pseudosequential file. Groups of records are stored in blocks, which have a capacity of holding a specified amount of data. For example, the blocks in Figure 9.14 can store up to 3150 pieces of data. The first block, starting at address 1345, is in sequential order.

The master file in Figure 9.14 stores individual blocks of records in sequential order. This is *not* a sequential file, however, since all the records are not stored in physically adjacent positions, but you might wish to think of it as a file of separate full or partially full blocks, each in sequential order.

The adjacent blocks are not in ascending order. For example, to pursue a logical ascending sequence, the record following 1115 at the end of the first block is in the block at address 1349.

Searching for Records

Since each block in this type of organization is always in sequential order, it is no longer necessary to have an index entry for every record. Instead, only

Figure 9.14. Index sequential organization.

First scan index,

INDEX

Record key	Starting block address
1115	1345
1315	1349
1429	1346
1725	1350

then search appropriate block.

1345	1010	1011	1013	1014	1017	1019	1110	1113	1115					
1346	1316	1317	1321	1323	1324	1410	1414	1415	1417	1418	1419	1427	1428	1429
1349	1117	1121	1120	1210	1211	1212	1215	1217	1218	1221	1310	1310	1313	1315
1350	1510	1521	1522	1617	1619	1620	1721	1724	1725					
Overflow blocks														

the highest or lowest key value for any record in the block is necessary in an index entry. This means that *only one* index entry is necessary for each block.

We will use the highest key value method to show how index sequential (or ISAM, which stands for indexed sequential access method) files are used. Suppose the program wants to find the record with the key value of 1323. How is it located when the file is stored using an indexed sequential organization? The program first accesses the *index,* starting with the beginning record. It compares the key in the index record to the search key: 1323 versus 1115. Since 1115 is the highest value in the first block and 1323 is a higher value, the program knows the desired record is not on that track. It reads the next index record. (Notice that the master file has not yet been accessed; only the index is being used.)

Next the program compares 1323 and 1315, the highest key value in the next block. Since 1323 is still a higher value, the program knows the record is not on that block, so it can ignore it. It reads the next index record and compares its key with the search key: 1429 versus 1323. This time the search key is lower than the highest key value on that track, so it knows the record should be on that track. The program tells the system to start reading records at address 1346 and comparing the keys with the search key: record 1, 1316 versus 1323; record 2, 1317 versus 1323; record 3, 1321 versus 1323; record 4, 1323 versus 1323—the keys match and the program knows that it has found the desired record. It can read the record and start whatever processing is necessary.

Using the index saves search time. Three short index records and three data records are read before the desired record is found. Without the index, the system would search through all the records in the first block (9), all the records in the second block (14), and 3 records in the third block, or a total of 26 records, before finding the desired one. Even in this small-file example, the difference is significant. Imagine the time savings when working with a file tens of thousands of records long.

Some of the blocks in the illustrations are not entirely full. This is common since analysts working with systems when files are expected to grow specify that unused space be left in each block to accommodate the growth. Typically blocks are 50 to 75 percent full when the file is first created.

File Maintenance under ISAM

As records are added to indexed sequential files, the system inserts them in such a way as to preserve the sequential nature of each block. For example, if records with keys of 1015, 1020, and 1322 are added to the master file, they will be inserted in the blocks starting at address 1345 and 1346 because the range of keys for them is in those blocks. Figure 9.15 shows that record 1015 was inserted after the previously stored 1014, 1020 after 1019, and 1322 after 1321. In each case the block was automatically resorted by the ISAM software. As records are added, others are, in effect, moved down to make space for them to maintain the sequence.

INDEX	
Record key	Starting block address
1115	1345
1315	1349
1429	1346
1725	1350

Add the following records to the master file
1015
1020
1322

Delete the following records from the master file
1014
1113
1313
1619

Change the following records in the master file
1100
1415

1345	1010	1011	1013	@	1015	1017	1019	1020	1100 (Changed)	@	1115			
1346	1316	1317	1321	1322	1323	1324	1410	1414	1415 (Changed)	1417	1418	1419	1427	1428
1349	1117	1121	1120	1210	1211	1212	1215	1217	1218	1221	1310	1310	@	1315
1350	1510	1521	1522	1617	@	1620	1721	1724	1725					
Overflow blocks	1429													

Figure 9.15. Index sequential file after updating.

Adding record 1322 points out another feature of indexed sequential files. When a record is added to a track that is already full, the last record on the track no longer has a home (1429 in the illustration). To handle these situations, a separate overflow area is maintained. When resorting caused the insertion of 1322, it moved each other record down one position, pushing 1429 "off the end." Then it stored 1429 in the first available position in the overflow. It did not find space for 1429 on the next block, as that could displace another record causing a series of other moves. Using an overflow area is a better solution since it displaces only one record.

How does the system find record 1429 when it is needed for processing? First the program searches the index, as described above, to determine the proper block. (When 1429 was moved to the overflow area, it did not change the entry for the block and record in the index.) Next the proper block is scanned one record at a time and record keys are checked to find the one with a value of 1429. When the end of the block is reached and 1429 has not been found, the system automatically goes to the overflow area and scans it until 1429 is found.

Changing and deleting records use the same search procedures. A change is made to a record and it is replaced in its original location. When a record is deleted, it is no longer accessible by the program. However, the space that a deleted record occupied is not reused. It remains unavailable for storing any other record. In the illustration deleted records are marked with the symbol "@" to represent the deletion for use.

Indexes occupy extra space, but they provide a faster method of locating records. They also permit entry into the middle of a file to retrieve one record or to begin processing the remainder of the file in sequential order. Because of the necessity to go first to the index to find a record and back to the index at the end of one block to find where the next block starts, ISAM is neither true sequential nor is it true direct access. But it is a compromise—a compromise paid for with extra space for the index, allocated but unused storage area in a block, and extra time to find a specific record when compared with the rate at which a single record can be located using direct addressing.

An additional feature of ISAM files is the flexibility to process the file in either way (sequentially or randomly), depending on the requirement at the time. For example, have you ever considered how you would design a file structure for a bank card system? Bank card systems must be capable of providing quick responses to requests from cardholders wanting information about their accounts. This need suggests a direct access file, keyed on the unique customer number, to retrieve the record. However, when the bank card processing group must prepare monthly statements, each record must be examined to determine whether to print a statement. This need suggests a sequential organization. Fortunately, ISAM allows one file to be used in both ways. This flexibility is the reason ISAM is used in so many business processing systems.

An alternative to ISAM is becoming increasingly popular. VSAM, which stands for *virtual sequential access method,* indexes records on multiple data items. By having multiple indexes, it is possible to retrieve data directly in several ways or to access records in the midst of the file using different entry criteria. Like ISAM, VSAM indexes and record storage activities are handled by the indexing software. The programmer does not have to build or maintain the indexes.

SYSTEMS DEVELOPMENT INVOLVING DATABASES

In many applications, the need for flexibility of storage and retrieval is essential. The guidelines presented in the preceeding section are very effective for the design of systems, based on master files, where the file structures of sequential, random, and indexed sequential will meet user needs. They are the most effective ways of organizing and storing data in transaction systems where each transaction is processed to update a record in the master file. However, when the purpose of the system is the support of management decision making and the same data is used in multiple applications, the analyst may find that these methods of file organization are not adequate.

This section discusses the concepts associated with databases and database management systems, and the software used to develop and use a database. It will also examine the file and database processing and storage methods. The design in systems that involve databases will be explored in detail.

Database Concepts

When the information systems are developed primarily for use in transaction processing, the analyst is able to anticipate the information requirements that will be made of the system and to develop reports and procedures that will meet the requirements. The reports are generally in a fixed format and the contents are predetermined. Similarly, individual data items, record keys, are used to identify one transaction or one entity uniquely from another. In turn the record key is used to help organize the records when they are stored in master files. The combination of record key and processing requirements is analyzed to determine which file structure (sequential, random, or indexed) is most efficient for the storage and retrieval of the data.

SHARED DATA

In management decision making where it is not always possible to anticipate information requirements in advance, the three file structures, which are also called *storage structures,* may not be the most efficient way to retrieve data. Managers do not deal with situations that require identifying one transaction from another, where they retrieve records by specifying a record key or where large groups of data are processed at one time to update files—common transaction processing activities. Instead, they are more concerned with answers to inquiries or special analyses providing information that cannot be retrieved using simple record keys.

For example, in a commercial laundry it is important to know the quantity of individual items each customer has on hand or has been given. The laundry lends the items to customers, who pay to clean them each time they are used. In other words, the rent is collected in the form of laundry charges. One customer may rent several sizes and colors of tablecloths and napkins. Another customer may rent bedsheets, pillowcases, and towels. Still another may rent hospital gowns and blankets, as well as sheets and pillowcases. The customers pay only for cleaning the items they use. When each delivery is made, the driver provides a priced delivery slip to the customer. At the end of the month, the customer also receives a statement, showing the number of deliveries and the costs of each throughout the month, as well as a record of any payments made or credits received by the customer during the period.

This example demonstrates two common transaction processing systems: inventory control, showing the assignment of linen inventories to customers, and accounts receivable, including the posting of sales and payment transactions, and the production of statements (and other reports).

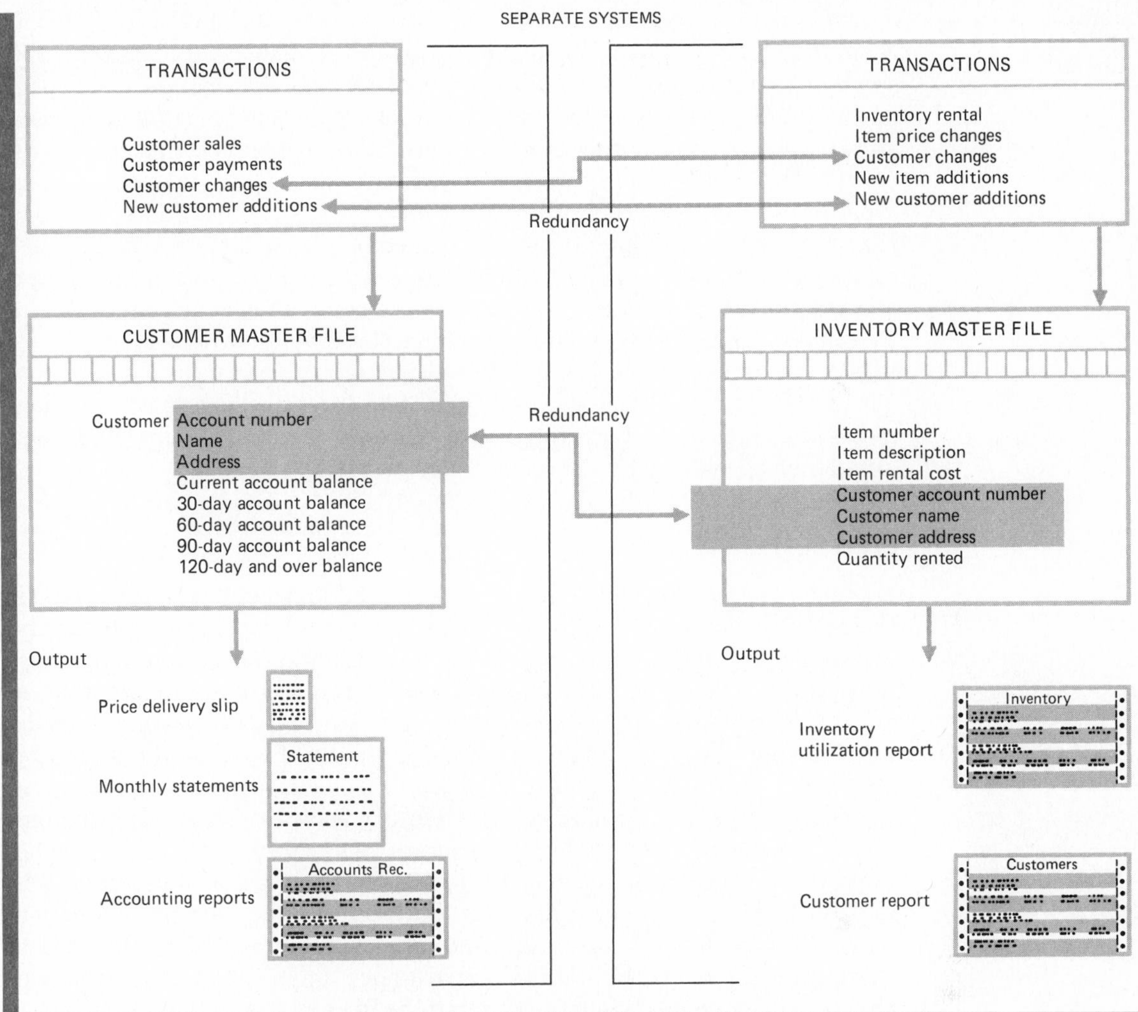

Figure 9.16. Inefficient file design in stand-alone information systems.

Each system can be developed on a stand-alone basis, where accounts receivable data is stored separately from inventory data (Figure 9.16). The first information systems that organizations develop are independent transaction processing systems. However as more systems are developed and their usefulness to management increases, there is often a need for some to be integrated to allow the sharing of information by more than one application. Similarly, management's need to receive answers to inquiries and special analyses begins to affect system design.

REDUNDANCY AND INTEGRITY

In the laundry example, if each system is developed independently, customer name and address information will be stored in each master file: at least once for each customer in the inventory master file and once for each customer in the accounts receivable file. There is obvious duplication of the same information in several files when many applications are developed, each depending on its own master file. In addition to requiring extra storage, unnecessary duplication of information, which is called *redundancy,* may also reduce the *integrity* of the information. That is, when particular types of information are duplicated in several master files, there is a good chance that the details will not always agree. If, for instance, a customer notifies an employee in the accounts receivable department of an address change, the adjustment may be made to the receivables master file but the information may not be communicated to the inventory department so its master file gets updated. The two files do not agree, and a user will not know which file is correct. The result is loss of data integrity. While this problem may sometimes be corrected by better office procedures, it may be avoided altogether by reducing data redundancy across files.

DATA RETRIEVAL

Management wants to have information available when it is needed, even if the requirement is a new one for which no current report can provide the necessary information. Many times the most useful information to management will not be retrieved using record keys. Secondary attributes (that is, nonkey data items) may be more important for many management needs. For instance, in the laundry example, with the inventory file stored on magnetic disk using an index sequential organization, how would a response be produced to a management inquiry such as: "How many customers do we have who rent tablecloths from us?" Or, consider the more complex inquiry: "Who are our customers who have been given more than 100 napkins?" These examples are representative of the requests managers make when dealing with planning and control problems. But the answers to the questions, when the data is stored under an ISAM organization, can only be determined by stepping through the file and examining every record to determine whether the customer rents tablecloths or napkins. The traditional sequential, random, and indexed storage structures, although very efficient for transaction processing, do not provide enough flexibility to assist in decision situations. The necessary information is not always available.

Database Methods

A *database* is a stored collection of data, organized on the basis of relationships in the data rather than the convenience of storage structures. It is not a replacement for files. Even in the most advanced database environments, files continue to play an important role. Data will still be captured in transaction files, and master files will continue to be important in many applications.

A *database management system* is a large program that provides more flexibility in the storage and retrieval of data and production of information. It may be an extension of a programming language, whereby a programming language, such as COBOL or FORTRAN, is extended to include database management commands. (This is called a *host language* database system.) Or, it may be an entirely new language developed to support database management. (This method is called a *self-contained* database system.)

SCHEMA

The use of database management systems does not eliminate the need for computer programs. As Figure 9.17 shows, the database management system is a bridge between the application program, which determines what data is needed and how it is processed, and the operating system of the computer, which is responsible for placing data on the magnetic storage devices. A *schema* defines the database and a *subschema* defines the *portion* of the database that a specific program will use. (Typically programs use only a section of the database.) To retrieve data from the database:

1 The application program determines what data is needed and communicates the need to the database management system.
2 The database management system determines that the data requested is in fact stored in the database (even though it may be stored under a different name, an alias). The data must be defined in the subschema (this indicates that the program is allowed to retrieve it) and in the schema (this indicates that the data is in fact in the database).
3 The database management system instructs the operating system to locate and retrieve the data from the specific location on the magnetic disk (or whatever device it is stored on).
4 A copy of the data is given to the application program for processing.

The database management system is a bridge between the application program and the stored data. It permits *data independence,* meaning that the application program can change without affecting the stored data. Under ordinary master file arrangements, if the program changes in such a way that the arrangement of the data retrieved or stored is modified, the master files must be recreated and restructured. With data independence, changes may occur in one data store or data use without affecting the other. A data dictionary is embedded in the data management system through the schema and subschema to ensure that data is properly defined and described and that duplicate names (aliases) do not result in redundant data storage or loss of data integrity.

DATA STRUCTURES

Database management systems do not replace the traditional storage structures. Even though information systems may use database methods,

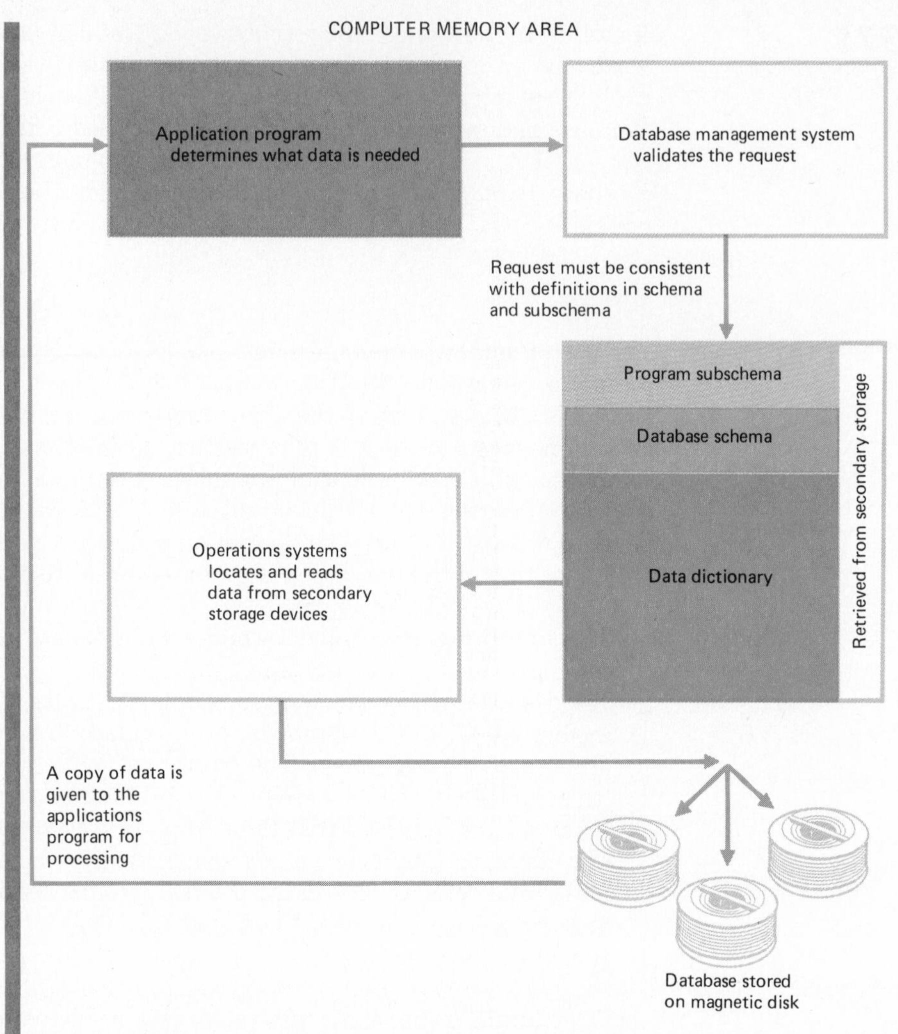

Figure 9.17. Interaction between application program and database.

the data will still be stored under sequential, random, or indexed organizations. That will not change since they are based on the way the computer hardware operates to store and retrieve data. However, more sophisticated data structures will emerge to provide the flexibility that we have emphasized.

Multilist

Database systems use one of several methods for logically structuring the data. *Multilists* link common items together in a file. A multilist is like a chain, where each link is a record meeting one of the requirements specified by the user through an application program. For instance, in the laundry example, one list of importance to management is the list of all users of

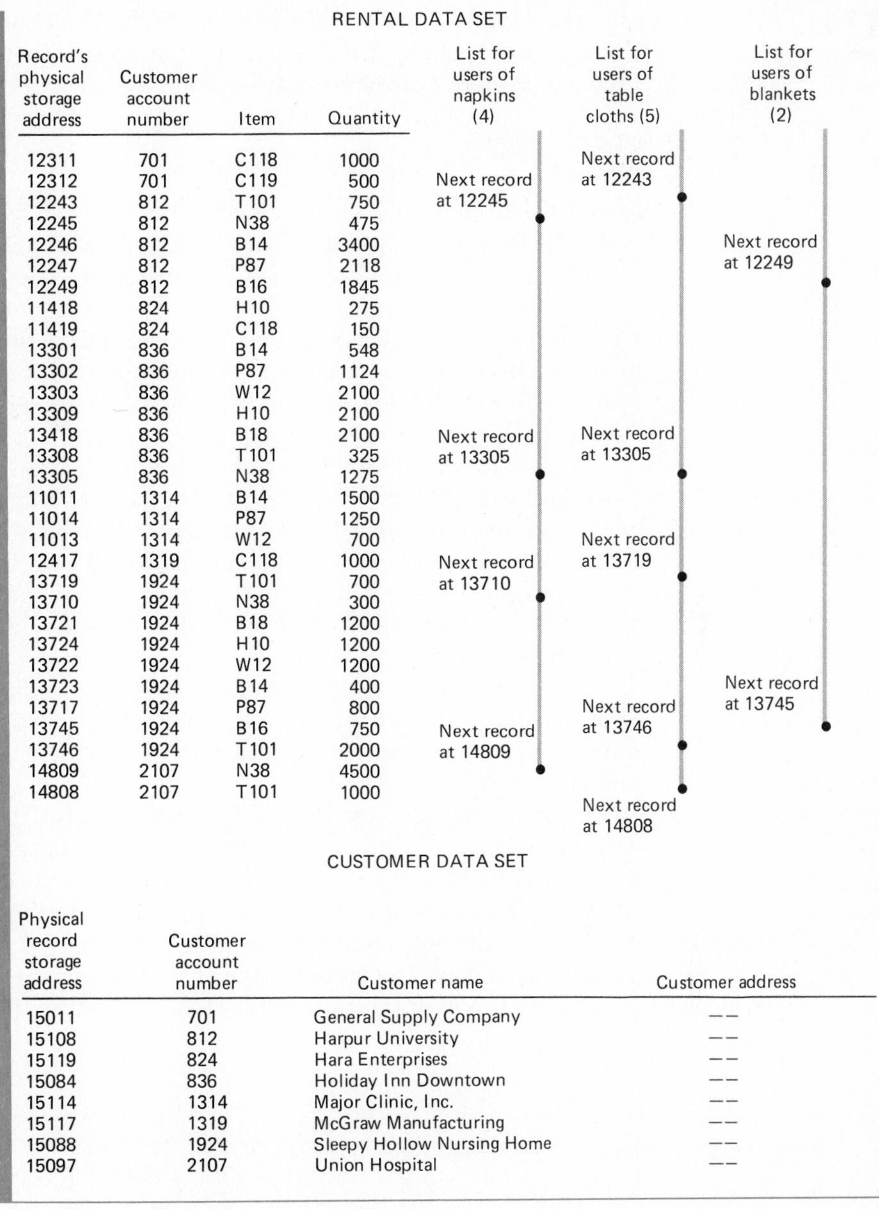

RENTAL DATA SET

Record's physical storage address	Customer account number	Item	Quantity	List for users of napkins (4)	List for users of table cloths (5)	List for users of blankets (2)
12311	701	C118	1000		Next record at 12243	
12312	701	C119	500	Next record at 12245		
12243	812	T101	750			
12245	812	N38	475			
12246	812	B14	3400			Next record at 12249
12247	812	P87	2118			
12249	812	B16	1845			
11418	824	H10	275			
11419	824	C118	150			
13301	836	B14	548			
13302	836	P87	1124			
13303	836	W12	2100			
13309	836	H10	2100			
13418	836	B18	2100	Next record at 13305	Next record at 13305	
13308	836	T101	325			
13305	836	N38	1275			
11011	1314	B14	1500			
11014	1314	P87	1250			
11013	1314	W12	700		Next record at 13719	
12417	1319	C118	1000	Next record at 13710		
13719	1924	T101	700			
13710	1924	N38	300			
13721	1924	B18	1200			
13724	1924	H10	1200			
13722	1924	W12	1200			
13723	1924	B14	400			Next record at 13745
13717	1924	P87	800		Next record at 13746	
13745	1924	B16	750	Next record at 14809		
13746	1924	T101	2000			
14809	2107	N38	4500			
14808	2107	T101	1000		Next record at 14808	

CUSTOMER DATA SET

Physical record storage address	Customer account number	Customer name	Customer address
15011	701	General Supply Company	--
15108	812	Harpur University	--
15119	824	Hara Enterprises	--
15084	836	Holiday Inn Downtown	--
15114	1314	Major Clinic, Inc.	--
15117	1319	McGraw Manufacturing	--
15088	1924	Sleepy Hollow Nursing Home	--
15097	2107	Union Hospital	--

Figure 9.18. Multilist data structure for laundry example.

tablecloths (Figure 9.18). Notice that the records themselves are not moved around. Instead, all the records that have a specified attribute (such as user of tablecloths) are logically linked together. The storage address of the next record in sequence is included in a record to continue the list, in the same way as links in a chain. The only difference is that, in an actual chain, the links are physically adjacent to one another, while in the list in a database, they are logically linked.

The "multi" in multilist refers to the fact that many lists can run through a database. In the laundry database, there are lists based on products rented, customer location, and account status.

Inverted File

The other type of data structure commonly used in database management systems is an *inverted file*. This approach uses an index to store information about the location of records having particular attributes. In a fully inverted file, there is one index for type of data item in the data set. Figure 9.19 shows an index for items rented, using the data from the previous example. Each record in the index contains the storage addresses of each record in the file that meets the attribute. For instance, the record for users of tablecloths contains five addresses; this indicates that there are five records in the database for users of tablecloths.

Some data items in a database will probably never be used to retrieve data. The street address or telephone number of a customer laundry is not ordinarily used to identify one customer from another or as a basis for responding to management inquiries. Therefore, an index will not be built for those data items. When all attributes are not indexed, the database is not fully inverted but rather partially inverted, a more common data structure.

Some database systems also include "count" information in the index. Since the addresses of individual records are part of the index record, the number of items meeting a particular requirement can quickly be determined by counting the addresses. If the request posed by a program is "How many customers do we have who rent napkins?", the answer can be determined by examining only the index. The data records themselves need not be examined.

Complex inquiries, where more than one attribute is specified, can be answered under either the multilist or inverted file data structures. First one list of items is assembled, either by following the links in a chain or by examining the appropriate index. Then the list for the second attribute is

Item index	Location
B14	12246, 13301, 11011, 13723
B16	12249, 13745
B18	13418, 13721
C118	12311, 11419, 12417
C119	12312,
H10	11418, 13309, 13724
N38	12245, 13305, 13710, 14809
P87	12247, 13302, 11014, 13717
T101	12243, 13308, 13719, 13746, 14808
W12	13303, 11013, 13722

(Addresses refer to physical storage addresses shown in Figure 9.18)

Figure 9.19. Inverted file data structure for laundry example.

examined. Those addresses or items that appear on both lists meet the requirement. Those that are on just one do not.

Relational Table

Recent developments in database management have produced a data structure called the *relational table*. The database systems that are centered around this data structure are termed relational databases. This method uses a data structure that is a two-dimensional table. The rows of the table loosely correspond to records and the columns to data items. The tables are logical, not physical. Therefore, the data is stored in the same way as discussed earlier.

When a request for information is made, the system produces a table containing the information. For example, in the laundry example, if a manager wishes to determine who uses napkins, the system will produce a table containing the names of all users of napkins. (Physically the file does not change.) However, as with the other data structures, the user is not aware that a table is formed, as the system does this invisibly in the course of producing the response.

Relational databases are a method whose time has come. As the information systems community continues to introduce them, the systems analyst should learn their features and how they will affect systems design.

Design in a Database Environment

Many systems analysts develop systems that involve database management systems and databases. This section discusses the considerations the analysts must address in these cases.

In most organizations where databases are used and managed well, a separate database management staff oversees the design and development of the database itself. The database management staff defines the schema, maintains the data dictionary, and enforces standards for data (such as name, type, length, and usage). Therefore, analysts do not design databases.

The systems analyst must still determine the information requirements and program processing specifications. They in turn are translated into the contents of the subschema. The *subschema* is the logical definition of the data from the database that the program will use. It consists of data names and descriptions, and is a subset of the schema. For each database there is a single schema (Figure 9.20), but there may be many subschemas. Each information systems application that uses the database may have a different subschema.

The systems analyst is responsible for determining how data will be linked together to meet user requirements. For example, in the laundry example, the analysts must decide that it is necessary to link accounts receivable and inventory data together. They must also determine that inquiries will be made on such items as item rented, color of item, account status, and type of customer. Then they must design a coding scheme that

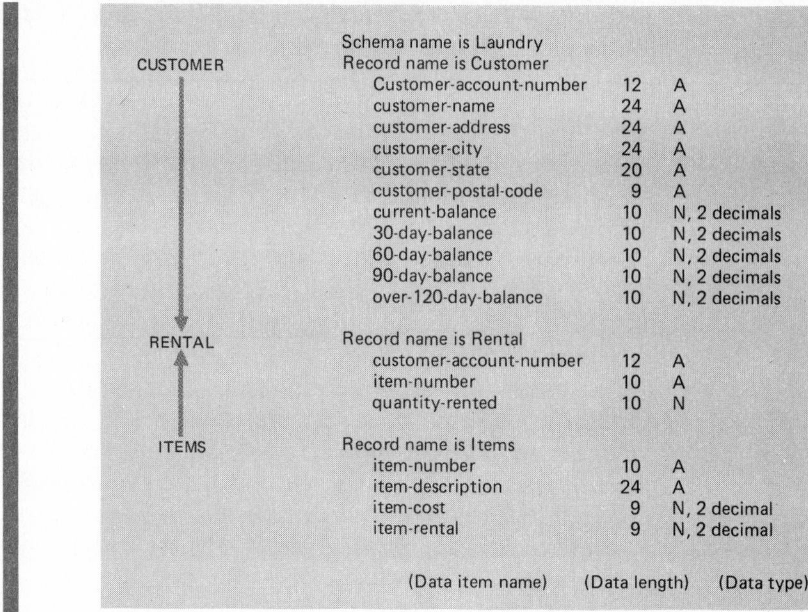

Schema name is Laundry

(Data item name)	(Data length)	(Data type)
Record name is Customer		
Customer-account-number	12	A
customer-name	24	A
customer-address	24	A
customer-city	24	A
customer-state	20	A
customer-postal-code	9	A
current-balance	10	N, 2 decimals
30-day-balance	10	N, 2 decimals
60-day-balance	10	N, 2 decimals
90-day-balance	10	N, 2 decimals
over-120-day-balance	10	N, 2 decimals
Record name is Rental		
customer-account-number	12	A
item-number	10	A
quantity-rented	10	N
Record name is Items		
item-number	10	A
item-description	24	A
item-cost	9	N, 2 decimal
item-rental	9	N, 2 decimal

Figure 9.20. Schema for laundry example.

uniquely identifies each item, as we have already emphasized. Carefully executed requirements analysis enables them to anticipate complex inquiries and provide methods for responding to them.

Record structures are determined by the systems analysts. Knowing that specific data items are needed to provide important user information continues to be the analysts' responsibility. However, in a database environment, the record structures are *logical* structures, meaning the way the program will see the data. The actual physical structures, that is, the way the system stores the data, may be different. (Differences between specific database management systems will tend to produce varying logical designs. These features must be learned through training in the capabilities of the specific system.) The database management system will assist in making the necessary transaction or reformatting of data to give the program what is expected. The structure of the data should follow the guidelines for length and type, specified in the data dictionary.

If the system will involve an existing database, the analysts must:

1 Familiarize themselves with the database schema.
2 Review the data standards and specifications in the data dictionary.
3 Determine logical data requirements and, working with the data administration staff, develop a subschema that conforms to the schema, while providing the data required by the information system.
4 Identify and design any master or transaction files needed by the information system but which are not part of the existing database.
5 For all entities, whether data about them is in a database or in separate

files, determine appropriate identification, coding, and validation schemes and proper processing procedures.

6 Consider the concerns for the design of input and output methods, which do not change.

If the analysts are working with a system where a new database will be developed, all of the above steps are necessary. In addition, close interaction with the database management staff will be required to establish the schema, data definitions, and data dictionary.

Database management systems do not replace the principles of systems design that we have discussed. Rather they provide the analyst with an additional tool to use in developing systems which provide managers with essential information. Questions about user requirements guide any decision concerning systems design or use of database software. The objective of the design is to provide the right information at the right time. Using database management systems is not an objective, but a means to an end.

Chapter 10 will examine the actual storage of data on auxiliary storage devices in file and database environments.

SUMMARY

Information systems are organized around files to accumulate and store data for processing. Files contain related records of data, describing entities of importance to the organization. The records themselves may be designed according to a fixed- or variable-length format, depending on the nature of the application and the amount of storage space available. Fixed-length records may use more storage, but they simplify programming and processing requirements.

The major types of files used in information systems are master, transaction, table, and report files. Master files are permanent files that exist for the life of the system, although they must be kept up to date to be useful. As events occur that affect or involve the organization, data describing them is captured into transaction files. The transaction files are in turn processed against the master file to bring them up to date. Table files are sometimes used to store reference data, used when processing transactions or producing output. Reference files, in contrast, accumulate output spooled to magnetic disk temporarily until it can be printed or produced on the appropriate output device.

All files are stored under a file organization. The two ways of storing records are by position or by address. The simplest way, sequential organization, is the only way records can be stored on magnetic tape. Each record is stored in the next available position. When direct access devices, such as magnetic disk, are used, records can be stored sequentially or under direct access or indexed organizations. Each of these organizations uses storage addresses to identify specific locations of records or blocks of data. The address consists of cylinder, surface, and sector numbers—specific areas of the disk that the system can locate quickly.

There are two direct access organizations. Direct addressing means that the record key corresponds exactly to a storage address. However, since record keys do not usually meet this requirement, hashing is often used to provide direct access capability. Under hashing, a storage address is derived by applying a key transformation algorithm that divides, extracts, or folds the record key. In some cases, synonyms develop, that is, keys produce the same address. A separate area of storage, called the overflow area, is reserved to store synonyms that occur in a file. The number of synonyms can be controlled by carefully developing the hashing algorithm.

Indexed file organizations use a separate file, the index, that keeps track of record keys and storage addresses of records in the master file. To find a record, the program first scans the index and then retrieves the record from the master file in the location specified by the index. The index makes it possible to process the file randomly or sequentially. Indexed organizations are index sequential, the most common, and index nonsequential.

When the purpose of the information system is the support of management inquiries and it is not feasible to retrieve data by specifying record keys, database systems may be used. The database management system is a program that bridges the file structures that store the data and the data structures that represent data needs of users. A schema defines the logical view of the database, and application programs use subschemas that are subsets of the schema. The database management system makes it possible to maintain independence between the logical database definition (through the schema and subschema) and the way the data is physically stored. The multilist and inverted-file data structures are the means by which data is logically organized to meet user requirements.

Analysts developing a system that includes a database must work with data administrators to determine how data is stored and what methods will be used for its retrieval and conversion to a format that the program needs. Analysts are still responsible for identifying and satisfying user requirements. However, they do so by drawing on the data stored in the database and by developing independent master and transaction files where appropriate.

KEYWORDS

Detached index
Direct access organization
Direct addressing
Division by prime
Extraction
Fixed-length record
Folding
Hashing
Index
Index nonsequential
Index sequential
Key transformation
Master file
Overflow
Physical record
Physical record key
Report file
Search key
Sequential organization
Spooling
Squaring
Synonym
Table file
Transaction file
Variable-length record

REVIEW QUESTIONS

1 What are the basic components of a file? Give an example of each. Explain how files differ.
2 Compare and contrast the types of files used in information systems. When is each type of file used?
3 What are record keys? Do all files rely on the use of record keys for storage or retrieval of data?
4 Explain the difference between a search key and a record key.
5 How do sequential and direct access organizations differ?
6 Discuss the different methods of storing data, using direct access organizations. Which direct access method is most frequently used? Why?
7 Explain the meaning of the following terms: hashing, synonym, overflow area, and physical record key.
8 What characterizes indexed files? What advantages do indexed sequential files offer in information processing systems? What disadvantages do they offer?
9 Is the index in an ISAM file part of the file or is it separate? How is it maintained as records are added to, or deleted from, a master file?
10 What purposes do databases serve in comparison with master files?
11 What is the difference between a database and a database management system? For what reasons do organizations choose to invest in database management systems?
12 Explain the difference between a schema and a subschema, between a host language system and a self-contained system, and between an application program and a database management system.
13 How do data structures and storage structures vary? What purpose does each serve in an information system?
14 What is the relation between a database management system, operating system, and application program?
15 How does the responsibility of the systems analyst for design change in a database environment?

APPLICATION PROBLEMS FOR CHAPTER 9

1 The New York State Trade Adjustment Assistance Center (TAAC) was established by the Economic Development Administration to assist firms in New York state whose businesses have been significantly affected by imports in certain produce areas. An important part of TAAC's operation is centered around an outreach program, aimed at notifying potential TAAC clients that they may be eligible for federal trade assistance. The outreach program works in the following manner: When new federal legislation affecting trade is passed by the national congress, TAAC studies it and tries to determine how many of the firms in its area could be helped by the legislation. Usually the legislation is written in such a way that it pertains only to firms producing certain specific types of products (for example, leather goods).

At various times, TAAC personnel will need to group firms by such categories as county of location, products manufactured or sold, dollar amount of yearly sales, number of employees, and postal zip code. TAAC has assigned each firm a unique identification number. There are currently approximately 3000 firms included in this paper file. However, it is expected that in the next 2 to 3 months, this number will increase to 10,000.

The TAAC director is considering whether to automate this file on a computer system. At the present time TAAC has no computer facilities. However, it is willing to invest in computer equipment to automate the file and to develop a flexible retrieval system.

a If the file would be processed, say 6 to 12 times per week, to retrieve information and produce reports, would it make sense to automate the system? Other than information retrieval, what other uses could be made of the file; that is, based on the description of TAAC above, how else could the file be processed?

b Under what storage structure should the master file be organized? What should be the record key? Explain your rationale for each.

c If a database system with inverted file or multilist capabilities is acquired, how should the additional capabilities be used to retrieve data?

d The director is considering whether a microcomputer will provide the capability needed to handle the center's needs. Each record in the system will require 350 characters of storage. Assuming that all programs will be stored on one floppy disk and the capacity of each disk is 1200K, will the system provide enough storage if it contains four disk drives? Show how you arrived at your answer. (Also explain how you will handle the problem of data being stored across more than one disk.)

2 Master file records with record keys, as shown below, are stored under an indexed sequential access method (ISAM) organization. Each track has the capacity to store six records. A separate overflow area is available but currently does not contain any records.

TRACK ADDRESS						
11008	1457	1501	1503	1519	1527	1528
11009	1987	1989	1994	1999		
11012	1628	1641	1642	1651	1680	
11014	1377	1378	1394	1395	1397	1399
11015	2018	2020	2021			

a Show the contents of the index for the above file.

b Process the following transaction data in the order in which it is given. Show the master file and index after updating the file with the transactions.

Add	1529
Add	1520
Change	1642
Delete	1378
Add	1627
Change	1394
Delete	1519
Add	1504
Add	1378
Add	1502

Use overflow storage if necessary.

c Using the revised file, explain how the system locates the record with the key of 1529.

3 The Cider Mill Playhouse theater wants to develop an automated box office system for speeding the processing of ticket sales. The theater runs 7 days per week, when it is showing productions. On many days, two performances are given. There are three general ticket prices, which vary depending on seat location. Reduced prices are charged for daytime performances. In addition, students and elderly patrons receive reduced prices from the normal ticket price for the performances they attend.

At any one time tickets for over 50 different performances will be on sale. A record of the theater seats sold and those available for sale at each performance is continually updated as sales are made.

The theater management will purchase whatever computer equipment is needed to operate the automated system as it is convinced the benefits exceed the costs. Therefore, either disk or magnetic tape storage will be available if needed.

a What files will be used to operate this system? Briefly describe their contents. What storage structure will each use?
b What is the record key for each file in *a*?
c Since ticket prices vary as described, how will management be certain of the proper amount of funds to collect for each performance?

4 An accounting system will be designed to produce monthly statements, summarizing customer account balances and activities. The systems analyst is planning to establish separate files consisting of (1) the customer master file, containing customer name and balance information, (2) payments and adjustments file, containing all payment and adjustment transactions entered into the system during the month as they occur, and (3) a sales transactions file, consisting of the total amount of each transaction, accumulated in the order of occurrence during the month. The record key in all cases is the customer account number. Other data in the transaction files include the date and amount of the transaction, and, in the case of the payments and adjustments file, a code indicating that the transaction is a payment or an adjustment.

The analyst wishes to produce a statement that has the starting balance printed at the top, followed by a list of all transactions in the order in which they occurred. For each transaction, the system will print either CHARGE, PAYMENT, or ADJUSTMENT, depending on the type of transaction. To print the transactions in the proper order, data from the two transactions files will have to be interspersed since the analyst does not want to first print all payments for a customer and then all sales. At the bottom of the statement, a new account balance will be printed.

a Based on the information provided, under what storage structure should each file be organized? (The computer systems configuration includes only magnetic disk and diskettes for use as secondary storage.)
b Discuss the processing procedure needed to print the account statements in the manner described. Be sure to indicate how the system will intersperse the printing of the different transactions and how the system will determine when all the transactions for a specific customer have been processed so that it can begin the next customer statement. (Use symbols or graphic notation to describe processing if necessary.)

5 A company that sells products to over 1000 regular customers provides an individual price for each item to every customer who purchases it, depending on the quantity the customer has historically purchased and the distance the customer is from the company location. The company sells 150 different items. As a systems analyst, you are responsible for structuring the data storage for a proposed system to assist in customer billing.

The following characteristics of the business are pertinent:

- Each customer receives, for every item it regularly purchases, a special price that management determines and will give to the systems operator. The price of each item is permanently stored, with the item identification number, as a default item price for the customer. No customer has more than 20 default items included in its purchase list.
- A master item list, consisting of 150 entries, contains the item identification numbers and descriptions of all products the firm sells.
- When the firm produces invoices for the customer, for each item sold it prints the item number, item description, and special price for the customer.

Management wants to be able to determine, on an inquiry basis, all prices currently quoted for a specific item and to know the customers receiving the prices. It also wants to be able to receive a complete price list of all items and all prices and customers who have quotes for the item. The report should list items in ascending order and group all customers for an item together.

Neither the number of customers nor the various items the company sells change often. Prices are adjusted no more than four times annually, although the changes seldom all occur at one time.

a Describe the master and transaction files needed for the system described above. The company does not have a database system, but has sufficient disk storage to handle your design, but storage should not be wasted. Processing speed and response to inquiries is important. The computer configuration in use includes four disk drives.

b Management is considering the purchase of a database management system for use with other existing information systems it has developed. Show how you would design the above system if a database system is available for your use. Explain why your design is different.

6 The Family Department Store, which has major facilities in several cities, is automating its charge account (accounts receivable) system. There are currently approximately 25,000 accounts. Each account has a seven-digit account number, the first and second digits indicating the store at which the account was opened.

When customers make credit purchases, the customer assistant makes an impression of the card number on a multipart sales slip. The customer also signs the form, which details each individual item purchased, the quantity of each, and the cost. Each transaction is given a unique identification number.

Sales transactions will be posted to a master file weekly, at which time the balance due will be adjusted, depending on payments made and purchase transactions received. Once a month the file will be processed to prepare invoices for mailing to customers. The invoice will list the customer's name and address, account number, balance due, finance charge, and minimum amount due. The invoice will also list each individual transaction by showing the date, transaction number, transaction details, and store location.

In addition to being processed monthly to produce the invoice, the file will also be used to respond to customer inquiries about account balances. In these cases, it is expected that customers will give their account numbers to the employee. The numbers will be input to the system for use by the program in retrieving the customers' records of information.

a What storage structure should be used for the file of customer records?

b Describe *two* ways to store transaction records and to process them against the main record for updating the balance due information. In one, include the records as part of the master file, and, in the other, store them separately. Explain how processing and invoice generation would occur in each case. What factors would determine your actual selection of one approach or the other?

c How would you handle customer inquiries about their account balances if they do not provide their account numbers?

d What processing mode(s) should be used for the file-oriented activities described above?

7 The State Personnel Office is responsible for maintaining the records of all administrative personnel employed in the state agencies. Records contain all personal data, including a unique employee identification number. The record also contains the following data: all job skills for the employee, pay grade, employment location by district as well as specific facility/agency, and seniority rating (that is, position or rank).

a How should the file be organized if it is regularly going to be used to assemble a list of all persons having a combination of a certain job skill, seniority level, and pay grade?

b How should the file be organized if it will be used only for payroll purposes and mailing information to individuals at their homes (where mailings will be made only for a certain region, not to all agency employees)?

c What advantages would be gained if a database management system is part of the system?

CHAPTER 10 AUXILIARY STORAGE DEVICES

QUESTIONS TO GUIDE YOU THROUGH THE CHAPTER

- In what ways do storage capabilities on magnetic tape and disk vary?
- How does the system find specific positions for storing or retrieving data?
- What factors determine the efficiency of auxiliary storage devices for storing or retrieving data?
- What does an address in auxiliary storage consist of?
- When should analysts expect damage or loss of data?

Business information systems are centered around the use of auxiliary storage devices to store important data. Computer main memory, although constantly expanding in capacity and dropping in price, is usually not large enough to accommodate the large volume of data used in many application systems, even in large computer environments. Also systems analysts and management desire to store data off-line and away from the computer system. The file organizations discussed in the previous chapter are stored on auxiliary storage devices (also called secondary storage).

This chapter describes magnetic tape and magnetic disk, the most common storage devices. It points out their technical features and discusses how they are used for storage, retrieval, and processing of records in files. Precautions the analysts and systems operators must take to protect the organization by providing additional copies of important files will also be discussed.

MAGNETIC TAPE

Magnetic tape is one of the best-known and least-expensive mediums for storing data on systems of all sizes. This method of auxiliary storage has specific advantages and disadvantages that analysts must weigh when determining whether to use it for the storage of files. This section first describes the physical characteristics of magnetic tape and then examines how files of data are actually stored on it.

Principles of Magnetic-Tape Storage

Magnetic tape consists of thin strips of mylar plastic coated on one side with tiny iron oxide particles, which can be used to store data. The particles can be moved around magnetically by a tape drive (as subsequently discussed) to represent data.

The magnetic tape is in 2400-foot reels (Figure 10.1), although shorter reels can be purchased if desired. When small microcomputers and personal computers were introduced during the 1970s, use of cassettes and ⅛-inch tape, rather than the traditional ¾-inch width, was introduced. A 2400-foot

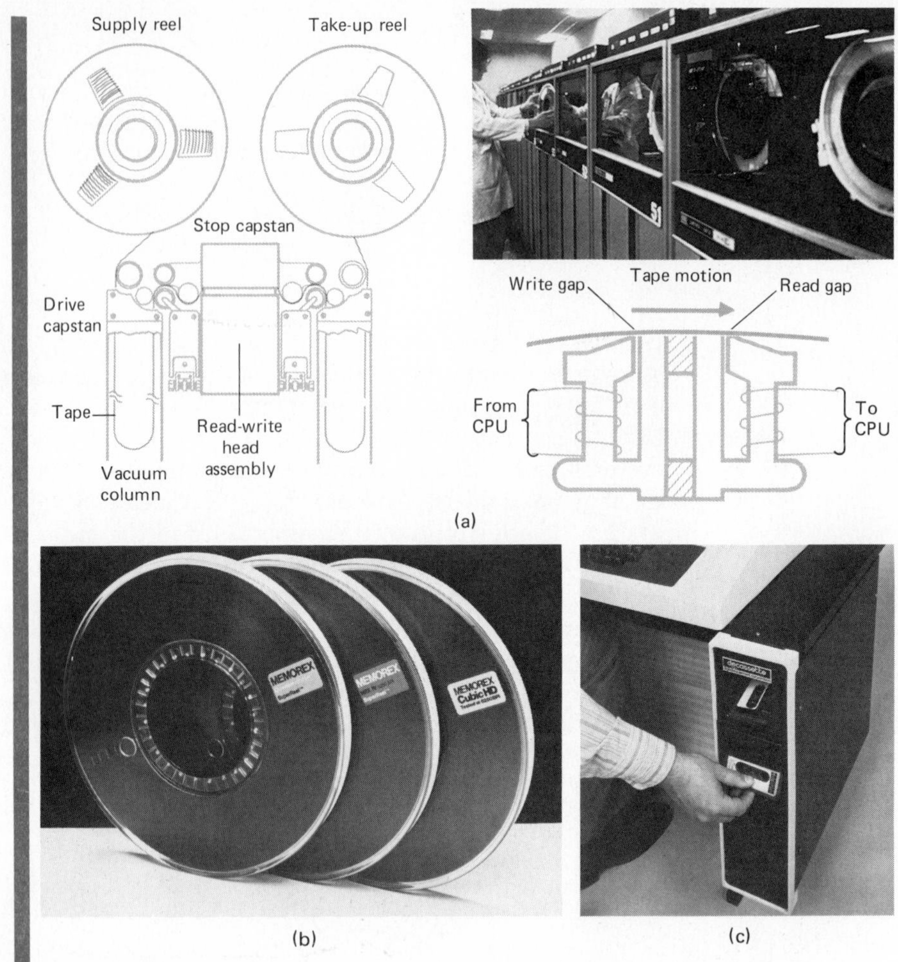

Figure 10.1. (*a*) Magnetic tape drive (Photo courtesy of Control Data Corporation) and (*b*) (*c*) tapes for data storage (*left*, Courtesy Memorex Corporation; *right*, photo courtesy of Digital Equipment Corporation).

reel of magnetic tape costs approximately $20, and a cassette costs less than $10. Both types of tape store data according to the principles outlined in this section.

Data is recorded by a *tape drive* that serves two purposes: It moves the tape so data received from the central processing unit can be stored (written) or so it can be read and sent to the CPU. It also translates data into spots on the tape that represent the data values. The tape drive is essential, since data is read from, or written to, the tape only when the tape is actually being moved.

Data on magnetic tape is stored by using a coding scheme (Figure 10.2) that consists of 7 or 9 bits, depending on the manufacturer of the computer system. For example, International Business Machines (IBM) computers use 9 bits to store data, while those manufactured by Control Data Corporation use 7. Each group of 7 or 9 bits codes one character of data, as

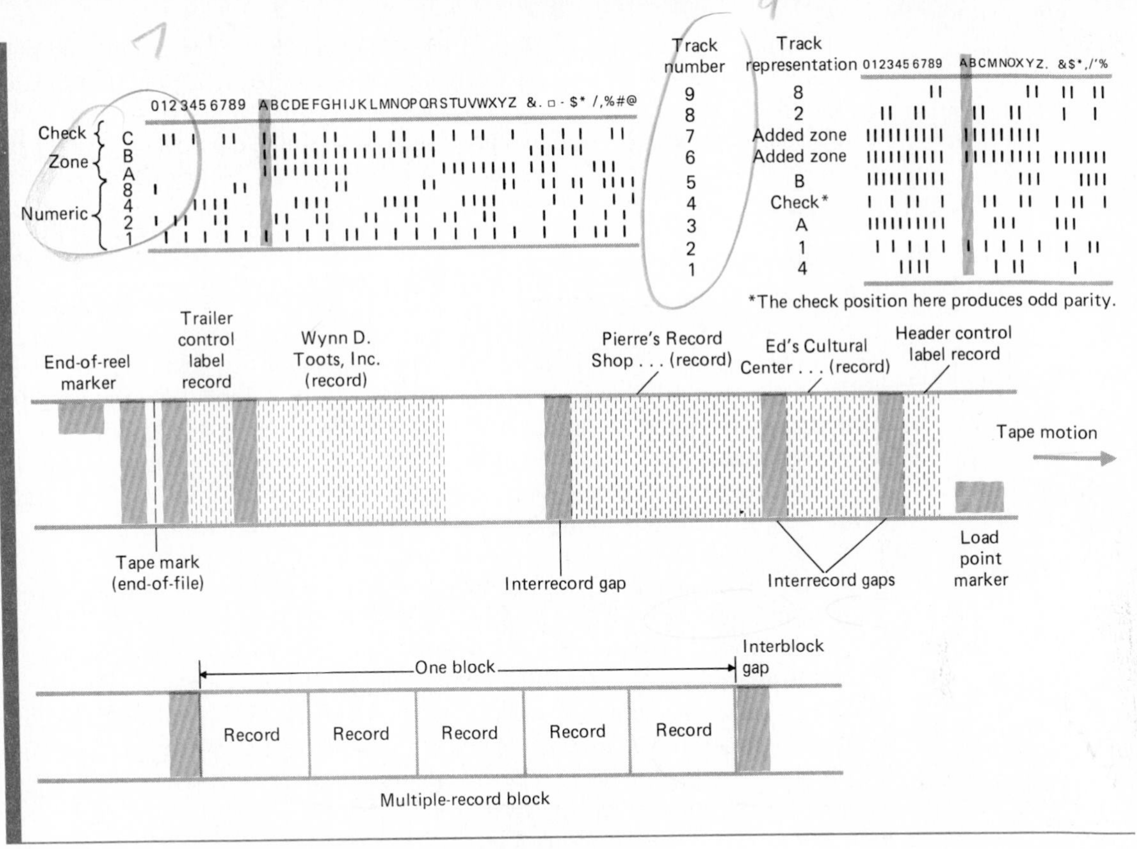

Figure 10.2. Magnetic tape coding scheme.

illustrated in Figure 10.2. The cross section on the tape is called a *frame*, while the group of 7 or 9 bits stores one *byte* of data.

Data runs linearly along the tape on tracks. Using the above format, then, magnetic-tape systems are 7- or 9-track tapes. This feature is fixed and cannot be changed by analysts or programmers. A tape system records in either 7- or 9-track format, but not both.

One of the bits in the illustration in Figure 10.2 is marked as a *parity bit*. A parity bit is actually an extra bit, not needed to store the data itself but added to assist in the detection of errors, on the rare occasions when they occur.

There are two parity schemes: even or odd. Under *even parity*, an even number of bits (that is, 2, 4, 6, or 8—numbers divisible by 2 without a remainder—in the case of a 9-track tape system) must be turned on for every character of data stored. Under the 9-track format, to store the character A, for example, bits 0, 1, and 7 must be turned on—an odd number. If the system is recording using even parity, the extra bit, the parity bit, is turned on (set to 1) to make an even number. Every time the data is read, the system counts the number of bits that are on. If data is recorded using even parity and in a character read there are an odd number of bits on, the system knows an error occurred and can signal this to the computer operator, who decides whether to continue processing.

Under odd parity the above process is reversed. The parity bit is set to one only when an even number of data bits are ones.

Storing Data on Magnetic Tape

Data is stored along the length of the tape at a specified density, measured in bytes per inch. One byte stores one character, as indicated in Figure 10.2. The *recording density* of a system is the number of bytes stored per inch (BPI). Standard BPI density on mainframe systems are 1600 and 6250, although some older systems are still in use that store data at 556 or 800 bytes per inch.

The recording density of a particular model tape drive is fixed and cannot be altered, but many have been built with the option of storing at either of two densities. The programmer, in the job control language of a computer program, instructs the tape drive to record data at either of the built-in density capabilities, such as 1600 or 6250 BPI.

Data is read from, or written to, the tape only when the tape is being moved forward by the tape drive. Data is read in *blocks* or *physical records*. To read a block of data, the tape is moved forward so the data passes the read-write heads of the tape drive. The tape stops and is restarted when the system tells the tape drive to read the next physical record. (This is the same principle as a home tape recorder. Music or voice is heard only when the tape is moving. When it stops, nothing plays.)

Each time the tape stops and restarts, it takes a very small fraction of a second, during which time no data is read. This means that whatever is on the tape in that spot will be missed. The high recording density increases the amount of data that could be overlooked. To allow space for the tape drive to stop and restart tape movement without losing data, interblock gaps separate each block (Figure 10.3). An *interblock gap* (also called *interrecord gap)* is a length of tape, 0.3 inch on current tape drives, that is totally blank. Its sole purpose is to separate blocks of data and to allow space for starting and stopping.

Figure 10.3. Format of sequential file on magnetic tape.

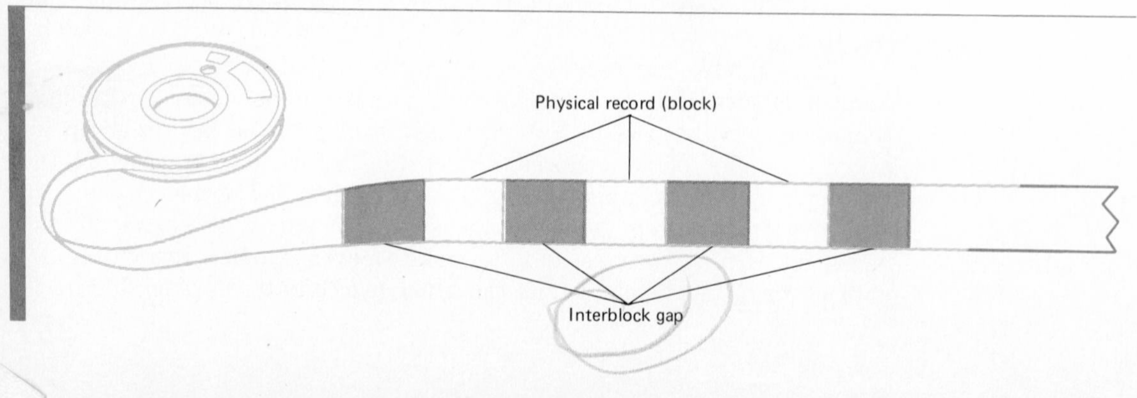

SPACE DETERMINATION

To demonstrate how data is stored on magnetic tape, we will calculate the amount of space needed to store a sample file of records. Analysts frequently make this calculation when determining storage requirements during systems design. The file will consist of 15,000 records and each record will be 175 bytes long.

The first step is to determine the amount of space required to store one record. For each record, space is needed for the data and for the interblock gap. The record is 175 characters stored at a recording density of 6250 BPI, which leads to the determination that 0.028 inch of tape are needed plus the space for the interblock gap (0.3 inch), or a total 0.328 inch, for each record (Figure 10.4).

To determine the space needed for storing the entire file, multiply the space for one record (0.328 inch) by the number of records in the file. In this example, that is 4920 inches, or about 17 percent of the reel of 2400 feet (28,800 inches) of tape.

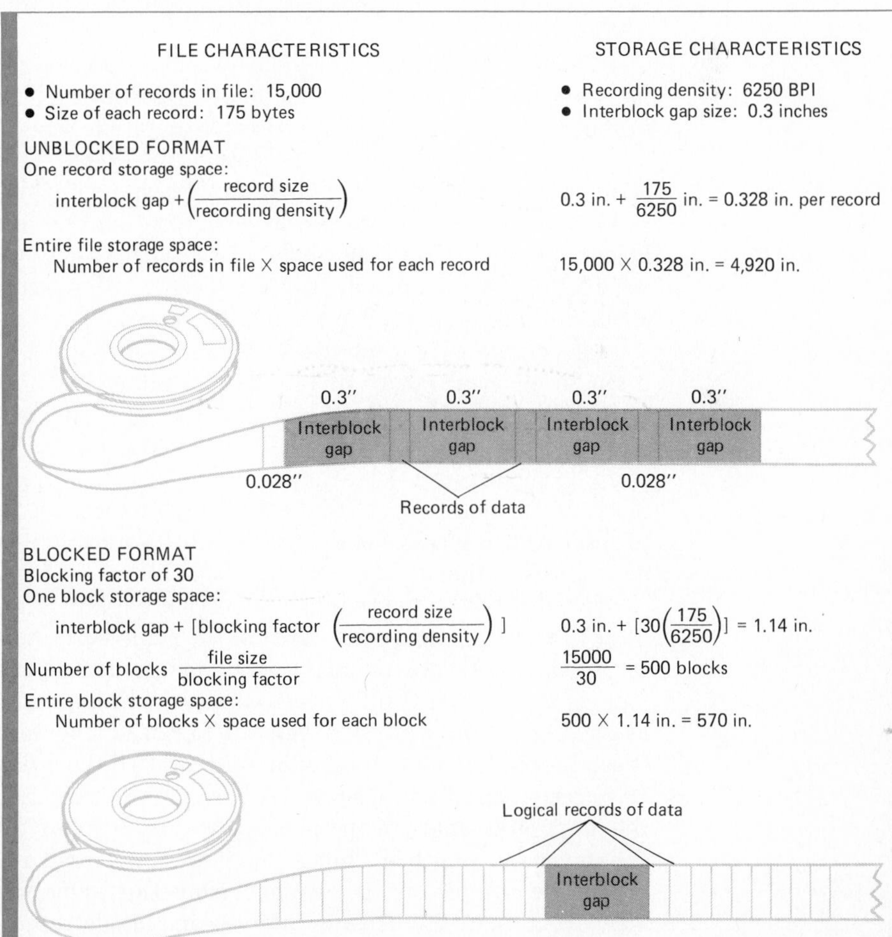

FILE CHARACTERISTICS
• Number of records in file: 15,000
• Size of each record: 175 bytes
STORAGE CHARACTERISTICS
• Recording density: 6250 BPI
• Interblock gap size: 0.3 inches
UNBLOCKED FORMAT
One record storage space:
interblock gap + (record size / recording density)
0.3 in. + 175/6250 in. = 0.328 in. per record
Entire file storage space:
Number of records in file X space used for each record
15,000 X 0.328 in. = 4,920 in.
0.3″
Interblock gap
0.3″
Interblock gap
0.3″
Interblock gap
0.3″
Interblock gap
0.028″
0.028″
Records of data
BLOCKED FORMAT
Blocking factor of 30
One block storage space:
interblock gap + [blocking factor (record size / recording density)]
0.3 in. + [30(175/6250)] = 1.14 in.
Number of blocks file size / blocking factor
15000/30 = 500 blocks
Entire block storage space:
Number of blocks X space used for each block
500 X 1.14 in. = 570 in.
Logical records of data
Interblock gap

Figure 10.4. Blocked and unblocked data storage on magnetic tape.

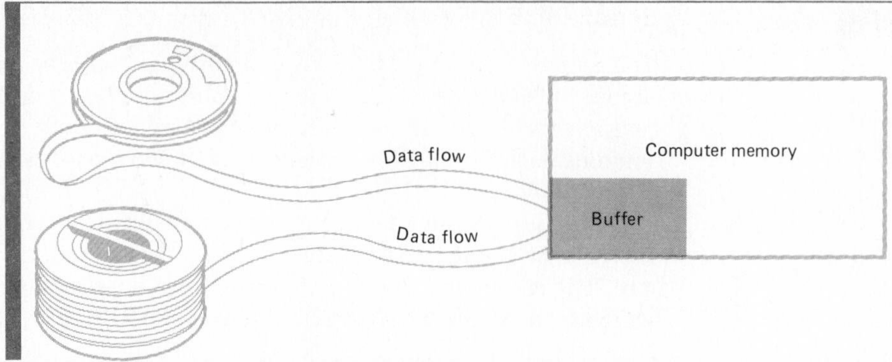

Figure 10.5. Buffer for input/output activities.

BLOCKING

Compared with the amount of space needed to store 15,000 paper records, magnetic tape does indeed provide concise storage of records. However, it is evident in Figure 10.4 that more space is needed for the interblock gap than for the data itself.

To make better use of storage space (and to speed the processing of the file, as will be examined in a moment), systems analysts usually reduce the number of interblock gaps required through blocking.

As indicated earlier in this section, the system reads and writes blocks of physical records of data. You know now that a physical record is whatever is surrounded by two interblock gaps, whether one byte of data or a much larger amount. Users, however, deal with *logical* records. That is, the records people use (such as medical records, sales records, invoices, or bank checks) in a systems sense are logical records.

Blocking occurs when the system stores multiple logical records within a single physical record or blank. The number of records in the block is termed the *blocking factor*. If, in storing a file of medical records on magnetic tape, the analyst specifies a blocking factor of 30, the system will store 30 medical records (the logical record in this example) within every block. If the block stores 75, the blocking factor is 75. If it stores 1, the term to describe this storage is *unblocked*. The first example we used pertained to an unblocked file.

Several additional points will further explain data storage on tape. All blocks in a file on magnetic tape use the same blocking factor. Thus, if one is recorded with a blocking factor of 30, all are blocked at 30. A block can be as long as the analyst thinks necessary, providing it can be read into memory at one time. When physical records are read, they are transmitted into a special input-output section of memory, called the *buffer*. The buffer (Figure 10.5) has a specified capacity. (It varies from computer to computer.) Thus the maximum length of any block is the number of bytes the buffer can hold. Whatever the length of a block, the system will read all of it and then pause.

If the sample file is changed from the unblocked specification used above to a blocking factor of 30, we can calculate the space savings to see whether it is significant. To store a single physical record with a blocking factor of 30, the space needed for one record (175/6250) is multiplied by the blocking factor and the space for the interblock gap is added to the result. As Figure 10.4 shows, space for each block is now 1.14 inches of tape. Blocking reduced the amount of interblock gap space for 30 records by 8.7 inches (29 blocks at 0.3 inch each).

The file of 15,000 records, when stored 30 records to a block, consists of 15,000/30 = 500 blocks. Thus the entire file requires 500 × 1.14 = 570 inches of tape, instead of the previous 4920 inches.

Timing Determination

In addition to being able to determine space needs, analysts also often want to know how long a particular application will run, i.e., how many seconds, minutes, or hours it will take to process the file. Once the blocking factor and space needs are determined, it is a simple process to calculate read time.

The time it takes to read a file of data (not including processing time in the CPU) is governed by the size of the logical and physical records, size of the interblock gap, recording density, and transfer rate of the tape drive. The *transfer rate* is the speed at which data can be transferred from secondary storage, magnetic tape in this case, into memory (or vice versa). The rate is determined and supplied by the manufacturer.

The following formulas are used to determine tape processing speeds.

$$\text{Tape speed (in inches per second)} = \frac{\text{transfer rate (bytes per second)}}{\text{recording density (BPI)}}$$

$$\text{Time per block of data} = \frac{\text{bytes per block of data}}{\text{transfer rate (bytes per second)}}$$

$$\text{Interblock gap time} = \frac{\text{size of interblock gap}}{\text{tape speed}}$$

Using the sample file from the earlier example, the time to read through a file of records on magnetic tape can quickly be determined, providing the transfer rate for the tape drive is known. In this example the system transfers at a rate of 320,000 bytes per second. The appropriate calculations produce results indicating that

$$\text{Tape speed} = \frac{320{,}000}{6250} = 51.2 \text{ inches per second}$$

$$\text{Time for each block of data} = \frac{5{,}250 \text{ bytes per block } (30 \times 175)}{320{,}000 \text{ bytes per second}} = 0.0164 \text{ second per block}$$

$$\text{Time for each interblock gap} = \frac{0.3}{51.2} = 0.0059 \text{ second per gap}$$

For the entire file, containing 500 blocks, the time is

$$\underset{\text{Blocks}}{500}\ (\underset{\text{data time}}{0.0164} + \underset{\text{gap time}}{0.0059}) = 11.15 \text{ seconds (read, but not processed)}$$

These steps should be repeated every time the analysts find a need to time the tape-reading requirement for a system during design and implementation. The section on magnetic-disk processing will develop similar information.

Sequential File Processing

The most efficient way to process transaction and master files is by having them both in the same sequence. In this way records need be read only one time. Since the master file is usually larger than the transaction file and is the more permanent of the two, design specifications should state that the transaction file is sorted into the same order as the master file before any other processing takes place. (Transactions will not occur in the same order as in the master file. For example, customers will not arrive in alphabetical or identification-number order.) The result of a sort process, using a utility sort program, is a sorted transaction file ready for further processing.

Figure 10.6 shows the partial contents of master, transaction, and sorted transaction files. As this illustration points out, the sorted transaction file is in the same alphabetical sequence as the master file.

FILE UPDATING

To update a master file, the three possible transactions are *adding* new records, *deleting* existing records, or *changing* the contents of existing master file records. When updating master files, a new master file is created, containing the results of the update activities. However, the previous master file is not destroyed. Furthermore it is not possible to add or delete records in a sequential master file without producing a new copy of the master on a different reel of tape.

We will step through the activities that occur in updating the master file in Figure 10.6 to produce the result shown in Figure 10.6*b*. The transaction file contents actually control the update process. The records it contains select those master file records to be updated and those to remain unchanged. Under the control of the computer program, the system reads into memory the first block of records on the transaction file and the first block on the master file. In the example, the master file is blocked at 10 and the transaction file is unblocked. Therefore, when the first records are read in, a copy of the transaction record with a key of 01-0112 is read into memory, along with the first block of 10 master file records (key values of 01-0100 through 02-0418). Next the system compares the transaction record key of 01-0112 with each of the master records in memory until it equals or exceeds them. In the example, the transaction and master keys match on record 3 of the in-memory block. The master record is changed according to the contents of the transaction record.

The next transaction record is copied into memory and the system continues to compare the remaining master records in memory. Since the transaction file has been sorted into master file order, the system does not have to backtrack and recheck any earlier master file records. Without the

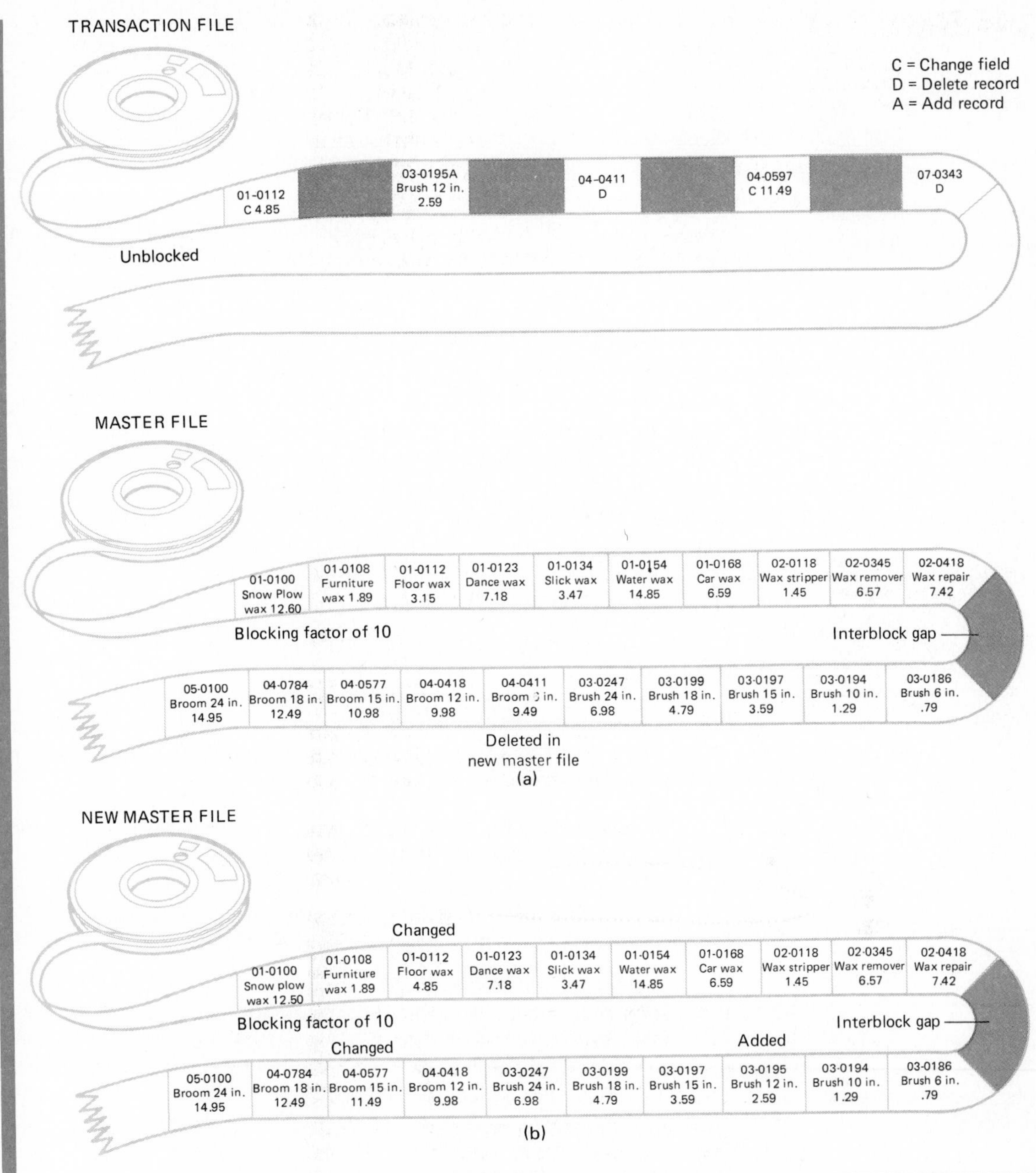

Figure 10.6. Sequential file updating process.

presort step, the master file would be reexamined from the beginning. No other records in the master file block in memory match the current transaction key, so the system writes the block to the new master file tape, incorporating the changes already made. The original master file remains unchanged. Then a copy of the next block of records on the master file (key values 03-0186 through 05-0100) is read into memory and the comparison with the transaction record key continues.

The master file key exceeds the transaction key after the second record in this block. According to the transaction record, a new record is to be added to the master file. The system inserts this record, maintaining the sequence.

The next transaction file record is copied into memory. It matches on the sixth record of the master file block. Since this is a deletion transaction, this record, with a key of 04-0411, will not be retained in the new copy of the master file.

Now the fourth transaction record is copied into memory and the comparison continues. When the master and transaction keys match on 04-0577, the change prescribed in the transaction record is made to the master record in memory.

Throughout the entire update process, the transaction file controls what happens next. The system takes care of maintaining proper blocking for the master file automatically. Neither the programmer nor the analyst have to specify how to carry that out, as it is taken care of by the operating system.

Figure 10.6*b* shows the results of the processing. The original sequence of the old master is preserved in the new master file.

ERROR HANDLING

During the file processing, error checks are made continually. The following types of errors can occur if the input data is not properly validated or if erroneous transactions are included in the transaction file:

1 Attempting to add records to a master file when the record is already stored in the file and duplicate keys are not allowed
2 Attempting to delete records that are not stored in the file
3 Attempting to change the contents of records that are not stored in the file (search key does not match any key in the file)

Whenever errors are found, they should be pointed out on a separate printed error report, with messages that report the error and show the record key affected.

DIRECT ACCESS DEVICES

Magnetic-disk systems are direct access devices. This means that the record can be written to, or read from, a specific location on the disk, unlike with magnetic tape, where records are found by scanning the tape. This section describes the features of magnetic-disk systems and distinguishes between the different types of disks. It looks at the characteristics of magnetic disks in detail and describes how storage locations are determined, what addresses consist of, and how the system uses each to process files.

Types of Magnetic Disks

Magnetic-disk systems are the most widely known direct access devices used on computers. They are used with computers of all sizes, from small personal computers to large mainframe systems. Magnetic disks fall into two general categories, which we call hard and flexible media.

HARD DISK

This type of magnetic disk consists of a metal plate coated with an iron oxide material (like magnetic tape) that can be used to store data. Hard disks on small systems may be as small as 5 inches in diameter, while those used on large mainframe systems are usually 13 inches, about the size of a long-playing phonograph record.

The magnetically coated plates are used in the three types of hard disks (Figure 10.7):

1 *Disk Pack.* A set of metal plates mounted on a spindle, approximately ½ inch apart. The number of plates varies from 4 to 10, depending on the system for which they are manufactured. The entire pack is carried together; individual plates cannot be removed by the user.
2 *Disk Cartridge.* A single metal plate contained in a plastic protective cover. The height of a disk cartridge, including the cover, is approximately 1 to 2 inches.
3 *Winchester Disk.* A special type of disk cartridge or disk pack in which the mechanism for reading and writing to the disk is sealed in the same

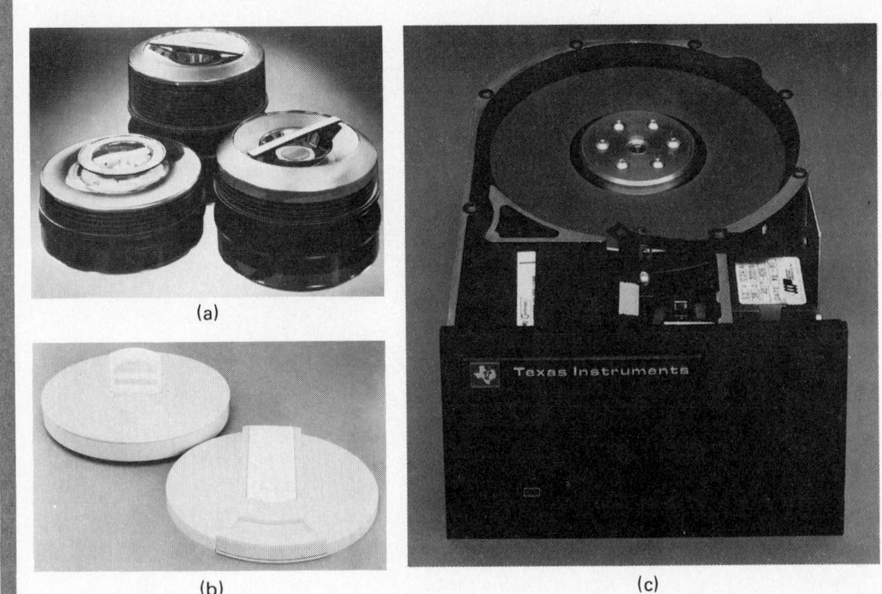

Figure 10.7. Assorted magnetic disk storage devices. [(*a*) and (*b*) Courtesy of 3M; (*c*) courtesy of Texas Instruments, Inc.]

unit with the plates (normally it is not) to protect against dust and improve processing performance.

Hard disks range in price from several hundred dollars for disk cartridges, the least expensive, to several thousand dollars for sealed Winchester disk systems.

FLEXIBLE DISKETTE

Flexible diskettes (Figure 10.8) are, as their name indicates, bendable. They are made of a soft plasticlike material containing a magnetic coating that will store coded data. The disk, which is very thin (less than 1/32 inch), will bend if held by the edge. It is mounted in a fiber jacket that protects its surface from damage and dust. "Diskette" therefore refers to the plastic disk and the fiber jacket.

Floppy disk cartridge disk systems are also being developed. The disks are sealed in a hard plastic casing to protect the media from dust and fingerprints.

The most common diskettes are either 5¼ or 8 inches in diameter, although 3-inch versions have been introduced.

Flexible diskettes are in most widespread use on personal computers, small business systems, minicomputers, and word processing systems. However, they can be used with systems of any size.

Figure 10.8. Assorted flexible diskettes. (Photo courtesy of BASF Corporation)

Magnetic-Disk Characteristics

We will look at the features of magnetic disks in detail to see how they store data and why direct access to records is possible with disks, while it is not with magnetic tape. The formatting of the disk permits organized data storage.

DISK LAYOUT AND OPERATION

Data is written to, or read from, magnetic disks (or diskettes) only when they are being rotated by the *disk drive* (Figure 10.9). Disk rotation varies depending on the size and manufacturer of the drive, but ranges from approximately 200 to several thousand revolutions per minute.

Writing and reading occurs through read-write *heads* that electronically sense the data from the disk surface. The heads, mounted on movable access arms, slide back and forth across the disk surface to locate data. Although they are very close to the surface of the disk (Figure 10.10), they should never touch the surface. (If they do, a situation called a *head crash* occurs, in which the disk is usually damaged, and data will surely be lost as a result.)

Normally the read-write heads are part of the disk drive unit. However, in Winchester systems, the heads are sealed in the same package as the disk pack. As indicated earlier, the reason is to protect against dust and dirt and improve access speed.

Data is stored on the disk surface in one of many tracks. A track is a concentric circle that has a fixed storage capacity, measured in bytes per track. Small diskettes have as few as 34 tracks per surface, while large packs have several hundred tracks per surface (Figure 10.11). Each track is identified by a number (starting from 0 and ascending by increments of 1) and a surface number. (Note that in disk packs, the very top surface of the upper disk and the very bottom surface of the lower disk often are not used in order to prevent data loss due to surface damage.)

In disk packs both the upper and lower surfaces of each disk store data.

(a)

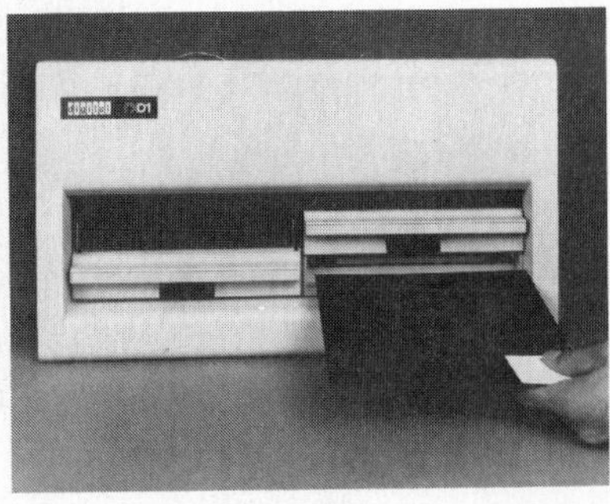

(b)

Figure 10.9. Magnetic disk drives for (*a*) hard (courtesy Control Data Corporation) and (*b*) flexible disks (photo courtesy of Digital Equipment Corporation).

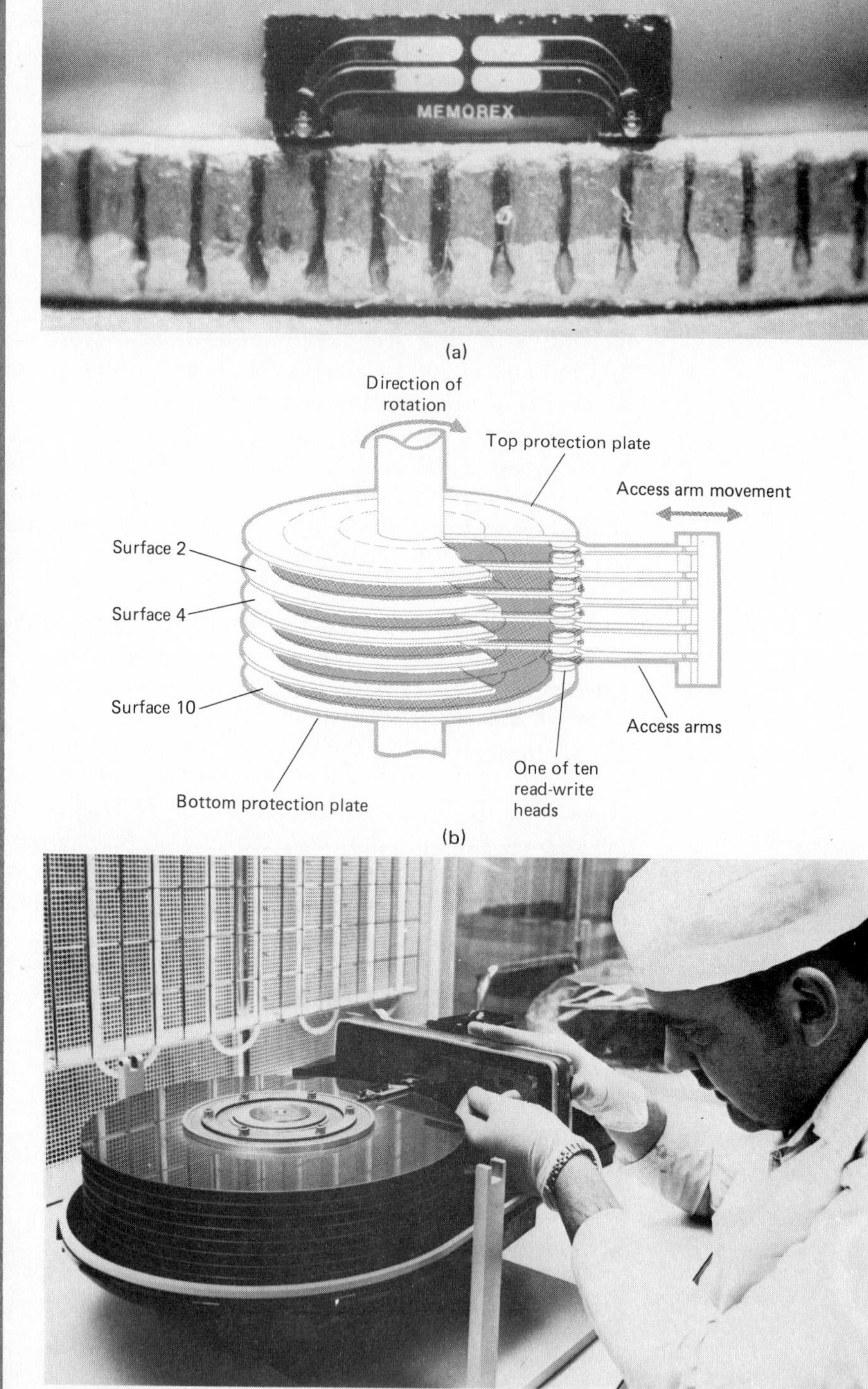

Figure 10.10. (*a*) magnetic disk read/write heads on a dime's edge and (*b*) (*c*) examples of the access arm. [(*a*) and (*c*) Courtesy of Memorex Corporation]

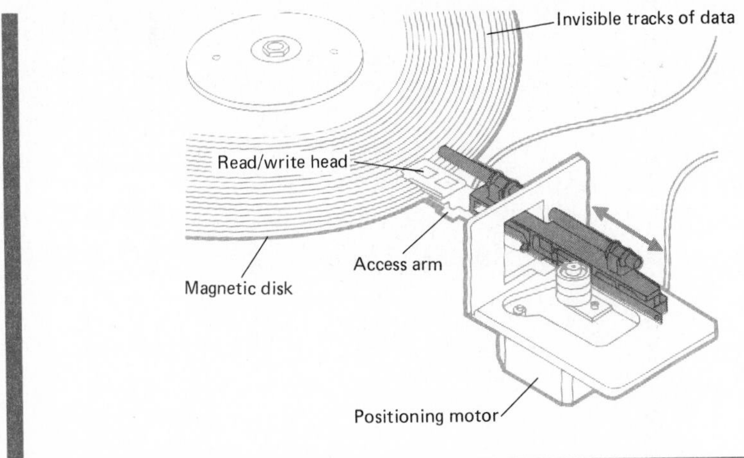

Figure 10.11.
Magnetic disk layout.

Disk cartridges and flexible diskettes may be either single- or double-sided for storage.

The read-write heads on a disk are mounted on an access arm. All heads move together. The heads on each surface can reference one track on that surface. Therefore, if there are, say, 20 accessible surfaces in the disk pack, 1 on each recording surface, when the access arm is positioned, the system can write or read to or from any of the 20 tracks. The tracks that can be referenced at one time from one specific position are collectively referred to as a *cylinder*.

To access a specific record, the program must determine and specify the cylinder and surface where the record is located. This concept is an important aspect of addressing in direct access devices. There are two addressing methods, which we refer to as track and sector addressing.

TRACK/CYLINDER ADDRESSING

The most widely used addressing form on large computers uses a track/cylinder addressing concept. The track is considered one large storage bucket. A detailed description of the layout of the track will make this concept more meaningful.

Index Point

The general layout of a track under the track/cylinder concept, shown in Figure 10.12, consists of an index point, home address, track descriptor record, and data records. The *index point* signals the start of a track. All tracks on the disk are synchronized to the index point. When the system senses this point, it knows a new rotation of the disk has started. The index point is sensed by the disk mechanism, not by the read-write heads.

When disks are *initialized*, that is prepared for use, a special utility program identifies the format of the disk by writing tracks on the disk

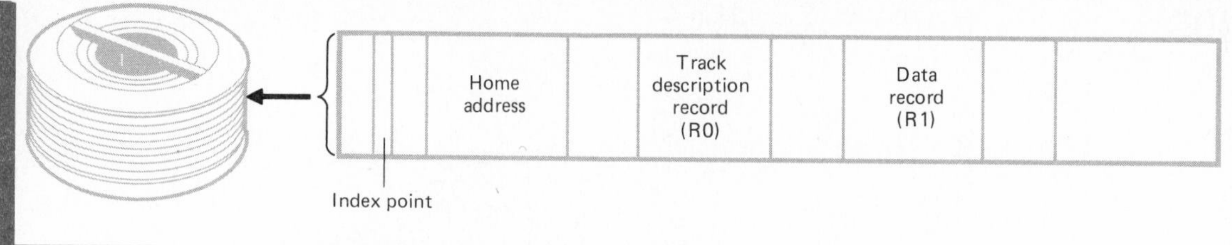

Figure 10.12. Magnetic disk track layout.

magnetically. (The tracks are not visible as there are no grooves or physical marks on the surface.)

Home Address

During initialization, the system writes the *home address* on the track. (If for some reason the system cannot write a home address, the disk is unusable.) The home address consists of four separate pieces of information (Figure 10.13).

The flag byte indicates whether the track is a primary or alternate track. The cylinder and read-write head number together identify a specific track on the disk. This feature is essential for the direct- and hash-addressing methods discussed in Chapter 9. A hashing algorithm, for example, must produce an address that corresponds to one of the cylinder-head-number combinations, stored in the home address. The check bytes are for error detection and function like the parity bit we discussed in conjunction with magnetic-tape storage.

The system automatically leaves short gaps between the index point, home address, and records on the track. Their size is determined by the system and cannot be adjusted by the programmer or analyst.

Track Descriptor Record

The next record on the track is the *track descriptor record* (Figure 10.14). This record, sometimes also called *record zero,* carries information that describes how the data on the remaining part of the track is organized. Nine different elements of information are included. The flag byte, cylinder number, and read-write head number serve the same purpose as just described. They are repeated in the track descriptor record, so that data on the track can be moved from a primary to alternate track should the need

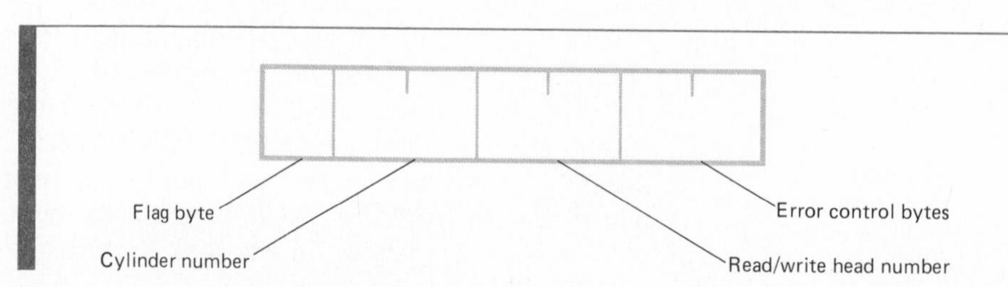

Figure 10.13. Detailed view of home address.

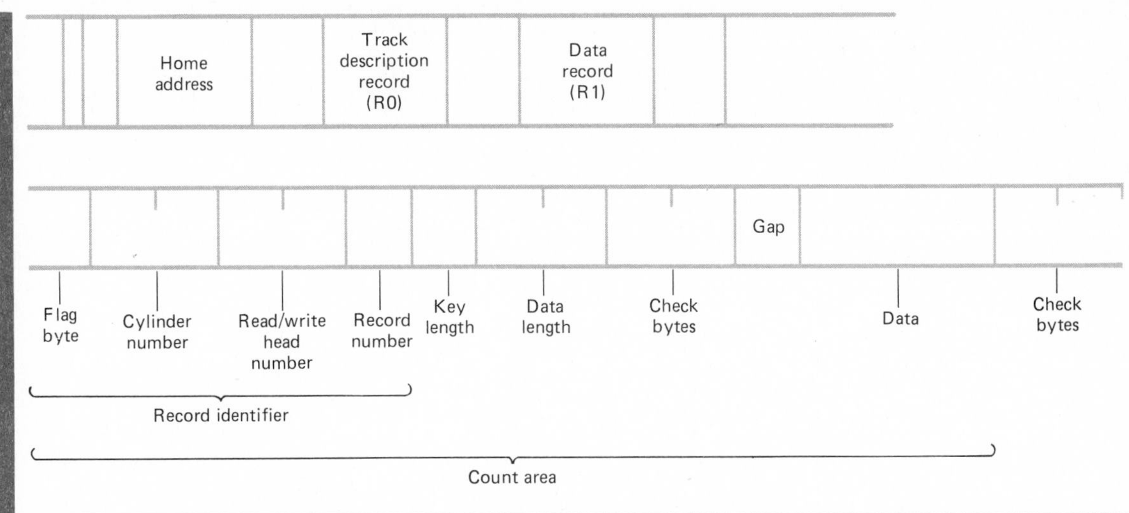

Figure 10.14. Track descriptor record.

arise. This gives the system all the information it needs to use the data that follows.

The *record number* is the sequence number of the record on the track. The first record on the track, number 0, is the track descriptor record. Its position is the reason why it is sometimes called record zero.

The cylinder, head, and record numbers comprise the record identifier and serve the purpose their name indicates: they make it possible to distinguish one record on a disk from another. The record identifier, along with the data-length details, describes the count area.

The *key-length byte* and *data-length bytes* in the record key and data areas of each record respectively describe the amount of space taken up by each. As will be shown later, the data-length bytes are instrumental in storing variable-length records.

Following check bytes for error control is the data area of the record. There is no data in the track descriptor record. However, every other record that follows the record has the same format and includes data.

General Formats

Data stored on the track can be recorded in two general formats (see Figure 10.15). The *count data format* pertains to a file of records that do not contain a physical record key. As described earlier, the file that stores data without physical keys is a sequential file. Sequential files can be stored on magnetic disk, as well as on tape.

The count key data format is used for all keyed data. There are five possible count key data formats. These combinations make possible the storage of fixed- and variable-length records, under blocked and unblocked

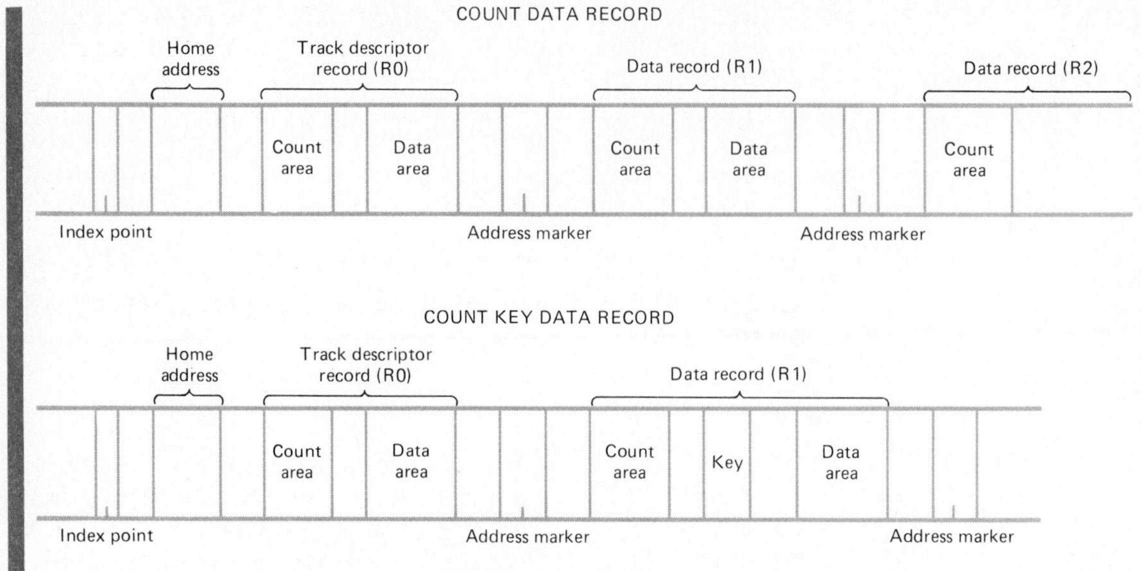

Figure 10.15. Magnetic disk record formats.

forms. An undefined format is also specified for any keyed record that does not pertain to one of the above formats.

TRACK/SECTOR ADDRESSING

The sector method of addressing on magnetic disk divides each track into a specific number of fixed-length blocks, called *sectors* (Figure 10.16). This method is used almost exclusively on floppy disk systems, as well as on many larger hard-disk systems, although in the latter it is not as common as the open track addressing method. In order to locate a record, the program must instruct the system to load from the appropriate cylinder, surface, and sector.

Each sector on a track has a fixed storage capacity. The innermost sectors (and tracks) hold the same number of bytes of data as the sectors on

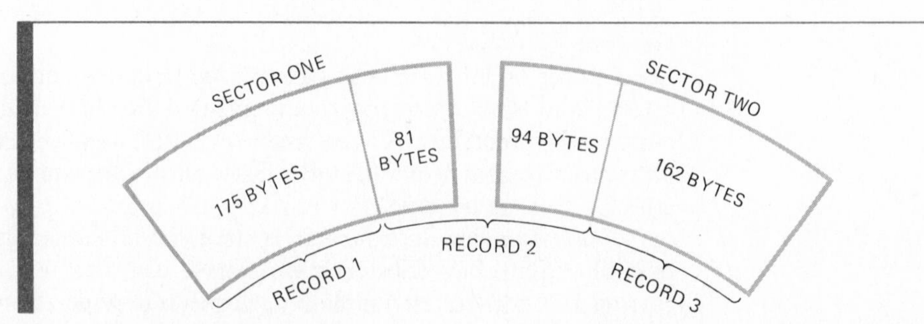

Figure 10.16. Sector spanning.

the outer tracks. Common sector capacities are 128 bytes per sector (called *single density),* 256 bytes per sector *(double density),* and 512 bytes per sector *(quad density).*

The operating system typically takes care of automatically blocking records to make maximum use of storage. If the record length is not evenly divisible by the sector length, the system automatically spans records across sectors. Figure 10.16 illustrates how 175-character logical records are stored using sector spanning.

Record lengths for variable-length records are possible through the inclusion of a record length field at the beginning of each record, as shown in the illustration.

DISK STORAGE CAPACITY

Disk storage is governed by the capacity of each track on the disk. This is a stated feature over which the analyst has no control. Track capacity may be stated as the number of bytes that a track can contain, in the case of track/cylinder addressing, or the number of sectors per track, along with a sector capacity, for track/sector addressing.

In track/cylinder addressing, the number of physical records that can be placed on a track depends on whether there are keys in the record and the size of the records, as well as the track capacity. The analyst determines the size of all records, except the track descriptor record and home address.

Often charts, such as those in Table 10.1, are provided by the equipment manufacturer to aid in disk space utilization. For this example, a file of 15,000 keyed records of 175 bytes each (including a key of 10 bytes) will be stored. The capacity of the track on the disk in this example is 13, 165 bytes. There are 19 tracks per cylinder.

Using the chart in Table 10.1, we find that, for any record requiring between 175 and 185 bytes of storage, including key length, the system can store 35 records per track, or 665 records per cylinder. Therefore, to store the file of 15,000 records, a total of 23 (15,000/665) cylinders, or 428 (15,000/35) tracks, must be allocated.

Blocking will change the required allocation, as it makes more efficient use of space. If a blocking factor of 15 is used in this example, there are 2625 bytes per block. The chart in Table 10.1 shows that four 15-record blocks, that is 60 logical records, can be stored on each track, or 1140 records in each cylinder. Now, owing to blocking, only 13 cylinders (15,000/1,140) are needed.

For systems using tracks with track/sector addressing, an effective estimate of how many tracks are needed can be found by dividing track capacity by record size. Thus, on a disk with a track capacity of 6,656 bytes, 38 complete records of 175 bytes each can be stored. A total of 395 tracks (15,000/38) is needed to store the 15,000 records. If the disk in this example contains 12 tracks per cylinder, the analyst can quickly determine that 33 cylinders should be allocated for the file.

When sizing a file, as above, it is important to take into account the

Table 10.1

CAPACITIES WITH KEYS

BYTES PER RECORD		RECORDS PER				BYTES PER PACK	
MINIMUM	MAXIMUM	TRACK	CYLINDER	PACK	FACILITY	MINIMUM	MAXIMUM
2	2	68	1292	521968	4175744	1043936	1043936
3	5	67	1273	514292	4114336	1542876	2571460
6	8	66	1254	506616	4052928	3039696	4052928
9	11	65	1235	498940	3991520	4490460	5488340
12	14	64	1216	491264	3930112	5895168	6877696
15	17	63	1197	483588	3868704	7253820	8220996
18	21	62	1178	475912	3807296	8566416	9994152
22	24	61	1159	468236	3745888	10301192	11237664
25	28	60	1140	460560	3684480	11514000	12895680
29	32	59	1121	452884	3623072	13133636	14492288
33	35	58	1102	445208	3561664	14691864	15582280
36	39	57	1083	437532	3500256	15775152	17063744
40	44	56	1064	429856	3438848	17194240	18913664
45	48	55	1045	422180	3377440	18998096	20264640
49	52	54	1026	414504	3316032	20310688	21554208
53	57	53	1007	406828	3254624	21561872	32189184
58	62	52	988	399152	3193216	23150816	24747424
63	67	51	969	391476	3131808	24662976	26228880
68	72	50	950	383800	3070400	26098400	27633600
73	77	49	931	376124	3008992	27457040	28961536
78	83	48	912	368448	3254624	28738944	30581184
84	89	47	893	360772	2886176	30304848	32108704
90	95	46	874	353096	2824768	31778640	33544112
96	101	45	855	345420	2763360	33160320	34887408
102	108	44	836	337744	2701952	34449888	36476352
109	115	43	817	330068	2640544	35977408	37957808
116	122	42	798	322392	2579136	37397472	39331824
123	130	41	779	314716	2517728	38710064	40913072
131	138	40	760	307040	2456320	40222240	42371520
139	146	39	741	299364	2394912	41611584	43707136
147	155	38	722	291688	2333504	42878128	45211632
156	164	37	703	284012	2272096	44305872	46577968
165	174	36	684	276036	2210688	45595440	48082464
175	185	35	665	268660	2149280	47015488	49702096
186	196	34	646	260984	2087872	48543024	51152864
197	207	33	627	253308	2026464	49901664	52434752
208	220	32	608	245632	1965056	51091456	54039040
221	233	31	589	237956	1903648	52588272	55443744
234	247	30	570	230280	1842240	53885520	56879152
248	262	29	551	222604	1780832	55205792	58322240

(Table 10.1 continues on next page)

Table 10.1 ***(Continued)***

CAPACITIES WITHOUT KEYS

BYTES PER RECORD		RECORDS PER				BYTES PER PACK	
MINIMUM	MAXIMUM	TRACK	CYLINDER	PACK	FACILITY	MINIMUM	MAXIMUM
263	279	28	532	214928	1719424	56526064	59964912
280	296	27	513	207252	1658016	58030560	61346592
297	315	26	494	199576	1596608	59274064	62866432
316	335	25	475	191900	1535200	60640400	64286496
336	357	24	456	184224	1473792	61899264	65767968
358	381	23	437	176548	1412384	63204176	67264784
382	407	22	418	168872	1350976	64509104	68730896
408	435	21	399	161196	1289568	65767968	70120256
436	467	20	380	153520	1228160	66934720	71693840
468	501	19	361	145844	1166752	68254992	73067840
502	540	18	342	138168	1105344	69360336	74610720
541	583	17	323	130492	1043936	70596160	76076832
584	631	16	304	122816	982528	71724544	77496896
632	686	15	285	115140	921120	72768480	78986032
687	749	14	266	107464	859712	73827760	80490528
750	821	13	247	99788	798304	74840992	81925936
822	906	12	228	92112	736896	75716064	83453472
907	1005	11	209	84436	675488	76583440	84858176
1006	1125	10	190	76760	614080	77220560	86354992
1126	1271	9	171	69084	552672	77788576	87805760
1272	1454	8	152	61408	491264	78110976	89287232
1455	1689	7	133	53732	429856	78180048	90753344
1690	2003	6	114	46056	368448	77834640	92250160
2004	2442	5	95	38380	307040	76913520	93723952
2443	3100	4	76	30704	245632	75009872	95182400
3101	4197	3	57	23028	184224	71409824	96648512
4198	6398	2	38	15352	122816	64447696	98114624
6392	12974	1	19	7676	61408	49064992	99588416
CAPACITIES WITHOUT KEYS							
1	2	96	1824	736896	5895168	736896	1473792
3	3	95	1805	729220	5833760	2187660	2187660
4	5	94	1786	721544	5772352	2886176	3607720
6	6	93	1767	713868	5710944	4283208	4283208
7	8	92	1748	706192	5649536	4943344	5649536
9	9	91	1729	698516	5588128	6286644	6286644
10	11	90	1710	690840	5526720	6908400	7299240
12	12	89	1691	683164	5465312	8197968	8197968
13	14	88	1672	675488	5403904	8781344	9456832
15	16	87	1653	667812	5342496	10017180	10684992

(Table 10.1 continues on next page)

Table 10.1 *(Continued)*

CAPACITIES WITHOUT KEYS

BYTES PER RECORD		RECORDS PER				BYTES PER PACK	
MINIMUM	MAXIMUM	TRACK	CYLINDER	PACK	FACILITY	MINIMUM	MAXIMUM
17	18	86	1634	660136	5281088	11222312	11882448
19	19	85	1615	652460	5219680	12396740	12396740
20	21	84	1596	644784	5158272	12895680	13540464
22	23	83	1577	637108	5096864	14016376	14653484
24	25	82	1558	629432	5035456	15106368	15735800
26	27	81	1539	621756	4974048	16165656	16787408
28	29	80	1520	614080	4912640	17194240	17808320
30	31	79	1501	606404	4851232	18192112	18798512
32	33	78	1482	598728	4789824	19159296	19758016
34	35	77	1463	591052	4728416	20095760	20686816
36	38	76	1444	583376	4667008	21001536	22168288
39	40	75	1425	575700	4605600	22452288	23028000
41	42	74	1406	568024	4544192	23288976	23857008
43	45	73	1387	560348	4482784	24094960	25215648
46	47	72	1368	552672	4421376	25422912	25975584
48	50	71	1349	544996	4359968	26159808	27249792
51	53	70	1330	537320	4298560	27403312	28477952
54	55	69	1311	529644	4237152	28600768	29130416
56	58	68	1292	521968	4175744	29230208	30274144
59	61	67	1273	514292	4114336	30343216	31371808
62	64	66	1254	506616	4052928	31410192	32423424
65	67	65	1235	498940	3991520	32431088	33428976
68	70	64	1216	491264	3930112	33405952	34388480
71	73	63	1197	483588	3868704	34334736	35301920
74	77	62	1178	475912	3807296	35217488	36645216
78	80	61	1159	468236	3745888	36522400	37458880
81	84	60	1140	460560	3684480	37305360	38687040
85	88	59	1121	452884	3623072	38495136	39853792
89	91	58	1102	445208	3561664	39623504	40513920
92	95	57	1083	437532	3500256	40252944	41565536
96	100	56	1064	429856	3438848	41266176	42985600
101	104	55	1045	422180	3377440	42640176	43906720
105	108	54	1026	414504	3316032	43522912	44766432
109	113	53	1007	406828	3254624	44344240	45971552
114	118	52	988	399152	3193216	45503328	47099936
119	123	51	969	391476	3131808	46585632	48151536
124	128	50	950	383800	3070400	47591200	49126400
129	133	49	931	376124	3008992	48519984	50024480
134	139	48	912	368448	2947584	49372032	51214272
140	145	47	893	360772	2886176	50508080	52311936

(Table 10.1 continues on next page)

Table 10.1 ***(Continued)***

CAPACITIES WITHOUT KEYS

BYTES PER RECORD		RECORDS PER				BYTES PER PACK	
MINIMUM	MAXIMUM	TRACK	CYLINDER	PACK	FACILITY	MINIMUM	MAXIMUM
146	151	46	874	353096	2824768	51552016	53317488
152	157	45	855	345420	2763360	52503840	54230928
158	164	44	836	337744	2701952	53363552	55390016
165	171	43	817	330068	2640544	54461216	56441616
172	178	42	798	322392	2579136	55451424	57385776
179	186	41	779	314716	2517728	56334160	58537168
187	194	40	760	307040	2456320	57416480	59565760
195	202	39	741	299364	2394912	58375968	60471520
203	211	38	722	291688	2333504	59212656	61546160
212	220	37	703	284012	2272096	60210544	62482640
221	230	36	684	276336	2210688	61070256	63557280
231	241	35	665	268660	2149280	62060448	64747056
242	252	34	646	260984	2087872	63158128	65767968
253	263	33	627	253308	2026464	64086912	66620000
264	276	32	608	245632	1965056	64846848	67794432
277	289	31	589	237956	1903648	65913808	68769280
290	303	30	570	230280	1842240	66781200	69774832
304	318	29	551	222604	1780832	67671616	70788064
319	335	28	532	214928	1719424	68562032	72000880
336	352	27	513	207252	1658016	69636672	72952704
353	371	26	494	199576	1596608	70450320	74042688
372	391	25	475	191900	1535200	71386800	75032896
392	413	24	456	184224	1473792	72215808	76084512
414	437	23	437	176548	1412384	73090864	77151472
438	463	22	418	168872	1350976	73965936	78187728
464	491	21	399	161196	1289568	74794944	79147232
492	523	20	380	153520	1228160	75531840	80290960
524	557	19	361	145844	1166752	76422256	81235104
558	596	18	342	138168	1105344	77097744	82348128
597	639	17	323	130492	1043936	77903712	83384384
640	687	16	304	122816	982528	78602240	84374592
688	742	15	285	115140	921120	79216320	85433872
743	805	14	266	107464	859712	79845744	86508512
806	877	13	247	99788	798304	80429120	87514064
878	962	12	228	92112	736896	80874336	88611744
963	1061	11	209	84436	675488	81311856	89586592
1062	1181	10	190	76760	614080	81519120	90653552
1182	1327	9	171	69084	552672	81657280	91674464
1328	1510	8	152	61408	491264	81549824	92726080

(Table 10.1 continues on next page)

Table 10.1 *(Continued)*

CAPACITIES WITHOUT KEYS

BYTES PER RECORD		RECORDS PER				BYTES PER PACK	
MINIMUM	MAXIMUM	TRACK	CYLINDER	PACK	FACILITY	MINIMUM	MAXIMUM
1511	1745	7	133	53732	429856	81189040	93762336
1746	2059	6	114	46056	368448	80413776	94829296
2060	2498	5	95	38380	307040	79062800	95873232
2499	3156	4	76	30704	245632	76729296	96901824
3157	4253	3	57	23028	184224	72699392	97938080
4254	6447	2	38	15352	122816	65307408	98974336
6448	13030	1	19	7676	61408	49494848	100018272

Track Capacity

The number of records that can be recorded on a track depends on the record size. The following equation is used to determine the number of equal length records per track. Home address and standard RO space are accounted for.

$$\text{Number of equal length records per track} = \frac{13{,}165 \quad \text{(track capacity)}}{135 + C + KL + DL \quad \text{(bytes per record)}}$$

where

C = 0 if KL = 0
56 if KL ≠ 0
KL = key length
DL = data length

expected growth of the file. Once a file is created, it should contain enough available space to accommodate the addition of new records. The analyst must determine the average growth rate for an organization during the systems investigation and allocate enough storage to handle the growth for several months or years, depending on the nature of the application.

TIMING DETERMINATION

The time it takes to retrieve a record from disk is a function of the operating characteristics of the disk drive and the data location. Whenever the program instructs the system to read a record, there is a delay in initiating the read, due to rotation of the disk. Read or write processes always start after the index point has been sensed, so the system knows that it has found the start of a cylinder. The delay is termed *latency time* or *rotational delay.* A typical latency time is approximately 0.01 second.

A second component of read-write time, associated with disk operation, is the time it takes the disk unit to position the read-write heads on the proper cylinder. *Seek time,* as the time for positioning the heads is called, varies depending on where the access arm is currently positioned. Vendors usually supply this operating time as the maximum (the time it takes to move the heads from the outermost cylinder to the innermost one), minimum (the time it takes to move from one cylinder to the next adjacent one), and average seek time. In evaluating read-write activities, average seek time is generally the best time to use.

Access time (the time to locate the proper record, but not to read or write it) typically is in the range of 35 to 60 milliseconds, the greatest portion being for seek time. (If the disk unit access time is 35 milliseconds, the latency time will typically be 0.010 second and the seek time 0.025 second. (A *millisecond* is 0.001 second.)

The other component of disk processing is the *data rate*, the rate at which data is read. Vendors quote these speeds in two ways: number of bytes per second or number of seconds per byte. If the data rate on the disk is 806 kilobytes per second (as for the IBM 3330 disk system), it takes 1.24 microseconds per byte.

To read a set of 817 records (unblocked), each 109 characters long (including key length), from a middle cylinder when the access arm is positioned at track 0 on a disk with the access times quoted above, the result is determined as follows:

$$\begin{aligned}&\text{Seek time} + \text{rotational delay} + \text{data rate time for}\\ &\qquad\qquad\qquad\qquad\qquad\qquad\qquad\qquad \text{817 records} = \text{read time}\\ &0.030 + (817 \times 0.0084) + (817 \times 109)(0.00000124) = 0.30 + 6.862 + 0.110\\ &\qquad\qquad\qquad\qquad\qquad\qquad\qquad\qquad\qquad = 7.272 \text{ seconds}\end{aligned}$$

Information necessary to estimate read-write time from disks is provided in systems manuals supplied by the manufacturers of the disk systems.

BACKUP AND RECOVERY OF FILES

Information systems are not immune to problems that can lead to accidental loss of data. Therefore, analysts are concerned with the preservation of both transaction and master file data. The concern starts during the design phase and continues throughout the life of the system.

Potential Causes of Data Loss

The analyst must assume the worst can happen when designing backup procedures for systems files. It is generally true that, soon after a system is installed (and often even before implementation is complete), something will happen to cause the loss of data. Some reasons for needing backup are the result of normal use of the system, but many are not.

Components in computer systems do wear out and need replacement. Equipment is normally maintained on a regular scheduled basis, calling for repair or replacement of parts and components after specific time intervals. But even under the best preventive maintenance schedules, components can fail and cause the loss of data.

Magnetic-tape and -disk storage media will also wear out after periods of use. Hard disks have much longer life then flexible diskettes, although both will last for months and years if properly handled and protected from dust and fingerprints. The magnetic coating may no longer store data in spots on its surface or the metal plates in disk units may become uneven, although the latter is not a frequent occurrence.

Failures also occur owing to the improper processing of data or operator error. Processing the wrong disk or tape or accidentally erasing a file of data may destroy the data completely. Unless the organization maintains backup copies of data, it may be in serious trouble. Imagine, for example, an organization that does not maintain copies of its accounts receivable files, with average balances of several hundred thousands of dollars, and accidentally damages or erases the master file. Without the ability to recreate the file, the organization will lose the money.

Software failures may lead to data loss, even in programs that have been in use for months or years. (Chapter 12 examines the problem of software reliability in detail.)

Natural disasters, such as fire, flood, or earthquake, can also result in data loss unless precautions are taken. Sudden power fluctuations or outages during systems processing may damage files.

In summary, the reasons data may be lost or damaged are many, including equipment failure, wearing out of components or storage media, operator error or improper processing of data, software failure, power outages, or natural disaster. The analyst must design effective backup procedures to protect the organization against these occurrences.

Backup Methods

Backup files are extra copies of any file made for use in case the current file is destroyed. They duplicate the original set of data. There are several effective methods for maintaining backup copies.

When designing sequential file systems, the analyst has a ready-made, virtually automatic, backup scheme available owing to the nature of the file system itself. As pointed out earlier, when a sequential file is changed through updating that adds and deletes records, a new file is created. In other words, there are then two generations of files, the new master file and the old master file with transaction file processes.

GENERATIONS OF MASTER FILES

In sequential file systems a common and highly effective method for maintaining backup copies, using the natural generations of files, is the *grandparent-parent-child* technique (Figure 10.17). Because of the normal update cycle for sequential files, two generations of master files normally exist. The grandparent technique expands this to at least three generations. A daily processing example will show the usefulness of this technique. Transactions are accumulated each day and processed the next day to

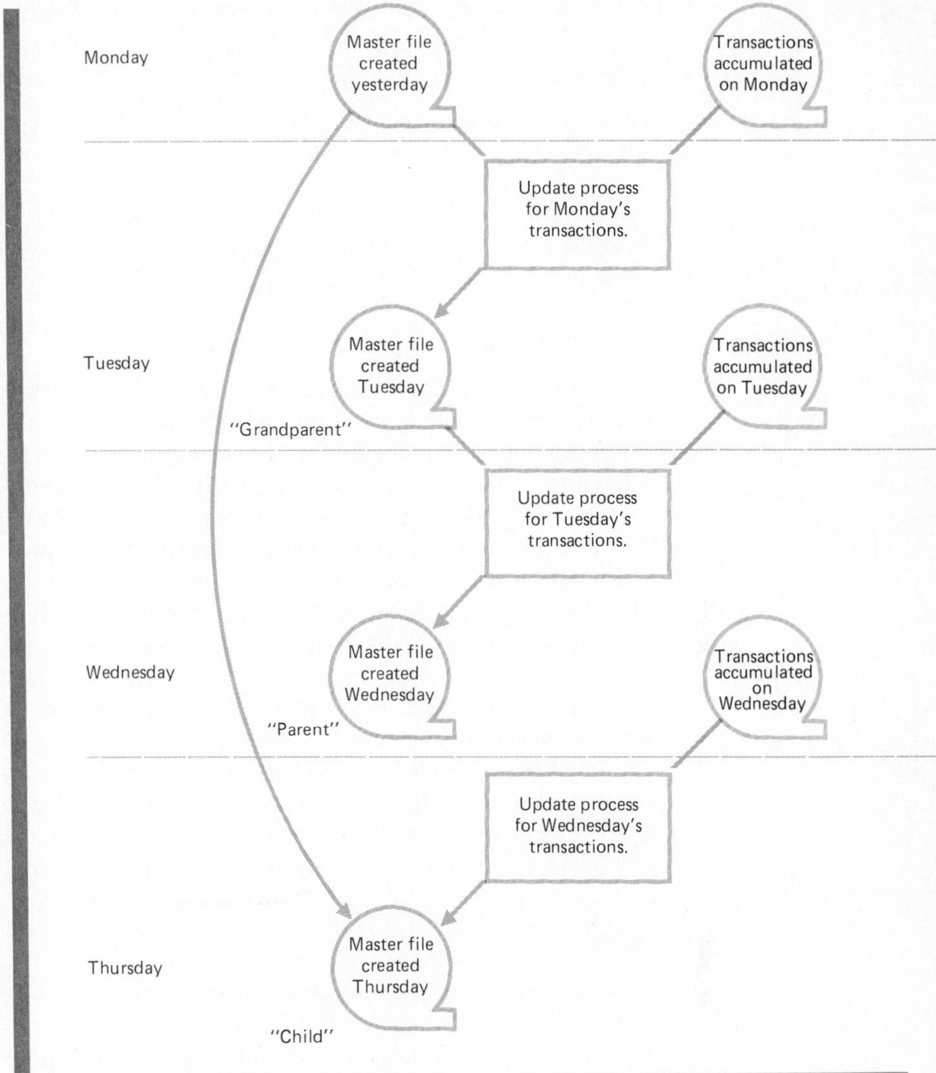

Figure 10.17. Generation backup system for sequential files.

update the master file. This means that those transactions accumulated on Monday will be processed on Tuesday and a new version of the master file produced. The input for Tuesday's processing is the master file from Monday and Monday's transactions. The output is a new master file.

On Wednesday, Tuesday's master file is updated with the transactions accumulated on Tuesday and a new copy of the master file is produced, although the versions from Monday and Tuesday are still retained.

On Thursday, the tape containing Monday's version of the master file is erased and reused to store the new version; Wednesday's master file is updated with the transactions from Wednesday.

At this point there are three generations of master files:

Thursday's master file (the child) created from Wednesday's master

Wednesday's master file (the parent of Thursday's) created from Tuesday's master

Tuesday's master file (the grandparent of Thursday's) created from Monday's master

Should the Thursday version be damaged or found to be improperly processed, it can be recreated by reprocessing the parent to produce a new version of Thursday's transactions.

MASTER FILE DUMPS

In systems using direct access master files, the generation method is not possible. Since records are updated in place on the "live" master file, copies of the previous day's file do not automatically exist. To ensure the existence of backup copies, analysts must specify other methods.

Dumping files is the process of duplicating a file to create another copy of it. A separate systems program is run that reads data from the master file and writes a copy of the data to a backup disk. Analysts may specify that only files are duplicated, or they may design procedures to copy the entire disk (involving multiple files and programs) to another backup disk. In either case, the dump provides an additional copy, while leaving the original version unaltered. The original copy is used in further processing, but the backup copy remains unchanged.

The transaction files are kept for a specified time, perhaps a few days or 1 to 2 weeks, depending on the organization. If at any time the current copy of the master file is damaged or erased, a copy can be processed and updated with the transactions accumulated since the last dump was made.

RECORD IMAGE COPIES

In very large systems, regular file dumping is not possible. The United States Social Security Administration, for instance, maintains several hundred million records in its database, as do many other government agencies. Making dumps of entire files or databases is therefore prohibitive in terms of time (it would take days to copy them) and cost.

An alternative backup method relies on the presence of transaction files coupled with copies of the master file records that are changed during processing. *Before images,* copies of the master file record before it is changed, and *after images,* copies of the record after the change is made, provide enough information to reconstruct records if they are damaged or lost.

If it is found that certain records were changed improperly, the transactions can be run in reverse to restore them to a point at which they are known to have been correct. This process is termed *rollback.*

Similarly, if necessary, backup copies of records (created as before images) can be made current by reprocessing them with copies of transactions. This process is called *bringing forward* the files.

It is the analysts' responsibility to design procedures for making backup copies of files and for using them to restore the system to a current status. At some point the backup copies will be needed. There is little question about that.

SUMMARY

Systems files are stored on a storage medium. The most common media are magnetic tape and magnetic disk. Each stores physical records that contain one or more logical records. When multiple logical records, such as sales invoices, pay checks, or inventory records, are stored within one physical record, it is called blocking. Blocking saves space and speeds processing.

When sequential files, on either magnetic tape or disk, are updated, a new copy of the master file is produced. However, when direct access or indexed files are updated, the changes are made in the file and no new copy is produced. This is possible because of the physical record keys used within direct access and indexed files; there are no physical keys in sequential files.

To protect against the loss of data, systems analysts design backup procedures. Duplicate copies of data are made to ensure that a copy of the records will always exist, even if the main copy is damaged or destroyed; there is always a chance this will happen owing to error, equipment or software failure, or natural disaster. When using sequential files, generations of copies provide adequate backup. However, when the files are stored under direct access or indexed organization, a method of dumping files or making before and after images is needed. The analysts must assume that backup copies will be needed sooner or later. Keeping the system running is essential.

The next chapter will examine the implications of processing files in on-line environments.

CASE STUDY FOR CHAPTER 10
FILE DESIGN FOR ORDER ENTRY AND ACCOUNTS RECEIVABLE PROCESSING

The selection of files and access methods for the system at Valley Industries was aimed at providing efficient processing capability, while minimizing the redundancy between files. Since there is a constant relationship between order entry, invoicing, and accounts receivable, the files were also designed to reflect the interrelationship, as will be shown.

This design used ordinary file storage structures. A database management system was not used. However, there are explicit links between files and methods of chaining files together, which will be pointed out when used.

The section that follows discusses the master, table, report, and transaction files for this system. The storage structures for each are identified and the record keys are noted. In addition, the record contents are listed. The data names correspond to those used in the data dictionary that was initially constructed during the requirements determination activities. The data dictionary contains specifications of data type and length.

MASTER FILES

Valley Industries' order entry and accounts receivable system is a traditional one, in the sense of relying on master files to store data about the ongoing elements of the system. This system centers around three entities: customers, orders, and product items. Three master files, each interrelated with the others, make up the core of the new system. They are:

1 Customer master
2 Item master
3 Open order master

Figure C10.1 shows the interrelationships of master files and information processing activities.

CUSTOMER MASTER FILE

The *customer master file* holds all data relating to the customer, including accounts receivable information. By using this file, information about the

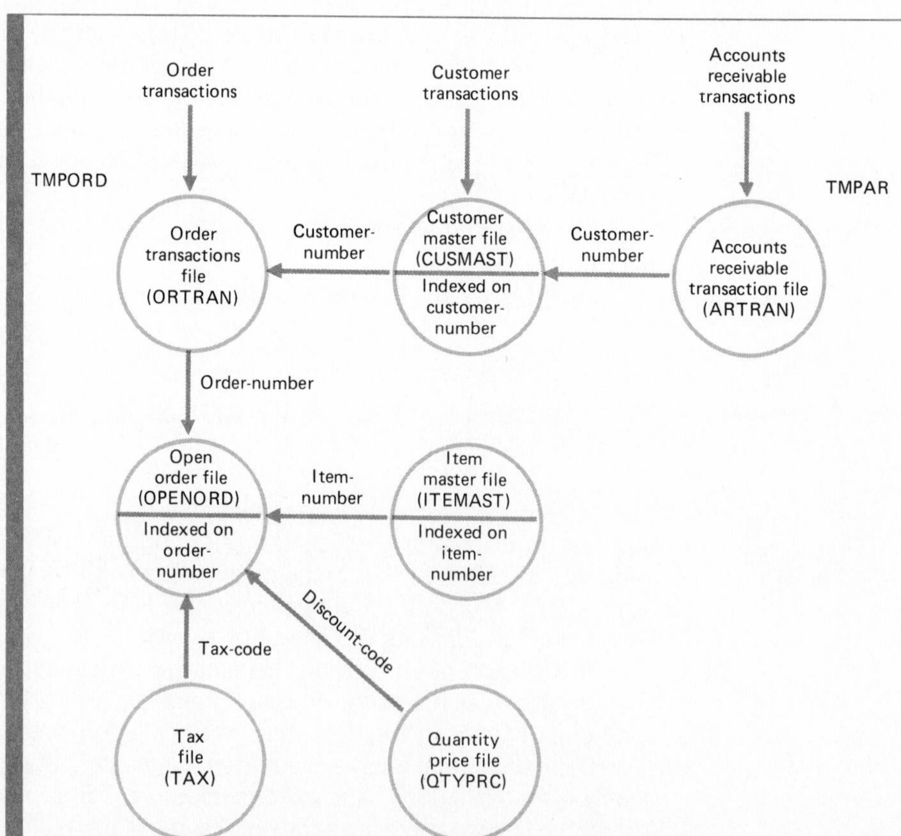

Figure C10.1 File chaining and interrelationships.

customer, such as name, billing address, shipping address, and telephone number, can be retrieved. In addition, credit information, including credit limit and account balance, is available. The file also stores the aging information regarding the customer's balance—data that allows the user to determine how current the customer's account is and whether payments on prior orders are overdue.

Each customer record also contains a count of open orders for the customer. This field, which changes when orders are placed or settled, permits rapid responses to inquiries from users wanting to determine how many orders a customer currently has in process. Since the count is maintained in the customer record, the system does not have to search through the entire open order file to count the orders for each customer.

The customer master file is an indexed file. The record key is the customer number. This file will be used in both order entry and invoicing activities. Financial data will be maintained through accounts receivable activities.

Contents of the master file are:

CUSTOMER-NUMBER
CUSTOMER-NAME
BILL-TO-ADDRESS
SHIP-TO-ADDRESS
TELEPHONE
CREDIT-LIMIT
REP-NUMBER
ACCOUNT-BALANCE
ACCOUNT-STATUS
CURRENT-DUE
PAST-30
PAST-60
PAST-90
PAST-120
OPEN-ORDER-COUNT

ITEM MASTER FILE

The *item master file* contains data about all items manufactured by Valley Industries. Whether the item is a standard item or one that has been specially manufactured for a particular customer, its details are recorded in this file. The file is indexed by item number.

The contents of the item master file are:

ITEM-NUMBER
DESCRIPTION
ENGINEERING-DRAWING-NUMBER
ENG-CHARGE

TOOLING
ADDITIONAL-REMARKS
ORDER-QUANTITY
ITEM-COST
UNIT-WEIGHT

OPEN ORDER MASTER FILE

The *open order master file* contains data describing all outstanding orders. One of the design decisions for this file concerned how much customer data to store in the file for each order. It was decided to store only the data item CUSTOMER-NUMBER in the order file (even though when the order is entered the data entry person must verify the customer name and address). The CUSTOMER-NUMBER serves as a link to the customer master file to retrieve name and address information when it is needed. The use of CUSTOMER-NUMBER as the key for the customer master file makes this chaining between files possible. (It also permits the inclusion of only the customer number, rather than all name and address information, in the invoice file, as discussed later.)

The open order file also contains data to tell Valley personnel the status of an order that has been placed into production, and it includes the production order number. Since it is expected that an additional manufacturing site will open in the near future, the design allows for tracking the production location of the order. A data item for that purpose is included.

The contents of the open order master file are:

ORDER-NUMBER
ORDER-DATE
CUSTOMER-NUMBER
ITEM-NUMBER
DESCRIPTION
ORDER-QUANTITY
ITEM-COST
DISCOUNT-CODE
TAX-CODE
ENG-CHARGE
TOOLING
ADDITIONAL-REMARKS
REQUIRED-DATE
TERMS
VALLEY-JOB-NUMBER
COMPLETION-STATUS
PRODUCTION-LOCATION

Retrieval of records from the file will be by order, production order, or customer number. However, the primary index will be on the record key of order number.

TABLE FILES

Systems analysts must be concerned with the way their design will accommodate changes brought about by normal business activities. In the Valley Industries system, two table files were established to provide the ability to change the company's quantity-pricing structure and to respond quickly to changes in state taxation laws.

QUANTITY-PRICE FILE

Prior to undertaking the current systems development effort, the quantity-pricing algorithm in use was very complex. The new design uses quantity ordered and discount percentage to determine the amount of the discount. Therefore, the company is not dependent on any single person to determine discounts. The algorithm will be included in the new system and will use the quantity-price table file.

The contents of the file are:

ITEM-NUMBER
QUANTITY-BREAK-1
QUANTITY-BREAK-2
QUANTITY-BREAK-3
QUANTITY-BREAK-4
QUANTITY-BREAK-5
QUANTITY-DISCOUNT-1
QUANTITY-DISCOUNT-2
QUANTITY-DISCOUNT-3
QUANTITY-DISCOUNT-4
QUANTITY-DISCOUNT-5

The direct-access file uses the item number as the record key.

TAX FILE

The tax file contains the details on taxing for the collection and reporting of sales tax amounts. The customer record will contain a tax code that pertains to all the customer transactions. When an invoice is prepared, the sales tax will be calculated by the system. The tax rate will be retrieved from the tax file by using the code included in the customer master record.

The analysts have assumed changes will occur in tax rates. If a certain tax rate changes, the rate associated with a specific code can be adjusted in the tax file only. The customer records will not change.

The contents of the tax file are:

TAX-CODE

TAX-BODY-NAME

TAX-RATE

The tax code is the key for this direct access file.

REPORT FILES

The order entry system is designed to use three report files. When order processing or accounting transactions occur that are designed to produce a high volume of output, the system will store the output in a report file. The report file is later dumped to the printer to produce the paper versions of the output. The systems operator determines when to print the output. However, this design feature has the additional advantage of allowing the user to determine that the output is correct before actual printing occurs. Report files for acknowledgements, invoices and bills of lading, and statements are included in the design.

ACKNOWLEDGEMENT FILE

When customer orders are received and approved, Valley Industries sends the customer an acknowledgement that verifies the order has been received and approved. The acknowledgement also restates all pertinent details of the order.

The file contents for each order are:

CUSTOMER-NUMBER

BILL-TO-ADDRESS

SHIP-TO-ADDRESS

PURCHASE-ORDER-NUMBER

The file contents for each item within an order are:

ORDER-NUMBER

ORDER-DATE

REQUIRED-DATE

ITEM-NUMBER

DESCRIPTION

ORDER-QUANTITY

ITEM-PRICE

QUANTITY-DISCOUNT

ENG-CHARGE

ADDITIONAL-REMARKS

Although Valley Industries treats every item a customer orders as a single order, the customers themselves do not. They may give a sales representative a purchase order that requests several different items. Therefore, the acknowledgement will include a confirmation of all items the customer ordered using a specific purchase order, whenever possible. The report file contains header information (such as customer number, name, and address) and details for each item.

The file is organized sequentially. It may be produced in two orders: postal-code order (for mailing purposes) or customer order.

INVOICE AND BILL-OF-LADING FILES

The invoices and bills of lading (shipping papers) are identical, except for the form on which they are printed. The bill of lading contains additional preprinted instructions to the shippers, stating their responsibilities.

Contents of this file include:

Header Information (at the beginning of the invoice or bill of lading)
CUSTOMER-NUMBER
CUSTOMER-NAME
BILL-TO-ADDRESS
SHIP-TO-ADDRESS
ORDER-NUMBER
ORDER-DATE
SHIPPING-METHOD
TERMS
Transaction Information (for each item invoiced)
ITEM-NUMBER
DESCRIPTION
ITEM-QUANTITY-SHIPPED
ITEM-COST
ITEM-COST-EXTENSION
Footer Information
TOTAL-TAXES
TOTAL-INVOICE

STATEMENT FILE

At the end of each monthly period, statements of account balances are prepared and distributed to the customers. The statement file is extracted from the transaction and customer master files. Each statement summarizes the different transactions that have taken place during the period. The four types of transactions affecting the customer account balance are adjustments, invoices, finance charges, and payments. The contents of the statement file vary, depending on the type of transaction record.

Header Information (at the beginning of the statement)
CUSTOMER-NUMBER
CUSTOMER-NAME

BILL-TO-ADDRESS
SHIP-TO-ADDRESS
TELEPHONE
REP-NUMBER
ACCOUNT-BALANCE (before processing)
CREDIT-LIMIT
Footer Information (at the end of the statement)
ACCOUNT-BALANCE (after processing the month's transactions)
CURRENT-DUE
PAST-30
PAST-60
PAST-90
PAST-120
DELINQUENT-AMOUNT
TOTAL-TRANSACTION-PAYMENTS
TOTAL-TRANSACTION-INVOICES
TOTAL-TRANSACTION-ADJUSTMENTS
Transaction Information (body of the statement)
TRANSACTION-DATE
TRANSACTION-TYPE
TRANSACTION-REFERENCE-NUMBER
TRANSACTION-AMOUNT
TRANSACTION-ACCOUNT-BALANCE

The TRANSACTION-REFERENCE-NUMBER is the invoice number, customer check number, or Valley adjustment number, depending on the type of transaction. The TOTAL-TRANSACTION-PAYMENTS, TOTAL-TRANSACTION-INVOICES, AND TOTAL-TRANSACTION-ADJUSTMENTS fields are the sums of each type of transaction shown on the statement.

This report file is stored sequentially. It may be produced in two orders: postal-code order (for mailing purposes) or customer order.

TRANSACTION FILES

The master files in the Valley Industries system can be updated either through transaction files or direct entry, depending on the specific master file in question and the nature of the change. There are two transaction files for entering order and invoice data and accounts receivable transactions. Changes to customer demographic data are made through direct entry.

ORDER TRANSACTION FILE

The order transaction file contains records created by order entry, order maintenance, and invoice transactions. The file is used to update the order master file, print acknowledgements, and produce invoices and bills of lading.

The file contains several record types and fields for auditing and control of transaction batches:

For control
BATCH-NUMBER
WORKSTATION-IDENTIFICATION
DATE
BATCH-RECORD-NUMBER
For transaction data
CUSTOMER-NUMBER
ORDER-NUMBER
CUSTOMER-NUMBER
PURCHASE-ORDER-NUMBER
TAX-CODE
ORDER-DATE
INVOICE-NUMBER or CHECK-NUMBER or CREDIT-NUMBER
TRANSACTION-TYPE
ITEM-NUMBER
DESCRIPTION
ORDER-QUANTITY
ITEM-COST
DISCOUNT CODE
TAX-CODE
ENG-CHARGE
ADDITIONAL-REMARKS
REQUIRED-DATE

This file is chained to the customer master file through the CUSTOMER-NUMBER. It is stored sequentially by batch and uses a secondary key of customer number.

ACCOUNTS RECEIVABLE TRANSACTION FILE

The *accounts receivable transaction file* captures all transactions that affect the accounts receivable file. Transactions include payments, adjustments, and charges through invoices. The format of the file is generalized to handle each type of transaction. A code (TRANSACTION-TYPE) indicates the nature of the transaction. The CUSTOMER-NUMBER is the link to the customer master file.

The contents of the accounts receivable transaction file are:

CUSTOMER-NUMBER
TRANSACTION-DATE (supplied by systems calendar)
TRANSACTION-TYPE

TRANSACTION-REFERENCE-NUMBER
TRANSACTION-AMOUNT

The TRANSACTION-REFERENCE-NUMBER is the invoice number, customer check number, or Valley adjustment number, depending on the type of transaction.

This file is stored sequentially as transactions are submitted for processing.

CUSTOMER TRANSACTION FILE

Customer transactions are processed directly against the customer master file. New customers are entered on-line; adjustments to names, addresses, and so on, are entered through the keyboard; and the data is stored directly in the master file. Hence this system does not use a transaction file for updating customer information. (Using such a transaction file would be a common practice with batch processing systems.)

As will be shown in the processing design, other very temporary files will be created by the system. Edit files, having the same image as the files from which the data for them is extracted, will be produced as well.

KEYWORDS

After image
Before image
Block
Blocking factor
Cylinder
Dump
Hard disk
Head crash
Home address
Index point
Interblock gap
Interrecord gap
Latency time
Parity bit
Rotational delay
Sector
Track
Track descriptor record
Transfer rate
Winchester disk

REVIEW QUESTIONS

1 How are records of data structured when stored on magnetic tape? How does the system read records on magnetic tape?
2 What methods are used to detect recording or reading errors when data is stored on magnetic tape? How does this change between 7- and 9-track formats?
3 In what way can the systems analyst or computer programmer affect the amount of space required to store a file of data on magnetic tape? Do any of the considerations in questions 1, 2, and 3 affect the time it takes to read data from the tape to the CPU? To process the data after it is read?
4 What factors determine read-write time when using magnetic tape? Which ones are under the control of the programmer or analyst? Which ones are not?
5 How do physical and logical records vary? Are they ever the same? Explain the reason for your answer.
6 Discuss the process of adding or

deleting records stored on magnetic tape. Is the process efficient or inefficient? Explain.

7 Distinguish between the different types of magnetic disk. Which types are most common on microcomputers? On mainframe systems?

8 There are several characteristics of magnetic disks that are an integral part of addresses used for storage and retrieval of data. What are they and how are they used in disk addressing?

9 What are the two general methods of storing records on a disk track? Why do systems use different methods? Which method is more common on systems of differing sizes?

10 Explain the meaning of the following terms: count data format, count key data format, index point, track descriptor record, and record zero.

11 Describe the process of reading a record from magnetic disk. What factors influence the amount of time this process takes?

12 How do backup methods vary when files are stored on magnetic tape and on magnetic disk?

13 Discuss the meaning and purpose of rolling back and bringing forward a file.

APPLICATION PROBLEMS FOR CHAPTER 10

1 A file containing 115,000 records will be stored on magnetic tape at a recording density of 6250 bytes per inch. The size of each fixed-length record is 340 characters. The interblock gap is 0.3 inch.

a How much space is needed to store the entire file if it is unblocked? What percentage of a 2400-foot reel of magnetic tape is occupied by the file?

b If the file is stored using a blocking factor of 75, what length of tape will be needed to store the entire file?

c Assume that the data transfer rate is 320 bits per second and one record will be processed from every physical record. If the processing time is 0.00001 second, how long will it take to read and process the entire file?

2 A master file will be stored on magnetic tape at a recording density of 1600 bytes per inch. The file of data contains 1.2 million records of 450 characters each. The interblock gap is 0.3 inch and the blocking factor is 60.

a How much space does each logical record require? How much space is required by each physical record?

b How many reels of tape will be required to store the file?

c What savings and benefits will be gained if the recording density is changed to 6250 BPI?

3 A sorted transaction file contains records that include the record keys and change codes shown below. The codes C, A, and D represent the processing activities change the record, add the record, and delete the record. The master file is in sequential order, based on the record key.

Transaction File:

| 1027 A | 1030 C | 1030 C | 1039 D | 1039 D | 1052 A |
1052 A | 1100 A | 1237 A |

Master File:

| 1020 | 102721030 | 1034 | 1039 | 051 | 1104 | 1237 | 1486 |

a Show the revised master file after processing the transactions in the transaction file. Indicate any error messages the system should produce.

b How would the process and results change if the master file were organized under a direct-access organization?

4 Magnetic-tape storage requires the systems analyst to select the recording density and blocking factors. If there is a file of 60,000 records, each 185 characters in length, depending on the physical and storage features of the tape system that will store this file, substantial variations will arise in storage space and processing time. Determine, for the different conditions given below, the following space and timing factors: (1) records per block, (2) time per block, (3) number of blocks in the file, (4) block length, (5) amount of tape needed, (6) tape speed, (7) interblock gap time, and (8) time taken to process the file.

A single buffer operation will be used and can hold whatever size block is being processed. You may assume that there is no delay due to processing between the reading of physical blocks from the file. The interblock gap is 0.3 inch.

	TRANSFER RATE (BYTES/SECOND)	DENSITY	BLOCKING FACTOR
a	60,000	1600	20
b	320,000	800	10
c	180,000	6250	25
d	60,000	6250	20
e	150,000	1600	10

5 A systems analyst is planning to store a master file on magnetic disk under an IBM format. The fixed-length records are 160 characters each and will be blocked at 45 records per block.

a Show the track layout for the file described above.

b If the track capacity is 35,616 bytes, how many records can be stored on each track?

6 A 1 million-character file consisting of 5000 records, each requiring 200 characters of data, will be stored on flexible diskettes using sector spanning. The diskettes are double-sided and contain 76 tracks per side. Each track has a capacity of 7946 bytes.

a How many records can be stored on a single track?

b How many tracks are needed to store the entire file?

c If the disk is only single-sided, can the data be stored on the disk? Explain.

7 The access time for a magnetic-disk unit consists of a rotational delay of 0.010 second and a seek time of 0.025 second. The data rate for the disk unit is 806 kilobytes per second.

A master file consisting of 20,000 records will be stored by using direct addressing. Each record is 150 characters in length.

a How long will it take to locate and read the first record in the file?

b If the processing speed is faster than the time it takes to locate and read a single record, how long will it take to read and process the entire file?

8 A file of 75,000 records is stored on magnetic disk under a random organization. Records are stored in blocks of 10 records each. Processing time is 30 microseconds and access time per block is 30 milliseconds. For each block, read time is 40 milliseconds and write time is 75 milliseconds.

A file of 7000 fifty-character records will be processed against the master file to update selected records. The transaction file is stored on magnetic tape at 6250 BPI, 750-character blocks, with a transfer time of 120,000 bytes per second. The interblock gap is 0.3 inch. The transaction file is already in sorted order.

a How long will this update process take?

b What would change if the master file were stored under indexed sequential organization?

CHAPTER 11

DESIGN IN ON-LINE AND DISTRIBUTED ENVIRONMENTS

QUESTIONS TO GUIDE YOU THROUGH THE CHAPTER

- What questions should analysts ask when studying the need for on-line and distributed systems?
- How is data transmitted from one location to another?
- What steps occur in sending or receiving data?
- Are there different methods of data transmission?
- How do the types of components connected to data networks vary?
- When should local and long-distance networks be designed?
- What questions should analysts ask when studying the need for on-line and distributed systems?
- How does file processing differ in on-line environments?
- In what ways must an on-line system be safeguarded against user activities?

Information systems are increasingly being developed to receive and process data using on-line methods. Batch processing is an effective processing mode in many situations, while on-line is preferred in others. The analyst must determine when to use either processing mode. In addition, as computers have become cheaper and smaller, they are being used in increasing numbers. People have become interested in interconnecting them in simple ways and in sophisticated networks.

This chapter focuses on systems design in an on-line environment or when communication is involved in the transmission or receipt of data for processing. The characteristics of on-line and distributed systems are first discussed, and then the questions the analyst addresses when designing the methods of interaction between user and system are carefully examined.

If the analyst decides to use data communication features in a systems design, the analyst must also select communication equipment, acquire data communication lines, and specify the method for linking the system into the communication network. In addition, the processing methods and procedures will vary from those where communication is not involved.

At the end of this chapter you should know when to select on-line processing, how to design communication-based systems, and how to process files in a communications environment. You should also know when to use distributed processing and how it differs from on-line processing.

CHARACTERISTICS

The characteristics of on-line and distributed systems determine when each should be used. This section discusses those characteristics.

On-Line Systems

On-line systems are those information systems that enable the user to directly interact with the computer while processing is taking place. Users want this capability in order to take advantage of several distinct features, while analysts often design using on-line mode to handle multiple tasks in the system at the same time.

INTERACTIVE COMPUTING

Interactive systems link the computer system and user to permit the submission of data, requests for information, or requests for processing with direct feedback of results or responses to the user. In a sense the computer and user carry on a conversation where the individual enters a command to the computer and the system responds with a request for further clarification, executes the request, or sends a message, such as an error message, to the requestor. The interactive dialogue determines what the system will do.

A typical conversation for signing onto an interactive system and printing a report is shown in the following dialogue:

Computer:	ENTER YOUR FIRST NAME.
User:	JIM
Computer:	ENTER YOUR LAST NAME.
User:	JOHNSON
Computer:	WHAT IS YOUR PASSWORD?
User:	OKEEDOKE
Computer:	WHAT REPORT DO YOU WISH TO PRINT?
User:	CURRENT SALES
Computer:	DO YOU WISH A SUMMARY (S) OR DETAIL (D) SALES REPORT?
User:	S
Computer:	THE REPORT YOU REQUESTED IS NOW PRINTING.

Many systems also use a menu of choices, as discussed in Chapter 8. The dialogue in a menu-based system is more brief since interaction is achieved by user entry of single numbers or letters to instruct the system. Both approaches, however, permit the user to control processing in on-line mode.

REASONS FOR ON-LINE PROCESSING

Batch processing systems are characterized by delay, the amount of time elapsing between the capture of data either on a source document or in machine readable form. (See Chapter 8 for a detailed discussion of data capture.) Systems analysts design batch-oriented systems when the delay is desirable or at least acceptable. For example, in payroll systems where checks are prepared on a weekly or biweekly basis, the delay in processing from week to week is very acceptable. There is usually no reason to process more than once a week.

In other situations, delay is intolerable, such as when processing airline reservations or bank deposits and withdrawals, or retrieving law enforcement information. In fact, delay in processing a request for information could be very costly. These applications are best suited for on-line processing. On-line systems will provide the quick responses needed to meet user requirements.

A second advantage of on-line processing is the ability to capture data as events are occurring. If users enter transaction data into the system when activities are taking place and the system immediately processes it, individuals will always have current results available. In some cases, processing can take place so quickly that the events are influenced as they are occurring. For example, suppose you are ordering merchandise from a salesperson in a catalog order store that uses on-line terminals to accept customer requests. The salesperson enters the information on items you wish to purchase into the terminal while you are standing at the counter. For each item, a response is displayed on the terminal telling whether the item is available or out of stock. The fact that you find out immediately whether the item you want is in stock influences your final purchase. When something is out of stock, you may decide to purchase something else in its place. In fact, you may modify your request and ask the salesperson to enter an order for a different item. A response will again be received on the availability of that item.

Some on-line systems allow multiple users to use the system at the same time. They may all feel they are using the system by themselves because their requests are accepted and processed quickly and without any visible evidence that other persons are submitting work at the same time. In some cases, on-line systems are designed to link multiple users together. They may interact directly, as discussed later in this chapter, or indirectly through a central computer system.

The remainder of this section discusses on-line systems and how they process data. Decisions analysts must make when designing them are also pointed out.

MULTITASKING

Computer systems are *task-oriented:* they process requests from users; that is, they complete the necessary tasks that together meet the request submitted from the user. Each request is a task or event requiring processing. For example, for an airline reservation, the request submitted by a reservation agent in the Boston airport to determine the space availability on Flight 307 on December 22 is a task for the system to handle. Under the control of the software, the system examines the request and determines it is valid. Then it decides what processing is needed and carries it out: The proper file is accessed and the record for flight 307 for the appropriate day is copied into memory and examined. Using the data just retrieved, the program determines that space is available on the flight and sends a message to the agent in Boston that a reservation may be made. When the message is sent, the task is completed (Figure 11.1).

The user interacts through a terminal linked to the system by communication lines, as discussed later in the chapter.

The computer hardware and software in on-line systems may have the capability of handling only one terminal submitting requests. However, it is more likely that on-line systems will handle multiple tasks. If the system accepts and processes several tasks *concurrently* over a short time span, it is an example of *multiprogramming*. That is, the system may have several tasks in memory, but only one is being handled at a time (Figure 11.2). Some systems interleave the processing of tasks and work on several partially completed tasks almost at the same time. If a request requires the retrieval of data from disk storage, the system may initiate the retrieval and, while needed records are being located and retrieved, may start handling another task. When the first job completes the input of data, processing the second task is interrupted and the CPU shifts its attention back to the first task to continue processing and finish it (unless it is interrupted again).

Under multiprogramming, only one job is being handled at a time.

Figure 11.1. On-line interaction between system and user.

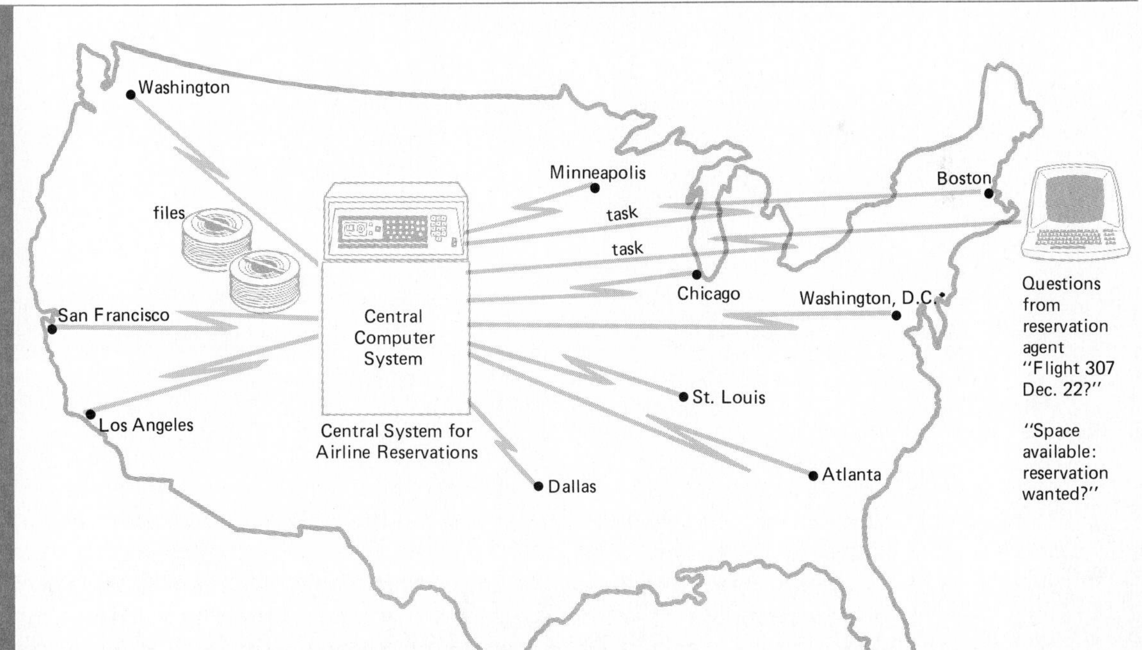

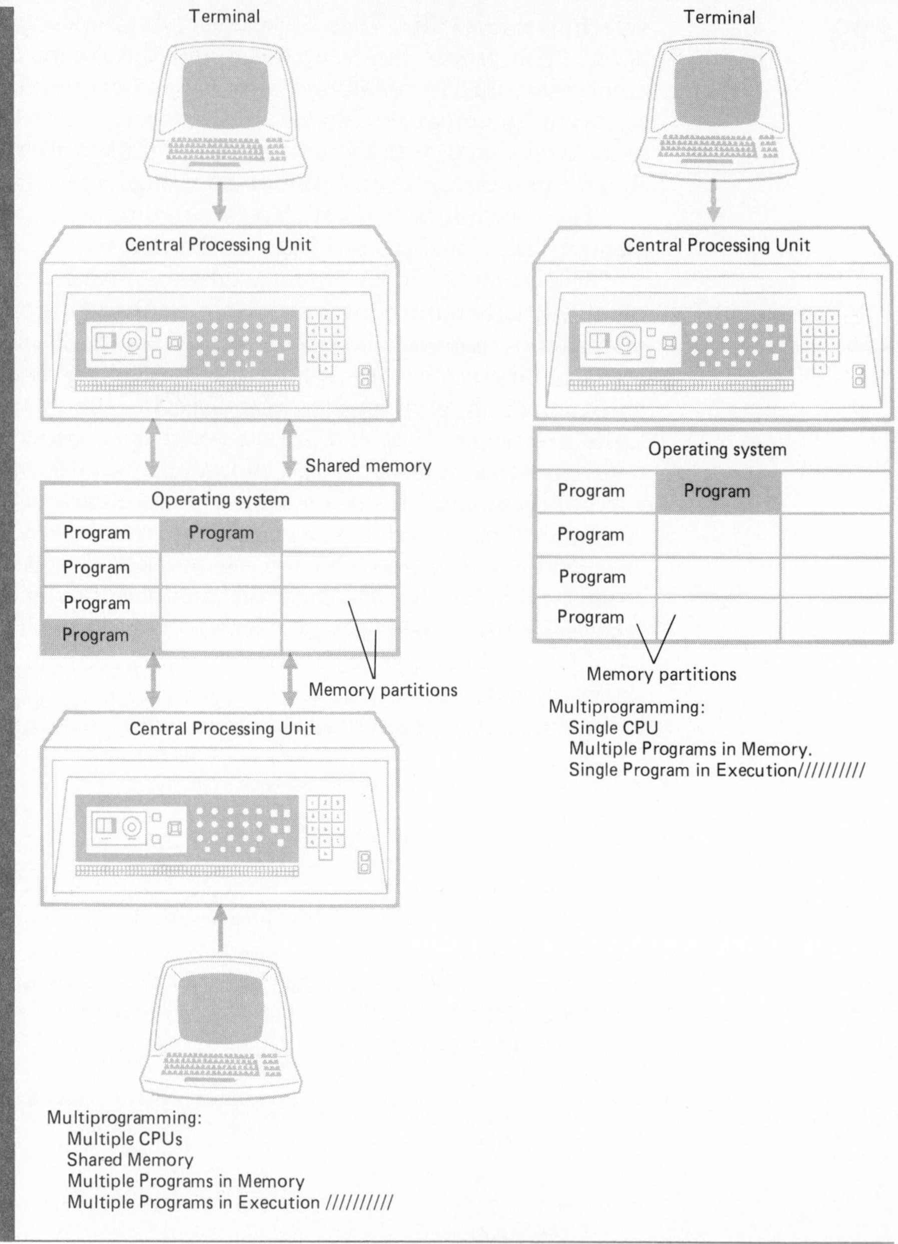

Figure 11.2.
Multiple task handling.

However, during the period of a few seconds or minutes, several tasks may be handled.

If the system is capable of processing multiple tasks *simultaneously*, it is an example of *multiprocessing*. Two or more central processing units share a common memory and execute programs in parallel. In other words, two different programs can execute at the same instant.

On-line processing can occur on computers of all sizes, whether micro or mainframe. In the past, multiprogramming and multiprocessing were only possible on large mainframe computers. However, now even these processing methods are possible on small computer systems. Thus systems analysts have many options available to them if they wish to design an on-line system in order to meet a particular processing requirement.

Distributed Systems

The ability to connect users to computer processing through communication methods is essential to organizations since it makes computer access available to all persons who need it, with a reasonable investment in hardware and software. However, there are many instances where a user wants to process data at a specific location, such as at a sales office away from corporate headquarters, and then periodically send data to a computer system at the headquarters location. In many instances, organizations already have several computers in operation, often at different, widely separated locations. In addition, communication costs are increasing, while the cost of computers is decreasing. It is now becoming feasible to place computers at each location where data is collected or information is needed. Mainframe computers are 10 to 15 times faster than small computers, but they also cost as much as 1000 times more. This imbalance has led to the serious consideration of using collections of small computers. All these are reasons for the analyst to consider distributed systems.

CONCEPT OF A DISTRIBUTED SYSTEM

A *distributed system* interconnects locations that have computer capability to capture and store data, to process data, and to send data and information to other systems, such as a central system at a headquarters location (Figure 11.3). The range of computing capability varies. Some locations use terminals, others microcomputers, and still others large computer systems. There is no requirement that all equipment be from the same manufacturer. In fact it is expected that several makes of autonomous hardware will be involved. This allows users to have the type of equipment most suitable for their needs.

All locations—they are called *nodes* in a distributed system—have the ability to capture and process data where events are occurring. In other words, if a specific location uses a minicomputer, users enter data and process it in their minicomputer. They receive rapid responses to inquiries, store data in the system, and prepare reports as the need arises. However, they can also transmit data or reports from their system to another one linked into the *network,* the collection of interconnected systems.

For example, large organizations are establishing networks to interconnect multiple sales and manufacturing locations (Figure 11.4). Sales, accounting, and technical information are readily accessible from multiple locations. Even word processing facilities are linked into the network.

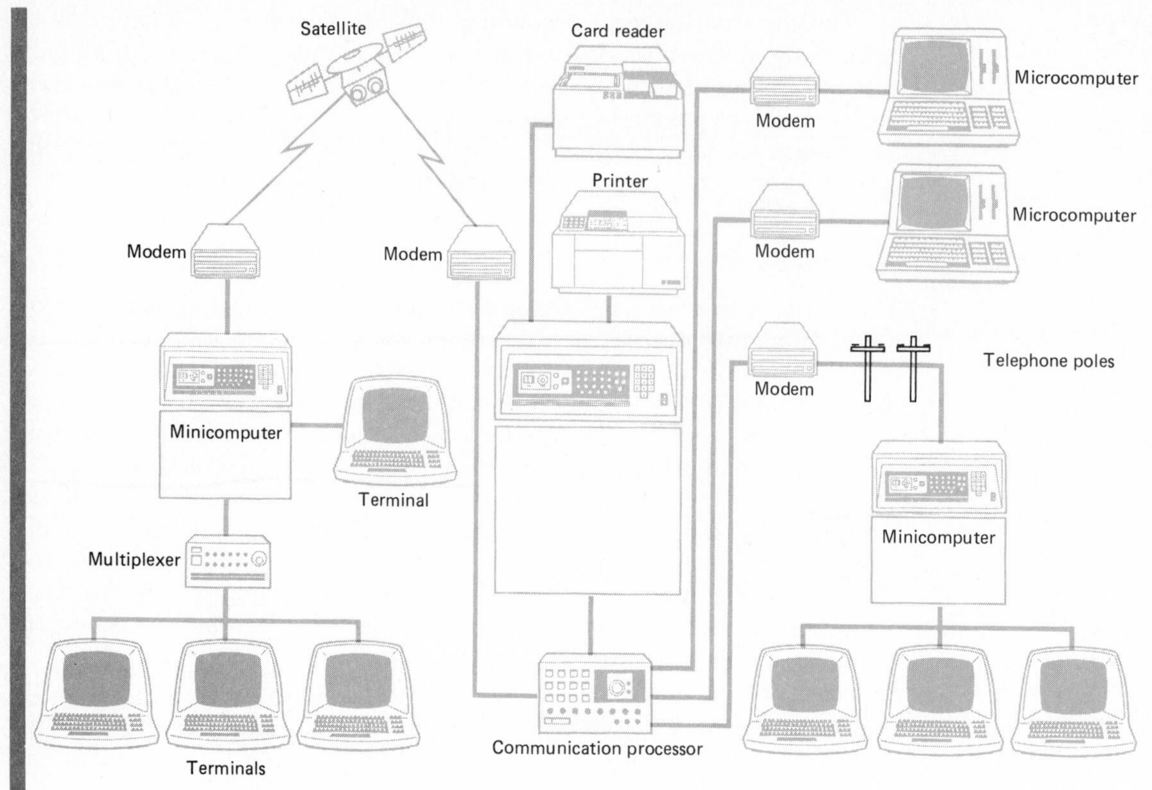

Figure 11.3. Components in a distributed system.

Corporate management at the top of the network is able to interact with other locations in the network while having its own independent information system. At the same time, terminals at field sales offices are able to access information in the system.

TYPES OF DISTRIBUTED SYSTEMS

Analysts use four different network designs for distributed systems: point-to-point, hierarchial, star, and ring networks. These types, which will now be discussed, are illustrated in Figure 11.5.

Point-to-Point

On-line computer systems are usually *point-to-point systems.* That is, terminals or data entry stations at one location are directly connected to a system in another location. The locations are the points in point-to-point systems. One machine is a terminal and the other a computer.

In distributed environments, point-to-point systems are linked together as a *network,* several interconnected locations able to communicate with each other. Each node in the location has equipment that transmits or

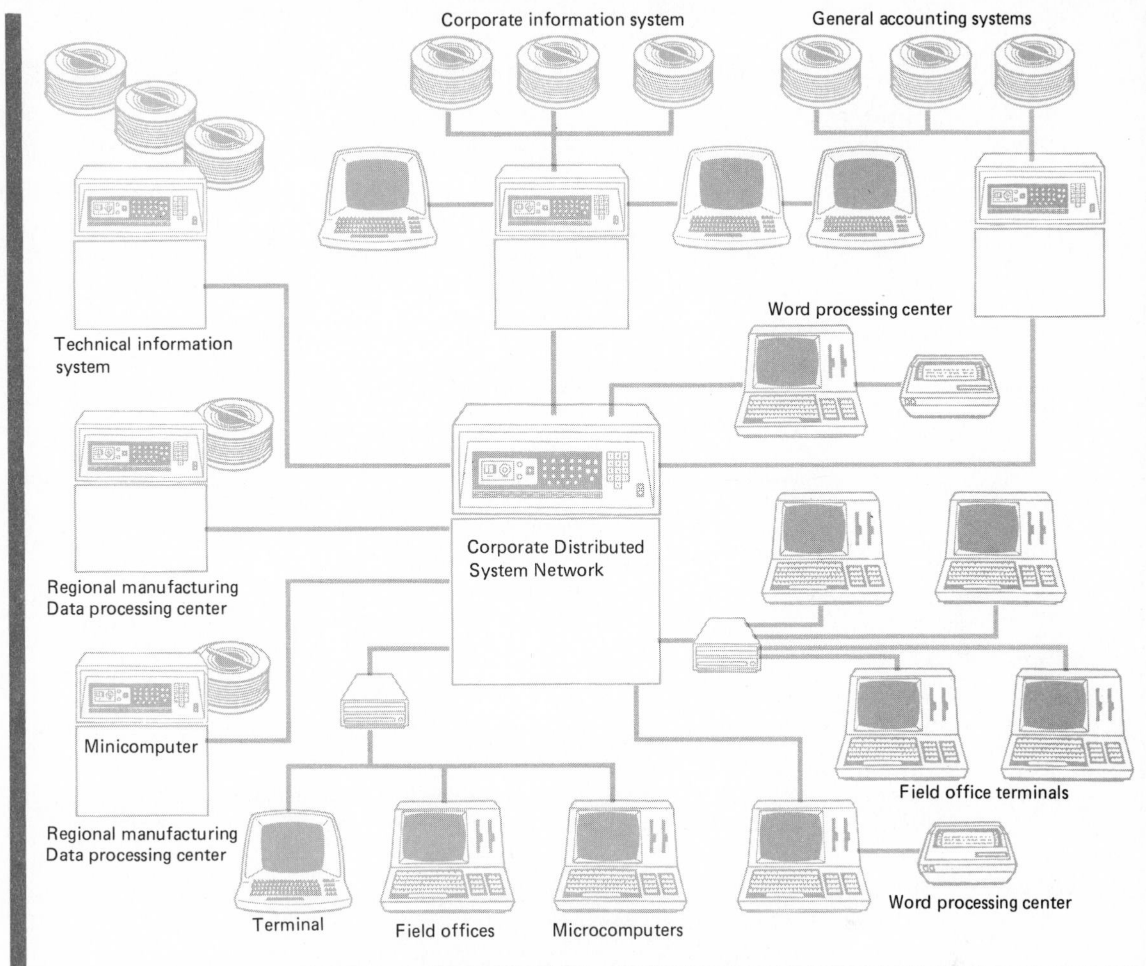

Figure 11.4. Distributed system for multilocation organization.

receives data. Some may store and process data and others may not. Two computers are said to be interconnected if they can exchange information.

If the volume of data transmission is high, point-to-point systems using dedicated communication lines are efficient since the communication line is busy much of the time. However, in systems where that is not the case, analysts often design *multidrop* lines that share a single communication line between several locations. Although only one location can send data at a time, so that the other locations must wait until the sender is finished, all locations can receive data simultaneously.

Many nodes can share a single communication line. Depending on the amount of use for the line, 20 or 30 locations can be interconnected if necessary.

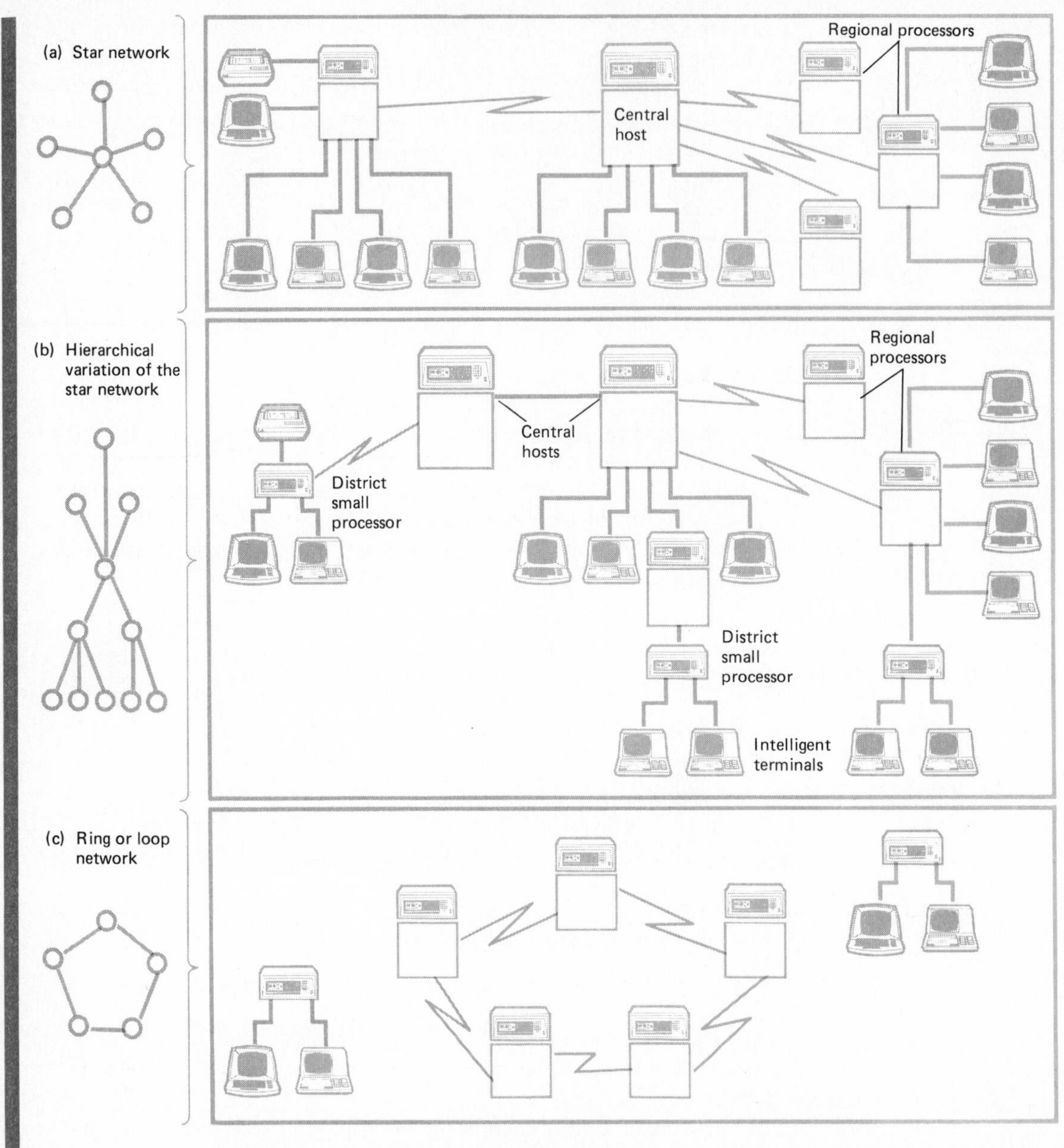

Figure 11.5. Types of distributed systems.

Hierarchial Networks

Some distributed systems, called *hierarchial networks,* are configured to have multiple levels of systems interconnected with one another. A large system interconnects with several other systems. Each lower-level system interconnects additional systems or terminals. They in turn are connected with still other systems.

Communication in a hierarchial network does *not* take place between systems on the same level. Instead the transmission of data occurs between systems at different levels (Figure 11.6).

This type of distributed system, the most common of the ones discussed in this section, is frequently used in organizations where headquarters communicates with regional offices. Regional offices in turn interact with district offices, which in turn communicate through terminals in field offices.

Star Networks

Processing nodes in a *star network* interconnect directly with a central system. In other words, each terminal, small computer, or large mainframe can communicate only with the central site and not with other nodes in the network. If it is desired to transmit information from one node to another, it can be done only by sending the details to the central node, which in turn sends them to the destination. The name given to this configuration describes its appearance, as shown in Figure 11.5.

Figure 11.6. Multilevel hierarchy in distributed system.

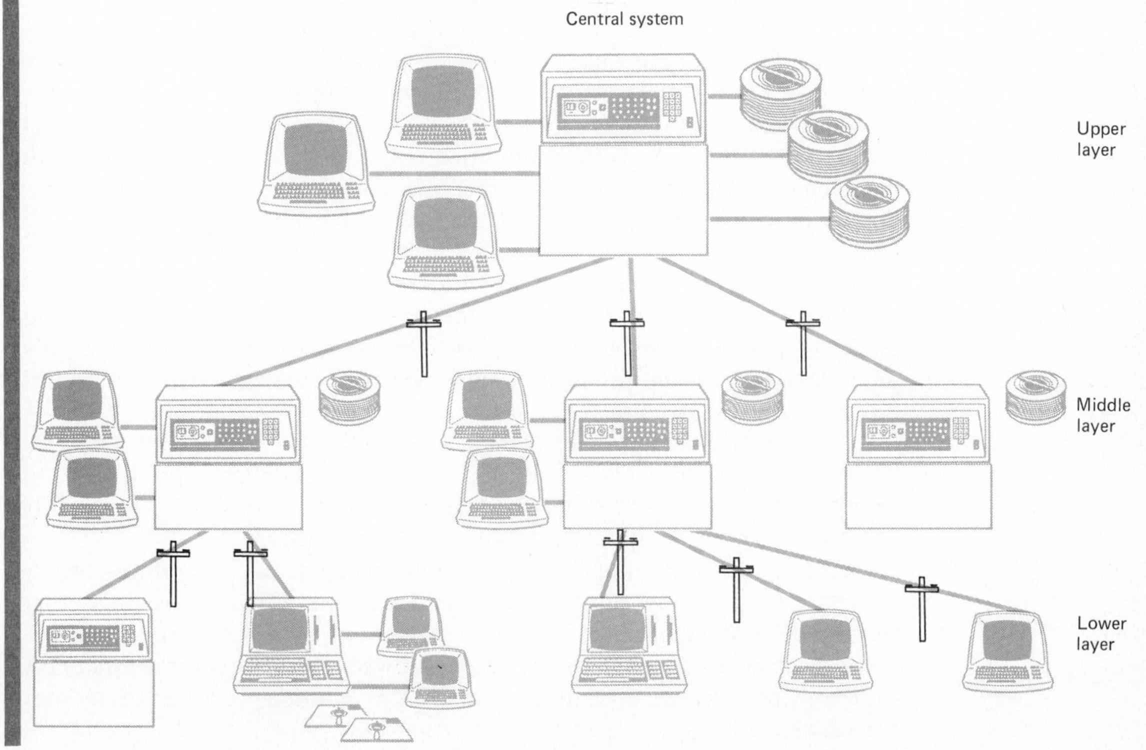

Ordinary telephone conversations involve a star network. When you dial a number, you send data to the local telephone exchange. It in turn routes your message to another exchange and to the party you are calling. Direct calling without going through the telephone company exchange is not possible.

Ring Networks

A *ring network* (also called *loop network)* permits direct communication between nodes and with the central computer. In other words, the central site does not handle data transmitted from one node to another.

If the telephone system used a loop or ring network, calling either through the telephone exchange or directly to the party to whom you wish to speak would be possible.

REASONS FOR DISTRIBUTED PROCESSING

Analysts design distributed systems when users need local processing with the ability to send results elsewhere, when it is important to use different equipment and have it linked through communication, or when load or software sharing is desirable.

Local Processing with Communication Capability

Analysts design distributed systems when it is desirable or necessary to capture and process data locally but also to communicate with other locations. For example, data from transactions occurring can be captured by direct entry into a microcomputer or a terminal connected to a minicomputer and stored on magnetic disk. At the end of the day, summary reports on transactions that have occurred are printed, but the stored transaction data remains on disk. Changes and corrections to transactions are made as they appear necessary after the transaction register is scanned.

If the system is, for example, a retail system (Figure 11.7), the transaction files can be processed at the end of the month to produce monthly statements for mailing to customers. At the same time, customer accounts are updated to show new purchases, payments, credits, and adjustments, and to produce a new account balance. All this is still happening at the local level.

Periodically throughout the month, information on inventory levels can be sent to a central system at the regional warehouse that handles all purchasing of merchandise for the firm. This process may be daily, weekly, or at whatever time interval management finds appropriate.

At the end of the month, the national and regional sales offices receive reports generated by the local system that summarize sales, inventory, payments, and accounts receivable information. In this way the central office receives all the information it needs, while the local offices are able to capture and process operating data in the manner best-suited to their activities.

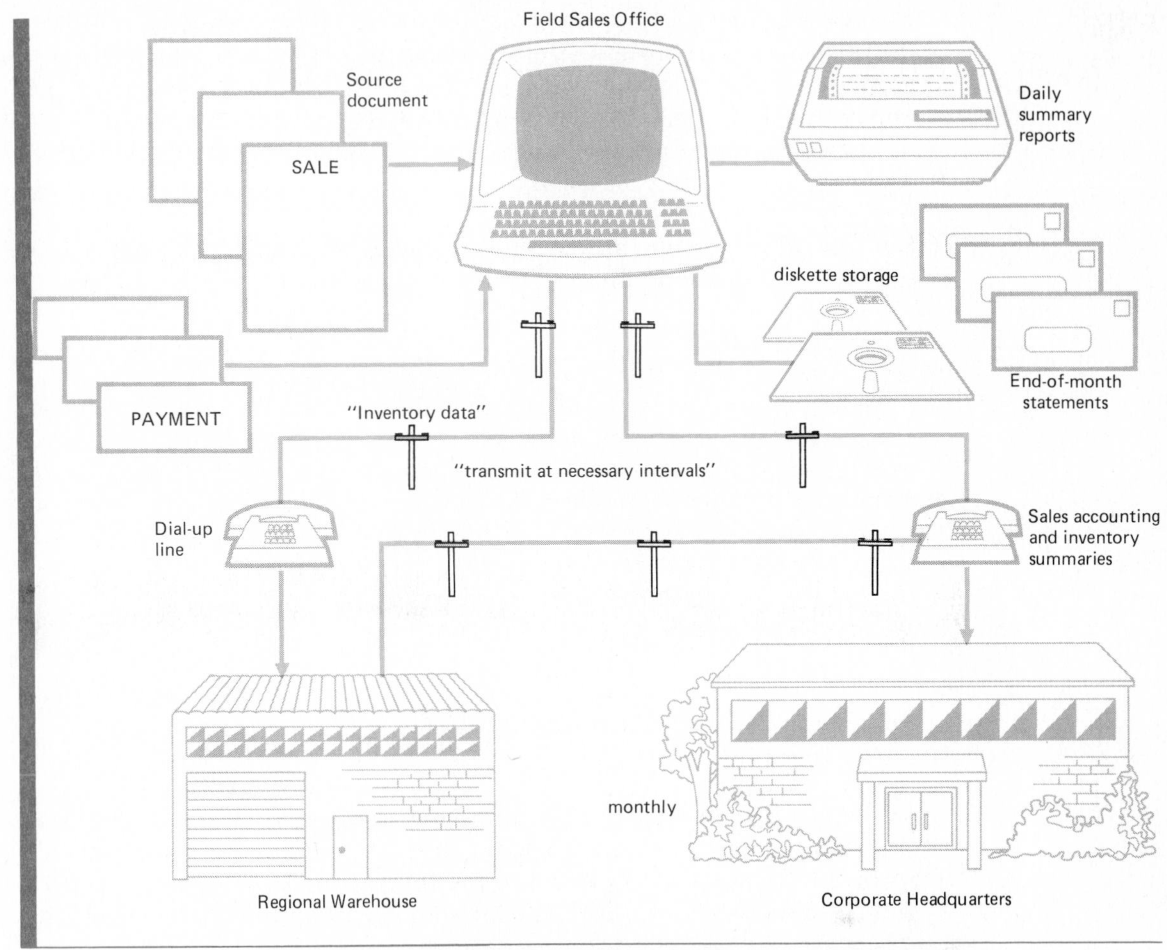

Figure 11.7. Multiple levels of data usage in a distributed retail system.

Linking Different Makes of Equipment

There are few limits on the brands of equipment needed to operate in a distributed environment. The size system needed can vary dramatically between nodes in a common network. Even the software will be different. In this way, local operations can be tailored to their own unique characteristics.

At the same time, through the many communication capabilities discussed later in this chapter, the data or local processing results can be transmitted throughout the network to other systems of different sizes or even made by other manufacturers.

Sharing Loads

Often some systems will be very busy with backlogs of work, while others have little processing going on. An important advantage of distributed systems is the ability to share work between sites. *Load sharing,* as this is called, permits one site to transport data to another node, through communication lines, and have it processed there. The results are stored at the remote site and recalled to the originator when the system is free.

Load sharing also provides operating reliability by ensuring that other equipment is available for use if the local system is inoperable. Processing can be done elsewhere in the network and results retrieved when the system is again running. Sometimes a terminal is kept on hand to link with other systems when the local computer system is unusable.

Sharing Software

Sometimes software is the reason for developing distributed systems. Some software packages only run on certain makes or sizes of equipment. Budget constraints may also prohibit one site from purchasing expensive software packages. However, if another site in a network has a specific package on its system, users in a distributed system are usually able to run the software.

Software sharing permits a remote user to access the computer system at another node, enter data, and have it run on the remote computer using the software stored on that system. As the results are generated, they are stored and later *downloaded* (transmitted back) to the originating system.

COMMUNICATION CONSIDERATIONS

On-line and distributed systems transfer data and information between the user and processing site by one of several communication methods. The analyst is responsible for selecting the means of communication to be used, acquiring the necessary communication equipment, services, and software, and coordinating the installation. Often outside agencies are involved in this phase of a development project.

This section discusses methods of data communication and cabling in on-line systems. The features of the different methods are pointed out and how to select the best method and what steps are necessary to install communication capability are emphasized.

Methods of Data Communication

Data can be communicated over ordinary telephone lines by using microwave facilities or earth satellite. Voice-grade telephone lines are the most frequently used method of communication, although the other methods, particularly satellite, are increasing in usage.

COMMUNICATION LINES

Communication lines are the most commonly thought of method for transmitting data. But the types and speeds of lines and the interconnection of line and computer should be planned carefully to ensure that users receive the services and responses they need.

Selecting Lines

They are most frequently used in a point-to-point form to interconnect two different locations. The analyst must select switched or leased lines. *Switched* lines are used on a temporary basis by dialing the number of the remote system. The common carrier, such as a public telephone company, connects to the two locations for the duration of the call. When the call is completed, the link is broken. The next time a new connection is made using different lines. The carrier selects and maintains the line connection.

Leased lines are dedicated to the transmission of data between two locations. That is, they provide a permanent path for the transmission of data from one location to another that exists whether data is being sent or not. The user rents the line by the month and pays a fixed amount, whether it is used very little or a great deal.

The analyst selects dial-up or leased lines depending on the (1) amount of data to be transmitted and (2) reliability of lines. Deciding between the cost of the two line alternatives is a simple matter of economics. By determining the average connect time (the number of minutes the line will be used during a month) and multiplying it by the cost per minute (which the carrier will provide on request), the analyst can calculate the cost of using a dial-up line. (It may be necessary to adjust the cost by the time of day data will be transmitted: evening rates are much lower.) The carrier will also provide the cost of a leased line on request. This cost varies by the location of each processing site: the carrier prices lines by distance between their exchanges. (The exchange is the first three digits of a local telephone number.)

Assume that an organization has estimated that it will transmit data over telephone lines for approximately 15 minutes per day at an average cost of $0.85 per minute. The system will be used every business day, or 20 days per month. The cost of local dial-up service is therefore $12.75 per day or $255 per month. In comparison, the cost to lease a local telephone line between two locations within this organization is $235 per month. The leased line is available for use 24 hours per day. In this example, it is clearly to the organization's advantage to lease the line rather than pay dial-up charges.

A second consideration is the reliability of the telephone lines. Some locations have better quality communication lines than others. This is important for the analyst to determine, since low-quality lines will have distortion and noise in transmission, which will result in the communication of faulty data, extraneous characters, or lost signals. In dial-up systems, neither analyst nor user control the line used for the call or its quality. Therefore, in an area where there is a high likelihood of transmission noise, the analyst should specify leased lines. The cost may be slightly higher for low-volume users, but the cost of bad data or poor transmission may far exceed line costs.

In cases where the need for continual communication is high, it may be advisable to specify the use of leased line with a dial backup. If the leased line fails for any reason, the user can continue to submit and receive data by temporarily using a dial-up line.

Connecting to Lines

Ordinary telephone communication lines transmit analog data. However, computers are digital devices and therefore transmit digital data. Although many carriers are establishing digital networks specifically for the transmission of digital data, analog lines are still the most commonly used form for data communication. To connect computers and analog lines, *modems* (also called *data sets*) are used. A modem, a contraction of modulator-demodulator, on the sending end converts digital signals from the computer into analog form for transmission. When the data is received on the other end, it is converted from analog to digital form so the receiving computer can process it.

Modems range in cost from approximately 100 to several thousand dollars, depending on quality, method of connection, and amount of intelligence built into them. *Acoustic couplers,* the least costly type, require the user to dial the proper telephone number on the telephone and then place the hand piece into rubber cups that hold the hearing and speaking ends (Figure 11.8). Sound devices in the coupler receive and send out signals through the phone piece.

Direct-connect modems are preferred because they are connected into

(a) (b) (c) (d)

Figure 11.8. Communication devices to connect computer components to telephone lines. [(*a*), (*c*), and (*d*) Courtesy Anderson Jacobson, Inc. and (*b*) Courtesy of ComData Corporation]

the communication line and make actual contact with it. As a result, the quality of transmission is clearer and cleaner, with little noise or distortion. Several different types of direct-connect modems can be specified. *Card modems* fit into special slots in the computer and make direct contact with the circuitry of the system. They are connected to the telephone network through an ordinary length of telephone wire. *Smart modems,* which may be card modems, or separate from the computer system and connected by a special cable, have built in intelligence. A small microprocessor is built into the modem to handle such routine operations as dialing the telephone number of the location to which the system is going to send data, answering the telephone and making connection with another location that is sending data to be received, or determining when the connection is made between two locations. Smart modems can also determine when a dial-up line is busy, when there is no answer on the other end, and when the carrier line disconnects. The term "smart" is very appropriate since this type of modem is in a sense a computer in itself. In spite of their capabilities, smart modems are relatively inexpensive; their prices start at approximately $200.

Line Characteristics

Communications lines vary in the speed at which they transport data and in their transmission direction. There are also different transmission protocols.

The rate at which data is transmitted is measured in *baud,* bits of data per second. The range of common baud rates is from 110 to 19,200 baud. Many microcomputer users, for example, use dial-up lines to communicate with other users at rates of 110, 300, 600, and 1200 baud. Their systems can generally operate at faster speeds, but the most inexpensive modems are available for these communication rates.

Common business transmission rates are 1200, 1800, 2400, and 4800 baud. By comparison, when terminals are directly connected to the CPU, with coaxial cable, not telephone lines, they communicate at 9,600 and 19,200 baud.

Voice-grade lines handle data transmission up to 9600 bits per second. The transmission itself may be either asynchronous or synchronous. In *asynchronous* transmission, data is transmitted one character at a time by using start and stop bits. That is, data bits are preceded and followed by special start-stop sequences. *Synchronous* transmission is continuous. A clock (usually in the modem) governs transmission by determining when each data bit is sent. Since transmission is timed, no start-stop sequences are needed.

Synchronous transmission is more efficient than asynchronous because more data can be sent in an interval of time. Most communication over 2000 baud is synchronous, and virtually all transmission under 1200 baud is asynchronous.

Conditioning

The type of line determines the direction of data transmission. There are three types of lines. *Simplex* lines transmit data in one direction only

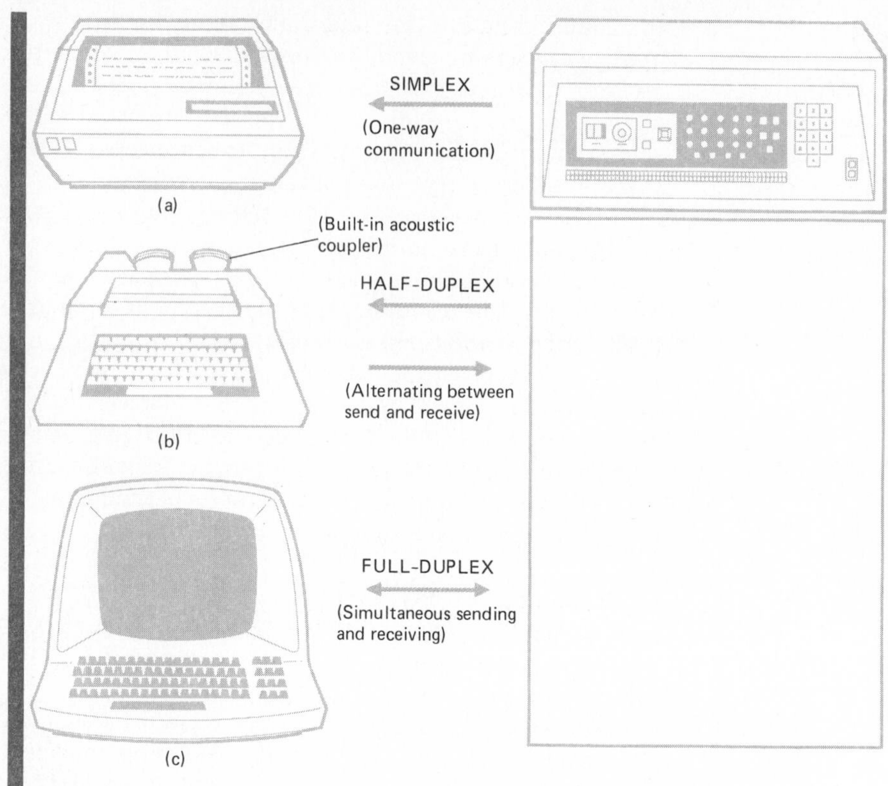

Figure 11.9. Types of transmission lines.

(Figure 11.9). If it is necessary to transmit data in two directions and only simplex lines are available, two such lines will be required—one transmitting in each direction (i.e., to and from a location).

Half-duplex lines carry data in one direction at a time. However, the lines can be reversed to transmit in the opposite direction. Therefore, they *can* transmit in two directions, but not at the same time.

Duplex or *full-duplex* lines transmit in two directions simultaneously. This type of line is most efficient because it allows a site to both transmit and receive at the same time.

Analysts and communication technicians often use the terms two wire, twisted pair, and four wire when discussing data communication. It is easy to keep up with this terminology if you relate it to ordinary voice-grade lines and the direction of transmission. Voice-grade lines in a dial-up switched network are generally two-line combinations, also called a twisted-pair line. Most leased lines are four-wire. Four-wire lines are always full-duplex. However, two-wire lines can be either half- or full-duplex. (Although many persons think that two-wire lines can only transmit half-duplex, there are special modems that support full-duplex on two-wire lines.)

There is still one other concern in selecting data communication lines—line conditioning. *Line conditioning* refers to a process in which the carrier uses filters to minimize interference and delay in a line. With increased conditioning, faster transmission rates are possible. The carriers offer several different types of conditioning, depending on the speed of transmission required.

Line conditioning is only possible on leased lines that are dedicated to a particular set of sites. It is not possible to purchase line conditioning on dial-up lines since the connections between two points vary from call to call.

The maximum speed on voice-grade, dial-up lines is 3600 to 4800 bits per second. If leased, conditioned lines are used, speeds up to 9600 bits per second can be attained. Furthermore, when leased lines are used, analysts can specify either point-to-point or multipoint configurations.

SELECTING THE RIGHT COMMUNICATION CONFIGURATION

To demonstrate the procedure for selecting and acquiring the proper communication configuration, we will work with an example installation. A major metropolitan hospital has decided to install a computer system in the hospital records section with terminals in each of three suburban satellite locations (Figure 11.10). The terminals will be used to enter data about new patients and treatment of those visiting the clinic and to retrieve data from the database at the hospital. The analyst has verified that the necessary communications software is available and that there is an available port on the computer to handle communication with the three locations. (A *port* is a communication entry point into the CPU. All external devices, including printers, terminals, and communication devices, transmit and receive data through ports. Since the system has a specific and limited number of them—sometimes as few as one or two—the analyst must be sure ports for communication are available before starting the design.)

Speed of interaction is important in this system. Therefore, the analyst determined that a minimum speed of 1800 baud is necessary. The computer system accepts asynchronous communication. However, in working with the carrier, the analyst decided to use a 2400-baud rate with synchronous communication. This determination was based on the fact that at 1800 baud conditioned lines are necessary, while at 2400 baud synchronous they are not. The combination of higher transmission speed, synchronous transmission, and not needing conditioning led to the selection of the 2400-baud line. Since the clinics operate around the clock and there is a need for continual interaction with the system, the analyst decided to use a leased line. The telephone company will use two 2-wire lines to provide the desired full-duplex line.

Direct-connect modems were selected to handle communication. At the clinic end, the modem is connected by cable to the CRT and directly linked to the telephone line. On the computer end, rack modems were selected and will be mounted in a separate cabinet in the computer room. A separate cable will connect the modems to the computer. Since the lines will handle synchronous communication and the computer uses asynchronous communication, a synchronous-to-asynchronous converter is used.

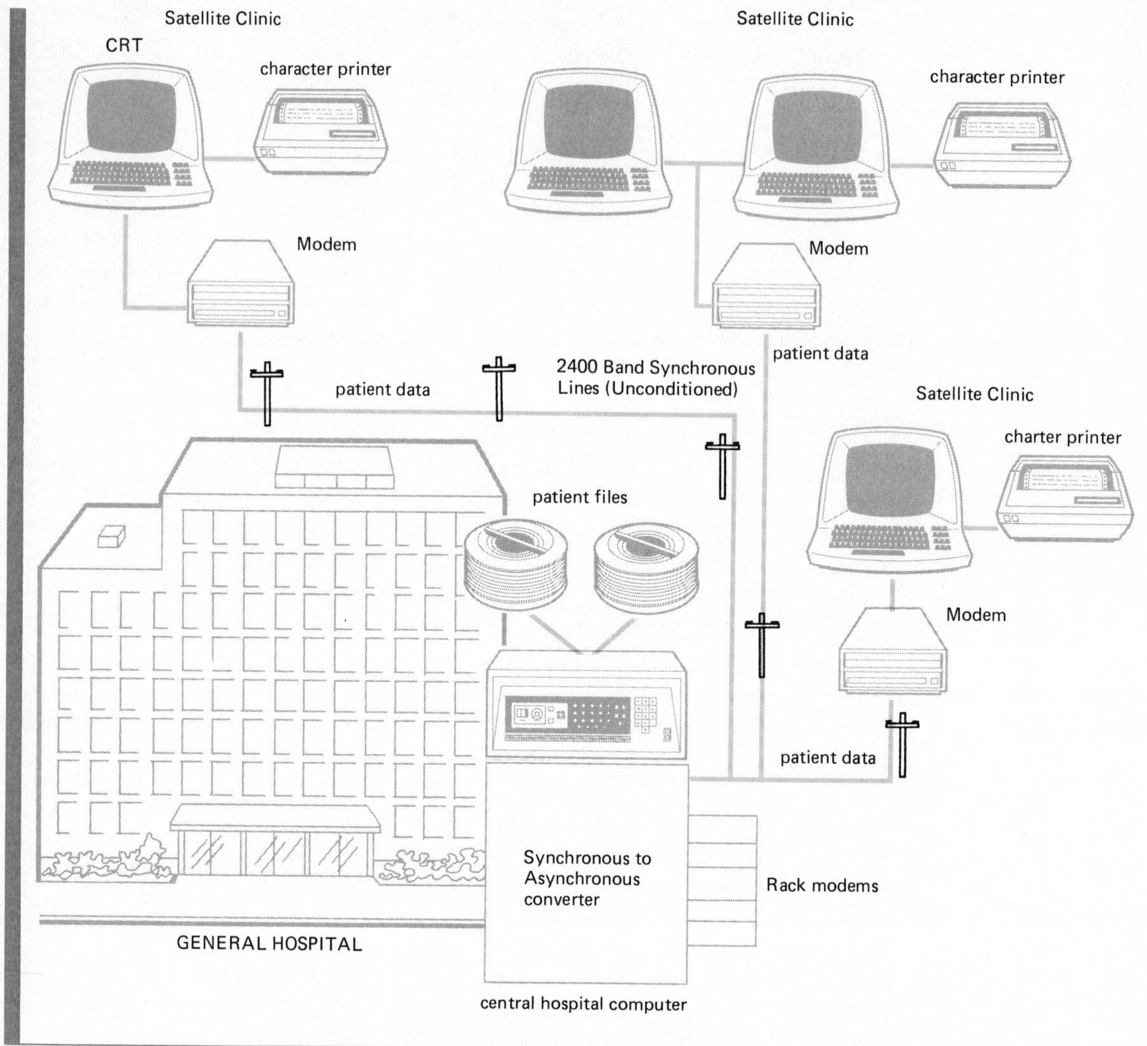

Figure 11.10. Medical system with voice-grade communication lines.

The analyst learned that the telephone company required 30 working days to prepare the lines and install them. Therefore, they were ordered 6 weeks before the planned systems installation date. The cost of each line from the clinic to the central site is approximately $200 per month, although this varies for each location.

This process is typical of what analysts do when specifying communication details in an on-line system.

MANAGING DATA COMMUNICATION

The activities of managing a communication system require additional software and processing time. Transferring and briefly storing data, as well as receiving transmission, uses central processor time and systems that do little data communication, this causes no prob er, in large communication systems, it is possible to use over one central processor time just to handle communication. To free up t *front-end processor* is often added to the configuration. It is a pre that interacts with both the CPU and the communication network ure 11.11). The front-end processor has the capability to identify terminals sending data, receive and assemble sets of data, and detect errors in transmission. Since front-end processors range in cost from $40,000 to $100,000, they are used only with large and medium-sized computer systems that process a high volume of communication traffic.

If terminals are not submitting data continually, the transmission line will be available for use by other terminals. For instance, in the hospital system example, it may be desirable to have several terminals or printers at each location. To do so will not mean that a separate line is needed for each device. Instead a *multiplexor,* a device that enables several devices to share a line, can be installed. The multiplexor scans each device to collect and transmit data on a single line to the CPU. It also communicates transmissions from the CPU to the appropriate terminal linked to the multiplexor. The devices are *polled,* periodically asked whether there is any data to transmit.

SATELLITE COMMUNICATION

The demand for data communication facilities is rising at an increasing rate. At the same time, communication costs are increasing substantially.

Figure 11.11. Communication devices—front end processor and multiplexor.

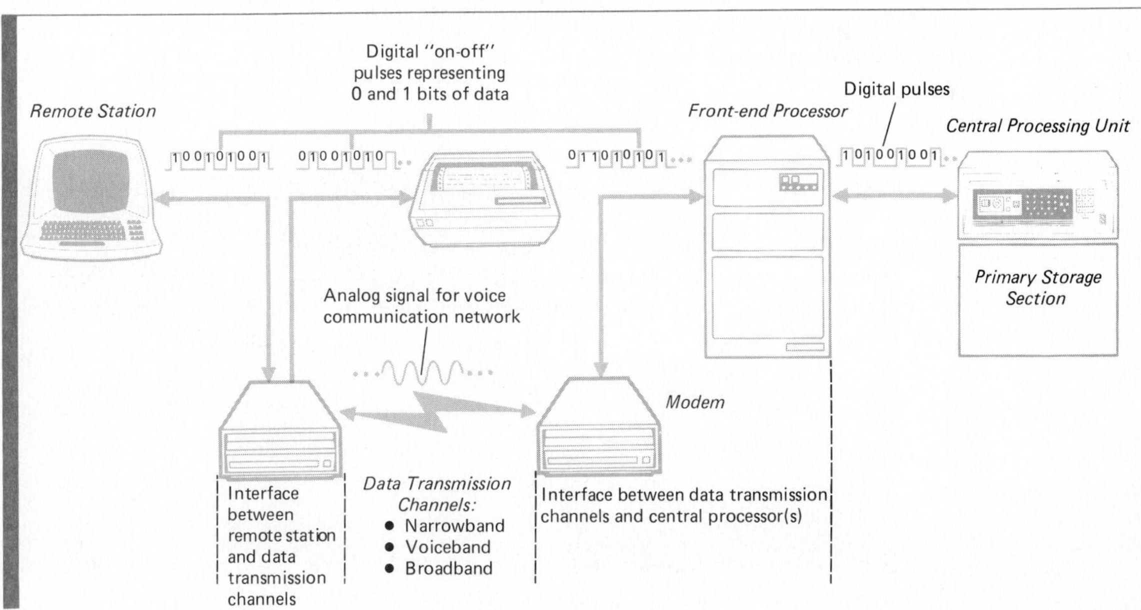

This has led organizations to examine other methods of data transmission. The use of communication satellites is a method whose time has come.

Federal agencies in the United States and elsewhere have been working with satellites for many years. You have also undoubtedly seen television programs that have been transmitted live via satellite. (The majority of overseas telephone communication is also handled by satellite, without the user ever being aware of it.) These uses of the satellite have treated it like an orbiting repeater station: the signal it receives is retransmitted at a precise angle to reach the intended destination. Transatlantic satellites, for example, connect carrier offices on each side of the ocean (point-to-point transmission).

The cost of satellites, millions of dollars each, prohibited organizations from acquiring their own satellites. However, there is an ongoing series of developments in satellite communication that is increasing the likelihood of their use by many organizations.

The cost of ground stations, that is, the necessary communication equipment needed to transmit and receive satellite data (Figure 11.12), has dropped to a point where industrial, educational, and public organizations can buy in. Antennas are being placed on rooftops to enable them to communicate with orbiting satellites or with ground stations that in turn transmit satellite data.

Satellites (or ground stations for satellites) poll users waiting to transmit data. As the data is received, it is retransmitted.

Several major universities have formed networks. Among the best known is ARPANET, which connects institutions in England and throughout the United States. The University of Hawaii also developed the ALOHA system. The best known emerging commercial system is being developed by Satellite Business Systems, a joint subsidiary of IBM, Aetna Insurance Company, and COMSAT. Other firms will be launching their own satellites for commercial use.

(a)

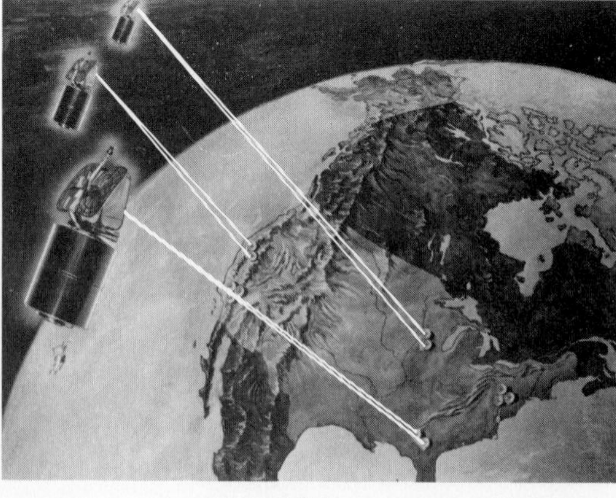

(b)

Figure 11.12. (*a*) Ground station (courtesy Western Union Corporation) and (*b*) communication satellite (reproduced with permission of AT & T).

MICROWAVE COMMUNICATION

Microwave transmission is often used as an alternative to the communication of data over cable. Data in coded form is transmitted through the air. It is passed along from one station to another in a "line of sight" until it reaches its destination. It may pass through a series of earth stations before it finally reaches the receiving station. When physical objects block the signals and prohibit direct transmission, satellites are used to relay the signals.

VALUE-ADDED CARRIERS

During normal voice conversations, it is unusual for there to be long pauses in the conversation during which no words are being sent over the lines. However, in data communication, it is just the opposite. Lines may be busy for brief periods, and, for other lengthy periods, no data is transmitted. In a sense then these lines have unused capacity.

Value-added carriers have established a service that meets the increasing demands for data communication. By constructing their own networks of leased lines and reselling them to users, they are able to provide a relatively inexpensive service in a limited geographic area. To use the service, the organization must pay a membership fee and usage charges, based on the amount of communication they require. In addition, they must establish their own communication links, using modems and communication software as discussed.

There is no limit to the size system or type of equipment that can be linked into a value-added network. Current members use systems ranging from terminals costing under $500 to large mainframe systems costing over $1 million each. Yet both use the same system to send data in the same manner. Value-added carriers are opening the world of data communication to many organizations and individuals who have not considered its use before.

The best known general-purpose value-added networks are operated by Telenet and Tymnet. In Canada, the Datapac network is growing in services offered and use. Others are emerging to link personal computers or to perform special services requested by individual organizations.

The strategies used for data transmission in value-added networks are packet switching and message switching. When ordinary dial-up voice lines are used to transmit data (or voice conversation), the system establishes a single connection that is sustained throughout the call. *Circuit switching,* as this type of transmission is called, links a line coming into a switching system from the caller and a line from the switching system to the destination. The same connection is used throughout the transmission. When you make a personal telephone call, for example, the line is constant throughout the call, although when you make the next call, you will use a different set of circuits.

Message switching does not rely on a single transmission path (Figure 11.13). Instead, data is sent a block at a time from switching office to

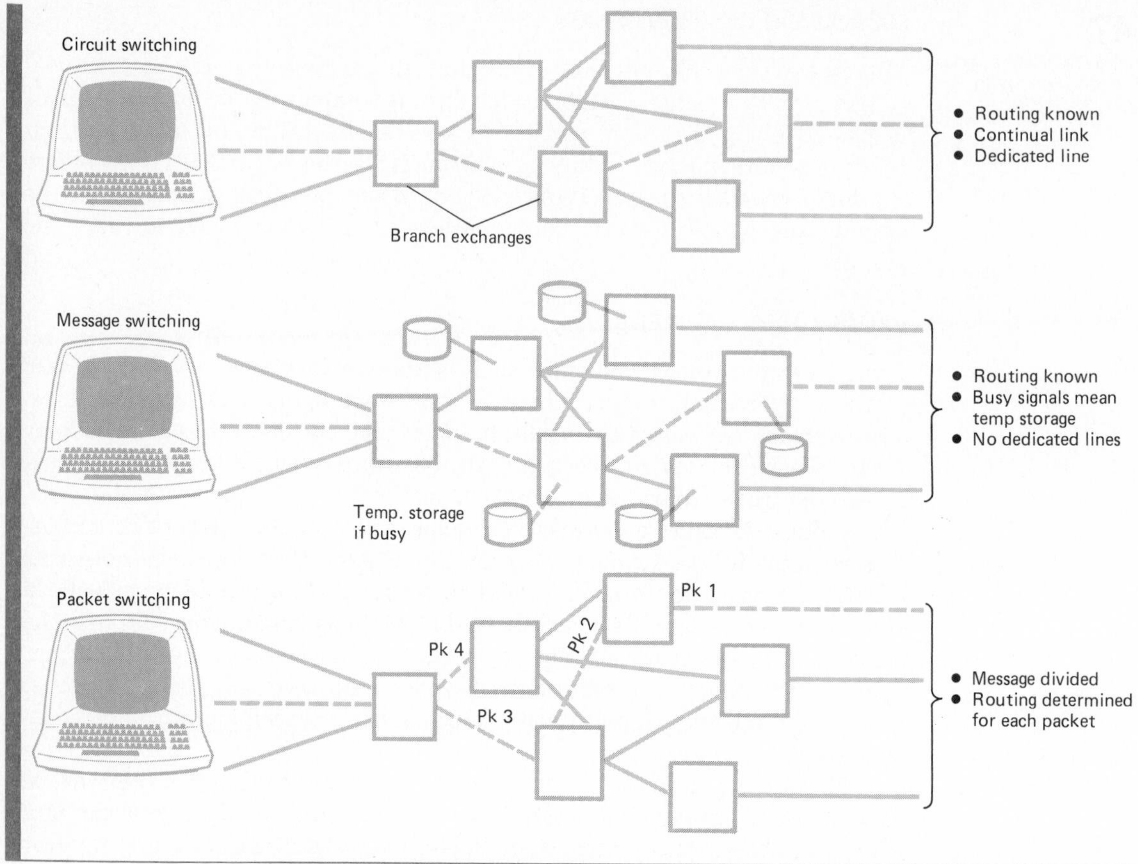

Figure 11.13. Data movement in distributed systems.

switching office. At each switching office, the data is briefly stored, inspected for errors, and then retransmitted to the next switching office. There is no limit to the block size transmitted under message switching. Because of the intermediate storage of the message, however, the phrase *store and forward transmission* is sometimes used to describe this method.

In *packet switching,* block size is limited. Therefore messages are transmitted in several blocks, each moving separately, even along different transmission paths. (Packets can arrive in the wrong order, so the system must reorder them at their destination.) These features ensure that no single user can monopolize one transmission line—a factor that is not controlled in message switching. For this reason, computer networks are most often packet-switched. Sometimes circuit switching is used, but message switching is not advisable.

The analyst considering packet switching and value-added networks should check with the carriers for the charging algorithms used, which include the number of bytes of data transmitted and the connect time to the system. With packet carriers, distance generally does not matter except in international communication. However, with circuit switching, charges are determined by time of use and distance of transmission, not amount of data transmitted.

Other questions analysts should address before designing a system around value-added networks are as follows:

1 Are dedicated lines needed to access the network? If so, what is their cost?
2 Are special types of dedicated equipment needed to connect to the network?
3 Is it necessary to share equipment in the carrier's computer (such as public access ports)?

Value-added networks are likely to increase as communication costs increase and organizations wish to take advantage of the remarkable growth in telecommunication technology.

Standards are developing to guide analysts in the development and use of networks. IBM has released specifications for its SNA network, and the X25 public network from International Standards Organization (ISO) is used by Tymnet and Telenet, systems for transmitting large amounts of data over long distances.

DIRECT COMPUTER CONNECTIONS

Not all data communication need use public carrier facilities or involve long distances. Systems interconnecting data processing components near each other can be linked through their own dedicated lines. This factor also allows organizations to establish local area networks.

Cable-to-Equipment Connections

In fact, when terminals and computers are linked together in a building or the distance between them is short, say several thousand feet, direct connections should be made between cables. To interconnect a terminal to a central processing unit at the opposite end of an office building, a simple coaxial cable, wire with a protective shielding to prevent static or electrical interference, can be strung through the ceiling or floor to transmit data (Figure 11.14). A simple connector on each end is used to plug the equipment and line together.

Local Area Networks

A local area network is a collection of data processing devices interconnected through cable and designed to send and receive data transmitted over comparatively short distances. The data transmitted through a local area network may be electronic mail (messages and notes), manuscripts, and reports, as well as computer files and software.

One distinction between local area networks and large networks is distance, as pointed out. However, cable, rather than carrier services, is

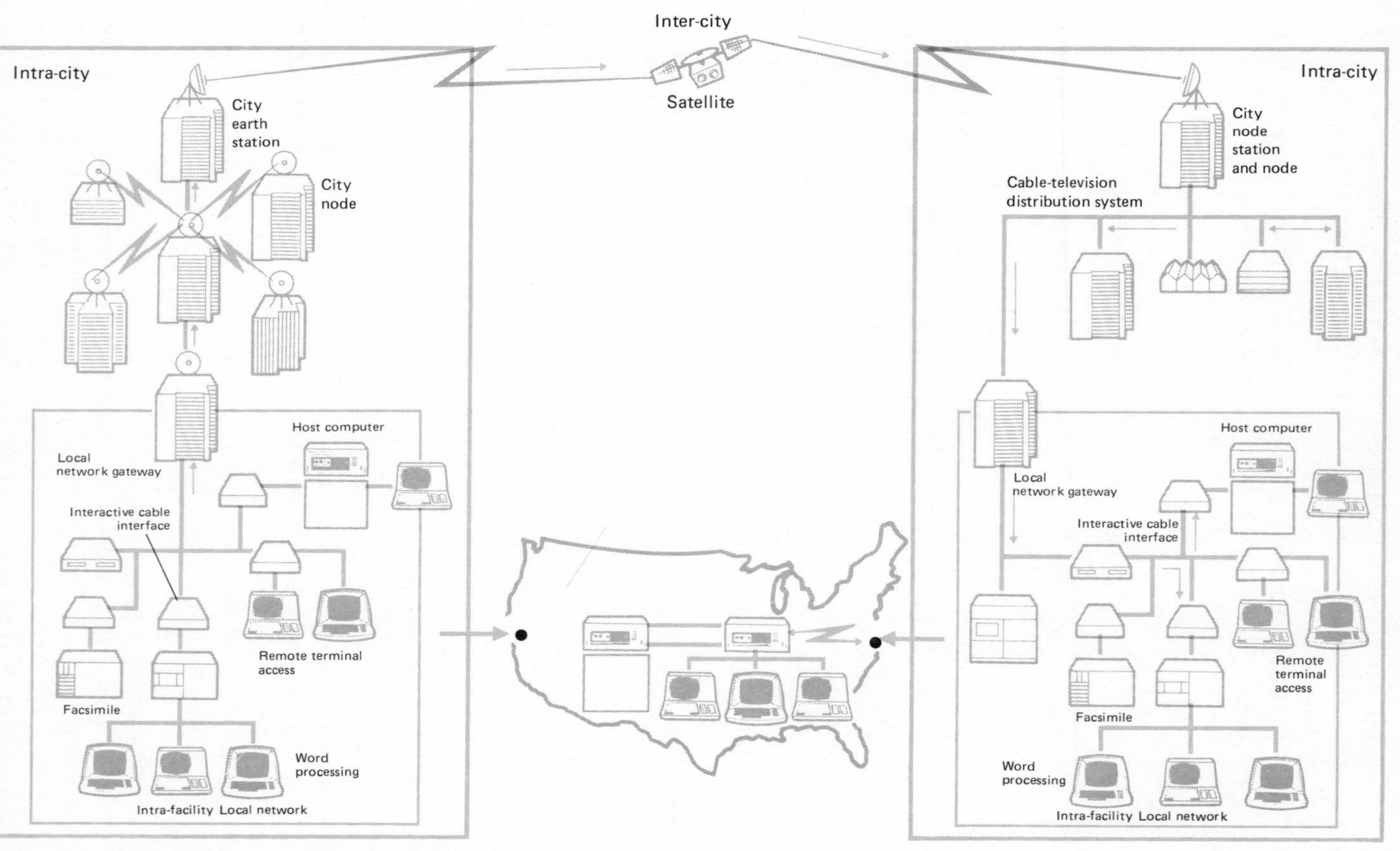

Figure 11.14. Local and network connected by coaxial cable.

used. The data transfer rate in local networks ranges up to 10 megabits per second of information moving between users. Xerox's widely promoted Ethernet is the most expensive, but fastest network system. It works well for large-scale systems that employ minicomputers in the network. However, it is more powerful than necessary for microcomputers. Slower-speed systems, transmitting at typical rates of 250 kilobaud to 1 megabit per second, are emerging for microcomputers.

In addition to twisted-pair lines, baseband and broadband coaxial cables are used in the construction of local area networks. Baseband coaxial cable permits any number of users to be linked into a network with the capability of transmitting the equivalent of 500 pages of text per second. However, only one user can access the system at a time.

Broadband coaxial networks use multiple cables that allow multiple users to transmit and receive data more quickly. This type of cable even permits the integration of voice and video transmission. It is the method that many cable television companies are exploring in large cities.

The analyst must determine the need for speed and multiple users, and the distance for transmission. These factors will then help select the proper method of creating a local area network. The decision about the network itself remains dependent on the need to link nearby, but multilocation, users together to send and receive data and information.

FILE PROCESSING IN A COMMUNICATIONS ENVIRONMENT

When information systems involve communications, the analyst must design special precautions to ensure that data is processed properly and protected adequately. This section discusses questions of processing validation, file storage methods, and updating concerns.

Processing Validation

As described earlier, when systems are used by persons linked to the computer system only by communications lines, it is difficult to tell who the user is. Therefore the analyst must build in extra precautions for validating user and transaction.

TRANSACTION VALIDATION

Terminals and computers located at remote sites have the full capability of sending anything over communication lines that can be entered through the keyboard, including data, processing requests, or commands to instruct the system to take a particular action. Inexperienced analysts tend to assume users will submit only valid transactions. Experienced analysts, many of whom have learned the hard way by making mistakes, assume that invalid data will be submitted either accidentally or intentionally. They assemble design specifications calling for verification of each submission from a user site to ensure it is acceptable to the system.

Transaction validation is the examination of input from a remote site to determine if it is acceptable for processing on the system. A transaction may be new data to be stored in the system, data to update an existing record, or a request to retrieve data (print a report or display answers to an inquiry) from the system.

The system must verify that it is capable of processing the request. For example, if a user enters a request to retrieve sales data while using a personnel system, the transaction is invalid. However, unless the system is designed to detect that this is an invalid request, refuse to process it, and alert the user through an error message, the system could crash. *Crashing* occurs when the program attempts to process a request that it has not anticipated, that is, an undefined operation. Unless the design specifies how to handle undefined operations, all processing will stop and the system will have to be restarted (with the likelihood that there will be loss of data in memory at the time it crashed).

For example, a hotel reservation system is designed to process three different types of transactions, including adding reservations to the system, changing reservations, and retrieving reservations. The user requests these transactions by entering the keywords of ADD, CHG, and RET respectively. If any of the keywords are entered, properly spelled, the system will initiate the appropriate action. However, if the user enters DEL, which is not a valid keyword, the system must recognize that it is not valid and send the message UNABLE TO PROCESS REQUEST: COMMAND NOT VALID, or whatever message the analyst developed, back to the user. Some systems are designed to display just a "?" when errors occur. Such messages, as discussed in Chapter 8, are inadequate to assist the user.

USER IDENTIFICATION AND AUTHORIZATION

Transaction validation is performed in conjunction with identification of the user. Several different levels of user identification are needed to protect a system fully from accidental loss of data and unauthorized use.

As the user signs onto the system, the first level of identification takes place. The dialogue in Figure 11.15 shows that, when individuals first sign onto the system, they identify themselves by providing an individual password that uniquely identifies them or a general password that all authorized users should know. (The general password is changed periodically by supervisors to protect against unauthorized users who accidentally learn it.) In some systems, it is also necessary to provide an approved account number against which usage costs will be charged.

Even if an authorized user is signed onto the system and attempting to submit a transaction the system is able to process, the combination of user and transaction may not be valid. In other words, analysts can specify additional levels of protection that require individuals to prove they have authorization. In Figure 11.15 the mere fact that the user has provided the sign-on password is not sufficient to change account balances or to print detailed profit and loss information. The additional passwords TOPHAT and BIGAPPLE must be supplied. Even if the original sign-on password

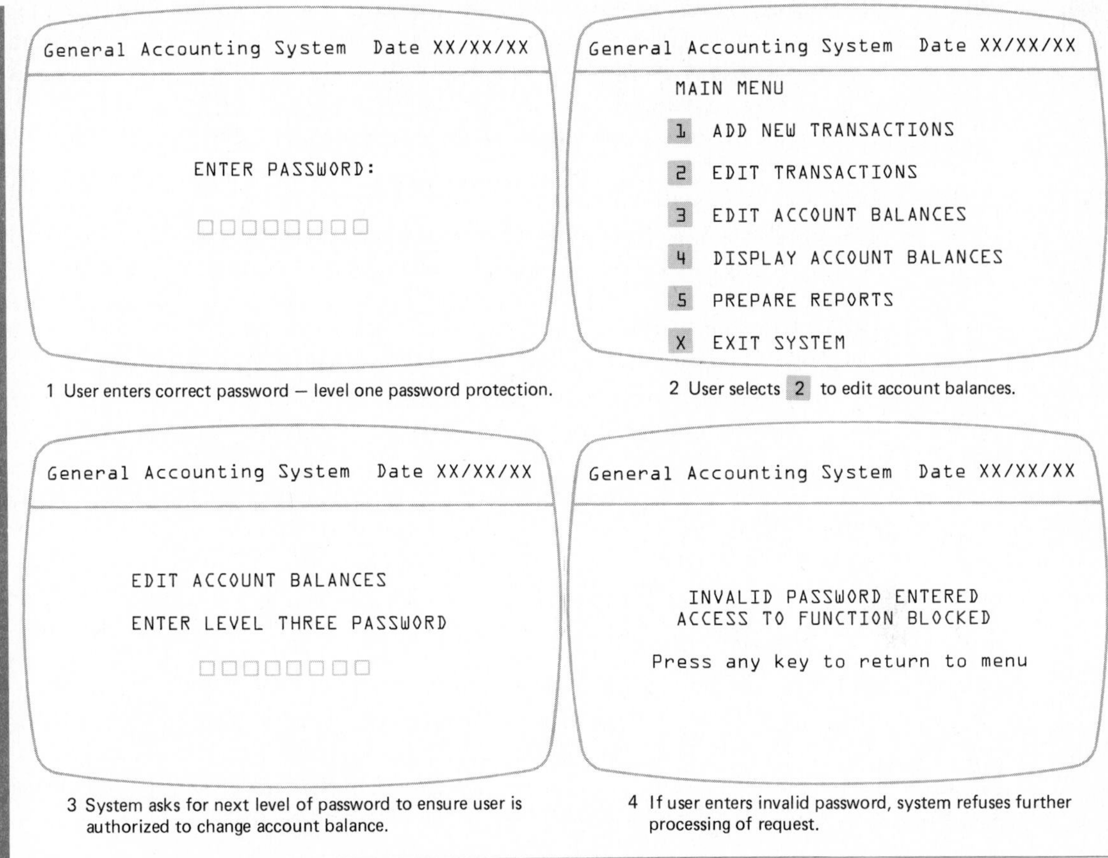
General Accounting System Date XX/XX/XX
ENTER PASSWORD:
1 User enters correct password — level one password protection.
General Accounting System Date XX/XX/XX
MAIN MENU
1 ADD NEW TRANSACTIONS
2 EDIT TRANSACTIONS
3 EDIT ACCOUNT BALANCES
4 DISPLAY ACCOUNT BALANCES
5 PREPARE REPORTS
X EXIT SYSTEM
2 User selects 2 to edit account balances.
General Accounting System Date XX/XX/XX
EDIT ACCOUNT BALANCES
ENTER LEVEL THREE PASSWORD
3 System asks for next level of password to ensure user is authorized to change account balance.
General Accounting System Date XX/XX/XX
INVALID PASSWORD ENTERED
ACCESS TO FUNCTION BLOCKED
Press any key to return to menu
4 If user enters invalid password, system refuses further processing of request.

Figure 11.15. Password protection built into on-line system at multiple levels.

SAFEGARD was entered earlier, failure to enter the second- and third-level passwords will result in displaying the message USER NOT AUTHORIZED TO PERFORM REQUESTED FUNCTION.

This system is menu-driven. To invoke a function, the individual enters the number corresponding to the activity displayed on the menu. (See Chapter 8 for a detailed discussion of menu-driven systems.) When the function number is entered, the password identification is requested. When it is not provided, the error message is supplied, and the menu is re-displayed. Analysts sometimes design systems so that the user is automatically signed off if an invalid request is made. However, this is an extreme action since honest mistakes in keying (typing mistakes) will occur. A better approach is allowing individuals to reenter the password a second or third time and, if still incorrect, to terminate processing then.

Audit Trail

In on-line systems, unlike batch environments, there may not be copies of input source documents to fall back on if the system fails during processing.

It is also possible for on-line users to sign onto a system, alter data stored in files, and sign off again, without leaving a visible clue to what happened. Unless the analyst develops an audit trail, no such protection exists in on-line and distributed systems.

An *audit trail* is designed to permit tracing any input record or process performed on a system back to its original source. One way of accomplishing this is by automatically maintaining a transaction log. The details of each transaction are recorded in a separate transaction file on the system (Figure 11.16). Before and after images, as discussed in Chapter 9, will provide information on how the record was changed. The storage of these details is automatic and invisible to the user, about whom information should also be stored so that it is clear who conducted the transaction. If the system has an internal clock, each transaction is also time-stamped to tell when it

Figure 11.16. Audit trail protects against loss of data.

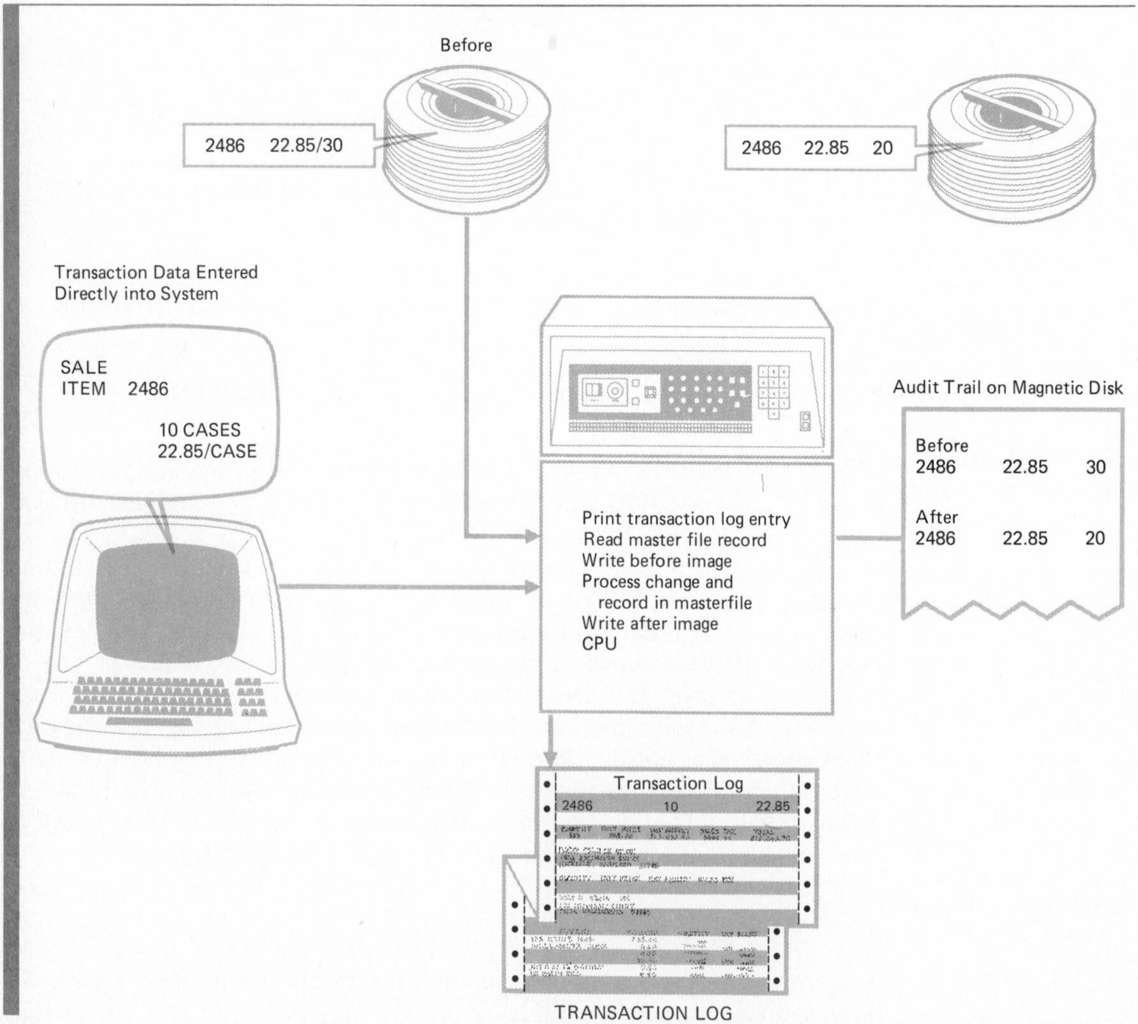

occurred. If the need arises to audit a particular record in a file, it is relatively easy to determine who submitted the transaction, when it occurred, what data the transaction contained, and how the master file record was modified. In other words, there is a complete trail of the entire transaction and its effect on the system.

Another form of audit trail presumes that storing transaction data on magnetic disk is not fully reliable. For example, in some small business systems, if the system is turned off, perhaps through a power failure, before the data captured on disk during an editing session has been backed up, it will be lost completely. (Some computer systems use disk systems in which the read-write heads drop down to the disk surface when the power is turned off. In these systems, users must remove the disk *before* powering down or they will lose data.)

Printing a copy of the transaction before processing it is one of the best ways to protect against data loss. Then, if anything happens during the on-line session, a backup copy of the master file can be mounted and the transaction data reentered by using the printed transaction list.

Users many miles away have no way of knowing when a malfunction occurs. As long as they can continue to enter transactions, they have every reason to believe the system is operating correctly. Therefore, the analyst must anticipate these problems and provide protection against them for the user. The analyst is responsible for safeguarding the integrity of a system by providing ways to audit its use.

File Handling

Since one of the aims of on-line processing is to provide data capture while events are taking place, special attention must be given to file structures and file handling activities.

When it is expected that the system will process many inquiries or it is essential to have immediate updating of records as transactions occur, direct-access or indexed organizations are appropriate. Furthermore, they must be mounted on disk drives that are operating. There is time neither to find, mount, and load magnetic tapes containing master file data nor to read through the tape to find the proper record. In an airline system, for example, passengers are not willing to wait the 5 to 15 minutes (or more) that would elapse while an operator carries out the indicated steps.

If a system is not dedicated to a single function, many different disks may be mounted and running. As a request is received from a user, the system examines and validates it, locates the proper program (also stored on magnetic disk), determines the needed files, prepares them, and begins processing. If the application is running in a multiprogramming or multiprocessing environment, processing may be interrupted several times to handle other requests. However, the disks and files keep operating, while waiting for the next request.

Magnetic-tape files may however have a place to accumulate the details of the transactions, that is, to store the audit trail previously discussed.

In *on-line updating* the system accepts and verifies the data as it is received. Then the transactions are processed against the master file to produce the desired changes. Audit trail records are also written.

If the request is for the retrieval of information to respond to an inquiry, the necessary data is located and processed and the response sent to the requestor. Sometimes the requests are for printed reports. Even if the data is immediately located and processed, the report may not be printed at that instant. Spooling of data into report files may delay the final printing of the report, even though all processing is complete.

When systems are not only on-line but produce results in time to affect events as they are happening, we say they are *real-time*. Instantaneous results of submitting and receiving answers to requests in an airline system mean it is operating in real-time. The system that accepts and processes data, but does not produce instantaneous results, is on-line, but not real-time.

When instantaneous results are not essential, *deferred on-line processing* is often specified in a design. Transactions are accepted through terminals or from nodes in a distributed network, and the data is stored in files. This is on-line data capture. However, actual processing of the data is deferred until a later time, when the system is available for processing.

Many banking systems use deferred on-line teller systems. When you make a deposit or withdrawal, the teller enters your account number and the transaction details directly into the system through the special terminal at the bank window. A record is made of your transaction for audit purposes.

(a)

(b)

Figure 11.17. Food store scanner for price data entry. (Courtesy of NCR Corporation)

However, the actual update processing for your account may not take place immediately. Some banks defer morning processing until noon and afternoon processing until the close of the business day. Others defer all updates until the end of the day. (Procedures for providing the necessary security to protect against repeated withdrawals from the same account at different branch locations must be carefully worked out to prevent overdrawing.)

In many grocery stores, point-of-sale systems centered around laser scanners capture data in an on-line mode. The scanner reads the universal product, or bar, codes on packages and translates them into digital stock numbers. The price and description for the product is retrieved from disk storage and printed on the terminal register tape (Figure 11.17). If the system immediately updates the inventory records for each item rung up, it is operating in an on-line mode. However, if the sales details are recorded in a transaction file and processed against the inventory master in the evening, it is a deferred on-line system.

SUMMARY

On-line systems are characterized by the direct entry of data into the computer system. User and system interact as data is submitted and results prepared. On-line systems avoid the delay built into batch processing systems, while allowing users to control when processing occurs. Some systems are capable of multiprocess—the name given to the ability to handle several user jobs at the same time. Multiprocessing systems process jobs concurrently, while those that multitask are capable of executing several jobs simultaneously.

Distributed systems interconnect computer devices at different locations to permit local processing of data and still allow transmitting data or making summary reports to other locations, such as organization headquarters. Load sharing and software sharing are also possible, even though the computing equipment at each node in the network may be of a different make. The different types of distributed systems, including point-to-point, hierarchial, star, and ring or loop networks, vary according to whether data can be transmitted directly from one site to another or must be sent through a central node in the system. Hierarchial networks are the most common in business, while star networks are typical of those used to transmit voice telephone conversations.

Data communication lines, one common method of transmitting data, use either dial-up or leased telephone lines that are connected to computer equipment through modems. Voice-grade lines vary in transmission speed from 100 to 9600 baud, depending on the speed specified by the analyst. The two methods of transmitting data are synchronous, which is controlled by a clock, and asynchronous, in which start and stop signals are sent along with the data. Most communication over 2000 baud is synchronous. Simplex lines carry data in one direction only. However, the more common lines are half-duplex, on which data is transmitted in two directions, one direction at a time, or full-duplex, on which transmission occurs in both directions simultaneously.

Other methods of data transmission use satellite and microwave facilities. Value-added carriers provide packet switching services that improve the usage of the line by carrying more data than a single user normally would.

Some organizations are developing their own networks, called local area networks. They are being used to link different computer systems together for such purposes as electronic mail and systems component sharing. Office buildings are being wired with cable to interconnect computer equipment.

When analysts develop on-line systems, they must consider additional file processing details. The validation of user and processing requests takes on additional importance since the user is not visible to the systems operator and therefore cannot be readily identified as a valid user. Transactions must also be validated to protect against illegal or unexpected processing requests. When transactions are submitted and processed on-line, audit trails become an essential method of preserving systems reliability and integrity. Even if processing is deferred to a time after initial data capture, protections are needed to safeguard the data and the system against loss of integrity.

It is generally expected that the combination of increased communication cost and falling hardware prices will expand the use of on-line and distributed systems in organizations of all types.

CASE STUDY FOR CHAPTER 11
COMMUNICATION CAPABILITIES

The on-line features of Valley Industries require the installation of communication capabilities that will support the planned input and output of data and information. The System/34 has specific communication capabilities around which the communication plan must be designed. Two specific types of communication methods will be used for the system.

SYSTEM/34 COMMUNICATION CAPABILITIES

The System/34 used by Valley Industries has five communication ports to which external devices can be attached. Two ports are currently in use. A high-speed printer is attached to one port. Two display terminals are attached to the other.

The ability to attach multiple terminals to a single port is made possible by a "cable-through" feature, in which multiple terminals are connected in series on the communication line. Since display terminals are seldom transmitting data at the same time, data is interleaved on the line as it is sent from the terminal to the central processor (or vice versa).

ORDER ENTRY AND ACCOUNTS RECEIVABLE COMMUNICATION

Three display terminals will be added to the current systems configuration to support the new order entry and accounts receivable system. Two will be located in the accounting department for handling customer orders and account transactions. The other terminal will be installed in the manufacturing supervisor's office, where it will be used to monitor and update order status records.

Since all three terminals are located within the Valley Industries' building, data communication will be handled using coaxial cable. (Common carrier telephone lines are not necessary.) The coaxial cables will be strung from the central processor to each department where terminals will be installed. The terminals are directly connected to the communication cable with screw-on connectors (Figure C11.1).

Data transmission speeds can be varied from slow speeds of 110 baud to very rapid speeds of 19,200 baud. The operating speed used in the Valley system is 9600 baud. This speed permits the instantaneous display of data on the display screen.

The accounting terminals will share the same communication cable and

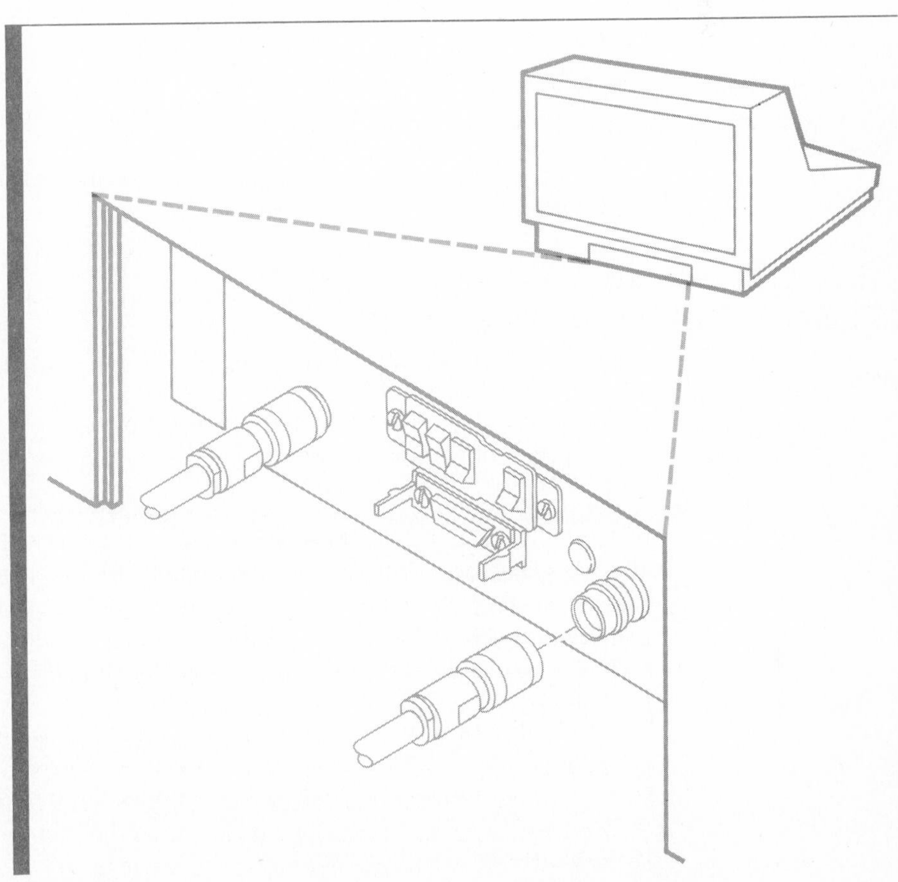

Figure C11.1 Cable connection to terminals permitting communication of data.

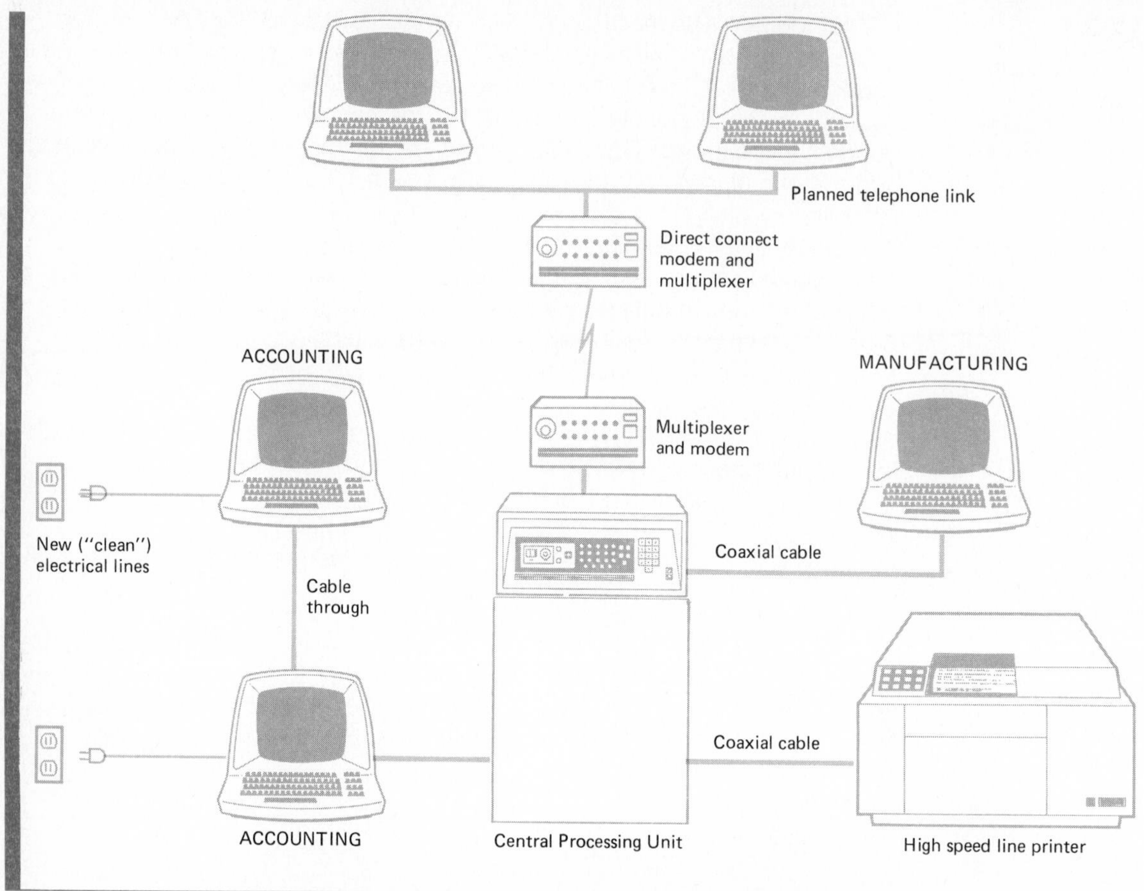

Figure C11.2 Configuration and cabling for equipment in new order processing system.

send and receive data from the same port. The manufacturing terminal will be connected to a separate port, although the terminal has a cable-through feature and can later share a line with other terminals if the need arises.

Figure C11.2 shows the configuration and cabling for the system.

FUTURE REMOTE TELECOMMUNICATION

The high likelihood that Valley management will open additional production facilities in the near future has been taken into account in communication planning for the new system. Therefore, systems analysts have ensured that additional ports are available to permit support of other locations by using two communication ports on the computer system.

When the new facilities are opened, terminals will be connected to the computer system using common carrier telephone lines. Leased lines capable of full-duplex transmission are anticipated, and data will be transmitted at either 2400 or 4800 baud. Owing to the System/34's design, synchronous transmission will be necessary.

It is likely that management and staff at the new production facilities will require more than one terminal. Therefore, in addition to modems on each end that connect the communication line to the computer components, a multiplexor will be installed. A four-channel multiplexor will permit up to four terminals to share the same telephone line. Although unlikely, if more terminals are needed, a multiplexor with more channels can be installed.

Each terminal will be connected to the multiplexor by its own separate cable.

The communication of data between terminal and computer, from in-house locations and planned remote facilities, is a well-proven method of transferring order and accounting data from place to place. It is highly preferable to the alternative of courier or messenger service.

KEYWORDS

Acoustic coupler
Asynchronous transmission
Baud
Data set
Deferred on-line
Direct-connect modem
Duplex
Full duplex
Front-end processor
Half duplex
Hierarchial network
Line conditioning
Local area network
Loop network
Multidrop line
Multiplexor
Multiprocessing
Multiprogramming
Point to point
Port
Ring network
Simplex
Smart modem
Star network
Switched line
Synchronous transmission

REVIEW QUESTIONS

1 What characteristics typify on-line systems? How do on-line and batch modes differ?
2 What reasons justify on-line processing?
3 Define the following terms: multitasking, multiprocessing, and multiprogramming. How is each related to on-line processing?
4 How do distributed and on-line systems vary? In what ways are they the same?
5 What are the characteristics of each of the types of distributed systems?
6 Why are organizations becoming increasingly interested in distributed systems? Are distributed and local area networks different? Explain your answer.
7 How do users in distributed environments share software? Loads?
8 What advantages and disadvantages are associated with switched and leased lines? What are the maximum transmission rates of each?
9 In what ways can computer components and communication lines be linked together? Explain the purposes and unique characteristics of each type of device?
10 How does data communication using dial-up lines work? Explain.

11 Contrast synchronous and asynchronous transmission. When is each most likely to be used?

12 How do the different types of communication lines vary?

13 What functions do each of the following serve: Front-end processor, multiplexor, and coaxial cable?

14 Distinguish between common carrier, circuit, packet, and message switching. Which is recommended for value-added systems?

15 Explain the service provided by value-added carriers. How is this service provided? Why should analysts consider using value-added carriers?

16 What unique file and transaction processing questions must be addressed by analysts working with on-line systems?

17 In what ways does an audit trail safeguard both data and the organization in an on-line environment?

18 Does file handling occur differently in on-line and batch environments?

19 What purpose is achieved by deferred on-line processing?

APPLICATION PROBLEMS FOR CHAPTER 11

1 Which type of distributed system does each of the following represent? (If it is not a distributed system, indicate why it is not.)

   a A group of microcomputers that can communicate directly with one another by using dial-up telephone service

   b A set of terminals that can interact directly with the home office computer system to enter and retrieve data from the corporate database

   c Regional offices connected directly to the corporate office and transmitting and receiving sales, accounting, and manufacturing data; district offices interacting with field offices where sales agents use terminals, and with regional offices where data is shared; and software residing on the regional office computer and used to execute special management analyses

   d Many northeastern medical institutions able to communicate directly with one another both to transmit data and receive information

   e A variety of computer devices, including terminals, microcomputers, and mainframe systems, that send and receive messages from individual locations by using the communication capabilities of a powerful computer system that routes all messages to the proper location

2 A manager is trying to decide whether to develop a distributed system or a series of stand-alone systems. Currently many locations in the company have computer systems, although the make and size vary significantly. All have potential communication capability, even though they are not currently involved in data communication activities. The work each computer processes currently produces results used only at that location.

The corporate information systems staff has watched the advances throughout the industry in data communication and distributed processing and knows it is a proven technology. The staff is involved in the design of a system at the corporate level that requires that the remote company locations transmit sales and manufacturing data to the corporate data processing center on a weekly and monthly basis. All data needs will be identified in advance and become part of a routine operating procedure involving the electronic transfer of data over common carrier lines. It is not anticipated that load or software sharing will be needed. However, staff members believe that other systems will be developed in the future that will require the periodic transmission of specific business data.

   a If all data will be transmitted using telecommunication services, must the firm develop a distributed processing system? Explain.

b What features, if any, characterize the situation described as one meriting distributed processing?

3 The information systems manager for a medium-sized organization is deciding how to provide data communication services linking a new customer service center to the computer system located at the home office. The manager must decide whether to lease a common carrier line or use dial-up service at ordinary rates. The communication software needed for either alternative has already been acquired by the company.

a What factors should the manager examine in deciding between the alternatives?

b Assume the cost of a leased line that will meet the company's requirements is $240 per month. In contrast, the daytime message rate for dial-up service averages $0.06 per minute. If the typical usage of the telephone lines under the dial-up option will be 4 hours per day for 20 work days per month, which of these two options should be selected? Explain.

4 The communication of data between computer and user locations can take place at varying speeds and using differing protocols. A systems analyst is trying to decide between designing a system to use 2400- or 1800-baud rates. What factors should the analyst consider to make this decision?

5 The business manager of a medical clinic is coordinating the expansion of the current medical records system. The existing system has been in use at the clinic for several years. Recently the clinic's board of directors approved plans to open its first satellite clinic at a location approximately 20 miles away from the main office. A terminal will be placed at the location that will enable medical staff members to interact with the computer center at the main clinic to retrieve patient data and submit changes and diagnostic information to the computer that will process it to update the patient's records. A printer will also be installed at the satellite clinic to provide paper copies of patient records when staff members request them.

a What steps should the business manager take to ensure that the data communication needs discussed will be met? Identify all equipment, software, and communication methods the manager must acquire or arrange.

b What communication line alternatives should the manager consider? Discuss the criteria the manager should use to select the proper alternative.

c If the business manager decides that four terminals should be installed at the satellite clinic rather than one, but does not want to increase the cost of communication lines needed, what communication equipment besides the terminals will be required?

6 Many companies employ salespersons who are based at locations around the country, hundreds, even thousands, of miles away from the home office. It is necessary for the salespersons to mail or telephone the orders of merchandise requested by customers so they can be processed at the home office. However, the excessive delay in receipt of mailed orders and the cost of lengthy long-distance telephone calls are both growing concerns to many sales managers.

To improve customer service and reduce long-distance telephone costs, many sales managers are turning to data communication methods. Small terminals which sales personnel can easily carry in briefcases can be used to transmit the data over ordinary telephone lines. Sales data can be keyed into the small terminals and transmitted directly to company headquarters.

a In addition to the terminals, what hardware and software must be used to handle the transmission of sales orders? Consider both the sending of orders by the salespersons and their receipt and processing at the home office.

b Can transmission over telephone lines at long-distance rates be accomplished at a lower cost than the same number of orders transmitted verbally over telephone lines? Explain the reason for your answer.

PART FOUR

QUALITY ASSURANCE AND IMPLEMENTATION

CHAPTER 12

SYSTEMS ENGINEERING AND QUALITY ASSURANCE

QUESTIONS TO GUIDE YOU THROUGH THE CHAPTER

- What is quality assurance?
- How are computer programs tested?
- Are software errors and software failures different?
- Why is software maintenance performed? How frequently is it required?
- What design procedures should be followed to produce quality software?
- What tools can be used to design and document software?
- Is there more than one right way to test software?

More critical functions in business, organizations, and everyday activities are being automated, and we are placing more trust in what is automated. This realization puts an increasing burden on systems analysts to ensure the systems they develop are of adequate quality. The quality of a system depends on its design, development, testing, and implementation. A weakness in any of these areas will seriously jeopardize the quality and therefore the value of the system to its users.

This chapter discusses those design considerations that lead to reliable systems. The design objectives for reliability and maintainability are discussed first and then the design guidelines and practices. Specific tools for use by the analyst to enhance reliability and maintainability are also discussed. Methods for design and documentation are presented.

The last part of this chapter examines quality assurance and testing of systems and software. It will be seen how philosophies, strategies, and techniques are combined to produce the reliable software that both analyst and user desire.

DESIGN OBJECTIVES

The two operational design objectives continually sought by developers are systems reliability and maintainability. This section focuses on the importance of these objectives and ways to achieve them.

Systems Reliability

A *reliable system* is one that does not produce dangerous or costly failures when used in a reasonable manner, that is, in a manner that a typical user expects is normal. This definition recognizes that systems may not always be used in the ways that designers expect. Users and business operations change. However, there are steps analysts can take to ensure that the system is reliable when it is installed and that the reliability can be maintained after implementation.

APPROACHES TO RELIABILITY

There are two levels of reliability. The first is that the system is meeting the right requirements. If, for instance, it is expected to have specific security features or controls built into it by the users, but the design fails to specify them and permits the loss of funds or merchandise for a lengthy time before someone detects the problem, the system is not reliable. Reliability at the design level is only possible if a thorough and effective determination of systems requirements was performed by the analyst. A careful and thorough systems study is needed to satisfy this aspect of reliability. We have already discussed many aspects of systems studies.

The second level of systems reliability is the actual working of the system delivered to the user. At this level, systems reliability is interwoven with software engineering and development.

An *error* occurs whenever the system does not produce the expected output. While it is true that no program is ever fully debugged or fully tested or can be proven correct—a fact that startles many users and aspiring programmers—errors are not limited to the correct use of programming syntax alone.

The computing industry, largely through the work of Glenford Myers, has come to distinguish between errors and failures. A *failure* is the occurrence of a software error, weighted by its seriousness. For example, if an inventory program is developed so that it truncates rather than rounds half cents when calculating the value of materials on hand, it is an error if specifications call for rounding. But it may be of no consequence to the user, who in fact does not consider this a failure. However, if the program regularly skips certain items or indicates they are out of stock when in fact the records show they are in stock, it is a serious failure.

Error Avoidance

There are three approaches to reliability (Table 12.1). Under *error avoidance,* developers and programmers make every attempt to prevent errors

TABLE 12.1

APPROACHES TO RELIABILITY

APPROACH	DESCRIPTION	EXAMPLE
ERROR AVOIDANCE	Prevents errors from occurring in the software.	Is impossible in large systems.
ERROR DETECTION AND CORRECTION	Recognizes errors when they are encountered and corrects the error or the effect of the error so the system does not fail.	Traps and modifies illegal arithmetic steps; Compensates for unexpected data values.
ERROR TOLERANCE	Recognizes errors when they occur, but enables the system to keep running through degraded performance or by applying rules that instruct the system how to continue processing.	Shuts down part of system. Does not perform some processing but keeps the system operational.

from occurring at all. The structured methods and techniques discussed later in this chapter are aimed at meeting that objective. The greater emphasis on early and careful identification of user requirements is another way this objective is pursued.

Analysts must assume that it is impossible to achieve this objective. Errors will occur despite the best efforts of very competent people.

Error Detection and Correction

This method uses design features that detect errors and make necessary changes to correct either the error while the program is in use or the effect on the user, so that a failure does not occur. Earlier, in Chapter 9, correcting user errors, such as misspelling keywords or entering invalid commands, was discussed. Error detection in programs is handled in a similar manner. For example, a program that calculates the productivity of a waiter or waitress in a restaurant by dividing the total revenue from meals served into the hours worked should not fail when employees do not serve anything. When a blinding snowstorm prevents customers from coming to a restaurant, employees will accumulate working time but will not have sales. The program should detect the divide-by-zero error and correct for it in order to keep the system running properly. Unfortunately, many programs fail when a situation like this one occurs. Even though it may not happen for several years after the system is installed, the error is there from the day of development. The failure occurs later.

Error Tolerance

Error tolerance strategies keep the system running even in the presence of errors. The United States NASA space agency, for example, designs its systems to be error tolerant through the use of redundant hardware. In one space program, redundant on-board computers and computer voting are used to process data in parallel, so results can be compared. Two computers process the data on location, course correction, and fuel use and compare the results with those produced by two other computers processing the same data. A fifth computer is even available to break a tie should one occur. There is even a sixth computer stowed away in a quickly accessible storage compartment if it is needed to replace one of the others that has been damaged or failed.

Another manner of error tolerance is through degraded processing. The user receives less service than the system was designed to provide, but that is considered a better alternative in some cases than having no service at all. For example, many electric power generation and distribution facilities in North America are computer-controlled. Suppose that on a record breaking hot day the system becomes overloaded and the computer control center is unable to correctly process allocation data and keep up with the power demands. Rather than risk damaging the power distribution network, the computer automatically shuts down part of the network. By providing degraded service, the computer tolerated a software error without failing.

CAUSES OF ERRORS

The software aspects of systems design are different from concerns about hardware reliability. In hardware, for example, a *design error* is produced in every copy of the item that is manufactured. However, application systems are often unique and design errors are not widely distributed. Of course, if you are working on a system that will be sold commercially, there is considerable concern over development and marketing of a software package that is rampant with design errors.

Manufacturing errors are introduced during the actual production process. They are not a property of the design and, in fact, may not be in every item produced. Manufacturing errors may only exist in items made during a specific time period, either because of unknown problems with material quality or mistakes made by people newly assigned to a step in the process. In software systems, the equivalent of manufacturing errors is the small chance that, when disk or tape copies of programs are made for distribution, errors will be introduced. This seldom occurs, however, and is not a problem that should be a major concern to the analyst.

Hardware failures occur as equipment is used and begins to wear out. There is no equivalent in software. That is, we do not find software unusable because it is worn out. The medium on which it is carried (such as magnetic tape or disk) may become worn or damaged, but the software will not.

Therefore, the primary software problem is designing and developing software that will not fail. Remember it is impossible to prove that there are no errors in a particular system.

The causes of errors that interest the analyst are (1) not getting the right requirements, (2) not getting the requirements right, and (3) not translating the requirements in a clear and understandable manner so that programmers implement them properly.

The earlier chapters on systems analysis describe the methods for conducting an effective systems study and identifying the right requirements. The design techniques and guidelines for output, input, file, and processing design will, properly applied, ensure that the requirements are right.

The transition from systems design to software development is an additional opportunity for introducing errors. They are called *translation errors* and are the result of the programmer not properly understanding or interpreting the design specifications produced by analysts. Conversely, they also occur when analysts force programmers to translate specifications that are incomplete. In the latter case, the programmer is forced to make design decisions while coding the software.

When misunderstandings exist and implementation occurs before they are detected, maintenance needs result. Of course, this is not the only reason systems maintenance occurs, as the next section discusses.

Systems Maintenance

When systems are installed, they generally are used for long periods of time. The average life of a system is 4 to 6 years, with the oldest applications often in use for over 10 years. However, this period of use brings with it the need to continually maintain the system. Because of the use a system receives after it is fully implemented, analysts must take precautions to ensure that the *need* for maintenance is controlled through design and testing and the *ability* to perform it is provided through proper design practices.

ISSUES IN MAINTENANCE

Many private, university, and government studies have been conducted to learn about maintenance requirements for information systems. The studies have generally concluded that:

1 From 60 to 90 percent of the overall cost of software during the life of a system is spent on maintenance (Figure 12.1).
2 Often maintenance is not done very efficiently. In documented cases, the cost of maintenance when measured on a per instruction basis is more than 50 times the cost of developing it in the first place (Boehm).
3 Software demand is growing at a faster rate than supply. Many programmers are spending more time on systems maintenance than on new development. Studies have documented that in some sites, two-thirds of the programmers are spending their time on the maintenance of software (GSA). There is a backlog of new development work. Moreover, there is a *hidden backlog,* requests for development work that users will not bother even to submit because they know it will be years before development can begin.

Several studies of maintenance have examined the type of tasks performed under maintenance (Lientz, Swanson, and Tompkins). Table 12.2

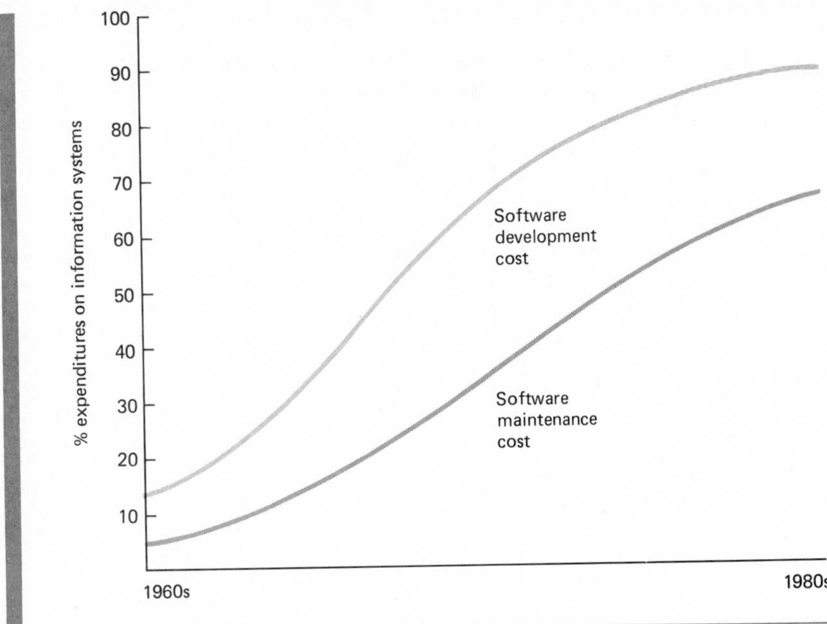

Figure 12.1. Trends in software and maintenance costs.

summarizes the broad classes of maintenance found in information systems environments. Once systems are installed, debugging and correcting errors or failures on an emergency basis is comparatively low: less than one-fifth of the tasks are for correction.

Information systems and the organizations they serve are in a constant state of flux. Therefore the maintenance of systems also involves adaptations of earlier versions of the software. Approximately one-fifth of all maintenance is performed to accommodate changes in reports, files, and data. This statistic also includes adaptations required when new hardware or software is installed in a particular processing center.

The greatest amount of maintenance work is for user enhancement, improved documentation, or recoding systems components for greater efficiency. Sixty percent of all maintenance is for this purpose. Yet, many of the tasks in this category can be avoided if systems engineering is carried out properly.

TABLE 12.2

TYPES OF SYSTEM MAINTENANCE

CATEGORY	ACTIVITY	RELATIVE FREQUENCY
CORRECTIVE	Emergency fixes, routine debugging	20%
ADAPTIVE	Accommodation of changes to data and files, and to hardware and system software	20%
PERFECTIVE	User enhancement, improved documentation, recoding for computational efficiency	60%

DESIGNING FOR MAINTAINABILITY

The keys to reducing the need for maintenance, while making it possible to do essential tasks more efficiently, are:

1 More accurately defining user requirements during systems development
2 Assembling better systems documentation
3 Using more effective methods for designing processing logic and communicating it to project team members
4 Making better use of existing tools and techniques
5 Managing the systems engineering process effectively

Design, as indicated by the above comments, is both a process and a product. The design practices followed for software dramatically affect the maintainability of a system: good design practices produce a product that can be maintained.

Design Practices

A well-structured design will meet the requirements outlined above. A *structured system* is one that is developed from the top down and modular. The modules themselves are relatively simple. This means that they have minimal effect on other modules in the system. The connections between modules are limited and the interaction of data is minimal.

TOP-DOWN STRUCTURE

Top-down methods are used throughout the analysis and design process. During the analysis stage, the value of using a top-down approach, starting at the general levels to gain an understanding of the system and gradually moving down to levels of greater detail, was discussed. In the process of moving from the top downward, each component was "exploded" into greater detail. One data flow diagram became several at the next lower level (Figure 12.2).

During the discussion of input and menu design, a top-down approach was also emphasized. The main menu contains several choices. Making one choice produces another menu, where more detailed options are presented to the user. This capability provides users with an easy-to-understand method for using the system and selecting options. They do not have to make all decisions together but instead can make one at a time.

The top-down method is also widely used in systems engineering and software design. Each function the system will perform is first identified and then developed in greater detail.

For example, an accounting system consists of many separate modules that are invoked one at a time as users indicate the particular function they wish to perform (Figure 12.3). Each upper-level module in turn leads to

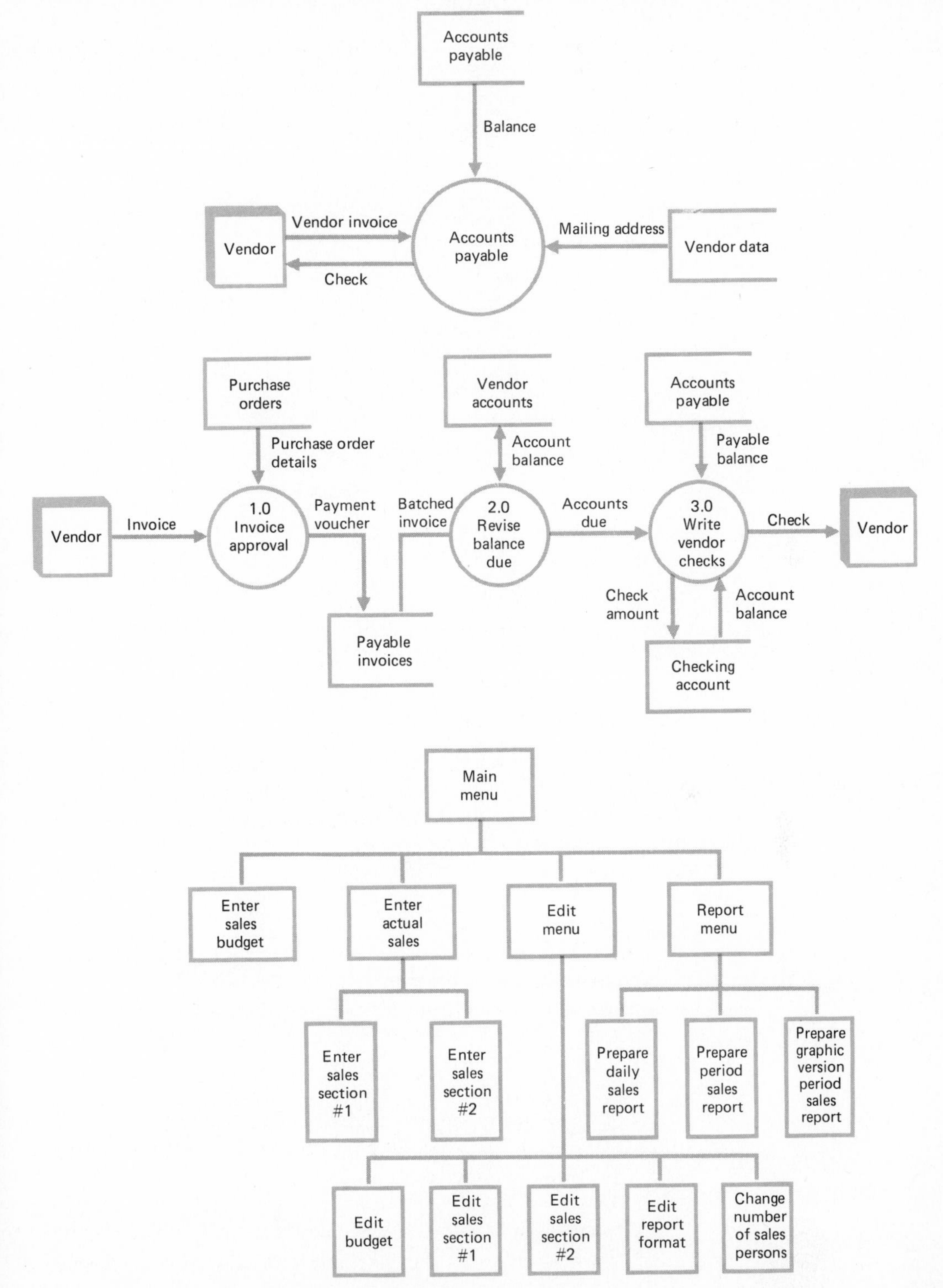

Figure 12.2. Top-down methods.

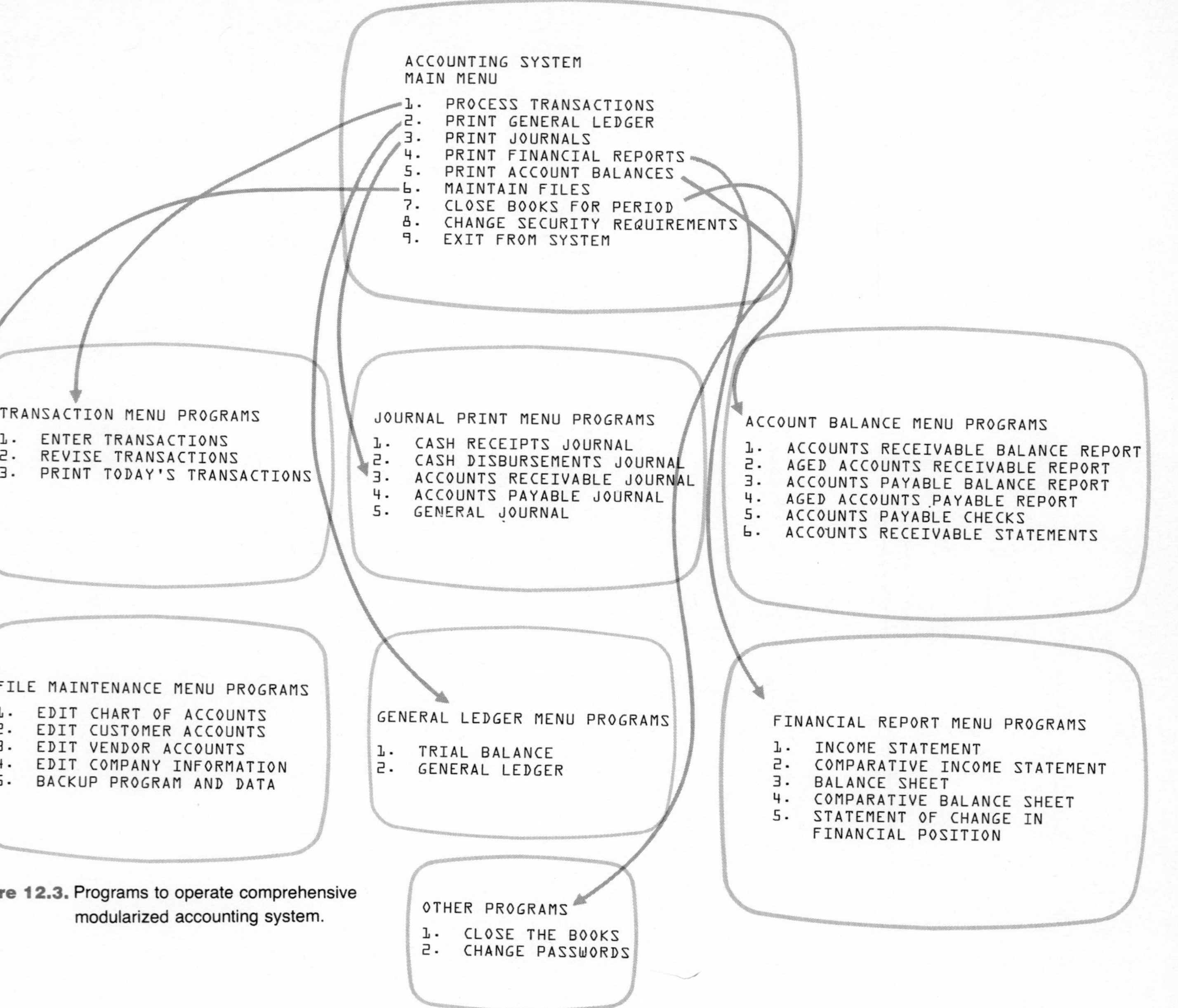

ACCOUNTING SYSTEM
MAIN MENU
1. PROCESS TRANSACTIONS
2. PRINT GENERAL LEDGER
3. PRINT JOURNALS
4. PRINT FINANCIAL REPORTS
5. PRINT ACCOUNT BALANCES
6. MAINTAIN FILES
7. CLOSE BOOKS FOR PERIOD
8. CHANGE SECURITY REQUIREMENTS
9. EXIT FROM SYSTEM
TRANSACTION MENU PROGRAMS
1. ENTER TRANSACTIONS
2. REVISE TRANSACTIONS
3. PRINT TODAY'S TRANSACTIONS
JOURNAL PRINT MENU PROGRAMS
1. CASH RECEIPTS JOURNAL
2. CASH DISBURSEMENTS JOURNAL
3. ACCOUNTS RECEIVABLE JOURNAL
4. ACCOUNTS PAYABLE JOURNAL
5. GENERAL JOURNAL
ACCOUNT BALANCE MENU PROGRAMS
1. ACCOUNTS RECEIVABLE BALANCE REPORT
2. AGED ACCOUNTS RECEIVABLE REPORT
3. ACCOUNTS PAYABLE BALANCE REPORT
4. AGED ACCOUNTS PAYABLE REPORT
5. ACCOUNTS PAYABLE CHECKS
6. ACCOUNTS RECEIVABLE STATEMENTS
FILE MAINTENANCE MENU PROGRAMS
1. EDIT CHART OF ACCOUNTS
2. EDIT CUSTOMER ACCOUNTS
3. EDIT VENDOR ACCOUNTS
4. EDIT COMPANY INFORMATION
5. BACKUP PROGRAM AND DATA
GENERAL LEDGER MENU PROGRAMS
1. TRIAL BALANCE
2. GENERAL LEDGER
FINANCIAL REPORT MENU PROGRAMS
1. INCOME STATEMENT
2. COMPARATIVE INCOME STATEMENT
3. BALANCE SHEET
4. COMPARATIVE BALANCE SHEET
5. STATEMENT OF CHANGE IN
FINANCIAL POSITION
OTHER PROGRAMS
1. CLOSE THE BOOKS
2. CHANGE PASSWORDS

Figure 12.3. Programs to operate comprehensive modularized accounting system.

using one of several lower-level modules until the desired function is performed.

MODULARITY

Using the top-down approach to planning the software for a system is no guarantee that errors will be avoided or that the system will be maintainable. In properly modularized systems, the contents of the module are so designed that they perform a specific function and are more easily understood by people than systems designed by other methods. There are four general types of module contents (Table 12.3), which are discussed below in order of most to least desirable (Stevens, Myers, and Constantine).

Module contents are not related to each other. The least-desirable type of grouping consists of steps that do not perform any complete function or that do not logically go together. This extreme case can arise if programmers work to strict rules and divide modules into sections of 50 statements each (or some other imposed limit). Thus input, output, calculation, and file-handling activities are performed in a single module. If this case occurs, it is usually created by the programmer working without explicit design specifications or a clear understanding of how to handle a task.

Module contents may also be grouped together because they logically go together. If analysts specify a module that handles all input or all output operations or one that handles all order-processing activities regardless of type of customer or data-handling needs for each customer, they are using logical grouping.

The elements may also be related by the *time* at which they are performed. That is, they logically seem to go together and are performed at

TABLE 12.3

TYPES OF PROGRAM MODULE GROUPINGS

	CONTENTS OF MODULE	EXPLANATION
BEST	Module Contents Determined by Function Performed	All activities in a module have the same single purpose, i.e., perform a single function. Examples: calculate finance charge on an account balance; edit a transaction.
↕	Module Contents Determined by Data Used	All elements in the module refer to the same data or files. Examples: printing, displaying, and copying data from a common file.
	Module Contents Determined by Logic of Processing	All steps are performed together or handle the same functions. Examples: all input operations, all output operations, and all initialization activities.
WORST	Module Contents Not Closely Related	Modules are developed by size or number of instructions (results from programming to rule). Examples: all modules are no more than 50 statements in length; all modules must fit on a single page.

the same time. If the analysts specify a module that initializes all variables and opens files, it is logically bound. This level of modularity is better than the first type because all the elements are executable at one time.

Modules that are logically bound are difficult to modify because the cost will be shared for each type of activity. Even the simplest change can affect all types of transactions. A better solution is to separate each type of transaction into its own module.

Module contents may also be determined by the data used. A module in which the contents refer to the same data is better than one that is developed only on the basis of processing logic. For example, a module may be designed so all operations on a set of data are performed at one time: a file is prepared to be printed on paper, spooled to disk, and also duplicated for backup purposes. A module that reads the next transaction and updates the master file by adding, deleting, or changing records, including the error checking required for each type of function, shares a common set of data. This type of binding is better than the other types discussed, but it is not as good as functional grouping.

Functional grouping occurs when all elements of a module have a single goal or function. The design objective is to attain modules with functional contents. If modules have only a single function, it is easy to determine whether the module is performing its function properly. Functional grouping also permits more thorough testing of the module. If changes are needed at a later time, analysts and programmers can quickly determine how the module is constructed, processes data, and interacts with other modules in the system.

The emphasis on reliability and maintainability is constant throughout systems development.

SOFTWARE DESIGN AND DOCUMENTATION TOOLS

Well-designed, modular software is more likely to meet the maintenance, reliability, and testing requirements outlined in this chapter. Three specific tools are discussed in this section: structured flowcharts, HIPO diagrams, and Warnier/Orr diagrams.

Structured Flowcharts

Structured flowcharts, also called *Nassi Schneiderman charts,* are graphic tools that force the designer to structure software that is both modular and top-down. It provides a structure that can be retained by programmers who develop the application software. Organization responsibilities vary. In some organizations, analysts are responsible for developing module logic, while in others that responsibility is delegated to the programmer. In either case, the programmer should be well versed on the use of structured flowcharts.

BASIC ELEMENTS

There are three basic elements used in developing structured flowcharts: process, decision, and iteration. (There are many similarities between these elements and the components used in structured English. See Chapter 5.)

Process

Simple processes or steps in a program are represented by a rectangular box, the *process symbol.* This symbol represents initialization of values, input and output activities, and calls to execute other procedures.

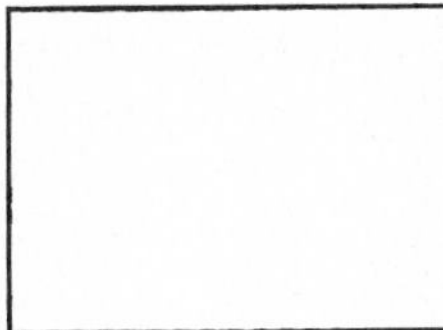

A name or brief description written in the box states the purpose of the process. The succession of steps is shown using several process boxes.

Decision

The decision symbol represents alternative conditions that can occur for which the program must have a manner of handling them. They show the equivalent of the IF-THEN-ELSE structures discussed under structured English and common in many programming languages. As examples will show, the decision symbol may show actions for more than two alternatives at the same time.

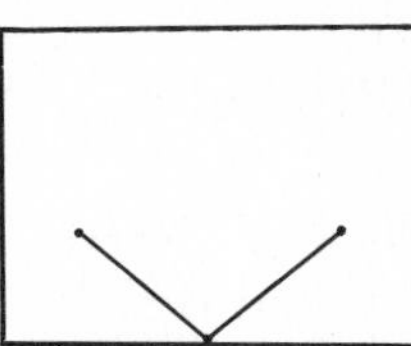

Iteration

The iteration symbol represents looping and repetition of operations *while* a certain condition exists or *until* a condition exists. The form of the iteration symbol clearly shows the scope of the iteration, including all processes and decisions that are contained within the loop. The left-hand portion of the symbol shows the path of repetition to follow until the conditions controlling the iteration are satisfied.

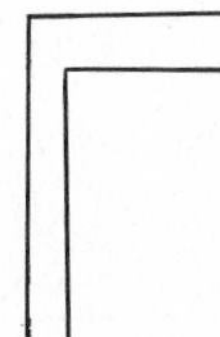

USING STRUCTURED FLOWCHARTS

Structured flowcharts use no arrows or continuations on separate pages. Each structured flowchart is shown on a single sheet of paper (or single display screen if developed on-line).

When designing a structured flowchart, the analyst specifies the logic in a top-down fashion. The first consideration in a process or decision is the top element. The second in sequence is the next one shown, and so forth. Similarly, there is a single exit from the process.

The analyst begins with a major process and introduces other symbols to subdivide the process. Each process is named, but, if the name is not underlined, it is a reference to some other diagram or description. This simple convention makes it possible to link together easily different procedures that are performed to complete an entire activity.

Figure 12.4 shows the steps needed to produce customer invoices during a monthly processing cycle. The structure chart reads from top to bottom and left to right. Each activity is nested within the iteration and alternative processes of which it is a part. In addition, each condition is clearly shown.

Individual parts of processes are often further described in lower-level diagrams. For example, the purchase, payment, debit, and credit transactions are identified in the module described in Figure 12.4, but individual modules are referenced to handle the processing for each type of transaction.

MONTHLY INVOICE PROCESSING

DO MONTHLY FOR EACH CUSTOMER:

Clear purchases, payments, current balance,

print month name, beginning balance.

DO FOR EACH TRANSACTION:

Print date of preparation,

old transaction date ← transaction date

End of transaction = false

Do for each transaction record

Case of transaction

Purchase	Payment	Debit	Credit
Cust. purch. = cust. purch. + amt.	Cust. pay. = cust. pay. + amt.		
Curr. bal. = curr. bal. + amt.	Curr. bal. = curr. bal. – amt.	Curr. bal. = curr. bal. + amt.	Curr. bal. = curr. bal. – amt.

Get next transaction record

Print curr. bal., cust. purch., cust. pay.

Beg. balance ← current balance

Figure 12.4. Structure chart for monthly invoicing.

An important use of structured flowcharts for the designer concerned about verifying systems specifications against planned software logic is to identify conditions and procedures followed when the conditions exist. The fact that the structure chart is easy to read will enable the analyst to determine whether the debit adjustment transaction, for example, has been added by the programmer or is a part of the original systems specifications.

HIPO

HIPO is another commonly used method for developing systems software. An acronym for *hierarchial input process output,* this method was developed by IBM for its large, complex operating systems.

PURPOSE

The assumption on which HIPO is based is that it is easy to lose track of the intended function of a system or component in a large system. This is one reason why it is difficult to compare existing systems against their original specifications (and therefore why failures can occur even in systems that are technically well-formulated). Single functions from the user's view often may extend across several modules. The concern of the analyst then is understanding, describing, and documenting the modules and their interaction in a way that provides sufficient detail but does not lose sight of the larger picture.

HIPO diagrams are graphic, rather than prose or narrative, descriptions of the system. They assist the analyst in answering three guiding questions:

1 *What* does the system or module do? (Asked when designing the system.)
2 *How* does it do it? (Asked when reviewing the code for testing or maintenance.)
3 *What* are the inputs and outputs? (Asked when reviewing the code for testing or maintenance.)

A HIPO description for a system consists of the visual table of contents and the functional diagrams.

VISUAL TABLE OF CONTENTS

The *visual table of contents* (or *VTOC*) shows the relation between each of the documents making up a HIPO package. It consists of a hierarchy chart that identifies the modules in a system by number and in relation to each other (Figure 12.5) and gives a brief description of each module. The numbers in the contents section correspond to those in the organization section.

The modules are in increasing detail. Depending on the complexity of the system, three to five levels of modules are typical.

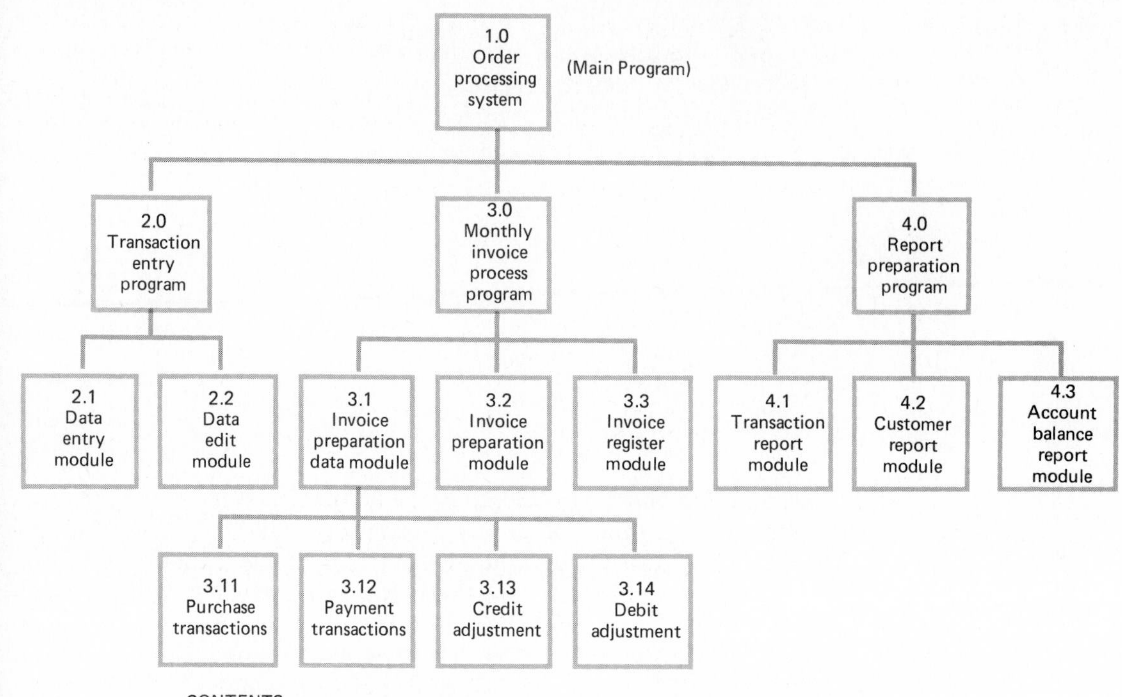

CONTENTS

1.0 ORDER PROCESSING SYSTEMS (MAIN PROGRAM)
Controls all processing. Invokes programs to handle data entry, monthly processing of records, and and printing of reports.

2.0 TRANSACTION ENTRY PROGRAM
Controls all data entry and editing of data already stored. Includes purchase, payment, and adjustment function data.

2.1 DATA ENTRY MODULE
Performs entry and validation of input data for purchases, payments, and credit or debit adjustments.

2.2 DATA EDIT MODULE
Performs retrieval and editing of previously stored transaction data for purchases, payments, and credit or debit adjustments. Allows changes to data or deletion or transaction record.

3.0 MONTHLY INVOICE PROCESS PROGRAM
Controls all invoice processing steps using transaction data entered during month

3.1 INVOICE PREPARATION DATA MODULE
Performs monthly processing of transaction data to prepare for printing of invoices. Calls separate modules for handling purchase, payment, and adjustment transactions.

3.2 INVOICE PREPARATION MODULE
Prints invoices on preprinted statement forms. Must be done only after invoice data has been prepared by module 3.1.

3.3 INVOICE REGISTER MODULE
Prints a detailed journal of invoices by number in ascending order. Must be done only after invoice data has been prepared by module 3.1.

4.0 REPORT PREPARATION PROGRAM
Controls all report printing for transaction, customer, and account balance reports.

4.1 TRANSACTION REPORT MODULE
Prints a detailed listing of all transactions entered during month in order of assigned transaction number.

4.2 CUSTOMER REPORT MODULE
Prints listing of all customers and demographic information in alphabetical and account number order.

4.3 ACCOUNT BALANCE REPORT MODULE
Prints listing of all accounts with nonzero balance in descending order. Includes aging information.

Figure 12.5. HIPO visual table of contents.

FUNCTIONAL DIAGRAMS

use on the lowest level only!

There is one diagram for each box in the VTOC. Each diagram shows input and output (right to left or top to bottom), major processes, movement of data, and control points. Traditional flowchart symbols represent media, such as punched cards, magnetic tape, magnetic disk, and printed output. A solid arrow shows control paths, and an open arrow identifies data flow.

The illustration in Figure 12.5 is an overview of the system, representing the top-level box in the VTOC. The numbers on the lower portion of the diagram indicate where more detail will be found; that is, they reference to other document numbers. For instance, document 3.11 will explain the purchase transaction process in greater detail.

Some functional diagrams will contain other intermediate diagrams (Figure 12.6). But they also show external data, as well as internally developed data (such as tables in the invoice example) and the step in the procedure where the data is used. A data dictionary description can be attached to further explain the data elements used in a process.

HIPO diagrams are effective for documenting a system. They also aid designers and force them to think about how specifications will be met and where activities and components must be linked together. However, they

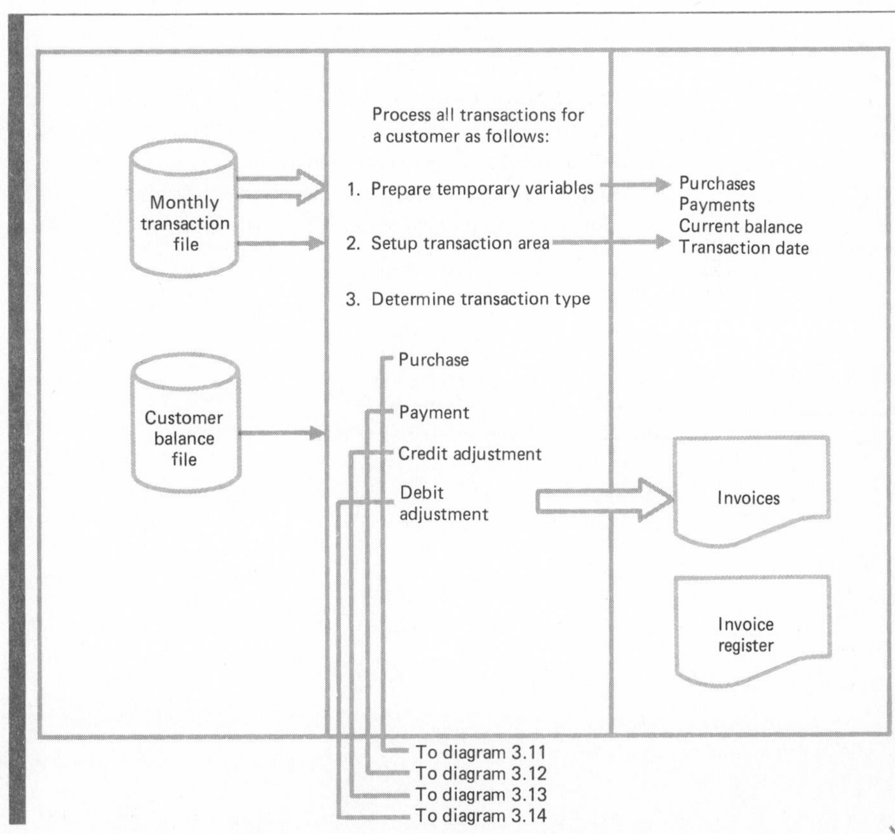

Figure 12.6. HIPO functional diagram for monthly invoice processing.

X

rely on a set of specialized symbols that need explanation to use, an extra concern when compared to the simplicity of, for example, data flow diagrams. They are not as easy to use for communication purposes as many would like. And, of course, they do not guarantee error-free systems. Hence, their greatest strength is the documentation of a system.

Warnier/Orr Diagrams

Warnier/Orr diagrams (also known as *logical construction of programs/ logical construction of systems)* were initially developed in France by Jean-Dominique Warnier and in the United States by Kenneth Orr. This method aids the design of program structures by identifying the output and processing results and then working backwards to determine the steps and combinations of input needed to produce them. The simple graphic methods used in Warnier/Orr diagrams make the levels in the system evident and the movement of the data between them vivid.

BASIC ELEMENTS

Warnier/Orr diagrams show the processes and sequences in which they are performed. Each process is defined in a hierarchial manner. That is, it consists of sets of subprocesses that define it. At each level, the process is shown in a bracket that groups its components (Figure 12.7). Since a process may have many different subprocesses, a Warnier/Orr diagram is a set of brackets that shows each level of the system.

Critical factors in software definition and development are iteration or repetition and alternation. Warnier/Orr diagrams show this very well. For example, in developing an invoicing system, there are processes that occur for each transaction, each day, and each month. As shown in Figure 12.8,

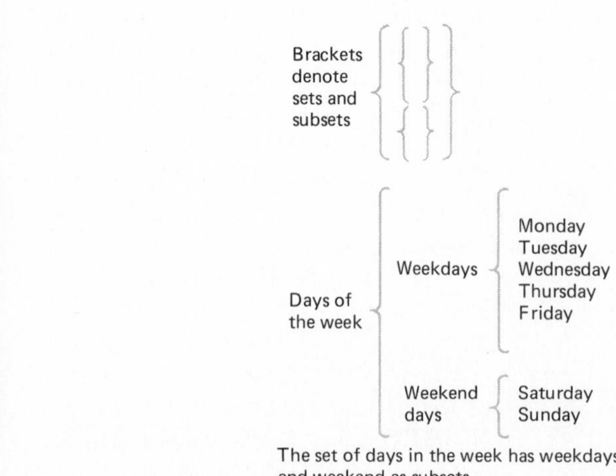

Figure 12.7. Set notation used in Warnier/Orr diagrams.

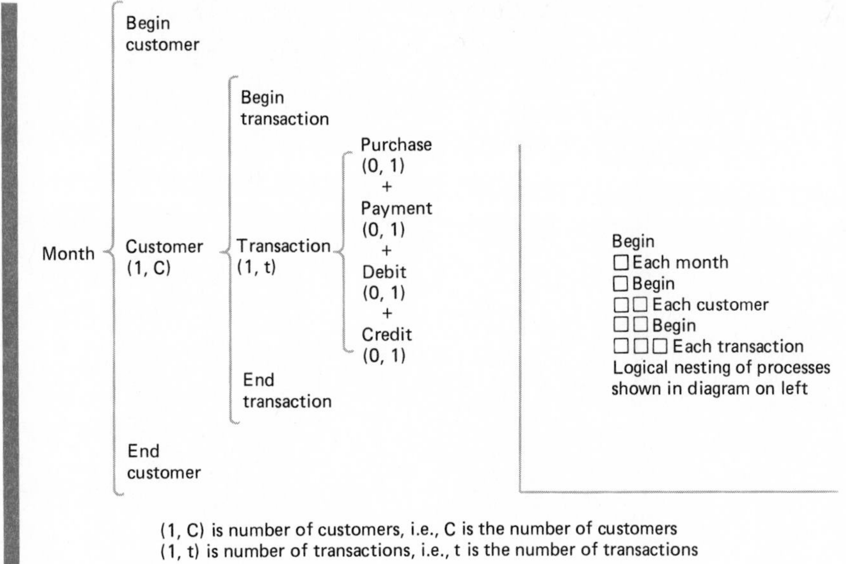
Begin customer
Begin transaction
Purchase (0, 1)
+
Payment (0, 1)
+
Month
Customer (1, C)
Transaction (1, t)
Debit (0, 1)
+
Credit (0, 1)
End transaction
End customer
Begin
□Each month
□Begin
□□Each customer
□□Begin
□□□Each transaction
Logical nesting of processes shown in diagram on left
(1, C) is number of customers, i.e., C is the number of customers
(1, t) is number of transactions, i.e., t is the number of transactions

Figure 12.8. Processes in monthly invoice processing.

the repetition of each case is not only easy to identify but also quickly placed in a logical sequence.

In some situations, the only concern is whether a certain characteristic is present. The alternatives are that it is or it is not. The notation used to indicate that a condition does not exist is a single line over the condition name. For example, in Figure 12.9, the four transaction types of purchase, payment, debit adjustment, and credit adjustment are alternatives. The symbol "+" represents alternatives.

USING WARNIER/ORR DIAGRAMS

The ability to show the relation between processes and steps in a process is not unique to Warnier/Orr diagrams, nor is the use of iteration, alternation, or treatment of individual cases. Both the structured-flowcharts and structured-English methods do this equally well. However, the approach used to develop systems definitions with Warnier/Orr diagrams is different and fits well with those used in logical systems design.

To develop a Warnier/Orr diagram, the analyst works backwards, starting with systems output. That is, this method uses an output-oriented analysis. On paper, the development moves from left to right. First the intended output or results of processing are defined. At the next level, shown by inclusion within a bracket, the steps needed to produce the output are defined. Each step in turn is further defined. Additional brackets group the processes required to produce the result on the next level.

A completed Warnier/Orr diagram includes both process groupings and data requirements. As indicated in Figure 12.9, data elements are listed for

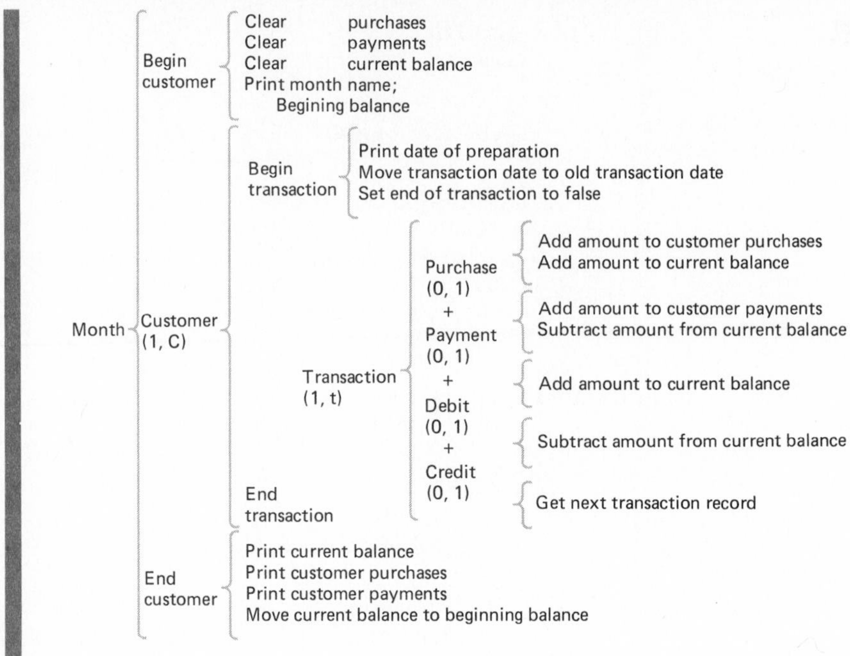

Figure 12.9. Data used in monthly invoice processing.

each process or process component. These data elements are the ones needed to determine which alternative or case should be handled by the system and to carry out the process. The analyst must determine where each data element originates, how it is used, and how individual elements are combined. When the definition is completed, a data structure for each process is documented. It, in turn, is used by the programmers, who work from the diagrams to code the software.

Warnier/Orr diagrams offer distinct advantages to systems experts. They are simple in appearance and easy to understand. Yet they are powerful design tools. They have the advantage of showing groupings of processes and the data that must be passed from level to level. In addition, the sequence of working backwards ensures that the system will be result-oriented. It is also a natural process. With structured flowcharts, for example, it is often necessary to determine the innermost steps before iterations and modularity issues can be addressed.

This method is useful for both data and process definition. It can be used for each independently, or both can be combined on the same diagram, as we did in the above example.

A powerful feature of Warnier/Orr diagrams is the way cycles are shown. The steps required to move from month to month in processing invoices, for example, are addressed in the diagram. The processing steps and report-preparation steps are clearly depicted, so that the individual using the diagram can readily visualize when steps are executed and what items are prepared to finish one monthly cycle and prepare for the next one. This aspect of systems processing is a critical one in a quality system.

QUALITY ASSURANCE

The techniques and guidelines introduced in the preceding section will, properly applied, produce well-designed, low-failure systems. However, even if the techniques are followed carefully, the analyst must not assume that necessary quality standards have been met.

Quality assurance is the review of software products and related documentation for completeness, correctness, reliability, and maintainability. And it, of course, includes assurance that the system meets the specifications and requirements for its intended use and performance.

Levels of Assurance

Analysts use four levels of quality assurance: testing, verification, validation, and certification.

TESTING

Systems testing is an expensive, but critical, process that may take as much as 50 percent of the budget for program development. The common view of testing is that it is performed to prove that there are no errors in a program. However, as indicated earlier, this is virtually impossible since analysts cannot prove that software is free and clear of errors.

Therefore, the most useful and practical approach is with the understanding that *testing* is the process of executing a program with the explicit intention of finding errors, that is, making the program fail. The testor, who may be an analyst, programmer, or specialist trained in software testing, is actually trying to make the program fail. A successful test, then, is one that finds an error.

Analysts know that an effective testing program does not guarantee systems reliability. Reliability is a design issue, as discussed earlier in this chapter. Therefore, reliability must be designed into the system. Developers cannot test for it. Later in this section, specific testing strategies will be discussed.

VERIFICATION AND VALIDATION

Like testing, *verification* is also intended to find errors. It is performed by executing a program in a simulated environment. *Validation* refers to the process of using software in a live environment in order to find errors.

When commercial systems are developed with the explicit intention of distributing them to dealers for sale or marketing them through company-owned field offices, they first go through verification, sometimes called *alpha testing*. The feedback from the validation phase generally produces changes in the software to deal with errors and failures that are uncovered. Then a set of user sites is selected that put the system into use on a live basis. These *beta test* sites use the system in day-to-day activities; they process live transactions and produce normal system output. The system is live in every sense of the word, except that the users are aware they are using a system that can fail. But the transactions that are entered and the persons using the system are real.

Validation may continue for several months. During the course of validating the system, failure may occur and the software will be changed. Continued use may produce additional failures and the need for still more changes.

CERTIFICATION

Software *certification* is an endorsement of the correctness of the program. This is an issue that is rising in importance for information systems applications. There is an increasing dependence on the purchase or lease of commercial software rather than on its in-house development. However, before analysts are willing to approve the acquisition of a package, they often require certification by the developer or an unbiased third party.

For example, selected accounting firms are now certifying that a software package in fact does what the vendor claims it does and in a proper manner. To so certify the software, the agency appoints a team of specialists who carefully examine the documentation for the system to determine what the vendor claims the system does and how it is accomplished. Then they test the software against those claims. If no serious discrepancies or failures are encountered, they will certify that the software does what the documentation claims (Figure 12.10). They do not, however, certify that the software is the right package for a certain organization. That responsibility remains with the organization and its team of analysts.

Testing Strategies

We have already indicated that the philosophy behind testing is to find errors. Test cases are devised with this purpose in mind. A *test case* is a set of data that the system will process as normal input. However, the data is created with the express intent of determining whether the system will process it correctly. For example, test cases for inventory handling should include situations where the quantities to be withdrawn from inventory exceed, equal, and are less than the actual quantities on hand. Each test case is designed with the intent of finding errors in the way the system will process it.

There are two general strategies for testing software. This section examines both, the strategies of code testing and specification testing.

CODE TESTING

The *code-testing* strategy examines the logic of the program. To follow this testing method, the analyst develops test cases that result in executing every instruction in the program or module. That is, every path through the program is tested. A *path* is a specific combination of conditions. For example, in the accounting systems example, one path through the system

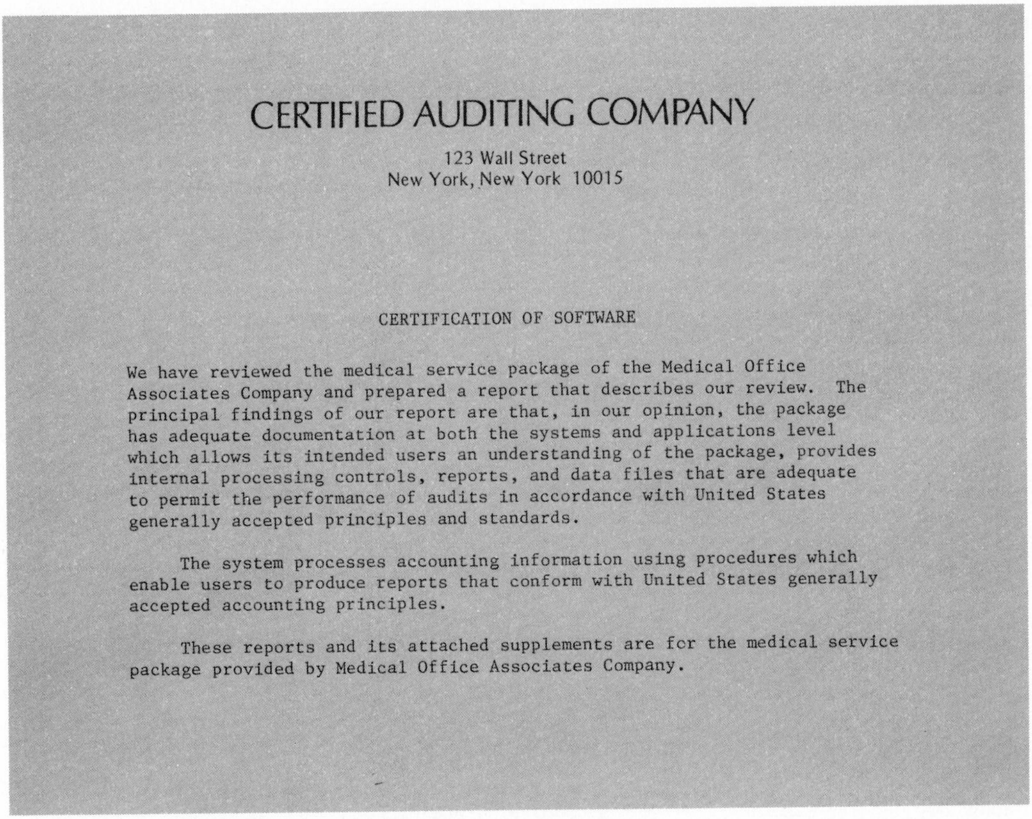

CERTIFIED AUDITING COMPANY

123 Wall Street
New York, New York 10015

CERTIFICATION OF SOFTWARE

We have reviewed the medical service package of the Medical Office Associates Company and prepared a report that describes our review. The principal findings of our report are that, in our opinion, the package has adequate documentation at both the systems and applications level which allows its intended users an understanding of the package, provides internal processing controls, reports, and data files that are adequate to permit the performance of audits in accordance with United States generally accepted principles and standards.

The system processes accounting information using procedures which enable users to produce reports that conform with United States generally accepted accounting principles.

These reports and its attached supplements are for the medical service package provided by Medical Office Associates Company.

Figure 12.10. Software certification statement.

is to change the account balances. The correct request is submitted, then proper passwords, data, and command entries (Figure 12.11).

On the surface, code testing seems to be an ideal method for testing software. The rationale that all software errors can be uncovered by checking every path in a program, however, is faulty. First of all, in even moderately large programs of the size used in typical business situations, it is virtually impossible to do exhaustive testing of this nature. Financial and time limitations alone will usually preclude executing every path through a program since there may be several thousand.

However, even if code testing can be performed in its entirety, it does not guarantee against software failures. This testing strategy does not indicate whether the code meets its specifications nor does it determine whether all aspects are even implemented. Code testing also does not check the range of data that the program will accept even though, when software failures occur in actual use, it is frequently because users submitted data outside of expected ranges (for example, a sales order for $1 million—the largest in the history of the organization).

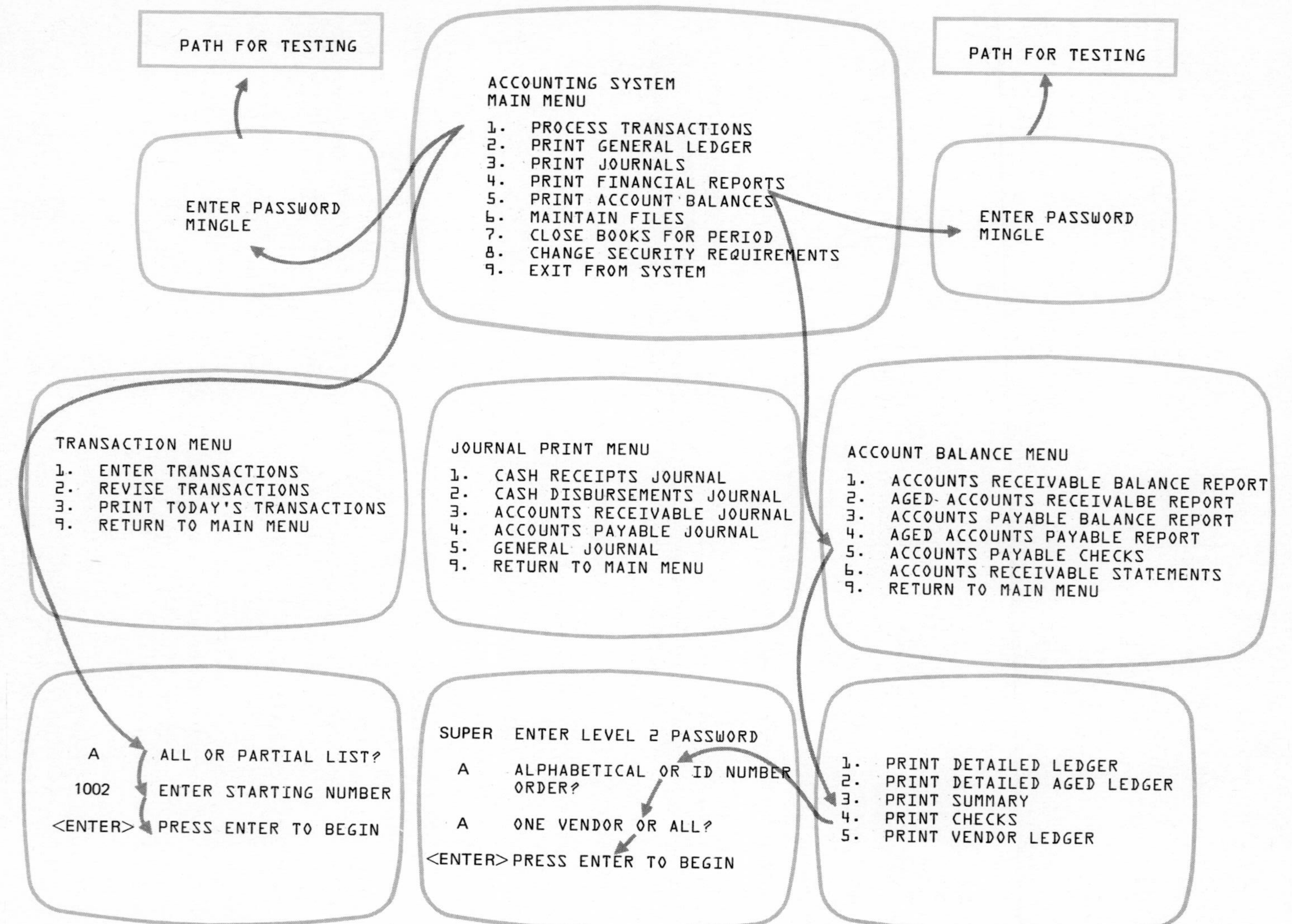

Figure 12.11. Data to test multiple paths through accounting system.

SPECIFICATION TESTING

To perform *specification testing,* the analyst examines the specifications stating what the program should do and how it should perform under various conditions. Then test cases are developed for each condition or combination of conditions and submitted for processing. By examining the results, the analyst can determine whether the program performs according to its specified requirements.

This strategy treats the program like a black box. That is, the analyst does not look into the program to study the code and is not concerned about whether every instruction or path through the program is tested. In that sense it is not complete testing. However, the assumption is that, if the program meets the specifications, it will not fail.

Neither testing strategy is ideal. However, specification testing is a better strategy since it focuses on the way software is expected to be used. It also shows once again how important the specifications developed by the analysts are throughout the entire systems development process.

TESTING PRACTICES

Regardless of which strategy the analyst follows, there are preferred practices to ensure that the testing is useful. The levels of tests and types of test data coupled with testing libraries are important aspects of the actual test process.

Levels of Tests

Systems are not designed as entire systems nor are they tested as single systems. The analyst must perform both unit and system testing.

UNIT TESTING

In unit testing the analyst tests the programs making up a system. (For this reason it is sometimes called *program testing* in contrast to systems testing, discussed in the next section.) The software units in a system are the modules and routines that are assembled and integrated to perform a specific function. In a large system, many modules at different levels are needed.

Unit testing focuses first on the modules, independently of one another, to locate errors. This enables the testor to detect errors in coding and logic that are contained within that module alone. Those resulting from the interaction between modules are initially avoided.

For example, a hotel information system consists of modules to handle reservations; guest checkin and checkout; restaurant, room service, and miscellaneous charges; convention activities; and accounts receivable billing. For each, it provides the ability to enter, change, or retrieve data and respond to inquiries or print reports.

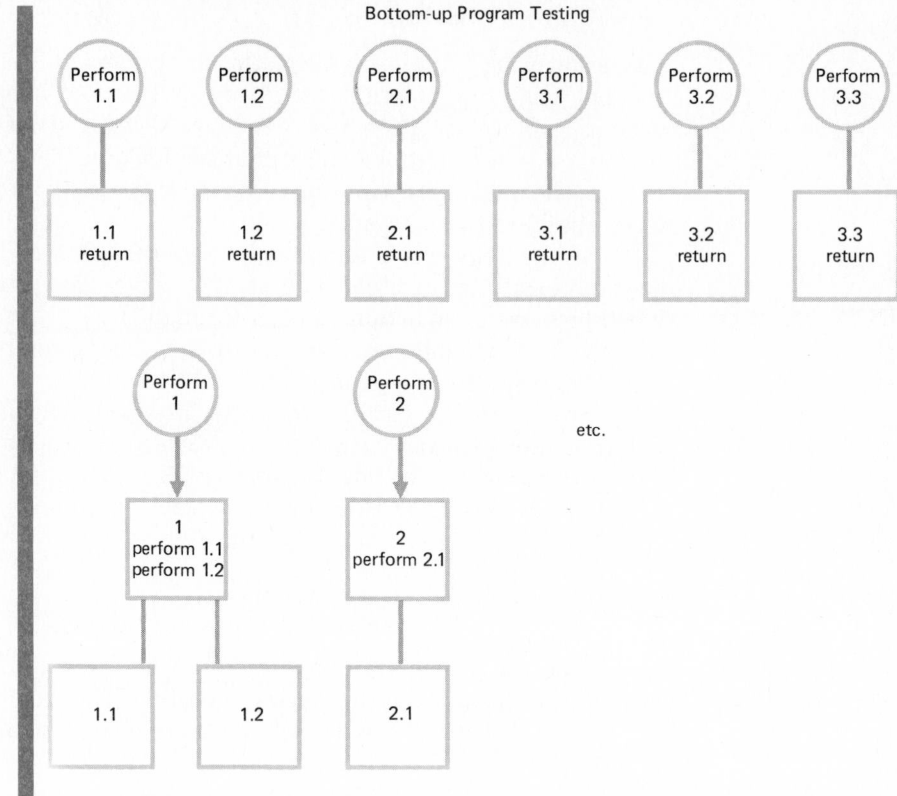

Figure 12.12. Alternate methods for unit testing.

The test cases needed for unit testing should exercise each condition and option. For example, test cases are needed to determine how the system handles attempts to check in guests who do and do not have reservations, as well as those who are changing the name on the reservation when a different person arrives than the one listed. Test cases for the checkout situations of paying the exact amount of the bill, only part of the bill, and more than the amount shown are also needed. Even checking out without making any payment at all must be included in a test case.

If the module receives input or generates output, test cases are also needed to test the range of values expected, including both valid and invalid data. What will happen in the hotel checkout example if a guest wishes to make a payment of $150,000 for an upcoming convention? Are the payment and printing modules designed to handle this amount? Testing for this question quickly detects existing errors.

If the module is designed to perform iterations, with specific processes contained within a loop, it is advisable to execute each boundary condition: 0 iterations, 1 iteration through the loop, and the maximum number of iterations through the loop. Of course it is always important to examine the results of testing, but special attention should be given to these conditions.

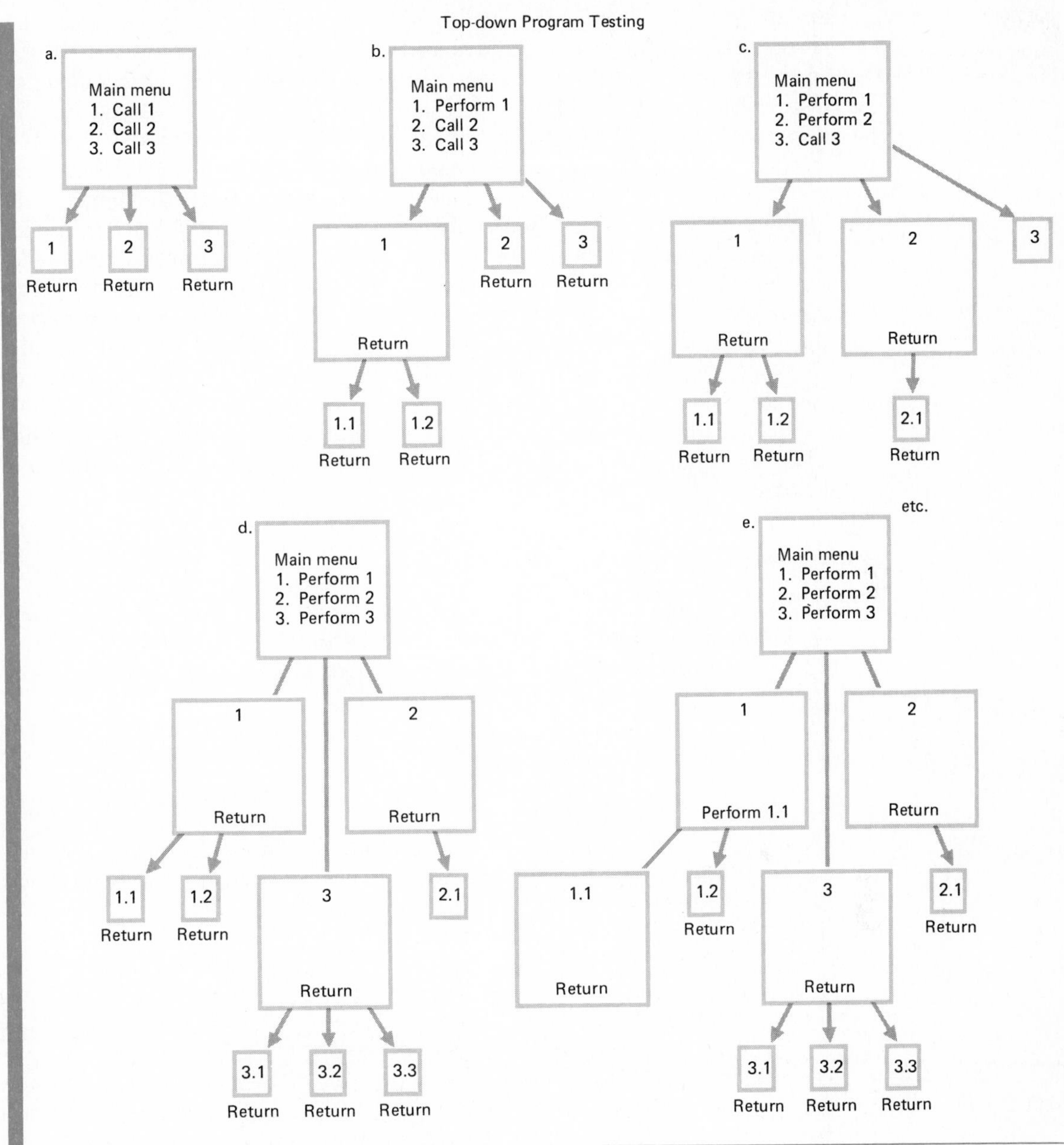

Figure 12.12. (*Continued*)

Analysts too often assume that a case of 0 iterations will automatically be handled properly; unfortunately that is a mistake.

Unit testing can be performed from the bottom up, starting with the smallest and lowest-level modules and proceeding one at a time. For each module in *bottom-up testing,* a short program (called a *driver program* because it drives or runs the module) executes the module and provides the needed data, so that the module is asked to perform in every way it will be when embedded within the larger system. When bottom-level modules are tested, attention turns to those on the next level (Figure 12.12) that use the lower-level ones. They are tested individually and then linked with the previously examined lower-level modules.

Top-down testing, as the name implies, begins with the upper-level modules. However, since the detailed activities usually performed in lower-level routines are not provided (because those routines are not being tested), stubs are written. A *stub* is a module shell that can be called by the upper-level module and, when reached properly, will return a message to the calling module, indicating that proper interaction occurred (Figure 12.13). No attempt is made to verify the correctness of the lower-level module.

Often top-down testing plans are combined with bottom-up testing. That is, some lower-level modules are unit-tested and integrated into a top-down testing program.

SYSTEMS TESTING

Systems testing does not test the software per se but rather the integration of each module in the system. It also tests to find discrepancies between the system and its original objective, current specifications, and systems docu-

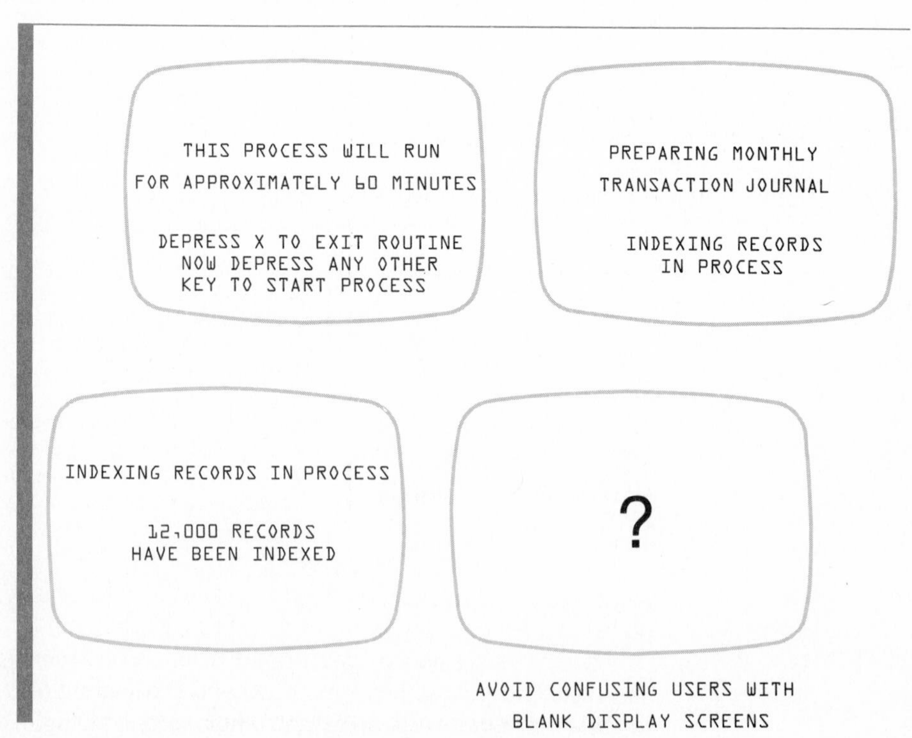

Figure 12.13.
Special system tests.

mentation. The primary concern is the compatibility of individual modules. Analysts are trying to find areas where modules have been designed with different specifications for data length, type, and data element name. For example, one module may expect the data item for customer identification number to be a numeric field, while other modules expect it to be a character data item. The system itself may not report this as an error, but the output may show unexpected results. If a record created and stored in one module, using the identification number as a numeric field, is later sought on retrieval with the expectation that it will be a character field, the field will not be recognized and the message REQUESTED RECORD NOT FOUND will be displayed.

Systems testing must also verify that file sizes are adequate and indices have been built properly. Sorting and reindexing procedures assumed to be present in lower-level modules must be tested at the systems level to see that they in fact exist and achieve the results modules expect.

SPECIAL SYSTEMS TESTS

There are other tests that are in a special category since they do not focus on the normal running of the system. Six tests are essential (Table 12.4).

TABLE 12.4

SPECIAL SYSTEMS TESTS

TYPE OF TEST	DESCRIPTION
PEAK LOAD TEST	Determine whether the system will handle the volume of activities that occur when the system is at the peak of its processing demand. EXAMPLE: All terminals are active at the same time.
STORAGE TESTING	Determine the capacity of the system to store transaction data on a disk or in other files. EXAMPLE: Verify documentation statements that the system will store 10,000 records of 383 bytes length on a single, flexible disk.
PERFORMANCE TIME TESTING	Determine the length of time system used by the system to process transaction data. EXAMPLE: Response time for inquiry when system is fully loaded with operating data.
RECOVERY TESTING	Determine ability of user to recover data or restart system after failure. EXAMPLE: Load backup copy of data and resume processing without data or integrity loss.
PROCEDURE TESTING	Determine clarity of documentation on operation and use of system by having users do exactly what manuals request. EXAMPLE: Powering down system at end of week or responding to paper-out light on printer.
HUMAN FACTORS TESTING	Determine how users will use the system when processing data or preparing reports. EXAMPLE: Activities of user when there is not an immediate response to an inquiry.

Peak Load Testing

There are critical times in many systems, particularly on-line systems. For example, in a banking system, analysts want to know what will happen if all tellers sign on at their terminals at the same time before the start of the 10 a.m. business day. Will the system handle them one at a time without incident, will it attempt to handle all of them at once and be so confused it "locks up" and must be restarted, or will terminal addresses be lost? The only sure way to find out is to test for it. The same situations can arise when tellers sign out during lunch periods and at the end of the day, so testing is looking at real situations.

Storage Testing

Analysts specify a capacity for the system when it is designed and constructed. Capacities are measured in terms of the number of records that a disk will handle or a file can contain. These capacities are linked to disk space and the size of indices, record keys, and so on. But they too must be tested. If the documentation for a new system to be run on a microcomputer claims that a disk file can store up to 10,000 records each 393 bytes long, the claim must be verified before implementation.

Storage testing often requires entering data (see the discussion below on live versus synthetic data) until the capacity is reached. Comparing the actual and claimed capacities will verify the accuracy of the documentation on the one hand and allow a judgment about actual capacity at the same time. Many, many systems are never tested in this way. Users find out too late that claims made during installation are not true: there is not enough storage capacity for transactions and master file records.

Performance Time Testing

When analysts are developing a design, their concerns are more on reports, inputs, files, and processing sequences than on performance time, although this changes with experience. During simple unit and systems testing, relatively small sets of data are used to find errors or cause failures. Therefore, users frequently only find out how slow or fast the response time of the system is after it has been installed and loaded up with data. That may be too late. (Systems are rarely too fast for users.)

Performance time testing is conducted prior to implementation to determine how long it takes to receive a response to an inquiry, make a backup copy of a file, or send a transmission and receive a response. It also includes test runs to time reindexing or resorting of large files of the size the system will have during a typical run or to prepare a report.

A system that runs well with only a handful of test transactions may be unacceptably slow when fully loaded. And the time to know about this is prior to implementation, when adjustments can be more easily made. Once files are fully loaded and the user is relying on the system for daily activities, it is difficult to pull it back and begin large-scale changes. The user needs the system and the analyst will not want to risk the loss of live data.

Recovery Testing

Analysts must always assume that the system will fail and data will be damaged or lost. Even though plans and procedures are written to cover these situations, they also must be tested. By creating a failure or data loss event where the users are forced to reload and recover from a backup copy, analysts can readily determine whether recovery procedures are adequate. The best-designed plans usually are adjusted or augmented after this test.

Procedure Testing

Documentation and run manuals telling the user how to perform certain functions are tested quite easily by asking the user to follow them exactly through a series of events. It is surprising how not putting in comments about when to depress the enter key, to remove diskettes before powering down, or what to do when the paper-out light on the printer lights up raises questions.

There is of course no substitute for a well-designed set of procedure manuals. Analysts concentrate on the major and critical details of a systems design and include them in the documentation. They also pay attention to the little details, such as those mentioned above, when designing the system. But often descriptions of the details do not get into the documentation. This type of testing not only shows where they are needed but also where they are wrong, that is, where actions suggested in the documentation do not match those that must really be taken to make the system run.

Human Factors Testing

What do users do if, after submitting a transaction through a terminal, the screen goes blank while the data is being processed? They may not take the actions the analyst wants or expects, instead responding in unusual ways, they may depress the send key several times, turn the power on the terminal off and back on, unplug the telephone and replug it, redial the computer center, or beat on the terminal. Obviously they will do just about anything if the analyst has not given them some message on the screen to indicate that their request has been received, it is being processed, and there will be a short delay. This is what human factors testing is all about—finding answers to questions about how people will react to the system in ways not anticipated. And as a general rule, as strange as the above actions may sound, the people are right.

It is the responsibility of the analyst to anticipate questions that will arise in the mind of the users as they interact with the system. If a screen will go blank during transaction processing, the analyst should make sure it displays a message informing the user that processing is occurring. Even that is not enough if the delay will be more than a second or two. For processing that will take long periods, the analyst should have the screen give the user a message telling approximately *how long* it will take and providing *an option to cancel the request*. The user may decide to have that 1-hour job run some other time, when the system is not so busy.

If the system is going into a long sorting step, the analyst should keep the user informed about how much of the sort is completed. Users appreciate systems displaying the numbers of records sorted or the percentages completed.

Also the analyst should be sure to *watch* how people enter data. Do they use different key strokes from those anticipated (such as the top row of numbers on the typewriter pad rather than those on the numeric key pad)? Are any key strokes awkward and therefore error-prone (for example, having to hold down the shift key with the little finger while depressing the "+" key with the index finger).

How will the user of a system feel after working with the system for a lengthy period of time? Glare on the screen or simply too much detail on one display is physically and mentally irritating. Slight modifications in the display contents or the location of the equipment are important human factor concerns that dramatically affect the user and, therefore, the system over time.

These simple testing questions are of monumental importance and extremely helpful in finding flaws that can cause the system to fail. Some analysts will find these flaws the hard way—through bad experiences. It is difficult to forget the system that was damaged because a user banged on the terminal when data was submitted and accepted by the system without displaying a response. But, following the guidelines above, the analyst can avoid those situations.

Designing Test Data

There are two fundamentally different sources of test data, live and artificial. Both have distinct advantages and disadvantages for the testor.

USING LIVE TEST DATA

Live test data is that which is actually extracted from organization files. After a system is partially constructed, programmers or analysts often ask users to key in a set of data from their normal activities. For example, in an general ledger accounting system, they may ask someone from the accounting staff to enter the chart of account numbers and a set of account balances, along with transactions affecting those accounts. Then the systems person uses this data as a way to partially test the system. In other instances, programmers or analysts will extract a set of live data from the files and have it entered themselves.

It is difficult to obtain live data in sufficient amounts to conduct extensive testing. And, although it is realistic data that will show how the system will perform for the typical processing requirements, assuming the live data entered is in fact typical, it generally will not test all the combinations or formats that can enter the system. The bias toward typical values then does not provide a true systems test and in fact ignores the cases most likely to cause systems failure.

USING ARTIFICIAL TEST DATA

Artificial test data is created solely for test purposes since it can be generated to test all combinations of formats and values. In other words, the artificial data, which can quickly be prepared by a data-generating utility program in the information systems department, makes possible the testing of all logic and controls paths through the program.

The most effective test programs use artificial test data generated by persons other than those who wrote the programs. Often an independent team of testors formulates a testing plan using the systems specifications.

Testing Libraries

To assure that all systems are properly tested, many organizations establish test libraries. A *testing library* is a set of data developed to thoroughly test a system of programs. It is stored in machine-readable form, usually on magnetic disk, and used by all persons who are involved with a particular system.

For example, a large inventory system consists of hundreds of computer programs. All share common data and file formats. Each will also process similar transactions. It will sometimes update records and other times retrieve data to respond to inquiries or prepare reports and documents. Because these programs are interdependent and process-related transactions, it makes sense to use a common set of data to test each program.

Testing libraries are not just for initial testing. As the system evolves and programs are modified and maintained, they must be retested. The testing library should be maintained throughout the life of the system so that, as each change is made, reliable data is again available to test the system.

SUMMARY

The quality of an information system depends on its design, development, testing, and implementation. One aspect of systems quality is its reliability. A system is reliable if it does not produce dangerous or costly failures when used in a reasonable manner. This definition distinguishes between software errors, when the system does not produce the expected results, and failures, the occurrences of software errors. It is virtually impossible to develop software that can be proven to be error free. Thus the strategy of error avoidance is not acceptable, and instead software developers use the strategy of error detection and correction or error tolerance. Both these strategies are useful for keeping the system operating and preventing failure. Unlike hardware where manufacturing and equipment failures occur, software failures are the result of design errors that were introduced when specifications were formulated and software written.

An additional aspect of quality assurance is avoiding the need for enhancement on the one hand and developing software that is maintainable on the other. The need for maintenance is very high and impedes new developments. The greatest amount of maintenance is for user enhancement and improved documentation—tasks that can be avoided or reduced in frequency through proper systems engineering.

The use of top-down and modular designs will produce a well-structured system. This approach results in simple modules where the connections with other modules are apparent. These features ease the need for maintenance, while at the same time ensuring it is easier to perform when required.

Maintenance and quality assurance needs are also better met when any of three structured development and documentation tools are used. All use graphic notation to describe systems or module components. Structured flowcharts, also called Nassi/Schneiderman diagrams, define modules in a system using the three basic process, decision, and iteration structures. Each is assembled in a top-down fashion to specify the logic of a module or system.

HIPO (hierarchial input process output) is also a graphic diagram of the system and consists of a visual table of contents that describes the system overall, and a set of functional diagrams. Each diagram shows input, output, processing steps, and data flow. HIPO diagrams are very effective for documenting a system.

Warnier/Orr diagrams show the hierarchial relations among processes and their subprocesses. They also show the repetition and iteration of processes very explicitly. To develop a Warnier/Orr diagram, the analyst works backwards, starting with the system's output and defining the system in increasing detail. Data requirements are added for each process. These simple and easy-to-understand diagrams are an excellent way of showing the relations among the processes that make up a system.

Quality assurance also includes testing to ensure the system performs properly and meets its requirements. Special cases of testing are validation, verification, and certification. The purpose of testing is to find errors, not to prove correctness. Test cases, using live or artificial data, are processed by the software, and errors are reported.

Two testing strategies, neither ideal or sufficient, are used. In code testing, the analyst develops test cases to execute every instruction and path in a program. Under specification testing, the analyst examines the program specifications and then writes test data to determine how the program operates under specific conditions.

The two levels of testing are unit testing and systems testing. In the first, the analyst, using one of the above strategies, tests the programs making up a system. In contrast, systems testing is aimed at finding discrepancies between the system and its original objectives.

Six special tests are peak load, storage, performance time, recovery, procedure, and human factors testing. Each focuses on finding operation flaws in the system to prevent its failure.

Both live and artificial data are used to test the system. Some organizations store the data in libraries to ensure all related systems are able to process a common set of carefully prepared test data.

Failures in testing show up quickly when the system is implemented. System implementation is discussed in the next chapter.

CASE STUDY FOR CHAPTER 12
SYSTEMS PROCESSING FOR ORDER ENTRY AND ACCOUNTS RECEIVABLE

The processing activities for Valley Industries fall into the two major categories of order processing and accounts receivable management. We will examine the processing using these two categories. An overview of the processing design is discussed first. Then the individual program modules are identified and examined in relation to their selection from the systems menu. Abbreviated system diagrams are presented to graphically explain processing.

PROCESSING OVERVIEW

The system for Valley Industries is centered around monthly activity cycles, such as sending out customer statements or producing monthly reports. Therefore the design must include adequate procedures to allow users to produce the reports and end the month properly. The processing design for this system explicitly provides for month-ending activities and for the closing of accounting records to reset totals and balances for the next month. The initiation of this activity is under the control of the user. This is a preferred alternative to using the systems clock to trigger the automatic closing of books, a practice that gives the user no discretion to delay activities until errors are found and corrected or additional late transactions are posted. Well-designed systems follow the practice used here.

Throughout the processing activities, security provisions are built into the system. All users are required to identify themselves properly and indicate they have authorization to perform the activity they are requesting. The password and validation procedure designed into this system will be indicated by a "Main Menu Security and Options" symbol whenever user validation is performed.

In some cases, temporary systems files are produced to carry out a process. In other cases, sorting activities are required to resequence a temporary file. They will also be graphically pointed out when used.

SYSTEMS PROCESSING

Processing is initiated from one of the menu screens shown in Figure C12.1. (They were originally explained in the discussion of the design of input at the end of Chapter 8.) By entering the number preceding each menu entry, the user invokes the programs necessary to carry out the activity. Each of the programs is discussed in relation to the menu number the user enters. For

```
Screen #1
ORDER ENTRY AND INVOICING
MAIN MENU

1  Order Processing
2  Inquiry
3  Reports
4  Monthly Close
5  File Maintenance
6  File Listings
```

```
Screen #2
ORDER ENTRY AND INVOICING
ORDER PROCESSING
 1  Order Entry
 2  Invoice Summary
 3  Order Maintenance
 4  Order Release
 5  Diskette Order Entry
 6  Batch Update
 7  Ready-to-Ship Notice
 8  Order Cards
 9  Acknowledgments
10  Invoices
11  Bills of Lading
12  Return to Main Menu
```

```
Screen #11
ACCOUNTS RECEIVABLE
MAIN MENU

1  Transaction Processing
2  Period Closing
3  Statements
4  Delinquency Notices
5  Aged Trial Balance
6  Customer Inquiry
```

```
Screen #12
ACCOUNTS RECEIVABLE
Transaction Processing

1  Receipts/Adjs Entry
2  Invoice/Credit Memos Entry
3  Process Unposted Transactions
4  Return to Main Menu
```

Figure C12.1. Menus for initiation of system processing.

On-line order entry programs provide input screens for data entry and verification of:

- order header information
- item and order comments
- item entry
- order entry status, providing for:
  - display current order and batch status
  - end order with on-line update
  - end order with delayed (batch) update
  - cancel order
  - end batch
  - delete batch

Order number is automatically generated by the system, credit status is verified, orders are priced, and quantity discounts are applied. It is run several times daily — once for each batch of orders.

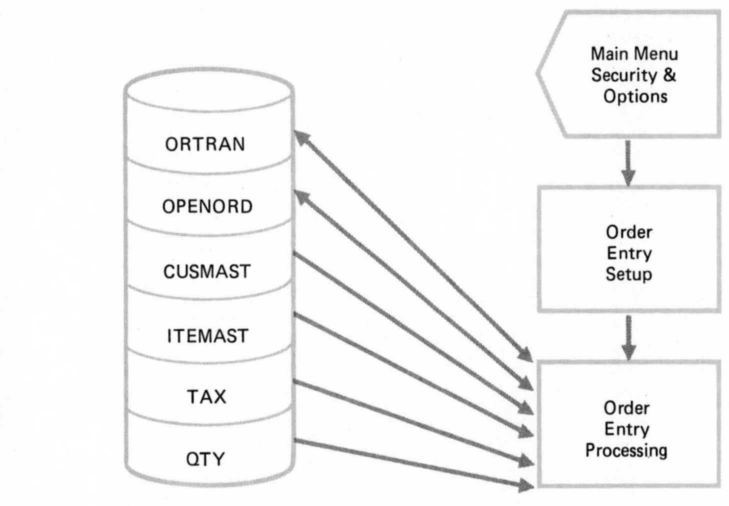

Figure C12.2.
Top-down methods.

This option will only be used to expedite a priority order — normal processing will be by batch update. Order is posted from ORTRAN to OPENORD and master files are updated at the end of order entry. Routine is called from work station. If there are errors, the order is not posted. During normal batch update, the order is processed again to produce update report.

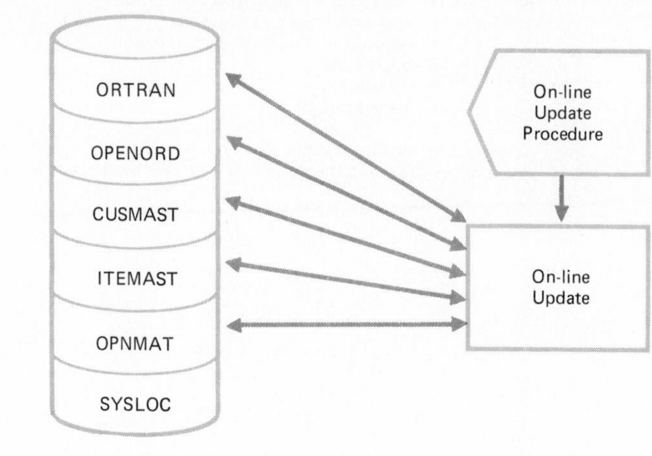

This module was added to the system for valley in order to print a periodic report of invoices prepared.

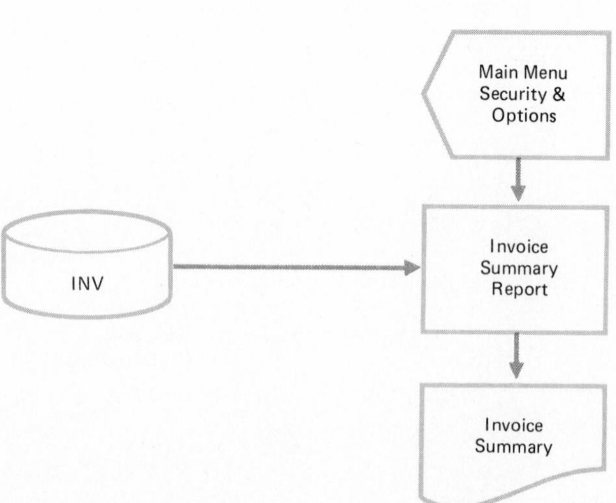

Figure C12.2. (*Continued*)

This program provides for on-line updating of customer order and detail information. OPENORD is updated and a record is written to ORTRAN for an audit trail. This is run as needed to update customer and order information.

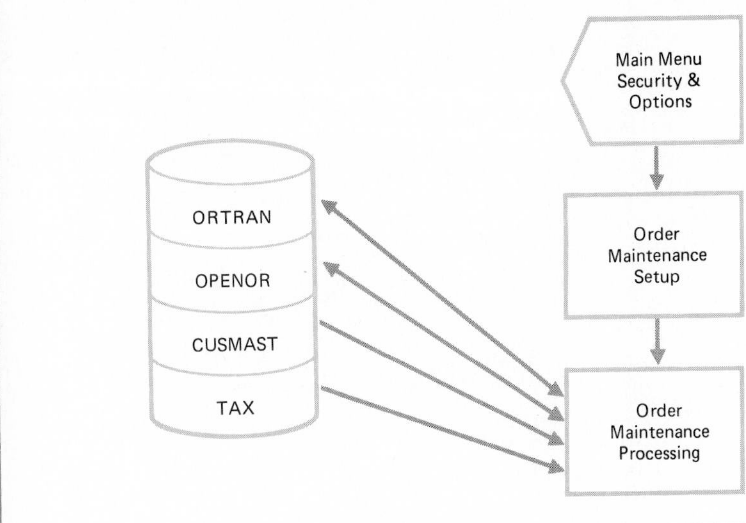

At the work station, an order to be released for invoicing is selected from open orders. Customers and item information are displayed. Changes to pricing and quantity shipped can be made. Order information and changes are verified. Program creates ORTRAN to release records from master file for input to updating and invoicing. It is run daily at least once – to release each batch of orders to be invoiced.

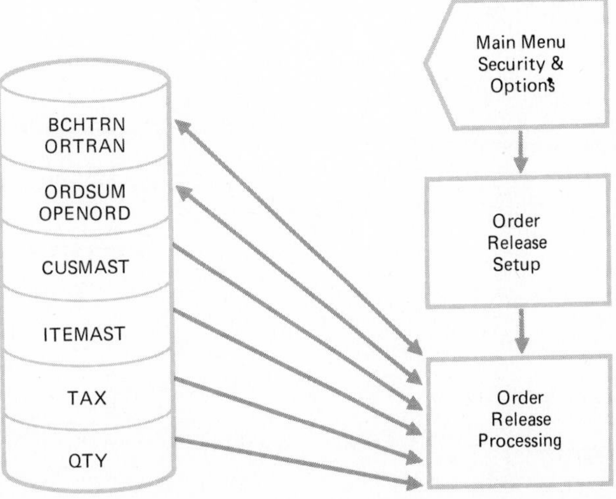

Figure C12.2. (*Continued*)

An alternative procedure for batch entry of orders will be used for daily processing at Valley. Orders are written to TMPORD and edited; accepted and rejected orders are listed. ORTRAN records are produced for accepted orders.

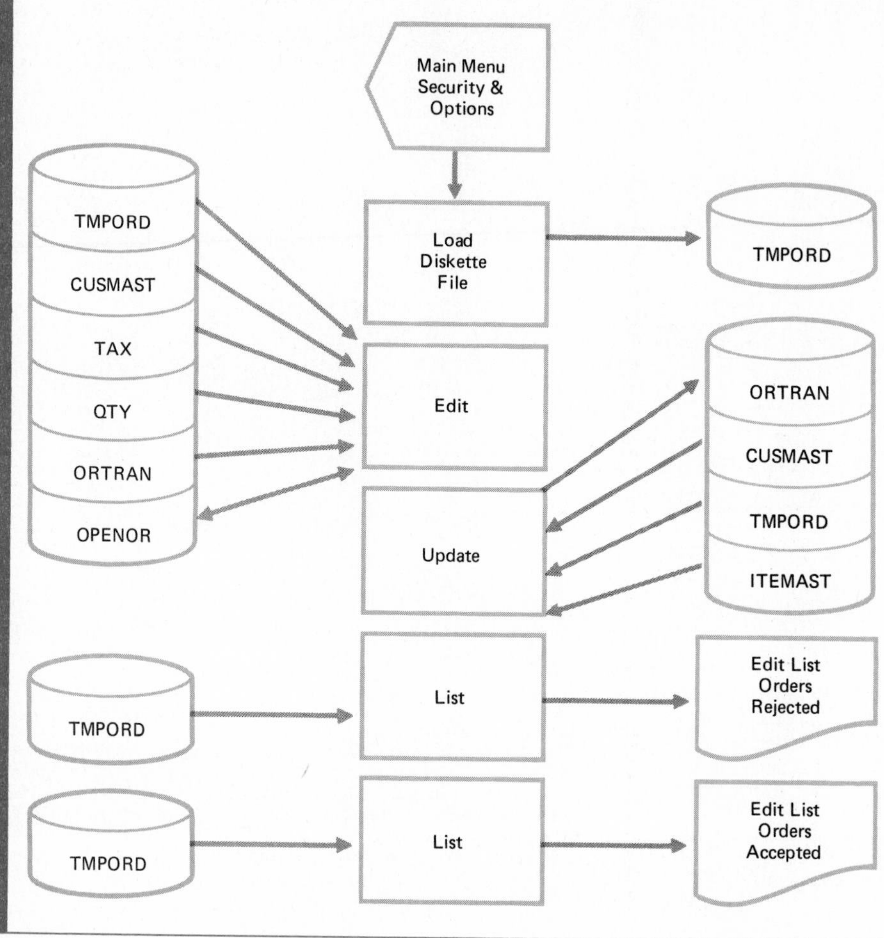

Figure C12.2.
(Continued)

This program consists of:
- entry batch update to process standard order entry batches and update master files from ORTRAN
- maintenance batch update which processes changes to OPENORD from ORTRAN
- release batch update which processes batches from ORTRAN which have been released for invoicing

When an order released fro invoicing is shipped, all master files are updated to remove the order from the system. An update edit report called the Batch Update Register is produced. It is run at least once daily.

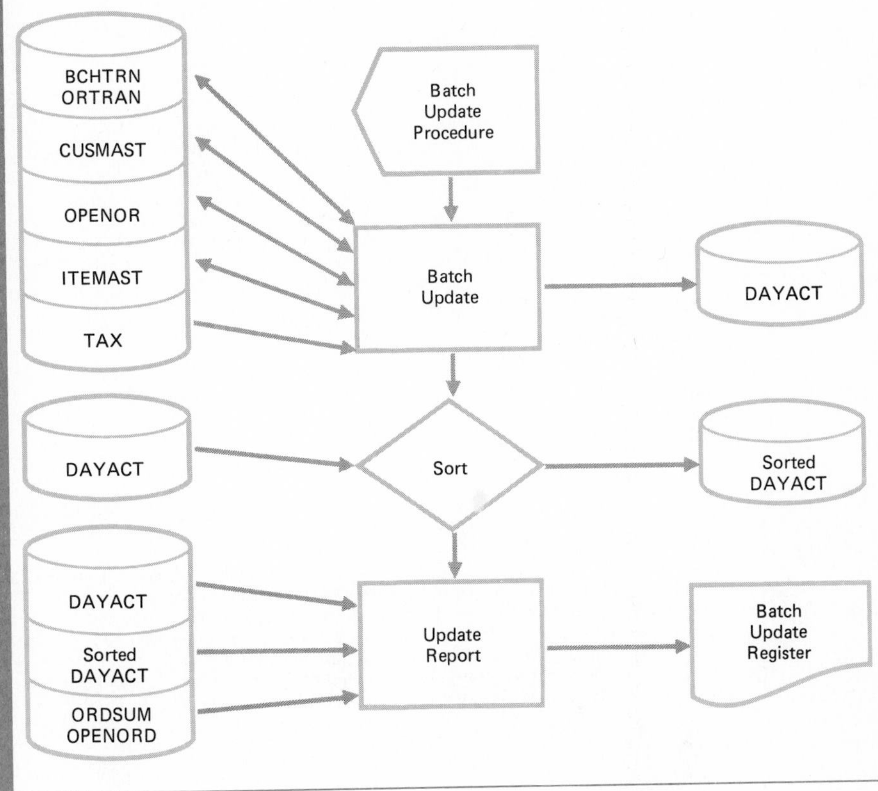

Figure C12.2.
(*Continued*)

This program creates a temporary file on disk and produces Ready-to-Ship Notice by order and location. Errors (customer information that does not correspond to master files) are noted for exception handling. The notice is used for on-line invoice processing at main office. The program must be run at least once daily for batch of orders ready to ship.

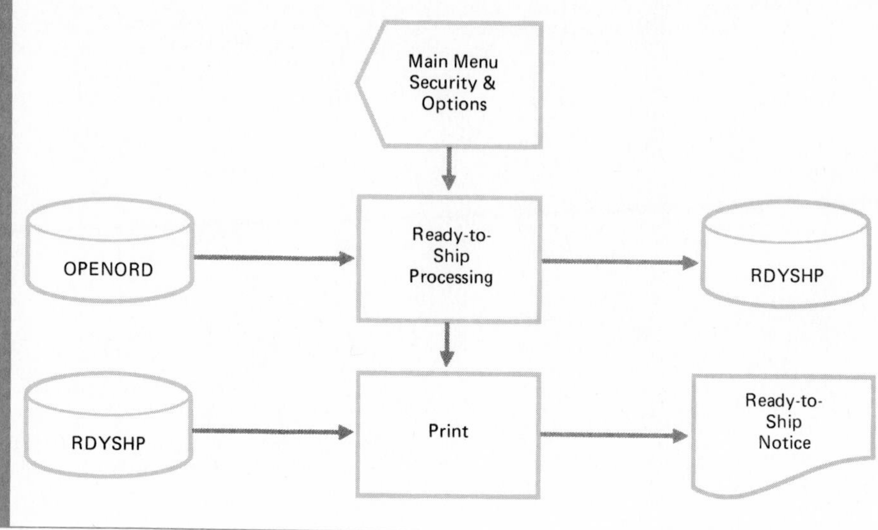

This program was added to the system to print Valley's order cards from ORTRAN at the time of master file update (or they may be selected later from the master file. The Order Cards will also be directed to the work station printers at the remote manufacturing locations where auxilliary production locations are developed. In addition to supplying production information, the Order Card serves as a turnaround document to note quantity shipped for invoicing. First options are specified on an input screen (including Order Cards by location); then a report file is extracted. This program runs at least once daily for each batch update, including order entry batches.

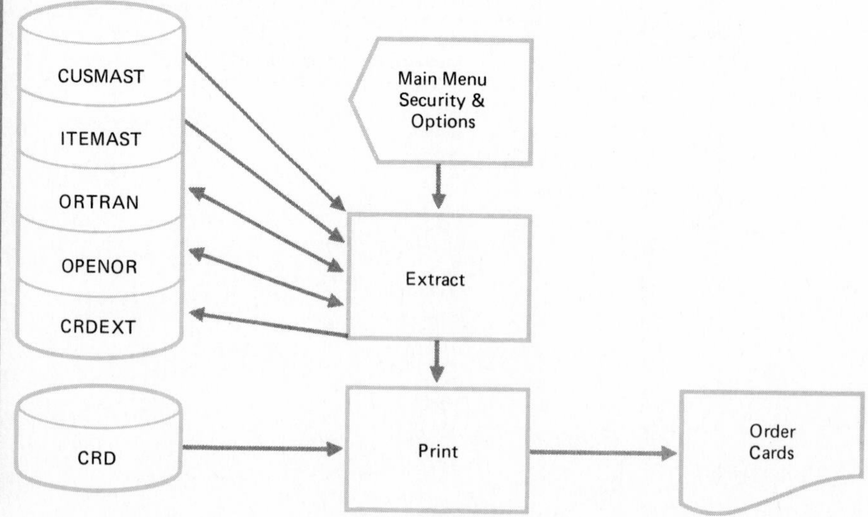

Figure C12.2.
(Continued)

This program prints customer order acknowledgements from ORTRAN order entry records when batch is released for updating. It is run at least once daily to print acknowledgements for each batch of orders entered. An extract file is created and then the acknowledgements are printed.

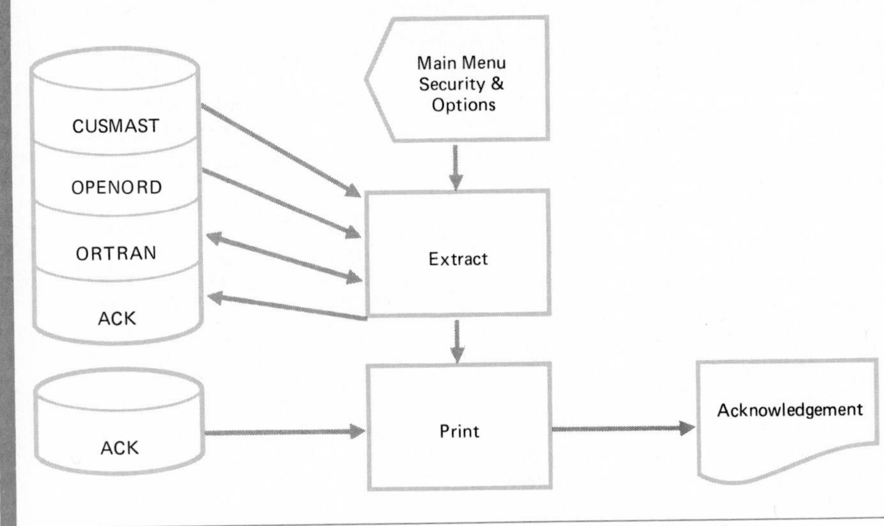

This program is initiated at work stations to print the invoices, which are mailed to customers. It builds an Invoice/Bill of Loading Report file. It is run at least once daily for each batch of invoices.

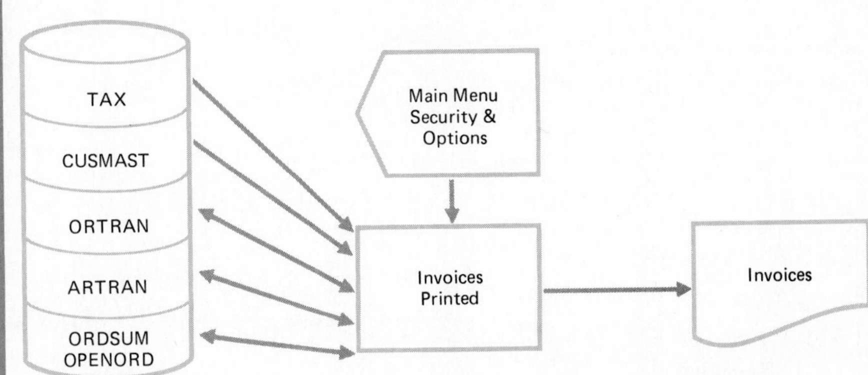

Figure C12.2. *(Continued)*

These two programs link Invoicing to Accounts Receivable. After invoices are printed, the invoice records are posted to the Accounts Receivable transaction (ARTRAN). A report, Apply Invoices to Master Files, produces customer and final totals. The Invoice Register program prints the Invoice Register and updates the Customer Master (CUSMAST). It is run at least once daily for each batch of invoices.

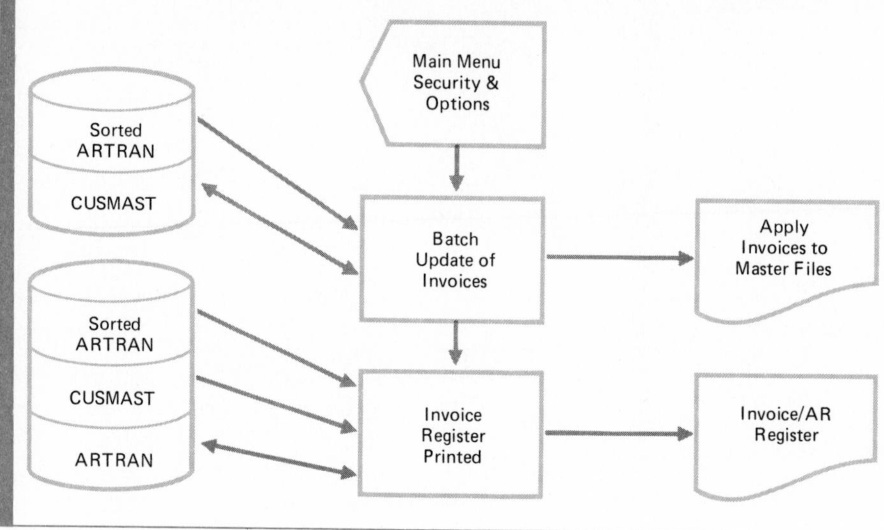

This program, called from the work stations, extracts records from the INVOICE/BILL OF LADING report file and then prints Bills of Lading. Bills of Lading, which contain invoicing information, are printed during the invoice cycle, are used as packing slips.

Main Menu
Security &
Options

OPENORD

BCHTRN
ORTRAN

CUSMAST

Extract

INV

INV

Print

Bills of
Lading

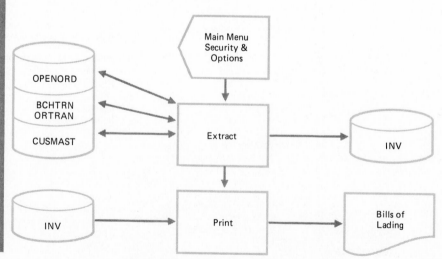

Figure C12.2.
(*Continued*)

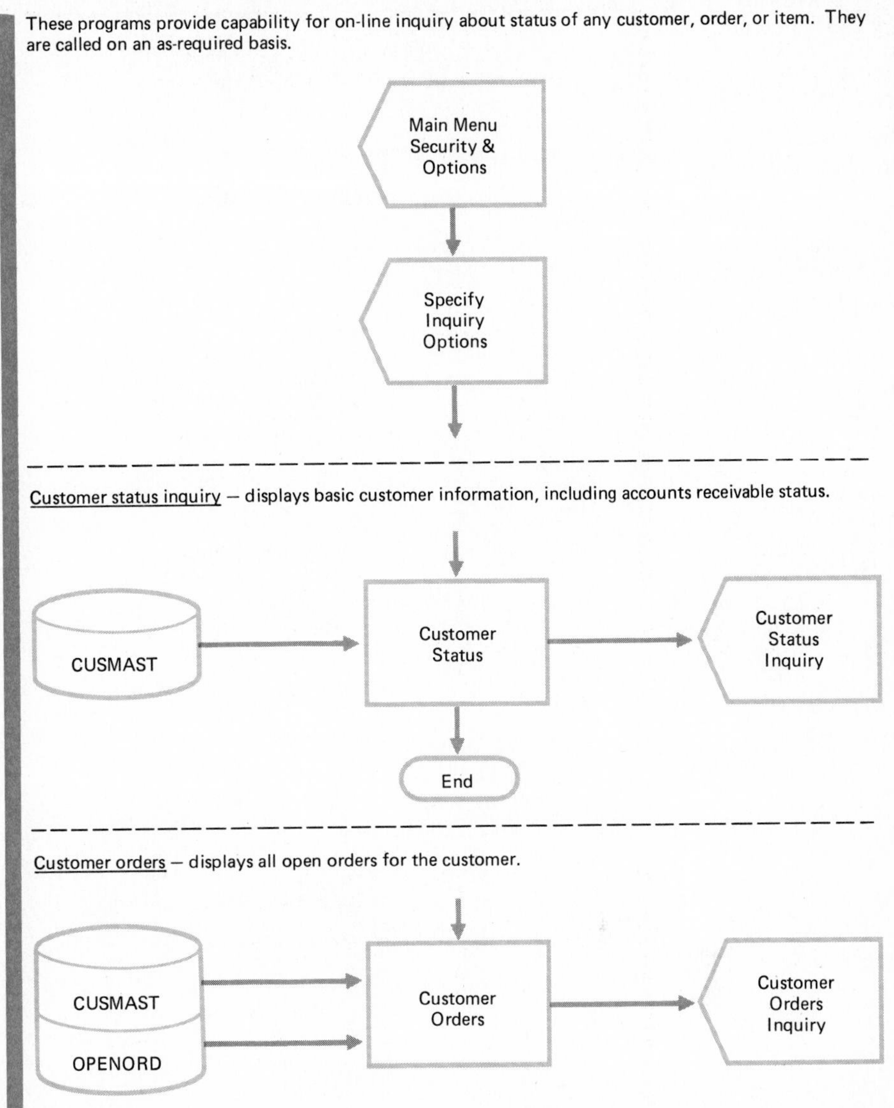
These programs provide capability for on-line inquiry about status of any customer, order, or item. They are called on an as-required basis.
Main Menu Security & Options
Specify Inquiry Options
Customer status inquiry — displays basic customer information, including accounts receivable status.
CUSMAST
Customer Status
Customer Status Inquiry
End
Customer orders — displays all open orders for the customer.
CUSMAST
OPENORD
Customer Orders
Customer Orders Inquiry

Figure C12.2. (*Continued*)

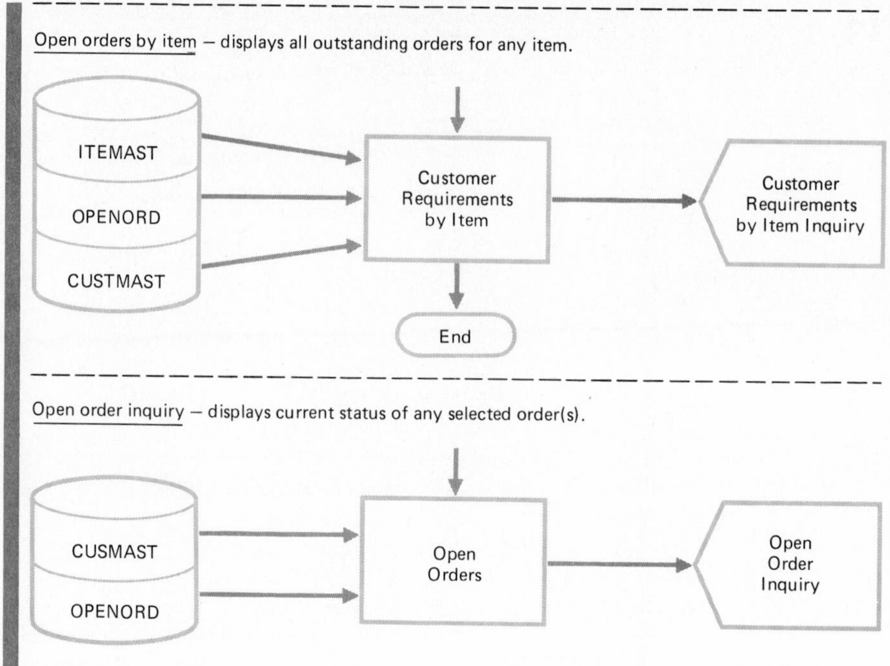

Figure C12.2.
(*Continued*)

These programs are called from the work station to extract the records needed and print the three different types of order status reports. These reports are run as required, except for the Open Orders by Customer, which is run on a regular weekly basis. The other two reports are: Open Orders by Date, and Open Orders by Item.

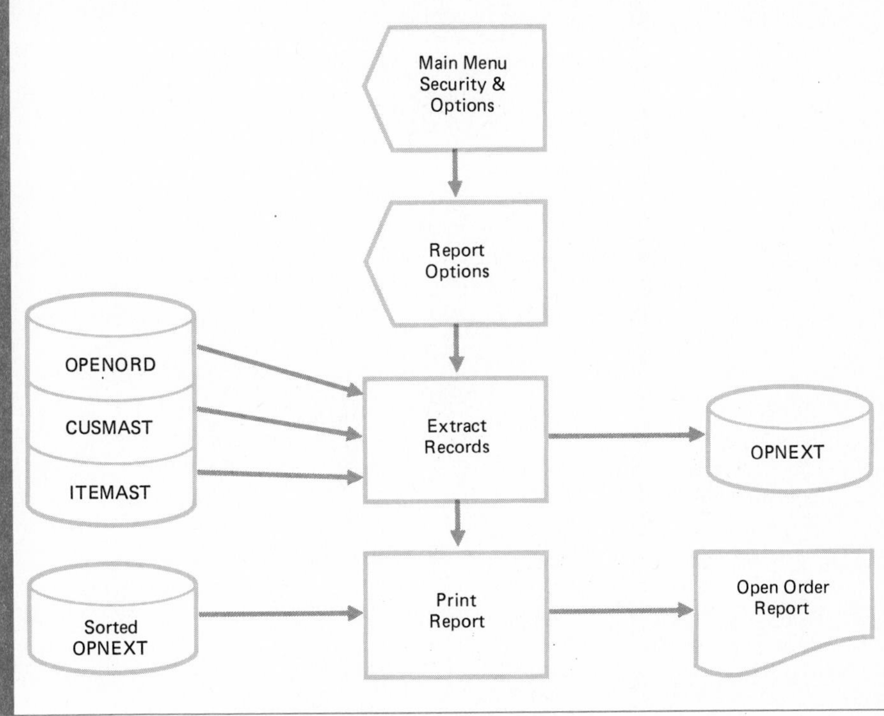

Figure C12.2. *(Continued)*

Taxing body reports are produced showing total taxable amounts by invoice or total amount due to each taxing body. The needed information is extracted to a temporary file and then printed. Taxing body codes are specified in the Tax File (TAX). Tax summary records are written to the taxing extract file. This file is reformatted for the new month at monthly closing.

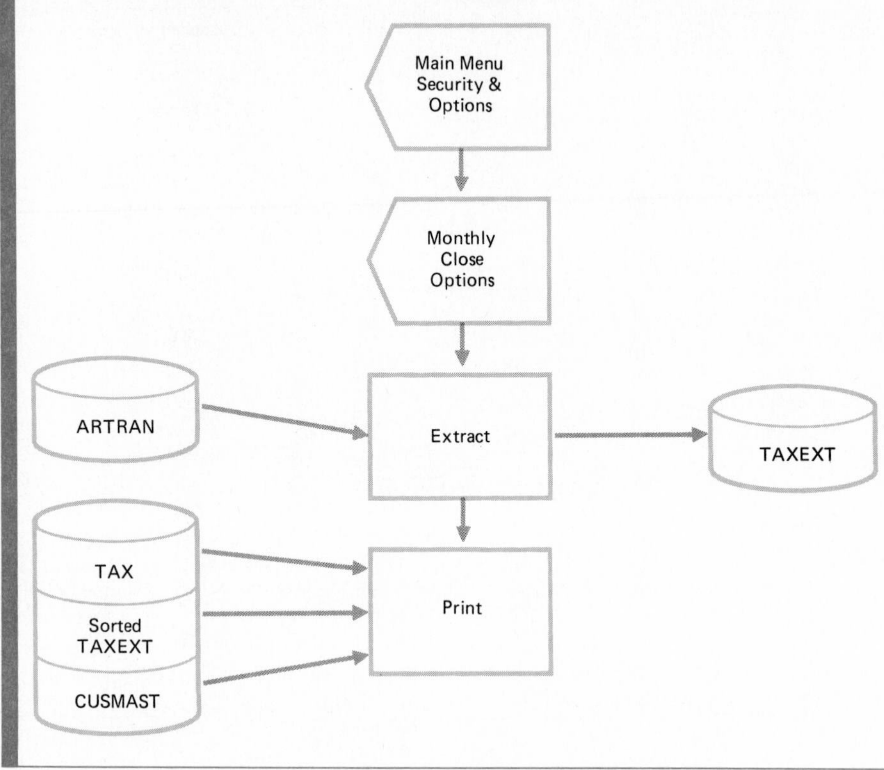

Figure C12.2. *(Continued)*

Other report programs include listings of the master files and an Item Price List from the quantity and item master files.

These programs are called from the work station to:

1. Enter cash receipts and adjustments, edit the transactions, build a batch segment on the Accounts Receivable Transaction File (ARTRAN), and update the Customer Master file (CUSMAST).
2. Enter invoices and credit memos, edit the transactions, and build a batch segment on ARTRAN. Invoices, in standard processing, will be posted to ARTRAN and CUSMAST during the invoice cycle.

Data entry displays for cash receipts and adjustments include: company, customer, cash receipt, adjustment, cash and adjustment post, and batch status. Data entry displays for invoice and credit memos include: company, customer, invoice, and batch status. Programs are run daily for each batch of transactions.

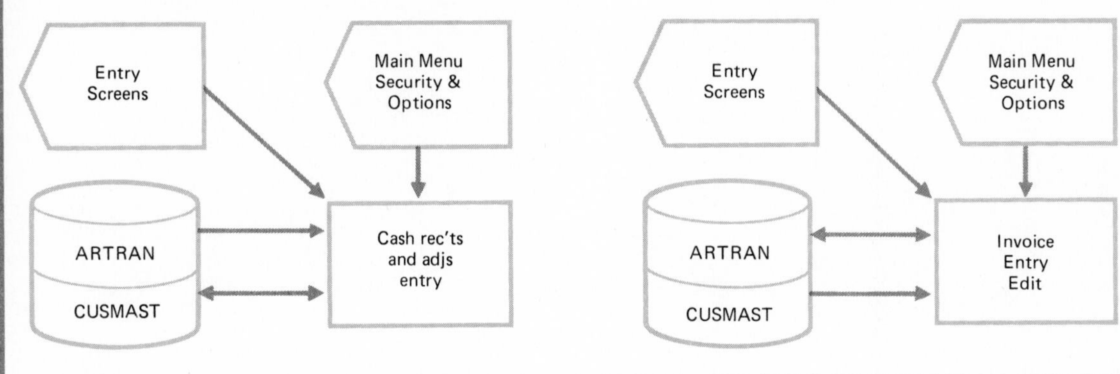

Figure C12.2. *(Continued)*

This same program can also be called from Order Entry and Invoicing, Order Processing Menu, option (10). It is called to post any daily transactions not posted during invoicing on the accounts receivable on-line update. Batch segments are first extracted from the Accounts Receivable Transactions File (ARTRAN). Unposted invoices or credit memos are posted to the Customer Master File (CUSMAS). The listing Apply Invoices to Master List is produced. Then the extract file is sorted to produce a Cash and Adjustments Register and the Invoice and Credit Memo Register. Programs are run at least once daily to post batches of transactions and/or to print the transaction registers.

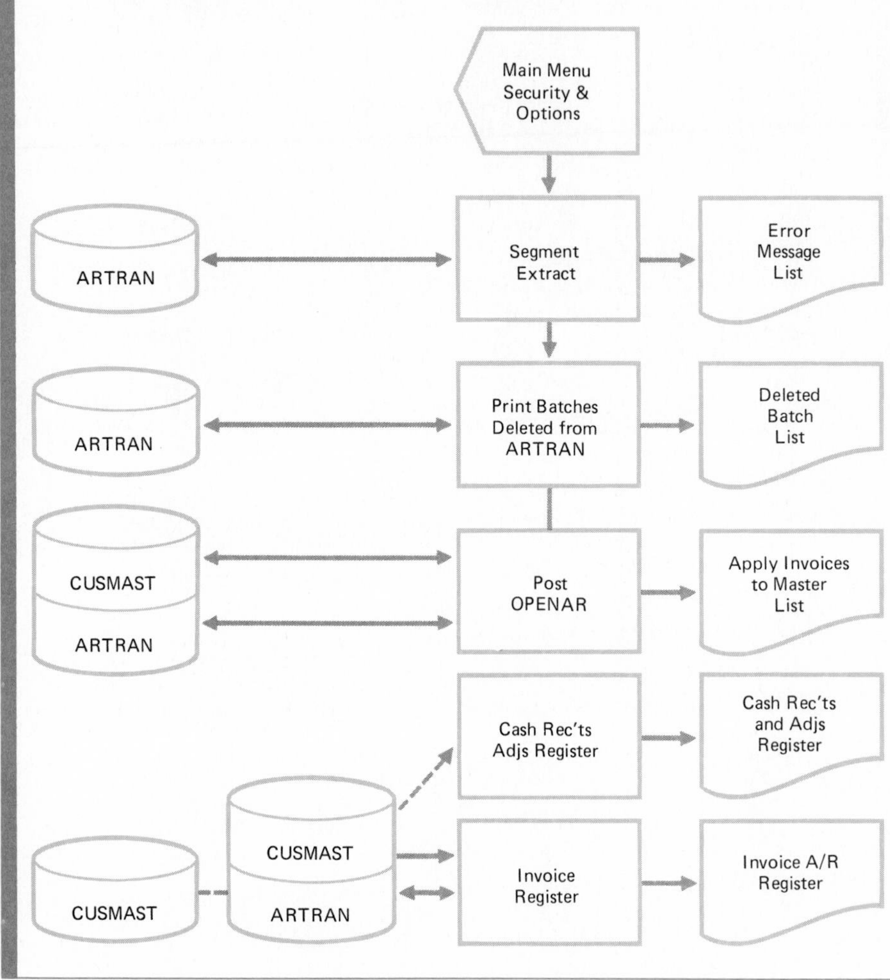

Figure C12.2.
(Continued)

The system for Valley's uses standard calendar month periods. During the closing run, service charges are calculated and the Customer Master file is updated. The transactions are aged and new account balances are created. A statement report file is created. The Customer Master Accounts receivable totals are updated and reports are produced if desired.

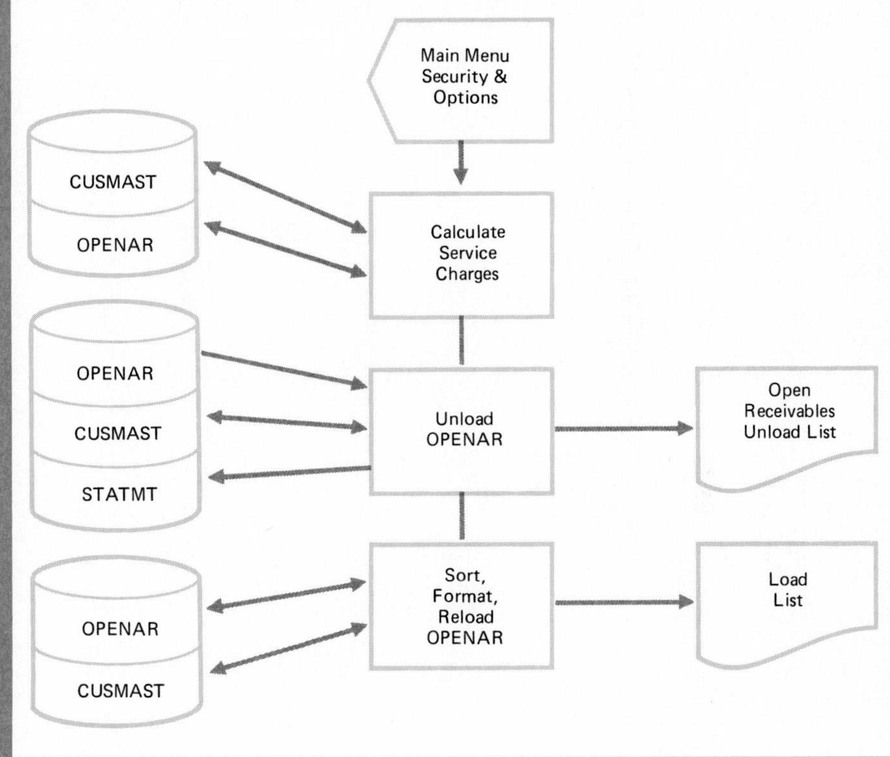

Figure C12.2. (*Continued*)

Statements are printed during period closing after accounts are aged. They are printed from temporary files created during the closing process. The files are deleted after all statements are printed.

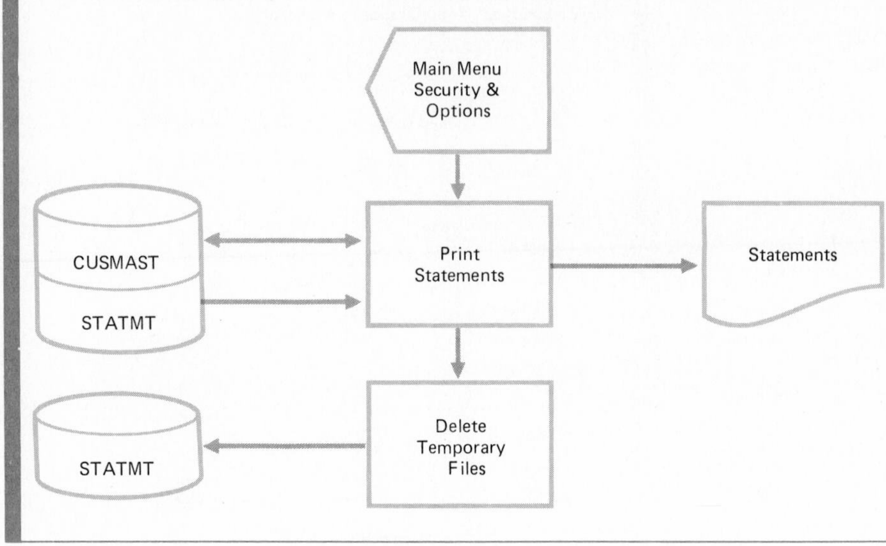

Delinquency notices are printed at period closing for all accounts with amounts over the specified delinquent period.

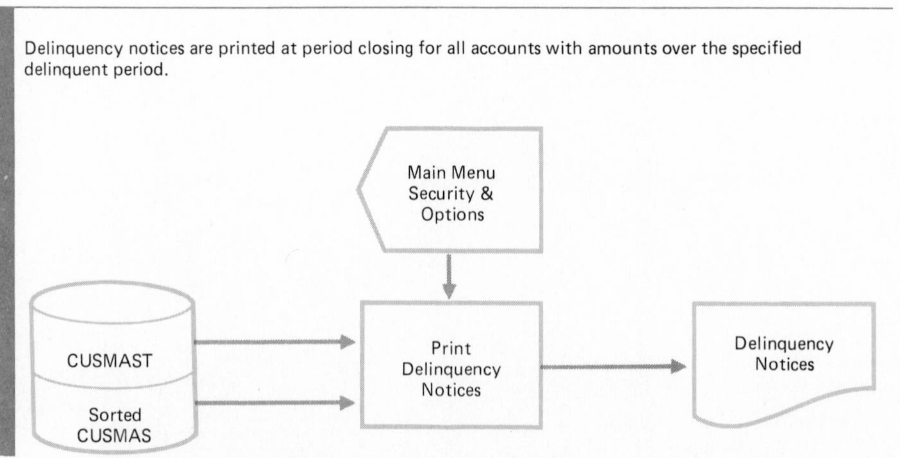

Figure C12.2.
(Continued)

The Aged Trial Balance is printed at period closing after aging of accounts and before statements. It shows aging by 30 day periods.

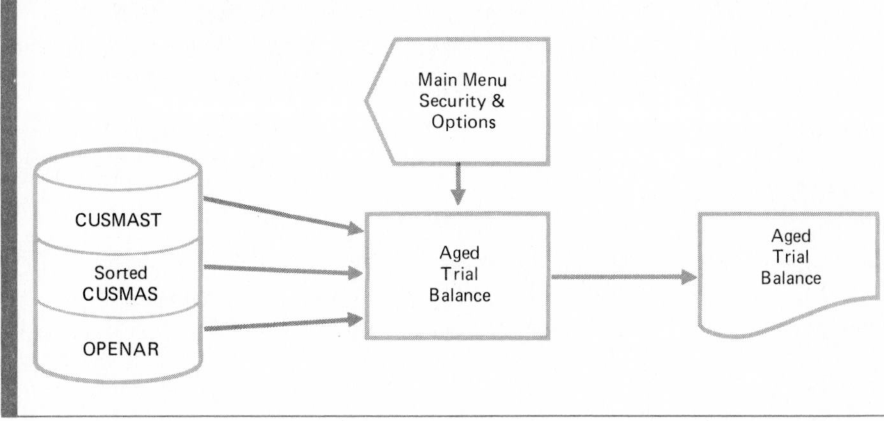

This program allows entry of customer number or numbers and displays in response customer master data and detail information from the Customer Master File (CUSMAST). On-line accounts receivable inquiry is run as required.

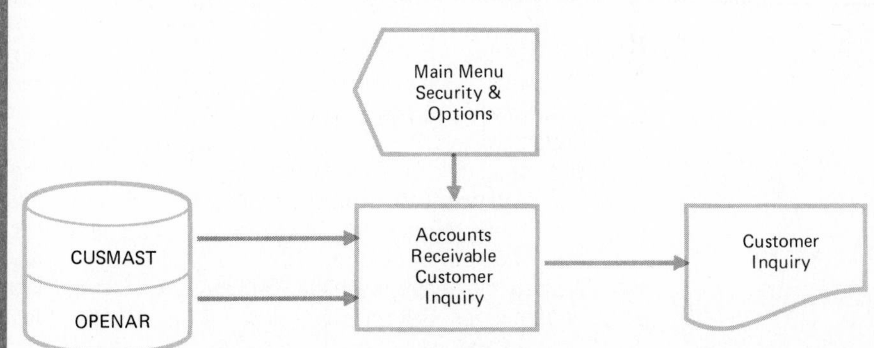

Figure C12.2. (*Continued*)

each, a brief explanation of the program function is presented along with an abbreviated HIPO diagram that shows the files used with each program and the output produced. When necessary, temporary internal files are also indicated. The design also indicates where sorting activities are required prior to the editing or production of output documents.

KEYWORDS

Alpha testing
Beta testing
Bottom-up testing
Certification
Code testing
Design error
Error
Error tolerance
Failure
Hardware failure
HIPO
Manufacturing error
Module strength
Nassi/Schneiderman diagram
Quality assurance
Reliability
Specification testing
Structured flowchart
Structured system
Test case
Testing library
Top-down testing
Unit testing
Validation
Verification
Visual table of contents

REVIEW QUESTIONS

1 What is system reliability? Discuss the approaches to system reliability, pointing out the advantages and disadvantages of each. Which approach is preferred? Why?
2 How do software and hardware errors differ?
3 Into what categories are system maintenance activities divided? What is the relative frequency of each?
4 What levels of modularity characterize software? How do the different levels vary?
5 Discuss the concept of structured flowcharts. What are the components or elements used in structured flowcharts?
6 What is HIPO? Discuss the concept and its components. How does HIPO differ from structured flowcharts? From Warnier/Orr diagrams?
7 Discuss the features of Warnier/Orr diagrams for system development. What are the advantages of the diagrams as design tools compared to other design methods discussed in this chapter?
8 What is quality assurance as it pertains to software? Why is it an important aspect of system engineering?
9 Discuss the most common types of quality assurance. Give examples of each type.
10 What is the purpose of software testing? Explain using examples.
11 How do code testing and specification testing differ? Explain the purpose of each.
12 What are the levels of system testing? Identify and explain each.
13 Discuss the six special system tests. Explain the purpose of each. Give examples to show the purpose of the test.
14 Should system testing use live or artificial test data? Explain the reasoning behind your answer.

APPLICATION PROBLEMS FOR CHAPTER 12

1 A common opinion of managers who are users of computer-based information systems is that software is very expensive and therefore it should be foolproof. It should not fail. Some persons even go so far as to say that they will not purchase another system again until the vendor will guarantee it will not fail.

a Is this an unreasonable position for management to take? Is a manager wrong to expect foolproof software if it is very expensive? Explain the reasons for your answers.

b If you must design a system for a manager who expects you to guarantee it will not fail, how will you handle the situation, that is, what will you tell the manager expecting this of you?

2 The process of updating sequential files is a common one in all automated information systems, regardless of the file media used to store transaction and master file data. If the transaction file is sorted into the same order as the master file, the steps are well known:

Prepare the master file for use.

Prepare the transaction file for processing.

Read a master file record.

Read a transaction file record.

If the master file and transaction file keys match, the master record is changed and written back to memory, and new master and transaction records are read into memory.

If the transaction file key is less than the master file key a record is created and written to the master file, and the next transaction file record is read.

If the transaction file key is greater than the master file record key, the master record is written to the new file, the next master record is read, and the process is repeated.

The above process is repeated until there are no more transaction or master file records. Then the files are closed.

a Develop a structured flowchart for the file processing procedure described.

b Develop a Warnier/Orr diagram for the procedure.

c How will each change if it is assumed that

(1) There may be more than one transaction to apply against a specific master file record.

(2) The master file is organized under a direct-addressing organization.

3 A common design pattern used when individuals must interact with an on-line system through display screens uses a series of menus. Each menu informs the user of the options that may be exercised at that point. In one system, the user signs on by entering the keyword STARTUP (any other keyword is an error) and the system responds by displaying the main systems menu. The options on the main menu are to add new records to the file, edit existing records, generate reports, re-index the main file, or exit from the system.

If the user selects the report option, another menu is presented from which the user can select one of four reports. After the report is selected, another display asks the user to determine whether the report should be in alphabetical, numerical, or chronological order.

The user can leave the system from any menu or can return to the next higher-level menu. The exit is achieved by depressing x or X. Moving from menu to menu is done by depressing m or M. All options are selected by number (1, 2, 3, 4, etc.).

a Develop a HIPO visual table of contents for this systems design.
b Describe the process using a Warnier/Orr diagram.
c Show the system sign-on and menu selection process in the form of a structured flowchart.

4 The documents firms produce to ship manufactured goods to customers are often called "shipping paper." Likewise, the system that produces the documents is referred to as a shipping-paper system. One particular system utilizes a shipping file to produce the proper documents for the transportation of goods to the customers. The customers are classified on the basis of a single two-character code that describes the type of customer and manner of shipment to be used. If the shipping code is BK, DV, or CN, the program adds a new shipping record to the shipping transaction file, a file created for later use by another module in the system. If the shipping code is DA and the destination is a production plant code DA, or if the shipping code is HH and the destination is a production plant with code DA, then a transaction record is also added to the shipping transaction file. The other instance where the system must create a shipping transaction record is if the order code is QZ5.

For these situations and for any other codes, an invoice is produced by the system (in addition to the creation of the shipping transaction records described). The quantity on hand in the finished goods inventory file is reduced by the number of units invoiced when the shipping document is prepared. If the item number on the shipping document does not agree with any item number in the inventory file, the file is not changed and an error message is produced. However, the shipping document is still prepared as described.

a Develop a HIPO diagram showing the input, process, and output for the shipping system as it has been described.
b Show the logic for the system using Warnier/Orr diagrams.
c Compare the diagrams developed in *a* and *b*. What advantages does one method offer over the other? What are the disadvantages of each method?

5 An analyst designed a management reporting system that provides a single-page report summarizing the day's sales and expenses. The activities of each of three major departments are reported along with a total for all combined departments.

In addition, the system reports accumulated year-to-date sales for each department and in toto. It does this by retrieving the sales from the previous day and adding the current day's sales to that total. The new total is then stored along with the current day's data.

The system is designed so that there is one large record of data for each day. In a normal year, the file thus contains 365 days. Each record number is the numerical day of the year. For instance, the data for January 1 is stored in record 1, January 31 in record 31, February 1 in record 32, and so on. When the user signs onto the system, the current date must be entered. The system in turn translates this into a numeric date for the year.

If the current date is January 31, the system will retrieve year-to-date sales from record 30 (for January 30) and add the 31st sales to it to form a new year-to-date total as of January 31. That total will be stored as part of record 31, but record 30 is not changed. At the end of the year, the system rolls over. In other words, after December 31, the system starts to reuse the file by beginning with record 1 (for January 1).

Develop test cases to determine whether the system is properly retrieving data from the previous day. Specify all the combinations of dates that are needed to ensure that the previous day's retrieval is working properly. Do not forget leap year, in which there are 29 days in February and 366 days in the year.

6 A payroll system has been developed to give incentive pay to employees meeting certain performance levels. A $500 merit pay allowance will be permanently added to those employees who are recommended for merit pay by their supervisor and

whose current pay levels are less than $30,000. If their salary levels are above $30,000 and they are recommended for merit increases, the amount of the increase is $250 rather than $500. For any employee who has an annual salary of less than $10,000, the amount of the merit increase is doubled.

a List all of the conditions this program must handle.
b Identify any error conditions that must be detected.
c Write test cases to validate the processing for all allowable combinations and to detect any invalid conditions the program may encounter.

7 Write the set of test cases you feel are necessary to adequately test the file update procedure described in question 3.

CHAPTER 13 SYSTEMS IMPLEMENTATION

QUESTIONS TO GUIDE YOU THROUGH THE CHAPTER

- What concerns should user and operator training address?
- How do training methods vary between organizations?
- What aspects of systems conversion are most difficult to manage?
- Are there varying conversion strategies?
- How do analysts ensure conversion is completed properly and accurately?
- Why is postimplementation review necessary when systems are installed?
- What methods are used to review systems after implementation?

Implementation includes all those activities that take place to convert from the old system to the new. The new system may be totally new, replacing an existing manual or automated system, or it may be a major modification to an existing system. In either case, proper implementation is essential to provide a reliable system to meet organization requirements. Successful implementation may not guarantee improvement in the organization (that is a design question), but improper installation will prevent it.

We discuss the three aspects of implementation, including training personnel, conversion procedures, and postimplementation review. In each area, the particular aspects are discussed, along with the methods of handling each aspect efficiently and effectively.

TRAINING

Even well-designed and technically elegant systems succeed or fail because of the way they are operated and used. Therefore, the quality of training the personnel involved with the system in various capacities helps or hinders, and may even prevent, the successful implementation of an information system. Those who will be associated with or affected by the system must know in detail what their roles will be, how they may use the system, and what the system will or will not do. Both systems operators and users need training (Figure 13.1).

Training Systems Operators

Many systems depend on computer center personnel, who are responsible for keeping the equipment running as well as providing the necessary support service. Their training must ensure they are able to handle all possible operations, both routine and extraordinary. Operator training must also involve data preparation personnel, such as keypunch staff and data entry persons.

If the system calls for the installation of new equipment, such as a new computer system, special terminals, or different data entry equipment, the

	TRAINING SYSTEMS PERSONNEL	TRAINING USER PERSONNEL
PARTICIPANTS	Data preparation personnel Data entry personnel Computer operators	All direct and indirect users
AREAS OF EMPHASIS	Equipment usage Equipment troubleshooting Computer-run procedures Computer-run timing Activity scheduling System maintenance	Equipment usage (where applicable) Equipment troubleshooting (where applicable) Application familiarization Data capture and coding Data handling: addition of records deletion of records editing of records Information retrieval Information utilization

TRAINING METHODS

IN-SERVICE AND VENDOR PROVIDED:	Equipment usage "Hands-on" operation Software features and controls
IN-HOUSE:	Same as above, but may be tailored to user firm. May use audio and visual instructional material; special training manuals; or special software.

Figure 13.1. System training activities.

operators' training should include such fundamental steps as how to turn the equipment on and use it, how to power it down, and what is normal operation and use. The operators should also be instructed in the common malfunctions that can occur, how to recognize them, and what steps to take when they arise. As part of their training, they should be given both a troubleshooting list that identifies possible problems and remedies for them, as well as the names and telephone numbers of individuals to contact when unexpected or unusual problems arise.

Training also involves familiarization with run procedures, that is working through the sequence of activities needed to use a new system on an ongoing basis. Operators become familiar with the actions they need to take, such as mounting magnetic disks or tapes, copying files, changing printer forms, or turning on communication systems, and when they must occur. In addition, they find out how long applications will run under normal conditions. This is important both to enable them to plan work activities and to identify systems running longer or shorter than expected–a frequent sign that there are problems with the run.

User Training

User training may involve equipment use, particularly in the case where, say, a microcomputer is in use and the individual is both operator and user. In these cases, users must be instructed first in how to operate the equipment. Questions that seem trivial to the analyst, such as how to turn on a terminal, how to insert a diskette into a microcomputer, or when it is safe to turn off equipment without danger of data loss, are significant problems to new users who fear computers.

User training must also instruct individuals in troubleshooting the system, determining whether a problem arising is caused by the equipment or software or by something they have done in using the system. Including a troubleshooting guide in systems documentation will provide a useful reference long after the training period is over. There is nothing more frustrating than working with a system, encountering a problem, and not being able to determine whether it is your fault or a problem with the system itself. The place to prevent this frustration is during training.

Most user training deals with the operation of the system itself. Training in data coding emphasizes the methods to be followed in capturing data from transactions or preparing data needed for decision support activities. For example, in an accounting system, it may be important to translate customer names into customer account numbers that are input as part of the accounting transaction (Figure 13.2). Users must be trained so they know how to determine the customer account number, that it is four digits in length, and that there are no alphabetic characters in it.

Data handling activities receiving the most attention in user training

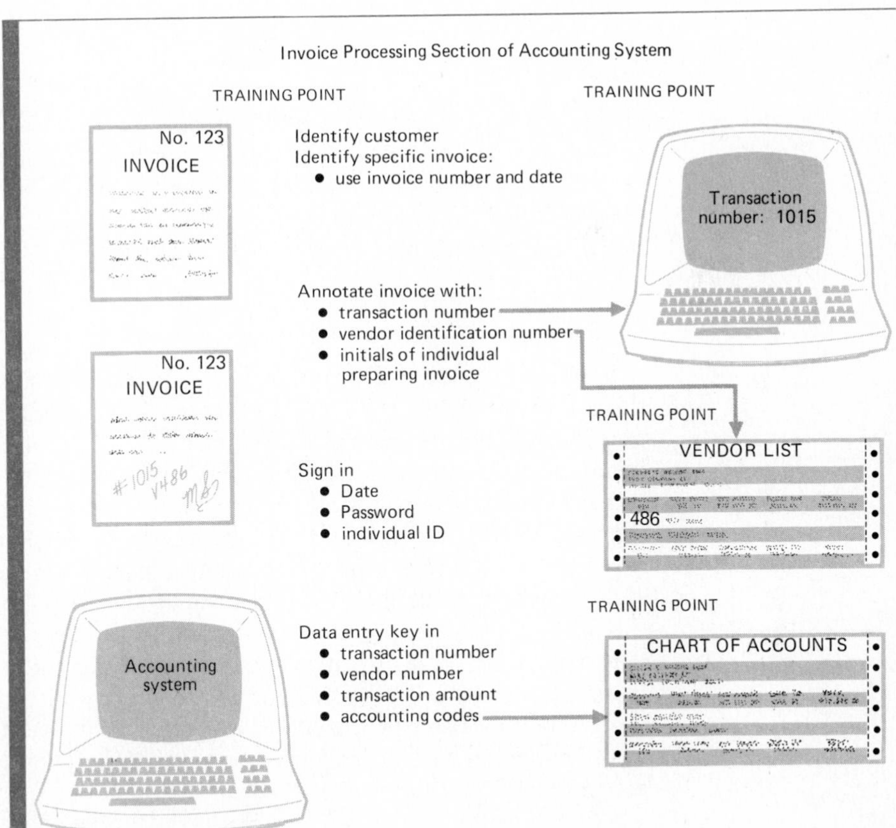

Figure 13.2. Training points for accounting system data entry.

are adding data (how to store new transactions), editing data (how to change previously stored data), formulating inquiries (finding specific records or getting responses to questions), and deleting records of data. The bulk of systems use involves this set of activities, so it follows that most training time will be devoted to this area.

From time to time, users will have to prepare disks, load paper into printers, or change ribbons on printers. No training program is complete without some time devoted to systems maintenance activities. If a microcomputer or data entry system will use disks, users should be instructed in the method of formatting and testing disks. They should also actually perform ribbon changes, equipment cleaning, and so on. It is not enough to simply include this information in a manual, even though that is essential for later reference.

As the above discussion demonstrates, there are two aspects to user training: familiarization with the processing system itself (that is, the equipment used for data entry or processing) and training in using the application (that is, the software that accepts the data, processes it, and produces the results). Weaknesses in either aspect of training are likely to lead to awkward situations that produce user frustration, errors, or both. Good documentation, although essential, does not substitute for training. There is no substitute for hands-on operation of the system while learning its use.

Training Methods

The training of operators and users may be achieved in several different ways. Activities may take place at vendor locations; at rented facilities, for example, in hotels or on university campuses; or in-house at the employees' organizations. The methods and content of the training often vary, depending on the source and location of the training.

VENDOR AND IN-SERVICE TRAINING

Often the best source of training on equipment is from the vendor supplying the equipment. Most vendors offer large educational and training programs as part of their services. In some cases, it is for a charge, but in many instances it is free. For example, IBM offers complimentary 2- and 3-day courses to purchasers of many of their mini- and mainframe computers. The courses, offered by experienced trainers and sales personnel, cover all aspects of using the equipment, from how to turn it on and off, to the storage and removal of data, to handling malfunctions. This training is hands-on, so the participants actually use the system in the presence of the trainers. If questions arise, they are quickly answered. Since the system is intended for training, there is not generally a rush to get training out of the way so that the productive use of the system can start. This could happen if training were conducted at the organization's location, a danger that installation personnel must guard against.

If special software, such as a teleprocessing package or database management system, is being installed, sending personnel to off-site short courses providing in-depth training is preferable. These courses, which are generally provided for a fee, include personnel from many organizations which are acquiring or using the same system. The benefit of sharing questions, problems, and experiences with persons from other companies is a valuable one. The personal contacts made during the sessions frequently last for years, with the continual sharing of information benefiting both parties. Often short courses involve additional time and costs for travel to other cities.

IN-HOUSE TRAINING

The advantage of offering training for the system on-site is that the instruction can be tailored to the organization where it is being offered and focused on special procedures used, growth planned, and problems arisen. Often the vendors or training companies will negotiate fees and charges that are more economical and enable the organization to involve more personnel in the training program than possible when travel is required.

There are also disadvantages. The mere fact that employees are in their own surroundings is a distraction, since telephone calls and emergencies can disrupt training sessions. Moreover, when outside firms come on-site, they may present courses that emphasize general concepts but lack sufficient hands-on training. The training coordinator must recognize this possibility and deal with it in advance to ensure that the course content will meet operating needs.

In-house training can also be offered through special purchased instruction material. A variety of professional training programs on special topics can be rented or purchased from computer training firms, such as Edutronics (McGraw-Hill, Inc.); Deltak, Inc.; Professional Development, Inc.; and Learning Corporation of America. Other vendors offer printed and audiovisual programmed instruction materials that are either self-instructional or supplement other training activities.

However there is no substitute for hands-on experiences. Training manuals are acceptable for familiarization, but the experiences of actually using the equipment, making mistakes, or encountering unexpected situations are the best and most lasting way of learning.

Training manuals take one of two approaches. Some have the user work through different activities step by step. For example, the checklist in Figure 13.3 lists the steps necessary to implement a system using flexible diskettes. Each individual step is listed in the proper order.

The other common approach is to create a case study example that includes all frequently encountered situations that the system is able to handle and the users should be able to handle. Then the users must use the system to handle the actual situations, that is, enter data as required, process the data, and prepare reports. If the system is inquiry-oriented, the case study should require the users to pose and receive responses to

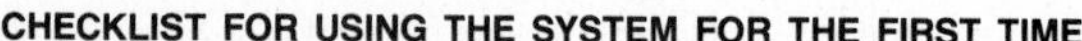

CHECKLIST FOR USING THE SYSTEM FOR THE FIRST TIME

_____ **1.** Turn on the power to the computer.

_____ **2.** Insert the master diskette in disk drive 1.

_____ **3.** You should receive the command prompt "A>" which indicates that the system is ready for your input.

_____ **4.** Enter the command "DIR" to list the files on the disk. Verify that the names of 14 files are displayed.

_____ **5.** Insert a blank diskette in drive 2.

_____ **6.** Enter the command "FORMAT" to begin initializing the blank disk for use. When the system asks which drive to format, enter "2". The initialization process will take approximately 1 minute.

_____ **7.** Test the newly formatted disk using the command "DISKTEST".

_____ **8.** Copy the contents of the master disk to the new disk using the command "COPY DISK 1 TO DISK 2".

_____ **9.** Copy the operating system to the new disk using the command "COPY SYSTEM TO DISK 2".

_____ **10.** You are now ready to begin using the new system. Put the master disk away. Use the copy you have just made for all activities.

Figure 13.3. Training checklist for preparing a small system for initial use.

inquiries. Figure 13.4 includes a partial case study that will train individuals to use an accounting system. Sample data and individual transactions are included, so individuals both use the system and receive immediate feedback about the correctness of their actions. If the results they produce do not match those provided in the training guide, the individuals will know mistakes were made.

During training, systems personnel should be alert for comments made by users or problems that users frequently encounter. Although human factors testing, performed earlier, is intended to detect difficulties, some problems may not occur until inexperienced users are directly interacting with the system. Awkward keying requirements to enter data, unexpected transactions, or unusual ways of preparing transactions may still arise during training. The trainer must be certain to involve systems personnel when problems in the design are found while assisting users who are reluctant to change from their old ways to new methods required to use the system. Of course, the trainer must first be certain that the new methods are in fact necessary and an improvement over current methods.

CONVERSION

Conversion is the process of changing from the old system to the new one. In this section, we discuss the methods of performing systems conversion and the procedures used to ensure it is performed properly.

Conversion Methods

There are four methods of handling a systems conversion (Table 13.1). Each method should be considered in light of the opportunities it offers and problems that it may cause. However, some situations force one method to be used over others, even though other methods may be more beneficial. In

DEMONSTRATION APPLICATION FOR YOUR NEW ACCOUNTING SYSTEM

To familiarize you with the system you have acquired, we will develop a sample application in which you enter data, retrieve information in response to inquiries, and produce reports. The activities you perform for the sample are similar to those you will perform every day in normal use of the system.

Follow each of the steps described below. You cannot damage the equipment even if you make a mistake, so don't be afraid to try something if you are in doubt whether it is correct.

1 Begin each day's work by entering the command:

STARTUP <RETURN>

(The <RETURN> key may be labeled <ENTER> on your terminal)

This starts the system and prepares it to accept your entries.

2 The first thing it asks you is today's date. For this session, we will input the data of April 15, 1986. Enter the date in the format:

04-15-1986

Use the backspace key (usually found in the upper right-hand corner of the keyboard) to backup and rekey a number if you wish to change what you have entered.

Each transaction entered throughout the day will automatically be annotated with this date for later referral.

3 The main menu appears as shown on the preceding page. Notice at the bottom of the screen there is a flashing message:

DISKETTE NOT YET INITIALIZED FOR YOUR COMPANY

The message is telling you that company information, such as name and address, has not yet been entered and that the system cannot be used until that information is provided. You must provide this information only in the very beginning when the system is used for the first time. The details will be stored after that and always referenced by the system when needed.

We will initialize the system next.

Number 5 on the menu will invoke the routine to initialize company information. Depress the number 5 key and press <RETURN>. Key in the following information in the blanks that appear on the screen:

BOULDER MANUFACTURING CO.
131 JAMES STREET
ATLANTA
GEORGIA
30303

Check your entries with the information above for spelling and capitalization. This information will be printed on all reports, statements, and checks that the system produces. Use the arrow keys to skip the cursor (the blinking spot of light that points to where each character of data will appear) up and down on the screen. Enter your corrections right over the existing data and the changes will appear on the screen.

Press the <ESC> (escape) key when you have finished.

4 Next a form is displayed that asks you to fill in the fiscal year and period ending dates for the company. Your accounting period can be for any length. For our sample company, enter the following information after the data headings on the screen:

TODAY'S DATE: 04-15-1986
PERIOD ENDING: 04-30-1986
LAST PERIOD ENDING: 03-31-1986
FISCAL YEAR END: 12-31-1986

Again, use the arrow keys to move the cursor when you want to make corrections. Press <ESC> when you are finished and the main menu will again appear.

5 The next step . . .

Figure 13.4. Narrative for case approach to system training.

TABLE 13.1

METHODS OF SYSTEMS CONVERSION

METHOD	DESCRIPTION	ADVANTAGES	DISADVANTAGES
PARALLEL SYSTEMS	The old system is operated along with the new system.	Offers greatest security. The old system can take over if errors are found in the new system or if usage problems occur.	Doubles operating costs. The new system may not get fair try.
DIRECT CONVERSATION	The old system is replaced by the new one. The organization relies fully on the new system.	Forces users to make the new system work. There are immediate benefits from new methods and controls.	There is no other system to fall back on if difficulties arise with new system. Requires the most careful planning.
PILOT SYSTEM	Working version of system implemented in one part of the organization. Based on feedback, changes are made and the system is installed in the rest of the organization by one of the other methods.	Provides experience and live test before implementation.	May give the impression that the old system is unreliable and not error free.
PHASE-IN	Gradually implement system across all users.	Allows some users to take advantage of the system early. Allows training and installation without unnecessary use of resources.	A long phase-in causes user problems whether the project goes well (overenthusiasm) or not (resistance and lack of fair trial).

general, systems conversion should be accomplished as quickly as possible. Long conversion periods increase the possible frustration and difficulty of the task for all persons involved, including both analysts and users.

PARALLEL SYSTEMS

The most secure method of converting from an old to new system is to run both systems in *parallel*. That is, users continue to operate the old system in the accustomed manner but they also begin using the new system. This method is the safest conversion approach since it guarantees that, should problems arise in using the new system, such as errors in processing or inability to handle certain types of transactions, the organization can still fall back to the old system without loss of time, revenue, or service.

The disadvantages of the parallel systems approach are significant. First of all, the system costs double since there are now two sets of systems costs. In some instances it is necessary to hire temporary personnel to assist in operating both systems in parallel. Second, the fact that users know they can fall back to the old ways may be a disadvantage if there is potential resistance to the change or if users prefer the old system. In other words, the new system may not get a fair trial.

All in all, the parallel method of systems conversion offers the most secure implementation plan if things go wrong, but the costs and risks to a fair trial cannot be overlooked.

DIRECT CUTOVER

The *direct cutover* method converts from the old to the new system abruptly, sometimes over a weekend or even overnight. The old system is used until a planned conversion day. Then it is replaced by the new system. There are no parallel activities.

If the analyst must make the change and wants to ensure that the new system fully replaces the old one so that users do not rely on the previous methods, direct cutover will accomplish this goal. Psychologically, it forces all users to make the new system work; they do not have any other method to fall back on.

The advantage of not having a fallback system can turn into a disadvantage if serious problems with the new system arise. In some instances, organizations even stop operations when problems arise so that difficulties can be corrected.

One organization allocated its entire accounting staff to entering data to start a new automated system. The task took approximately 3 weeks, during which time none of the regular accounting business that was to be converted to the new system was performed. Therefore, a 3-week backlog of work developed. However, that was expected and management planned to authorize overtime work and the hiring of temporary assistance to catch up after conversion. Approximately 2 days before the direct cutover was planned, a senior manager realized that the accounting department was not planning to preserve the accounts receivable aging. The manager stopped the conversion. As a result, the accounting staff had to catch up on the 3-weeks work and reschedule the conversion to a date 1 month later, when many of the previous steps had to be restarted. The system was finally implemented 3 months later, after much extra work, overtime, and staff frustration because of the way the cutover was handled.

This was a particularly drastic step. It would have been doubly bad if the steps were taken because of technical problems needing correction. If users know that a system was halted once because of difficulties, they may not be fully confident that the system will be reliable even if analysts tell them the problems have been corrected. And the time it takes to redo work stopped because of the conversion can be both lengthy and costly, and never recaptured.

Direct cutover requires careful advanced planning. Training sessions must be scheduled and maintained. The installation of all equipment must be on time, with ample days allowed in the schedule to correct any difficulties that occur. Any site preparation must be complete before the conversion can be done.

Direct conversions are quite common, particularly with purchased or turnkey systems. For example, a hotel operating 24 hours a day decided to install an automated reservation system. The entire system was implemented during a 1-week period that included setting up the computer system, loading the software, and testing the system. During the week, a separate training crew worked with all the accounting and front desk personnel to familiarize them with the operation and use of the system. These activities occurred Monday through Saturday. On Sunday, all personnel were brought in to enter reservations, guest charges, and accounting information into the new system so it coincided with the current system. On Sunday evening, after the close of business for the day, the new system was started and used permanently. The old paper reservation files were removed, and the cash registers and bookkeeping machines were replaced with the terminals. The new system became live at midnight on Sunday. There was no old system to fall back on.

PILOT APPROACH

When new systems also involve new techniques or drastic changes in organization performance, the *pilot* approach is often preferred. In this method, a working version of the system is implemented in one part of the organization, such as a single work area or department. The users in this area typically know that they are piloting a new system and changes may be made to improve the system.

When the system is deemed complete, it is installed throughout the organization, either all at once (direct cutover) or gradually (phase-in).

This approach has the advantage of providing a sound proving ground before full implementation. However, if the implementation is not properly handled, users may develop the impression that the system continues to have problems and cannot be relied on. For example, they may feel that the difficulties they had for 2 or 3 weeks may in fact not be gone just because the analysts claim they are.

PHASE-IN METHOD

The *phase-in* method is used when it is not possible to install a new system throughout an organization all at once. The conversion of files, training of personnel, or arrival of equipment may force the staging of the implementation over a period of time, ranging from weeks to months. Some users will begin to take advantage of the new system before others.

For example, a medical system aimed at linking 10 or 15 different clinics to a hospital may phase in over a year. The work required to convert paper patient and insurance records to files stored on magnetic disks requires 2 to 3 weeks for each clinic. A week of training users is also required for each clinic. Therefore, the analysts may phase this system in one clinic at a time, allowing 3 to 4 weeks for each conversion. It is conceivable in this system that the full conversion will be phased over 1 year.

Long phase-in periods create difficulties for analysts, whether the conversions go well or not. If the system is working well, early users will communicate their enthusiasm to others who are waiting for implementation. In fact, enthusiasm may reach such a high level that when a group of users does finally receive the system, there is a letdown. In the clinic example, for instance, the medical staff may exaggerate the time savings from not having to search for medical records or manually prepare insurance claims that will be handled by the new system. Later, when conversion occurs, the staff finds out that the system, even though working properly, does not do the processing instantly. The disappointment is understandable.

On the other hand, if there are problems early in the phased implementation, word of difficulties will spread also. Then the users may expect difficulties when they are converted and react negatively to the smallest mistakes, even their own. When systems will be phased in, they must work well on the first conversion and all that follow.

Conversion Plan

The *conversion plan* includes a description of all the activities that must occur to implement the new system and put it into operation. It identifies the persons responsible for each activity and includes a timetable stating when each activity will occur.

During the preimplementation stages, when the conversion is in planning, analysts should assemble a list of all tasks, including the following:

1. List all files for conversion.
2. Identify all data required to build new files during conversion.
3. List all new documents and procedures that go into use during conversion.
4. Identify all controls to be used during conversion. Establish procedures for cross-checking the old and new systems. Determine how team members will know if something has *not* been completed properly.
5. Assign responsibility for each activity.
6. Verify conversion schedules.

The conversion plan should anticipate possible problems and ways to deal with them. Among the most frequently occurring problems are missing documents, mixed data formats between current and new files, errors in data translation, missing data or lost files, and situations that were overlooked during systems development. The conversion manager must guard against the omission of steps in the conversion. A checklist (Table 13.2) will prevent missed steps. Personnel absences must also be expected and adequate fallback plans specified.

Conversion timing is difficult since there are so many aspects of the conversion, ranging from the installation of equipment to the ordering of forms and supplies. Some of the activities in the conversion actually begin

TABLE 13.2

INSTALLATION CHECKLIST

I. Hardware

A. Electrical outlets

___ 1. CPU

___ 2. Console

___ 3. Modem(s)

___ 4. Work stations/printers

B. Cabling

___ 1. Cable and connectors for local devices

___ 2. Telephone lines to remote site(s)

___ 3. Cable and connectors for remote device(s)

C. Supplies

___ 1. Diskettes

___ 2. Magazines for diskettes

___ 3. Printer ribbons

___ *a.* Systems printer

___ *b.* Character printer(s)

___ 4. Stock paper

___ 5. Binders

___ *a.* Manuals

___ *b.* Reports

D. Planning forms

___ 1. System/34 installation planning chart

___ 2. Local work-station network diagram

___ 3. Remote work-station network diagram

E. Device installation

___ 1. CPU

___ 2. Systems printer

___ 3. Console

___ 4. Modem(s)

___ 5. Local work-stations/printers

___ 6. Remote work-stations/printers

F. Systems software

___ 1. Microcode

___ 2. SSP systems configuration

___ 3. Utilities

___ *a.* DFU

___ *b.* SORT

___ *c.* WSU

___ *d.* SEU

___ *e.* SDA

___ 4. RPG

___ 5. Apply PTF's

___ 6. Backup system

___ *a.* #LIBRARY

___ *b.* RPG

G. Systems security

___ 1. Passwords

___ 2. Menu security

___ 3. List security file

___ 4. Backup security file

INSTALLATION CHECKLIST

II. Accounts receivable system

____ A. Signed copy of contract
____ B. Installation survey
____ C. Installation timetable
D. Request test files from existing system
____ 1. Names/addresses
____ 2. Balances
____ 3. Transactions
____ 4. Other: ________
____ 5. File layouts

E. Forms
____ 1. Patient registration
____ 2. Charge ticket(s)
____ 3. Labels
____ 4. Change of information
____ 5. Account adjustment
____ 6. Insurance/itemized statement request
____ 7. Receipt/payment journal
____ 8. Check-digit labels
____ 9. Batch control slips
____ 10. Batch control log
____ 11. A/R control log
____ 12. Masterfile updates
____ 13. Initial statements
____ 14. Follow-up statements
____ 15. Blank/imprinted letter quality
____ *a.* Company account statements
____ *b.* Collection letters
____ *c.* Requested itemized statements
____ 16. Message inserts for statements
____ 17. Statement envelopes
____ 18. Return envelopes
____ 19. Collection work card
____ 20. Patient recall
____ 21. Insurance
____ *a.* Medicare
____ *b.* Welfare
____ *c.* Blue Shield
____ *d.* AMA
____ *e.* Other: ________

F. Programming instructions
____ 1. Conversion
____ 2. Insurance
____ 3. Other: ________

G. Train personnel
____ 1. Systems operators
____ 2. Data entry
____ 3. Registration/reception
____ 4. Cashiering
____ 5. Medical records
____ 6. Business office
____ 7. Insurance
____ 8. Credit/collections
____ 9. Satellite offices
____ 10. Other: ________

TABLE 13.2 *(Continued)*

INSTALLATION CHECKLIST

____ H. Initialize scratch diskettes
I. Build program libraries
____ 1. Source
____ 2. Object
____ 3. Conversion
J. Set controls
____ 1. Systems control information (ARCTL)—ARP902
____ 2. File size definitions—FLMENU
____ 3. Backup object library
K. Build master files
____ 1. Client/control
____ 2. Location/facilities
____ 3. Doctor
____ 4. Insurance company
____ 5. Notice
____ 6. Diagnosis
____ 7. Charge
____ 8. Payment/adjustment
____ 9. Modifier
____ 10. Backup master files
L. Build A/R files
____ 1. AR.ACCT
____ 2. AR.MAST
____ 3. AR.PATS (family only)
____ 4. AR.HIST
____ 5. AR.KHIST
____ 6. AR.MTD—ARP030
____ 7. AR.XREF—FLMENU, build patient cross reference
____ 8. AR.PREF (family only)—FLMENU, build patient cross reference
____ 9. Backup A/R files
M. Reconcile balances converted
____ 1. Check cross-foot errors—BALARM
____ 2. Correct cross-foot errors—ARFOOT
____ 3. Run analysis report for aging (process)
____ 4. Run A/R control totals—ARP040
____ 5. Prepare A/R conversion balance reconciliation and obtain signatures
____ 6. Backup AR.MAST file if corrections made to balances in M.2
____ N. Establish daily balancing controls
O. Begin normal operations
____ 1. Real-time registration
____ 2. Batching charges, payments, adjustments
____ 3. Data entry, auditing, posting, balancing
____ 4. Daily backup
____ 5. Automatic insurance
____ 6. Request insurance/itemized statements
____ 7. Master file maintenance
____ P. Statement processing
____ Q. Month-end processing (must run ARP072A and ARP073A prior to first month end)

while the system is under development. For example, if new equipment is required, it must usually be ordered at least 90 days prior to the required delivery date. Preprinted forms require from 6 to 14 weeks lead time in order to have them designed and printed. (Chapter 14 discusses project management and techniques for planning and monitoring systems development activities.)

When many persons are involved in the conversion, someone from the systems department should be appointed as conversion manager. This individual is the contact person for outside vendors and for managers and user personnel. The conversion manager is also responsible for checking all arrangements, reviewing conversion plans, verifying the delivery of equipment, software, forms, and supplies, and preparing the site.

Site Preparation

Analysts often work with vendor personnel to outline site preparation guidelines. The customer or systems engineers will present a list of specifications for the electrical wiring and outlets (Figure 13.5), air conditioning needs, humidity controls, and space requirements (Figure 13.6). It is best to have the site preparation completed prior to the arrival of the equipment. Vendors are reluctant to deliver equipment when construction work is still in progress.

If the system is a microcomputer, little site preparation work is needed. However, the electrical lines should be checked to ensure they are free of static or power fluctuations. It is a good idea to install a "clean" line that is

WIRING SPECIFICATIONS

1 Power Requirements:
120 VAC, 60 Hz, @30A, Single Phase.

2 Wiring Considerations:
- All computer equipment outlets must be on the same phase and same circuit.
- **No other applicances or circuits shall be permitted on the computer circuit.**
- The ground should be a minimum of #10AWG, either soldered at breaks and splices, or where the code prohibits soldering, splice-free, and looped over the ground screws at each outlet.
- The ground run must return *directly* to a good earth bond and not to other branch grounds.
- If possible, (a ground-fault interrupter) and a surge suppressor should be installed at the breaker box.

3 Outlet Type:
Three-wire, duplex. The standard variety; *not* the twist-lock style.

4 Special Equipment:
In order to help prevent other equipment from being installed on the computer circuit, orange "Hospital" outlets should be used.

5 Number of outlets per equipment site:
Central Processor: 4 (2 duplex)
Each Terminal: 1 duplex
Each Printer: 1 duplex—This may be eliminated if the printer is to sit directly adjacent to the central processor or one of the terminals.

Further information may be obtained by contacting the computer hardware maintenance department.

Figure 13.5. Sample electrical specifications for site preparation.

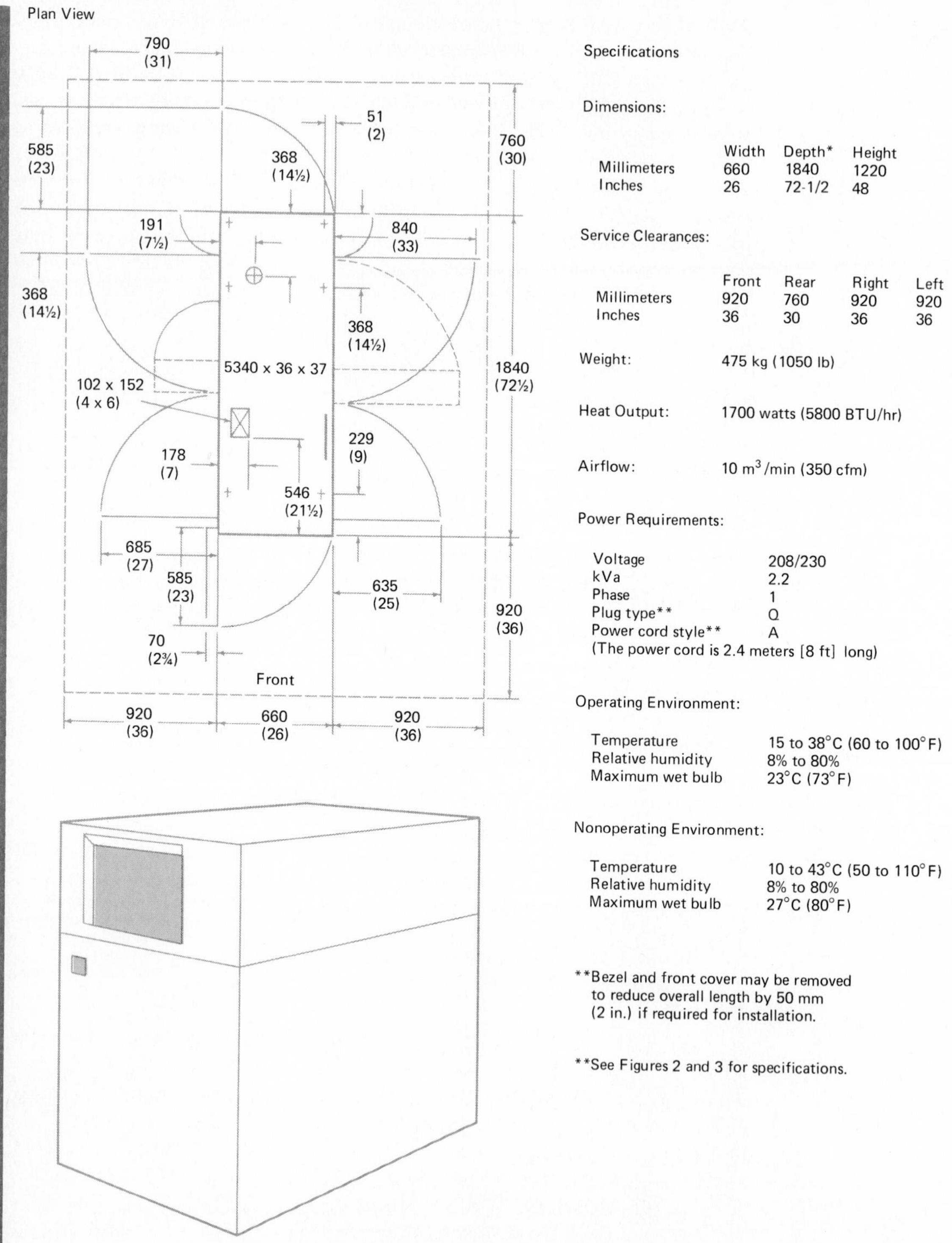

Specifications

Dimensions:

	Width	Depth*	Height
Millimeters	660	1840	1220
Inches	26	72-1/2	48

Service Clearances:

	Front	Rear	Right	Left
Millimeters	920	760	920	920
Inches	36	30	36	36

Weight:	475 kg (1050 lb)
Heat Output:	1700 watts (5800 BTU/hr)
Airflow:	10 m^3/min (350 cfm)

Power Requirements:

Voltage	208/230
kVa	2.2
Phase	1
Plug type**	Q
Power cord style**	A

(The power cord is 2.4 meters [8 ft] long)

Operating Environment:

Temperature	15 to 38°C (60 to 100°F)
Relative humidity	8% to 80%
Maximum wet bulb	23°C (73°F)

Nonoperating Environment:

Temperature	10 to 43°C (50 to 110°F)
Relative humidity	8% to 80%
Maximum wet bulb	27°C (80°F)

**Bezel and front cover may be removed to reduce overall length by 50 mm (2 in.) if required for installation.

**See Figures 2 and 3 for specifications.

Figure 13.6. Environmental specifications for IBM System/34 Computer system.

not shared by any other equipment. Such machines as electric typewriters and office copiers can interfere with computer operations.

Static electricity is one of the most common foes of computers. Carpet on the floors around computer rooms should be avoided whenever possible since it can create static that in turn is carried by operators. When they touch computer equipment, the static charge can be transferred to the terminal or computer and cause the introduction of errors in the data or, in some cases, accidental erasure of the data. Highly waxed floors produce the same effect.

If carpet is necessary, it should be the antistatic type that will not allow static buildup. Antistatic mats can also be installed around terminals and computers to eliminate the problem.

The site layout should allow ample space for moving equipment in and setting it for normal operation. Vendors will provide clearance requirements for performing service and maintenance and for air circulation. These requirements must be strictly adhered to or warranties can be voided and maintenance discontinued until specifications are met.

Data and File Preparation

Along with training, the most time consuming aspect of conversion generally involves the preparation of data and systems master files. If a system is starting from scratch, all the necessary data will have to be entered into the system, often by manual methods. For example, to convert from a manual medical records system to an automated system, several thousand patient records will have to be keyed into the system from the paper charts. Depending on the number of persons who will be assigned this data entry task, 2 to 3 weeks calendar time will be required in a moderate-size system of, say, 7500 records. In addition, table files for insurance codes, medical procedure codes, and diagnostic information will have to be entered. The tasks are not difficult, but they do take time.

During conversion, it is vital that precautions be included so that no records are overlooked or improperly entered. The controls suggested include record counts, financial accumulations, hash totals, and comparison of systems balances.

RECORD COUNTS

The most basic control is to ensure that all records are entered in the system. The batch control methods outlined in Chapter 8 for day-to-day transaction entry should also be used during conversion. Records in groups of 50 or 100 each, for example, are prepared. Each batch is numbered. This method enables the conversion manager to ensure that all records in a batch are entered (the number counted by the system should equal the number in the batch) and that each batch is processed.

At the end of the conversion process, the number of records in the system's master files must equal the number of records in the old system.

However, unless batch methods are used, the existence of a missing-record problem is not known until the end of the data entry operation. Then it is difficult to determine precisely where the problem occurred. With the batch method, one can quickly detect a problem and correct it before moving ahead.

PREESTABLISHED FINANCIAL TOTALS

In addition to ensuring all records are converted to the new files, conversion managers must verify their financial accuracy. Each batch should have a financial total of account balances, wage accumulations, inventory totals, or order quantities. The overall systems balance before the conversion must be compared with the balance on the new system at the end of the conversion.

PREESTABLISHED HASH TOTALS

Hash totals, summations on nonfinancial fields, offer additional protection during conversion. The sums of the account numbers, part identification numbers, or patient numbers are by themselves meaningless. However, they offer one more conversion control. If the hash total calculated by the system for records entered does not agree with a preestablished total, it is a signal to the data entry staff that there is an input problem to correct before cutover.

SITUATIONS INVOLVING DATA TRANSMISSION

When data enters the system during conversion by means of terminals at other locations, extra precautions are included in the conversion. Every transaction must be identified with a sequence number to provide a method for ensuring that each transaction submitted is received and included in the new files. Thus transaction counts provide protection against data loss. Knowing that 1200 transactions were sent from a remote terminal allows the analyst to verify that the same number entered the system.

A common practice when terminal submissions are used during conversion calls for the accumulation of records from each location into separate files. When transmission is completed, the records are inspected for errors resulting from operator mistakes or noise during transmission, as well as for completeness. Only after the file has been proofed and verified is the data combined with the system's master files.

The batch and transaction totals just described are equally important in systems involving communication as in batch environments. Therefore, record counts, financial totals, and hash totals continue to be necessary.

POSTIMPLEMENTATION REVIEW

After the system is implemented and conversion is complete, a review of the system is conducted by users and analysts alike. Not only is this a normal tendency, but it should be a formal process to determine how well the system is working, how it has been accepted, and whether adjustments are needed.

The review is also important to gather information for the maintenance of the system. Since no system is really ever complete, it will be maintained as changes are required because of internal developments, such as new users or business activities, and external developments, such as new legal requirements, industry standards, or competition. The postimplementation review provides the first source of information for maintenance requirements.

This section discusses the analysis questions to raise and methods to acquire review information.

Review Questions

The most fundamental concern during postimplementation review is determining whether the system has met its objective. That is, analysts want to know if the performance level of users is improved and the system is producing the result intended. If either is not, one may question whether the system can be considered successful.

The system's output quality merits special attention. The concerns raised during analysis and design about the accuracy of information, timeliness of presentation, completeness, and appropriateness of format continue to indicate systems quality. Reports that are awkward to use or do not contain sufficient information to be useful may need redesign. Or the review may reveal that information previously thought unnecessary must be provided after all. This question may in turn affect input requirements.

Ease of use and the tendency toward errors in input are fundamental questions for the analyst to address during this review. Is the system easy to use? Are there adequate safeguards to prevent errors in input and to detect, report, and correct them if they occur? If the answers to these questions are not favorable, the reliability and quality of the entire system may be suspect.

User confidence is generally also an indicator of systems quality. The confidence users, managers, and operators have in the system are sure to affect its longevity and use. Can an analyst really expect users who are not confident in the system's reliability to draw on it in critical decisions? It is unlikely. But, if evaluators find that confidence levels are not adequate, they must also determine why. The questions of accuracy, completeness, timeliness, and usability continue to be central to the review.

Ease of use and benefits of use balance each other. It is generally found that systems that are easy to use and provide distinct benefits are accepted and well-received by people. However, even if using a system provides better performance but the system itself is awkward to use, it is not uncommon to find that the system will be avoided. Thus ease of use is as important an attribute as reliability.

In some cases, unsuitable systems components may be found during postimplementation review. For example, a system whose throughput time is excessive may be traced to the amount of time required to print output. Changing printers may eliminate the problem. Data preparation bottlenecks may be traced to insufficient terminals or data entry stations.

What does it cost to use the system? Throughout the process of analysis and design, we have emphasized both development and operational costs. How accurate were the cost estimates? Are operating costs higher than expected? Are the time costs excessive? If they differ dramatically (too high or too low) from the estimates, the reason may be due to improper systems usage. Unintended steps may have been added or essential steps missed, or it may be that prior estimates were inaccurate. In any event, the underlying causes should be explained.

Audit tests will reveal weaknesses in the system and in its future reliability. The four primary audit areas are (1) systems controls, both financial and nonfinancial; (2) protection against unauthorized access or usage; (3) security of hardware and software; and (4) provisions for backup and recovers.

Table 13.3 summarizes postimplementation review questions.

Review Methods

In general, the data collection methods of questionnaire, interview, observation, sampling, and record inspection are most useful for collecting details about the new system.

In addition, supplemental methods will reveal additional information to evaluators. For example, *event* (critical incident) *logging* requires users to record unusual or unexpected events that impact the system. These events

TABLE 13.3

QUESTIONS FOR EVALUATION OF INFORMATION SYSTEMS.

ISSUES TO CONSIDER IN THE EVALUATION OF INFORMATION SYSTEMS*
1. How have information systems changed the cost of operation?
2. How have information systems changed the way in which operations are performed?
3. How have information systems changed the accuracy of information that users receive?
4. How have information systems changed the timeliness of information and reports users receive?
5. How have information systems brought about organization changes? Are these changes for the better or for the worse?
6. How have information systems changed the completeness of the information?
7. How have information systems changed control or centralization? What is the effect of such changes?
8. How have information systems changed the attitudes of systems users or persons affected by the system?
9. How have information systems changed the number of users?
10. How have information systems changed the interactions between members of the organization?
11. How have information systems changed productivity?
12. How have information systems changed the effort that must be expended to receive information for decision making?

*These evaluations should be performed both before and after installation of an information systems application.

may reflect incidents that the system cannot handle because of incomplete design or activities that are not occurring in the prescribed manner. For example, when an order entry system is installed, users may find that they are not able to override the product prices retrieved by the system. The frequency of the incident reveals its importance to the organization. However, it may also reveal either that users are attempting to discount prices to certain customers or that, when quantity purchases are made, provisions must exist for quoting special prices. In either case, the situation must be made known to analysts evaluating the implemented system.

Impact evaluation determines how systems affect or change the areas of the organization in which they are installed. If new systems are proposed and developed on the basis of increased speed, decreased errors, better integration of activities, reduced data redundancy, or improved productivity, systems should be evaluated against these expectations. Sampling records for errors, assessing the quantity of throughput, or observing users will provide concrete statistics of the effects of the system.

The impact of the system should also be compared with financial costs and benefits. Even if greater productivity is achieved with a new system, management wants to know whether the costs of achieving the changes produce the intended financial, service, or competitive advantages. During the systems proposal stage, the expectations of costs and benefits were developed. After implementation, the system is reviewed to compare the actual costs and benefits with the expectations.

How do users and other persons affected by a new system, such as customers, suppliers, or internal managers, feel about the new system? This simple question reveals much about the future usefulness of the system. (A system that is strongly disliked may not be in use long unless adjustments are made.) *Attitude surveys*, data collections of ideas and opinions about a system, provide this information. Whether through questionnaires, the most frequent attitude survey method, or personal interviews, attitude surveys reveal the people side of the system. Pertinent questions probe individuals' feelings about the changes in the amount of work they perform, quality of their efforts, quality of the service to customers or patients, ease of use, or acceptance of the system by coworkers.

These review methods emphasize the importance of collecting both quantitative and subjective data to determine the suitability of the system. There is no substitute for effective review. Introspection and supposition have no place in systems development, even after the system is implemented.

SUMMARY

Implementing a system, whether a new one or an existing one that has been modified, consists of the three primary activities of training, conversion, and postimplementation review. Training involves both system operators and users who will use the new system either by providing data, receiving information, or actually operating the equipment.

Training the systems operators includes not only how to use the equipment, but also how to diagnose malfunctions and what steps to take when they occur. Training also involves instruction in systems run procedures and normal operating activities, such as loading files, changing printer forms, and initiating data communication.

Most user training deals with the operation of the system itself, with the most attention given to data handling procedures. It is imperative that users are properly trained in methods of adding transactions, editing data, formulating inquiries, and deleting records. No training is complete without familiarization with simple systems maintenance activities. Weaknesses in any aspect of training are likely to lead to awkward situations that produce user frustration and errors.

Training may be achieved through vendor and in-service assistance or in-house activities. Most vendors offer special courses on their premises as part of normal service. Whether complimentary or paid for, they are usually an excellent source of hands-on training. Off-site short courses are good sources of specialized training when in-depth knowledge is required in a specific topical area, such as data communication or database management.

On-site training may be arranged if large groups of persons must be trained in an organization. This method may be the most efficient when compared with the time and cost of travel for many persons. However, the disadvantage of distracting telephone calls, business emergencies, and other interruptions must not be overlooked.

High-quality training is an essential, although not sufficient, step in systems implementation. The conversion itself must also be carefully planned and executed. Conversion is the process of changing from an old system to a new one. Four methods are common: parallel systems, direct cutover, pilot approach, and systems phase-in. Parallel systems offer the greatest security in installation, while direct cutover provides the highest risk. When systems involve large parts of the organization, the phase-in method, where conversion occurs gradually, say a department at a time, is common. When new methods or ideas need to be tried out, the pilot approach is often used: one area of the organization uses the system and provides feedback to the analysts. When the system is ready for implementation, one of the other conversion methods is selected to install the system.

The conversion plan describes all the activities that must occur to implement the new system and put it into operation. It identifies the tasks and assigns the responsibilities for carrying them out. The conversion plan should also anticipate the most common problems, such as missing documents, incorrect data formats, lost data, and unanticipated systems requirements, and provide ways for dealing with them when they occur.

A major aspect of conversion is the preparation of the systems site. Preparation activities include electrical and air-condition preparation, site layout, and installation of the equipment. Many vendors provide site specifications that must be satisfied before they will install the equipment.

Data and file preparation consumes a large proportion of conversion time. Not only must the data be converted to a format acceptable in the new system, but analysts must ensure that it is done without loss of detail or accuracy. By using record counts, financial controls, and hash totals, analysts are able to detect and correct problems quickly, before they get out of control, even if data transmission is involved in the conversion.

After the system is implemented and the conversion is complete, a review should be conducted to determine whether the system is meeting expectations and where improvements are needed. Systems quality, user confidence, and operating statistics are assessed through such techniques as event logging, impact evaluation, and attitude surveys. The data collection methods used during analysis are equally effective during postimplementation review. The review not only assesses how well the current system is designed and implemented, but also is a valuable source of information that can be applied to the next systems project.

CASE STUDY FOR CHAPTER 13
VALLEY SYSTEMS CONVERSION AND IMPLEMENTATION

The primary activities associated with the conversion of the existing order processing system to the new one are installation, training, conversion of files, and cutover. The plan of each activity is examined in the discussion that follows.

INSTALLATION

The existence of the System/34 at Valley Industries meant that it was unnecessary to do extensive site planning or arrange for the delivery of an entire computer system. However, since new terminals were needed, systems staff members did coordinate their installation. The terminals themselves were ordered from the manufacturer 8 weeks in advance of the time they would be needed. (The vendor indicated the normal delivery time was 3 to 5 weeks.) Therefore, the equipment arrived well in advance of the implementation date.

Prior to the arrival of the equipment, electricians were contacted to assist in the site preparation. New electrical lines were installed in the accounting office for the two terminals to be used in order processing and accounts receivable maintenance. A new electrical line was also installed in the manufacturing area for that terminal. The new lines were not essential; however, the analysts were unsure what other devices were attached to existing electrical lines and wished to avoid any chance of electrical interference from equipment and machines in the building.

The electrical contractor also strung coaxial communication cables from the central processor site to the terminal locations. Connectors were installed on the cable ends to fasten them to the equipment.

All electrical work was completed in 2 days. An engineer from IBM was on the premises the second day to connect the terminals, reconfigure the computer system to recognize the additional terminals, and test all equipment for proper functioning. No difficulties were encountered.

COMPUTER SUPPLIES

Computer supplies needed for the new application were also ordered in advance of the date they were required. Supplies consisted of additional disks and storage cases for the disks, both of which were received 1 week after they were ordered.

Paper supplies required the longest lead time. Preprinted monthly statements, showing the Valley logo, address, and other pertinent information, were ordered 8 weeks in advance. The stationery for order acknowledgements and new mailing envelopes required 4 weeks. Cases of blank paper were readily available and arrived in under 1 week.

TRAINING ACTIVITIES

Three types of training were conducted to familiarize personnel with the details of the new system. Systems operators, direct users, and managers received training in systems utilization.

OPERATOR TRAINING

The systems operators, who were already very familiar with the System/34, were introduced to the order processing system. After a general overview of its purpose and use, they discussed run procedures with the systems analysts. The following procedures were discussed:

1 *Daily run activities*, including when the system would be in operation, the files needed to run the system, and the specific diskettes to be mounted on the system. Backup procedures for copying files were examined and a color coding scheme agreed on to distinguish data disks for one day from those of other days.
2 *Periodic report preparation*, including the forms and documents needed for printing purposes. It was noted that accounting personnel will indicate when to run a report and that systems personnel are responsible for ensuring the proper forms are loaded on the printer.
3 *Emergency procedures*, including indicators that a process is taking longer than usual or that data is not recording properly. Specific restart procedures were discussed to ensure that operators will be able to recover from any problems that arise, whether due to user mistake, operator error, or equipment malfunctions.

All systems operation procedures are stored in a run manual that will be updated when changes occur.

DIRECT USERS

Direct users for the new system include the staff members who process incoming orders, maintain accounts receivable, and use terminals in the manufacturing department. Each person, although generally familiar with computer reports used in Valley activities, was inexperienced in actual hands-on systems utilization. They attended a 2-day course offered by IBM, System/34 Operating Concepts. The course was designed to familiarize display station operators on the basic operating concepts of the System/34. It included hands-on training with a working computer system and demonstration problems. In addition, a self-study course, System/34 Operations, was purchased. The course further acquainted the staff members with systems operating details.

The remainder of the training was conducted by the systems analysts who designed the new system. Data entry procedures were discussed and tested. Some adjustments were made on the basis of recommendations from the accounting staff. Credit and collection activities were also tested using demonstration data.

Both manufacturing and order entry personnel spent a great deal of time making inquiries to retrieve information and records, editing previously entered data, and running reports. Throughout the entire series of activities, troubleshooting activities were emphasized. Users became familiar with methods of determining when the system was not performing as expected and whether the operators caused the result or if there was a systems problem. Many questions were raised during this portion of the training.

A joint meeting was also held with systems operators to answer any user questions concerning backup procedures and daily and monthly running schedules and to agree on the expectations of each group for the other. The meeting was productive.

MANAGEMENT USERS

Mr. Olson attended a special training session for managers offered by IBM. The 2-day course, Data Processing Concepts, is intended to introduce managers to computer concepts, controls, and procedures. The course lays the foundation for changing from manual to automated systems.

A morning-long training session was also held with all management personnel, except the president, who was out of town, to familiarize them with the capabilities of the new system. Sample reports were prepared and distributed at the meeting. A long question-and-answer session gave all persons a chance to discuss concerns and offer suggestions freely.

CONVERSION

A direct cutover to the new system was planned and scheduled to coincide with the end of the calendar month. After the prior month was completed and manual accounting statements sent, the new files were loaded and prepared to go into full usage.

The three master files that were converted from manual to computer form were the customer, item master, and open order files. The manual records for each served as the basis for the new file. Records were grouped into numbered batches, and personnel keyed the data into the system through the display terminals. Audit and control procedures for each file included:

1 *Customer master file* Numbered batches of 50 records each. Hash totals on customer numbers. Financial totals on current balances. Accounts that had been sent to a collection agency were not entered into the new system.

2 *Open order file* Numbered batches of 50 records each. Hash total on order number. All orders were entered into the system.
3 *Item master file* Numbered batches of 50 records each. Hash totals on item numbers.

A temporary office assistant helped in the batching and accumulation of hash totals. The actual records were entered by the accounting staff members. Batch totals were accumulated during data entry and compared with the manual totals.

The entry of data to build the master files took nearly 3 days. During that time, new orders were accepted but not processed. At the end of the conversion, they were entered into the system. By the end of the next day, all work was processed and up-to-date.

POSTIMPLEMENTATION EVALUATION

The systems analysts remained with the project through the implementation stage to assure a smooth transition process. Programmers were also available if their services were needed.

The implementation was well-planned, and the entire event went smoothly. The system has been in use for some time, but virtually no problems have been encountered. Analysts and management jointly wish to review the system after 6 months. The objectives of the postimplementation review will be to:

1 Determine whether the systems goals and objectives have been achieved.
2 Determine whether personnel procedures, operating activities, and order controls have improved.
3 Determine whether user service requirements have been met, while simultaneously reducing errors and costs.
4 Determine whether known or unexpected limitations of the system need attention.

All indications are that the new system was well-received and will meet the performance objectives that led to its development in the first place.

What do you think the postimplementation review will show?

KEYWORDS

Attitude survey
Conversion
Conversion plan
Direct cutover
Event logging
Impact evaluation
Parallel systems
Phase-in
Pilot systems
Postimplementation review

REVIEW QUESTIONS

1 What is the purpose of systems training? How do user and operator training differ?
2 What advantages and disadvantages do in-house and in-service training offer? Discuss the role hardware and software vendors play in user training? In operator training?

3 What is the relation between conversion and systems implementation?
4 What methods are used for systems conversion? Briefly describe each.
5 Describe the purpose and contents of a conversion plan.
6 What is site preparation? Describe the concerns and activities associated with it. Who is responsible for site preparation?
7 How do conversion managers ensure that files and data are properly converted during implementation? Discuss the purpose of each method.
8 Why are controls needed on data transfer during conversion? What problems are most frequent?
9 Discuss the concerns of analysts during postimplementation review. Is this review important if the system has been properly implemented and favorably received by users?
10 What methods are used in postimplementation review? What is the purpose of each?

APPLICATION PROBLEMS FOR CHAPTER 13

1 A large antique dealer with four different stores is planning to install an automated inventory system. The system will allow the continual monitoring of items on hand, order, or backorder and rapid entering of newly received quantities into the inventory record. A central computer system, located at the main store which serves as the management headquarters, will store all information. Individual stores will be connected to the computer system through terminals and dedicated telephone communication lines. The users will retrieve information by entering information about the specific item wanted or the class of items of interest. If the user wishes to search a class of items, the display screen will show a full screen of information and then pause until a key is depressed indicating that the next screen of information can be displayed.

A particularly important aspect of the store operations is that each store maintains its own inventory of unique items. All items are individually serial-numbered, classified by type of item (such as chair), style (such as Chippendale), and age (in years). Separate records are kept for the items that each store has. That is, in the current manual system there are four separate inventory books, one for each store, that is kept at the store itself. It a customer is seeking a particular type of item, the sales assistant first shows the items that are available at that store. If the customer wants to know about other items or if the store does not have the desired item, the sales assistant then telephones the other stores and asks them whether they have the desired items. When calls are received, the salespersons must stop what they are doing and check their records. (Sometimes they are able to respond from memory, without checking stock records, although errors do occur when this is done.)

The analyst responsible for implementing the system is considering how to install the system. Each store has approximately 25 employees who must receive systems training. The 10 management employees will also need systems training. Thus, training plans must provide for 110 persons. Each training session will run approximately 3 days, and a single session can handle no more than 10 people since it requires hands-on activities right at the computer terminal.

The telephone company will install all the communication lines at the same time. All computer equipment will arrive together and be installed as soon as it arrives. The software portion of the system is well-proven and in use at many other similar companies.

a Should the analyst plan the implementation of all stores at one time, say during the week following the completion of training, or should the stores be phased in one at a time? What factors underlie your recommendation?

b If the systems design is altered to use a central inventory that includes all items, but lists the store at which the item is located (rather than four separate store inventories), will your implementation recommendation change? Explain.

2 The manager of a speciality store is contemplating when to install a computer-based sales and inventory system. The system will assist in capturing sales information, including customer names and addresses, that will be used as the basis for future mailing lists. It will also provide for the constant updating of inventory items. As items are sold, they are removed from the inventory records. At the same time, the system will contain information about items on order and the date on which items are expected to arrive, which can usually be estimated very accurately.

The speciality store does approximately 60 percent of its annual business between November 1 and January 1 each year. That is also the time when it gets the greatest amount of its new customers.

The manager knows that, if accurate information is not available about items in inventory or accurate arrival dates cannot be given to customers, significant sales will be lost. Each item the store sells is expensive, often priced over $100. Under the current manual system, inventory problems are both frustrating and costly. The 18 store employees are anxious for improvement, although they are concerned about whether the computer will be the answer and are unsure of how difficult it will be to learn how to use the system.

Assume that it is now July 1. The hardware and software for the new system can be ordered immediately. The suppliers estimate it will take 90 days for all necessary components to arrive. They also want 1 week to install and test the equipment and the programs to run the system and another week to train the personnel. Then all company inventory records must be entered into the new system through the on-line terminals. Supplier sales personnel estimate that the process will take about 2 weeks.

a Show the sequence of activities (by the week), using a bar or milestone chart (see Chapter 14). Assume that there will be no overlap in activities.

b The manager must decide whether to sign the contract now and seek implementation in time for the heavy shopping season beginning on November 1 or delay implementation until after January 1, when the level of business activity is at its slowest for the entire year. What are the advantages and disadvantages of each alternative?

c What would you recommend if you were the analyst? Why?

3 A new accounts receivable system will be implemented in a large company. The main reason for developing and installing the system is to improve the accuracy of the accounts receivable records, which average $1 million at the end of each month, and to provide more information for use in managing the receivables to improve collections and reduce the accounts receivable balance.

Under the new system, reports will be provided on which customers have overdue balances, how long the balances have been overdue, and when the last payments were made by the customers. The system will also provide controls that will prevent persons entering accounts receivable data from making errors.

One of the greatest problems with the current manual system is the error rate. At the present time there are accounts totaling over $200,000 in value for which only customer names and balances are available (there are no supporting sales or payment transactions) or which are being disputed by customers, who say they have made payments but did not receive credit for them, who are being charged for purchases they did not make, or who want full proof they are the ones responsible for the balance before they will make payment.

Management is insistent on installing the new system so that it is accurate and provides uniform information on all accounts and accounts balances. But it is not sure how to handle the $200,000 of problem accounts. Two approaches seem most reasonable: (1) enter all accounts information, including the problem accounts, into the new system, but include annotations in the accounts that are disputed or (2) keep the problem accounts separate from the new system (in essence, run two separate systems) and handle them independently from the automated system.

Which strategy should be adopted? Why?

4 An airline is changing from its current automated reservation and ticketing system to a new system that will use more powerful computers that are manufactured by another company, and new software that stores and processes data in a different way from that of the old system. All files in the current system are stored on computer media and are highly accurate. The files include those listed below.

Airline flight schedules	Each flight is identified by a unique number.
Airline personnel file	Each individual is identified by an employee identification number.
Airline reservation file	Each entry contains the passenger name, flight data, flight number, ticket cost, and class of service.
Travel agent file	Each entry contains the identification number, name, commission rate, and current account balance for each travel agent registered with the airline.

a Discuss the steps you would take to handle the systems conversion, paying particular attention to the validation process you would use for transferring the files listed to the new system.

b How can the transfer of data from one system to another be achieved without keying all the records manually? The formats of the current and new files are not compatible, and the storage media used on one system will not work on the other.

c If the alternatives for the actual conversion are to use either parallel systems or the direct cutover method, which method would you recommend? Why?

PART FIVE

INFORMATION SYSTEMS ADMINISTRATION

CHAPTER 14 MANAGEMENT OF INFORMATION SYSTEMS DEVELOPMENT

QUESTIONS TO GUIDE YOU THROUGH THE CHAPTER

- How do analysts estimate the amount of time needed to develop an information system?
- What factors determine program development time?
- Is it possible to estimate the effect of personnel experience in program development time?
- What methods are most frequently used to manage systems projects?
- How do team practices enable managers to best utilize project personnel?
- In what ways do project personnel ensure the right system is developed in the right way?

Successful information systems projects are successfully managed. In contrast, systems projects may go awry if time is not estimated properly, development plans do not take into account the critical nature of some tasks, and personnel are not utilized efficiently or effectively. This chapter discusses methods for estimating and managing project schedules. It will show how development time estimates are formulated, combined into working schedules, and used for the evaluation of performance. Systems development is inherently a team effort, as has been indicated repeatedly. This chapter shows how teams are organized and managed and points out how design and development reviews assist in achieving the desired quality and performance standards in the completed systems.

The first part of this chapter will emphasize management of the programming and physical development of the system. The last section discusses structured walkthroughs, a review method that can be applied to requirements analysis, design, and development to maintain systems quality throughout all systems development activities.

ESTIMATION AND MANAGEMENT OF DEVELOPMENT TIME

Poorly planned systems projects will not meet the schedule and will disappoint enthusiastic users. In some organizations, late developments are the rule, while, in other firms, they are the exception. Those projects that are developed on time have common characteristics: (1) a carefully formulated estimation of time requirements, (2) a means for management to monitor progress, (3) a means for comparing actual against planned performance, and (4) sufficient information to deal with problems when they arise. Each of these characteristics is discussed in this section.

Estimating Time Requirements

One of the most difficult aspects of project management is the formulation of estimates of the time required to develop a system. Estimates are, as their name suggests, approximations of the hours, days, or months of effort needed to produce the desired system. Their accuracy is in large part dependent on the skills, knowledge, and experience of the person preparing the estimates, usually the project manager. As will be shown, they are in many cases determined by factors, like the individual analysts' and programmers' abilities, systems complexity, and interruptions not directly related to the project, that are not directly under the control of the project manager.

METHODS OF TIME ESTIMATING

There are three common methods of estimating project development times. The *historical method* is based on careful records that are maintained on previous development efforts. The records indicate the characteristics of the program or project, task assignments, personnel time requirements, and any problems or unusual occurrences. When new projects are proposed, they are compared with the records on file to match planned with past efforts to estimate expected development time. The maintenance of records is a time-consuming process that many organizations prefer to avoid. This method is only as good as the records, and even then it is useful only if the proposed project fits the characteristics of a prior development.

Experience is said to be the best teacher. The *intuitive method* relies on the experience of senior personnel who estimate, on the basis of their personal experiences, expected development time. This method is sometimes described as an educated guess, the education portion being the prior experience of the individual making the estimate. Intuition differs from the historical approach in that documented cases and detailed records are not used.

The intuitive method is the most widely used approach. However, few people are able to estimate with high levels of accuracy. Its use is therefore due to the fact it is a quick and convenient method of deriving an estimate.

The *standard formula* method offers a more concrete approach to estimation. Individual factors that affect development time most drastically are identified and quantified. Such factors as personnel characteristics, systems details, and project complexity are assigned individual weights. An arithmetic formula specifies how to relate the individual elements to produce an estimate of development time in hours, days, or weeks. There have been numerous attempts at effective formula development, including highly publicized efforts by several large computer vendors. However, all are viewed with a certain amount of skepticism. We will develop a programming estimate, using an IBM formula, later in this section. However, many organizations have suggested standards or procedures for estimating development time.

Project time estimates are necessary for informing management of when a project will be finished and the system implemented. But, in addition, time estimates are needed to assist the project manager in scheduling personnel on various tasks to be performed or in making staff adjustments later, should the need arise. Project time estimates include two types of time requirements: project hour requirements and calendar time requirements.

PROJECT HOUR REQUIREMENTS

Project hour requirements are the time needs to conduct a systems investigation, formulate the logical design, code the software and prepare files, develop test data, test the software, and order and install the equipment. In other words, each activity associated with the development of an information system requires an amount of time that must be estimated and incorporated into the project schedule.

Estimating Systems Activity Times

Systems investigation time is determined from the number of persons to be interviewed and the time to develop, circulate, receive, and analyze questionnaire data, conduct observations, and inspect records. Although the analyst is dependent on other persons (that is, those who are interviewed or who must complete and return questionnaires), in many ways estimating investigation time is less complicated than estimating other systems activities.

Logical designs involve the creativity of the analyst and also require the development of many systems details, such as report definitions, file organizations, input validation and control methods, and run procedures. They are more difficult to estimate than analysis activities.

However, in most systems the greatest difficulty in formulating gross time requirements is in estimating the time for software programming and testing. Developing program logic requires approximately 35 percent of the total program time, as does testing and debugging (Figure 14.1). Actual coding and development of test data requires 25 percent of the time. Documentation requires approximately 5 percent of the project time allocation (IBM). This estimate is dependent on three major components:

1 Level of programmer expertise
2 Level of program complexity
3 Level of programmer understanding for the specific program

Programmer experience and expertise varies greatly from individual to individual. Large projects will involve programmer trainees, experienced personnel, and highly seasoned veterans. The project manager must consider the level of expertise when assigning individuals to specific tasks and estimating the time each person will need for a particular task.

Identifying Program Development Variables

Some project managers use a system of weights to evaluate an individual's skills and associate them with project time requirements. The criteria used include:

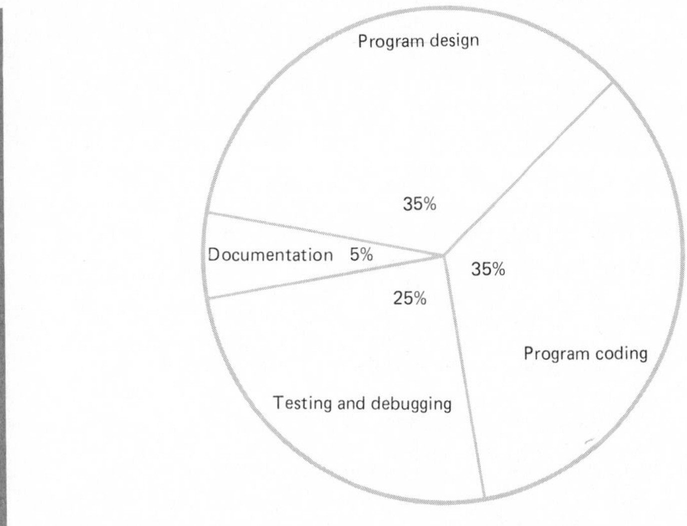

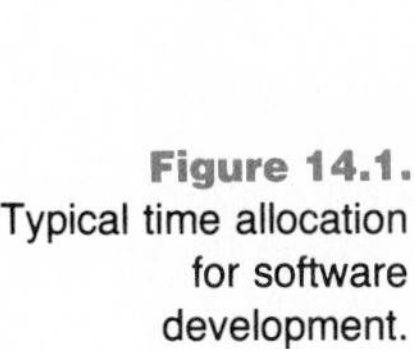

Figure 14.1. Typical time allocation for software development.

1 Knowledge of the programming language to be used for the project
2 Experience with the computer system on which the system will run
3 Programming experience
4 Logic ability
5 Creativity and imagination
6 Patience
7 Maturity
8 Persistence
9 Education

Each individual is assigned a weight, typically between 1 and 5, based on the individual's attributes in each of the above categories. For example, a new programmer will usually be evaluated as a 1 or 2 in terms of programming experience, while a seasoned veteran as a rule is rated a 5.

In general, analysts should assume that a programmer trainee requires three to four times more time to develop a program than a veteran programmer with 5 to 7 years experience. In contrast, a senior programmer with substantial and varied experience needs approximately 50 to 75 percent less time than a veteran programmer.

Program complexity is a measure of the level of systems features, such as input and output methods, and the difficulty of program logic that will be embedded in the software. For example, a program that reads a single type of punched card, updates a sequential file on magnetic tape, and prints a listing of each transaction processed is not as complex as an on-line system accepting variable types of input from multiple locations. If several files are involved or distributed processing is used, program complexity may be judged even greater.

The variables making up program complexity (modified from a system proposed by IBM) include the following:

VARIABLE	WEIGHT
TYPE OF INPUT	
Single card	1
Multiple card	2
Single data item, direct input	1
Multiple data item, direct input	2
Magnetic input (tape, disk, MICR, etc., see Type of files)	1
TYPE OF OUTPUT	
Printer, one line per record	1
Printer, multiple lines per record	2
Display, single screen, single line	2
Display, single screen, multiple line	3
Display, multiple screen	4
Punched card, single format	1
Punched card, multiple format	2
Magnetic output (see Type of files)	
TYPE OF FILES	
Sequential file, single-record type	1
multiple-record type	2
variable-length record	3
Indexed sequential file, single-record type	2
multiple-record types	3
Virtual sequential file	4
Direct-access file, single-record type	3
multiple-record type	4
PROGRAMMING LANGUAGE (SEE TABLE 14.1)	

Each factor relevant to a program is assigned a weight, lower numbers for attributes that involve the least complexity and higher numbers for those that involve the most. A 1-to-5 scale is often used for these weights. Figure 14.2 demonstrates the use of this weighting system for a system using index sequential files and error reporting.

The programmers' knowledge of the system or program they must develop may span several levels (IBM):

1. Detailed knowledge of the required job
2. General knowledge of the required job
3. General knowledge of related subjects
4. No job or general knowledge of related subjects

Further weighting is assessed depending on the knowledge needed to perform the job. For instance an individual who has high job knowledge in a situation that only requires a moderate level of such knowledge will be evaluated differently than one who has high job knowledge in a system that demands high knowledge (Table 14.2).

Calculating Programming Time Estimates

Each program must be evaluated independently of the others. To determine the number of days for each program, the project manager must combine the

TABLE 14.1

WEIGHTS FOR PROGRAM PROCESSING CHARACTERISTICS (COURTESY OF INTERNATIONAL BUSINESS MACHINES CORPORATION)

PROGRAMMING SYSTEM	FUNCTION	Weighting Points			Range[1]	
		SIMPLE	COMPLEX	VERY COMPLEX	MIN.	MAX.
COBOL	• Restructure data	1	3	4		
	• Condition checking	1	4	7		
	• Data retrieval & presentation	2	5	8		
	• Calculate	1	3	5		
	• Linkage	1	2	3		
	Total	6	17	27	4	27
Assembler language	• Restructure data	4	5	6		
	• Condition checking	4	7	9		
	• Data retrieval & presentation	4	7	9		
	• Calculate	3	5	8		
	• Linkage	2	3	5		
	Total	17	27	37	12	37
IBM utility programs (sort, file-to-file, copy-restore, etc.)	• Control card changes only	1	N/A	N/A		
	• Own coding required	2	3	4		
	Total	3	3	4		
RPG		2	8	13		
PL/I	• Restructure data[2]	1	2	4		
	• Condition checking[3]	.5	3	6		
	• Data retrieval & presentation[4]	.5	4	8		
	• Calculate[5]	1	2	4		
	• Linkage[6]	.5	1	2		
	Total	5.5	20	37	2	24

[1]Range represents the minimum and maximum weighting that can be developed from the proper use of these tables applied to a single program. Such weights should be evaluated for historical accuracy to better make such estimates.

[2]Restructure data—Combining, condensing, rearranging, and deleting data and file updating.

[3]Condition checking—Control checks, such as header and trailer label routines, reasonableness checks, limit checks, and error routines associated with these procedures.

[4]Data retrieval and presentation—Unique file search for specific records, table lookup, randomizing techniques for record access, and indexing associated with these activities.

[5]Calculate—Arithmetic computations of all types, excluding simple steps taken in connection with one of the other categories (for example, add 1 to a counter).

[6]Linkage—Program overlay routines, check-point and restart procedures, and routines required to permit program to interface with a programming system or with another program or program module.

PROGRAM CHARACTERISTICS	WEIGHT
INPUT FEATURES	
Index sequential; one type of record	2
Sequential file of transactions on magnetic tape	1
Sequential file of error exception data on magnetic disk	1
OUTPUT FEATURES	
Single format output listing	1
Single format transaction listing	1
Single format error report	1
	7
COMPLEXITY	
COBOL language; moderate complexity	17
PROGRAMMER CHARACTERISTICS	
Programmer experience factor	3.5
Programmer job knowledge	0.75
PRODUCTION LOSS FACTOR	60%
FORMULA RESULT:	[(17 + 7) × (3.5 × 0.75)] × 1.60 = 100.8 days

Figure 14.2. Program development time using estimation formula.

data identified above. If a quantitative approach is followed strictly, the program complexity is multiplied by the sum of programmer experience and understanding. In the example in Figure 14.2, the program characteristics result in weights totaling 7. The COBOL program, assessed to be of moderate complexity using the features outlined in Table 14.1, has weights of 17. The program itself requires general, but not detailed, knowledge by the programmer, who in this example is assumed to be a trainee. In addition, it is estimated that an additional 60 percent will be added to pure programming time because of meetings and lost time. Using the formula in Figure 14.2, a total estimate of 100 days is produced for the sample program.

Estimates can be sensitive to errors. Therefore, some managers prefer to use an estimate that combines individual estimates of earliest, latest, and most likely development time. They are combined in a formula to produce a new estimate:

$$\text{Estimate} = \frac{\text{most pessimistic} + 4 \times (\text{most likely}) + \text{most optimistic}}{6}$$

In some organizations, the use of a specific formula is required to

TABLE 14.2

SAMPLE PROGRAMMER PRODUCTIVITY GUIDELINES

(*a*) Programmer's Experience Level (Courtesy of International Business Machines Corporation)

PROGRAMMING POSITION	OVERALL PROGRAMMING EXPERIENCE	PERSON DAYS PER PROGRAM: WEIGHT POINT
Senior programmer	Experience in writing and implementing many programs on varied types of equipment. Very experienced in particular computer configuration and programming system.	0.50–0.75
Programmer	Experience in writing and implementing programs of various complexities. Experience with particular computer configuration and programming system.	1.00–1.50
Apprentice	Written and implemented several programs. Limited experience with particular configuration and programming system.	2.00–3.00
Trainee	Completed programming school. Written academic training programs. Very limited experience.	3.50–4.00

(*b*) Job Knowledge Chart (Courtesy of International Business Machines Corporation)

	Job knowledge required		
JOB KNOWLEDGE AVAILABLE	MUCH	SOME	NONE
Detailed knowledge of this job	0.75	0.25	0.00
Good general knowledge of this job with fragmentary detailed knowledge	1.25	0.50	0.00
Fair general knowledge of this job but little or no detailed knowledge	1.50	0.75	0.00
No job knowledge but general knowledge of related subjects	1.75	1.00	0.25
No job knowledge and no general knowledge of related subjects	2.00	1.25	0.25

develop estimates that can be presented to management. Each organization has its own policy for estimation procedures.

CALENDAR TIME REQUIREMENTS

Merely identifying project time requirements does not produce the number of days, weeks, or months to build into the project schedule. It is only one factor. In most systems projects, additional time is used on project activities. Management meetings, project reviews, education and training, interaction with users, sick time, vacations and holidays, and computer systems unavailability extend the schedule beyond the previous estimates. In fact, in large systems projects, the additional time needed for these activities extends the total development time from 50 to 100 percent.

Based on these criteria, a project that is estimated to require 250 days programming time will take from 375 to 500 project days.

A *project day* (sometimes called a person day) is used to measure the number of days a project will require on the basis of the work one individual can do during 1 day. The number of persons working on the project affects the calendar time, although not proportionally. Adding more people to a project reduces the total calendar time, but nonproject time must be allowed.

Three methods are commonly used to plan calendar time requirements: bar, milestone, and PERT charts.

Bar Charts

The simplest planning uses bar charts that show each activity in a systems project and the amount of time it will take. This method, developed by Henry L. Gantt (the charts are sometimes called *Gantt charts),* uses bars to indicate the amount of time spent on each task (Figure 14.3). The analyst first identifies each task and estimates the amount of time needed for it. When this information is transferred to the bar chart, the tasks are listed from top to bottom on the left side of the chart in the order in which they will be undertaken. Calendar time is shown from left to right. A horizontal bar is marked on the chart for each task, indicating when it starts and when it is expected to be completed. Thus, the first task in Figure 14.3 is planned to take 2 weeks. Three separate activities, beginning in the third week, require from 2 to 4 weeks each. The absence of a bar means no work is associated with the activity during a particular time period.

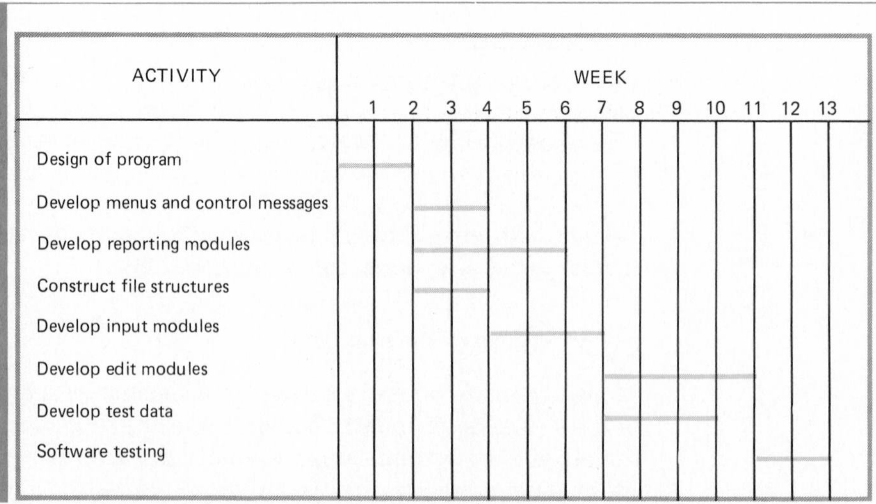

Figure 14.3. Bar chart information system development plan.

Bar charts are most manageable when the project consists of a limited number of tasks or activities. Otherwise the size of the chart becomes unwieldy and includes so many bars that it is difficult to use the information.

Frequently several levels of charts will be used to communicate planning information. An overall planning chart shows the major activities. An individual responsible for an entire project will want a more general chart than the chief programmer, for example, who must subdivide each major task into smaller tasks, that are individually managed and controlled. Thus how finely task details are shown on bar charts depends on the way the chart will be used.

Milestone Charts

All projects have significant events, called *milestones,* that mark significant points in their development. They represent difficult hurdles to be passed or critical tasks that must be completed on time. Milestone charts show the significant events in completing a project and the sequence in which they must be completed. They differ from bar charts because they represent completion points, not individual tasks to be undertaken.

For example, significant milestones in completing a systems implementation include the arrival of the equipment, installation of the equipment, completion of user training, conversion of files, and cutover to the new system.

Progress in a project is measured by comparing the status of an activity with a milestone or completion time; this allows the project manager to keep the project on time. The disadvantage of this method is its total emphasis on time, rather than on the interdependencies of tasks and events or monitoring of project costs. The developer must also be sure to use milestones that are significant and measureable. Milestones such as interviews 50 percent completed, coding half done, or analysts comfortable with logical design are not useful and should be avoided.

PERT Charts

The most sophisticated planning method is the Program Evaluation and Review Technique (PERT). This method, developed in 1958 by the U.S. Navy and Booze, Allen, and Hamilton, a management consulting firm, has been used in many complex projects requiring careful planning and management. In developing the Polaris weapons system the Navy needed a method to schedule and integrate thousands of industrial and scientific activities, a procedure for determining the project's progress, and a way to evaluate the effect of changes in the completion schedule. PERT was devised to meet this challenge. It was successful in aiding the Navy to complete the Polaris weapons system 2 years ahead of schedule, when other Navy projects, not using PERT, were running behind schedule and over budget.

Although the best approach to project management is to break the project into small, manageable pieces, there is a danger of losing sight of the overall project while supervising the smaller tasks. Project activities are usually interdependent. However, the interdependence of tasks is not evident in the bar-chart or milestone methods. The critical tasks, those that must be completed on time and in a specific sequence, are also not evident. A project manager wants to: indicate the individual activities and the time needed for each, show the interrelationship of activities, identify the proper sequence, give time estimations, isolate areas where potential problems or delays may occur (and indicate those areas needing the closest monitoring and supervision), and have a means of monitoring progress on the project. It may be necessary to know, for example, what the effect of delaying a certain activity is on the project as a whole, or for which activity there is the least tolerance for delay. Properly developed PERT charts provide this information. Bar charts merely imply task interdependence.

Projects consist of events and activities. The PERT chart uses nodes and paths (or arcs) to represent the interrelation of project activities (Figure 14.4). The nodes represent events, and the paths show the activities that are required to move ahead from one event to another. The numbers in parentheses indicate the amount of time needed to perform each activity. In a large project, the network of lines and nodes will be extensive.

The PERT chart is most valuable when a project is being planned and designed. When the network is finished, it is studied to determine the *critical path,* that is the path from beginning to end, over which the total time required will be greater than for any other path (shown in color in Figure 14.5). If activities along this path are not completed on time, the entire project will be late. Hence management attention should be continually directed to these activities.

PERT also shows the interdependencies of the tasks and assists in answering three common management questions:

1. What other activities must precede or be completed before the initiation of a specific activity?
2. What other activities can be done while a specific activity is in progress?
3. What activities cannot be started until after the completion of a specific activity?

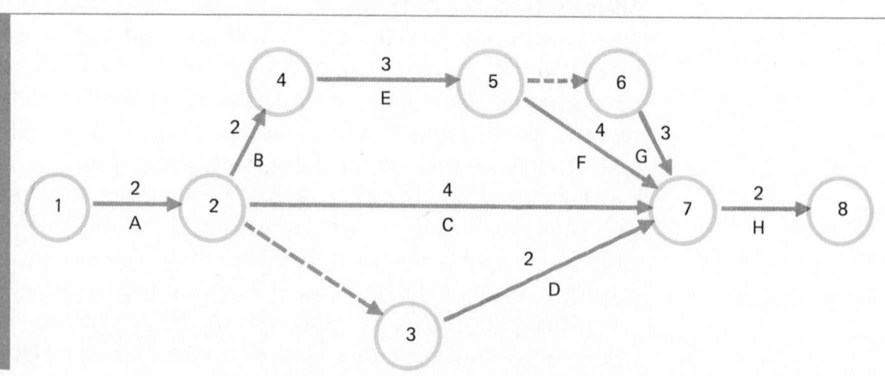

Figure 14.4. Sample information system development PERT chart.

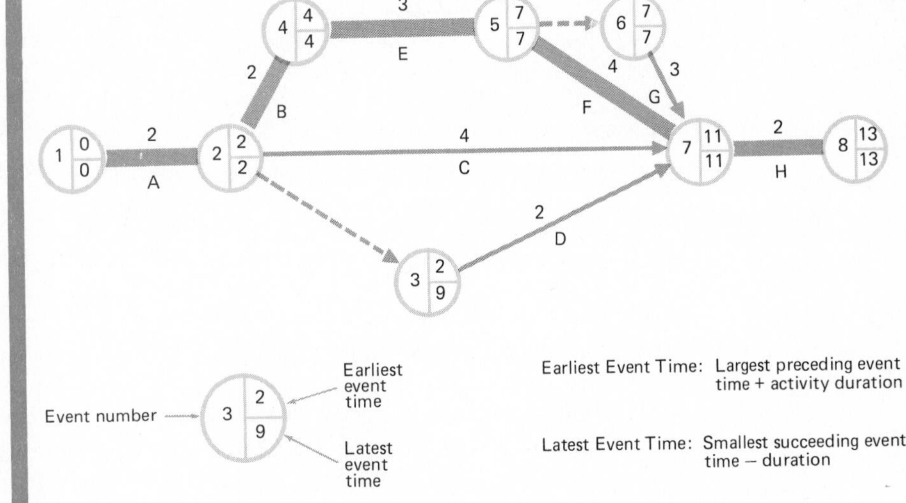

Figure 14.5. Activity times in PERT network.

To develop a PERT network for an information systems project, the tasks and times associated with each activity must be identified first. The time for each activity is the *duration*. Next, the sequence of activities must be identified and the places where specific tasks must precede others and where certain activities may occur simultaneously with others noted. This information is shown in the network developed in Figure 14.5: the lines represent activities A through H and the number on each line is the number of weeks the project manager expects that activity to take (that is, the activity duration). The lengths of the lines themselves have no significance.

In this example, events 2-4, 2-7, and 2-3 cannot begin before task A is completed, as indicated by the location of the events on the network. The dotted line between events 2 and 3 has special significance. No time is associated with the dotted line, and it does not have a task identification (a letter or a name) assigned. When there is a dependency between two events, but no time or resources are consumed, it is called a *dummy activity*. Before task D in Figure 14.5 can begin, event 2 must be completed. Similarly, event 5 must occur before activity G may be undertaken. The dummy activities can therefore be used to link parallel activities. (Activities C and D can occur in parallel.)

The next step is to analyze the project schedule. We want to know (1) how early the event can begin and (2) how late the event can begin without affecting the overall project schedule. The earliest event time (denoted ET) is 0 for the first event. For the others it is the *highest sum of the activity duration and ET of any immediately preceding event*. For example, four activities immediately precede event 7. The ET is computed by examining the ET and duration time for each preceding event.

ACTIVITY	PRECEDING ET	DURATION	CALCULATED ET
3–7	2	3	5
2–7	2	4	6
5–7	7	4	11
6–7	7	3	10

Since event 7 cannot begin until all preceding events are completed, our concern is with the largest time factor, 11 in this case. Figure 14.5 shows the ET for the entire network. A frequently used notation shows the ET in the upper right part of the node and the LT in the lower right portion.

The latest event time (LT) is the latest time at which the event can begin *without delaying* the project. To determine this time, it is necessary to work backwards through the network, starting from the right. The latest time is the *smallest difference between the LT of the terminal event minus the activity duration time.*

For example, to determine the LT for event 7, the LT of the following node, number 8 in Figure 14.5, is noted as 13. Subtracting the duration time, the latest event time is determined as 13 − 2 = 11. The lower right number in node 7 is shown as 11.

To determine the latest starting time for event 2, the computations are:

ACTIVITY	SUCCEEDING LT	DURATION	CALCULATED LT
2–4	4	2	2
2–7	11	4	7

Since the smallest LT is 2, this time becomes the LT for event 2.

The *critical path* is the set of activities that managers must monitor most closely. It identifies the events that must be begun and completed on time and require no more than the estimated duration time; otherwise the entire project will be delayed.

In Figure 14.5 the critical path is shown in color. It was determined by linking together all the nodes where the ET and LT are equal, meaning there is no room for change or deviation. That is, there is no *slack time.*

The amount of slack time associated with an event can be shown formally by subtracting the duration time and ET of the initial node from the LT of the terminal node. For example, for event 3-7, the slack time is 7 weeks (11 − 2 − 2 = 7). This means that activity 3-7 can begin anytime from the second to the ninth week, and, if the duration time of 2 weeks is maintained, the project will be on schedule. Knowing that there is this flexibility may ease personnel scheduling.

PERT charts are most useful in design, as indicated. In large systems, it is difficult to keep the charts maintained and updated to show the exact status of all activities. For this reason, many managers use a combination of charts: PERT charts to plan development and show interdependencies and bar charts to show calendar schedules.

PERSONNEL AND DEVELOPMENT MANAGEMENT

Developing reliable schedules does not guarantee project success. The project must still be managed. Personnel must be assigned and properly used. At the same time, the development must meet specifications and follow guidelines for quality assurance. This section discusses the utilization of personnel and the use of structured walkthroughs throughout the development process.

Project Team Concepts

Systems development and computer programming in particular are typically considered individual activities. However, from a management viewpoint, it is essential to provide for the departure of key personnel on whom an organization is highly dependent, provide training for new or rising personnel, and ensure that the best people are used for specific jobs. In this section, we discuss team concepts, with special emphasis on the programming activities of systems development. However, the team concept applies throughout the systems development process. Three variations of the team concept are discussed: chief-programmer teams, specialist teams, and leaderless teams (Figure 14.6).

CHIEF-PROGRAMMER TEAMS

The chief-programmer team consists of a chief programmer, a backup programmer, and support personnel. The *chief programmer* is a highly experienced and skilled programmer who performs all the design tasks for the project and writes the program code for all the critical modules in a

Figure 14.6 Characteristics of team programming arrangements.

	CHIEF PROGRAMMER TEAM	**SPECIALIST TEAM**	**LEADERLESS TEAM**
Team Members:	Chief Programmer Backup Programmer(s) Programming Librarian	Chief Programmer Backup Programmer(s) Administrator Toolsmith Test Specialist Documentation Editor Programming Librarian Other specialists as needed	Membership same as either other format. Leadership depends on the project.
Characteristics:	Chief programmer formulates design tasks and writes code for all critical modules in system. Also performs integration and testing of team's code. Serves as primary contact for users and other teams.	Common core of team members stays together throughout project. Administrative support added to handle budgets, facilities, and computer arrangements. Specialists added as needed for specific tasks.	Team members' assignments and leadership roles change from project to project. The team stays together from project to project.

system. This person also integrates and tests the team's code. In large projects, communication between users and development teams is time-consuming and occasionally even confusing, particularly if a specific user is working with several team members at the same time or if different team members individually contact the same users repeatedly. To avoid frustrating and confusing communication, the chief programmer is the primary contact for users and other teams.

The *backup programmer,* who has similar skills but less experience, performs such activities as researching design alternatives and development strategies. This person also participates in software design, program coding, and test planning. The *programming librarian,* generally not someone with programming or design experience, is responsible for maintaining both the external program library and the internal documentation library.

The *external program library* consists of source code sets, object modules, and temporary drivers, as well as test data and job control language procedures. It is maintained in printed form, usually in a set of binders. The librarian's responsibility is to keep the library updated with copies of each item provided by the programmers as changes are made. The *internal library* serves as an archive of information, a backup for the programmers in the event the external program library is damaged or destroyed.

The chief-programmer team concept gets senior-level people back into the mainstream of programming and systems development. Too often good technical people are promoted up and into management tasks. In many cases they are much better technicians than managers. And, they may be happier in development roles. The chief-programmer team method provides for both advancement and the opportunity to continue in development roles.

Under this structure, teams are adjustable, so that specialists may be added as needed for a project. The team will vary in size and personnel from job to job and thus have the flexibility needed for different tasks. At the same time, it is an effective way to provide training and experience for junior personnel or individuals in training. The librarian role provides for regular and painless maintenance of systems documentation.

Of course, backup programmers may want to move ahead to chief-programmer roles. Chief programmers may still need management training. If these concerns are not met, the advantages of the team concept may be reduced or even lost.

SPECIALIST TEAMS

A frequent variation on the team format, the *specialist team,* includes specialists as the need arises, as its name indicates. A common core of team members stays together for the entire project. Each member has a special assignment that takes advantage of his or her talents. In addition to the chief and backup programmers, an administrator is responsible for budgets, arranging physical space and machine time, and dealing with personnel difficulties. A documentation editor edits the documentation and supervises its production, while the librarian manages the systems libraries and archives. A *toolsmith* is responsible for designing and developing or acquiring any special programming or testing tools needed, while a *test specialist* writes all test cases and develops test drivers.

The specialist team offers similar advantages to the chief-programmer team, but involves individuals who have specific expertise, benefiting the team, the individual, and the project. Specialists are usually members of several project teams at the same time.

LEADERLESS TEAMS

Some organizations have modified the chief-programmer concept by establishing teams that have no permanent leader. Particular team members rise to leadership on an informal basis for different projects, depending on the nature of the task and their own abilities. The team members allocate work assignments among them, on the basis of their talents. Unlike the other programming teams, this team stays together from project to project; it is not automatically disbanded after each system is completed.

Leaderless teams are not in widespread use, although the concept does have advantages. However, many organizations feel that someone must be appointed with specific management responsibility for the project—an aspect that is explicitly excluded in leaderless teams.

Structured Walkthroughs

A *structured walkthrough* is a review of a system or its software by persons involved in the development effort. The participants are generally at the same level in the organization; that is, they are analysts or programmer-analysts. Typically department managers of, say, marketing or manufacturing are not involved in the review even though they may be the eventual recipients of the system. Sometimes structured walkthroughs are called *peer reviews* because the participants are colleagues at the same level in the organization.

CHARACTERISTICS

The purpose of walkthroughs is to find areas where improvement can be made in the system or the development process. Team members do not place blame for any problems encountered. To do so negates the possible benefits from the process. It should be viewed by programmers and analysts as an opportunity to receive assistance, not as an obstacle to be avoided or put up with.

Similarly, the review session does not result in the correction of errors or changes in specifications. Those activities remain the responsibility of the developers. Hence the emphasis is constantly on review, not repair.

The walkthrough concept recognizes that systems development is a team process. The participants, with the possible exception of participants from user departments, are those individuals who are actually involved in the development of the system or production of software.

The individuals who formulated the design specifications or created the program code are, as you would expect, part of the review team. A moderator is sometimes chosen to lead the review, although many organizations prefer to have the analyst or designer who formulated the specifications or program lead the session, since they have greater familiarity with the item being reviewed. In either case, someone must be responsible for keeping the review focused on the subject of the meeting.

A scribe or recorder is also needed to capture the details of the discussion and the ideas raised. The walkthrough leader or the sponsoring programmers or analysts may not be able to jot down all the points aired by the participants. Therefore, appointing another individual to record all the relevant details usually ensures this occurs in a more complete and objective fashion.

Systems managers are increasingly discovering the benefits of establishing standards for data names, module determination, and data item size and type. The time to start enforcing these standards is at the design stage. Therefore, they should be emphasized during walkthrough sessions.

Maintenance should also be addressed during walkthroughs. The issues of coding standards, modularity, and documentation are key determinants of supporting later maintenance needs. It is becoming increasingly common to find organizations that will not accept new software for installation until it has been approved by software maintenance teams. In such an organization, a participant from the quality control or maintenance team should be an active participant in each structured walkthrough.

The walkthrough team must be large enough to deal with the subject of the review in a meaningful way, but not so large that it cannot accomplish anything. Generally no more than 7 to 9 persons should be involved, including the individuals who actually developed the product under review, the recorder, and the review leader. On the other hand, a review team of only two or three people will not generally provide enough independent idea generation and objectivity to produce the intended results.

As a general rule, management is not directly involved in structured walkthrough sessions. Its participation could actually jeopardize the intent of the review by preventing persons from speaking out about problems they see in a project. Management is often interpreted to mean evaluation. Many times the result is that individuals attempt to perfect their product before the review session so that they look good in the eyes of management. Managers may feel that raising many questions, identifying mistakes, or suggesting changes indicates that the individual whose work is under review is incompetent. Therefore, it is best to provide management with reports summarizing the review session rather than to have managers participate (Figure 14.7). The most appropriate type of report will communicate that a review of the specific project or product was conducted, who attended, and what action the team took. It need not summarize errors that were found, modifications suggested, or revisions needed.

Summary of Walkthrough/Review

Date ________
Time ________

Project/Contract No. ________________
Project Name ________________
Unit/Section/Module Reviewed ________________
Brief description of above ________________

Participants

________________ Leader-Phone

Results

[ ] ACCEPT IN CURRENT FORM

[ ] REJECT – MAJOR REVISIONS NEEDED

[ ] ACCEPT WITH MINOR MODIFICATION

[ ] REJECT – REDEVELOPMENT NEEDED

[ ] REVIEW NOT COMPLETED

Discussion/Recommendations

Attachments

________________ Leader Signature

Figure 14.7. Sample form for reporting results of walkthrough sessions.

Structured reviews rarely exceed 90 minutes duration.

The structured walkthrough can be used throughout the systems development process as a constructive and cost-effective management tool, after the detailed investigation (requirements review), following design (design review), and during program development (code review and testing review).

REQUIREMENTS REVIEW

A *requirements review* is a walkthrough conducted to examine the requirements specifications formulated by the analyst. Also called a *specification review,* this walkthrough is aimed at examining the functions, activities, and processes that the new system will handle. It is conducted after the completion of the detailed investigation and emphasizes the information and processing requirements the proposed design should handle. If there are inconsistencies among the requirements stated by the users and those the analyst is proposing to meet through the new system or if there are vague specifications, the walkthrough should uncover them so they can be dealt with.

The requirements review, like all walkthroughs, is conducted using a written document that participants read and study prior to the actual walkthrough. This description must spell out the system and its requirements and how key components in the system relate to one another. It should also identify the persons in key positions who will use or influence the new system. It is vitally important that sources and uses of information also be described and evaluated.

In addition to the narrative, the most effective requirements reviews also use data flow diagrams, decision tables, or data dictionaries to assist in describing and understanding the processes, data captured and used, and storage requirements. Organizations will vary in the particular form of description they use, but they all use one or more of these methods to communicate the requirements for review.

DESIGN REVIEW

Design reviews, as the name suggests, focus on design specifications for meeting previously identified systems requirements. The information supplied about the design prior to the session may be communicated using HIPO charts, structured flowcharts, Warnier/Orr diagrams, screen designs, or document layouts. In other words, the logical design of the system is communicated to the participants so they can prepare for the review.

The purpose of this type of walkthrough is to determine whether the proposed design will meet the requirements in an effective and efficient way. If the participants find discrepancies between the design and requirements, they will point them out and discuss them. However, it is not the purpose of the walkthrough to redesign portions of the system. That responsibility remains with the analyst assigned to the project.

CODE REVIEW

Structured walkthroughs were first used to review the program code; they worked so well that the process was expanded to the other types discussed in this section. A *code review* is a structured walkthrough conducted to examine the program code developed in a system, along with its documentation. It is used for new systems and for systems under maintenance.

As a general rule, a code review does not deal with an entire software system, but rather with individual modules or major components in a program. The code itself is compared with the original specifications or requirements to determine whether they are being satisfied. Discovering that a portion of a code does not agree with the original specifications or finding problems or mistakes that originated with the earlier requirements analysis is not uncommon. Although finding that a program or design must be modified can be frustrating, it is better to realize it during the review than after the system is implemented. Costs will be lower, changes easier, and more important, users will receive the proper system.

When programs are reviewed, the participants also assess the execution efficiency, use of standard data names and modules, and program errors. Obvious errors, such as syntax errors and blatant logic errors, can even be jotted down ahead of time by team members and submitted to the recorder and thus save meeting time. Other errors may merit discussion and examination during the review. Figure 14.8 shows a checklist that can be used for noting problems and their severity. Missing details, unnecessary components, and major and minor errors are easily pointed out using such a checklist.

When applied to maintenance projects, the process is the same, except

Walkthrough/Review Checklist

Project/Contract No. ____________________
Project Name ____________________

Review Category	Problem Detected (check all that apply)			
	Absent	Unnec	Error	Major*
Backup procedures				
Error messages				
Execution time				
External documentation				
Internal documentation				
Input validation				
Interface mechanism				
Procedural logic				
Passing of data				
Meets design specifications				
Meets user/problem specifications				
Meets coding standards				
Meets data standards				
Maintainability				
Storage use				
Test data				
Test procedure				
Test for end conditions				
Test for all possible conditions				
Test drop through				
Transfer of control				
Visible structure				

*Major error that will cause failure or crash

Figure 14.8. Sample checklist for guiding review activities.

that some of the program code already existed prior to undertaking the maintenance work. The importance of comparing the code with the requirements or specifications is no less important when changes are made to an existing system than when the project is a new system.

TESTING REVIEW

Perhaps the least common use of the structured walkthrough is for the analysis of testing programs. Yet the same benefits of peer review can be realized in this development activity. In fact, errors undetected during unit and systems testing will likely remain with the system when it is implemented. These are the errors that will cause nightmares for users and analysts alike.

Participants in testing reviews do not actually examine the output from test runs or search for errors that have been detected by using a set of test data. Instead they focus on the testing strategy that will be used and assess its suitability for detecting critical systems errors. Walkthrough participants also assist in developing test data that can detect design or software errors. Since the purpose of testing is finding errors, not proving program correctness, the assistance of the walkthrough team in developing effective test cases can be extremely helpful in detecting unknown errors. The team's ability to approach a system with a fresh look, since it has not been working with it every day, will usually bring new ideas and questions that are converted into test cases.

APPROVAL AUTHORITY

In many organizations, the team that conducts a structured walkthrough has the final approval authority over the project at that phase. If the team does not approve the specifications, the design, or the code, problems identified by team members must be fixed before further development can occur. When major changes are required, the team may request a final review before acceptance is granted. However, if the changes are less crucial, it may accept verbal or written notification they are complete and not conduct an additional review.

Some organizations require unanimous approval of all team members before a project is approved. Others establish strict voting rules. For example, in some cases a simple majority of voter approval is needed. In still others, the formality depends on the nature of the problem or change suggested. Design questions may require full-team approval, while questions of programming style or execution efficiency may be resolved by majority approval.

Merely conducting structured walkthroughs does not guarantee that a program or system will be better than if no walkthrough is conducted at all. This method is successful only if the sessions are properly managed and the suggestions followed by analysts and programmers. Management support, as with so many systems development activities, is essential.

SUMMARY

To meet important development schedules, information system projects must be planned carefully. The time required to develop a system may be estimated using historical records of the effort needed to develop other similar projects. Sometimes experience or intuition is the basis of estimates. A third method uses a standard formula that takes into account program and personnel characteristics.

Both project hour requirements, the number of personnel hours needed to develop a system, and the number of calendar days are important. The methods above are aimed at determining personnel hours. To estimate and visually show calendar times, the analyst may use bar charts that identify the amount of time each activity in the project will take, or milestone charts that mark significant points in development. The most sophisticated planning method, PERT (planning evaluation and review technique), allows analysts to identify and assess the interdependence of activities in a project. Overall project time is identified along with the critical path, the set of activities from beginning to end over which the total time required will be greater than for any other path. Activities on the critical path should be monitored carefully by management for timely project completion.

Personnel management is also a concern of project managers. Often systems analysts and programmers work in teams rather than as individuals. Team programming and system development provides training opportunities for inexperienced personnel while allowing individuals to use their talents and abilities in effective ways. Three common types of teams are chief programmer, specialist, and leaderless teams. They vary in the nature of personnel comprising the team, in the responsibilities assigned to individuals, and by whether they consist of temporary or permanent members.

Structured walkthroughs are often employed to enhance system quality and to provide guidance to systems analysts and programmers. A walkthrough, also called a peer review, is an opportunity for an individual to receive assistance from colleagues. Depending on the type of review, system specifications, computer programs, or software testing plans are reviewed in sessions lasting up to 90 minutes. The review session does not result in correction of errors or changes in specifications. Those activities remain the responsibility of the developer and occur after the review session is completed.

The walkthrough is a team activity. However, as a general rule, management is not directly involved in a walkthrough session. Rather, managers are provided with reports summarizing review sessions. The report summarizes the nature of the review, indicates who attended, and what action was taken.

The management of a systems project is an important aspect of the overall development effort. If the system is delivered late or if steps are not taken by analysts and managers to ensure that it is high quality, the users will surely be disappointed. The system may even fail. The guidelines mentioned in this chapter provide the basis for sound project management.

KEYWORDS

Chief-programmer team
Code review
Critical path
Design review
Dummy activity
External program library
Gantt chart
Internal program library
Leaderless team
Milestone
PERT
Requirements review
Slack time
Specialist team
Structured walkthrough
Testing review

REVIEW QUESTIONS

1 What methods are used to estimate program development time? Briefly describe the advantages and disadvantages of each one.
2 Compare the two types of time requirements associated with project development. Is one type more important than the other? Explain your answer.
3 What are the proportions of total program development time typically required by each activity comprising software programming and testing? What factors affect these estimates?
4 How do veteran and inexperienced programmer time requirements vary?
5 What factors are determinants of program complexity? How is each utilized to estimate program development time? What other influences must be considered when formulating time estimates?
6 When there is uncertainty over programming time estimates, how is a single usable estimate determined?
7 Discuss the similarities and differences between bar, milestone, and PERT charts.
8 What is the purpose of PERT? What components comprise a PERT chart?
9 When is PERT most valuable for project management? Why is this so?
10 Compare and contrast the three common programming team concepts? Why will an organization select one over the others?
11 How do internal and external program libraries vary? Are both needed? Explain.
12 For what purposes do project managers use structured walkthroughs? What guidelines ensure meaningful results?

APPLICATION PROBLEMS FOR CHAPTER 14

1 A computer program for an on-line system that will be written in the COBOL language has the following characteristics:
  a A table file containing reference information will be stored on magnetic disk.
  b A direct entry transaction file will be stored sequentially on magnetic disk. The

record format will vary depending on the type of transaction. Two formats will be used, but both will use fixed-length records of the same size.

c The master file, consisting of a single record format, will be stored using an index sequential access method.

d The system will produce a transaction report, a master file listing in either alphabetical or numerical order, and a summary report for management. In addition, through on-line inquiry, information can be retrieved and presented visually. Each inquiry will produce a response that utilizes two different screens.

This system requires a moderate general knowledge of the business activities it will support, but not detailed knowledge. Two highly experienced programmers will be assigned to develop the software. Both are experienced with the computer configuration that will be used, but neither is considered a senior programmer.

If the productivity factor is 75 percent, how long should it take to develop this program using the two programmers equally? Use the guidelines discussed in this chapter for calculating the estimate. How should this estimate be used in comparison with other estimates that may be developed using historical records or intuition?

2 A system to aid a retail sales firm in sales and inventory management has been designed and programming is about to begin. The system will be on-line, using data communication methods over leased telephone lines. The project manager has identified the following steps in the development of software and the most likely times. They are listed in the expected order of starting.

Overall control modules	2 weeks
Sales portion of system	
Input module	1 week
Edit module	3 weeks
Reporting module	2 weeks
File development	2 weeks
Software testing	2 weeks
Inventory portion of system	
Input module	2 weeks
Edit module	6 weeks
Reporting module	4 weeks
Inventory reorder module	2 weeks
Physical inventory module	1 week
Software testing	3 weeks
Systems testing	2 weeks

Data communication lines must be ordered at least 6 weeks before needed. They will be required to perform system testing. All equipment needed to develop and operate the system is already on-site.

a Develop bar and milestone charts for the project. Use week numbers (1, 2, 3, . . .) to show calendar periods.

b Develop a PERT chart for the system, using the time estimates provided above. The development of the two portions of the system can occur simultaneously. Data communication lines can be installed independently of programming activities. Show the earliest and latest time estimates for each activity.

c Examine the PERT chart to determine where there is slack time.

d Are there any dummy activities in this development effort? If so, identify them and indicate why they are dummy activities.

3 The following information on an information systems project has been prepared by the manager of the information systems development:

The PERT chart for this system is shown below:

S ⟶ 1 ⟶ 2 ⟶ 5 ⟶ 9

EVENT	DESCRIPTION
0	Beginning project
1	Prepare development plan
2	Prepare systems specification
3	Install computer equipment
4	Prepare and test computer software
5	Conduct systems testing
6	Prepare training program
7	Conduct systems training
8	Prepare conversion plan
9	Implement and test system

a Complete the following table for the PERT chart:

EVENT	EARLIEST TIME	LATEST TIME	SLACK TIME
1			
2			
3			
4			
5			
6			
7			
8			
9			

What is the critical path for the project? Why is this set of activities significant to the project manager?

4 The senior executive who supervises information systems development at the corporate level is concerned about the amount of time spent on structured walkthroughs. The executive, who feels that walkthroughs may not be a productive use of time, has indicated that it is appropriate to have brief meetings but the amount of time preparing for structured walkthroughs seems excessive. In addition, the executive feels the best people are used repeatedly in many of the walkthroughs. Therefore, they are not productive in systems development activities.

a How would you respond to the executive regarding the usefulness and purpose of structured walkthroughs? Give examples to demonstrate your response.

b Would you make any changes in the use of walkthroughs based on the comments and information provided by the executive? Explain.

CHAPTER 15 HARDWARE AND SOFTWARE SELECTION

QUESTIONS TO GUIDE YOU THROUGH THE CHAPTER

- How do analysts compare the capabilities of different computer systems?
- What factors must be considered when acquiring computer hardware and software?
- How is information about computer speed and capacity acquired?
- Does the purchase of new software mean the organization will own it?
- Are there options to purchasing equipment from computer manufacturers?
- How does the acquisition of software differ from the acquisition of hardware?
- What protection should the organization seek in a contract for software?

The many different sizes and types of computing resources put a burden on the analyst who must select or recommend the source of hardware, software, or services. This chapter examines the considerations in acquiring hardware and software.

There are many makes and sizes of computer equipment. Therefore, the analyst must use a systematic way of evaluating and selecting equipment, paying attention to both the equipment and the method of acquiring it. Increasingly, the analyst is selecting commercial software that meets specific system needs. When an organization purchases software, it becomes highly dependent on the software supplier. Therefore, the analyst must examine all the important issues before committing the organization.

The information may be generated as a result of sales calls made by the supplier's staff or of written requests for proposals (RFP), invitations sent to suppliers describing the organization's needs and asking for sales proposals.

When you complete this chapter, you will know what factors to consider when selecting and contracting for hardware, software, or services.

HARDWARE ACQUISITION

Computer systems often are purchased out of habit or because of someone's recommendation. This is particularly true for the inexperienced analyst who is not familiar with the questions to ask when making a wise selection and purchase decision. This section discusses those questions. It explores the factors of importance when determining equipment size and capacity needs and discusses methods for comparing different systems. The financial factors of purchasing and leasing systems and contracting for service and maintenance will also be examined.

Determining Size and Capacity Requirements

Since computers range in size from small microcomputers to large mainframe systems, the number of options to choose from when selecting a system is obviously very large. Even within the lines of a single manufacturer, there are many different models and configurations from which to select. How then does the analyst determine which system to use when a new computer will be acquired?

The starting point in an equipment decision process is the size and capacity requirements. One particular computer system may be appropriate for one workload and inappropriate for another. Systems capacity is a frequent determiner. Relevant features to consider include such aspects as:

1 Internal memory size
2 Cycle speed of system for processing
3 Number of channels for input, output, and communication
4 Characteristics of display and communication components
5 Types and numbers of auxiliary storage units that can be attached
6 Systems support and utility software provided or available

Frequently software needs dictate the minimum configuration required. For instance, if a particular program to be run on a microcomputer requires, say, 256 kilobytes of storage, the feasible list of candidates will exclude all those systems, regardless of their attractiveness, that do not have or cannot be easily configured to have a memory of at least 256 kilobytes.

All systems have limits, depending on what they are designed for. The limits may or may not be a factor in a particular selection decision. For example, some systems will only communicate data in a bisynchronous fashion. If the system has other attractive features and will not be used for data communication or teleprocessing, the bisynchronous feature may be of little concern. However, if the primary application for the computer will require synchronous transmission of ASCII data (see Chapter 11), the bisynchronous limitation is important. Likewise, the fact that a particular minicomputer is limited to five ports for connecting terminals and printers may be too restrictive in a teleprocessing system that is designed to link 23 sites together through terminals and communication lines.

As indicated, software needs often dictate hardware requirements, such as internal memory sizes, communication ports, disk capacity, and the ability to use magnetic tape. (Not all computers allow the connection of magnetic tape subsystems.) Vendors are reliable sources of configuration requirements. They will provide minimum configuration requirements needed to use their software properly. Trade newspapers and magazines provide regular distribution of information about hardware and software requirements. In addition, purchased subscription sources regularly update looseleaf binders that contain details about alternative systems configurations, purchase and lease costs, operating specifications, and user comments. These services, which cost several hundred dollars yearly, provide monthly updates and telephone assistance when searching for computer operating details.

Auxiliary storage capacity is generally determined by file storage and processing needs. To estimate disk storage needed for a system, the analyst must consider the space needed for each master file, the space for programs and software, including systems software, and the method by which backup copies will be made. When using flexible diskettes on a small business system (Figure 15.1), the analyst must determine whether master and transaction files will be maintained on the same diskette and on which diskette programs will be stored. Backup considerations, as well as file size, guide the decision about how many disk drives are needed. In the example, three disk drives are used to allow ample space for the master file today and expansion tomorrow. This configuration also provides a way to make backup copies of all disks.

Computer Evaluation and Measurement

Often comparisons are made between different computer systems on the basis of actual performance data. Benchmark data, generated by using synthetic programs, is more effective than simply comparing technical specifications.

BENCHMARKING

A *benchmark* is the application of synthetic programs to emulate the actual processing work handled by a computer system. Benchmark programs permit the submission of a mix of jobs that are representative of the users' projected work load. They also demonstrate data storage equipment tech-

FILE SPECIFICATIONS

Master file requirements:	396 kilobytes
Transaction file requirements:	
If accumulated and processed daily:	90 kilobytes
If accumulated and processed weekly:	450 kilobytes

DISK AND DISK DRIVE SPECIFICATIONS

Flexible diskette with double density capacity of 596 kilobytes; from 1 to 4 drives may be included in configuration.

CONFIGURATION AND SPACE USAGE PLAN

Disk Drive 1 to contain programs
Master file will be stored on disk and will use Drive 2
Transaction file will be stored on disk and will use Drive 3
Data backup will be from Drive 2 to Drive 3 always:

DRIVE 2	DRIVE 3
Master file	Backup copy of master file
Transaction file	Backup copy of transaction file
Programs	Backup copy of programs

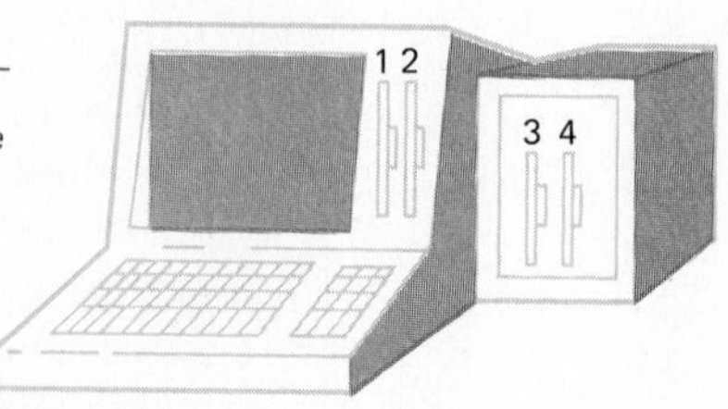

System configuration will include 3 disk drives based on this analysis.

Figure 15.1. Disk utilization plan for small computer system.

niques and provide the opportunity to test specific functions performed by the system. Through this technique, the limitations of the equipment become apparent early in the acquisition process. Sometimes user organizations will insist that the results are attached to the sales contract, formally stating that a specific number of transactions can be processed in a given period of time, the response to an inquiry will be within a stated amount of time, and so forth.

Benchmarks can be run in virtually any type of systems environment, including batch and on-line job streams, and with the users linked to the system directly or through telecommunication methods. As the next section discusses, the jobs can be simulated through synthetic programs.

Common benchmarks are the speed of the central processor, with typical instructions executed in a set of programs, as well as multiple streams of jobs in a multiprogramming environment. The same benchmark run on several different computers will make speed and performance differences attributable to the central processor apparent. Table 15.1 shows a comparison of results using repeated additions, subtractions, and detections of transaction mismatches. The differences in processing speeds is quite apparent.

Benchmarks also may be centered around an expected language mix for the programs that will be run, a mix of different types of programs, and applications having widely varying input and output volumes and requirements. The response time for sending and receiving data from terminals is an additional benchmark for the comparison of systems.

Sometimes, rather than running actual benchmark jobs on computer systems, systems simulators are used to determine performance differences. In commercial systems simulators, the workload of a system is defined in terms of, say, how many input and output operations there are, how many instructions are utilized in a computation, and the order in which work is processed. The specifications are fed into a simulator that stores data about the characteristics of particular equipment (such as instruction speed, channel capacity, and read-write times). The simulator in turn processes the data against the operating characteristics and prepares a report of the expected results as if the actual computer were used. Then the systems characteristics can be changed to mimic another model of computer and a

TABLE 15.1

SAMPLE BENCHMARK FOR COMPARING COMPUTER SYSTEMS

BENCHMARK: Execution of 1 million instructions using identical arithmetic instructions.

COMPUTER SYSTEM	COBOL PROGRAM	FORTRAN PROGRAM	PL/I PROGRAM
1	385*	419	451
2	368	535	342
3	308	437	267

*Speeds in instructions per second.

new set of performance data produced for comparison. The time and expense of running actual benchmark programs on a computer is of concern to analysts and vendors alike. Thus, the use of commercial simulators is an attractive alternative.

DESIGN OF SYNTHETIC PROGRAMS

A *synthetic job* is a program written to exercise a computer's resources in a way that allows the analyst to imitate the expected job stream and determine the results. Then the artificial job stream can be adjusted and rerun to determine the impact. The process can be repeated as many times as necessary to see which tasks a comparison set of computers handles well and which it does not handle as well.

The synthetic jobs may be adjusted to produce the same type of activity as actual programs, including perhaps random access of files, sequential searching of files with varying size records, input and output activities, and file accessing in varying random patterns. The types of hardware and software features that are often simulated are listed in Figure 15.2.

COMPARISON OF BENCHMARKS

Although some comparison on the basis of equipment performance is better than no comparison at all, there are drawbacks to the use of benchmarks. First of all, the comparisons are on purely quantitative grounds. They do not relate the learning time needed to become accustomed to the system or the quality of the systems software (such as the quality of the diagnostics produced during compilation or the efficiency of the object code produced).

In addition, benchmarks do not provide reasonable assurances that programs currently being used on an existing system can be converted to the new system or that the new machine will run them efficiently even if they are converted. Vendors may also make sales claims that a specific system will handle additional tasks that another system cannot do. Benchmarks will not directly verify these statements. Therefore, the purchaser may insist that certain sales claims are attached in writing to the sales contract.

Are benchmarks needed? They are, but the analyst must recognize what they do and do not indicate.

HARDWARE	SOFTWARE
CPU processing speed	Scheduling algorithm
Memory access speed	Compilation algorithm
Interrupt handling abilities	Code efficiency
Peripheral channel speed	Virtual storage management algorithm
Card reader speed	File handling efficiency
Printer speeds	Interrupt handling
Seek time for magnetic disk	Indexing methods
Rotational delay for magnetic disk	Multiple buffer handling
Communication speeds	Communication processing procedures

Figure 15.2. Representative benchmarks for hardware and software.

Plug-Compatible Equipment

Frequently analysts, for reasons of cost, consider equipment for a particular make of computer that is not manufactured by the computer vendor. Such equipment is called *plug-compatible* equipment. A second company specializes in manufacturing systems components, such as printers, disk drives, or memory units, that can be connected to a vendor's system in place of the same equipment manufactured by the vendor. The central processing unit does not care or know that it is not the same make.

The benefit of plug-compatible equipment is the lower cost of an item, compared with that of a major computer vendor. Because firms specializing in specific components can develop manufacturing expertise or may not have the same level of investment in research and development—they are duplicating a component developed by another firm—they are able to offer the same product at a lower cost.

There is a large market for plug-compatible equipment because of price differences. But the analyst must ensure that the equipment will meet necessary quality levels, that it will perform as well as (or possibly better than) the original equipment, and that the computer vendor will not disallow warranties and service agreements on the rest of the system. There is a danger that some service people employed by the vendor will blame malfunctions on the "foreign" equipment attached to the system. Therefore, the analyst must reach agreements on maintenance responsibilities and methods for resolving disputes about malfunction.

Financial Factors

The acquisition of and payment for a computer system are usually handled through one of three common methods: rental, lease, or purchase. Determining which one is right depends on the characteristics and plans of the organization at the time the acquisition will be made. One way is not better than the others at all times. (Table 15.2 summarizes the features of each method.)

RENTAL

Computer rental is for the short-term use of a system, generally from 1 to 12 months. Each month a payment is made for the use of the equipment. Both the user and supplier have the option of canceling the rental with advanced notice, usually 30 or 60 days ahead of the termination date.

Because the commitment is short-term, the renter has a great deal of flexibility. The decision to purchase a system can be delayed until financing is adequate, a new generation of equipment is available, or such time as the organization wishes, for whatever reason. This may be particularly important when an organization is in the midst of planned rapid growth, where it will outgrow a specific system in a brief period; when important reorganizations of divisions and departments that will affect computing resources are in progress; or when the enterprise is in a dynamic change period.

TABLE 15.2

COMPARISON OF COMPUTER SYSTEMS FINANCING OPTIONS

METHOD OF ACQUISITION	ADVANTAGES	DISADVANTAGES
RENTAL	Short-term commitment. High level of flexibility. Does not require cash up-front.	Most expensive option. Little control of equipment change. Not all vendors will rent.
LEASE	Predetermined payments for fixed period. Does not require cash up-front. Usually better service from vendor than under rental. Little risk of obsolescence. Less expensive than rental.	More expensive than purchase. May have limitations on hours of equipment use.
PURCHASE	Least cost in long run. Distinct tax advantages if a profit-making firm. A business investment. Full control over equipment use.	Risk of obsolescence. Permanent commitment. Full responsibility for all problems. Greater early cash requirements than other options.

Compared with other acquisition methods, rental is the most expensive. The monthly payments are higher, and the organization does not receive any tax or ownership benefits, other than being able to deduct the monthly rental as a business expense. The equipment received is often used, although the rental agreement should be written in such a way that the renter is assured of having a system that runs properly and will be maintained adequately. The short-notice cancellation provision may not provide enough security for the renter to plan on the continued availability of the system. For this reason, rental is typically a short-term solution, perhaps while waiting for the official announcement and delivery of a new system. The opportunity to rent computers is not always available: many firms refuse to tie up capital or equipment for short-term rentals. The analyst must ensure that rental systems are even available before making such a decision. Not all suppliers offer short-term rentals.

LEASE

A *lease* is a commitment to use a system for a specific period of time, generally from 3 to 7 years. Payments are predetermined and do not change throughout the course of the lease. Depending on the terms of the lease, payments are monthly, quarterly, semiannual, or annual and include the cost of equipment service and maintenance. At the end of the lease period, the lessor does not own the equipment. (If that is the case, the Internal Revenue Service considers the agreement a conditional sale and the entire transaction must then be treated as a purchase.)

Compared with rental, leasing is less expensive. Because there is a longer commitment, the supplier will generally provide better service and the user can count on the presence of the system. Leasing protects against technical obsolescence, always a concern when purchasing computer equipment. If the lease term is short, the lessor can upgrade to a more powerful system at the end of the lease. However, if the equipment is leased from a computer manufacturer, it is usually possible to upgrade to a larger system even though the lease has not expired, providing the system is acquired from the same manufacturer.

No capital investment is required to lease a computer system. Yet specific tax advantages can be gained. In addition to deducting the cost of the lease as a business expense, a tax credit for the investment, which directly lowers the income tax a business pays, can be passed from the equipment owner to the lessor. In some cases, the title for the equipment can even be passed to the lessor. Legal assistance is needed to investigate the terms and conditions allowed by the Internal Revenue Service at the time such a transaction is considered.

PURCHASE

The ownership of computers through outright purchase is the most common method of computer acquisition and is increasing in popularity as lease costs are rising. Over time, the purchase option is frequently the lowest cost, especially in light of the tax advantages that can be gained.

Under purchase, the organization takes title to the equipment. Of course the money for the purchase must be taken from operating funds or borrowed. And, in a sense the organization is locked in since it is more difficult to change to a different computer system; either the system must be sold or arrangements must be negotiated to trade it in on a different computer.

The organization must acquire its own maintenance service (for parts and labor), usually from the manufacturer, and pay the monthly charges. The charges will fluctuate from year to year. In addition, if the equipment was financed with a loan, the periodic payment on the loan must be made. The cash outflow still may be lower than renting or leasing, depending on the terms arranged by the purchaser. In return for the outgoing cash, specific tax advantages are gained through purchase:

1 The monthly maintenance charges are deductible as a business expense.
2 Interest on any loan financing the purchase is deductible as a business expense.
3 An investment tax credit may be taken on the purchase; this lowers the amount of income taxes paid by the organization.
4 The cost of the equipment can be depreciated over time; this also lowers the taxable income and therefore the income taxes paid.
5 Local, state, and federal taxes paid on the purchase are deductible from income taxes.

Table 15.3 compares the cost of owning a computer system under each of the three methods over a 5-year period. The purchase option indicates the

TABLE 15.3

COMPARISON OF COMPUTER ACQUISITION COST ALTERNATIVES

	RENTAL	LEASE	ACQUISITION
BASIC SYSTEM			$189,678*
MONTHLY PAYMENT	$ 6,807	$ 4,846	$ 4,817
MONTHLY MAINTENANCE	1,225	—	1,225
YEARLY COST	$ 98,631	$ 58,152	$ 72,504
5-YEAR TOTAL COST	$493,155	$290,760	$362,520 Additional tax savings. Will own the system.

*No downpayment, 18% interest rate, monthly payments.

use of depreciation to reduce taxes. In a sense then, depreciation deductions on income tax reduces the cost of the computer to the organization. Normally this benefit is not possible under lease agreements and it is never feasible for short-term rentals. (The use of monthly expenditure estimates to calculate project costs and benefits are also discussed in Chapter 6.) Of course the tax benefits described only apply to firms that operate for profit. Nonprofit firms that do not pay income taxes do not receive tax benefits from computer purchases.

Maintenance and Support

An additional factor in hardware decisions concerns the maintenance and support of the system after it is installed. Primary concerns are the source of maintenance, terms, and response times.

MAINTENANCE SOURCE

Once the system is delivered and installed, there is a brief warranty period during which time the sales unit is responsible for maintenance. Often this is a 90-day period, although the specific terms are a subject for contract negotiation, discussed later in this chapter. After that time, the purchaser has the option of acquiring maintenance from various sources.

The most common source of maintenance for new equipment is from the sales firm. If a mainframe or minicomputer system is purchased through the manufacturer's sales force, there is also generally a maintenance support group that will provide service for a standard price. Large companies set national maintenance costs that are adjusted on an annual or semiannual basis. If the system is a micro- or personal computer, the dealer will generally provide maintenance as a chargeable service. (If personal computers are purchased from mail-order houses, the buyer may pay a lower purchase price, but may lose the convenience of local service. Lower service costs are one reason some mail-order firms are able to provide lower purchase prices.)

Service is also available from companies specializing in providing maintenance service. *Third-party* maintenance companies, as these firms are called, frequently provide service in smaller communities, where manufacturers do not find it cost-effective to maintain an office. In addition, sellers of turnkey systems, who deliver and install working hardware and software combinations but do not manufacture the equipment themselves, suggest the use of specific third-party maintenance firms whom they work with directly and inform of changes in hardware, software, and suggested maintenance procedures. When a used computer system is purchased from an independent sales organization, the purchaser may have no choice but to use a third-party maintenance firm. Many manufacturers will not service equipment they did not sell.

TERMS

In formulating a maintenance agreement, the terms of the agreement are as important as the cost itself. The contract may be written to cover both labor and parts (all parts regardless of the number needed or their cost), labor and an allowance for parts, or labor only with parts charges added on as needed. Which type of contract is desired depends on the expenditures the organization is willing to make in comparison with how frequently it feels service will be required. The labor-and-parts form is the most common with large systems.

The analyst should also consider how maintenance costs will change. Large manufacturers have established policies of adjusting their maintenance charges on an annual or semiannual basis and frequently will not change these policies for any customer. Other suppliers and service companies will offer open-ended contracts that allow the adjustment of charges at any time with 30 days notice. Frequently analysts negotiating services with these companies will seek a cap on maintenance. That is, they will seek agreement, in writing, that the maintenance costs will not increase by any more than a stated maximum amount during a specific time period, such as a calendar year. This type of protection ensures that the supplier cannot take advantage of the user who is totally dependent on the service agency. Most service companies are very reputable, but good business practice dictates that adequate protection should always be sought in contracting for services.

SERVICE AND RESPONSE

Maintenance support is of course only useful if it is available when it is needed. Two concerns in maintenance are the response time when service is requested and the hours of support.

When a telephone call is placed for emergency maintenance, will a technician or engineer be dispatched immediately? That may be unlikely. However, the user has a right to expect a reasonable response time when an emergency call is made. Often organizations specify in the contract that the response to a telephone call must be made within 2 hours. Others specify same-day response, and still others accept response no later than the next morning. The dependency the user organization has on the computer system will dictate how these terms are negotiated. An on-line system that is in use around the clock, 24 hours a day, will need much quicker response than one that is used intermittently for batch processing.

When smaller desktop and microcomputers are in use, an alternative to on-site support is available in the form of carry-in service: The user delivers the computer to the dealer or maintenance agency for repair. Often service while you wait or same-day service is possible. For problems requiring longer repair times, a rental system may be available.

Repair service is often provided only during normal working hours. If an organization wishes evening service or around-the-clock coverage, it is usually available for an extra charge, say 10 to 50 percent additional cost.

We have been emphasizing repair service only. However, equally important is the need for performing preventive maintenance, the routine service of cleaning and adjusting the equipment to prevent breakdowns. Whenever contracting for maintenance, a schedule of preventive maintenance must be agreed on in advance. Manufacturers have suggested preventive maintenance cycles and procedures. This information should be filed in the systems department and included in service agreements.

In all instances, the stocking of sufficient spare parts is important. Good service is impossible if spare parts are not available. User organizations will want to obtain sufficient assurances about adequate parts inventories in advance.

OPTIONS TO IN-HOUSE SYSTEMS

Two less-frequent options for computer support are the use of service bureaus or facilities management companies. A *service bureau* is a company that owns computer facilities and makes them available to users for a charge. The user submits processing that is done at the service bureau on the bureau's computer systems. In some cases, organizations interact directly with the computer through terminals located in the users' offices. There is usually a monthly cost plus a charge that varies depending on the amount of time the user is in communication with the system. Additional fees may be charges for storing data, mounting magnetic disks and tapes, or printing pages.

Some service bureaus will provide data processing services. The bureau prepares the data for input, handles all processing, and may even provide pickup and delivery service. Custom programming is available for a charge.

The use of service bureaus is very common in accounting and payroll applications. Often firms which want automatic data processing services in these areas but do not want to purchase equipment or hire systems personnel will contract with a service bureau. However, as computer costs continue to drop and high-quality commercial software is available, the reliance of some firms on service bureaus may change.

Facilities management companies provide a service to companies wishing to develop information systems capabilities but not to maintain a staff of operators, analysts, and programmers. Under this option, the user organization may purchase a computer system and then contract with a facilities management firm to operate the computer and provide the service *on the organization's premises.* The facilities management company provides the information systems expertise and personnel for a fee. It also develops software or acquires commercial software to meet the organization's needs.

Through facilities management, an organization can obtain professional information processing service without investing time and resources in managing a systems staff. It also receives the benefits of owning a computer system.

SOFTWARE SELECTION

Many of the same concerns addressed in the selection of hardware apply to software. The determination of whether commercial software is right for a particular task and the arrangement of contractual terms are the responsibilities of the user organization.

Evaluation of Software

One of the most difficult tasks in selecting software, after systems requirements are known, is determining whether a particular software package fits the requirements. For those that do, further scrutiny is needed to determine their desirability in comparison with other candidates. This section first summarizes the application requirements questions and then suggests more detailed comparisons.

APPLICATION REQUIREMENTS QUESTIONS

Whenever analysts evaluate possible software for adoption, they do so by comparing software features with previously developed application requirements. You should recall that representative requirements questions include:

What transactions and what data about each transaction must be handled?

What reports, documents, and other output must the system produce?

What files and databases drive the system? What transaction files are needed to maintain them?

What is the volume of data to be stored? What volume of transactions will be processed?

Are there unique features about this application that require special consideration when selecting software?

What inquiry requirements must the software support?

What future enhancements are possible and will be supported?

What hardware and communication features does the software require?
What are the limitations on the software?

By working from this basic set of questions, coupled with mandated cost and expenditure limitations, the analyst is able to remove from consideration quickly those packages that do not meet requirements. Then it is necessary to examine the remaining candidates for adoption further on the basis of such other attributes as flexibility, parameterization, capacity, and vendor support.

FLEXIBILITY

The flexibility of a software system includes the ability to meet changing requirements and varying user needs. Software that is flexible is generally more valuable than a program that is totally inflexible, although excessive flexibility is not good either, as that requires the user or analyst to define many things in the system that could be included in the design as a standard feature.

Areas where flexibility is wanted are data storage, reporting and options, definition of parameters, and data input. In addition, the flexibility of software may vary by the types of hardware it will support. For example, an interactive mailing list program, designed so the operator enters data through a CRT keyboard, should be designed to allow the use of one- or two-line street addresses (Figure 15.3). Business addresses typically require more than one line, so there is room to enter the name of the company, street address, and department or mail stop, in addition to the individual's name and the city, state, and zip code. On the other hand, a well-designed system will also not require the operator to provide two address lines when only one is needed. The second one may be left blank.

Output flexibility is equally important. Although the programming logic is more complicated, the software should determine the presence of one or two lines of address data and adjust the output format accordingly. If you receive computer-prepared mailing labels that have a blank line in the middle of the label, it is a sure sign that the system used was not flexible enough to adapt to the data it processed.

A well-designed mailing system will surely provide both mailing labels and printed reports listing file contents. But it should also provide them in alphabetical and zip-code order for mailing. (The postal service provides a reduced postage rate as an incentive for submitting large mailings, of over 200 pieces, in ascending zip-code order.) A full list of the master contents, including items that are stored in the system but not included on mailing labels (such as telephone numbers or employee classifications), is a useful report that can also be produced in alphabetical order, in zip-code order, or on a selective basis using the categories built into the system.

Still additional flexibility is made possible by the size of the mailing labels (Figure 15.4) that can be used and the number across that can be printed. Depending on the preferences of users and the supplies they have,

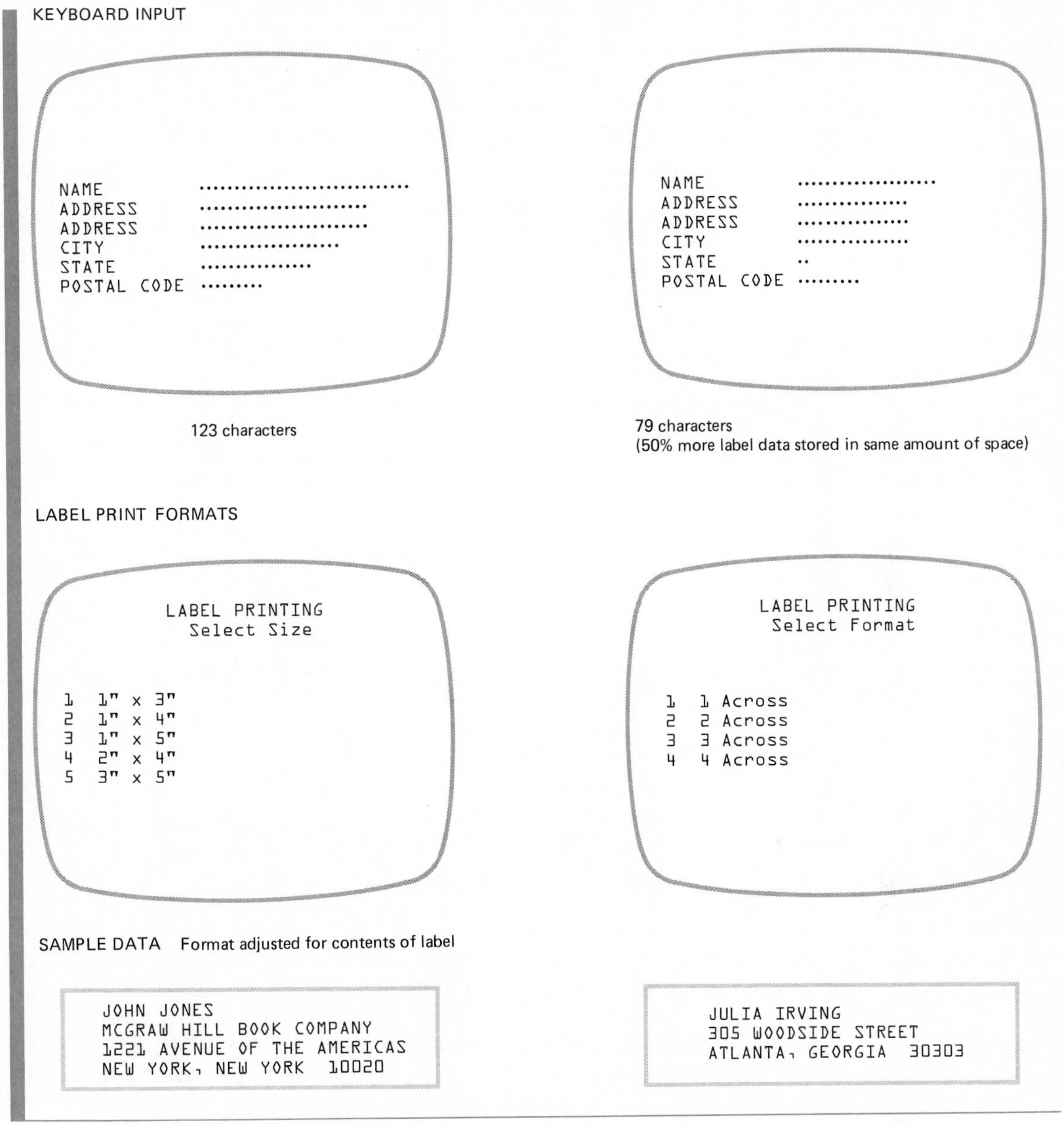

KEYBOARD INPUT

```
NAME          ..............................
ADDRESS       ........................
ADDRESS       ........................
CITY          ....................
STATE         ................
POSTAL CODE   .........
```

123 characters

```
NAME          ....................
ADDRESS       ................
ADDRESS       ................
CITY          ................
STATE         ..
POSTAL CODE   .........
```

79 characters
(50% more label data stored in same amount of space)

LABEL PRINT FORMATS

```
        LABEL PRINTING
          Select Size

1  1" x 3"
2  1" x 4"
3  1" x 5"
4  2" x 4"
5  3" x 5"
```

```
        LABEL PRINTING
         Select Format

1  1 Across
2  2 Across
3  3 Across
4  4 Across
```

SAMPLE DATA   Format adjusted for contents of label

```
JOHN JONES
MCGRAW HILL BOOK COMPANY
1221 AVENUE OF THE AMERICAS
NEW YORK, NEW YORK  10020
```

```
JULIA IRVING
305 WOODSIDE STREET
ATLANTA, GEORGIA  30303
```

Figure 15.3. Example of input/output/storage flexibility in mailing list system.

labels may vary in size from 1 × 3 up to 3 × 5 inches and be printed 1, 2, 3, or 4 across.

Suppose the user does not want to store a two-line address or wants to have shorter field lengths as a trade-off for increasing the number of records that can be stored. The capability to instruct the system to handle one of the optional formats is another dimension to software flexibility.

LICENSE AGREEMENT FOR McGRAW-HILL EDUCATIONAL SOFTWARE

This agreement gives you, the customer, certain benefits, rights and obligations. By using the software, you indicate that you have read, understood, and will comply with the terms. To obtain the full benefits and rights due you, return the card below.

Here's what McGraw-Hill expects of you:

1. McGraw-Hill licenses and authorizes you to use the software specified below only on a microcomputer located within your own facilities.
2. You will abide by the Copyright Law of the United States. This law provides you with the right to make only one back-up copy. It prohibits you from making any additional copies, except as expressly provided by McGraw-Hill. In the event that the software is protected against copying in such a way that it cannot be duplicated, McGraw-Hill will provide you with one back-up copy at minimal or no charge.
3. You will not prepare derivative works based on the software because that is also not permitted under Copyright Law. For example, you cannot prepare an alternative hardware version or format based on the existing software.

Here's what to expect from McGraw-Hill:

1. If you believe the diskette is defective, we will try to diagnose the problem over our Microcomputer Software Hotline: Call toll free, 800-223-4180, Monday through Friday, 8:30 A.M.-4:30 P.M. EST. (N.Y. residents call 212-997-2646, collect.) If the diskette is defective, we will replace it at no charge. We cannot, however, offer free replacement of diskettes damaged through normal wear and tear, or lost while in your possession.

(Continued on reverse side)

- - - - - - - - Tear here and mail - - - - - - - -

Your Name/Title ________ Date ________
Institution ________ Department ________
Address ________
City ________ State ________ Zip Code ________
Telephone ( ) ________ Date of Purchase ________
Program Information:
Title ________
Author ________
ISBN Code No. 0-07- _ _ _ _ _ - _
Type(s) of Microcomputers in Use ________
Number of Computers ________ Used in Grades/Courses ________
Remarks (please note any specific needs you may have): ________

2. If you have a problem with the operation of our software, we will advise you via our Microcomputer Software Hotline: Call toll free, 800-223-4180, Monday through Friday, 8:30 A.M.-4:30 P.M. EST. (N.Y. residents call 212-997-2646, collect.) Of course, McGraw-Hill does not warrant that the software will satisfy your requirements, that the operation of the software will be uninterrupted or error-free, or that program defects in the software can be corrected. Except as described in this agreement, software and diskettes are distributed "as is" without warranties of any kind, either express or implied, including, but not limited to, implied warranties of merchantability and fitness for a particular purpose or use.
3. Your name will be placed on our priority mailing list, and you will receive a periodic update notice of McGraw-Hill's newly released educational software, plus timely information on any special software offers.
4. Additional rights and benefits may come with the specific software package you have purchased. Consult the teacher support materials that come with this program, or contact the McGraw-Hill representative in your area.

7/82

- - - - - - - - - - - - - - - -

NO POSTAGE NECESSARY IF MAILED IN THE UNITED STATES

BUSINESS REPLY CARD
FIRST CLASS PERMIT NO. 26 NEW YORK, N.Y.

POSTAGE WILL BE PAID BY ADDRESSEE

MICROCOMPUTER SOFTWARE HOTLINE
McGRAW-HILL BOOK COMPANY 28th Floor
1221 Avenue of the Americas
New York, New York 10020

Figure 15.4. Sample software license agreement.

AUDIT AND RELIABILITY PROVISIONS

Users often have a tendency to trust systems more than they should, to the extent they frequently believe the results produced through a computer-based information system without sufficient skepticism. Therefore, the need to ensure that adequate controls are included in the system is an essential step in the selection of software. Auditors must have the ability to validate reports and output and to test the authenticity and accuracy of data and information.

Specific audit and control procedures of interest include the abilities to:

- Trace a transaction through each processing step by having the capability to examine intermediate data values produced during processing.
- Print selectively records and transactions in the system that meet certain criteria (such as a highly active account or a high-balance account) to validate the accuracy and authenticity of both transactions and results.

- Maintain a constant balance in the system when financial matters are involved and to report the fact that the system either is or is not in balance.
- Produce a detailed journal of all transactions and the effect of the transactions on account balances or master file records.
- Provide sufficient controls on input, such as batch and transaction controls and counts.

Systems reliability means that the data is reliable, that it is accurate and believable. It also includes the element of security. The analyst evaluates security by determining the method and suitability of protecting the system against unauthorized use. Ensuring that the system has passwords is not sufficient access protection. Multiple levels of passwords are often needed to allow different staff members access to those files and databases or capabilities they need. That is, since not all persons require the same level of access, many security systems utilize multiple levels of passwords that control the level of entry into the system an individual is allowed: to retrieve reports the individual is authorized to receive, to submit transaction data for processing, to change account balances or correct data in files, or to change current security provisions and passwords.

The technical security features are not adequate if passwords or other security methods are displayed whenever they are used. For example, if the password one must enter to access the system is displayed on a visual display whenever it is entered, security will not be maintained for long. Someone will quickly read the password from the screen as it is entered. Some systems even have such poor security that they print the user, account number, and password on output when the computer produces it!

CAPACITY

Systems capacity refers to the number of files that can be stored and the amount of data that each file will hold. To show complete capacity, it may be necessary to consider the specific hardware on which the software will be used. However, capacity also depends on the language in which the software is written. The language is sometimes a procedural language, such as COBOL, PL/I, BASIC, or PASCAL. But it may be a database system, a system for automatic or computer-assisted generation of software, or a file management system. Other limitations affect the overall systems capacity, although they may be disguised as a result of the above software aids. Capacity is also determined by:

- The maximum size of each record measured in number of bytes
- The maximum size of the file measured in number of bytes
- The maximum size of the file measured in number of fields per record
- The number of files that can be active at one time
- The number of files that can be registered in a file directory

For example, suppose that two systems have identical characteristics, allowing the storage of 1000 characters in a single data item. The file itself will hold up to 64,000 records. The first system allows 128 fields per record. The second allows 64 fields per record. In addition, the first allows only two files to be open and active at one time. The second allows 64 records per file and 8 files to be open and active simultaneously. You would quickly determine that there is greater capacity in the second system. If all other factors are equal and the capacity is important now or for expansion, the wise decision will lead to the selection of the second system.

VENDOR SUPPORT

When purchasing commercial software from a vendor, the analyst always evaluates the services provided. As with hardware, it is not enough to know that the quality of the item purchased is adequate. Software also needs to be maintained, and the analyst must determine who will perform the maintenance and for what cost *before the purchase agreement is signed*. In addition, the terms of the maintenance must be detailed. These include:

- How frequently will software maintenance be performed? That is, will new versions be provided on a regular basis? Will there be a charge for updates?
- If there is a monthly maintenance fee, what services does it cover? What services are excluded?
- Will the software developer provide custom programming to tailor specific aspects of the software to the demonstrated needs of the user? At what cost? At what priority, that is how soon after agreement is reached will the programming be started and finished?
- What agreements are there for controlling increases in maintenance fees?
- How will disputes about software maintenance needs be resolved?
- During what hours are software support services available? What are the provisions for receiving emergency support when needed beyond regular hours?

Even though some software sales agents will avoid answering these questions, the reliable ones will not; they may even volunteer the information before the question is asked. In either case, the analyst is responsible for raising the questions and getting the answers.

Vendor support also includes the training that is supplied when a system is acquired. Depending on the vendor, it may be complimentary or for a fee, and at the user's site or another location. If the system is a turnkey system, where the vendor provides in-house training and installation, the contract should clearly state the number of hours of training supplied and the number of personnel who will be included in the training. Generally the number of days on-site are also specified.

As this section indicates, support after purchase is an essential part of the selection process. Good software that is not maintained in a dynamic environment will soon cease to be so good!

Software Contract

All terms and capabilities discussed in this section may be included in a software contract. Unless the contract includes all agreements, including verbal promises, it may be difficult to prove them after the system is installed or personnel changed.

Contract negotiation is a legal process and should involve an organization lawyer and financial expert. Since hardware and software firms negotiate contracts regularly, they are often better negotiators than systems analysts or data processing managers. Having the lawyer draft the contract or modify one suggested by the vendor is a more effective method.

Two types of software contract are drawn:

- Outlining the terms of leasing a software package. Often when organizations acquire software, they only receive the right to use it for a fee, whether one time or for some time interval. A paid-up license (see Figure 15.4) allows the organization to use the software indefinitely. But since it does not own it, the business cannot sell it, give it away, or distribute copies.
- Outlining the terms of a custom programming assignment, wherein the organization contracts with an independent agency or agent to produce software. The terms may state that the work will be done for a fixed fee; for the cost of the work to the developer plus a specific percentage of the cost that is added to the cost, giving the developer a profit; or for a fixed amount and a specific calendar or hourly duration.

The contract should clearly fix the ownership of the software so there is no dispute at a later time and, if a lease or service is involved, state when the contract is terminated.

Since there will often be a period of time between the formulation of a software agreement and the date on which it is actually available for use, the terms must protect the organization by specifying when and how testing will be completed and when full implementation will occur. There must be no question when implementation is complete. Often this point is fixed as the time the first statements are printed, in an accounting application, or when the first month's reports are produced, in others.

Payment is also frequently tied to implementation. A common pattern followed when large, expensive software systems are purchased is to split payment: a one-third downpayment when the contract is signed, another one-third when the software is delivered, and the final-one third when implementation is completed.

A final consideration, often overlooked in software contracting, is the protection needed when dealing with some software firms. An organization that is making a commitment to a software system must be assured that the software will continue to be available and that it will be maintained, regardless of what happens to the supplier (who may sell the software, be acquired by another company, or go out of business through sale or bankruptcy). Because there is always the possibility that one of the above may occur unexpectedly, attorneys involved in contract negotiation request that the seller provide the source code and program listings, or store a copy of the program with an independent third party who will make it available if the seller goes out of business. Similarly, the attorney will want to ensure that the software will be available for the purchaser if the seller goes out of business. An attorney should ensure that the software will be available for the purchaser if there is a dispute over maintenance and enhancement, where the purchaser wishes to contract for its own maintenance. These issues are complex and require an extensive legal background. For this reason, legal advice should always be sought in contract negotiation.

Throughout this chapter we have emphasized the importance of hardware and software acquisition. Even though systems analysts properly analyze information requirements and formulate an effective logical design, the system will still be dependent on having the right hardware and software combination. Therefore, this process is as important as any other step associated with systems development. Unfortunately, it lacks the glitter and spectacle of other aspects of systems development. Many programs that educate systems analysts do not touch on many of the issues discussed in this chapter, even though they are vital to real-world information systems.

SUMMARY

The decision to acquire computer hardware or software must be handled like any other business decision. Alternatives are considered and the features of each are compared with organization requirements. For each there are specific questions about systems capability, after-purchase service and protection, and costs.

When purchasing computer hardware, the size and capacity of the system is assessed against the requirements of the application. Features, such as the number of terminals that the system will support, the speed of processing, and the equipment that can be attached, are fundamentals that the analyst cannot overlook. Frequently published information is available through subscription services to supplement that provided by the vendor and other users. In addition, benchmarks can be derived to show how a specific system will process a specific mixture of jobs. If the same benchmarks are run on several different systems, the analyst gathers data that makes more direct comparison feasible. However, benchmarks only show quantitative data. The analyst must still evaluate the ease with which the system can be used, quality of support from the vendor, and any other factors that the organization feels essential, even though not assessed through benchmarks.

Computer acquisition may occur through rental, lease, or direct purchase. Rental and lease are similar, except that, since the rental period is usually much shorter than a lease period, up to approximately 18 months compared with a lease period that may be as long as 7 years, the monthly charge is higher. Both rental and lease charges may be deducted from income as a business expense for profit-making organizations.

If the computer is purchased, the organization owns the equipment and can depreciate its cost over a period of years and months as allowed by the Internal Revenue Service. It can also deduct the cost of interest if the equipment is purchased through loan financing, and it is eligible for a credit on income taxes. Monthly maintenance costs are also deductible. The purchase of equipment results in overall lower cost than rental or lease.

When contracting for maintenance, the organization should be sure it knows who will provide the maintenance and what the terms of the maintenance agreement include: labor, parts and labor, or some other arrangement. The response time when a call for maintenance is needed must also be specified, along with a schedule for preventive maintenance.

The selection of software is done with the same care used in the selection of hardware. That is, application requirements are compared with software features. Particular attention is paid to the flexibility of the software, its capacity, and the extent of audit and reliability features. And the after-purchase support and maintenance provided by the vendor must not be overlooked since the purchaser is highly dependent on the vendor for continued support. Legal assistance is advisable when contracting for software to ensure that the organization is fully protected and will have adequate software capability even if the vendor changes or goes out of business.

There is no substitute for the careful selection of hardware and software. Effective analysis and design practices are of course essential. But they must be matched with the proper equipment and suitable software. This chapter outlined the most important considerations in this area.

KEYWORDS

Benchmark
Facilities management
Lease
Plug-compatible
Service bureau
Synthetic program
Third-party maintenance

REVIEW QUESTIONS

1 What factors determine the size and capacity requirements of a computer system? How is information about the differences between systems acquired?

2 What is a benchmark? Give examples of some benchmarks. How are they determined? Who develops them?

3 Discuss the reliability of benchmark

data in comparing computers of different sizes and makes. Indicate why you feel they should or should not be used when evaluating different computer systems.

4 Why do some organizations consider plug-compatible equipment when purchasing hardware? What are the advantages and disadvantages of plug-compatible components?

5 Discuss the financial methods of computer acquisition, comparing the similarities and differences of each method.

6 Which methods of financing computer acquisitions are the least and the most expensive in the short term? In the long term? Explain the role federal income taxes play in your answer.

7 How do service bureaus and facilities managements differ? What is the benefit of each to the organization needing computer service?

8 Why are maintenance agreements so important when purchasing or leasing a computer system? What terms should the purchaser discuss when arranging for maintenance.

9 The ability to tailor software to fit a specific application is an important factor in selecting one program over another. What are some representative factors that demonstrate flexibility in software?

10 Discuss the importance of audit features in software. How is auditability assured?

11 How is the capacity of software evaluated? With what aspects of the systems requirements data does the analyst compare capacity data to determine whether a specific program will have sufficient capacity to meet requirements?

12 Outline the concerns a purchaser should have when contracting for software. Explain the importance of each concern.

13 When an organization pays for software, does it generally own the software? Explain the reason for your answer.

APPLICATION PROBLEMS FOR CHAPTER 15

1 Many small business owners consider the purchase of a business microcomputer for use in processing payroll data and preparing employee paychecks. However, other small business persons feel payroll processing activities should not be automated but should be handled manually or sent to a service bureau that will perform all the work needed to calculate pay, determine proper payroll taxes, prepare paychecks, and maintain payroll records.

One business owner is contemplating whether to purchase a business microcomputer to handle the company payroll or send it to a service bureau. The cost of the computer, including sufficient disk storage to maintain all required records for the company's 250 employees, is $10,000. A printer will cost an additional $3000 and the payroll software and operating system another $1000. The service bureau alternative will cost $0.50 for each employee check. All payroll records will be maintained by the service bureau as part of the per-check charge. End-of-year withholding tax forms will also be prepared free of charge. In both cases, payroll checks are prepared for all employees every week.

a Construct a cost-benefit analysis for the two alternatives outlined above. Assume that the current cost of money is 22 percent and the microcomputer has a useful life of 3 years. Which alternative is the better investment if the business microcomputer will be depreciated fully over 3 years on an equal month-by-month basis and every $2 of depreciation reduces the amount of taxes the business pays by $1? Explain the reason for your answer, with specific cost comparisons.

b In addition to cost, what other factors should the business owner consider in making the payroll processing decision?

2 A business owner is contemplating purchasing a computer system for processing sales, inventory, and accounting data. Currently the firm, which is very successful and has a high profit margin, maintains all records manually. Employees firmly believe that the installation of computer processing facilities will assist them in their jobs and would welcome the benefits of automation. Management too believes that better business performance would result from improved information and transaction processing control.

The owner, on the one hand, is willing to make the investment but, on the other, believes that computer systems are decreasing in cost and increasing in capability. Business periodicals, newspapers, and even business colleagues all tell the owner that a better and more powerful system will be available *next year* for less money than a currently available computer. Hence the owner is planning to wait for one more year, as he has for the last year and the year prior to that, before purchasing the system.

As you know, the owner is correct in the sense that computer systems are decreasing in cost and increasing in processing ability. Every business person contemplating the acquisition of a computer, regardless of size or cost, faces the same dilemma. What factors should an owner consider when deciding whether to wait? Is "next year" always a better time to purchase the system?

3 A manager must decide whether to purchase or rent a computer system. The firm, which is growing rapidly and expanding to other locations, does not now use computer processing but is at the point where the advantages of computer information systems must be acquired simply to remain competitive. The computer system needed to meet business requirements over the next 12 months will cost $50,000 to purchase and an additional $22,500 for software, training, and installation. For tax purposes, the useful life of the system is 5 years. Monthly maintenance costs will be $600. If purchased, the system will be financed for the full purchase price at a 16 percent interest rate.

As an alternative, the firm may rent the system for $2800 per month.

Leasing for a 5-year period is also under consideration. The monthly cost of the 5-year lease is $2100.

a Which alternative is the most financially beneficial one? Be sure to consider and show all appropriate costs for each of the three options.

b What benefits does rental offer in the situation described? Can the same benefits be achieved by leasing?

BIBLIOGRAPHY

INFORMATION PROCESSING

Benjamin, Robert I.: "Information Technology in the 1990s: A Long Range Planning Scenario," *MIS Quarterly,* **6,** 2, June 1982, pp. 11–31.

Branscomb, Lewis M.: "Bringing Computing to People: The Broadening Challenge," *Computer,* **15,** 7, July 1982, pp. 68–75.

Champagne, George A.: "Perspectives on Business Data Processing," *Computer,* **13,** 11, November 1980, pp. 84–99.

Galbraith, Jay: *Organization Design,* Reading, MA: Addison-Wesley, 1977.

Kling, Rob: "Social Analyses of Computing: Theoretical Perspectives in Recent Empirical Research," *Computing Surveys,* **12,** 1, March 1980, pp. 61–110.

Olson, Margrethe H.: "Remote Office Work: Changing Work Patterns in Space and Time," *Communications of the ACM,* **26,** 3, March 1983, pp. 182–187.

Rockart, John F.: "Chief Executives Define Their Own Data Needs," *Harvard Business Review,* **57,** 2, March–April 1979, pp. 81–91.

REQUIREMENTS DETERMINATION

Davis, Gordon B.: "Strategies for Information Requirements Determination," *IBM Systems Journal,* **21,** 1, 1982, pp. 4–30.

Decision Tables: A Systems Analysis and Documentation Technique, GF20–8102–0, White Plains, NY: IBM, 1962.

DeMarco, Tom: *Structured Analysis and System Specification,* Englewood Cliffs, NJ: Prentice-Hall, 1979.

Fitzgerald, Jerry, Ardra F. Fitzgerald, and Warren D. Stallings, Jr.: *Fundamentals of Systems Analysis,* 2d ed., John Wiley and Sons, 1981.

Gane, Chris and Trish Sarson: *Structured Systems Analysis: Tools and Techniques,* Englewood Cliffs, NJ: Prentice-Hall, 1979.

HIPO-A Design Aid and Documentation Technique, GC20–1851, White Plains, NY: IBM, 1974.

Katzan, H.: *Systems Design and Documentation: An Introduction to the HIPO Method,* NY: Van Nostrand Reinhold Co., 1976.

McDaniel, H.: *An Introduction to Decision Logic Tables,* Princeton, NJ: Petrocelli Books, 1978.

Naumann, J. David, Gordon B. Davis, and James D. McKeen: "Determining Information Requirements: A Contingency Method for Selection of a Requirements Assurance Strategy," *The Journal of Systems and Software,* **1,** 1980, pp. 273–281.

Orr, Kenneth T.: *Structured Requirements Definition,* Topeka, KS: Ken Orr and Associates, 1981.

Orr, Kenneth T.: *Structured Systems Development,* NY: Yourdon Press, 1977.

Pollack, S. L., H. T. Hick, Jr., and W. F. Harrison: *Decision Tables: Theory and Practice,* NY: Wiley-Interscience, 1971.

Senn, James A.: "A Management View of Systems Analysts: Failures and Shortcomings," MIS Quarterly, **2,** 3, September 1978.

Taggert, William M., Jr., and Marvin O. Tharp, "A Survey of Information Requirements Analysis Techniques," *Computing Surveys,* **8,** 1, March 1976, pp. 1–15.

Weinberg, Victor: *Structured Analysis,* NY: Yourdon Press, 1978.

Yourdon, Edward: *Managing the Structured Techniques,* 2d ed., NY: Yourdon Press, 1979.

SYSTEMS DESIGNS

Benbasat, Izak, A. Dexter, and R. Mantha: "An Experimental Study of the Human/Computer Interface," *Communications of the ACM,* **24,** 11, November 1981, pp. 752–762.

Bradley, James: *File and Data Base Techniques,* NY: Holt, Rinehart, and Winston, 1982.

Cardenas, Alfonso F. and William P. Grafton: "Challenges and Requirements For New Application Generators," *Proceedings of National Computer Conference,* 1982, pp. 341–349.

Chen, Peter: *The Entity-Relationship Approach to Logical Data Base Design,* Wellesley, MA: Q.E.D. Information Sciences, 1977.

Dickson, Gary W., James A. Senn, and Norman L. Chervany: "Research in MIS: The Minnesota Experiments," *Management Science,* **23,** 9, May 1977, pp. 913–923.

Doll, Dixon R.: *Data Communications: Facilities, Networks, and Systems Design,* NY: Wiley-Interscience, 1978.

Dwyer, Barry: "One More Time—How to Update a Master File," *Communications of the ACM* **24,** 1, January 1981, pp. 3–8.

Gore, M., and J. Stubbe: *Elements of Systems Analysis for Business Data Processing,* 3d ed., Dubuque, IA: William C. Brown, 1982.

Grochow, Jerold M.: "Application Generators: An Introduction," *Proceedings of the National Computer Conference,* 1982, pp. 389–392.

Keen, Peter G. W.: "Information Systems and Organization Change," *Communications of the ACM,* **24,** 1, January 1981, pp. 24–33.

King, John Leske and Edward L. Schrems: "Cost Benefit Analysis in Information Systems Development and Operation," *Computing Surveys,* **10,** 1, March 1978, pp. 19–34.

Kroenke, David: *Database Processing,* Chicago, IL: Science Research Associates, 2d ed., 1983.

Management Planning Guide for a Manual of Data Processing Standards, GC20–1670–2, White Plains, NY: IBM.

Martin, James: *Computer Data-Base Organization,* Englewood Cliffs, NJ: Prentice-Hall, 1977.

Martin, James: *Computer Networks and Distributed Processing,* Englewood Cliffs, NJ: Prentice-Hall, 1981.

Mason, Richard L. and Ian I. Mitroff: "A Program for Research on MIS," *Management Science,* **19,** 5, January 1973, pp. 475–485.

McCracken, Daniel D.: *A Guide to NOMAD for Application Development,* Reading, MA: Addison-Wesley, 1980.

Myers, Ware: "Computer Graphics: The Need for Graphics Design," (parts one and two) *Computer,* **14,** 6 and **14,** 7, June and July 1981, pp. 86–92 and 82–88.

Naumann, Justus D. and A. Milton Jenkins: "Prototyping: The New Paradigm for Systems Development," *MIS Quarterly,* **6,** 3, September 1982, pp. 29–44.

Page-Jones, Meilir: *The Practical Guide to Structured Systems Design,* NY: The Yourdon Press, 1980.

Planning for an IBM Data Processing System, 4th ed., GF20–6088–3, White Plains, NY: IBM, 1970.

Senn, James A.: *Information Systems in Management,* 2d ed., Belmont, CA: Wadsworth Publishing Company, 1982.

Senn, James A. and Virginia R. Gibson, "Risks of Investment in Microcomputers for Small Business Management," *Journal of Small Business Managements,* **19,** 3, July 1981, pp. 24–32.

Spiegel, Mitchell G., "Prototyping: An Approach to Information and Communication System Design," *Performance and Evaluation Review,* **10.1,** Spring 1981 pp. 9–19.

Zelkowitz, Marvin V.: "A Case Study in Rapid Prototyping," *Software-Practice and Experience,* **10,** 1980, pp. 1037–1042.

Zmud, Robert W.: "Individual Differences and MIS Success: A Review of the Empirical Literature," *Management Science,* **29,** 10, October 1979, pp. 966–979.

SYSTEM DEVELOPMENT

Baker, E. T. and H. D. Mills: *Datamation,* **19,** 12, December 1973, pp. 58–61.

Boehm, Barry: "Software Engineering," *IEEE Transactions on Computers,* **25,** 12, December 1976, pp. 1226–1241.

Boehm, Barry: "Software and Its Impact: A Quantitative Assessment," *Datamation,* **19,** 5, May 1973, pp. 48–59.

Brooks, Frederick P., Jr.: *The Mythical Man Month,* Reading, MA: Addison-Wesley, 1978.

Cardenas, A. F.: "Technology for Automatic Generation of Application Programs: A Pragmatic View," *MIS Quarterly,* **1,** 3, September 1977, pp. 49–72.

Higgins, David A.: *Program Design and Construction,* Englewood Cliffs, NJ: Prentice-Hall, 1979.

Howden, William E.: "Contemporary Software Development Environments," *Communication of the ACM,* **25,** 5, May 1982, pp. 318–329.

Jackson, Michael A.: *Principles of Program Design,* NY: Academic Press, 1975.

Lientz, Bennet P. and E. Burton Swanson: *Software Maintenance Management,* Reading, MA: Addison-Wesley, 1980.

Management Planning Guide for a Manual of Data Processing Standards, GC20–1670–2, White Plains, NY: IBM.

Metzger, Philip W.: *Managing a Programming Project,* 2d ed., Englewood Cliffs, NJ: Prentice-Hall, 1981.

Mills, Harlan D.: "Principles of Software Engineering," *IBM Systems Journal,* **19,** 4, December 1980, pp. 414–420.

Myers, Glenford J.: *The Art of Software Testing,* NY: Wiley-Interscience, 1979.

Myers, Glenford J.: *Software Reliability,* NY, John Wiley and Sons, 1976.

Nassi, I., and B. Schneiderman: "Flowchart Techniques for Structured Programming," *SIGPLAN Notices,* **8,** 8, August 1973, pp. 12–26.

Peters, Lawrence J.: *Software Design: Methods and Techniques,* NY: Yourdon Press, 1981.

Stevens, W. P., G. L. Myers, and L. L. Constantine: "Structured Design," *IBM Systems Journal,* **13,** 2, May 1974, pp. 115–139.

Yourdon, Edward and Larry L. Constantine: *Structured Design,* Englewood Cliffs, NJ: Prentice-Hall, 1979.

Warnier, Jean Dominique: *Logical Construction of Programs,* NY: Van Nostrand Reinhold Company, 1974.

Wasserman, Anthony I. and Steven Gutz: "The Future of Programming," *Communications of the ACM,* **25,** 3, March 1982, pp. 196–206.

INDEX

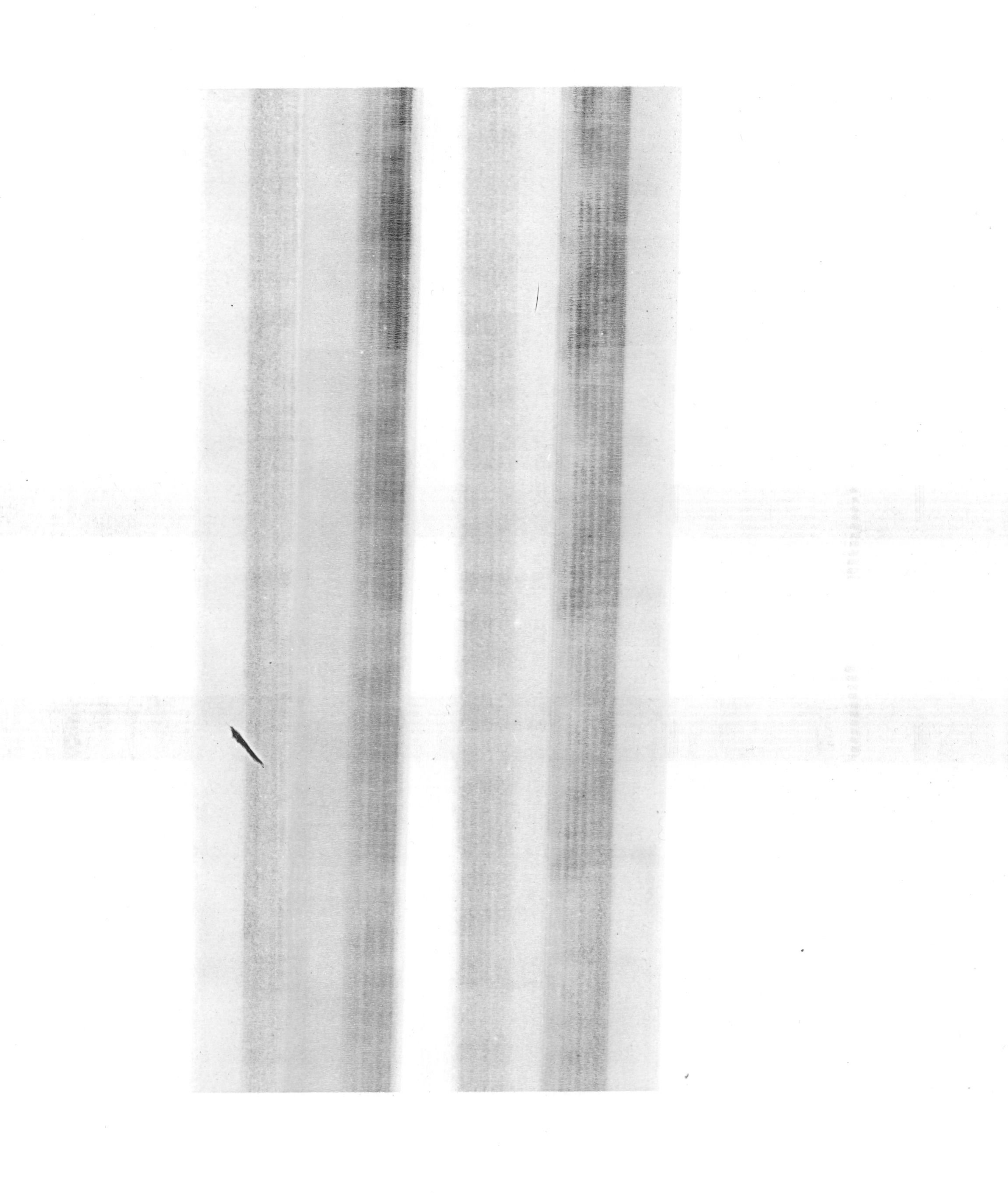